T0319973

Market Research
Best Practice

Market Research Best Practice

30 Visions for the Future

A compilation of discussion papers, case studies and methodologies from ESOMAR

ESOMAR WORLD RESEARCH PUBLICATION

Edited by

Peter Mouncey
Frank Wimmer

John Wiley & Sons, Ltd

Other Wiley Editorial Offices

John Wiley & Sons Inc., 111 River Street, Hoboken, NJ 07030, USA

Jossey-Bass, 989 Market Street, San Francisco, CA 94103-1741, USA

Wiley-VCH Verlag GmbH, Boschstr. 12, D-69469 Weinheim, Germany

John Wiley & Sons Australia Ltd, 42 McDougall Street, Milton, Queensland 4064, Australia

John Wiley & Sons (Asia) Pte Ltd, 2 Clementi Loop #02-01, Jin Xing Distripark, Singapore
129809

John Wiley & Sons Canada Ltd, 6045 Freemont Blvd, Mississauga, ONT, L5R 4J3, Canada

Wiley also publishes its books in a variety of electronic formats. Some content that appears
in print may not be available is electronic books.

Library of Congress Cataloguing-in-Publication Data

Market research best practice / edited by Peter Mouncey, Frank Wimmer.
     p.   cm.
  Includes bibliographical references and index.
  ISBN 978-0-470-06527-3 (cloth : alk. paper)
  1. Marketing research.   I. Mouncey, Peter.   II. Wimmer, Frank.
  HF5415.2.B4587 2007
  658.8′3—dc22

                                                        2006036082

British Library Cataloguing in Publication Data

A catalogue record for this book is available from the British Library

ISBN   978-0-470-06527-3 (HB)

Typeset in 11/13pt Bembo by TechBooks, New Delhi, India
Printed and bound in Great Britain by TJ International Ltd, Padstow, Cornwall, UK
This book is printed on acid-free paper responsibly manufactured from sustainable forestry
in which at least two trees are planted for each one used for paper production.

Contents

PART SIX: BEST PRACTICE CASE STUDIES

Contributors

EDITORS

Peter Mouncey (FMRS, F IDM)

e-mail: peter.mouncey@zen.co.uk

Before 2000, Peter was a member of the senior management team responsible for Group Marketing Services and CRM strategy at the Automobile Association. After 29 years he left to be an independent marketing services consultant and is a Senior Associate Consultant for Marketing Best Practice. Also as a Visiting Fellow of Cranfield University School of Management, Peter teaches and researches various marketing topics, and has a role as a Director of the Return on Marketing Investment Research Club. He is also Director of Research at the Institute of Direct Marketing.

Peter is a Fellow of both the Market Research Society (MRS) and the Institute of Direct Marketing (IDM); he is a former Chairman of the MRS and a past member of the IDM Council. Peter has also chaired the Association of Users of Research Agencies and the Research Development Foundation. He is a long-term member of the MRS Market Research Standards Board and has worked with the MRS, and other market research industry bodies, on developing and implementing strategy in response to the Data Protection Act 1998 and writing the Society's guidelines on this topic. He also runs seminars on data privacy and survey research.

Peter is Executive Editor of the *International Journal of Market Research* (the journal of the MRS) and also serves on the Executive editorial board of the IDM journal. Peter has presented, and written, many papers on market research, database marketing, CRM and related topics.

Professor Dr Frank Wimmer

e-mail: frank.wimmer@sowi.uni-bamberg.de

Frank, born in 1944, is Professor of Business Administration and, in particular, Marketing at the University of Bamberg. Frank is also a member of the advisory committee of the GfK Association (GfK Nürnberg e.V.), which is the parent institution of the GfK Group. As a non-profit organization it aims to promote basic research, cooperation with scientific institutions and the training of marketing executives and market researchers. Frank is also chief editor of the *Yearbook of Marketing and Consumer Research*, published four times per year in German and once in English by the GfK Association.

After obtaining his diploma-degree in business administration at the University of Erlangen-Nürnberg, Frank was associated on a freelance basis with an institute for psychological market research in Nürnberg (today the Psyma Group). From 1970 until 1983, he was a research assistant in the marketing department at the University of Erlangen-Nürnberg. In 1975 he completed his doctoral thesis, and in 1983 he wrote his post-doctoral thesis on the behaviour of socially weak and older consumers. From 1983 until 1985 he was acting Head of Marketing at the University of Hannover before moving in 1985 to the University of Bamberg.

Frank is inter alia Academic Vice President of the 'European Management and Business Sciences Consortium' (EMBS, an exclusive network of European universities), Coordinator of International Relations at the Faculty of Social Sciences, Economics and Business Administration and Academic Head of the Nürnberg Academy for Marketing (NAA). His work focuses on Marketing Intelligence and on qualitative methods of market research/consumer insights, city and regional marketing and ecological marketing.

AUTHORS

Catherine Jill Argall

e-mail: catherine.argall@medicareaustralia.gov.au

Catherine Argall is Chief Executive Officer of Medicare Australia. Medicare Australia is Australia's leading health claims and payments agency. Formerly, Catherine was the General Manager of the Child Support

Agency. Today, Australia's Child Support Agency is acknowledged as a service leader both internationally and nationally. Over a career of 30 years, Catherine has served Australian Governments in positions in other departments, including Finance, Veterans' Affairs and Administrative Services. She was awarded the Public Service Medal (PSM) in 1995 for 'outstanding public service as General Manager, Australian Property Group and in the area of public sector management'.

Malcolm Baker

e-mail: baker@brsgroup.com

Malcolm Baker is a native of the UK, where he began his research career working for Research International, in those days the research arm of Unilever. In 1984 he founded the B/R/S Group in California, which quickly became a leading national provider of innovative qualitative services. From 2000–2004 he headed up Research International's global qualitative practice, the world's largest community of qualitative professionals. Malcolm is a specialist in consumer psychology and branding and communications. He has published several papers on branding, and in 2004 was the winner of ESOMAR'S Annual Carla Monti Award for his paper 'Managing Global Brands to Meet Local Expectations'. He is also a three-time Atticus award winner, WPP's annual awards for innovative, published thinking.

David Bakken

e-mail: dbakken@harrisinteractive.com

David Bakken has worked in marketing research and consulting for more than 20 years. He specializes in understanding the dynamics of buyer decision-making. His areas of expertise include new product development and sales forecasting, market segmentation and market positioning. Prior to joining Harris Interactive in 2000, David was Vice President of Stratford Associates Marketing Research, Inc. David has held positions with Gordon S. Black Corporation, with the ASSESSOR™ Simulated Test Marketing division of Information Resources, Inc. and A. T. & T. David received his BA in Psychology from the University of Michigan and his PhD in Social Psychology from Boston University. He is the author of several papers and articles related to marketing research and speaks frequently at major MR conferences, including the Advanced Research Techniques Forum (sponsored by the American Marketing Association), Sawtooth Software conferences, and selected ESOMAR conferences.

Jill Barnes

e-mail: jill.barnes@csplc.com

She was born and raised in Johannesburg, South Africa and obtained an MA degree (cum laude) from Unisa in 1991 in Research Psychology. Jill started working on the supplier side of the market research business and has subsequently worked for various companies, including Coca-Cola and Tiger Brands, the biggest local FMCG company in sub-Saharan Africa. Her passion is research in emerging markets and she has extensive experience in working in Africa and across a wide number of categories, including food, personal care, home care, beverages and confectionery, pharmaceutical and financial services. She currently leads the Market Research team at Tiger Brands.

Christine Blache

e-mail: cblache@9aplus.com

Having studied Music in NYC and Business in Paris, Christine Blache has an MBA from ESCP/EAP, France. After a few years as a TV documentary producer, Christine started 9A+, her own consulting business in New Media and was among a handful of key players in France's Internet Revolution. In 2003, Christine joined the creative team of PortiCo Research, an ethnographic marketing research company, as a Consultant, bringing her love for innovation to the international team.

Vanessa Briese

e-mail: vanessa@heartbeat.com.au

Vanessa began her career in 1996 in the publishing industry in marketing, sales and new business development before moving on to media planning. She joined Heartbeat at the beginning of 2003 to pursue her keen interest in understanding what drives consumers and why. Since joining, Vanessa has focused her energy and passion on researching the youth market in Australia and is seen frequently commentating on trends in the media. She holds a Bachelor of Commerce degree from the University of Sydney.

Rex Briggs

e-mail: rex.briggs@marketingevolution.com

Rex Briggs is the founder and CEO of Marketing Evolution, a marketing research consulting firm with offices in New York and California, and with clients in more than 20 countries around the world. Rex has more than 15 years' experience specifically in marketing research: he started his career at the strategic market research consulting firm Yankelovich

Partners, where his clients included McKinsey & Company, IBM, Toyota and Nissan. He has been honoured with the Atticus Award for his work in Direct Marketing, the Tenagra Award for outstanding contribution to branding and the Fernanda Monti award for his work in customer relation marketing (CRM). Rex pioneered the leading methodologies for cross-media marketing measurement. Recently Rex co-authored the book, *What Sticks: Why Most Advertising Fails and How to Guarantee Yours Succeeds.*

Paul Buckley
e-mail: Paul.Buckley@avon.com
Paul Buckley is currently Market Research Director – Europe, Middle East and Africa for the Avon Company, which he joined in January 2006. He is responsible for the full range of qualitative and quantitative research work undertaken by the company in the region, working closely with the Global Marketing team in New York. When the chapter was written, he was Vice President, Research & Evaluation at Allied Domecq, where he spent six years. Prior to that, he held a variety of market research and NPD positions, first at Unilever (1982–1993) and subsequently Coca-Cola (1993–1999). Paul holds a First Class Honours degree in Mathematics from Cambridge University.

Peter Bycroft
e-mail: peter.bycroft@cordia.com.au
Professor Peter Bycroft is the Managing Director of Corporate Diagnostics Pty Ltd and an Adjunct Professor in the Faculty of Arts and Social Sciences at the University of the Sunshine Coast, Queensland, Australia. Peter is an Environmental Psychologist and a recognized expert in market research, quality management and improving organizational performance. He is widely recognized as one of Australia's leading authorities in strategic evaluation, having developed customized evaluation protocols for many Australian Government organizations. Peter has been a member of the Australasian Evaluation Society's (AES) National Awards Committee since 2000, and was appointed Chairperson of that Committee in 2005.

Gert de Nooij
e-mail: g.j.denooij@scanmar.nl
Dr Gert Jan de Nooij is currently a Managing Partner at Scanmar BV. He started his career at Phillips doing marketing modelling forecasting. After

that he became an Assistant Professor of Marketing at Tilburg University. After five years in the academic world, he decided to join GfK as Market Research Director AGB Panels (currently GfK Panel Services Benelux). This was followed by another academic position, this time as Assistant Professor of Market Research at Nijenrode University. Dr de Nooij has been published by ESOMAR as well as in the *Journal of Economic Psychology*, *Tijdschrift voor Marketing* and *Jaarboek MOA*.

Pia de Wit

e-mail: pia-de.wit@unilever.com
Pia's background is in Food and Dietetics, in Market Research and in Social Psychology. She has worked for Unilever Research & Development in The Netherlands for many years, focusing on consumer perception and behaviour.

Ioannis (John) Dimopoulos

e-mail: john.dimopoulos@reckittbenckiser.com
Ioannis (John) Dimopoulos is currently a Senior Vice President and Global Director of Market Research at Reckitt Benckiser plc. Originally from Australia, John has been based in the UK since January 2000, when he was appointed to lead the Global Market Research Function. With a Business Degree Major in Marketing (1987, University of New South Wales – Australia), John has worked on the client side of the market research industry for over 18 years. His first role was at Procter & Gamble, which he joined in January 1988, working across all the categories in the Australia and NZ operation, as well as the ASIA Region, where in 1995–96 he held market research responsibility for the Pantene Brand and Hair Care Conditioner Development. He joined Reckitt & Colman plc in February 1997, and became a member of the newly formed Global Market Research Leadership Team. In October 1998, his role expanded to include East Asia. During the merger discussions (late 1999), John played a key role in helping to influence the structure and role of the Market Research Function, which led to his current appointment.

Emre Erdoğan

e-mail: emre.erdogan@infakto.com.tr
Dr Emre Erdoğan was born in Istanbul in 1971. He graduated from the Galatasaray Lisesi and Political Sciences Department of the Bogazici University. He completed his MA and PhD in the same department. He worked as project manager in IMV-SAM (1997–2000) and

STRATEJI|MORI (2000–2003) and became one of the founders of the Infakto RW (2003). He is an expert on quantitative techniques, sampling and political methodology and the author of numerous papers about marketing research and Turkish politics. He is currently teaching social statistics courses at Istanbul Bilgi University, Department of Political Sciences.

Britt-Marie Eriksson

e-mail: ittizz@telia.com

Britt-Marie has a bachelor's degree in business, which concentrated on international marketing, together with a master's degree in Economics from the University of Lund. She has broad experience in the building industry, and in particular, in working with end consumers. Her work experience includes looking at different living issues for Skanska Nya Hem. Here, concepts such as storage, lighting, ease of cleaning and other indoor design issues were key to her research. She now works as Marketing Manager for Lafarge Roofing, an international company in the building sector. Here she has continued to work with segmentation studies with focus group researchers and is today implementing a B2C thinking and orientation into the company. She also drives and manages both internal and external projects internationally in branding and communication.

Karl Feld

e-mail: karl.feld@d3systems.com

Mr Feld serves as Research Manager at D3 Systems, where he directs market, opinion, media and programme evaluation research activities in Eurasia and North Africa. Prior to joining D3, Mr Feld held management positions at several large research organizations. He began his career specializing in research in post-conflict environments, and has deep research experience in over ten industries. Mr Feld earned an MA from Georgetown University's School of Foreign Service, a BA from Ripon College and also holds the ESOMAR/MRA Principles of Marketing Research Certificate. He is internationally published on multimodal techniques and has won several industry awards.

Lena Gilchrist

e-mail: lena.gilchrist@ipsos.se

Lena Gilchrist is the Country Manager for Ipsos in Sweden. Lena has been working in market research for over 20 years, is well experienced in the area of consumer insight and brand management and has a lot of practical experience from a wide spread of clients and industries on how to integrate insight in the client's organization. Lena also has a long history of teaching at Stockholm University and Bergs School of Communication. She has a degree in Economics and Marketing from Stockholm University.

Sangeeta Gupta

e-mail: sangeetagupta10@gmail.com

Sangeeta Gupta is a seasoned hand in the market research business in India. After an auspicious beginning in qualitative research, she moved for a short while to account planning at FCB Ulka, came back to her first love, qualitative research, for almost a decade, and later held responsibility for the total customized research branch operations for ACNielsen at Delhi for five years. She then worked briefly as an independent consultant in the areas of leadership and innovation, and currently holds responsibility for consumer insights at Pepsico in India.

An active participant at various local and international conferences and seminars, Sangeeta has contributed to the world of research in two significant ways. One, she has developed/adapted new techniques in qualitative research from anthropology, psychology to semiotics; and two, has been an enthusiastic and effective advocate of combining research methods/data sources (qualitative, quantitative, published data etc...) to effectively garner insights for a vast variety of marketing problems.

Nic Hall

e-mail: n.hall@research-int.com

Nic Hall is a qualified Chemical Engineer, with postgraduate courses in German as well as Marketing and Business related topics. After two years with Mobil Oil in Johannesburg, South Africa, working in Marketing Services, Marketing and Sales, he joined Unilever Foods in Durban, where he held a marketing position for five years. Nic joined Research International South Africa in 1983 as a Research Executive. In 1990 he was appointed a Director of the South African company and one of its six owners. He moved to the UK in 1997. He is currently a Senior Director in RIUK, with a particular focus on RI's Global Solution – Market Strategy. Nic is a past Chairman of a regional branch of the South African Market Research Association. Publications include several papers presented to SAMRA and to various ESOMAR conferences, where he has twice won awards for the best paper at a conference.

Kristin Hickey

e-mail: kristinh@theleadingedge.com.au

Kristin has been with The Leading Edge for eight years, working across a range of clients including Fosters Australia, Australia Post, Fonterra Brands, GSK, Nestlé, Microsoft, George Weston Foods, and Yum! Kristin's career represents a combination of academia, management consulting and market research. She lectured for a number of years at Bond University on the topics of management, marketing and corporate strategy. Kristin has a BA (Hons), an MBA and undertook a PhD in Customer Service – a field in which she has authored two books. Kristin's background and experience helped develop the Value Architect role within The Leading Edge – a position designed to deliver solutions to clients that are well beyond the scope of market research. As such, Kristin has a depth of understanding of customer satisfaction and an unrivalled knowledge on how to translate customer research data into meaningful and measurable business strategies. She has presented at ESOMAR Congresses in 2002, 2003 and 2005, where her most recent paper won the 'Fernanda Monti Best Overall Paper Award'.

Karen Hofman

e-mail: khofman@porticoresearch.com

Karen Hofman is Senior Research Analyst/Project Manager based in Montreal, Canada for PortiCo Research, United States. Since 1998 her ethnographic analyses have ranged from global syntheses to the particularities of domestic ethnic markets, from new product development to the conflicting perspectives in service relationships and market segmentation. Prior experience includes real estate development feasibility analysis, as well as academic research in anthropology and psychology on language transmission, cultural change and learning theories. She has a BA in anthropology and economics from McGill University, Canada, and an MSc in anthropology from Université de Montréal, Canada.

Jan Hofmeyr

e-mail: JN.Hofmeyr@iafrica.com

Jan Hofmeyr (PhD) is currently the International Director of Innovation for Synovate's Brand and Communications practice. Before joining Synovate in 2006, Jan ran The Customer Equity Company, a TNS-owned company responsible for marketing the Conversion Model. Jan is perhaps best known for developing the Conversion Model in the late 1980s. Together with Butch Rice, he turned it into the most widely used measure of commitment in the world. Jan has worked for most of the world's leading brands in most of their leading markets. He is the author of four books, including *Commitment-Led Marketing* (with Butch Rice). Jan lives and works in Cape Town, South Africa.

Siegfried Högl

e-mail: siegfried.hoegl@gfk.com

Siegfried Högl is Managing Director of GfK Marktforschung GmbH, Germany. Additionally, he is a member of the GfK Custom Research Board and the ESOMAR Council. His research focus lies on the entire range of brand and communication research. Siegfried studied business management and economics at the University of Regensburg, with majors in marketing, statistics/econometrics and finance. His degree was awarded in 1980.

Oliver Hupp

e-mail: oliver.hupp@gfk.com

Dr Oliver Hupp is Division Manager at GfK Brand and Communication Research, GfK Marktforschung (Germany), where he has been employed since 1999. He is head of the team for research and development. His main focus areas are national and international brand positioning studies with TARGET® POSITIONING, brand performance analyses with BASS and financial brand valuation using the Advanced Brand Valuation Approach. He is responsible for the development of brand management tools as well as national and international client counselling in the field of brand positioning and evaluation. Oliver is the author of numerous publications concerned with the topics of brand management and brand valuation. Together with Siegfried Högl, he won the ESOMAR Best Methodological Paper Award in 2002 and 2003.

David Jenkinson

e-mail: kristinh@theleadingedge.com.au

David Jenkinson joined Fosters in 2004 with a charter to facilitate the organizational change necessary for the business to become a 'Consumer-Led' organization. As head of the i-Nova group, David is responsible for driving insight-based value creation across the group. This includes ensuring all frameworks, capabilities and processes to deliver growth are embedded across Beer, Wine, Spirits and Non-alcohol. To achieve this, the i-Nova group utilizes market research, foresight and scenario planning, strategy, decision support, and insights-based innovation. David holds an MBA, an MSc in Management Sciences and a BSc. He has nearly 20 years' experience in the marketing industry, including six years in the field of strategic marketing working with British Airways and Mars in Europe and eleven years as Regional Strategy Planning Director at Y&R advertising where he worked across a diverse range of clients both internationally and domestically. His speciality areas of expertise include the development of brand equity models and strategic brand consultancy.

Edeltraud Kaltenbach

e-mail: edeltraud.kaltenbach@maritzresearch.de

Edeltraud Kaltenbach is Senior Research Executive at Maritz Research in Hamburg, Germany. After studying economics with a focus on marketing and psychology at the University of Cologne and Tokyo University, Edeltraud started her research career at GfK in Milan, where she worked as an Account Manager. In 1995, after two and a half years at GfK, Edeltraud moved on to work at Infomark Research & Consultancy in Milan, where she was leading qualitative projects for clients from various sectors. In 1998, Edeltraud joined Maritz Research's branch in Hamburg, Germany. As a Senior Researcher, Edeltraud works on qualitative research projects for many of Maritz Research's clients. Maritz Research is focused on the Automotive, Pharmaceutical, Hospitality, Finance, Telecommunication and Technology industries.

Mansoor Khan

e-mail: mansoor.khan@tns-global.com

Mansoor Khan is International TV Development Director, TNS (UK). His initial education and training was in engineering, graduating from the University of North London; later, he joined the UK's Engineering Council and gained professional status. Mansoor has also been educated in the field of Management Studies and holds an extensive range of postgraduate qualifications, including an MBA from London. With early career stints at Scotland Yard (Metropolitan Police) and then at Hitachi UK, Mansoor has been at TNS for the last 16 years, where he has held various posts in management. Specializing in international TV audience measurement, he has been responsible for the project management and start-up of many TAM services globally.

Sjoerd Koornstra

e-mail: sjoerd.koornstra@heineken.nl

Sjoerd Koornstra is International Market Research Manager for Africa and the Middle East within Heineken. In this position, he is focusing on embedding research within the business process, structuring the Marketing/Sales information household infrastructure and applying regional brand health and portfolio analysis. He has broad international experience, and has been active in several market-research-related areas for 20 years. Sjoerd has held international positions in the field of Marketing Research, Knowledge Management and Marketing Information Technology and has also been project manager for the Heineken Brand Dashboard. He has a master's degree in applied econometrics in business administration.

Derek Leddie

e-mail: derekl@theleadingedge.com.au

Derek Leddie is the CEO and founding partner of The Leading Edge. Under Derek's leadership, The Leading Edge has, since 1990, grown from two people to over 100, expanding geographically both in Australia and overseas. Within Australia, The Leading Edge is seen as the research category leader in breaking new ground with an offer that combines consumer expertise with brand building, the innovation process and business building market frameworks. Derek holds a Bachelor of Business Degree from Kuringai University, with, majors in Marketing, Computing and Economics. He has over 15 years' experience in marketing and in both quantitative and qualitative research. His skills are very much focused on developing, via marketing research, optimal management and marketing solutions.

Omar Mahmoud

e-mail: omarmahmoudom@yahoo.com

Omar has over twenty years' experience in market research and marketing services, for UNICEF, Procter & Gamble and Novartis. He has held global, regional and local positions in Western Europe, the Middle East and Africa, and North America and is currently Associate Director in P&G's Consumer & Market Knowledge department. Omar has taught Market Research, Marketing and Business Thinking at The International University in Geneva. His areas of expertise include innovation and initiative success, advertising research, price research, concept development, thinking and decision-making. He is a member of the ESOMAR

Professional Standards Committee and an Advisory Board Member of *Admap* magazine. He has been published in *Admap*, *Research World* and *Market Leader*, and is a contributor to *Admap's* 'On marketing' column.

Daryl Maloney McCall

e-mail: daryl.maloney@insightmarketing.com.au

Daryl has over 20 years' experience in research management and marketing consulting, and is a co-founder and Director of Insight Marketing Systems. As VP of Sales & Marketing for 'Research Reporter – the marketing information management system', Daryl has consulted in over 40 market research departments in North America, UK/Europe and the Asia Pacific region. Prior to founding Insight Marketing Systems, Daryl worked as both a buyer and supplier of market research, and has extensive experience across a diverse range of marketing information areas including competitor intelligence, primary and secondary market research and geodemography. Daryl has worked for international companies including Shell Oil and Mintel, and consulted on a broad range of marketing management issues to numerous industry leaders such as Toyota, Kodak, AXA, Diners Club, IKEA and Australia Post. Daryl has a double major in Psychology (Science) from the University of Melbourne, Australia.

Lluís Martínez-Ribes

e-mail: lluis@martinez-ribes.com

Fascinated by retail innovation, a specialization pursued in 20 countries, Lluís combines his work at ESADE as Professor and former Marketing Department Head, with a selective consulting activity. With an MBA from ESADE and an MBA in Retailing from Stirling University (UK), Lluís is involved in Active Learning at Harvard Business School. He is a visiting lecturer at SDA Bocconi B.S. (Italy) and has also taught at Edinburgh University, Vienna University, HEC B.S. (France) and Goizueta B.S. (USA). Lluís is the author of various books and conference papers and leads courses such as 'Retail innovation' and 'Future Marketing Challenges'. He has been consultant to companies such as Bayer, Camper, Coca-Cola, Fagor, Goodyear, Danone, Habitat, Intersport, Sara Lee, Mattel, Mercadona, Olympic Committee, Prénatal, Unilever.

Lyn McGregor

e-mail: lyn.mcgregor@flamingo-international.com

Lyn joined the board at Flamingo International in 2003 to develop her experience in heading large global branding projects. During her time at Flamingo, Lyn has helped to broaden the range of strategic position-ing projects undertaken by the agency. Prior to joining Flamingo, Lyn received the award for the best 'Application of Research in 2003' from the Market Research Society in the UK for a paper written while she was Head of Insight at Added Value. Always passionately interested in developing strategic brand visions and positioning, as well as innova-tion and design development, Lyn moved to Added Value from Sys-tem Three in Scotland (now part of TNS), where she was head of the qualitative function. Prior to her commercial research career, Lyn lec-tured in Consumer Behaviour and Marketing Strategy on Masters Degree courses in Marketing and International Marketing at the University of Strathclyde.

Stephen Needel

e-mail: drsteve@advancedsimulations.com

Dr Stephen Needel is Managing Partner of US-based Advanced Sim-ulations. He formed, and manages, an international company that uses virtual reality simulations to study retailing, marketing and shopper con-sumption issues. As president of Simulation Research, he helped intro-duce virtual reality to the marketing research world. His previous jobs include Vice President for Product Development and for Analytical Ser-vices at A.C. Nielsen, as well as head of the Advanced Analytical Team at Information Resources. Earlier jobs included analytical roles at Burke Marketing Research and Quaker Oats and a lecturer at the University of Connecticut.

Selim Oktar

e-mail: selim.oktar@shift-istanbul.com

Selim Oktar earned his university degree from Boğaziçi University De-partment of Economics. After graduation, he worked for JWT as Head of Strategic Planning in the research department. In 1987, he founded STRATEJI Planning and Research, expanding to Stratej Mori later on. In 2000, the company was recognized as the most admired in the indus-try by the Istanbul Faculty of Communication. In 2001, the company merged with GfK and Selim became the CEO for Manajans Thompson. With more than 20 years of experience, Selim has consulted in the areas of Strategic Development, New Business and Market Development, Cor-porate Brand Management and Communication and Knowledge Man-agement. He also lectures and presents seminars at foundations like IDA Turkey and the Boğaziçi University.

Roger A. Parker

e-mail: roger.a.parker@boeing.com

Roger Parker is the Senior Marketing Scientist for the Marketing and Business Strategy unit of Boeing Commercial Airplanes, the group within the Boeing Company responsibility for the manufacture and sale of commercial jet aircraft. His primary responsibility is the development of advanced market research tools, and he is the Principal Investigator for a major research project developing an agent-based model of the world's airline industry, using discrete choice methods as the foundation of modelling agent behaviour. He has over 30 years' experience in market and public policy research and modelling within Boeing and as a long-time consultant.

Hilary Perkins

e-mail: Hilary.Perkins@beamglobal.com

Hilary Perkins has extensive experience in the spirits and wine industry, having worked for over 20 years at Allied Domecq and now heading up research and innovation at Beam Global Spirits and Wine. Additionally, she has an MBA and an interest in the family farming enterprise comprised of both organic dairy and beef and Pedigree Hereford cattle. With such a diverse background, one consuming interest is the need to understand what consumers want and why, to enable effective targeting for business success.

Jonathan Rabson

e-mail: j.rabson@researchreporter.com

Jonathan Rabson is currently European Director for Insight Marketing Systems (IMS), the developers of Research Reporter, the award-winning information management software for market researchers (www.researchreporter.com). Jonathan is responsible for developing the European market for Research Reporter, as well as configuring and supporting clients that have adopted the research portal application to help leverage the power of their marketing knowledge. With over 15 years' experience in technology solutions for market research, Jonathan was previously International Sales & Marketing Director at E-Tabs, and held senior roles in Global Account Management, Marketing and Training at SPSS and Quantime. A graduate in Computing Science from the University of London's Imperial College of Science and Technology, Jonathan also has a postgraduate degree from the University of London's Institute of Education. Jonathan's joint paper 'Getting Research Noticed at the

Corporate Top Table' with Daryl Maloney McCall (IMS) and Ioannis Dimopoulos (Reckitt Benckiser) won Best Methodological Paper at the ESOMAR Congress 2004.

Lucile Rameckers

e-mail: lucile.rameckers@philips.com

Lucile Rameckers is Senior Research Consultant at Philips Design, Eindhoven. She combines analytical, observational and creative methods to fully understand people's personal, cultural and social contexts, then communicates her findings in as vivid a manner as possible to multidisciplinary teams in various innovation projects. Lucile graduated in Consumer and Business Studies (1993, Wageningen University) – as part of which she attended the Smeal College of Business (1992, Pennsylvania State University). Before joining Philips in 1999, she worked at Belgium's University of Leuven in Applied Economics, and as project manager of Market Research for SKIM Analytical, a Rotterdam-based international market research agency.

John Rice

e-mail: mwbutchr@mweb.co.za

John 'Butch' Rice co-founded Research Surveys in 1979. Research Surveys is one of the largest research companies in South Africa. In 1990, together with Jan Hofmeyr, he set up an international marketing network for the Conversion Model, a model that measures the strength of the relationships between brands and consumers. He has published extensively in international publications, and co-authored the book *Commitment-Led Marketing – the Key to Brand Profits is in the Customer's Mind* with Jan Hofmeyr in 2000. He retired from his position as Joint Chairman of Research Surveys in 2000 and now spends his time consulting internationally.

Farheen Romani

e-mail: farheen.helim@lowemail.com

Farheen Romani serves as a Brand Planning Director at LOWE Lintas (India) Pvt, Ltd Mumbai. Farheen brings over five years of marketing research experience to her new role, and is responsible for strategic planning on the Lifebuoy brand for HLL. Prior to joining LOWE, Farheen was a research manager at AC Nielsen (India), where she was involved mostly in implementation of new research tools and techniques and their adaptation in the Indian market. Before that, she served as a senior research executive at TNS worldwide. Farheen holds an MBA degree from the University of Pune (India).

Corinne Rosinski

e-mail: corinne.rosinski@jpcr.be

Corinne Rosinski has been Managing Director of JPCR s.a. Belgium, her qualitative market research and consulting agency, since September 2004. Corinne joined Unilever Belgium in 1985, where she worked for 19 years in market research, marketing and sales. From 1999 to 2004, Corinne was Head of the Consumer and Market Insight department of Unilever Belgium. In five years, she contributed to a major evolution in the role of the market research department: from 'data provider' to 'consultant making impact' and to 'leadership for growth'. Corinne has also been President of the UBA (Union Belge des Annonceurs) Market Research Commission (2003–2004).

Xavier Roure

e-mail: xroure@plusfresc.es

Xavier holds a Masters in Marketing at Distributor Companies from ESADE (Escuela Superior de Administración y Dirección de Empresas), Barcelona and an MBA in Retailing from the Institute for Retail Studies, University of Stirling. He joined the Marketing Department of Super-mercats Pujol S.A as Junior Marketing Manager where he was involved in all the activities that are typical in a marketing department, specifically product management, loyalty programmes and category management in Supermercats PLUSFRESC. In January 2002 he became Manager of the Marketing Department. Xavier is now Marketing Director, where he has full responsibility for all instore developments, including staff management. He has collaborated in training programmes for several organizations, including ESADE, AECOC, Recoletos, Instituto de empresa, EHI-Retail network and ESOMAR.

Subhransu Rout

e-mail: subsan29@gmail.com or subhransu.rout@motorola.com

Subhransu holds an MBA specializing in Marketing with a Physics Honours graduation. "Why is blue called blue"? – This question from his 3 year old son got Subhransu to adopt a 'challenging the basics' mode of thinking. He took the 'technology' plunge from November 2006 and heads the Consumer Insights & Intelligence (CI&I) department of Motorola India Pvt. Ltd., Mobile Devices Division. He is also part of

Motorola's Global CI&I team. He began his market research career with MBA-GALLUP in 1995 and then moved on to IMRB/CSMM in 1996, wherein he held various key positions and handled a rich spectrum of clients. He joined Hindustan Lever Limited (Unilever India) in December 1999 and handled a variety of categories spanning Tea, Ice Creams, Popular Foods and Hair Care. In the Hair Care category, he was the Senior Regional CMI Manager (representing the Central Asia & China region on the global Unilever Hair Care CMI network) and was also the Global CMI Leader for Clear shampoo. He moved on to GlaxoSmithKline Consumer Health Care (GSKCH) India in September 2003 and set-up and headed the Consumer Insights department therein. This stint in GSKCH gave him a rich experience in Nutritional Health Care and OTC categories. Subhransu's singular passion is to use novel/differentiated insights to unlock growth opportunities for brands.

Hans-Willi Schroiff

e-mail: hans-willi.schroiff@henkel.com

Dr Hans-Willi Schroiff is Vice President of Market Research at Henkel KGaA, Germany. Previously he held various academic positions, finally as Assistant Professor of Psychology at RWTH Aachen. He is the author of numerous publications – both in Psychology and in Market Research, and a frequent speaker at international business schools, business events and conferences. Dr Schroiff is a member of the Executive Committee of the Marketing Science Institute (Boston). He is also Chairman of the Advisory Board for the German Internet Research Company Dialego (Aachen) and a member of the Advisory Board of ICW. Since 2003, he has lectured on MBA courses at the Marketing Department of RWTH Aachen.

Solveig Shapiro

e-mail: solveig@iafrica.com

Solveig is the Managing Partner in the Qualitative Consultancy, which was established in 1986 as the first specialist qualitative research practice in South Africa. She has many years' experience, covering many product fields, amongst the diverse peoples of Southern Africa, on both the buyer and supplier sides of the industry. She has twice been elected to the national council of SAMRA (the Southern African Marketing Research Association), where her portfolios included chairing the qualitative special interest group and the professional standards committee. She commutes between Johannesburg and Cape Town, and also travels extensively in the region.

David V. L. Smith

e-mail: david.smith@dvlsmithgroup.com

David Smith is CEO of DVL Smith Group, and a Professor at the University of Hertfordshire Business School. He is a Fellow, and former Chairman, of the UK Market Research Society and holds the Society's Silver Medal. He has won numerous awards from the Market Research Society, ESOMAR and other bodies. His Doctorate is from the Department of Organizational Psychology, Birkbeck College, University of London. He is a graduate member of the British Psychological Society, and a member of the Chartered Institute of Marketing and the Institute of Management Consultants. He is the author of *Inside Information – Making Sense of Marketing Data and The art* and *Science of Interpreting Market Research Evidence.*

Greet Sterenberg

e-mail: g.sterenberg@research-int.com

Greet Sterenberg is Global Director of Qualitative Space for Research International. She joined Research International Netherlands in 1995 as head of the Qualitative Unit and has, since 2000, been part of the Research International Head Office. Based in Amsterdam, her role is leading and growing the global qualitative offer to help clients gain a better understanding of consumers and customers, solve problems and develop knowledge to create successful brands and businesses. Key areas of expertise are Consumer understanding, Branding and Innovation. She has a degree in (medical) sociology and anthropology and more than 20 years of experience in marketing and market research. Before joining Research, she had several marketing and sales roles in the pharmaceutical industry. Since 2002, Greet has been the global coordinator of the Research International Observer, a bi–annual, own-funded qualitative study that runs in more than 45 countries. She regularly moderates seminars and client events around the world.

William Stone

e-mail: bill.stone@analyticalgroup.com

William and his company, WKS:CSM, specialize in integrated total customer quality management. Educated as a clinical psychologist, Bill has a 25-year career in market research and analysis, including senior positions at a number of recognized companies. His specialized knowledge in research strategies, modelling and process quality management (Six-Sigma, TQM, etc.) uniquely enables him to assist clients in building operational excellence and running smart businesses. Utilizing leading-edge assessment tools and processes, clients gain a detailed view of what is important, what they are doing right and where they need to focus resources to achieve market share and competitive position. Bill is a certified Six-Sigma Black Belt, and has served as an examiner for the State of Arizona Spirit of Excellence Awards, an Associate Professor at Arizona State University and has been recognized internationally for his published work in customer satisfaction.

Earl Taylor
e-mail: etaylor@msi.org
As Marketing Science Institute's CMO, Earl Taylor is responsible for recruiting and retaining corporate members who set priorities for, and fund, research by leading marketing academics. While a Senior Vice President at Research International, Earl conducted studies and published articles primarily on branding, co-authoring 'How Global Brands Compete' in the September 2004 *Harvard Business Review.* His and Lynn B. Upshaw's *The Masterbrand Mandate* (Wiley 2000) won WPP Group's Atticus 'Grand Prix' award. Earl has a PhD in sociology from Harvard University and a BA in psychology and sociology from Rice University.

Jem Wallis
e-mail: jem@heartbeat.com.au
Jem is co-founder and owner of Heartbeat. He is recognized internationally as a pioneer in new approaches to qualitative research and is passionate about challenging corporations and companies to think differently about customers, consumers and people. He is a regular conference speaker on social trends, and is an advisor to many multinational clients on strategy and consumer planning. Jem is currently leading Heartbeat's international expansion, with Brazil the first of a number of countries to benefit from the Heartbeat approach. He has an Honours degree in Psychology (BSc) from Nottingham University, UK and has been working in qualitative research for over 20 years.

Natalie Wearne
e-mail: natalie.wearne@tns-global.com
Natalie Wearne is currently a Senior Consultant in TNS's Australian-based social research arm. She has over ten years' experience conducting market research in the government sector, and has worked on major studies for many of the signature Australian Government agencies, including the Departments of Finance, Health, Defence and the Australian Taxation

Office. Natalie's key areas of interest and expertise include stakeholder satisfaction research, programme evaluation, brand health and social policy evaluation. She holds a Bachelor of Business in marketing and Honours in organizational psychology, and is accredited by the Australian Market and Social Research Society.

Ji-Seun You

e-mail: jiseunyou@lge.com

Ji-Seun You is Europe Product Planner for LG Electronics Inc., Germany. After her studies in International Business Studies with specialization in Finance & Risk Management, English and Spanish, she began her career in product planning in 2004 at LG Electronics. In her position she is, among other things, responsible for international surveys, new product developments and innovations and market observation for white goods.

We would like to acknowledge the following authors:

Tamsin Addison
Monica Bueno
Olof Eriksson
Ijaz Shafi Gilani
Michael O'Donohue
James Potocki
Sinéad Twomey

Foreword

We are delighted to present this best practice compilation of 30 ESOMAR World Research Papers, realized in cooperation with John Wiley & Sons.

Each of the selected papers, first presented at an ESOMAR event over the last ten years, is an authoritative and valuable reference in its own right on how to conduct research and how to use research to greatest effect. Each paper illustrates how the best research can truly support the objective and informed process of decision-making for business around the world.

Seen as a whole, we also wanted to go beyond pure methodology, and so chose papers which have made an important contribution to how research has developed as a discipline and which demonstrate those new skills which are so important for the evolution and vitality of the industry.

We're very grateful to our editorial team, Peter Mouncey of Cranfield University School of Management, UK and Frank Wimmer of GfK Nuremberg and University of Bamberg, Germany, respectively, for their thoughtful and passionate commitment to this project. The board of ESOMAR's Developing Talent initiative provided their ideas and guidance to ensure that the Best Practice papers lived up to the initiative's ideals and the objectives of stimulating the development of research skills for today's changing and increasingly demanding marketplace.

Finally, of course, our thanks go to all the authors who allowed their work to be reproduced here.

I hope you'll agree that ESOMAR's Book of Best Practice succeeds in showcasing the best the market research industry has to offer.

Véronique Jeannin
Director General
ESOMAR

Preface

When we first met at the outset of this project, we asked ourselves: 'what ideas, philosophies and concepts form the best practice for our industry?' A very daunting question and one not answered easily. There are important new challenges facing the market research industry. In particular, expectations have changed. We are moving from data-management to decision-facilitation; from an emphasis on methodology and tactical support to input at the strategic level.

Looking around, we decided that the collection of ESOMAR World Research Papers would certainly be the best place to find the material. We initially felt that we were faced with an overwhelming amount of material! Overall, we had an archive containing thousands of papers that had been presented at ESOMAR Congresses, conferences, seminars and workshops over many years. However, in reality, the agenda that we had to address narrowed the field down to papers written and presented within the last ten. In addition, the key relevant themes have tended to emerge only over this period. That still left hundreds of papers to sift through, so we concentrated our search on those papers selected for the *Excellence in International Market Research* book, published annually by ESOMAR from 2000–2005, and topped-up with additionally selected papers, particularly from more recent events.

Our belief was that by concentrating on certain criteria, we would succeed in our mission. We decided that the papers we selected had to:

- be evidence based, but provide interpretation from that evidence;
- be creative and innovative;
- contain methodological developments;
- provide background, context and new knowledge;
- demonstrate understanding of business and markets;
- clearly demonstrate impact and influence;
- be engagingly written;
- have international value or application.

We also defined the following six key part headings for the book:

- Facilitating Decision-making
- Knowledge Management
- New Methodologies
- Modelling
- Facilitating Diversity
- Best Practice Case Studies.

In one sense, all papers could be classified under the first heading . . . . a problem. We solved this by defining the papers in this part as being focused on the role of market research in developing corporate strategy–research in the boardroom. Integrating methods, data and knowledge management were quickly seen as an area of research which will surely be central both now and in the future. As business and society continue to expand communication channels based on the Internet and e-mail, more and more data are becoming available. Market research's response to this means blurring the borders between methodologies and working with increasing amounts of information. Doing this well will allow businesses to truly understand consumers and to keep them at the heart of the decision-making process.

Of course using scientific, statistical and analytical methods and techniques to gain insight or support decision-making means that new methodologies and models will certainly continue to form the heartbeat of market research. These techniques are vital to the continued growth and development of the industry, as these papers demonstrate.

Understanding a fast-paced changing world is also critical to our industry. We decided that research's abilities to understand human commonalities, as well as their differences, will be a cornerstone for our industry. Our section on diversity brings cross-cultural research into the spotlight.

We also decided to group all the case studies together rather than try and fit them to the other headings. We hope this will also help those readers who are interested particularly in finding examples of how market research can be applied to resolving business issues.

The book is aimed at three key audiences:

- marketers;
- academics;
- market researchers.

For all three, the aim is the same – to demonstrate the added value that market research can bring to business decision-making, whether you are a marketer wanting to understand what market research should deliver, an academic wanting to ensure that your syllabus reflects the strategic role that market research can play or a market researcher, either in an agency or client organization, looking for innovative and creative solutions that will help address the business issues faced by your clients.

Whether a marketer, academic, market researcher within a client organization or a research company, we hope you enjoy the book and find it interesting, challenging and useful. We certainly enjoyed putting it together.

Peter Mouncey
Frank Wimmer

Acknowledgement

We would like to thank all the authors who contributed to this publication. It was a pleasure and a privilege to read and review your work.

Peter Mouncey
Frank Wimmer
Angela Canin

Part One

Facilitating Decision-Making

Chapter One

Creating Maximum Value for the Client: Developing a New Strategic Role for Market Researchers

David V. L. Smith[a]

> *This chapter argues the case for market researchers extending their skill sets to embrace a range of business consultancy skills.*

INTRODUCTION

This chapter takes the view that much of the past frustration with the output of market research centres on our failure to extend our skill set into four key areas that are critically important to improving the quality of information-based decision-making. First, there is the skill required to work more holistically with qualitative and quantitative data in order to provide a rounded picture of the complexity of many of today's markets. Second, there are skills associated with knowing how to apply powerful business concepts and constructs in order to bring our consumer evidence alive. Third is the skill in knowing how to incorporate management hunch, intuition, flair and imagination into our data analysis. Fourth, there are the skills in knowing how to help decision-makers test

[a] CEO, DVL Smith Group and Professor, University of Hertfordshire Business School, UK.

Market Research Best Practice. Edited by P. Mouncey and F. Wimmer.
© 2007 John Wiley & Sons, Limited.

the safety of evidence-based decisions by applying various decision facilitation techniques. By extending market researchers' skills in these areas,
coupled with a greater focus on communicating with decision-makers in
an impactful way, we will dramatically improve the quality of the market
research offer to our clients. In order to make these ideas concrete, we
provide an illustrative case study example of these ideas in action. We
look at a project to assess a new high technology business communications device. We conclude the chapter by arguing that extending the
market research offer in this way is a 'win–win' for the market research
industry: we can continue to offer excellence in traditional market research but will be responding to the growing need to bridge the worlds
of data analysis and management intuition. In this way we can prevent
the industry from becoming a low cost commodity provider of data,
with other management service players picking up the responsibility for
explaining how our consumer data impacts on business decisions.

The calls for market research to be engaged more actively in helping
decision-makers make informed judgements has led to various research
agencies extending their traditional remit over the last decade or so to include various skills more traditionally associated with business and management consultancy. But an important point to make is that agencies
which have extended their traditional market research offer in this way
do not see themselves as 'top-down' management styled consultants ('we
have seen that problem before and would like to prescribe our solution to
your company'). Rather, they see themselves as essentially 'bottom-up'–
what we might call research information-based business consultants. Everything they do is founded on a detailed and research-led understanding
of what consumers in different markets are trying to tell us. The core of
their work remains knowing what is in the heads of consumers. This is
their power. But, in addition, they offer a broad set of strategic business
skills that allow critical customer-based insights to be used to maximum
advantage during the decision-making process.

SETTING THE VOICE OF THE CONSUMER IN THE DECISION-MAKING CONTEXT

Market research earned its spurs during the days when most businesses
were production, rather than consumer, led. In this era, individuals who
could be the 'voice of the customer' were seen as being of enormous
value. However, over the last few decades decision-makers – as their

own understanding of consumers has expanded – have raised the barrier in terms of their expectations of the feedback from market researchers. So today, market research that is presented exclusively, some would say naively, from solely the consumer perspective is often no longer tolerated. Decision-makers now want market researchers to explain exactly how the consumer perspective nestles within the complex business, technological and social context that underpins most commercial decision-making. They want to integrate the consumer fully into the commercial process. Today, it is much more important than in the past for market researchers to understand the business context for which they are providing the consumer perspective. Business success is primarily down to strategic excellence rather than tactical retrieval. Therefore, it is important for market researchers to understand leading edge thinking about what makes for success, and to recognize that latent consumer need is only part of the equation. For example, rather than simply jumping on the brand bandwagon and assuming that having one is all that is needed, researchers must be equipped to explain exactly why, and more importantly how, brand building should command its share of management time and investment. The brand's contribution as a corporate asset must be understood realistically, rather than assumed, if it is to be leveraged properly. And the wider commercial context that market researchers are expected to understand does not rest on having a good working knowledge of fundamental business concepts and a perspective on how leading edge strategic business thinking is evolving constantly. It also extends to understanding the technological context. Today, with the interconnectivity and convergence of so many different products, it is imperative for market researchers to have a full mastery of the technological environment, if they are properly to assess opportunities that might not fit with existing convention. We cannot rely on researched consumers, on their own, to be clear about what is happening around them. We have to be able to interpret their, by definition, naïve responses in an appropriate manner.

For today's market researchers to be taken seriously, they also need to have a perspective – a sound conceptual grasp – of how communications in our complex, chaotic, nonlinear and multimedia culture operate. They need to be at the forefront of challenging the received wisdom and leading the way in reconstructing their measurement systems to, for example, reflect the behaviour of decreasingly deferential and more streetwise, communications-aware consumers. Consumers today can read the writing on the wall – and elsewhere. Consumers now know how to pick up all the cues and clues about what brands represent. In short, it is a world that requires the researcher to take a properly holistic view of the different communication 'touch-points' that can impact on building brand reputations.

In sum, agencies that are extending their traditional offer to include more business consultancy skills are today attaching much more importance to understanding the wider context of the problem they are investigating. They know that 'context explains everything'. It is all about the 'panorama principle'. This tells us that, all other things being equal, in most investigations if there is a choice between going in for more detail or stepping back and understanding the big conceptual picture, then the latter, rather than the former, is likely to pay the greater dividends. It is the researchers' ability to see the 'wood for the trees', and to stand back and see the shapes and patterns at work that differentiate the consultancy-based agency from the more traditional data-centric market research supplier. The future is becoming less about drilling down into a more and more detailed understanding of the consumer evidence alone, and more about understanding the underlying structures that explain what is happening in society, technology and within organizations.

DEVELOPING A MORE HOLISTIC APPROACH TO MARKET RESEARCH ANALYSIS

The market research discipline grew out of classic social science methodologies. This set up the expectation that market research provides something close to 'scientifically objective' truth, whereas in reality what we do is no more than loosely follow some of these guiding principles to achieve what we might call a 'scientific approach' (this, by the way, is totally respectable). In short, the harsh reality is that, at best, market research is as much an art as it is a science. But everything is confused by the pressure we face as an industry, on the one hand, to deliver data that lives up to the quality 'gold' standard of 'correct' social science methodology, but, on the other hand, to respond to the realities and pressures of the modern business information world. This tension is seen in the frustration many market researchers experience in trying to make sense of the enormous breadth that is the reality of 21st century marketing data. With a few exceptions, the current market research literature looks rather tired and outdated because it does not look holistically at both the art *and* science of market research. One particular peculiarity of our technical literature is that it is devoted largely to the idea of analysing a *solitary* dataset, on the assumption that these data have been collected in a fairly orthodox way, thereby enabling the application of classic 'textbook' statistical tests. This rigid adherence to, now outdated, analytical concepts about the way we handle data is very frustrating for new look market research agencies genuinely keen to help business leaders make informed evidence-based decisions. They know, of course, that most decisions are based on multiple sources of data where the information rarely meets the requirements of orthodox methodology. The challenge, therefore, is to develop rigorous frameworks that allow us to understand information in a more holistic way. Here it is important to stress that the holistic approach does not mean that we have drifted into an 'anything goes' way of collecting and interpreting consumer data. The holistic researcher will follow a rigorous process akin to journeying along an 'information learning curve'. As they do so they will know that many of the data they are evaluating will be of questionable accuracy with no rigorous account of the method employed to assemble the data. None of this, though, disturbs today's experienced analysts. They are rapidly learning how to 'compensate' for these methodological inadequacies in their evidence. As they journey along the information learning curve they constantly evaluate each piece of evidence by referring to other prior knowledge. Critically, today's researchers do not suspend disbelief and assume or 'pretend' that the data have been collected using 'classic' methodologies. They are totally transparent with clients about the way they operate in today's imperfect information world. Specifically they are committed to developing holistic analysis frameworks that help them make sense of imperfect data and resolve the mismatch between the classic purist techniques still being used, and the messy evidence with which we typically have to work. (See Smith and Fletcher, 2004 for a comprehensive review of holistic analysis frameworks.)

CAPITALIZING ON THE GROWING INTERPRETIVE POWER OF MARKET RESEARCHERS

Today's breed of more business-consultancy-based market researchers are honest enough to state explicitly that 'not all respondents are created equal in their ability to contribute to the survey process'. They are transparent in arguing that it is legitimate, on occasions, to 'override' some of the consumer evidence by setting it in the context of everything else we know – the cumulative knowledge we have acquired over the years about the survey process. There is a growing confidence in taking into account the insights we now have about how attitudes are formed, and under what conditions they can be expected to fluctuate and change. In the early days of market research there was an inevitable tendency to be very nervous about overriding the literal feedback provided by consumers. Of course, the doyens of different forms of psychoanalytical-based qualitative research were always inviting us to look more deeply into exactly what people were saying. But much mainstream market research was conducted, and interpreted, largely on the premise that it was the market researcher's job to provide a straight reportage of the direct feedback being provided by consumers. But now, as our expertise of how people respond to surveys has grown, we are more confident in our ability to get underneath what our respondents are telling us. Therefore, it is important to pass our consumer data through various 'knowledge filters' (what we now know about the psychology of people's responses to surveys and how to interpret consumer feedback in this context). These are discussed in detail in Smith and Fletcher (2004), so here we simply make the point that new look market research agencies work in a transparent way with analytical holistic frameworks that openly juxtapose literal consumer feedback with what we know from years of experience about the robustness of the particular types of consumer feedback. This makes for more informed and less naïve market research. Business consultancy oriented agencies take the view that conceptual thinking – informed by the consumer evidence – is the most powerful way of solving problems. They know what key business concepts and principles will add most power to the consumer evidence. On occasions, this evaluation of the available concepts will place the consumer evidence centre stage in its more literal form. But in other situations such an evaluation may lead to a 'down weighting' of the consumer evidence, given what else we know about the issue under investigation.

HARNESSING THE POWER OF MANAGEMENT INTUITION

Seasoned market research veterans within our ranks will have been brought up in an era where market research represented 'detached objectivity'. As such, it was believed to be 'superior' to softer, more anecdotal and archetypal evidence. This reflects the way market research, as it sought to achieve credibility in the 1960s and 1970s, relegated management intuition and forced it to play second fiddle to the hard 'scientific' consumer data. But there has been an upsurge of interest in the 'scientific' basis for intuitive thought over the last decade or so. In fact, the topic of the power of intuitive thought has almost forced its way into the bestsellers' list. Goleman has sold millions of copies of his book *Emotional Intelligence*. And the idea of left (logical) and right (creative) brain thinking is now commonplace. Claxton's *Hare Brain, Tortoise Mind* is another popular text, as is Patricia Einstein's book on the wisdom of intuition, and Wiseman's *The Luck Factor*. On top of all this, we find a massive upsurge in what we might call the personal and business 'success' literature, much of which highlights the power of positive thinking and the value of marshalling positive energy to help deliver successful outcomes. Thus, we now know that 'informed' productive intuition can be cultivated; practice helps. We also know that there is scientific evidence that backs up the idea that our brains develop instincts during childhood that can serve us well in later life (this is about the laying down of 'somatic markers'). We also know that in certain situations – notably where there is ambiguity and uncertainty – the ability to think in a circular, unorthodox, nonlinear way about a problem can produce big breakthroughs. These days, we have also learnt to respect practical knowledge acquired by osmosis, and to be less 'sniffy' about individuals who can perform without being able to articulate the theoretical basis for what they are doing. So, in sum, we know that there is much to commend intuitive thought. It has many sound credentials and is no longer seen as some inconsequential irrelevance. It is now recognized formally as having the potential to make a substantial contribution in certain decision-making situations and, as such, needs to be managed accordingly. (See Smith, 2003, for a review of the role of intuition in decision-making.)

However, the attendant dangers of eschewing the hard data route and just going down the intuitive route are also now being recognized fully. We know that many decision-makers operate with rather flawed self-knowledge, often coupled with low levels of technical know-how. This means that when faced with uncertainty decision-makers have an instinctive predilection to fill this vacuum with what is simply erroneous or partial thinking. They will confidently present what they have concluded as 'powerful intuitive thought', whereas, in fact, it is often just plain wrong. Put another way, we know that decision-makers have a tendency to let lazy, partial and stereotypical thinking – based on false assumptions and sloppy technical knowledge – masquerade as true 'informed' intuition. So, the more business consultancy-oriented agency knows the importance of having rigorous checks and balances in place in order not to allow over zealous and erroneous 'intuition' to ride roughshod over the consumer evidence we have assembled painstakingly. The trick is to know when, like Henry Ford, to back your intuition ('If I had listened to my consumers, I would have invented a faster horse'), and when to be aware of the danger of not having proper checks and balances in place to curb any intuitive excesses. The following comment by Piers Brendan in his biography of Mussolini neatly illustrates the point. He writes of Mussolini: 'Anything that is not spontaneous intuition fails to attract and seduce him. In this way he creates around himself a dangerous atmosphere of messianic expectation, which he enjoys as a sign of blind faith in his ideas (Brendan, 2000).'

In summary, market researchers have recognized the need to adapt their approach to better reflect what we now know about the nature of intuitive creative thought and decide how best to factor this into the decision process. Specifically they have been active in finding checks and balances that allow us to combine flair and imagination with the hard consumer evidence. Here is not the place to detail the various frameworks that holistic researchers have developed to tackle the problem of pure consumer data being 'dumb', but management beliefs being 'blind'. But it can be confirmed that considerable effort is now going into developing analytical frameworks that embrace the power of management hunch, prior knowledge and intuition. It is no longer just dismissed as unfounded, risky or dangerous.

ADDING FLAIR AND IMAGINATION TO THE ANALYSIS PROCESS

Agencies, which are now placing an emphasis on acquiring more business consultancy skills, are becoming more confident than their predecessors in bringing flair, imagination and creativity into the data analysis process. Exactly what constitutes creativity in the market research context is a big topic; it is one that has been addressed elsewhere by the author (see Smith 2004). But the evidence suggests that market research agencies will benefit from including in the project team different types of creative individuals. We know, for example, there is creativity that is born out of the existence of a problem; necessity being the mother of invention (Barnes Wallace, inventor of the bouncing bomb, once said: 'There always has to be a problem first. I have never had a novel idea in my life.'). Then there is 'synthetic' creativity, using various, what we might call 'thinkertoys' in order to help individuals think outside the box (running brainstorming sessions using techniques to turn everything upside down and thereby generate a creative outcome). There is also creativity defined in terms of people's ability to see the emerging big picture that is just round the corner (for instance, Winston Churchill saw the likely emergence of the communist Iron Curtain). Then there is a form of creativity that is not just about having the analytical skills, but also the courage to push ahead with your observations and beliefs in the face of opposition from conventional thinking (Galileo and Darwin fall into this category of creativity). And then we have creativity as a form of charismatic entrepreneurial energy, the Stellios, Woodruffe and Branson types who have the drive to overcome practical obstacles being thrown in their way and power ideas through to a successful execution. And sitting in pride of place in the nobility of creativity is surely the ability to think clearly, deeply, intelligently, sensitively and perceptively about issues in order to generate a richer understanding about what is actually happening in our world.

Therefore we are beginning to find more market research agencies prepared to recruit into the analysis team brand development specialists who are able to add conceptual power to the evaluation of brands. Similarly, agencies are beginning to recruit communications specialists able to unravel the complexity of the way modern day marketing communications 'work'. The key is finding ways of retaining the rigour of orthodox data analysis, while still encouraging flair and imagination. It is about creating an environment within which both rigour and imagination are respected and can flourish.

BEING ENGAGED WITH, NOT DETACHED FROM, THE DECISION-MAKING PROCESS

We now know that many senior decision-makers, when listening to market research presentations, make their decisions in 'real time'. The notion of decision-takers sitting passively listening to market researchers present different 'building blocks' of desk, qualitative and quantitative evidence *before* thinking about what this means for them is increasingly misguided. The big decisions are being made as the presenter is speaking. Today decision-makers want presenters to start at the end by focusing on the overall implications of the evidence for the end decision. They want market researchers to be action oriented, to take risks, and to become involved and engaged in the decision. They do not want them to be detached from the data by drawing out arcane distinctions between the 'purist evidence' and the 'interpretation'. Many market researchers still tend to labour under the misapprehension that provided they have done an incredibly thorough job in collecting and analysing their data, then senior decision-makers will listen, and do justice, to their knowledge. Unfortunately, the world is not like this. Today, everyone has to fight when it comes to getting his or her message over. Thus, agencies seriously committed to putting market research in the vanguard of business decision-making are aware of the enormous power of 'corporate storytelling'. Stories are one way in which human beings make sense of the world; we are storytelling animals. Consultancy-based agencies have learnt that information presented as a story offers a number of important benefits. For instance, it is a delivery style that can help communicate the complex whole, and also one that aids comprehension. It enriches and involves and can be inspirational, while also providing an opportunity to entertain. It also enhances actionability and helps gain buy-in to the end decision. In short, consultancy style agencies know that a powerful way of presenting consumer survey evidence is to tell it as a narrative. We know that we are presenting data for an aggregate sample, but a simple technique that adds a bit of theatre and immediately brings presentations to life is to present data drawn from a total sample as if they form a story from a single customer.

And there is growing awareness of the value of market researchers developing various decision facilitation skills: helping decision-makers test the 'safety of the putative decisions'. First, there are the basic techniques: helping decision-makers think clearly, logically, deeply and dispassionately about the available evidence, and deciding whether the lessons about the flaws that we know characterize the way people go about applying information to decision-making have been applied. Are we deceiving ourselves about the apparent quality of a critical piece of consumer evidence? Are we trying too hard to believe something is true to validate our predetermined decision? Second, there are techniques we can apply to help decision-makers *stretch* their thinking. The goal here is to help decision-makers to think big and imaginatively: to assist them to reach out for more 'creative' interpretations of what the hard evidence might be telling us. For example, amongst various techniques we might use to get middle managers out of their tendency to default to a 'safety shot', rather than be more ambitious, would be to work through the consequences of what such a cautious approach to the market might mean in the longer term. The third set of techniques seeks to balance out the power of rigorous analysis and the potential of the imagination. Thus, the ultimate measure of the success of the holistic approach is its ability to stretch the decision-makers' imaginations and do justice to brilliant, intuitive thinking, whilst also ensuring that these creative insights are grounded in hard consumer evidence-based reality. This requires the application of various checks and balances. This could include, on the one hand, turning any extravagant, abstract, outrageous or woolly claims into concrete accounts of how this impacts on the key decision points. And, on the other hand, it could seek to lighten up certain data-literal decisions by getting the parties involved to go with the overall flow of the wider body of more intuitive-led 'evidence'.

We now illustrate the way in which market research agencies that have extended their offer to include various skills more traditionally associated with business consultancy might look at the introduction of a new communications device.

MAKING SENSE OF AN IMPERFECT WORLD TO DEVELOP THE 'PERFECT' BRAND: AN ILLUSTRATIVE CASE HISTORY

One of the leading new technology companies wanted help to explore the possibilities for capturing a slice of the burgeoning handheld multimedia messaging market. This is an exploding product territory that the company felt was rapidly in danger of becoming terminally hijacked by companies like Blackberry.

Following an intensive programme of product development, the company – who, for reasons of confidentiality, we must refer to as 'Newco' – had arrived at what it believed to be the perfect product to displace alternatives. The technology was working, the funding secured and the planning in process. All they needed was to perfect the brand, which they recognized they needed to build in order to realize the potential. Project 'Perfect' was born.

For a combination of reasons, Newco decided that it needed to launch 'Perfect' under a new and distinct identity. Although Newco's well-known, highly regarded and undeniably potent brand property was a head-brand option, it was felt that too overt an association could limit success. More importantly perhaps, and with an eye to the future, it was decided that the brand should lie within an entirely separate commercial operation.

Newco recognized at an early stage that, before any brand name, identity or communications strategy could be developed, a number of fundamental issues needed to be explored.

- Just how important is any eventual brand likely to be? To what extent will it lie behind customer decision-making and, therefore, what level of resource (in terms of time, effort and investment) should be allocated to its development?
- How should the brand be structured to most effectively create, capture and secure consumer demand?
- Where should Newco be looking for appropriate, and indeed competitive, brand attributes? What is currently driving brands in the sector and what could, with the appropriate application, come to drive the new brand's equity?
- Which elements of what we might call the 'touch-point' universe should Newco's marketing strategy be seeking to prioritize? How could Newco best take advantage of, and indeed orchestrate, the different messaging channels that collectively would produce the new brand's reputation and equity?

These questions presented Newco with a number of issues that precluded a 'traditional' market research solution.

- The market is still very new. It is not yet fully formed and the brand 'rules' are still being written. Any definition to emerge from an audit or examination of the opportunity defined by the extant competitive brand properties would be likely to be at best bland, and at worst, misleading.
- Relevant information was scarce and spread across a diverse range of sources. Whilst there was a substantial body of product research attesting to the technological leap that 'Perfect' represented, because of that – and the very newness of the sector – directly relevant data had to be teased from a variety of different places. This required not only a degree of 'detection skill' but also, and probably more importantly, a capacity to extrapolate meaning into a new space.
- Newco's management team possessed a considerable amount of accumulated knowledge and expertise. However, they did not have ready access to adequately focused consumer attitude and behaviour data and,

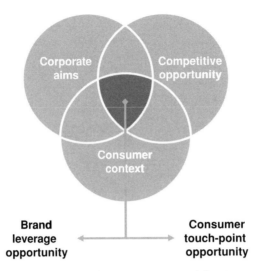

Figure 1.1 Overview of the learning programme created for Newco.

more importantly, data that were felt to be either sufficiently comprehensive or, given the rapid pace of market growth, suitably up to date.

Rather than take the more traditional approach and jump straight into blue-sky brand development – platform, name, identity and so forth – Newco decided that it was important to take time to explore these issues beforehand, and thereby create a more informed foundation for the branding process that was to follow.

Accordingly, we worked with them to create a learning programme that would make full use of existing knowledge. This was founded on objective consumer input and fully enrolled and involved the brand development team. This was a learning programme that, whilst founded on original consumer insight, would also draw in existing management expertise and create a framework to intuit answers to the questions that lay beyond the capabilities of immediately accessible consumer data.

It was an holistic learning programme that combined the needs of Newco's corporate aims with the competitive and consumer contexts, in order to first and foremost understand the potential for brand leverage and the application of the touch-points (Figure 1.1).

The learning programme was delivered through a five step process:

1. Desk research – a review of information residing in a variety of data sources, coupled with exploratory management and trade interviews.

2. Development team workshop – initiating the active involvement of
   the business development team in the learning process, thereby em-
   powering their contribution:
   – establishing working hypotheses and options for brand leverage;
   – defining the initial 'touch-point set'.
3. Dynamic consumer discovery groups:
   – simulating the market context;
   – exploring, testing and refining brand leverage options;
   – clarifying the touch-points;
   – identifying the core brand equity attribute options.
4. Quantitative research to validate the touch-point and competitive,
   equity opportunities.
5. Analysis and reporting.

In the course of the above programme, we tailored a number of different conceptual frameworks to help us evaluate the 'Perfect' brand in the
context of what, by definition, was a market whose structure was still to
be set properly. This allowed us to provide Newco with an objectively
reasoned and initially evidenced case for the new brand based on three
pillars. (Note: the following examples are for illustrative purposes only;
all data has been disguised to protect confidentiality.)

A structure for brand leverage

The first step of the learning programme was designed to develop a reasoned, and as far as possible, evidenced case for exactly how important the
brand was actually likely to be, i.e. the brand leverage. Then, building on
this, providing an explanation of the drivers that needed to be structured
for maximum impact.

In the course of the analysis, we identified that consumer choice of
'Perfect' would most probably be governed by six main drivers: quality,
visual impact, imagery, recommendation, price and familiarity. Allied
with that, we determined that the relative importance of those drivers
to the consumer universe as a whole was such that 'quality' accounted
for more than 30% of the influence, 'appearance' around 23%, 'image'
just under 20%, and so on (Figure 1.2). Finally, this phase of the analysis
established the extent to which each driver was likely to 'depend on
brand' which, in this instance, was expressed as a range from 'minimum
required' to 'maximum possible'.

Brand Leverage Structure

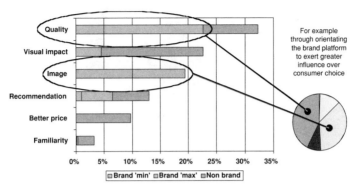

Figure 1.2   A structure of brand leverage.

With this knowledge we not only confirmed the potential importance of the required brand property to the eventual success of the business as a whole (and so helped rationalize the need for investment) but also, more importantly, established an initial foundation and framework for its brand platform.

A candidate for pool of equity attributes

Once the scale and location of brand reputation leverage had been established, the learning programme moved on to explore the equity attributes operating in the sector. These are the various components of brand reputations that are currently influencing consumer preference for one option over another. To do that, we identified, and then quantified, the contribution of the different elements making up the brand reputation universe that are most actively influencing choice of similar products (Figure 1.3). Those attributes, collectively defining the sector drivers, represented the starting point for planning the new brand's make up. They not only determined which attributes could be employed to greatest advantage (i.e. against a particular competitor) but also, and equally importantly, those that were 'free' (that is, not 'owned' by any competitor) and so arguably 'available'.

That insight, combined with the implications for branding that emerged from a parallel analysis of the corporate aims and intent created the basis for the definition of the brand platform.

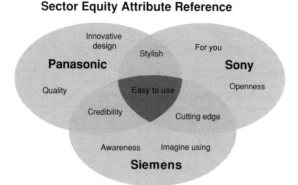

Figure 1.3 A candidate pool of equity attributes.

The touch–point opportunity map

There is an ever-widening appreciation that brand reputations are the result of every point of contact between the brand and the consumer, and therefore need to be managed in a correspondingly holistic sense if they are to be developed effectively and efficiently. This holistic approach takes in, for example, design, peer group 'comment', product performance ('satisfaction') and so on, as well as the more didactic traditional messaging channels such as above-the-line advertising. This understanding is leading brand managers to consider a far wider set of options than used to be the case. This is something that was judged to be particularly important for a high touch, high profile item such as 'Perfect'.

In view of that, the third component of the learning programme was designed to identify the touch-point opportunity map. This exposed the different points of contact exerting effect in the sector as well as quantifying their importance (in terms of contribution to consumer understanding) and their capacity to deliver relevant messages (Figure 1.4). Armed with this, Newco has been able to structure its brand communications plan in the most efficient and impactful manner. It has helped to decide more effectively which touch-points the company needed to concentrate its efforts on, as well as how to coordinate them for maximum impact.

In the course of this learning programme, Newco was provided with powerful guidance for both its forthcoming brand development and its initial communications strategy. Through joining reasoned and informed argument with market and consumer evidence it successfully completed what would otherwise have been a somewhat less than full picture.

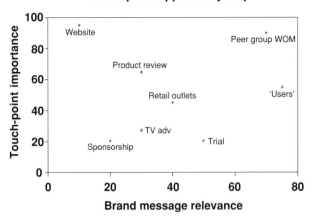

Figure 1.4 The touch-point opportunity map.

Moreover, it did that using a combination of analytical tools tailored to the specific circumstances – such as the Brand Leverage Matrix and Touch-Point Audit – and a framework to tap the intuition of those closest to the business, its owners and its managers.

THE VISION OF WHERE YOU WANT TO BE IS ANYONE'S GREATEST ASSET

The emergence of the new breed of business-consultancy-based market research agencies should be welcomed as a distinct 'win-win' for the market research industry. Unfortunately, however, this perception does not seem to be the general view within the market research industry, which harbours three central concerns about the development. First, there seems to be a concern that the arrival of market researchers who wish to be involved more actively in the decision process somehow implies that more orthodox data-centric market research is of less value. There is a feeling in some quarters that the holistic, more consultancy-styled approach compromises the 'science' of orthodox market research. So, will this threaten mainstream market research? We would say no. New look market research will not undercut the bedrock of the industry: the professional collection and analysis of market and consumer data remains at the heart of what we do. Second, the 'stretching' of a market researcher's data collection and analysis skills into the broader arena of business decision-making consultancy is seen by some as a 'bridge too far'. For some it is a development that represents the slippery slope into market research that places a 'dangerous' emphasis on flair, creativity and imagination, something with which they secretly feel deeply uncomfortable. The business consultancy approach is seen as being rather ephemeral and flaky – something that is seriously flawed with a lack of sound principles, grounded methodologies and solid reasoning. So, does the consultancy approach imply a lowering of methodological rigour? We would say no: it is simply replacing orthodox approaches with a more holistic approach that has its own rigour and set of inbuilt checks and balances. Third, there are concerns that the claims being made by the more business-focused agencies are not sustainable; how can we as an industry, provide the requisite bigger picture business skills? The task of recruiting talent that not only can analyse data, but can also help to demystify decisions, is seen as a Herculean challenge. And related to this is the issue of whether appropriate education and training programms can be developed to teach the skills needed for such an ambitious undertaking as extending the boundaries of traditional market research. Others simply seem to feel nervous about dabbling in complex and murky decision-making waters. Trying to establish exactly what is going on in the heads of senior decision-makers when they decide to do what they do is seen as someone else's bailiwick.

So, is the extended market research consultancy model sustainable? We say yes. As an industry we must recognize, and believe in, our strengths. If we continue to harbour self-deprecating fears about our capabilities, we will simply fall by the wayside and become commodity providers of low cost data. If market researchers are going to play a more prominent role in business decision-making, they must first believe that they have a contribution to make. Market researchers must believe in the powerful position they occupy within the management services arena. We are not seeking to replicate the excellent work already done by management consultants, who already have the powerful conceptual thinking toolkits needed to analyse business problems. The territory that new style market researchers seek to occupy still pivots around knowing what customer information *really* means. The focus remains on our in-depth understanding of consumer psychology. But this now needs to be set in the context of a greater appreciation of critical business concepts, and a greater confidence to engage creatively with decision-makers.

In summary, we are a superbly talented industry, but one that somehow wants to 'sabotage' our own efforts to integrate market research into the business decision-making process. This sabotage takes the form of a predilection to cling to a now outmoded notion of what market research is all about. Market research is no longer *just* about reporting what consumers say. Increasingly it is about helping clients demystify complex problems and make informed decisions. It is about combining our flair and imagination with our expertise in consumer market research. We are a fantastic industry, but one that is divided by a confused vision about what market research is now about. Therefore, we need to articulate clearly to senior business decision-takers what 'new', more consultancy-styled market research is now able to deliver. Perhaps ESOMAR should introduce a 'Charter' outlining the approach followed by today's more consultancy-oriented market researchers. Such a manifesto would demonstrate that today's 'new' market research is about the fusion of our traditional mastery of consumer data with imaginative multidisciplinary thinking that is focused firmly on helping clients achieve business success.

ACKNOWLEDGEMENT

The author would like to thank Simon Cole for his contribution to this chapter.

REFERENCES

Alexander, M. (2004), *As Above, So Below*. Proceedings of the Market Research Society Conference.

Amabile, T.M. (1996), *Creativity in Context*. Westview Press.

Arden, P. (2003), *It's not how good you are, it's how good you want to be*. Phaidon Press.

Baron, J. (1997), *Thinking and Deciding*. Cambridge University Press.

Bazerman, M. (2002), *Judgement in Managerial Decision Making* (Fifth edition). John Wiley, & Sons, Ltd.

Belbin, M.R. (2003), *Management Teams – Why they succeed or fail*. Butterworth Heinemann.

Brendan, P. (2000), *The Dark Valley: A Panorama of the 1930s*. Alfred A. Knopf.

Breuer, N.L. (1998), *The Power of Storytelling*. Workforce (December).

Buzan, T. (2001), *The Power of Creative Intelligence. 10 ways to tap into your creative genius*. Thorsons.

Claxton, G.L. (1997), *Hare Brain, Tortoise Mind: Why Intelligence Increases When You Think Less*. Fourth Estate.

DeBono, E. (2000), *New Thinking for the New Millennium*. Penguin Books.

Einstein, P. (1997), *Intuition, the path to inner wisdom: how to discover and use your greatest natural resource*. Vega.

Fletcher J. and Morgan, B. (2001), *Deeper into Brands*. Proceedings of the Market Research Society Conference.

Franzen, G. and Bouwman, M. (2001), *The Mental World of Brands*. WARC.

Goleman, D. (1997), *Emotional Intelligence: Why It Can Matter More Than IQ*. Bantam Books.

Harre, R. (1979), *Social Being*. Blackwell.

Harries, C. and Hardman, D. (2002), Decisions, Decisions. *The Psychologist*, 15(2), 65–67.

Harvard Business Review (1999), *Managing Uncertainty*. Harvard Business School Press.

Heath, R. (2001), *The Hidden Power of Advertising*. ADMAP Publications.

Hill, N. (1994), *Keys to Success*. Penguin Books.

Jackson, B. (2001), *Management Gurus and Management Fashions*. Routledge.

Johnson, S. (1998), *Who moved my cheese? An amazing way to deal with changing work and your life*. Random House.

Karlöf, B. (translated by Gilderson, A. J.) (1993), *Key Business Concepts: A Concise Guide*. Routledge.

Kaye, B. and Jacobson, B. (1999), True Tales and Tall Tales: The Power of Organisational Storytelling. *Training & Development* **53**(3), 45–50.

Kotler, P. and Trias de Bes, F. (2003), *Lateral Marketing: new techniques for finding breakthrough ideas*. John Wiley & Sons, Inc.

Leadbeater, C. (2002), *Up the Down Escalator*. Penguin Books.

Leonard, D. and Straus, S. (1999), Putting your Company's Whole Brain to Work in Harvard Business Review: *Breakthrough Thinking*. Harvard Business School Press.

Mahmoud, O. (2002), *The Operation Was Successful But The Patient Died: Why Research on Innovation is Successful Yet Innovations Fail*. Proceedings of the ESOMAR Congress.

Mainelli, M. and Harris, I. (2000), *Clean Business Cuisine: Now and Z/Yen*. Z/Yen Ltd.

McCoy, C.W. (2002), *Why didn't I think of that? Think the unthinkable and achieve creative greatness*. Prentice Hall.

Michalko, M. (1991), *Thinkertoys. A Handbook of Business Creativity*. TenSpeed Press.

Michaluk, G. (2002), *Riding the Storm: Strategic Planning in Turbulent Markets*. McGraw-Hill.

Nutt, P. (1997), Better Decision-Making: A Field Study. *Business Strategy Review*, **8**(4).

Ridderstrale, J. and Nordstorm, K. (2001) *Funky Business*. FT Prentice Hall.

Ridderstrale, J. and Nordstrom, K. (2004), *Karaoke Capitalism: Managing for Mankind*. FT Prentice Hall.

Sherrington, M. (2003), *Added Value: the alchemy of brand-led growth*. Palgrave Macmillan.

Smith, D.V.L (2003), *Factoring intuition into the analysis of market research evidence*. Proceedings of the ESOMAR Congress.

Smith, D.V.L. (2004), *What is creativity in market research?* Proceedings of Market Research Society BIG Conference 2004.

Smith, D.V.L and Dexter, A. (2001), *Whenever I Hear the Word Paradigm' I Reach for my Gun: How to Stop Talking and Start Walking*. Proceedings of the Market Research Society Conference.

Smith, D.V.L. and Fletcher, J.H. (2001), *Inside Information: Making Sense of Marketing Data*. John Wiley, & Sons, Ltd.

Smith, D.V.L and Fletcher, J.H. (2004), *The Art and Science of Interpreting Market Research Evidence*. John Wiley, & Sons, Ltd.

Stern, S. (2004), How to Make Creativity Contagious. *Management Today*, March, 52–57.

Sternberg, J.R. (Ed.) (2004), *The Handbook of Creativity*. Cambridge University Press.

Tourangeau, R., Rips, L.J. and Rasinski, K. (2000), *The Psychology of Survey Response*. Cambridge University Press.

Whitefield, P.R. (1975), *Creativity in Industry*. Penguin.

Wiseman, R. (2003), *The Luck Factor*. Century.

Chapter Two

The Heart Transplant: Making a Difference to Organizations by Putting the Consumer at the Heart of the Business

Kristin Hickey[a], Derek Leddie[b] and David Jenkinson[c]

We know that consumers are important to business success – most businesses struggle to get the consumer to the heart of their business. This chapter highlights the importance of this vision and identifies the key reasons why businesses continue to be product- or brand-focused, rather than truly consumer-centric.

INTRODUCTION

At best, most research organizations have become efficient at responding to qualitative and quantitative research briefs. The good ones have built relationships around a stream of project briefs, but this business model continues to under–deliver to the need of CEOs in marketing-driven organizations today – that is, '*How do I get the consumer at the heart of my*

[a]Value Architect, The Leading Edge.
[b]Chief Executive Officer, The Leading Edge.
[c]i-Nova Manager, Carlton United Beverages.

Market Research Best Practice. Edited by P. Mouncey and F. Wimmer.
© 2007 John Wiley & Sons, Limited.

business to drive a competitive advantage?' This is a very different mission and one that the market research industry is not currently geared for.

This chapter examines how the traditional role of consumer research within large organizations acts as a barrier to marketing innovation, passion and the financial momentum of its brand portfolio. Identification of these weaknesses has helped us to develop a new approach, which is currently being rolled out amongst our clients to replace a 'brand-centric' or 'marketing-centric' business heart with a truly 'consumer-centric' one. In order to achieve this, we have combined the rigour of quantitative market frameworks, robust financial value measures and forecasts, deep psychological understanding of individuals, 'tribes' and their situational values/motivations, and highly actionable innovation and brand planning tools. In addition, we have expanded the research role to help change organizational culture through bringing segments to life in a highly interactive, three dimensional way within the business.

Whilst this approach is neither quick nor easy, it can truly revolutionize the way marketing decisions are made within the organization. A live case study (Carlton United Beverages) will be used to illustrate the steps involved, as well as the enormous impact on the business strategy, structure and culture.

This chapter shares the passion of embarking on a challenging journey with clients in order to make a real and measurable difference to the way businesses view consumers and use consumer insights. We hope the audience will share this passion and walk away with a vision for a new research model that can replace a weakening marketing heart with a strong, healthy consumer-centric one.

THE HEART

The heartbeat had slowed to a dangerous level. The patient would inevitably die. Yet modern surgery now offers the opportunity for the inevitable to be reversed, promising the potential of renewed vitality and growth.

In our marketing environment today, the flailing heart – the damaged heart – is our preoccupation with brands; the new heart, the living, breathing consumer. Ironically, the former only exists in the minds and hearts of the latter, yet many businesses continue to be introverted in their perspective, driven by their branding or categories, rather than truly committing to understanding the world from a consumer perspective.

We know that consumers are important to business success, yet most businesses struggle to get the consumer truly to the heart of their business. This chapter highlights the importance of this epic vision and identifies the key reasons why businesses continue to be product-or brand-focused, rather than truly consumer-centric. We then present a new vision for re-search – one that redefines the traditional business model and research processes as impetus to monumental cultural revolution within an orga-nization. In doing so, we present a live case study and illustrate some of the tools, skills and processes that provide hope to those whose hearts may be failing.

THE NUMBER ONE NEED

Every year The Leading Edge interviews its clients – CEOs, Marketing Directors and Consumer Insight Directors – in an effort to keep abreast of market needs. Recent history reveals that clients in the Australian mar-ket have traditionally been technique focused – excited and passionate about buzz words such as semiotics, ethnography, hierarchical Bayes or web-based capabilities. It was, therefore, surprising to find that in the last two years, the number one need of senior management with respect to the market research industry has been, 'to get the consumer to the heart of our business'. Not only do managers see the benefits of this vi-sion as underpinning sustainable business growth, but they also agree that they are unlikely to gain any significant momentum through further con-sumer research. As one director comments, 'ideas are like a commodity, execution is a source of competitive advantage'.

Consumer-centricity, as we have coined it,[1] is not only seen as the Holy Grail because it is something new or different – in fact, quite the contrary is true, as building a business offer around the wants and needs of consumers is the fundamental premise on which the marketing discipline was built. Instead, consumer-centricity is seen as the Holy Grail because it remains so elusive. Few companies seem to have got it right, but there is common recognition amongst senior managers that, for those who are further down the track to achieving consumer-centricity, the competitive advantage is not only significant, but sustainable.

---

[1] Consumer-centricity is the development and implementation of a business model that ensures strategic planning processes are underpinned by strong consumer insight at all stages. The terms 'customer' and 'consumer' can be exchanged readily for applicability across both consumer and B2B markets.

There are three key reasons why managers see consumer-centricity as a source of sustainable competitive advantage. First, it allows an organization to get much closer to the consumer, thereby increasing the relevance of innovation, communications or other marketing. Second, it provides an element of consistent objectivity within a business. No longer are there push and pull effects between various departments based on opinions or differing priorities, as consumer insight and feedback provide incontestable direction. Third, consumer-centricity can be seen as a significant source of bargaining power with trade or retailers, particularly in situations where this bargaining power is being diminished through severe price competition or shelf space pressure.

In many ways, the market research industry is grateful that clients haven't quite managed to crack the 'Holy Grail' of consumer-centricity. While the need is heightened, businesses have already shown signs of increasing their expenditure on consumer insights, creating provisional buoyancy in the research industry. On closer review, this buoyancy should be a significant cause for concern for our industry, as it signals a significant increase in pressure on our industry to truly deliver to this principal need. Our industry holds itself up as expert in the field of consumer insights, yet, to date, we have failed to provide strong, compelling leadership for businesses searching for consumer-centricity. Our business models haven't adapted to facilitate the change required; our processes and products continue to change, but not at the rate expected by the marketing industry. More importantly, the competitive situation has changed – management consultants, marketing consultants, branding specialists and advertising agencies have begun encroaching on our space, fuelled by the unfulfilled needs of our clients and the relative sluggishness of our industry in taking responsibility for delivery to this need.

It is this realization that has prompted our interest in truly understanding what consumer-centricity looks like, and how our business model, processes and relationships must adapt to deliver to this contemporary business vision. Let us begin our investigation by further examining the nature of this 'Holy Grail' of modern business.

IN SEARCH OF THE HOLY GRAIL

If consumer-centricity truly is the Holy Grail, we need to know what it looks like. In simple terms, consumer-centricity is the term given to a business model that places the customer or consumer at the heart of strategic planning. For many organizations, this means a significant change in

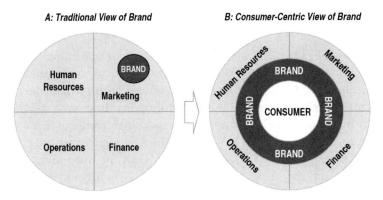

Figure 2.1 Consumer-centric business model.

the way the business thinks about the consumer and, consequently, the way it is structured, as illustrated in Figure 2.1.

In the first diagram, the functional structure underpins the way the business operates. Unfortunately, in this instance, the brand and its consumers are seen by employees as the domain of the marketing function, resulting in a strong silo effect and significant distance between the consumer and business decision-making.

The second diagram illustrates a different perspective – the structure within a consumer-centric organization, where the consumer is seen as the key to success and the brand represents any interaction the business has with its consumer. The advantages of this approach become clear when we reflect on the source of business revenue and profit. By placing the consumer at the heart of business planning, we are better equipped as a business to ensure that our products, our NPD pipeline, our brands and communication are all tapping into existing and emergent wants and needs. Whilst this sounds a very simplistic goal, it is one which not only translates into above-average market returns, but the internal culture and processes can often be harnessed as a sustainable source of competitive advantage over competitors.

In many ways, the second diagram represents the end goal in a consumer-centricity journey that is rarely simple, easy or fast, mainly because of the structural and cultural change required to support this new business model. During the course of this chapter, we will examine some of the key barriers to achieving consumer-centricity, then turn our attention to innovations in both research approaches and, more importantly, business models that facilitate this consumer-centricity revolution.

WHY SO ELUSIVE?

As we have already mentioned, most companies we encounter share this vision of being consume- or market-focused. At the same time, most, when questioned, don't hesitate to acknowledge that while they may have made some progress towards this vision, their business is still driven largely by financial goals, technological capabilities, competitor reactivity and historical category and brand focus. In Australia in particular, many FMCG businesses are additionally battling with the duopolistic retailer conditions and the subsequent diminishing bargaining power they face in the grocery world.

One of the biggest indicators of momentum towards this vision has been the restructuring of client – business models to reposition 'researchers' or 'research buyers' as consumer insight departments or planners. In many cases, this has been considerably more than simply a renaming exercise, with the insights division assuming new levels of responsibility and a different type of relationship with its internal customers. Whilst this transformation and commitment to change is apparent on the client side, it remains lacking on the supplier side, with few research businesses having adapted their business models accordingly.

Whether the transformation undertaken by clients has been negligible, or whether the parallel change in supply-side business models has been far too slow, one thing remains clear: despite murmurings of change within the marketing and research disciplines generally, business expectations of consumer-centricity continue to exceed actualization of this vision. We believe there are six key explanations or barriers in place reinforcing this elusiveness:

1. Lack of understanding of consumer-centricity.
2. Scope of change required.
3. Inability to 'visualize' the vision.
4. Absence of a clear critical path.
5. Lack of processes and personnel.
6. Absence of affordable business partners with relevant expertise and appropriate business models

Let us examine each of these barriers in turn.

Lack of understanding of consumer-centricity

In our interviews with CEOs and non-Marketing Directors, it became apparent that some senior managers did not truly understand the concept

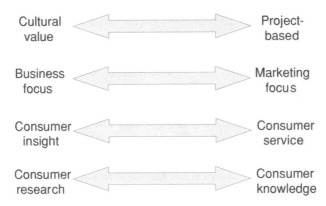

Figure 2.2   Disparity in understanding consumer-centricity.

of consumer-centricity, nor fully recognize its scope as a business vision. Four sources of disparity are illustrated in Figure 2.2.

The first source of disparity relates to whether the vision of consumer-centricity is embraced as a cultural goal or is seen as an independent project running in parallel with 'normal business activity'. Companies that recognized the vision as a significant transformation in both business model and culture were more likely to be further down the path towards a consumer-centric way of working than those who had delegated its responsibility to an individual person or department.

The second source of disparity lies in management's belief about where responsibility for consumer-centricity lies. Clearly, those who endorsed the task as being the responsibility of the marketing department alone were, ironically, propagating the structural handcuffs outlined earlier.

The third issue highlights a confusion between consumer-centricity and a business's efforts to provide reliable customer service (and the associated investment in continuous service improvement research). This view was very different from those CEOs who fundamentally believed not only in consumer insight, but also in consumer foresight. In the former case, managers believed that consumer-centricity was all about understanding service performance deficits and investing in continuous improvement of customer service. This 'deficits-approach' to business improvement is certainly commended, but it is very different from the proactive perspective adopted by endorsers of consumer insight. For these managers, consumer-centricity means beginning business planning processes with consumer truths and a robustly developed foresight about how consumer lives are changing and how this might affect consumer needs and behaviour designed to fulfil these needs. Clearly, the two perspectives are very different, not only in their start points, but in the magnitude of opportunity for big leaps forward versus small, incremental change. Whilst both are obviously necessary within any organization, the vision of consumer-centricity focuses on the more future-oriented perspective.

Finally, there is a marked difference between businesses that focus on the collection and warehousing of consumer research projects and those that invest in the continuous distillation and translation of those research debriefs into living and breathing consumer knowledge. In one instance, we were proudly informed of the 'vault' held in one organization – a filing system housing over $6million of ad hoc consumer research projects. Unfortunately, when questioned, we found that there was not a single reported insight or higher level learning that had made its way out of the vault and into the business for everyday focus, planning and deployment. In cases such as these, the difference between a focus on information *accumulation* and information *distillation* is an important step in truly understanding the principles of consumer-centricity (and ensuring the 'vault' of knowledge doesn't become an 'information prison').

Scope of change required

As a result of the divergence of perspectives and understanding of consumer-centricity, it is not surprising that managers have fundamentally different views on the scope of change required. Even for those who understand the bigger vision fully, most continue to fall into the trap of underestimating the time, the resource commitment and the difficulties of corporate change required to realize this vision. Often, we hear managers talk about investing heavily in consumer-centricity and being aware of the significance of change, yet few articulate this as a three- to five-year plan, which, in reality, it probably is. This underestimation is associated with high degrees of internal frustration, of under-resourcing and of insufficient change management planning designed to inform, engage and manage employees through this journey of change.

Inability to 'visualize' the vision

One of the key reasons for underestimating the scope of change required is that few managers have been able to articulate their vision to others fully. Certainly, it is easy enough to say, 'we want to have the customer at the heart of our business', but what does this mean in reality? What does it mean in terms of organizational structure, in terms of processes, in terms of research and development, or in terms of retailer relationships? What does it mean for individuals, for the way the business works and for long-term shareholder value?

Managers who are able to articulate their vision clearly in terms of long term organizational strategy, structure and relevant business division implications find themselves a step ahead in terms of making the vision work – simply because others are able to understand and, therefore share, the vision.

Absence of a critical path

Having a vision is one thing, having a clear plan of how to realize that vision is another. In our experience, clients who are able to develop a 'roadmap' or consumer-centricity blueprint, are generally in a much stronger position to ensure progress is made. Unfortunately, this doesn't happen very often in practice, lending itself to a climate of uncertainty and distinct lack of urgency in the business.

Lack of processes and personnel

In order to move from vision to reality, the business needs to ensure it has the right mix (and breadth) of personnel on board, supported by processes that reflect the consumer-centricity goal. Fast tracking towards change without these elements in place can lead to inconsistencies and a sense of desperation which transpires throughout the business. Unfortunately, a research or consulting partnership will generally be insufficient to drive the required change, as it means the passion, skills and intellectual property are not *owned* and, therefore embraced, by the business.

Lack of clearly positioned business partners

The traditional business partner for this type of journey is the management consultant. Unfortunately, as most of us are aware, employing top level consultants is often financially prohibitive and unlikely to be considered by businesses unless radical financial turnaround is required. Sadly, whilst many senior market researchers or strategic marketers have the ability to fulfil this need, few have cracked the processes or business model required to underpin this offer in its entirety. In view of this, we certainly hope this chapter sheds additional light and inspires the type of change required for our industry to compete effectively at this level.

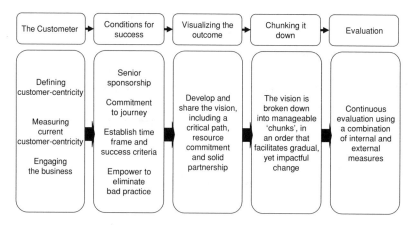

Figure 2.3   A systemic consumer-centricity revolution.

WHAT WE HAVE DONE TO OVERCOME THESE BARRIERS

Recognizing these barriers to consumer-centricity, The Leading Edge began to develop a process for a gradual, systemic consumer-centric revolution. The process has five key steps (Figure 2.3), which will be explained in further detail.

Step 1: The 'Custometer'

The first step is to evaluate the current consumer-centricity of the target business in order to size the task and tailor the process. We use a tested instrument for this purpose, called the 'Custometer'. The 'Custometer' represents a combination of (a) internal audit procedures, (b) staff feedback (either via stakeholder interviews or online questionnaire), (c) consumer feedback,[2] and (d) senior management perspective.

From these inputs, a consumer-centricity scorecard is developed and, in the case of Australian clients, this can be benchmarked against leading domestic and multinational businesses. Key components of the scorecard include:

- the degree to which consumer-centricity is endorsed as a company vision;
- the degree to which there is evidence of consumer-centricity in business, portfolio or brand strategy;

[2] If deemed applicable.

Custometer 2003: Company A Scorecard

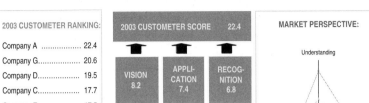

Figure 2.4   Example of Custometer scorecard.

- the degree to which consumer-centricity has recognized value within the current structure, culture, reward and recognition systems;
- an overall consumer-centricity rating along with key needs identified for the business.

An example of such a scorecard is shown in Figure 2.4.

Part of the reason for conducting this consumer-centricity audit upfront is to create a strong selling platform *within* the business. Explicitly mapping consumer-centricity scores and sizing the degree of change required virtually guarantees senior management support, particularly when expressed as a competitive deficit. Business engagement at this early stage is critical, and we encourage a full-day workshop with senior management to present the findings of the Custometer research, engage stakeholders in the need for a customer-centric journey and articulate clearly the benefits of undertaking this journey.

Step 2: Conditions for success

Once the business is committed to the consumer-centricity vision, we need to put measures in place that will overcome the six hurdles we identified earlier. The first of these is to ensure senior sponsorship – not just lip service, but true commitment, endorsement and responsibility for deploying the customer-centric vision. Ideally, this needs to come from the CEO or a divisional leader to truly make an impact on the business. This critical step will also make it easier to secure appropriate resources and empowerment along the way.

Having secured senior support (and budget commitment), it is important that all stakeholders acknowledge the length of the journey on which they are embarking. Getting support and commitment is one thing; expecting to retain it over a two- to three-year period is another. Ask stakeholders what they expect and be prepared to manage a change in these expectations as the business recognizes this is not a short-term turnaround project, but the beginning of a considerably more serious vision. If necessary, develop internal 'pledges' of commitment that recognize this, but be sure to revisit existing KPIs if the business expects a behavioural change.

Even once stakeholders recognize the scope of the journey they are about to embark on, it is still important for them to have accurate and realistic timeframes in place. If possible, translate this medium-term vision into three strategic horizons, as shown in Figure 2.5.

Horizon 1 will involve required infrastructure changes to facilitate the vision. These changes typically will create high degrees of internal change,

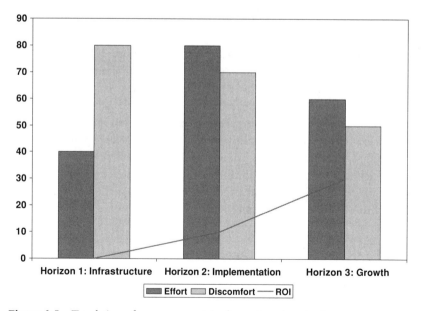

Figure 2.5　Translation of consumer-centric change into three horizons.

confusion and discomfort on the part of employees, but not necessarily effort, as most of this early responsibility will fall on the shoulders of the facilitating partner. In Horizon 2, change starts to kick in, with employees needing to embrace new processes, new ways of thinking, new tools and new perspectives of the market. Whilst still uncomfortable, this stage typically requires much greater effort on the part of employees relative to outside parties. By Horizon 3, one would hope that the business has settled into change and can begin to see the rewards of its efforts. Continued investment in understanding customers obviously continues, and the growth and development of employees finally begins to pay off with reduced levels of discomfort and the first strong signs of financial return.

Spelling out these three stages helps individuals to prepare for change whilst setting a clear and definitive perspective on how long this period of transition is likely to take. It is useful, at the same time, to begin thinking about success criteria – what would a successful result look like in the short (Horizon 1), medium (Horizon 2) and long term (Horizon 3)? What are the milestones the business should look forward to, so they can be celebrated collectively along the way? Remember, a journey without milestones is a tedious hike.

Finally, in terms of establishing optimal conditions for success, it is important to formalize authority and empowerment, as vision without empowerment will ultimately inhibit change. Ensure that someone is responsible for eliminating 'bad' practice within the business and that employees understand clearly the rationale for this empowerment and are truly prepared for behavioural change.

Step 3: Visualizing the outcome

At the beginning of the consumer-centricity journey, clients seem eager and ambitious. At the same time, few seem to have a tangible idea of 'what' they are building. The combination of a sense of major change and outcome uncertainty can lead to wheel spinning inside even the most organized business environment. Consequently, the task of visualizing the outcome is a critical one, synonymous with the development of an architectural blueprint prior to construction.

The following diagrams provide an example of what we mean by visualizing the outcome. On the one hand, we visualize what the ideal workflow would look like once the business has achieved its goal of consumer-centricity. Note, this is very different from visualizing the *journey* of transforming the organization to consumer-centricity

(Figure 2.6), as the latter really depends upon the outcomes of the initial Custometer results, organizational structure and support systems. This blueprint simply helps people understand the end goal and how this type of process is different and superior to what is already in place (which obviously needs further support than a single diagram). Having said that, this is NOT a blueprint for change, it should be noted that we have included, in italics, the various service offers The Leading Edge now provides to facilitate the building of this type of process outcome.

The second type of visualization is the ideal organizational structure and cultural requirements that will deliver this vision (Figure 2.7). This does not necessarily mean that this organizational structure is set in stone (or that it will even happen), but the documenting of proposed ideals helps the business to understand the rationale, the degree of change required as well as a summary of the cultural goals of a successful transition. Importantly, the structural vision also highlights the importance of the vision in terms of driving organizational change, rather than needing to work within the confines of the existing structure.

Step 4: Chunking it down

Having a vision and a blueprint is an excellent start, but we need to figure out where to start building! This step can often be the difference between success or failure. Some clients try to begin with a structural change, but often the right processes and people aren't in place to make this work effectively. Others choose to start with the 'tangibilization' stage – bringing the customers to life through theatre, video footage or immersion programmes – but often find that the business sees this as fun and interesting, but nothing really changes over time.

'Chunking it down' is the very technical term we give to breaking the blueprint down into a series of interrelated, systematic objectives. Moving from left to right through Figure 2.6, we can then see the steps as a manageable process and quickly develop an appropriate critical path or Gant chart. The order of these steps and the associated requirements are outlined in Table 2.1.

Step 5: Evaluation

Accompanying the journey must be a clear system of evaluation, so the key stakeholders, change managers and partners are truly accountable for customer-centric change. Evaluation systems need to be discussed and

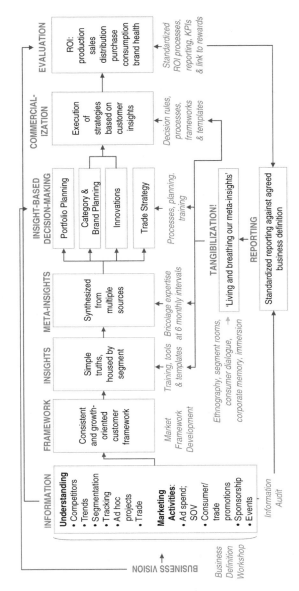

Figure 2.6 Visualization of consumer–centricity journey.

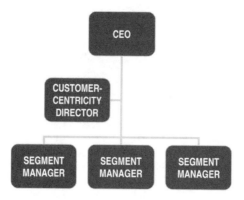

Culture of consumer passion across multi-functional business divisions!

Figure 2.7   Visualization of structural and cultural change required.

agreed to upfront, otherwise the business risks slow momentum in the early stages of transition.

Relevant KPIs need to be established, depending on what the business blueprint looks like, the agreed size of the challenge and the required steps involved. They may also need to take into account differing levels of influence to ensure those accountable are equally empowered to make change happen.

In all honesty, these five steps have been articulated only after each and every one of the preceding hurdles has tripped us up. Needless to say, there are likely to be many more hurdles to be encountered along the journey to consumer-centricity, given the importance of this need and the long-term nature of the transition required. The following case study provides a perspective on what the consumer-centricity journey, or the 'heart transplant', looks like in reality – a combination of rough roads, excitement, anticipation, disappointment and confusion, yet a journey that has inspired the development of this holistic approach to consumer-centricity and an increased confidence in our ability to deliver.

CASE STUDY – CUSTOMER-CENTRICITY REVOLUTION UNDERWAY AT CARLTON & UNITED BEVERAGES

Business situation

The business situation when we first embarked on consumer-centricity conversations with Carlton & United Beverages can best be described as

Table 2.1 Steps in the consumer-centricity journey.

Steps in order	Purpose	Involves
1. Business definition	To agree to a common perspective of what game the business competes in and what its long-term vision is.	Senior management workshop that documents business definition agreement and vision.
2. Information Audit	To review the existing information and insights to evaluate the utility of various information sources and optimize hard and soft information inputs for the business.	Review of information sources combined with stakeholder survey to evaluate investment vs usefulness to the business. Identification of gaps and development of information vision for immediate deployment.
3. Market framework development	To develop a shared view of the market, a common language and identification and prioritization of priority customer segments.	Development of a highly actionable and meaningful segmentation that predicts current and/or future behaviour and identifies clear business opportunities.
4. Insights training, tools and templates	To develop a process for ensuring that information is appropriately distilled and insights clearly separated from observations and hypotheses.	Development of specific templates, insights generation training, corporate memory (insights housing) and toolkit for input into planning processes.
5. Bricolage for meta-insights	To further distil a potentially growing number of insights down to their core essence, which we call 'meta-insights'.	Process of insight identification, mapping, questioning and finding deeper, more powerful insights through the combination of multiple sources.
6. Tangibiliza-tion	To bring customer meta-insights to life in an interactive and compelling way such that they become valued and treasured as a company asset.	Customer immersion programmes, segment rooms, visual boards, ethnography videos, consumer 'buddies', training in qualitative research techniques.
7. Insight-based decision making processes	To develop business planning processes that best leverage meta-insights in a proactive and consistent manner.	Combination of existing processes with best practice thinking around innovations, portfolio, category and brand planning for tailored and ownable processes and toolkits.
8. Commer-cialization	To develop 'go to market' frameworks and toolkits to ensure customer insights are not overlooked during stages of marketing plan implementation.	Development of commercialization toolkit including checks on opportunity sizing, understanding of customer and financial value impact.
9. Evaluation	To ensure that all marketing activities are objectively and robustly evaluated as input to future business decisions.	Development of internal systems for capturing and harnessing information; standardization of KPIs and objective procedures for their development (i.e. econometric modelling).
10. Reporting	To ensure that reporting throughout the business is based on a consistent framework with clearly understood and prioritized KPIs.	Development of appropriate KPIs, reporting system and multi-levelled scorecards for maximum flexibility.

'geared for change'. The virtual duopolistic structure of the Australian brewing market had shed all excess costs, streamlining manufacturing and distribution to a point where further cost savings were negligible. Despite such streamlining, neither player could realistically claim a significant nor sustainable cost advantage. Similarly, whilst equally competent, neither player could rely on technical expertise, on knowledge or human capital as a sustainable source of competitive advantage. In fact, the only source of sustainable advantage that the CEO could foresee was the development of a superior business perspective – a model, structure and associated processes that would deliver a unique and consumer-focused perspective to the business. The impetus for change was therefore strong – the seeds of which were planted firmly in the vision of the CEO, who briefed personally in this imposing challenge.

Crafted solution

We were briefed by John Murphy, the CEO, over two years ago. At the time, we developed what we believed was a comprehensive proposal, promising to deliver a market framework or consumer segmentation and to ensure full deployment of this segmentation solution through workshops, training, systems and processes. Specifically, the proposal included:

- A business immersion phase, including a series of senior stakeholder interviews to understand values, beliefs and visions held by individuals throughout the organization.
- An information review and audit phase which would help determine the usefulness of existing data sources in delivering to these needs.
- A qualitative research phase – expanding the lens of consideration to lifestyles, needs and recreational spend, rather than simply category-specific attitudes and beliefs.
- A diary analysis focused on understanding words, moods and time-specific occasions and behaviours.
- A robust quantitative research phase that covered the entire geography of Australia and the recreational behaviour and spend patterns of individuals over the last seven days.
- A series of workshops aimed at deployment initiatives within the business.

In addition to this proposal, as we embarked on the consumer-centricity journey (unidentified in those terms at the time), the scope of insight work expanded from a consumer segmentation to include:

- On- and off-premise behavioural understanding via:
  - ethnographic study;
  - in venue observation study;
  - customer (trade) interviews;
  - on-premise consumer interviews;
  - re-analysis of security camera footage inside venue.
- Category-specific segmentation solutions in the wine and spirits categories.

The combination of insights and learnings from these research endeavours have delivered some successes for the business, as well as some failures. The learnings from each are documented below.

Successes

When we initially embarked on this project with CUB, over 80% of all archived research projects were brand-focused. Brand building seemed to require further brand research and almost all business decisions seemed to be based around addressing existing brand weaknesses within the current portfolio. To say the business was brand-centric is surely an understatement – the company was so myopic in its brand focus that it seemed to be missing significant growth opportunities and often marketing a range of brands within its portfolio to the same consumer segment on virtually identical platforms.

Two years down the track, the new heart–that of the consumer–is beginning to kick in. Significant changes have been made to the business both in a physical sense and in the perspective it now adopts of the market. The following list illustrates some of the most significant changes that have contributed towards realizing the consumer-centricity vision:

- The business definition has changed from 'beer' to 'multibeverage'. In addition, the business recognized that its competitive set includes all forms of goods and services consumers purchase as part of their leisure consumption (i.e. discretionary income).
- An information audit has been conducted, the results of which have not only identified key deficit areas, but provided insight on how best to optimize return on information investment and management moving forward.
- A model explaining consumer behaviour has been built, providing a consistent understanding of consumer decision-making and highlighting opportunities for the business (Figure 2.8).

Figure 2.8   Example of explanatory consumer behaviour model.

- A consumer segmentation frame has been developed – a behavioural frame that stretches over the entire business, explaining fundamental differences in behaviour via a combination of highly actionable variables. This segmentation is sufficiently flexible that it allows the business to view the consumer segments and understand their key needs (a) across the business or (b) within category, brand or geographical region.

- This segmentation has been translated into a user-friendly Visual Basic-based Excel tool for easy navigation by internal users and partners. This segmentation tool allows users to access critical information and insights about consumer segments through a variety of 'sub-lenses' such as category, brand or geography. It helps highlight key segment needs which should become the basis of regular qualitative tracking to understand changes in these needs or the behaviours undertaken to fulfil them (Figure 2.9).

- A significant ethnography piece has been conducted and workshopped across the business to enable employees to become truly immersed in the lives of consumers within each segment. Myths and false beliefs have been partially dispelled using the combination of ethnography and consumer immersion programmes.

- A combined effect of the information audit and the segmentation study is the redesign of the business's primary category and brand tracking vehicle, which has now moved from a syndicated study to a single

Back To Main Menu	18-24 Year Olds	18-24yr Insights	Male Dashboard	Needs, Personality, Values	Beer	Research Design
			Female Dashboard	Occasions (On & Off Premise)	Spirits & RTDs	Personality Defn.
			Geographic Overview	Tastes & Alcohol Attitudes	Wine & Cider	

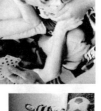

FOSTER'S GROUP
Inspiring Global Enjoyment

AUSTRALIA SNAPSHOT, 2004 – 18–24 YEAR OLDS

There are almost 1.8 million 18-24 year olds in Australia, 90% of whom are alcohol consumers. This group shares similar life challenges – in particular, the major challenge of transitioning from a child to an independent, self-sufficient adult. The adult world introduces a host of complexities, in particular, finding a home, a job and often making new friends. Whilst finding a job is important, work itself is considerably less important or valued than leisure activities. Of these, spending time with friends and love/sexual interests take priority and dominate leisure time. About one in four is a student and around the same proportion live at home with their parents. The general feel of this group, as a whole, is self-defining and optimistic.

18–24 year olds drink mainly on the (extended) weekends and often exhibit quite compensatory behaviour (either all or nothing). Drinking is about relaxing, socialising, celebrating or playing – it is about meeting people and having a good time – being part of something fun. 18–24 year olds are sophisticated in their social networks, being heavy users of mobile technology and text messaging. Their social groups are mixed gender, although males and females exhibit different consumption behaviour – males consuming beer and spirits primarily; females consuming RTDs, spirits or liqueurs. Males drink far more frequently than females (72% drink more than once a week vs 54% females) and are likely to be strong Endorsers of alcohol, while females can be Endorsers, or Passive Resistors. Income constraints dictate occasion-specific behaviour (i.e. drinking cheap alcohol before leaving home to go out), as well as venue and alcohol choice. For this reason, mainstream beers are popular. These consumers are even more price sensitive when challenged with spreading relatively small incomes across a broad range of leisure, fashion and other recreational choices.

Figure 2.9 Example of user-friendly delivery tools.

CUB CONSUMER DASHBOARD

The Leading Edge

	MALES 18-24	FEMALES 18-24	MALES 25-34	FEMALES 25-34	MALES 35-54	FEMALES 35-54	MALES 55+	FEMALES 55+
SEGMENT SIZE	6%	6%	10%	10%	19%	20%	14%	19%
TOTAL VOLUME	11%	5%	15%	8%	27%	14%	14% ↑	7% ↑
CUB SHARE[1] (RED) ex wine								
SEGMENT INSIGHTS (see attached)	· Peer inclusion · External focus · Journey of experiences · Binge & purge	· Peer inclusion · Self definition · Discovering · Passive resistance	· Hunter & protector · Male connectivity · Play escapes	· Assessing values · Return to family · Defining future	· Heightened responsibility · My castle, my world · Reassessment	· My nest, my world · Celebrate the everyday · Addressing fears	· My life, my time · Redefining masculinity · New responsibility	· Breaking the shackles · Explore and conquer · Self rediscovery
TOTAL DRINKS:								
Cider	1%	2%	1%	2%	2%	2%	1%	4%
Liqueur	10%		15%	9%	5%	5%	2%	4%
RTD	5%	41%	2%	20%	5%	19%	16%	45%
Spirits	83%	7%		6%		5%		5%
Wine		8%	76%	25%	85%	39%	77%	47%
Beer		41%		42%		32%		43%

Figure 2.10 Example of consumer-centric reporting dashboard.

source tracker, where measures can be integrated readily with ad hoc research as well as demographic and social trends.

- Subsegmentations have been conducted within each of the relevant drinks categories, allowing for greater detail in category marketing, yet sufficient synergies to facilitate a consistent total business view as per the consumer dashboard in Figure 2.10.

- For each category, a prioritization process and toolkit has been developed that provides a clear and objective means of identifying priority segments, understanding their needs and overlaying the core category 'pillars' or truths for additional insight. This process reveals rich insight about how the needs of the priority segments can best be met and evaluates the existing portfolio of brands in terms of their current and potential ability to deliver to these needs.

- A customer study has been conducted and a simple framework developed for linking the consumer and customer segmentations and key insights.

- The business has restructured from a functional to a category-based structure as an intermediary step towards a segment-based structure. Within this structural change, the consumer insights and innovation team (which has its own branding – i-Nova) has increased its size and status, representing a prime position on the Senior Leadership Team, reporting directly to the CEO and expanding by a headcount of six full-time employees in a contracting headcount business. This expansion in personnel has included the addition of one full time contractor to project manage change, two strategic planners, two innovations planners and one data analyst.

- An asset redesign – one of the existing meeting rooms is being converted into a 'segment room' to represent the life needs of one of our consumer segments. The renovations involved are extensive and include furniture, fittings, life-sized photos and images, music, clothing and décor to reflect this particular segment. Mini glass cubicles house real paraphernalia that reflect what the segment might have in their own homes, wallets or handbags, while journals and photo albums document 'typical' thoughts and issues this segment may be grappling with. Despite the clutter, the room remains highly functional for meetings or presentations – thus enabling continuous immersion for business planning to this segment. While this is still work in progress, the vision for the segment room is that it will be 'launched' by a representative from that segment (also one of our ethnography subjects) who will provide employees with a 'guided tour' of the room, sharing precious parts of their life, food, beverage and music tastes with the broader audience. We have found the philosophy of 'bringing the consumer *into* the business' far more successful with other clients than trying to engage employees to go out and interact with consumers in the outside world. Perhaps this is simply providing a safety net, but at least it has proven encouraging – particularly for corporate employees, who often live in suited castles protected from the real world.
- The most recent innovation is the expansion of our segmentation understanding to include an important third dimension of *occasion-specific needs*. Whilst the existing segmentation identifies key segment needs and how they are fulfilled currently, the purpose of this additional piece of work is to help develop a set of tools and processes for occasion-specific innovations and brand positioning opportunity. One innovative approach we have included is the development of category-specific visual themes to capture each of these occasion-specific needs. This is very different from the application of personality images or life needs seen previously by the industry, as the degree of time investment in development and validation of a set of category-specific needs for quantitative testing is truly innovative. An example of the needstates brought to life in visual themes, words, colour, music consumer quotations,

example occasions, animal and brand analogies currently being quantified via a robust online study (N = 2000), has already proven a valuable
investment for the business. Two examples are shown in Figure 2.11.

Learnings and implications for market research providers

In many ways we are still learning from this case study as we continue our
pursuit of consumer-centricity. In fact, the five steps outlined above have
only recently been developed in response to our learnings, as we began
the journey in a somewhat naïve way – particularly our underestimation
of the degree of structural and cultural change required truly to translate
a customer-centric vision into a reality. In many ways this should not
have been surprising, but at the time we truly believed that we could
help make this type of difference without systemic changes to our own
business model as a consumer insights specialist.

The key challenge a research partner faces in this endeavour is that,
whilst the skill sets required are not that different from those skill sets
associated with leading consultancies (professional facilitation, creativity,
research rigour, etc.), the business model to leverage these skills looks
remarkably different. The key differences and implications from a research
business perspective are outlined in Table 2.2.

To facilitate the effective integration and deployment of these new skills
and/or new applications of existing skills, we have employed a unique
structural design within our business. The key to this structural change
is the development of a specialist team of 'Value Architects' within the
business, who work towards building business value through the application of non-research skills to existing and new clients. Some of these
skills include communications strategy development, management consulting, brand and category planning and ideation. The key to the success
of this business unit has been a unique matrix structure where traditional
research consultants continue to 'own' the client relationship, freeing up
the Value Architects to work across clients on specialized projects such
as this one. By working with the research consultants, the Value Architect's time can be dedicated to the non-research demands, particularly in
the areas outlined above. At the same time, researchers are continuously
exposed to and gradually upskilled in these areas where applicable. Response to this initiative, both internally and externally, has been extremely
positive and profitable for the business and has allowed us to compete in
new territories that springboard off our core competency – consumer
insights.

Figure 2.11 Examples of tangibilization of insights.

Table 2.2 Implications for research business model.

Existing skills	Traditional business model	Customer-centric model	Future changes required to research business
Facilitation	Focus group moderation and client workshopping.	Translating a vision into a powerful impetus for business change.	Acquisition of change management skills.
Consumer segmentation	Statistical analysis to validate conceptual models developed in qualitative research.	Rigorous process to define actionable and meaningful solution that is congruent with stakeholder perspectives.	Internship periods required for consumer-centricity jobs.
Strategic thinking	Providing value to research results through on-the-job strategic thinking.	Translation of strategic thinking into tailor-made planning processes and tools.	Move from focus on thinking to application and deployment tools.
Creativity	Bringing consumer insights to life.	Translating consumer insights into business assets (i.e. segment room design).	Design relationships.
Training	Rarely used.	Required to upskill clients in application of tools or processes within their business.	Development of appropriate training manuals and toolkit.

Learnings and implications for clients

There have been numerous learnings from the client side as well – many that will ensure CUB's business not only embraces consumer-centricity, but understands and endorses fully the benefits and long-term implications. In many ways the changes already made within the CUB business show enormous courage and leadership, as they are clearly more significant and enduring than mere title changes or role modifications. The most significant changes are:

1. The change of organizational structure within the business away from brands to support a category-based portfolio strategy. Within the scope of this change, the role of insights and innovations has been elevated to hold a position on the senior leadership team, working closely with the CEO and senior business strategists. More importantly, the division itself has expanded through the investment in a full-time change management focus, employing analysts and strategic planners to ensure (a) internal competencies are developed and owned in this area,

and (b) consumer insights are integrated in the day-to-day planning activities of the category teams. Awareness of these changes has been heightened by the separate branding of the group (i-Nova) for application across different business units in an increasingly global and multibeverage group.

2. After almost two years, the focus on the consumer is finally permeating the business. One of the key changes supporting this initiative has been realigning decision-making power with the i-Nova group instead of with the brand or category managers. Effectively, this means that research is guided by the insights and innovations team, reducing investment 'wastage' and enforcing the need for clear insights where they may be lacking. This, combined with a new focus on consumer immersion at the beginning of brand or category projects, has heightened the importance of the consumer in the minds of the marketing and sales teams.

3. In line with the above changes, the business has undertaken the task of developing new intellectual property around insights-based planning processes. Whilst it may have been easier to tweak existing processes or look to other businesses to 'borrow' planning processes, the i-Nova group has embarked bravely on developing processes unique to its categories, brands and business situations. While the development of this toolkit is still very much work in progress, there has already been a significant shift in the way the group has been embraced by the brand and category teams.

It is still very much early days for CUB's journey to embrace the consumer-centricity vision. Further tools, reinforcement of insights-based decision-making and, importantly, financial returns and tools to measure them are still to be realized, yet the changes made by the business represent a notable step towards developing a way of working that is unique in its consumer and future focus.

CONCLUSION

Getting the customer to the heart of the business is the number one need of businesses today. Whilst consumer insights are still highly valued, there is a shared belief that further investment in research alone will not deliver to this need. Consequently, we must extend and expand our skills as researchers and adapt our business model truly to deliver to this vision.

This chapter has outlined our perspective on consumer-centricity, along with a structured approach to its delivery. Whilst the case study outlined is still very much a work in progress, it has been invaluable in helping us truly understand both the business impact of changing a brand-centric business into a consumer-centric one, and the necessary changes required in our own business model to facilitate this type of long-term cultural change. In this instance we have been fortunate to have had the opportunity to trial many of these skills and business model adaptations in strong partnership with Carlton & United Beverages, and look forward to further successes as their business slowly undergoes this significant transformation and the new heart kicks in.

Chapter Three

The Holistic Approach: Emphasizing the Importance of the Whole and the Interdependence of its Parts

Christine Blache[a] and Karen Hofman[b]

Corporate visionaries and qualitative research suppliers can obtain the best results from research by employing an holistic approach that brings key players into the discovery process. A checklist of actions indispensable to successful projects and innovation is proposed.

INTRODUCTION

As corporate visionaries work to get to know their consumer in a fast-changing environment wrought from global competition, where changes in the marketplace happen in the blink of an eye, they must break through the barriers raised by tight schedules, limited budgets and the resistance of soldiers of the status quo. What can be done? Strategic research managers turn to qualitative research as a source of innovation, but also in their quest for a new Grail in consumer research–getting quantitative results while using qualitative techniques.

[a] Consultant, PortiCo Research.
[b] Senior Research Analyst/Project Manager, PortiCo Research.

Market Research Best Practice. Edited by P. Mouncey and F. Wimmer.
© 2007 John Wiley & Sons, Limited.

But what kind of qualitative research can reap such results? Qualitative research that follows an holistic model – one which emphasizes the importance of the whole while simultaneously acknowledging the vital interdependence of its parts.

Through examples from our recent research, we will try to illustrate how companies and their research partners can obtain the best results by working openly and closely together. We will also explain how things can sometimes go wrong and what steps should be taken to avoid jeopardizing the success of a project in midstream. Finally, we will give our own definition of the Holistic Approach and propose a 'checklist' of actions we feel are indispensable to the conduct of successful research and innovation.

AN HOLISTIC APPROACH

When one considers the vast amount of money spent on research each year, and that the return on such investment may not always be up to par, it is no wonder smart research managers think that the time has come to start developing overarching research strategies, building from a solid yet nuanced understanding of the multifaceted consumer. How do we get this? Strong qualitative research done collaboratively.

As qualitative market research suppliers, we have found over the years that the projects which uncovered the most meaningful and actionable opportunities were built upon a broad-based multidimensional approach combined with a strong collaboration with the clients throughout the course of the entire research process. These were projects in which the client took an holistic approach internally, in their relationship with our market research team and in their approach to the design and evolution of the project.

The holistic approach has been, and is being, applied in many different industries; for example, the airline business. We all think we know what it takes for a plane trip to be completed successfully: we need adequate planning, coordination and communication from the beginning to the end. But now think about what else needs to go right in order for the plane ride to be a success. The things we don't normally concern ourselves with, but someone, say a pilot, would. We need to make sure that we have the proper plane size and power, that it will be able to fly safely, that the structure, the engine, the electronic gear and the landing equipment are all in good shape. During the flight we will have to stay in contact both with the ground and other aircraft in our airspace, as well as the people whose lives are in our hands in the cabin. All this until we have delivered our passengers safely to the gate. It is a strong relationship based on trust, during the entire process, with numerous teams, intermediaries and partners all operating behind the scenes.

With worldwide competition, tighter budgets and an educated and increasingly savvy consumer, the need for efficient results dictates that companies exert just as much dedication and care as an airline pilot would when bringing projects to life, to success.

CASE HISTORIES

PortiCo Research recently conducted two research projects for two different clients that, though on the surface similar, ended with radically different outcomes.

In the first case, while working on a project on innovation for the European branch of an international consumer goods company, we had a very active and strong collaboration with the client across all the different levels of the decision ladder from the onset of the research. As a result, the findings of the research easily climbed up the different levels of management, reaching the General Manager. At present, a new line of products is being developed by the company's R&D department.

In the second case, while working on a global project for a different international company, our teams were not united, and we have since learned that the research results are on a shelf somewhere, figuratively and maybe even literally. We are left trying to figure out if and how ties with the different actors on the project can be reconnected.

What happened?

The first project

How we got started

A little over a year ago, we were challenged by the new European Innovation Department of an international consumer goods company to conduct ethnographies to uncover opportunities for new product development.

While it is always great to be invited to play a role in the development of new products, at the same time we were concerned about the breadth of the study, and became even more so when we found out that the budget to accomplish this task was rather tight.

Our first meeting with the client was an extensive exchange around the idea of innovation – what it meant for them, why they were considering ethnography, what their ideas were in relation to reaching the consumers. What was their perception of their usual consumer? How did they perceive their brand at this moment in time? Where did they see their brand going in the near future? How innovative were they willing to be with their product? Could drastic changes be accepted in the renewal of certain lines of products? For our team, this kind of intellectual and emotional involvement is a key component of the early stages of research.

Regarding the scope of the project, we asked if we could narrow it down a bit, in order for us to have a greater focus. For example, we suggested we work around a specific age sample or household composition type, but the client asked that we keep the research as open as possible to gather as much information and insight as we could. They felt this was a rare opportunity to be out there with a blank canvas trying to uncover what could be the next innovative steps the company would take. Most of all they wanted to rid themselves of any preconceived ideas that might lead them in the wrong direction. We needed to deconstruct their initial vision in order to uncover new ideas. The challenge, however, was to come up with 'immediately actionable results'. They wanted the R&D department to start developing new products in the next few months. We agreed to this on two conditions:

- that the client be involved fully in and off the field from the very start of the research to the end;
- that the research be narrowed down halfway through the field work, based on our first findings.

They agreed.

What made things 'click' in the project?

Preparation phase

- The team that hired us was empowered to make decisions and carry them through. This gave them leverage and leeway in decision-making.
- Our team was involved very early on in the preparation. The clients expressed their needs, their expectations and their goals openly.
- 'Dreaming' was allowed. The clients started with very open minds and fought against preconceived ideas. They were ready to rid themselves of opinions that would prevent them from being receptive to new

findings. They brainstormed actively with us and pushed concepts hard during these discussions, constantly rethinking their product category on the whole.

- The clients provided us with a context: elements already in their possession, innovation benchmarks, trend watching, details of their recent successes and failures with innovation, etc.
- The clients also provided us with guidance on the company's culture, politics and general attitude towards qualitative research within the different departments of the company. They discussed what they had done before, what had worked or hadn't worked and why, where product development had to fit within their financial framework, what would go well within the company's culture and what wouldn't. They gave us examples of innovative developments that went as far as the prototype phase before they were considered too bold or too pricey. In other words, we had to come up with new, bold ideas, but they had to be grounded sufficiently if we were to be successful.
- In preparing the research, time was allowed for solid back and forth exchanges in defining the territory, the target, the scope and the type of subjects we wanted to explore, allowing for the elaboration of a solid and broad-reaching interview guide.
- The clients allowed for enough time. The emphasis was on getting it done right, not just quickly.

During research

- The project manager on the client side had several qualities that facilitated the in-field and analysis work:
  - he was internally respected and had leverage;
  - he was both attentive and open-minded;
  - he participated actively in exploring new angles and in challenging our findings to push the research further;
  - he engaged readily in our discussions about the most far-fetched ideas, leaving no stone unturned;
  - he was sufficiently knowledgeable on the company's brands and practices, allowing him to react immediately to ideas and findings;
  - He was present in the field and also made himself readily available during the analysis phase of our research.
- The complete management team on the client side agreed on several 'mid-term' brainstorm discussions to analyse the findings while still in the field. This allowed for:

- immediate feedback on the scope of the findings;
- the room to make adjustments;
- the opportunity to adjust the ongoing research based on initial insights;
- clear communication.

Disseminating the results

While our team was preparing the final deliverables, based on the topline analysis done by our ethnographers, the client organized an 'innovation workshop' that included both our team members and members of their R&D, marketing, communication, production and finance departments. This workshop was aimed at reviewing the results together, deciding which directions were the most interesting to take, brainstorming on the type of actions that could be taken from there, defining possible new lines of products and benchmarking these ideas against what was already developed in the company and what was available on the market. Our role was then to synthesize this workshop and prepare for a final presentation.

The clients' team had been involved in the entire process of the research, and so many people had been brought in at different levels that a formal presentation was almost unnecessary. The research material was already self-appropriated by the clients' team.

When the formal presentation took place, all the parameters, and most notably the political ones, were worked between the clients and us in order to facilitate the passage between 'research results' and 'product development' at a higher hierarchical level within the company. We actually co-presented the research as a team.

Conclusion

While still waiting for quantitative results on the consumer side regarding the new product development, the research was already considered successful by management within the company because of the success of the holistic team approach. This was accomplished thanks to the help of an open-minded management team which took a serious role both in guiding the research, involving its team and maintaining a proper balance between 'being generous and creative' and 'turning ideas into facts.' A paper was written internally by the project manager about the research and the paper was elected Notable Paper of the Month and distributed across all the departments of the company.

The second project

How we got started

The second project began as a global exploration of similarities and differences in consumer needs, values and practices around a broad theme central to this major international company's business. The division that commissioned this research was charged with bringing a new, globally-based way of thinking to the company's more traditional approach. As researchers, we were very excited to be contributing to the development of what promised to be a more holistic corporate vision.

We were brought into the project initially by a consulting agency that had an established relationship with the client. From the enthusiastic give-and-take of our initial meetings with the agency and the client, we anticipated a strong tripartite collaborative relationship that would stimulate thinking and be characterized by an openness to the reframing of preconceived (and perhaps culturally-biased) notions pertaining to the central theme.

Given this climate, we agreed to the open-ended subject of the research, anticipating increasing definition as the project developed. Faced with budget and time constraints, we worked with the client and consultant to build a research design that would allow the project to be completed in a specified timeframe, but that would require prompt client feedback along the way to keep the process moving smoothly.

Falling off track

With the approved design and objectives in hand, our two field teams set out to conduct fieldwork simultaneously in culturally disparate countries on two different continents.

Once in the field, the client and the consultant, overloaded with busy schedules, attended a limited number or none of the interviews. For similar reasons, no members of the client's in-country teams could attend the interviews. This situation gave us little opportunity to debrief with the client about our findings, either while in the field or thereafter. We were unable to fine-tune the focus of our research.

Trapped between the company's objective of being 'open and creative' in their thinking and strategic research, and the ensconced practice of demanding immediate development, the client's project managers were under a lot of pressure. This resulted in ambiguous communications and lack of client input. Situations arose where we were asked to provide findings that were neither incorporated in our agreed upon interview guide nor mentioned as mid-course adjustments while in the field.

While the project yielded rich results based on the stated objectives and the agreed-upon consumer targets, communication breakdowns and missteps in obtaining broad-based organizational buy-in compromised the acceptance of the research across organizational divisions.

Many of the problems we encountered seemed to stem from a sort of schizophrenia that arises in companies that want to change their approach in understanding and communicating with the consumer, but find themselves trapped in systems that pressure them for concrete and immediate quantitative results. Certainly not an holistic approach.

THE HOLISTIC APPROACH: STEPS AND ACTIONS FOR SUCCESSFUL PROJECTS WITH ACTIONABLE RESULTS

'Start your journey with a sense of destiny'
Gary Hamel in *Leading the Revolution*

The holistic model can be applied to many situations. One common application of holism is found in medicine, where one considers that traditional and unconventional methods can be used complementarily to help cure patients of what ails them.

Another use of holism has been applied to agriculture by Allan Savory. His 'Holistic Management' was designed to help farmers in Africa create a model of farming that takes into account economics, ecology and social responsibility.

Specializing in ethnography, we find this last example about agriculture particularly interesting. Having to deal with the complexity and desires of consumers who are more and more eager to lead meaningful lives and to express themselves through their choices, we feel it is essential to find a level of collaboration with clients that will be rich and deep, both on the organizational level and on the intellectual level. In the process, we must take into account economics, ecology and social responsibility.

Actions to take on the client side

In the quest for the Grail—the challenge of getting quantitative results using qualitative techniques—we have found that the most successful companies in reaching their goals are those who combine vision and passion with collaborative work and result-oriented actions.

How can top management involvement be essential in developing an overarching marketing research strategy?

On an emotional, social and political level

- Reinforce or reinvigorate the values of your company and brands. There is a strong emerging desire for meaningful and soulful products, brands and actions.
- Find a TRUE equation between what you say and what you do. This goes for:
  - your brand;
  - your products;
  - the way you run your company or division.

  For example, changing your strategy by launching a 'health food' line probably requires revisiting the way you buy resources, transform them and distribute them.
- Take into account that you are dealing with an educated and responsible consumer whose expectations are getting higher every day. This complexity has to be taken seriously, and the emergence of anti-marketers, anti 'ready-made' speeches, must encourage the development of over-arching politically and socially coherent strategies from companies and brands. Company policies both within and outside the organization may be deciding factors in consumer choice.
- Remember also that you are facing a global reorganization of both economic standards (some traditionally mature markets see their buying power decrease and need to make smart choices, while emerging economic giants create new opportunities) and family standards (the explosion of the 19th century family unit model in favour of a less formal, community-oriented model that's reshaping everything from habitat to education).
- Word travels fast:
  - you must be the one to promote the right idea;
  - the slightest mistake regarding ethics can immediately catch up with you;
  - you must design a highly collaborative organization that will both promote your messages and prevent crises.
- 'Share your dreams'. Elaborate a vision and share this vision with others in a clear and inspired way – be passionate and infect others with

your ideas in such a way that they will be excited about their work. Such excitement infuses your brands with energy, which then gets communicated to the consumer.

- Most of all keep an open mind at all times. The market researcher is often coming to the table with a fresh perspective that facilitates their seeing what is often overlooked by clients who have been conditioned by past findings. With a fresh perspective, market researchers can uncover the magic that will make consumers connect with a product more deeply.

From an organizational point of view

- Articulate your vision so that at least the strong lines (both in terms of directions and expected results) are clear to everyone.
- Communicate the message to the appropriately empowered management.
- Develop an overarching research strategy for the short, middle and long term. Use well-designed, broad-based ethnographic research to gain a firm grasp of your consumer market and provide a roadmap for future quantitative research.
- Make sure you will be able to provide the energy and investment that will match the scope of your vision (is everybody on the same agenda?).
- Estimate the scope and breadth of your project and select the appropriate methodology: you may not want to use a bazooka to kill a fly. In an overarching theme approach, you may want to set a solid base by using qualitative research methodologies that can capture important and often unanticipated or nuanced findings around the complexity of consumer motivations.
- Once in the field, allow for the development of as many angles as possible.
- Never lose sight of your long-term strategy and keep on communicating it during the entire length of the project.
- Validate the different steps on a regular basis–missing a step could mean additional time and stress.
- Allow sufficient timing for communications and synthesis of data throughout the process. Listen to the market researcher's ideal timing (it is not in our interest to have a project drag on longer than necessary, and we have experience in knowing what timeframes are most comfortable for progress).

- From global to local: INVOLVE YOUR TEAMS! They know a lot of things you don't and they will be extremely valuable both in contextualizing and relaying your ideas within vastly different cultural frameworks.
- Make sure that, within the company, all departments work on the same 'metrics'. If they don't, adjust the communication system among the departments to ensure a better flow of data and action.
- If you are going to use intermediaries for qualitative research, make sure you are in touch with all partners at regular intervals. Qualitative research is deep and thorough, and you don't want to miss out on the precious data as it is being extracted and analysed. Let it resonate regularly against the strategy you defined.
- Understand the benefits and limitations of using an intermediary consultant to coordinate research efforts (use is more common with international and/or strategic projects).
  - *Benefits*: larger projects need either a consultant or an empowered project manager to oversee all the efforts produced by all teams. Being at the same time aware of all steps of the research while being able to distance oneself, a good consultant can bring depth, vision and velocity to a project. A good consultant can unlock doors and keep the level of watchfulness and inspiration very high.
  - *Limitations*: Consultants will sometimes try to water down or soften the blow of bad news (e.g. on one project we were asked to do a video that softened the harsh findings, only to be later asked by the client to make it more biting so that upper management would truly understand the scope of the problem). Other times they might try to force findings into predetermined schema that do not necessarily reflect the organic structure and inter-linkages of the actual findings (e.g. on two international projects, we literally spent days trying to make our findings fit into the consultants' grids), which leads to inflexibility in the communication of findings.
- Use market researchers as sounding boards in helping to refine your research strategy. Their understanding of the complexity of the consumer experience can offer insights that help you build richer, more grounded and holistic research strategies. For example, a major American retailer for whom we had previously completed two successful projects approached us about conducting strategic research with its commercial customers. We developed a research proposal suggesting avenues of exploration that stimulated our client's thinking. The company came back to us with a far more elaborate research objective,

to which we proposed several ideal methodologies. After a few more rounds of discussion and rethinking, we persuaded our client to examine the constellation of relationships linking commercial and consumer customers. Ultimately, this proved key in getting at the heart of their research question.

Actions to take on the market research side

In this context, research companies' most significant role is to take the client a step further in sustaining a very high level of expectation and excellence, helping open as many doors as possible for innovative ideas and uncovering the conscience of the brand.

Be holistic on emotional, social and political levels

- Research companies need to be inspirational. The research company's role is to help the client be generous with its brand. There is a conscience beneath each brand that needs to be developed and revealed to the consumer. In a complex world with educated consumers, having the conscience of a company behind a brand is a major asset. The research company is there to provide the tools that will bridge the gap between the company's and its consumers' expectations.
- Research companies cannot be shy. They must keep their clients in tune with the deep shifts taking place in society and strongly voice the ideas emerging from the field.
- Research companies need to be bold and daring. Observation is not enough. It is the responsibility of research companies to offer new angles and be bold about it. They must be prepared to read between the lines of what consumers say, to get at underlying values, motivations and needs.
- Research companies need to be true partners. Ideas will remain mere ideas if they are not channelled through collaborative exchanges and expressed in actionable terms.

Be holistic in an organizational way

- Find your champion within the company. You will not obtain and sustain a strong relationship with the client without someone who can establish trust and quality exchanges.

- Privilege both analytical thinking and dreaming from day one until the very last day of the project.
- Keep angles wide open at all times.
- Process the results in a direction that is desirable, focused, validated, flexible and actionable.
- Encourage the client's project manager to teach you about the company's policies, politics and strategies.
- Encourage the client's project manager to be the promoter of your ideas.
- If you work through an intermediary, look for proper collaborative management that will help you reach the best win/win/win (client/intermediary/marketing company) situation.
  - Explain very early on the absolute necessity of having access to strategic information about the company's vision and goals. Insist on being briefed on the baseline understanding of the consumer, so that you can add to the client's knowledge base.
  - Install a communication network that will help you to communicate and discuss your findings and analysis during the entire duration of the project–involved intermediaries can become advocates of the findings.
- If it is known in advance that client feedback may be difficult/not always immediate, allow extra communication time in the schedule to avoid frustration/miscommunications on both sides.
- Be realistic about timing and methodology. Be wary of ambiguity and over-compromising in the interest of building a relationship.

CONCLUSION

Organizations today are ever more aware of the need to be generous, expressive and innovative – and the need to stay dynamic in a rapidly changing world. But to do so, they must harness their resources both internally and externally to unleash their creativity and gain momentum. Taking an holistic approach with their teams, their market researchers and their research strategies is the key to ensuring productive results that move from consumer insight to viable new products, brand positioning and marketing strategy.

Chapter Four

Integrating Decision-making and Marketing Intelligence: The Roadmap to the Boardroom

Selim Oktar[a] and Emre Erdoğan[b]

The industry has to be ready to respond to the increasing demands of customers by revising, reversing its business processes and exploiting technological opportunities. This chapter proposes a methodology to prepare the industry for the next phase.

INTRODUCTION

The marketing research industry is facing several challenges stemming from a changing business climate and the emergence of new actors. Unless a paradigmatic shift occurs, marketing research information is just one of numerous information sources facing today's decision-makers every day. Hints of such a paradigmatic shift are visible. Tomorrow's company will be customer-centric and armed with knowledge-management tools. The industry has to be ready to respond to the increasing demands of customers not only by revising, but also reversing, its business processes and

[a] President, KNEXTEP and board member, STRATEJI/GFK.
[b] Founder, Infakto RW.

Market Research Best Practice. Edited by P. Mouncey and F. Wimmer.
© 2007 John Wiley & Sons, Limited.

exploiting technological opportunities. This chapter proposes a methodology to prepare the industry for the next phase.

CHALLENGES TO CONVENTIONAL MARKETING RESEARCH

The marketing research industry experienced modest but healthy growth rates during the last half decade with average growth rates above 5% (ESOMAR, 2005). This does, however, mask serious criticisms, both from professionals and customers. In his seminal article, Gibson (2000) states:

> *'So, comic strips show marketing research as laughable, business authors find it irrelevant, academia separates itself, and even we researchers know something is wrong. Isn't it time we stop kidding ourselves with superficial talk about communications?'* (p. 3)

According to Gibson, marketing research fails to satisfy its potential users because it limits itself to describing the past, and does not try to estimate the future. Even the American Marketing Association declared a divorce between marketing research and scientific methods, by defining this service through these words:

> *'[Marketing research is] systematic gathering, recording, and analyzing of data about problems relating to the marketing of goods and services'* (p. 4).

This clear limitation of the industry, where *'data are already in existence, waiting to be collected'* avoids the scientific emphasis which was envisioned by practitioners, and general acceptance of this definition has created significant consequences. First of all, it impeded recruitment of new talents (p. 5). Marketing research education became limited to data gathering and analysing, rather than developing new models or theories (ibid.); new graduates emphasized implementation of sophisticated statistical models, rather than questioning their findings (p. 6), and all of these resulted in one of the most significant developments: marketing research's findings failed to predict the market, and credibility of the industry continuously declined over time.

Gibson argues that a redefinition of the industry by AMA in 1991 to include an emphasis on 'scientific methods', might be a fresh start for practitioners. However, according to Gibson, this redefinition has not been echoed in managerial rhetoric, and the industry is still identified with 'gathering, recording, and analyzing of data' (p. 7). Finally, Gibson says that in order to change the course of the industry, we have to change the definition, then the education and training of new talents (ibid.).

Marketing research professionals and intelligentsia are also aware of this crisis in the industry, and potential remedies are being discussed by them. In a recent issue of Shea and LeBourveau (2000), several professionals from marketing research companies and customers discussed the main hurdles they faced. According to them, hurdles may be grouped under three main headings: societal hurdles, business processes and organizational hurdles. Societal hurdles are listed as social and demographic changes which result in fragmented markets that squeeze marketing researchers:

> '*As researchers we are trying, but nobody has big enough budgets, no one has the background or mentality. We know this is a big business, but as a group, marketing researchers just don't have the tools and know-how to adequately address this.*' (p. 5)

The second societal hurdle is argued to be 'nonlinearity of the environment'. As a result of rapid technological change, customer profiles change rapidly and existing tools are not sufficient to understand and explain these new profiles. Moreover, according to the discussants, most marketing research professionals are far from being adapted to a changing paradigm (ibid.).

Business process hurdles are clearly visible in the demands of customers. First of all, the marketing research industry does not satisfy the demands of customers to reach 'every time to everything'. Second, the compressed time expectations of customers are not corresponded to by marketing research companies. Third, a changing dynamic environment requires dynamic decision-making models which are not included in the knowledge base of the industry (p. 8).

Organizational hurdles are the results of those listed above. The function of marketing research became limited to one of numerous information suppliers who were not included in decision-making processes (p.10). Second, the marketing research industry failed to recruit new talents, as Gibson argued above; human resources in the industry remained limited compared to rising competition from consultancy and IT firms (p. 11). Third, an increased number of data sources meant that marketing research firms failed to ensure a certain level of data quality.

In their seminal article, Monster and Pettit (2002) discuss threats and opportunities for our industry. According to them, globalization of the business and rapid technological innovations created significant pressures upon the industry, stemming from rising expectations of customers. Increased penetration of the Internet made global products available worldwide through online businesses. Consequently, globalization of the client sector created a demand for global marketing research data. Meanwhile, as a result of increasing and diversifying demands of customers of the marketing research industry, several competitors, including CRM providers and consulting integrators, business intelligence and OLAP tools, etc., emerged. According to Monster and Pettit, in order to struggle with these challenges, technological innovation is a necessity:

> '*As consolidation and globalization continue for both client and supplier, it will be imperative to have software capable of performing across the enterprise*' (p. 21)

Neal (2002) also discusses the existing situation of the industry and presents reasons behind this crisis. According to him, the problems of the marketing research industry are firstly dependent on underfunding of research activity (p. 2); secondly, the exclusion of market researchers from planning and decision-making processes (p. 3); thirdly the dissatisfaction of customers, who demand quick acquisition of results (ibid.); and forthly, the declining quality of research projects as a result of a human resources problem in the industry (p. 4) and alienation of employees from the scientific characteristic.

All of the above-named authors and marketing research professionals are aware of the crisis, independent of the diversity of their attributed reasons. Similarly, the solutions offered to the crisis are innumerable. Some authors propose to redefine marketing research activity, while some others argue for the use of technology and redefinition of our processes. Moreover, another common denominator for the intelligentsia of the market research industry is labelling the problems of the industry as symptomatic, rather than systematic. What is the difference?

Merriam-Webster defines symptomatic '*as being a symptom of a disease*', and a symptom as '*something that indicates the presence of bodily disorder*'. It means that the above-discussed problems are related to a 'disorder' of functioning of the industry, and that when this disorder is treated, these symptoms will disappear. How to treat, is a problem of business medicine, and when these measures are taken, there is no another obstacle to recovery. Epistemological problems of this 'symptomatic' approach are discussed broadly by French philosopher Foucault and followers.

On the other hand, systematic means *'relating to or consisting of a system'*, and a system is described as *'a regularly interacting or interdependent group of items forming a unified whole'*. The main difference between 'systematic' and 'symptomatic' approaches is that while a 'symptomatic' approach envisions an existing equilibrium point to which the body will return after recovery, a systematic approach explains the situation as a result of 'regular' interactions of members of the universe. It also considers an equilibrium point; however, a system may be in equilibrium at more than one point, and the two equilibrium points may differ in many characteristics.

From a systematic point of view, the current crisis in the industry will not be remedied by trying to recover our previous position. Our attempts to recover our previous situation will affect the environment, and other actors in the game will behave differently to their previous actions, since they have experienced a 'crisis' within the industry. As Heraclites says, *'you can't swim in the same water twice'*.

As market research professionals, we have to discuss what the system is, how it functions and what changed to push us to think about our sector. Then, after such systematic analysis, we can talk about the course of the industry and measures to be taken in order to make it stronger in the forthcoming new equilibrium.

In the following part of this chapter, a short discussion of the systematic evolution of the knowledge space in which we and our customers operate will take place.

THE KNOWLEDGE SPIRAL

As market research professionals we are living in the knowledge space. First of all, what we are producing – information about the customer, employee, market, etc. – is critical to the decision-making function of our customers. Even in the minimalist definition of our industry – 'acquiring marketing data and transforming it' – marketing research is an important component of the knowledge base of the company (Frishammar, 2002: p. 146). So, if we understand how the knowledge space operates, we can discuss our position in this space.

Figure 4.1 presents the theoretical evolution of the knowledge space in a limited time period. The y-axis of the graph represents the amount of data; it may be measured in terrabytes of data, numbers of pages or volumes of documents. The x-axis represents time. The dotted line is the demand function of decision-makers; in other words, the quantity

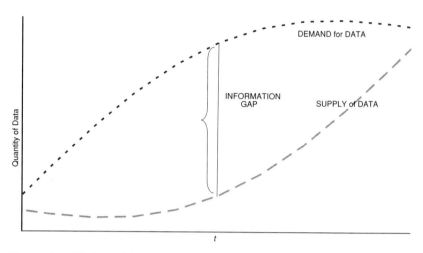

Figure 4.1   The knowledge space.

of data needed by decision-makers – or knowledge workers – to make decisions and to run their companies. The dashed line shows us the supply of data by different agents. These agents may be market researchers like us, internal suppliers of financial or operational data or other tangible or intangible data.

As the figure shows, we expect the demand curve of decision-makers to be a logarithmic shape, meaning that as time goes on, the decision-makers' marginal need for data decreases, and in the long run it becomes equal to zero. At the beginning, the decision-maker needs a huge amount of data in order to understand, control and manipulate the course of the company. While the engineer-manager F.W. Taylor needed a lot of data from production and compilation times of parts, time spent to package them, wages of workers, etc., all of these data are now in common use in almost every kind of managerial information system. If a radical shift in the knowledge production function of managers does not occur, the marginal contribution of additional available data will be insignificant.

On the contrary, the supply function will be exponential. Meaning that as time goes on, the amount of data available for decision-makers will increase exponentially, as a result of a very similar assumption: supply follows demand as a result of the invisible hand to satisfy excess demand. The shape of the function is not linear because when a supplier responds to excess demand, others will follow it. Since the good is information, mainstreaming will be quicker; other players would follow the leader much easier as a result of lacking or lower entry barriers. Consequently,

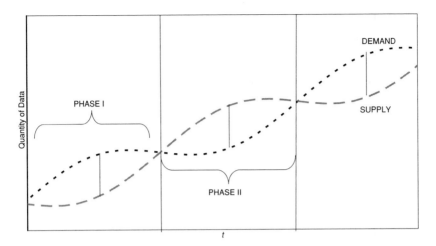

Figure 4.2   The knowledge spiral.

as time goes on, both the number of suppliers and the quantity of data supplied will increase and reach the equilibrium point, when supply equals demand. The area labelled 'information gap' in the figure describes times of crisis, when there is excess supply or demand of data.

When the above framework is applied to the historical evolution of decision-making processes, the graph is as shown in Figure 4.2.

The figure presents a dialectical relationship between demand for and supply of data over time. In the initial phase, the demand curve is logarithmic, and in the succeeding phases it takes a sinusoidal form with a positive slope. Similarly, the initially exponential supply curve also becomes a sinusoidal shape over time. This transformation of shapes is dependent on the evolution of management knowledge and information processing functions over time.

Phase I of Figure 4.2 is characterized by the development of modern/scientific management by F.W. Taylor. Taylor, an engineer and manager, published his experience in management under the title *Principle of Scientific Management* (1909). He described the main objectives of his approach as being the development of a scientific approach to production processes and allocation of sources, the division of labour between workers and managers and the motivation of workers through material benefits. This newly born professional manager had to collect a significant amount of data in order to control and manipulate his company – the individual performances of workers on the production line being the simplest among them. In the initial phase, the demand for data was limited to simple tangible information, such as accounting and production data. The evolution of Fordist mass production and the corresponding mass consumption led to the emergence of modern marketing. Increased production capacity, improved transportation facilities and intensified competition as a result of increased supply of similar goods from different producers pushed companies to develop marketing skills. The development of mass media in particular created a significant opportunity space for advertising and marketing campaigns (Witzel, 2000: p.7).

The first phase of the knowledge spiral continued until the late 1960s. The peak point in the information gap between demand and supply was the 1930s, in which the majority of reputable advertising agencies and marketing research companies were established. The legendary IT company, IBM had been founded in 1914, to produce 'business machines' to overcome the calculation complexities of new data. It was the first signal of exponential growth in the data supply. Enduring economic prosperity created a significant opportunity space for suppliers: the yearly average growth of personal income was 3% between 1950 and 1975; labour productivity and foreign trade doubled during this period (Glyn *et al.*, 1986).

Such a suitable environment resulted in huge increases in the supply of data. First of all, the number of data sources increased: financial, accounting and operational data were no longer the only sources. Marketing and product managers had to consider sales data, marketing research information and sectoral trends; the human resources department had to care about employees' performances and their satisfaction; high level managers had to have some idea about the overall course of their industries, macroeconomic developments and competitors' positions. Moreover, thanks to technological developments, and especially to the Moorian growth of processors, the information production capacity of data suppliers increased day by day (Wiig, 1997: p. 5).

However, this rapid increase in the supply of data was not matched by increased demand. Following the adoption of Max Weber's bureaucratic theory and the development of a basic human resources approach, this period was characterized by the settlement of the existing management paradigm. According to Clarke and Clegg (1998), until the 1970s there was no sign of a paradigm shift in management (p.17). Today, we are experiencing the second information crisis of the century, in which data supply significantly surpasses demand. The main characteristics of this crisis will be discussed next.

THE CRISIS OF TODAY AND THE MARKETING RESEARCH INDUSTRY

So far we have argued that today's crisis is one of oversupply. We experienced an equilibrium point in which demand for data equalled supply and a honeymoon period when large information technology conglomerates had substantial profits during the late 1970s and 1980s. Now, decision-makers are facing a significant information overflow.

In 2000, it was estimated that corporate data was growing between 75% and 150% per year, a pace that has probably not diminished since. The Gartner Group projects that by 2004, businesses will be managing 30 times more data than in 1999. In an almost startling finding, the School of Information Management and Systems at the University of California, Berkeley has determined that more information will be generated over the next three years than was created in the previous 300 000 years. Another Gartner Group study, released last year, found that the average company utilizes just 7% of the information stored in data warehouses (Microstrategy, 2002).

Of course this oversupply of data leads decision-makers to be much more conservative. Today's management theory literature is full of 'how to use data collected' or 'how to invest in IT smartly' articles (Balasubramanian *et al.*, 1999).

The most significant development which will affect demand for data and increase the productivity of the information collected is the evolution of knowledge management, which is defined as 'systematic management of knowledge', or as 'organizational capability that allows people to create, capture, share and leverage their collective knowledge to improve performance' (ibid.). The main objective of this discipline is to maximize the enterprise's knowledge-related effectiveness and returns from its knowledge assets and to renew constantly (Wiig, 1997: p.2).

The major problem for theoreticians of the discipline is integrating the huge amount of data accumulating in a company's knowledge base and developing new techniques to improve the efficiency of data collection and information production processes. Following Romer's contribution to the economic theory of growth, which argued that the emerging economy is based on ideas more than objects, and that there is 'enormous scope for discovering new ideas' is critical (Read, 1999: p. 5). Investment in making people knowledgeable in order to bring innovation has become crucial for enterprises (Wiig, 1997: p.5). The transformation of tacit knowledge in to explicit knowledge, and the process of accumulating it as part of the knowledge capital of the firm, is discussed and described in the earlier works of Nonaka (1997: p. 2).

The current crisis in the marketing research industry is highly dependent on the current situation of the information gap. Nevertheless, as shown in Figure 4.1, this gap will not be everlasting. Dynamic factors will push decision-makers to use and control the dataflow effectively. The first of these dynamic factors is the above-mentioned knowledge management concept. With the exploration of new ways of transforming information into knowledge, demand for data will be increased within a short time period.

Secondly, it seems that a paradigm shift in management science is occurring. According to Clarke and Clegg, new areas of intellectual inquiry became visible after the 1980s. These inquiries focused on organizational learning, flexible organizations, open communication, network organization, social responsibility, a stakeholder approach, etc. (Clarke and Clegg, 1998: pp. 50–56). Despite a multiplicity of reasons for this change, the consensual view of the management intelligentsia is that tomorrow's company will be very different than today's. It is a clear indicator of an incoming paradigm shift.

Thirdly, the rapid development of technological opportunities – in terms of CPUs, storage capacities, networking and the rise of the Internet – will also help managers to develop much more efficient information production methods. Firms are aware of these opportunities and the computer market grows continuously. Clarke and Clegg have stated that the average yearly investment of US firms in computers increased by 30–40% during the last two decades (ibid.: p.161).

When all of these factors are taken into consideration – intellectual investment in knowledge management, a changing managerial paradigm and use of enhanced technological capacities – it has to be expected that exponential growth of demand for data will take place within less than two decades. Of course, the winners of tomorrow will be the investors of today.

The specific situation of the marketing research industry is closely related to how it is attributed by decision-makers. Frishammar states that marketing research is only one of several sources of information for decision-makers, and its scope is limited to 'a mean by which the firm generates, transmits, and interprets information from the environment about or relating to the success of the firm's marketing plans' (Frishammar, 2002: p.148). One of the classical textbooks on marketing research defines the marketing research process as beginning with agreeing on the research process, which comprises a shared understanding between the manager and the researcher of the problems or opportunities to be studied, decision alternatives to be evaluated and users of the research results (ibid.). Such a definition limits the researcher to being a subcontractor and assumes that customers have perfect information and skills to delegate the research. It means a clear exclusion of professional researchers from the boardroom.

In order to satisfy the potential demand for data, the marketing research industry needs not only to revise its definition, but also its processes and its objectives. Especially since the new management paradigm creates a significant opportunity space for market researchers.

THE CUSTOMER CENTRIC ORGANIZATION AND A NEW ROLE FOR THE INDUSTRY

The New paradigm of management is characterized by its customer-centric approach. After a half-century long period of prosperity characterized by the rapid growth of industrial and service sectors and the decline of agriculture, enduring economic stability with an average annual growth rate of 4%, growth of real wages and productivity, the world economy experienced a series of crises (Glyn *et al.*, 1986: p. 9).

An important characteristic of the period was cited as follows: '*a fundamentally new development of the post-war period was that the massive growth in production was counterbalanced by an equal growth of consumption . . . .*' (p. 10). The capitalist mode of production was enforced by Fordism and Taylorism, and a corresponding mode of regulation. The economic climate was suitable for further growth as a result of the abundance of capital for investment and growing markets stemming from the increased purchasing power of workers (Lipietz *et al.*, 1995). Lower levels of inflation and increased world trade were enforcing an enduring economic prosperity (Glyn *et al.*, 1986: p.16).

Following the first and second oil crises, the world economy faced a serious crisis. During the 1970s, productivity decreased, profits declined and the inflation rates of advanced countries almost doubled. Mergers of international companies took place and competition intensified. Coupled with declining real wages, increased unemployment rates directly affected demand (ibid.: p. 42, 46, 50, 58). It was the end of the Golden Age.

The above-mentioned signal of a paradigm shift owes its existance to this crisis in Fordism. From a managerial perspective, the major implication of the crisis was the scarcity of customers. As a result of declining relative real wages, the average purchasing power of consumers declined over time. In the previous era, production increases as a result of increased productivity were matched by equivalent demand increases. Today, such an abundance of demand is not available. Intensified competition, the supply of similar goods from different companies and the selective attitude of customers have created significant pressure on companies that want to survive. The first fact pushing these firms to care about customers is simply stated as: 'cost of attracting a new consumer is 7 times higher than keeping an old one'. Retention and loyalty have become two important concepts, and a new approach has been developed under the name of relationship management. Relationship management focuses on increasing customer retention, establishing continuous customer contact, a high emphasis on customer service and a high level of commitment to meeting customer expectations (Baker and Cooper, 2002: p.15).

Such a paradigmatic shift has created significant emphasis on 'customer relationship management' (CRM). Boxwell (2000) outlines a common definition of CRM as follows:

> *'CRM will be taken to mean those processes involved in the identification of profitable customers and/or customer groups and the cultivation of relationship with these customers. The aim of such processes is to build customer loyalty, raise retention rates and therefore increase profitability.'* (p. 6)

Although CRM is a vision of management, it is often used as a kind of technological investment. Schultz categorizes approaches to CRM under two different headings. The first is the North American, version, which emphasizes the technology area, especially data management (Schultz, 2002: p.1). The second is labelled the Nordic Approach, and focuses much more on aligning the organization's resources in such a way that ongoing relationships are formed and maintained. Thus, the primary focus is on building customer loyalty and retention (ibid).

However, despite institutional attempts to underline the visionary role of the CRM approach, technology has continued to dominate the discipline. According to the Aberdeen Group, the total CRM market is expected to be increased to 24 bn USD in 2003 from 5.5 bn USD in 1998. The Gartner Group states that 28% of total costs are allocated to software investments, 23% to hardware purchases and 11% to telecom expenses. Only 38% of the total investment is allocated to 'services', which includes all kinds of services.

Table 4.1   Business decision matrix.

	Financial	Operational	Customer/ Intangible
Future (vision)			
Today (strategies /tactics)	**INTERNAL SYSTEMS**	**CRM**	**MR**
Past (performance)			

On the other hand, such investments do not add significant value for investor companies. As Brooke and Suntook (2002) state, '55–75% of CRM projects fall well short of their objectives, and unsuccessful CRM projects will increase to 80% by mid-2003' (p.60). The reasons for this failure are numerous and are discussed regularly.

The main point here is that the dynamics which allowed the CRM market to experience such growth also created a significant opportunity space for the research industry. First of all, the industry's more than 100 years of experience gave it an intangible knowledge about the customers. Though companies of today are trying to shift their orientation from transactional to customer-centric, the majority of marketing research questions are already focused on the customer. Consequently, the research industry may shift its focus to customer research, which has much more external linkages than marketing research.

In order to understand what an opportunity space has been provided to the industry, we have to make a short description of the decision-making processes of a company (Table 4.1).

The management of a company may take decisions related to the past, today and tomorrow. Decisions related to the past are limited to some performance indicators. Today's decisions are more focused on strategies and tactics, while tomorrow's decisions are about the vision of the company.

The data sources of a company may be threefold. The first is financial/accounting data flowing from sales and cost figures. The second is operational data, which includes delivery times, etc. Lastly, customer and intangible data are collected by customers through internal methods or marketing research.

When we place existing knowledge solutions in this matrix we observe that financial and operational data are collected and analysed by using internal systems, such as SAP. Information about customers is collected through CRM systems, but it is limited to past, and perhaps present, transactions of the customer. It does nor collect any information about potential customers, nor does it give any idea about the future behaviour of customers. A significant advantage of CRM systems is that they are easily integrated with legacy systems. Operational and financial data are almost already integrated through legacy systems. Advances in reporting software, such as BusinessObjects, ProClarity and Crystal Reports, allow integrated reporting of information collected by these different channels.

The role of conventional marketing research is limited to collection of information about customers and other intangible sources. Compared with CRM, marketing research has numerous advantages: first of all, while information gathered about customers through CRM systems is limited to transactions, marketing research brings significant information about values, attitudes and behaviours of both existing and potential customers. CRM systems also fail to give information about potential customers and competition. Secondly, estimation of future behaviour of customers by using only transaction data is not easy to implement, and even increasingly sophisticated statistical techniques have failed to develop comprehensive models. Thirdly, transactions on which CRM systems are based are highly dependent on the occurrence frequency of transactions, which may be affected by other factors.

These failures of CRM systems and the competitive advantage of the marketing research industry are well known and have been discussed in detail. The most important point here is that opportunities created for the industry by the customer-centric revolution are not limited to playing a bridging role between the market and the CRM systems. The emergence of the customer centric organization that is not only focusing on, but also existing to satisfy, customers' needs, creates a new type of consultancy for marketing research experts experienced with regard to the eye of the customer.

Challenges against such a shift in the role of market researchers are numerous. First of all, as argued above, market research data is not easy to integrate with other information sources, both internal and external ones. Secondly, the changing economic environment pushes decision-makers to speed up interpretation of information and transform it into action plans rapidly. The conventional business processes of the industry limit opportunities to respond to these demands. Thirdly, as argued above, information collected by the research industry is used generally to support marketing decisions. Consequently, the industry has to revise, and even change, its business processes to overcome these challenges.

REVERSING RESEARCH PROCESSES

The majority of problems with which the industry is faced stem from existing business processes. Conventional marketing research processes for a marketing research firm are described in Figure 4.3.

The diagram shows that the process starts with agreement on a research process, followed by establishing research objectives. The research project is then designed, data are collected, analysed and reported to the customer with strategic recommendations. According to the diagram, the role attributed to the marketing research company ends after reporting. The company does not show any interest in how the results are used by the customer, which kind of data (operational/financial, etc.) are used with the marketing research data, or which internal reports are produced by the customer by using these data. In short, the marketing research company has a limited idea about how data/information provided to the customer are transformed into knowledge. Furthermore, since the process starts with 'agreement on the research process', just after the customer decides to launch a research project, the marketing research agency has no idea about how this information will be used in the decision-making process. It signals a clear exclusion of marketing research firms from the decision-making.

This exclusion is a result of the Fordist-type production of marketing research information. In the previous phase, our information sources were limited. Production capacity (for example, computing capacity) was also restricted. Finally, our distribution channels were limited to only hard-copy reports. Moreover, our data collection and reporting processes were classical Fordist-type stock and queue processes, which resulted in considerable delays. Today, in the second phase of the knowledge spiral, our resources, production capacity and channels are no longer limited. Thanks to advanced segmentation techniques, it is not difficult to conduct surveys targeting the slightest segments. The technological revolution and commercialization of huge computers has allowed us to make sophisticated analyses. And, as a result of enlarged WWW technology, online reporting tools spreading out and presenting our results to our customers online is no longer a dream.

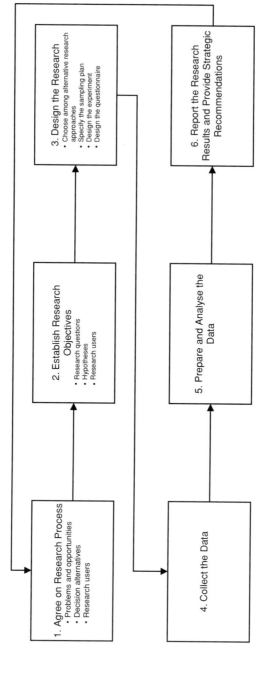

Figure 4.3 Conventional marketing research processes.

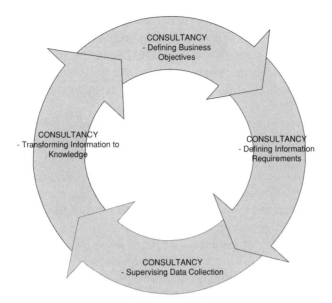

Figure 4.4 New processes.

Nevertheless, these technological avenues don't propose a new and different role for professional marketing researchers. As long as the above-stated processes are kept, technological innovations only speed up our job, they don't satisfy the expectations of customers. When the current challenges to the industry and the possible expansion of demand for data are considered, keeping existing business processes and trying to improve them will only satisfy today's expectations, and will fall short of tomorrow's. As members of the marketing research industry, we have to reverse our processes to be competitive in tomorrow's information market (Figure 4.4).

When reversing our processes, we should keep in mind that these new processes have to satisfy certain requirements. First of all, they have to make marketing research data easily integrable with other information sources to create a seamless flow of our business from data collection to reporting and thus eliminate stock and queue delays. Moreover, our new processes have to satisfy possible demand expansion which will create an extra load. The outputs of these processes have to be integrated with knowledge accumulation and create a basis for the knowledge capital of the firm. Lastly, these processes have to create another role for marketing research professionals, especially in the decision-making process.

Our proposed research process starts with analysing and understanding business objectives. These objectives may be generalized – such as increasing market share of the company, becoming the market leader, etc. – at the board level. What is important here is to explore the business objectives of other managerial levels, from strategic business units to operational ones.

When describing business objectives of companies, the most suitable methodology is questioning decision-makers about how they will decide and which information they need when they decide. A graphical exposition of information requirements also allows one to explore the integration of information from different sources. For example, a middle manager may want to see a line graphic of monthly sales and quarterly measured customer satisfaction. Or a financial manager may use a scatter plot of profitability of products and portfolio shares of these products. When the explorative study of business objectives is completed, a document of information requirements will be created.

This information requirements document needs to include some information about source (individuals, companies, internal or external data), timing (monthly, annually) and the expiration date of data to be collected. Moreover, the information requirements document will determine data-gathering methods. For example, in order to reach different segments or sources, different methods of data gathering may be employed. Thanks to technological innovations during the last decade, using the Internet, PDAs, tablet PCs and other tools is no longer a dream for market researchers.

Data collection methods may not be limited to the resources of the marketing research firms. In addition to operational and financial data from legacy systems, a pipeline to CRM systems may be established to facilitate integration of data. Moreover, the data-gathering process may be operated through the existing call centre of the company or may be outsourced to a data-gathering company. The information requirements document also helps to make an analysis of the knowledge base of the company. Which departments are using which metrics, at which managerial level? What importance is attributed to metrics by different managerial levels or departments? Which metrics, internal or external, are used altogether? All these questions may be answered by accumulating knowledge through the 'nervous system' of the company, and are included in the knowledge capital. On the other hand, the information requirements document will be a roadmap for the IT team of the company which is always faced with difficulties in understanding the needs of the business.

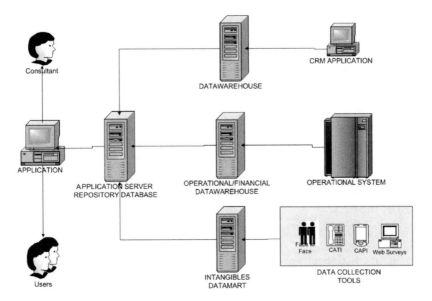

Figure 4.5   Provisioned data flow.

After setting up analyses which will be used by decision-makers and defining the information requirements document, the next step is arranging the data-gathering process. Since the cost of every piece of information is known – such as the per unit price of surveys, required technological investment, etc. – calculate an ROI (return on investment) for the overall information requirement of the company. Then, the board of the company may decide easily which information is worth collecting, and which may be postponed or cancelled. Another advantage of working with an information requirements document is that it can include alternatives for sources, timings and expiration dates, thus it becomes possible to estimate alternative budgets and ROIs.

Converting single-shot data-gathering attempts to such a continuous and seamless process (Figure 4.5) significantly decreases the cost of data gathering and reporting. By establishing a pool of users, companies may set up their respondent basis and reach to customers periodically by using panel or rolling sample methods. Or, the process may start with drawing a sample from CRM databases of the company – by using segments as clusters – and this sample may be used in data collection. Thus, reaching needed information with a probabilistic basis becomes possible, which is much cheaper than trying to collect information from the entire database.

The next step of the process is to prepare analyses which decision makers need in their jobs. The above mentioned information requirements document also includes information about which analyses will be used by decision-makers. When the project starts up, these analyses have to be ready following the first flow of data from internal or external sources. The role given to the consultant here is guiding interpretation of incoming data, exploring how decision-makers use these data and assisting on developing and setting up new analyses which aren't forecast in the first phase of the process. Furthermore, when collected information results in it birth of new business objectives, the consultant has to be in contact with decision-makers in order to revise information requirements and restart the cycle.

As may be easily seen, the overall process is highly technology dependent. The information requirements document has to be in an interactive form, in which decision-makers can easily express and visualize what they want to see. Moreover, this process has to be recorded and accumulated to contribute to the knowledge base of the company; consequently the lifecycle of information requirements will be observed and analysed by knowledge managers.

The technological basis of the process enforces itself after the compilation of the document. Attributes of data (expiration, source, etc.) have to be reserved in a relational database which allows control, coordination and optimization of data gathering. In addition, this database has to be a pool for collected data or be able to set up pipelines with legacy systems or CRM data warehouses. Data collected from different sources with different schedules have to be integrated and stored in this database. Thus, such a system has to have a sufficiently developed communication infrastructure with existing systems, enough storage capacity and highly developed processors to process data. Plus, such a system has to communicate with different data collection tools, from paper and pen, to PDAs and the Internet.

Technology plays an important role when decision-makers use the data collected and transform them in to information, then knowledge. Decision-makers will make their analysis visually, can create their reports by using these data in an integrated way with their documentation systems and communicate with their colleagues to share their findings. Then, all of their intellectual efforts have to be channelled and accumulated through the knowledge management system.

At first sight such a technological system may seem to be exaggerated and not easy to implement. However, many companies have the foundations of this system. As a result of extraordinary investments made in managerial information systems, operational and financial data are already digitalized and standardized. Many companies have made considerable investments in CRM systems and data warehouses, which enable them to accumulate operational and financial data in a customer basis. Several processes of the marketing research industry are automated: you can collect data from different platforms and integrate them through an online reporting tool. It is certain that the next decade will bring many further technological opportunities.

INTEGRATING MARKETING INTELLIGENCE WITH DECISION-MAKING

The critical point here is that we are putting forward a methodology for bridging the decision-making processes of corporations with business intelligence provided from different sources, from operational systems to marketing research. Furthermore, such a methodology will underline the above-discussed opportunities for our industry.

In order to deal with the difficulties of establishing such a bridge, we emphasize the 'metric' concept. Metrics are defined as 'indicators' or 'measurables' by MIS engineers, and used to compare and present universally a specific situation. A closer analysis of the historical evolution of managerial information systems shows how metrics are always embedded in these systems.

During the above-presented first phase of the knowledge spiral, managers were dealing with simple metrics from accounting and the operational system, such as profit, loss, delivery time. Then, with the expansion of bureaucracy in firms, activity-based costing produced several metrics. Implementation of ERP systems also contributed to the number of relevant metrics, through which managers can measure and compare performances of their companies. The most significant change came with the development of CRM systems. The CRM approach resulted in the emergence of customer-centric metrics. For example, before the CRM revolution, market share was a relevant metric for any company. As a result of the above-discussed scarcity of customers, valid portfolio share of a customer as a metric is emphasized by corporate management. The transition to a customer-centric organization may be summarized as the transformation of old, product-oriented metrics to customer-centric ones. Subsequently, when performance of the company is measured through customer-centric metrics, it is not surprising that a product orientation will be replaced by a customer-centric one.

Though the marketing research industry's major area of interest is the customer's point of view, it is not possible to argue that our industry had a knowledge accumulation of metrics. Instead of dealing with metrics, we emphasized hypotheses, questions, advanced statistical models and data collection. Consequently, our research questions became almost always firm-, sector- or country-specific. Moreover, the lack of a metric-oriented approach pushed the marketing research industry to talk and think about non-comparable measurements. And, since such a universality is absent, integrating marketing research data with operational, financial and other intangible information became difficult day by day.

However, a metrics approach is not far from being applicable in our industry. It is only a different approach of abstraction. For example, think about a customer satisfaction survey for the banking sector. The major question is: 'how satisfied are you with your X bank credit card?'. With this formulation, the question is both sector- and brand-specific. If we replace the brand with another one, it loses its brand specificity, while replacement of both brand and credit card makes it non sector-specific. From this perspective, we can talk about a metric of satisfaction, measured for credit cards of X bank, and there is only a minor difference between this survey and another one conducted for Toyota cars. Changing attributes are limited.

A metrics approach plays a significant role in our methodology, although qualitative and insight research should not be converted to such quantitative measurements. During the formation of the information requirements document, pushing customers to think on a metrics basis helped to integrate information flowing from different data sources. For example, he/she puts his/her business objective as having the highest share from portfolio of the most profitable segment of users. Here, we need two metrics, the first one is share from portfolio, and the second profitability of users. When we plot the shares of our customer and his/her competitors in this segment by using a bar chart, the information required for this business objective is constructed. Another example is that a product manager wishes to compare sales numbers and customer satisfaction of different products in order to satisfy his/her business objectives of creating the most satisfactory product and converting this satisfaction to sales. This may be visualized by using a scatter plot in which different products are plotted by using two different metrics.

Such a metric-oriented approach is critical for our industry. Establishment of a knowledge base composed of universal and comparable metrics, which are not culture-, industry- or brand-specific will create a significant competitive edge against other data suppliers. When globalization is taken into account, transnational companies will prefer such a knowledge base, which speeds up application and standardization of knowledge management, performance measurement, etc.

This knowledge base gives us rules for analyses, metrics and data collection methodology. For example, analyses made for a bank are usually similar to analyses of a customer from the car industry. Again, data collection methods can be converged for a customer of a research firm or the firm itself. Such a convergence will help the research firm decrease operational costs by an estimated 30%.

In order to apply this approach, we developed a software package with which decision-makers define their analyses without any data connection. When decision-makers define their business objectives, the researcher can transfer these objectives easily to metrics, analyses, rules and bases. Then this software produces an information requirements document, especially documenting which metrics are used by which departments, which metrics are used altogether, etc. This is a starting point of knowledge accumulation for a company. By using this package, customers define and visualize their analyses, without caring about data sources and neglecting whether data are internal or not. Then they can note the desired period and source of data collection. Consequently, it is not difficult to compile the above-discussed document.

CASE STUDY

As KNEXTEP, we had the opportunity to test this approach on one of our customers. The customer is an affiliate of the largest commercial bank in Turkey; it is operating in the securities market and has a customer base of 750 000 customers, making it the largest investment institution in the market. It is known as the most innovative institution in the market, since it was the first launcher of several securities products.

The customer, willing to develop such a knowledge management system, summarized its main target as 'keeping its leader position in the market, by improving its profitability'. Following a kick-off meeting and with the consent of the customer, several workshops were conducted at leader, business and operational levels. The major aim of these workshops

Table 4.2   Information requirements item example.

Business objective:	Increasing effectiveness of alternative distribution channels for mutual funds operations		
	Metrics	*Source*	*Period*
	Usage of ADCs in mutual funds operations	Internal Operational	Monthly
	Satisfaction from ADCs in mutual funds operations	External Marketing research firm	Biannually
	Cost of ADCs in mutual funds operations	Internal Financial/ERP	Variable

was to reverse our processes, as stated above. Thanks to these workshops, we had the opportunity to gain the consent of higher management, which was crucial in the rest of the process. The workshops endured for more than three months, and 17 workshops with participation of more than 50 people from different levels were organized. Four of these workshops were with leaders (CEO, general manager, assistant general managers), seven were with strategic business units, four with operational units and two with IT teams. Moreover, considerable time was allocated to the project team to develop the information requirements document.

During these workshops, the moderator pushed participants first to state their business objectives, and secondly to describe what information they needed and how they wanted to see it. Our software package was used to form the information requirements document. Our moderators tried to deconstruct the business objectives of participants from every managerial level. Table 4.2 shows the transformation of a business objective to an information requirement item which has to be collected from different sources.

After three months of intense discussion, a final document of information requirements had been compiled with the consensus of the project team, composed of customers and consultants. The information requirements document included 43 metrics and 120 analyses made by using these metrics. When segmentation and cross-comparison are taken into account, it is possible to estimate that this number will be augmented as customers use it.

When the document is analysed closely, it is possible to observe that the majority of these analyses are needed by strategic business units: more than 70% of analyses were requested by strategic business units, while this ratio was 51% for leaders and only 15% for operational units. The percentage of metrics to be obtained from internal sources of the company is 60, while this ratio is 26 for external sources, such as interviews, and 16% for third-party data such as overall trade volume of the bond market. 40% of metrics will be collected daily, the schedule for the remaining 60% varies between monthly and biannually. Among all metrics, only 40% of them are expected to be collected on a customer basis. An interesting finding is that all the information requests from the operational units are customer-based. It is a clear indicator of how operational units are much more customer oriented than other managerial levels. Another significant finding is that our client currently reaches only 10% of this information, despite its million-dollar investment in information technologies.

After finalization of the information requirements document, it was shared with the IT team of the bank. Today, they are putting together a schedule of implementation by using their prior investments and it is estimated that initial results will be taken within less than three months. An important point here is that the current project does not include the formation of online data collection, as a result of the client preferring to use its existing investment.

Making an evaluation of an unfinished project may lead to several fallacies. However, our project with the client showed that launching such a project outlined how customers (end users) are not satisfied with existing IT systems, and how they fail to receive the required informa-tion. Secondly, this project showed that multi-million IT investments fail to produce customer-centric reports. Thirdly, during workshops we of-ten observed that our client was product-oriented. A breakdown of the metrics shows that leaders and business unit managers are still product oriented.

The current stage of the project is focused on converting the collected metrics and analyses into customer-centric ones. The lower percentage of customer-centric metrics shows how there is a significant gap between the orientations of high-level management and strategic business units. Our active role in this conversion is another indicator of how marketing research professionals may guide and lead customers during this process.

CONCLUSION

We have argued that the marketing research industry is experiencing a crisis and that the intelligentsia of the industry are discussing the reasons for this crisis and remedies to be taken. However, a common characteristic of these discussions is accepting the crisis as a symptomatic one and missing its systematic nature. We propose that the current crisis in the industry is dependent on the existing information gap as a result of the dialectical relationship between demand for and supply of data. Though decision-makers of today are facing information overflow, within less than two decades, an explosion of demand has to be expected as a result of the above-discussed paradigmatic shift. However, in order to exploit the opportunities provided by the forthcoming demand explosion, the marketing research industry has to revise its processes.

We have proposed in this chapter a methodology to revise our business processes. This methodology, which starts with the definition of information requirements depending on business objectives and ends with the reconciliation of business objectives according to gathered information, is characterized by an intense use of technology, implying a metric approach to bridge information flow from different sources. Our methodology gives the market research professionals a consultant role in guiding transition to a customer-centric organization. Hence, marketing research's exclusion from decision-making processes will end, and the industry will have another mission with more added value.

We have had the opportunity to use this methodology with our customers, and one of them, which is an affiliate of the largest commercial bank in Turkey, helped us to verify our expectations and to draw some conclusions.

1. The board of the company has to be customer-centric-oriented. The nature of today's company ensures that lower levels of management are much more product oriented and such an identification creates the most significant obstacles to transition to a customer-centric company.
2. Even if the board is customer-centric, a lack of knowledge management vision in the company makes the process difficult to apply. Without such a vision, gains from such a transition will be relatively weak.
3. Integration with existing IT systems and the support of the IT team is crucial during the process. Application of the process without the participation of the IT team results in the emergence of an additional knowledge island.

4. Integration of internal data is very important. Without the support of these data, usage of marketing research information remains limited in terms of expressing its added value to decision-makers.

5. The project has to be initiated by a decision from the top-level management of the company, and has to be a part and initiator of a reform project. Hence, resistance against the project will be short-lived.

Finally, if the marketing research industry is willing to produce information which will be discussed in the boardroom, it has to be ready to forget what it has accumulated until today and revise its classical motto: 'Marketing intelligence is something more than the marriage of the science of sampling and the art of asking questions'.

REFERENCES

Baker, S. and Cooper, P. (2002), *Market Research: Mediating Between CRM and the Brand*, paper presented at the CRM Conference of ESOMAR, Prague.

Balasubramanian, P.R., Nochur, K., Henderson, J.C. and Kwan, M.M. (1999), Managing Process Knowledge for Decision Support, *Decision Support Systems*, **27**(1–2), 145–162.

Boxwell, L. (2000), Customer Relationship Management, unpublished manuscript.

Brooke C. and Suntook, F. (2002), *From Customer Research to CRM: How Understanding the Customer is the Cornerstone of effective CRM*, paper presented at the CRM Conference of ESOMAR, Prague.

Clarke, T. and Clegg, S. (1998), *Changing Paradigms: the Transformation of Management Knowledge for the 21st Century*, HarperCollinsBusiness Publishers.

ESOMAR (2002), Industry Report.

Frishammar, J. (2002), Characteristics in information processing approaches, *International Journal of Information Management*, **22**, 143–156.

Gibson, L. D. (2000), Quo Vadis, Marketing Research?, *Marketing Research*, **12**, 36–41.

Glyn, A., Hughes, A., Lipietz, A. and Singh, A. (1986), *The Rise and Fall of the Golden Age: An Historical Analysis of Post-War Capitalism in the Developed Market Economies*, Intervention to Seminar: Money, Finance And Trade Reform, of Wider/Unu, Helsinki, August.

Lipietz, A., Glyn, A., Hughes, A. and Singh, A. (1995), *Le Monde de l'après-Fordisme*, Presented at CNRS-INSERMIRESCO day of Precarisation and Globalization.

Microstrategy (2002), *Business Intelligence Software Engendering a Quiet Revolution in the Business Place*, White Paper.

Monster, R. W. and Pettit, R. C. (2002), *Global Market Research In The Internet Age: A report on the trends, current practices, and future of Net-centric research* paper presented AT THE Net Effects 5 Conference of ESOMAR, Berlin.

Neal, D. (2002), Getting serious about marketing research, *Marketing Research*, **14**(2), 24–28.

Nonaka, I. (1997), *Organizational Knowledge Creation*, paper Presented at the Knowledge Advantage Conference held November 11–12.

Read, W. H. (1999), *Knowledge As A Strategic Resource*, an incidental paper of the Program on the Information Policy.

Schultz, D. (2002), Two Faces of CRM, http://www.marketingpower.com/content2005 .phpession iD=59a9, last accessed on 10.10.2006.

Shea, C. and LeBourveau, C. (2000), Jumping the hurdles of marketing research, *Marketing Power*, **12**(3), 22–30.

Taylor, F.W. (1909, 2005), *Principles of Scientific Management*, 1st World Library Ltd.

Wiig, K. M. (1997), Knowledge Management: Where Did It Come From and Where Will It Go?, *Expert Systems With Applications*, **13**(1) pp. 1–14.

Witzel, M. (2000), Introduction, *Marketing* (Bristol: Thoemmes Press,), pp. vii–xxxvii. Available at http://www.thoemmes.com/economics/marketing_intro.htm.

World Bank (2001), *World Development Report 2000–2001: Attacking Poverty*, Oxford University Press.

Chapter Five

Market Research: A New Generation on the Go

Corinne Rosinski[a]

> *This chapter shows how the market research department's role can be transformed from being a mere provider of data that brings limited value, into becoming a strategic partner that offers crucial consumer insight and enables sound business decision, to be made.*

INTRODUCTION

Over the past few years, there has been a lot of discussion and debate around the role of market research within the industry. Many market researchers feel the need to move away from a position of being mere 'data providers' towards becoming real 'consultants adding value'.

In this chapter, we start addressing the problem with the most common criticism of market research. We then review 'the 5 golden rules to increase your impact'. These golden rules are our synthesis of what we have learned through 19 years of experience in the field of market research (both on the provider and client sides) and extensive readings (success case stories in the industry). We then illustrate, with our very concrete experience at Unilever Belgium, how we transformed the role from 'Researcher' to 'Consultant making real impact in the business' and to 'Leadership for growth'.

[a]Managing Director, JPCR s.a. Belgium.

Market Research Best Practice. Edited by P. Mouncey and F. Wimmer.
© 2007 John Wiley & Sons, Limited.

We explain what we believe have been the success factors in this remarkable journey: create an aspirational vision that announces the intended added value and involves the whole team; bring this vision to life within the company; develop, train and coach the team towards new competencies; give visibility to the department through central 'added-value' activities; use outstanding processes and tools for 'consumer understanding, consumer insights and creativity'; involve research agencies in a 'partnership spirit'.

In particular, we illustrate how we have used the 'Unilever Reconnect with the Consumer for Growth' programme to move from a business that is good at market research into a business that is 'world-class at consumer insight', and how it has helped us further strengthen our role in the organization . . . what we call our 'virtuous circle of success'.

The purpose of this chapter is to be practical and to provide the reader with concrete tips and recommendations, in order for the 'research role' to become much broader in the future.

COMMON CRITICISMS OF MARKET RESEARCHERS

In a recent paper from John Forsyth (2002), I was amazed by a chart about the image of market research among CEOs. On the question 'How useful is the information?', CEOs ranked 'Market Research' in last position, after 'Finance and Accounting', 'Marketing', 'Information Services' and 'Human Resources' (average rating: 1.8 on a 5-point scale)!

Common criticisms of research providers include: 'they are too data bound', 'they are too reactive, rigid and slow', 'they are insular, don't know our business', 'their presentations are valium', 'they are not integrative enough: they focus on one job at a time', 'they are not good at delivering or generating insights', etc.

In 2002, there was a big initiative (RELEAS) from Esomar, aimed at helping researchers increase their added value. It started with the 'Marco Polo travelogue' (Hofmans and Schellekens, 2002), which explored the 'research' world of both clients and providers. They discovered a troubled relationship between research providers and their clients. Marco Polo found that the research buyers (clients) lived on an island: lonely and isolated from both end users and providers. On one hand, they don't feel understood and accepted by the end users of research: end users do not understand the value that research can bring, that research takes time to be conducted and what the research process entails (complexity, costs, etc.). On the other hand, they feel that providers do not understand their needs and can't deliver what they want. According to them, providers don't have enough bright and experienced people who can serve them well, they lack creativity and innovation, they lack knowledge of their products and market as well as of their company. When interviewing providers, Marco Polo found they were trying desperately to cross the border that separated them from the client's territory and saw them failing. They complain that research buyers don't let them have sufficient access to the end users, that they are not sufficiently provided with business issues and research objectives, that the relationship with most clients is too 'project-based' and that the market research staff at the client side is not sufficiently educated in market research.

Marco Polo highlighted that such a troubled relationship between research providers and their clients might represent a risk for long-term growth and stability of the market research industry, because the added value of market research would be questioned. Marco Polo's travelogue called for concerted industry action *to put market research in the driver's seat for the future*. Since then, there have been a lot of forums, debate and papers within the industry (cf. Esomar RELEAS initiative).

In the next section we present our '5 golden rules' to increase your impact within the organization. Although we focus more on the clients' side, the principles remain valid for the providers' side as well.

THE 5 GOLDEN RULES TO INCREASE YOUR IMPACT

Rule 1: Create an aspirational vision that announces the intended added value

The first thing to do is to ask yourself some fundamental questions on the value you bring: 'What value does market research bring to the organization?', 'What would they be doing if market research were not present ?' 'What are the major strategic decisions taken by my company?' 'What was my role in these decisions?', 'How could I have had more impact?' (Dimopoulos, 2002).

Every successful leader has a clear vision of what he wants to achieve, of what his objectives are. The same rule applies for market research. If you want to be successful, you need to define your vision first. A 'vision statement' is an energizing picture, based on a view of the future, of what leadership wants the function to become. It contains the following key elements: a fundamental goal, a view of the future, an offering and the sources of competitive advantage. A few examples of vision statements related to market research:

Research relaunch initiative vision statement: 'To be the fundamental resource for business intelligence, knowledge, and tools that are used systematically for achieving higher levels of market performance and stakeholder value.'

McKinsey customer insight vision: 'To be the preeminent consultants generating deep customer and consumer insights to create innovative marketing and business solutions for our clients.'

Eli Lilly and Co-USA market research mission: 'Delivering insights that drive decision making.'

Unilever Consumer and Market Insight Key Vision: 'connecting the business with consumers' (the insight is: 'Great brands are connected with their consumers, average ones are not').

At Benckiser (UK), they have defined two levels to measure the success of market research: first through the success of the company, second through the innovation they deliver, and the insights that they have been able to leverage. Market research does not own the insights. Benckiser success in innovation is because of its systematic consumer-driven focus as a company. They do not care about who thought of the idea first... they are far more concerned with where it goes.

While defining such a vision statement is very important, it needs to be shared within the team and really be alive. Otherwise, it will only remain 'a beautiful sentence'. It also needs to be communicated properly within the organization. Let us conclude that it needs to inspire the teams every day.

Rule 2: Build more business capabilities – evolution of the market research role

Traditionally, market researchers are really experts in their field with a lot of analytical skills. What capabilities are essential to play a much bigger role and raise our impact in our organizations? We use the McKinsey model, which defines four types of role, with new competencies:

- **Project management** – this is the best known role for a market researcher. It is about planning and managing the market research budget, conducting market research projects to respond to the needs of your clients, recommending the best methodology according to the objectives, controlling the quality of the fieldwork and ensuring the data/information/results are used properly.

- **Voice of consumer** – this is already an evolution of the role – as market researcher, you ensure the consumer's voice is heard, especially if business expediency favours an alternative approach. You don't hesitate to take personal risks to press the consumer case. You want to develop deep consumer insights, not only from one single study, but in an integrated perspective.

- **Knowledge development** – you are a custodian of past and present research work. You proactively drive and motivate teams to use existing information, in order to avoid 'reinventing the wheel'. You know how to activate the research and consumer insights you have in appropriate forums. You also write summaries of learning on important consumer themes, when relevant.

- **Advisor to senior management** – you are consulted for advice on strategic decisions. You are included in key business meetings, even if there is no 'formal research' to conduct, because you are a 'respected advisor', an internal 'consumer guru'.

Of course, new skills and competencies are required to be able to play this bigger role: a balance of commercial awareness, marketing and marketing strategy knowledge, communication and assertivity skills, breakthrough thinking and proactivity. This will require a focus on training and coaching. We will come back to that in the second part of this chapter on our experience at Unilever.

As expressed by Ravi Parmeswar (2002), Vice President of Knowledge and Insights at the Coca-Cola company,

> 'Research cannot be called research anymore. It will be more about looking ahead at the consumer and the marketplace – strategic anticipation, identifying opportunities and how to leverage our core assets to leverage those opportunities, based on consumer needs and the marketplace . . . '.

Let us also quote Wil van den Berg (2002), Chief Marketing Officer at Philips Consumer Electronics:

> 'Market researchers tend to emphasize the technical part of their job, but I think they shoudn't do this. Of course we need people with excellent knowledge of techniques and methodology, but it is when they have a vision and judgement that researchers can make a difference.'

In order to stress the importance of this bigger role, there is a 're-branding' of 'research' in the industry (Chadwick, 2002). Here are a few examples of other titles used: Consumer and Market Insight Manager, Head of Consumer Insights, Head of Customer Understanding, Customer Knowledge and Strategy, Associate Director, Global Trends, Strategic Planning etc. Needless to say these new names are only meaningful if they are translated into a real change within the organization.

Rule 3: Broadly scope your target and services

If you want to achieve greater impact, ask yourself two questions (cf. Forsyth, 2002):

'Who are your customers?'
'What is the scope of your services?'

Traditionally, market research (on the client's side) has been a service department for Marketing, with two pillars of research: continuous research (retail and consumer panel mainly) and ad hoc research (e.g. consumer research to contribute to the development of the brands). For Marketing, there has been a tremendous evolution (e.g. bigger role cf. supra), new tools, e.g. Internet, Customer Relationship Marketing, where market research can offer added value.

With the increasing power of the trade and increased competition at points of sale, it has become more and more important to focus on the 'shopper' as well ('the consumer as a shopper'). According to POPAI's 'Consumer Habit Study–Belgium' (2001), 75% of purchase decisions are made at the point of sale. Market research has also become a key partner for Sales to conduct shopper research, help them in category management projects, business reviews, customer satisfaction surveys, etc.

As shown in Figure 5.1, the market research department can scope its customers even more broadly:

- **Product development** – they need the feedback of the consumers to develop the right products and innovations. It is a good idea to involve them in 'cross functional teams' so that the consumer dimension becomes more alive, and drives the development process.
- **Operations** – market research can play a valuable role by helping operations with sales forecasts, promotional effectiveness analysis etc.

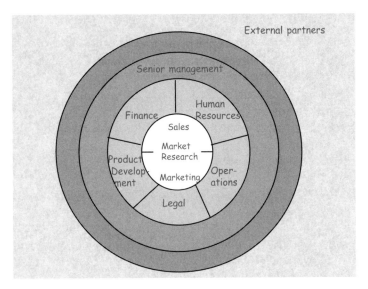

Figure 5.1   Who are your customers?

- **Human resources** – for instance, why not take the responsibility to lead 'employee satisfaction surveys'? Market research can also play an important role in the 'company culture'. We will come back to that in the second part of this chapter.
- **Finance** – market estimates, market and sales forecasts, competitive assessment . . . predictions for annual plans, budget management, etc.

As already mentioned, senior management is also a key potential customer: make sure you are involved sufficiently in the business and strategies to come up with the right 'advice', take the 'helicopter view' and try to spot new opportunities for the business. Speak the language they want to hear: people in the boardroom do not want 'research', they want 'solutions' to their problems. All too often, some very expensive 'strategic consultants' appear on the scene, while client-side researchers are in a unique position to contribute. The challenge is to gain acceptance and recognition from senior management.

As well as your customers inside your company, you need to think of *external partners* as well. A few examples are:

- **Advertising and media agencies** – market research often has a poor image among advertising agencies. One common criticism is that 'advertising tests kill creativity'. However, there are constructive ways to work effectively with advertising agencies. You can, for instance, involve them in consumer understanding and insights before the development of new campaigns (team work). Having an efficient communication tracking system is also very valuable. Again with all your knowledge, you should be a 'consultant' with valuable advice on communication strategies, and you should be involved in key meetings.

- **Retailers** – why not participate in business reviews with the clients, where you contribute with your 'objective knowledge' of the shopper?
- **External associations** – networking is important not only for your 'personal visibility', it is also a rich source of new insights and ideas. Quite often, a good 'address book' helps you get things done more efficiently. Of course, you will need to find the right balance in order not to be overloaded with external activities and networking. This is a matter of defining your priorities.

For all your (potential) customers, the question is: 'What is my role?', 'What value does or can market research bring to make better decisions?'

By broadening your scope in this way, your job will be richer and more motivating. You will also increase your impact in the organization (virtuous circle).

Rule 4: Focus on knowledge management and clear/actionable consumer insights

We need to increase the perceived value of market research. Although we buy 'data', our decision-makers are interested in 'solutions'. Let us first look at the '*Pyramid of understanding*' (Hastings, 2002) shown in Figure 5.2a.

Considering all the layers in turn:

- **Data** comprise the basic raw material of market research. The main concern for researchers when handling data is that they are valid, reliable and generalizable. Data on their own are rarely useful and insightful – even to researchers – therefore, they have to be analysed and reduced into information.
- **Information** describes something about a market and, as the pyramid suggests, there can often be large amounts of information in a research study that still needs to be reduced by considering carefully the original objectives of the research study.

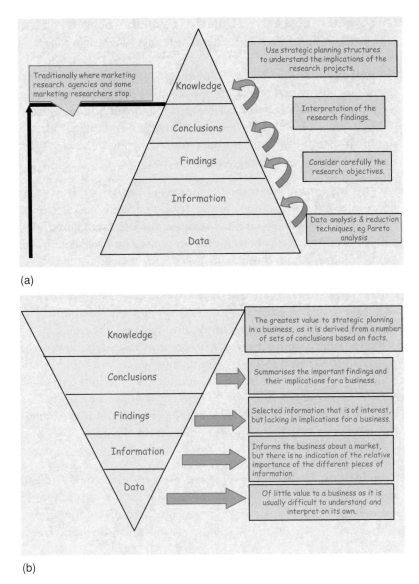

Figure 5.2 (a) The pyramid of understanding; (b) the value of understanding to a business.

- **Findings** are those pieces of information that answer a research question and they are usually of much more interest to internal clients. This is because we are dealing with far less material, where most of it is relevant to the problem that generated the need for research in the first place.

- **Conclusions** are an interpretation and a summary of the findings that represent the very essence of what that particular research project has to say.
- **Knowledge** is acquired from combining a series of conclusions from many different research projects and involves a sense of what action recommendations should be taken following the investment in market research. Inevitably this final stage involves using strategic planning structures such as usage and attitudes studies, the Porter Model, market attractiveness/business strength matrices, etc.

The last stage – moving from conclusions to knowledge – appears to involve skills that are traditionally not associated with market research, and yet this is a very crucial stage. Managing the last stage can transform a collection of projects gathering dust on shelves on to a strategic plan to guide an organization through a whole series of decisions in the short and long term.

Client-side researchers are in a unique position to make this transition as they have access to other research projects and a detailed knowledge of the client's business environment. As already stated, the challenge is to gain the recognition and acceptance of senior management, in order not to be beaten by expensive strategy consultants. We are in a better position to add value to the research results we produce: we are in the *consultancy business!*

Turning to the *value* of each layer in the pyramid, this is the opposite of the amount of material each layer contains (see Figure 5.2b). On the top, we have:

- **Conclusions**, because they represent the very essence of a research project and the decision-making implications for the organization.
- **Knowledge**, because it can guide the organization through a series of decisions in the short and long term and it can form the basis of strategic plans.

It is amazing how many researchers still flood an internal client with information, or, if they identify some findings, they fail to follow through with the implications for the business.

Therefore, *a balance of skills and competencies* is required to move from *data, information* and *findings* to *conclusions* and *knowledge*. Commercial and marketing knowledge is required at all levels of the pyramid. Moving from *data* to *information* and *findings* is likely to require more application of specialist knowledge and patient analysis. Moving from *findings* to *conclusions* and to *knowledge* is more likely to require competencies with regard to communication and assertiveness. We need to ensure we have the right talents in our market research teams!

Fresh thinking on market research presentations

We must present research in a manner that is challenging and action-oriented. Highly effective people (both from the client and agency-side) always start at the end (Table 5.1) (Smith, 2002):

Table 5.1   The best and worst in market research presentations.

The worst practice: 'No to boring building blocks of evidence'	**The best practice** 'Yes to an attacking/narrative true story'.
• 35 key findings from the research • 10 pages of methodology • every analysis conducted • narrow perspective: analyses just from that project	• the recommendation • methodology in appendix • only the analyses needed to support the recommendations • broad perspective: integrates analyses and insights from other projects as well.

Rule 5: Build good external relationships with partners

In order to maximize your impact within your organization, you don't just need the right talents in your team. You also need excellent 'partners' on the agency-side. What do we mean by 'excellent partners on the agency-side'?

First of all, they have to be a *consulting partner* rather than a 'data provider'. Even if you buy data (for example: retail panel, consumer panels), you need your agency to be able to draw conclusions and recommendations which are actionable for the business. You need them to have a 'strategic scope', integrate knowledge from previous research and sources. You want them to present results in an inspiring and engaging way. In order to be able to play this role, you need to integrate your agency into your business, involve them in key meetings where they can 'broaden their scope' and acquire a business perspective. Working in this way is very motivating for the agency: like you, they have more impact on the business, and this gives more sense to what they are doing.

You also expect your agency to be *service-minded*. But with a little extra, which is being able to challenge you when necessary (like you need to challenge your own internal clients when you do not agree). The last thing we want is the agency to become 'complacent'. By this we mean, for example, conducting meaningless research, or telling the client what he wants to hear. We need to work with integrity to add more value.

In certain cases, it is worth considering *Partnership agreements* with agencies, for instance in the case of using standard methodologies. This is particularly useful for quantitative research, like 'simulated test markets', 'advertising pre and post tests', etc. Advantages are: benchmarking, simplification and cost efficiencies. Of course, the agency has to remain competitive and very active to invest in further development, and the client needs to keep his eyes on the market, again to avoid the risk of becoming complacent.

In the case of qualitative research, I prefer to talk about *preferred partners*, but we should never give exclusivity here. Building expertise and thorough strategic knowledge is key (which pleads in favour of one partner), but fresh thinking and ideas are very important as well.

By building solid relationships with agencies (partners) as described above, you move to a *virtuous circle*:

- your agency enjoys working for you – you get the best talents and the best service;
- it helps you raise your impact in the organization.

Let us now look at our concrete experience at Unilever Belgium: how we managed to move the market research department from 'data provider' to 'consultant making a real impact' and 'leadership for growth'.

OUR PERSONAL EXPERIENCE AT UNILEVER BELGIUM: HOW WE TRANSFORMED THE ROLE OF THE MARKET RESEARCH DEPARTMENT FROM 'DATA PROVIDER' TO 'LEADERSHIP FOR GROWTH'

In 1999, we decided to merge the market research departments of the three Unilever Belgium divisions – Hartog-Union (brands such as Becel,

Bertolli, Calvé and Lipton), Iglo-Ola (frozen food: Iglo, and ice-cream: Ola-Magnum, Cornetto, Carte d'Or etc.) and Lever-Fabergé (home and personal care: Coral, Omo, Robijn, Cif, Dove, Axe, Rexona, Signal etc.). The Unilever Belgium market research department was born (April 1999)!

In five years, we managed to move from 'data provider' to 'consultant making a real impact' and even 'leadership for growth'. What were the different *key steps* in this evolution of our role in the organization? What are the *success factors* behind this virtuous circle?

Step 1: Towards an integrated market research department

Before deciding to merge the three departments, we had regular contact between the three heads of department in order to share best practices and find potential synergies. At that time, I was responsible for the market research department of Iglo-Ola. It was obvious in our discussions that we could gain more impact in the business by finding more synergies. We started preparing a proposal for the national management and looking at different scenarios, with 'pros' and 'cons'. We rapidly arrived at the conclusion that the best way forward was to go for one, *integrated* department.

The main *advantages* of having one integrated department were:

1. To *add more value* to the business – by maximizing the synergies between the three divisions (best practices, cross-fertilization of knowledge, 'Unileverage'), having one strong department with critical mass.
2. To make cost *savings* by using our internal resources more efficiently, by negotiating better contracts with our agencies, etc.

In the proposal for national management, we started very clearly by defining our mission in the company.

Mission Unilever Belgium market research department

General:

- To ensure that *consumer understanding* is at the heart of the company.
- To provide an *added-value service* for Marketing, Sales and Board Unibel (in the beginning, we identified those to be our main customers).
- To be a *partner* for strategy and decision-making.

We expressed this as follows:

'As market researchers, we want to be *partner-consultants* within our organizations, offering the best service and advice with real *added value*. We want to be a department in which each member works with *passion* to deliver the best information responding to the queries and the needs of our Marketing, Sales and Board colleagues. A department we are proud of because we *anticipate their needs* and we offer them the required information and tools to help them in their *business decisions*.'

(Th. van den Abelen, C. Bodart and C. Rosinski,
Market Research Unibel, January 1999).

Before explaining how we managed to bring this mission to life within the team and the company, let us discuss some important practical issues linked with the merger to one department.

One department, one boss

We all knew that by recommending one integrated department, there would be one boss only. I openly put that issue on the table: I was interested in the job of course, but what about my two colleagues? We were very lucky: they had other plans, so we could really work together in the same direction!

Organization and hierarchical reporting lines

After having examined different scenarios, we recommended a *bipolar* structure for the department:

- *Category Market Research Managers*, all dedicated to one division or business unit (according to the size), with the objective to become 'the consulting partner' of that division.
- the *Central cell* (which has subsequently been renamed the *Market Information Department*), which coordinates continuous research for the three divisions (central contact with agency, data quality and standard reporting, expertise and training, etc.) for better efficiency.

As a head of department, I was still responsible for one division as well (still Iglo-Ola, with the help of a trainee). My big challenge was to build a real team, make this department work and add more value to the business. In order to help me succeed, it was important that all team members became my direct reports, while still having 'dotted' reporting lines, towards the Marketing Directors of their divisions. This was not only important on paper, it was a strong recognition of our status and role within the organization. I also had the main responsibility for people management and development.

One department, one physical location

I can assure you there has been a lot of debate about the physical location of our department! Some directors wanted to have their Market Research Managers close to their Marketing department. We were very clear in saying that one physical place was the only way forward to achieve our ambitious objectives. And with hindsight we were right! The only discipline we needed was to have regular contact with the marketing (and sales etc.) teams, in order not to live 'isolated on an island'. This could happen through daily visits ('walk the talk', regular meetings, etc.). The advantages of being all together are numerous: stronger team building, stronger expertise level, synergies, 'cross-fertilization' of good initiatives, mutual coaching, better 'step-back' and efficacy (better than if you are in the same office as product managers who keep asking you questions), recognition of our 'consultant' status, etc.

One department, stronger talents and career opportunities

With the integration of the market research department, it became possible to have more career opportunities, still in market research. Even if my advice to people is to broaden their experience and move to 'the user's side' (marketing, sales) at a certain moment of their career (because it gives them a more practical business perspective), it has become possible to make several jobs in market research, with a good progression. There are entry jobs, junior and more senior functions, all in the same department.

By building a strong department, it has also been possible to hire excellent external talents and offer them attractive jobs. Again, a virtuous circle because these strong talents add a lot of value to the business, contribute to improving our image and increasing our impact in the organization, etc.

Now back to the second step: how we managed to build a solid and committed team.

Step 2: Aligning and motivating the team towards the vision and Bringing this mission to life within the company

Although we were very proud of the mission statement we had put on paper, I quickly realized that it was not alive for my brand new team! Why? Because it was not defined by the team itself! One key lesson is that you need to *involve the whole team* in defining the vision and mission statement.

Therefore, we organized a 'day out' (May 1999) with the complete team (12 people at that time). I put them in to two groups ('syndicates') and gave them a simple task: to make two drawings (see Figure 5.3a, b and c). The first drawing was to express how they felt at the time as market researchers ('As is'). The second how they wanted to feel in the future ('To be'). I then asked them to put words on these drawings. What happened? They used almost the same words as in our initial mission statement, but now it was stronger: it was built by the whole team (Figure 5.3d).

Now that the team really shared the same vision, mission and values, it was very important to bring it to life within the entire company. In June 1999 (one month after the 'day out'), we organized an *'open door day'*. This was a day where everybody in Unilever Belgium could visit us (in our brand new offices). Our objectives were the following:

- To *announce and share our vision*, mission and concrete objectives with the whole company.
- To install our image and give *visibility* to our department.
- To give *'ownership'* to the team and motivate them as 'one team' (every member of the team was active during that day: everybody presented some key messages, key objectives, etc.).
- To *'educate'* our clients: we developed the '*10 Commandments for a Good Partnership*' (see Figure 5.4).

During our day out, we found that one of the problems was that our internal clients (e.g. product managers) were not behaving in the way we

---→

Figure 5.3 Day out market research Unilever Belgium – drawings 'As is' figures and 'To be'. The 'as is' figures express some feelings of frustration about being 'a bottleneck': conflicts, a heavy workload, reactive. There is also no clear vision of our role within the company (a big question mark), too many data, too much focus on the consumer and brands but not enough on the shopper and the sales, etc. The 'to be' figures show a big light bulb (which has become our symbol): the fact that we are now all together makes us stronger. Together as market researchers of the three divisions, but also better integrated with marketing, sales, etc.

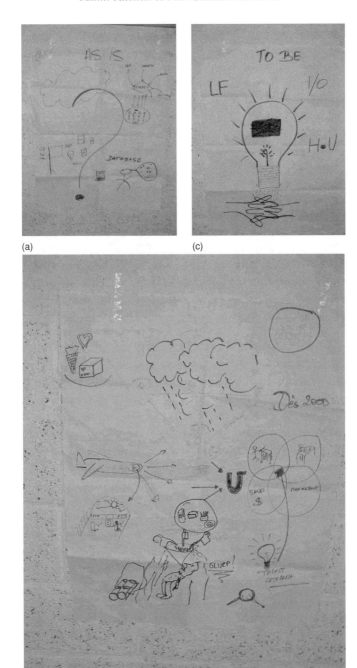

(a)

(c)

(b)

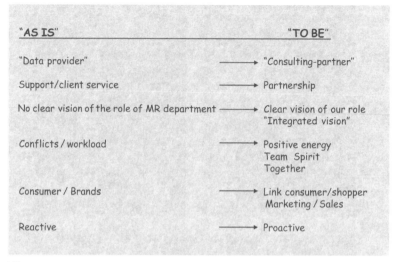

"AS IS"   "TO BE"

"Data provider"   ⟶ "Consulting-partner"

Support/client service   ⟶ Partnership

No clear vision of the role of MR department ⟶ Clear vision of our role
                                                "Integrated vision"

Conflicts / workload   ⟶ Positive energy
                                        Team Spirit
                                        Together

Consumer / Brands   ⟶ Link consumer/shopper
                                        Marketing / Sales

Reactive   ⟶ Proactive

(d)

(e)

Figure 5.3 *Continued*

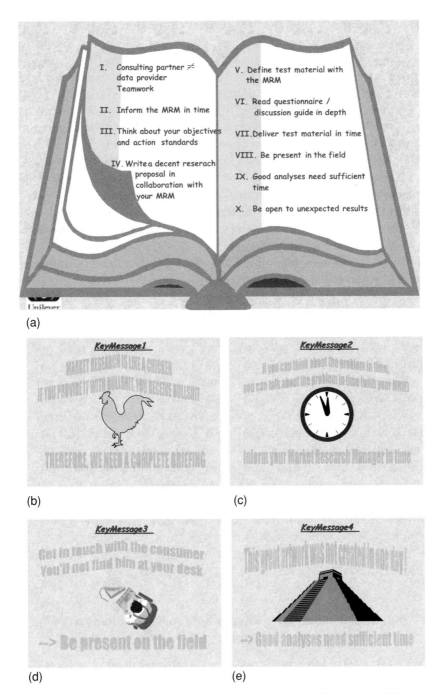

Figure 5.4 (a) The 10 commandments for a good partnership; (b)–(e) some of the key message posters displayed around the office.

wanted (examples: quick and dirty briefing, everything urgent, failing to involve us in designing test material, etc.). We found it a good idea to 'educate them' in an intelligent way by developing the 10 Commandments for a Good Partnership'. We put these 10 Commandments on big boards and also created a few posters with key messages, such as:

- 'Market research is like a chicken. If you provide it with bulls . . . , you receive bulls . . . Therefore, we need a complete briefing' (in June 1999, we were in the middle of the dioxin crisis, hence this analogy).
- 'If you can think about the problem in time, you can talk about the problem in time (with your market research manager). Therefore, inform your market research manager in time.'
- 'Get in touch with the consumer, you will not find him at your desk. Therefore, be present in the field.'
- 'This great artwork (we show the Egyptian pyramids) was not created in one day! Good analyses need sufficient time.'

All these posters were exposed and presented during our open door day. They stayed afterwards in our offices . . . a clever and fun way to remind our 'partners' to play the game . . . just in case they forgot! And it helped a lot.

Last but not least, we had a 'Golden book' in which every visitor could write a testimony, a few words to encourage us, etc. We received a lot of 'congratulations' and positive strokes, such as: 'Great initiative! Good luck to your fantastic team', 'An excellent start, go for it!', 'Super idea, super team, well done!', 'A great start, success guaranteed!', 'A wonderful team ready for excellence', 'Great! I promise I will follow your 10 commandments', etc. We also gave special T-shirts with our logo to each visitor. All of this has been a tremendous success: the Golden book has had about 150 visitors, we have generated a lot of positive word-of-mouth about our department, and a motivated team.

Now our challenge was to deliver, and really become the 'Consulting Partner' we wanted to be!

Step 3: Coaching the team towards the 'consultant making impact' role

When we merged the three market research departments, the team was quite heterogeneous in terms of experience: a mixture of new trainees, junior and senior market research managers. In order to move in the direction of 'Consulting Partner', it was important to work at three different levels:

- translating the vision and mission into clear plans;
- individual and team coaching to leverage the potential of the complete staff to play a bigger role in their division;
- team initiatives to give visibility to our department.

Translating the vision and mission into clear plans

All too often, a market research plan is an assembly of brand team bids rather than a coherent strategic plan to address fundamental knowledge gaps and business priorities. It was important to step back from the day-to-day and take stock of what we know and do not know. Together with the Marketing Directors, it was important to agree the 'Annual Strategic Understanding Plan' in order systematically to prioritize the budget behind strategically important projects. Although we would still keep some flexibility around these plan according to emerging business needs, this type of plan was key to focus our resources on the most added-value activities.

Individual and team coaching

The transformation of the role from 'Market Research Manager' to 'Consultant Making Impact' requires a shift in the type of activities:
More time is spent on:

- preparing and managing big scale strategic projects;
- mining the work for foresight and insight;
- synthesizing the multiple strands into actionable knowledge;
- raising the profile of consumers in the business;
- playing an 'advisor role' in business meetings.

And less time is spent on:

- administration;
- quality checking;
- method development;
- small-scale evaluative projects;
- repetitive research.

Within Unilever, this transformation of the MR function to a *more strategic/planning* role resulted in a rebranding of the function as CMI (consumer and market insight). Although we should not underestimate the expertise and specialist skills which are necessary to play this bigger role, we will concentrate here on two core *'leadership competencies'*, which have been a key focus within Unilever in the transformation of the role: 'seizing the future' and 'strategic influencing' (Unilever, 2002).

1. **Seizing the future** – 'Outstanding individuals are focused constantly on taking action to get to the future first. They monitor closely what is happening, both internally and externally, and take decisive action today to create new growth opportunities for tomorrow. In a world where being first into a market is key, they act with speed and decisiveness to stay ahead of the game, maximizing growth opportunities for the business.' What does this mean for CMI? To identify growth opportunities and push these proactively. It is important for CMI to do this, because we have the best perspective on trends and unmet needs and aspirations. It is a great way for us to 'fuel growth'.

2. **Strategic influencing** – 'Outstanding individuals use strategic influencing to build commitment to their growth agenda and to influence others without using hierarchical power to adopt a specific course of action. They use influencing strategies positively to orchestrate organizations'. What does this mean for CMI? To use our skills to build a persuasive case and find ways to influence decision-takers to adopt this. It is important for CMI to do this, because we do not have the hierarchical power, so we need to influence others if we want to have an effect, to make a 'difference' – if not, we will be 'back-room technicians'.

To achieve this transformation of the role, requires a lot of training and coaching, both at individual and team levels. As defined by Philippe Rosinski, an expert in coaching and leadership (Rosinski, 2003), 'Coaching is the art of facilitating the unleashing of people's potential to reach meaningful, important objectives.' As stressed by Rosinski, there are important key elements in this definition:

- concrete objectives: coaching is oriented towards concrete impact and results;
- important and meaningful for the coachees: the objectives must resonate with coachees' inner motives and values;

- potential: coaches are deeply convinced that people have more potential than they are currently able to display;
- facilitating: coaching is an interactive and developmental process where the coach enables coachees to find their own solutions;
- people: coaching can be applied to individuals and to teams;
- art: choosing an effective approach in a given situation.

Now here are the big lines of my 'coaching' approach:

1. At the *individual level* – according to a person's needs, I have regular 'coaching' meetings with them. I act as a 'facilitator' and help them find their own solutions and implement actions. I trust them and empower them to act as real managers in their respective teams. I don't need to be 'front line', unless they want me to be so. I always express pride in others' accomplishments and enjoy seeing my people grow. Everybody in my team knows that I put a lot of care into their own development plans and career opportunities, even if it is not the best solution for the department, because it can sometimes create discontinuity. But I am a firm believer that by putting a lot of attention on people in this way, they feel motivated and will do a great job. It is a real 'win-win' situation. On top of regular individual coaching meetings, we make a more formal review twice a year: a summary of performance, evaluation of 'skills' and 'competencies' and a personal development plan. Each individual has clear objectives with a concrete work plan.

2. At the *team level* – we have regular (once a month) staff meetings where we share 'best practices' and 'cross- fertilize' good initiatives so that we can leverage the team. We define the future together, which means the vision and top priorities for the department. 'Genuine commitment is found where team and individual objectives intersect. This creates congruence, a resonance, which is the basis for true synergy.' (Rosinski). We also organize regular days-out on specific topics to raise the potential of the teams and further consolidate 'team spirit'. We always try to find a good balance between 'business' and 'relational/team spirit' in these outdoor initiatives. Finally, there is also collective training on skills (consumer insight) and competencies (cf. supra).

Team initiatives to give visibility to our department

Once a year, we put together a *departmental work plan*, which reflects the key priorities of our department. This plan is agreed with the 'Marketing

Directors' Committee' (a forum which groups the Marketing Directors of the three divisions), and then cascaded in the different teams. This work plan gives common directions for the individual work plans (see above) and also includes *central team initiatives*.

One year after the 'open door day', we organized a *'Market Research Fair'* for the whole company to communicate our main achievements, to further stretch the vision and communicate our objectives and to further reinforce the team. Again, every team member was involved in this by owning a topic and moderating it (in special workshops run in parallel). I presented a short introduction in plenary, where I launched officially 'Reconnect with the Consumers', a major step in the evolution of our role towards growth (see below).

Since then, let us say that we organize one or two big events per year – *'central conferences'*– for the whole Unilever Belgium company in order to add value for the business and give visibility to our department. For example:

- 'The Teenagers'
- 'Trend Watching'
- 'A-brands versus private labels: survival of the fittest?'
- 'The Seniors'.

All these conferences have been great successes: with the collaboration of external and internal speakers, we managed to present each time a lot of new, holistic insights for the business. A good way to inspire the teams for their plans, while also giving strong credibility and visibility to our department.

Let us now concentrate on the Unilever major worldwide initiative, called 'Reconnect with the Consumers', which has helped raise our role further, and how we implemented it within Unilever Belgium.

Step 4: Implementing 'Reconnect with the Consumers for growth' (Unilever, 2002)

'Our growth depends on one thing above all others. Consumers. If we do not get better at understanding our consumers and meeting their needs, wants and aspirations, we will not grow. It's as simple as that'

Keki Dadiseth, Unilever HPC Division Director,
and Patrick Cescau, Unilever Foods Division Director.

The challenge

An international survey carried out in 2000 among Unilever managers and suppliers revealed that most of us rarely engaged directly with consumers, that we spent far too much effort on the evaluative and far too little on the illuminative:

> '*We use market research to eliminate risk (the well-known 'umbrella effect'), but not to illuminate opportunity.*'

Unilever's Path to Growth agenda demands a *significant increase in our rate of growth*. To get that growth we need a stream of consumer-relevant innovation brought to market fast – and that in turn calls for a change in the way we *connect with consumers*.

As shown in Figure 5.5, we want to put more focus on 'strategic understanding' and 'direct consumer contact', in order to generate better 'insights' and be able to make more intuitive decisions. That means we have less need for 'risk reduction research' and can be faster to market with more 'consumer-relevant' mixes.

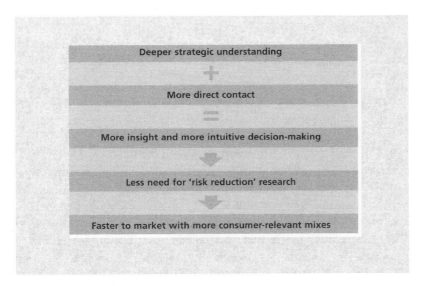

Figure 5.5 The goal: change to grow.

Our Unilever vision and goals

Our vision is: 'Growth of our leading brands driven by insightful people who have insightful ideas and are connected by powerful knowledge management and shared learning'.

Our key goals are:

- Faster and *more intuitive decision-making* based on greater consumer intimacy.
- A decisive shift in emphasis to *insight/foresight*, and of budget from the tactical/evaluative to the *strategic/illuminative*.
- A radical improvement in our retention and *sharing of knowledge*.
- Greater *simplicity* in all we do.

The tools for change

'Reconnect with Consumers' is a package developed by Unilever that pulls together smart ways of working from around the world. It is about turning from a business that is good at market research into a business that is *world-class at consumer insight*. It provides An interlocking set of new tools and disciplines designed to effect a step-change in how the consumer is put at the heart of our everyday working lives.

For the purpose of this chapter, we will focus on two pillars:

- direct consumer contacts;
- insight activation.

Before explaining the fundamentals of these tools, I want to emphasize that implementing 'Reconnect with the Consumers' has been very powerful in achieving the goals outlined above. The fact that it has been driven strongly by the CMI department with the full commitment of the top management gave us an outstanding booster in our role and impact within the company. We believed firmly it was the way to go, and the whole team was 100% committed.

Every CMI manager has been trained to fulfil this new, exciting vision, 'Connecting the business with the Consumers'. This meant in practice more focus on new roles, such as 'Consumer guru' (passionate about understanding the consumer – strong advisor for project leaders and senior management), 'Consumer voice' (put across the consumer case in business decisions), 'Consumer process expert' (on top of traditional research, manage a process to encourage direct consumer contact sessions, facilitate Insight Activators' projects, etc.), 'Guardian of consumer – knowledge' (access past insight and research work and bring it into current projects, share knowledge and fill gaps).

The importance of direct consumer contacts: a real eye opener!

One of the fundamentals of 'Reconnect with the Consumers' is that all of us should spend more time interacting directly with consumers – much more in most cases than we currently do. Typically, we underinvest in this because: we perceive ourselves as short of time, we assume that it is someone else's job (marketing, MR, the agency), we lack confidence in how to do it.

The prime purpose of direct consumer contact is to bring us *closer to consumers*, so we have a much greater feeling for how our brands fit in with their daily lives and we become even more consumer-focused.

The importance of 'connecting' with the consumers for effective marketing has become widely recognized within the industry . . . but is still not implemented enough in practice. Let us quote Jim Stengel, Global Marketing Officer from Procter & Gamble:

> *'Consumers are changing as so must we. As an industry, we are simply not doing enough to know our consumers and connect with them. We cannot easily reapply old strategies to this new consumer. Marketing strategies must be dynamic and holistic – to connect with her where and when she is most receptive.'*

Within Philips, market research played a big role in shifting from a 'product oriented' into a 'consumer- and market-driven company'.

> *'Philips had decided that it was too much driven by its technological know-how and heritage, and too little by a good sense of what consumers want'.*
>
> (Van den Berg, 2002)

Starting a real 'consumer reconnect' programme is a real step-change in the 'consumer mind' focus, as suggested by the testimonials below:

'The difference between sitting behind a mirror in a focus group and sitting talking to consumers face-to-face is a million miles.'

'It is a real eye opener!'

'Now you really see the consumers through their eyes, deep in their world – not through your own marketer subjectivity.'

'The importance of personal experience: what I hear I forget, what I see I remember, what I do I know.'

There are many possible forms of direct consumer contacts: face-to-face at home, accompanied shopping, connecting with him in different places (e.g. cinema, leisure park, petrol stations, going out, etc.). You can combine observations and interviewing. What can also be very insightful is to meet experts, who can give another perspective on the subject. For example, on a project for a deodorant, we met dermatologists, perfumery shop managers and psychologists.

We also organized an event for Unilever Belgium Marketers: 'Reconnect with the Youth'. We spent one Saturday afternoon, evening and night in different places with experts and consumers: trendy fashion stores, trendy DJ, trendy bars and discos to 'reconnect with Youth night life'. This event was very insightful and has inspired the 'underground launch' of Lipton Ice Tea Green in Belgium (how to start first with opinion leaders, trend setters and peers, before targeting the mass).

The message is also to be a consumer yourself (we sometimes forget), be curious and open-minded towards the world around you.

Training is very important before undertaking consumer interviews. We have developed a simple process of providing practical training for every person involved in this (The 10 golden rules for active listening). This gives them the confidence they need to get started and get the most out of their interviews. Of course, practice makes it even better. The feedback we have had so far has been unanimously positive: it is an enormous-step change in the consumer mind focus.

Since we started with this in 2001, the *success* of 'direct consumer contacts' is increasing continuously. Almost every function can be involved in projects. We started with Marketing. We then extended to Sales, advertising agencies, Development, Finance, etc. Every project we make with 'direct consumer contacts' is led by CMI Managers with very clear objectives and deliverables. Debriefings are facilitated by us in order to draw the best insights (see below).

It is worth mentioning that 'direct consumer contacts' are not a substitute for research. They are particularly useful in exploratory projects to gain understanding, to get started with all the team being involved (including advertising agency, development, pack design agency, if relevant, etc.). It can be productive in preparation for a big study (prepare stimulus material based on consumer insights), to learn about the relationship between the consumers and your brand. It is very motivating and stimulating for the whole team, and makes our discussions richer and more productive. As CMI Managers, the possibility of running 'direct consumer contacts' is now part of our *tool box*. We know when to advise it in the projects we run.

It is great to run direct consumer contacts. We also need the right tools to generate relevant *consumer insights.* According to the Unilever consumer understanding survey undertaken in 2000, 'Insight is the cornerstone of brand marketing, yet only 28% of us have a formal system for developing insight'.

The importance of insights

Good insights are the lifeblood and inspiration for successful brands and feed all marketing activities: brand key, innovations, communication and activation.

'An insight is a penetrating understanding which provides hooks or clues that lead to brand-building opportunities.' (definition from Unilever Marketing Academy).

'A brand identity insight is that element of all you know about the consumers and their needs which the brand is founded upon.'

'An insight is something you should feel in your guts, not just think in your head. It is a creative link from consumer understanding to market response.'

Consumer insights are opportunities to create value for consumers, to improve aspects of their lives, as shown by the examples below.

Dove (soap, shower and bath products):

— Consumer insight: soap leaves skin feeling tight and dry.
— Brand discriminator: Dove contains 1/4 hydrating cream, so it leaves your skin soft and smooth.

Axe (male deodorant and perfumery):

— Consumer insight: the 'mating game' is a major preoccupation for young men. Feeling, looking and smelling good is essential for success.
— Brand discriminator: Axe is a cool brand whose products are designed to help me get the girl.

Becel Pro-Activ (margarine):

— Consumer insight: understanding the consequences of having cholesterol is frightening.
— Brand discriminator: Becel pro-activ spread is a revolutionary spread enriched with plant sterols, an active ingredient which lowers cholesterol levels.

Lipton Ice Tea (beverages):

— Consumer insight: young people want it all – pleasure, excitement, goodness.
— Brand discriminator: with Lipton you can have it all, live life to the full and do yourself good.

The brands which have fully embraced the process of 'Reconnect with the Consumers' have shown the best results and impact on Unilever growth.

So what we need is great consumer understanding and insight: this is the basis for great brand marketing. Within Unilever, an excellent process has been developed to help generate great consumer insights and ideas: it is called the *Insight Activator*. For confidentiality reasons, we will limit ourselves in this chapter to the major principles of this approach and the benefits it provides. In particular, we will explain how we have implemented it within Unilever Belgium with great success, and how it has helped strengthen our role further in the organization.

The 'Insight Activator': a powerful tool

The Insight Activator is a set of *creative and inspiring tools* and techniques to generate superior consumer insights into their underlying needs and behaviours. It is used as the key tool on projects to gain a *better understanding of consumers*, through acquiring key insights from real consumers and then applying them to *building brands*. It assists in driving consumer and market insight into the heart of brand building and helps us develop insight platforms for accelerated brand growth.

The Insight Activator process has a series of stages:

- **Define the task (Briefing)** – whether it is to drive *brand positioning*, *innovation*, *communication* or *brand activation*. The briefing contains key information such as background, objectives, consumer target, deliverables, etc.
- **Enlist a strong team** – there must be a good balance between the number of people and the right mix of disciplines. The involvement of senior marketers is key (experience, support, sign-off). Typically, participants of the core team should be: the marketing team (including team leader/decision-maker), the CMI team (which facilitates the whole process), creative agencies, trade marketing, development.
- **Review existing knowledge** – we do not need to reinvent the wheel! Consult existing knowledge (reports, Internet, etc.), experience and

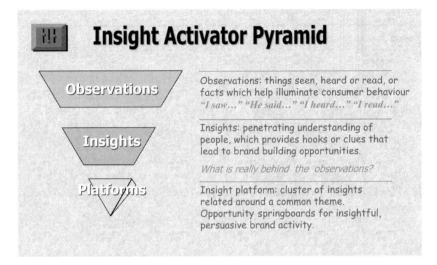

Figure 5.6 From observations to insight platforms.

trends in the light of the task, and clearly identify gaps and hypotheses before commissioning any new research.

- **Explore the world further** – expand understanding and stretch thinking using personal experience, direct consumer/experts contacts and, if necessary, commission new research.
- **Collect learning together** – make connections, cluster and craft them into *insight platforms*, via an intensive 'mix' workshop. Mixing all the observations, learning's and understanding together is really magic: it feels exhaustive, creative and satisfying for the whole team!
- **Select the most powerful insight platforms** – to answer the brief and use them as a springboard *for creativity to generate ideas* (product innovations, communication or brand activation).

During the Insight Activator process, we move from 'observations' to 'insights', and from 'insights' to 'insight platforms', as shown by Figure 5.6. An insight platform is a cluster of related insights around a common theme. A platform is richer and yields more opportunities than just one single insight. Insight platforms help us find many new and relevant ways to satisfy our consumers. Table 5.2 shows an example of an insight platform for oral care.

Great insight platforms are rich and ripe. They are inspiring, are expressed in clear consumer language, capture the essence of the insights, have an emotional hook and, if possible, a memorable headline.

Table 5.2   Insight platform for oral care.

Insight platform: 'Oral Care On the Go'
I need easier oral care because I'm always on the go.

Key supporting insights:
- My kids cannot brush their teeth at school.
- My kids tend to snack more and more.
- My children need extra oral care protection.
- After eating, I can't always brush my teeth as I would like because I don't have my brush with me.
- During the day, I often wish my mouth felt as fresh as after brushing.
- Sometimes kids do not even brush their teeth in the morning due to the rush and an unwillingness to do so.

Opportunity areas:
- Products which offer convenient oral care solutions (e.g. chewing gums).
- New types of oral care kits/packs for 'on the go', easy to put in the bag.
- Special 'on the go' solutions, quick and fun for kids.

Since we introduced the Insight Activator process in Belgium, we have conducted about eight projects on different brands, with different types of objectives: generate new product innovations, new communication, activation ideas, drive brand positioning, etc. All these projects have been driven and facilitated by the CMI team. All members of my team have been trained to facilitate the Insight Activator, and I have acted as a coach in all projects. I can tell you it was a real challenge and 'stretch' for my team. Some of them were afraid of not having the skills and experience required to facilitate this (especially running the big 'mix' workshop and creativity session). But with appropriate training and coaching, and by working 'step-by-step' through the different stages, they all managed to run these projects successfully, with great satisfaction from the whole team, starting with the decision-maker.

As shown in Figure 5.7, the *benefits* we have experienced from this process are numerous. In the first place, it helped us to complete the task, by generating great consumer insights and platforms, and from that, concrete ideas for the business. Moreover, it provided the whole team with a strategic framework and a thorough understanding for the long-term development of our brands. Compared to a process where one single person has a brilliant idea, we have a very powerful team process where everybody feels aligned and motivated (the amount of positive energy is incredible throughout the process!). Needless to say, this process also increases 'consumer focus', is by the way beneficial for personal development (active listening, creativity) and company cultural values

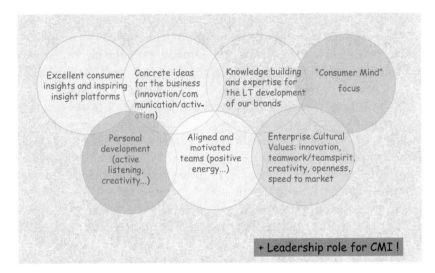

Figure 5.7 Insight Activation – key benefits.

(innovations, team spirit, speed to market). And finally, a tremendous benefit for us, CMI Managers, is that it put us centre stage, with a strong leadership role!

Step 5: Towards the 'leadership for growth role' and a virtuous circle of success for CMI

Implementing 'Reconnect with the Consumers', and in particular leading Insight Activator projects, has been a springboard for our CMI role. While gaining confidence in the process, we started to apply the process with *flexibility* for other strategic reviews. Some projects require a 'full Insight Activator', others can be done with a 'lighter approach'. With experience gained, we realized the approach can be done in modules, according to the objectives, and then it is less heavy (which is good for our Belgian market).

Here are a few examples of the types of project we are now leading, using the philosophy and tools from the Insight Activator in a flexible way:

- **Brand reviews** – we organize 'one day meetings' around our key brands, with multidisciplinary teams (marketing, trade marketing, advertising agency, media agency, ACNielsen [retail panel agency], GfK [consumer panel agency], ad hoc research agency). These one-day meetings take place out of the office, in a nice and inspiring location. The purpose is to review the brand thoroughly and to shape together the strategy and action plan for the future. Before the meeting, every team member is briefed by us in order to make a short, 'to the point' presentation on the brand, using their knowledge and expertise domain. All these presentations happen that day. We facilitate the meeting in order to make everybody active and contribute throughout the day. We ensure we finish the meeting with a common understanding of the key issues and next steps. Often, we organize direct consumer contact activities for every team member prior to the brand review in order to immerse them better in the subject.

- **Brand positioning workshops** – the purpose of this kind of workshop is to review current positioning of the brand and to shape together the future positioning. This is particularly useful when we feel there is a gap between the current/desired positioning and the current perception by the consumer. To make this kind of workshop very productive, we also organize some type of 'connect activities' prior to or during that day.
- **Consumer target workshops** – for example 'The Seniors'. The purpose of this kind of workshop is to gain better understanding of the consumer target (for example, seniors – which is key for the future, with the tremendous demographic shift!), and to define an action plan for our brands to better capitalize on the opportunities of this target group. Again, it is very powerful to have consumer connect activities either before or during the day.

We have run several strategic Days-out of this kind, with considerable success. All team members are very enthusiastic about it. It is a very efficient way to involve a whole team in an important subject, and to design the strategy and action plan together.

In January 2004 we made an internal satisfaction survey in order to evaluate the satisfaction towards our CMI department in general, and in particular towards 'Reconnect with the Consumers'. The results were very positive:

Most added-value CMI department:

To the question: 'In what way did the CMI department bring added-value?', the top spontaneous answers were:

Getting better insights (33%)/Insight Activator process (29%)
Nielsen/GFK Workshops (for Sales: 37%, Nielsen: 31%)
Qualitative research (27%)

Consumer trends (19%)
Getting to know the consumers (15%)
Helped me to have direct consumer contacts (15%).
Helps me to build the future of my brand (13%)
(Comment: Those who had already been involved in Insight Activators put it in first).

Reconnect with the consumer:
Big hits are:

CMI: focus growth and building future of our brands, adding value for the business
Direct consumer contacts: new insights through direct consumer contacts. Gives marketers (and sales) a new and relevant point of view, with a 'real life' focus
Insight Activators: improved the quality of insights and turned insights into actionable ideas. CMI are leading IA projects effectively
Conferences: added value for the business
Brand health review workshops.

The results were very motivating for us as a strong recognition of the added value we were delivering to the business. On this basis, we further stretched our vision, as illustrated in Figure 5.8.

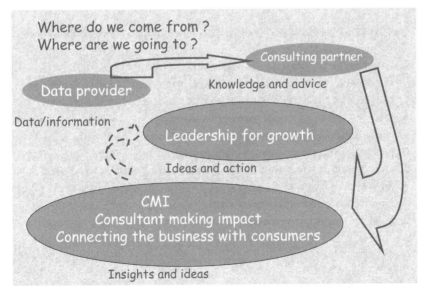

Figure 5.8 The virtuous circle.

In 1999, when we merged the MR departments from the three divisions, we were 'data provider' (data/information). We gradually moved to 'Consulting Partners', by focusing more on knowledge and advice. With 'Reconnect with the Consumers', we moved further to 'Consultants making impact' by 'connecting the business with the consumers' (CMI), and focusing on 'insights and ideas'. Now, we want to stretch ourselves further to *'Leadership for Growth'*, by leading team projects where we also ensure we generate concrete ideas and actions for the business. This vision, and the related CMI department work plan, have been endorsed fully by the senior management, which is again a sign of trust and strong encouragement for our initiatives.

Reviewing performance (like with our satisfaction survey) again proved useful at different levels: providing motivating feedback for the team, further building the department, gaining support and commitment from senior management, giving visibility to our department (all the users received the key results from the survey, as well as the derived vision and action plan). This is what we mean by building a *virtuous circle of success.*

Overall learning's: our success factors

Finally, what are the key success factors of this fantastic evolution of our role? We can summarize the lessons learnt in ten points, 'my 10 commandments':

1. Create an aspirational vision that announces the intended added value.
2. Involve the whole team in the vision.
3. Bring this vision to life within the company.
4. Develop, train and coach the team towards new competencies.
5. Give visibility to the department through central added-value activities.
6. The importance of direct consumer contacts.
7. Use the right tools and talents for powerful consumer insights.
8. Move to the virtuous circle.
9. Involve your agencies (partnership).
10. Don't be afraid to change!

I am particularly grateful to Unilever for having supported me at all times in the accomplishment of this great journey, and for allowing me to reveal some of the success factors today. We do hope the lessons and messages contained in this chapter will contribute to the further growth of our role in our organizations and to a bright future for our exciting profession.

Don't be afraid to change!

REFERENCES

Chadwick, S. (2002), *The client/provider dialogue. The vision.* Proceedings of the ESOMAR Conference: Managing Research for Profit, Gothenburg, Sweden.

Dimopoulos, J. (2002), *Understanding the contribution of research as a value driver.* Proceedings of the ESOMAR Conference: Managing Research for Profit, Gothenburg, Sweden.

Forsyth, J. (2002), *Generating more impact from marketing research.* Proceedings of the ESOMAR Conference: Managing Research for Profit, Gothenburg, Sweden.

Garcia-Gonzalez, J. (2002), *The role of market research in the increase of shareholder value.* Proceedings of the ESOMAR Conference: Managing Research for Profit, Gothenburg, Sweden.

Hastings, R. (2002), *People don't want market research. They want marketing solutions to marketing problems.* Proceedings of the ESOMAR Conference: Managing Research for Profit, Gothenburg, Sweden.

Havermans, J. (2004), Can market researchers compete with consultants? A seat at the board room table. *Research World,* January, 16–19.

Hofmans, M. and Schellekens, M. (2002), *The Marco Polo Travelogue,* Releas Initiative, ESOMAR.

Parmeswar, R. (2002), Coca-Cola–The Relationship Company. *Research World,* April, 8–9.

POPAI (2001), Consumer Buying Habits Survey, Belgium. *Retail Insights.*

Rosinski, P. (2003), *Coaching Across Cultures.* Nicholas Brealey Publishing.

Smith, D. (2002), *Spotlight on decision making. What is needed?* Proceedings of the ESOMAR Conference: Managing Research for Profit, Gothenburg, Sweden.

Stengel, J. (2003), *Consumers are Reinventing Marketing: Will you be in Touch or Left Behind?* Presentation given at World Federation of Advertisers Conference, Brussels, Belgium.

Unilever (2000), *Path to Growth. Leadership competencies for Growth* – internal documents.

Unilever (2002), *Reconnect with Consumers for Growth* – internal documents.

Van den Berg, W. (2002), Research is an integral process. *Research World,* February, 22–23.

Chapter Six

The Operation was Successful but the Patient Died: Why Research on Innovation is Successful yet Innovations Fail

Omar Mahmoud[a]

This chapter argues that new products fail because of individual and group irrationality. The chapter outlines the thinking errors, cites examples and provides recommendations for improving the decision-making process.

INTRODUCTION

'Everyone complains about his poor memory, nobody about his judgement.'
La Rochefoucauld

Most new products fail. Failure is attributed to the proposition (weak advertising, parity product, high price, etc.) or to the marketing plan (inadequate media, low distribution, etc.). This interpretation does not explain why failures continue in spite of the growing knowledge about factors

[a] Chief - Market Research, UNICEF Private Sector Division.

Market Research Best Practice. Edited by P. Mouncey and F. Wimmer.
© 2007 John Wiley & Sons, Limited.

driving success and failure, and following a rigorous product launch process.

Millions of species have lived on Earth over hundreds of millions of years. Yet it is estimated that about 99.99% of all species that have ever existed have disappeared (Ormerod, 2005). Too many creatures competing for limited resources. Survival of the fittest, and failure of the majority. Is something similar happening to new products? Yes.

Every year, thousands of new products and brands appear on store shelves. The problem is that most of the items introduced fail in the market and even end up being discontinued. Manufacturers lose millions of dollars making, distributing and marketing these products. Estimates of new introduction success rates range from a relatively high 30% to as low as less than 1%, depending on the country, category and definition of success (McMath, 1998). Business literature and internal corporate reviews that address this issue tend to focus on the product, marketing and organizational aspects of the business, citing examples of what are considered to be the reasons for failure and giving managers advice for success. But most of the advice is not of much help to managers. Managers of large and mid-sized corporations are aware of, and operate by, apparently sound management practices. They study their markets, listen to consumers, test their products before launching them and support the launch with strong marketing plans and heavy spending. Many companies even have new product launch systems in place. But new products continue to fail most of the time. Why?

The traditional explanations of new product failures can be classified into three types:

1. Inherent, or conceptual, initiative weakness. These include a technology-driven idea not built on real consumer needs, a product that does not deliver on a concept promise, a negative value perception by consumers, a narrowly defined small target group, a difficult habit to change, etc.
2. Weakness in the marketing plan. Marketing plans may suffer from low awareness generation due to low media spending, slow and low distribution build-up and inadequate initial promotion.
3. External market events. These may result from competitive preemption or strong competitive retaliation, negative public relations or word-of-mouth, or changes in the economic, trade or legal environments.

The above reasons for new product failure become more serious under flawed organizational structures and reward systems that widen the gap between the managers' interests and those of the company.

While we agree with most of these assessments, we judge them to be first causes that nevertheless require deeper explanations. Simply put, most of these reasons for product failure are known in advance, as most post mortem analyses show. Importantly, research for new product launches, including many validated simulated test market techniques, has a much higher success rate (i.e. predictability) than the rate of new product success. One could argue that the rate of new product success should at least be equal to the accuracy of new product research forecasting, if not higher, by assuming the lower ranges of the forecast in financial calculations.

We think that a critical and common reason for new product failure lies in managers' inability to think clearly and logically throughout the product launch cycle. It is taken for granted that all managers are smart and think straight. But, as thinking guru Edward De Bono explains, there is a difference between intelligence and thinking (De Bono, 1986, 1988). Using a car driving analogy, most managers have a good car motor (brain) but they don't always drive it well (think straight). Most managers make smart and cold decisions based on clear and adequate data. But, in reality, the data are often incomplete, grey and messy. Moreover, cognitive limitations, biases, emotions, interests and wishful thinking often prevent managers from making sound business decisions. They cease to think rationally. Rational thinking is defined as the thinking that leads to the conclusion that is most likely to be correct given the available knowledge at the time (Sutherland, 1992 p. 4).

Market researchers, in addition to conducting and developing new tools for market research, ought to lead the decision-making process within their organizations to ensure that their research efforts help their organizations achieve their ultimate business objectives.

While managers' irrationality applies to many aspects of running the business, this chapter focuses on business irrationality as it applies to new product introductions. These irrationalities are divided into cognitive, emotional, and group irrationalities. The chapter will cover each of these three types of irrationalities, citing examples from the psychology and business literature. It will also cover a number of thinking errors related to the misuse or abuse of market research. It will conclude by giving recommendations to improve companies' decision-making processes.

'We think, and it is true, but we think so badly that I often feel it would be better if we did not.'

Bertrand Russell

COGNITIVE REASONS

The availability error

'Man is a credulous animal and must believe something. In the absence of good grounds for belief, he will be satisfied with bad ones.'

Bertrand Russell

The availability error occurs when managers base their decisions on the most available information and not on *all* the evidence.

Information may be available because it is widely publicized, recent, dramatic or emotional. Examples of the availability error in our everyday lives include slowing down after seeing a car collision, fearing to fly after an air crash or thinking that one is more likely to die in an accident than due to a stroke. The availability error often leads us to draw illogical conclusions confidently. When asked whether there are more words ending with 'ing' or with 'n' as the letter before last, the majority of respondents select the logically impossible answer of 'ing', given that 'ing' is a subset of the words with 'n' as the penultimate letter. The reason for this irrationality is obvious – words with 'ing' are more available than words with 'n' before the last letter (Dawes, 1988 p. 99).

In business, the availability error occurs when decisions are based on the most recent focus group or a manager's spouse's opinion of a new product, as they may be more available to the manager's mind at the time of decision-making than tons of research data (Sutherland, 1992 pp.16–32; Kahneman *et al.*, 1993 pp. 163–178). Teams working on new initiatives start their research by doing qualitative research in which consumers are tortured until they confess that they like the new product. News spreads in the organization about how great the new initiative is. The team and management mindset shifts quickly from exploration to execution, with the remaining research seen as confirmatory of these early impressions.

Importantly, these available impressions are usually based on interactions with real people, with visual memories and verbatim reactions, making them more powerful and memorable than dry numbers in a management report (Pratkanis and Aronson, 2001 p. 173).

The 'penny wise' mentality is another example of the availability error in business. A company in a cost-saving mode may slash all budgets, including its market research budget by 20%. This reduction in a company's already tiny research budget of a few thousand dollars may result in taking undue risks on investments of millions of dollars. But this error occurs because the 20% savings are immediate or 'available', while the high risk associated with less research is not.

A variant on the availability error is to think that the available information is all we need to solve the problem at hand. In a school experiment, students were given a number of maths problems, including one that gave them the numbers of different animals on a ship and asked them to calculate the age of the captain (e.g. there are 12 cows, 16 sheep and 24 goats on a ship; how old is the captain?). About 70% of the students gave numerical answers and justified their response on the grounds that when you have a maths problem, you use the available numbers and mathematical signs to come up with the solution. While business cases may be less extreme, they often involve a similar mechanism. More data may be needed to answer a business question, but managers use what they have and think it is adequate. In everyday life, people have difficulty saying 'I don't know.' In the business world, many managers are reluctant to say 'I need more data.' In a machomarketing environment, it is often considered more important to make a decision than to assess whether one has enough information to make such a decision. It is, however, rational behaviour to seek more information when data is inadequate for decision-making.

> *A team that tested a new concentrated drink qualitatively in an underdeveloped market had a vivid picture of consumers' excitement about product performance in in-home visits, which had a stronger impact than negative quantitative data that arrived in reports and forecasts later on.*

First impressions: the anchoring effect

Managers must learn to avoid the anchoring effect by relying on more 'zero-based' thinking. The anchoring effect is another faulty form of reasoning, which occurs when our thinking is influenced by the first piece of information given to us. Two groups of respondents were asked to estimate the percentage of African countries that are members of the United Nations, and to indicate whether it is higher or lower than a given figure. That figure was 10% for one group and 65% for the second group. The resulting estimates were 25% for the first group and 45% for the second group.

In business, when managers are told that the initial results of a test market or product test are positive, they push the project ahead, even if subsequent and more comprehensive results contradict earlier data. When sales of a new product are estimated aggressively at around $100 million, 'conservative' revisions may bring it down to a lower number, but that number may still be much higher than a more realistic estimate had the original forecast been lower than $100 million. In other words, managers are often aware of the anchoring effect and make adjustments, but still adjust insufficiently. What managers need to do is to evaluate the new product economics using objective criteria and ignoring previous estimates.

The anchoring effect is a common tactic that managers use when re-questing budget funds for their project or department. If a manager wants to increase his budget from $1 million to $2 million, he asks for $4 million. The manager approving the budget assesses the budget from a base of $4 million rather than $1 million or $2 million. An approved budget of $2 million then looks like a budget cut compared to the requested $4 million, and fits with the company's cost-saving mode.

A new product launch team tested a product at three prices – Euro 5, Euro 6 and Euro 7. They got fairly positive results and a payout proposition at Euro 6. However, just before launch, economics dictated a Euro 8 pricing. The team went ahead driven by the initial, but now wrong, estimates.

It is too dark inside

'It used to be that people needed products to survive. Now products need people to survive.'

Nicholas Johnson

Clear thinking requires that managers seek to find out the facts, not to confirm their judgement. In one of the Nasrudin pleasantries, the following conversation takes place between the Middle Eastern sage, who was seen looking for something under the streetlight, and his neighbour:

Neighbour: What are you looking for?
Nasrudin: My house key.
Neighbour: Where did you lose it?
Nasrudin: Under the bed?
Neighbour: So, why aren't you looking for it inside the house?
Nasrudin: Oh! It's too dark inside.

In business, experts and managers agree in theory that products should be made based on consumer needs. In practice, however, companies often make what they are good at and then try to convince consumers that is what consumers need. Why? Because it is not easy to identify and make what consumers really need. It is easier for companies to make what they are good at, regardless of what consumers want. In theory, the consumer is king. In practice, the technology, trade or Wall Street are the real kings.

Managers then seek the information they need to prove that they are meeting consumers' needs. Surveys are designed to confirm what has been decided, not to find out what needs to be done. Using marketing doublespeak often obscures this reality. Instead of saying that a decision is purely judgemental and contradictory to consumer research findings, it is said to be a 'strategic decision' that is hard for young managers to understand.

A team invented a dishwashing gel to be used instead of using soap or washing powders, available at home and used for laundry, household cleaning and dishwashing: new technology and good aesthetics. The new technology was not addressing a real consumer need and required new usage and purchase habits. It failed.

Bull's eye objectives

Managers should make an effort to meet objectives and not create objectives that fit their efforts.

A man walked into a bar and noticed a bull's face drawn on the wall with an arrow in the middle of its eye. Impressed by the precision of the shot, the man asked the bar owner, 'How did you get the arrow exactly in the middle of the bull's eye?' The bar owner replied, 'I first shot the arrow, then I drew the bull's eye around the arrow.'

In business, companies start by setting aggressive objectives, such as having superior products or best value brands. They then translate those objectives into specific measures such as obtaining a higher product rating against the market leader in a consumer product test. It is often in this translation from objectives to measures that things go wrong. After failing to obtain a product advantage for a new soft drink in a blind in-home use test, managers may start trying different measures. They may test the product identified, add biasing statements to the test such as 'super refreshing drink', test among morning drinkers only or run a taste test in a central location instead of an in-home use test. Through trial and error, the product is likely to achieve an advantage among some consumer group in some kind of testing for some test measures. The product may have met its action standards or measures, but has it really met its objective?

A team developed a new chocolate with nuts bar providing superior taste. It tested it blind against existing products and got parity results. It repeated the testing context aided with different kinds of statements, tested among demographic subgroups, and finally found a small internal advantage among chocolate with nuts eaters. The product was a mediocre launch.

Non-stick (Teflon) facts

'So, we see best what we are supposed to see. We see poorly, or not at all, that data that does not fit into our paradigm.'

Joel Barker

Breakthrough changes come from facts managers don't like and often ignore. While the availability error produces a bias to the most available data, non-stick or Teflon facts are those data available to managers that are overlooked completely. Most managers talk about the importance of being first to introduce a new product. Data says otherwise. A published survey shows that out of 500 cases, only 11% of new brands were market leaders a few years later. About 47% of first entrants fail (Golder and Tellis, 1993; Tellis and Golder, 2002 pp. 40–56). This fact, however, is ignored completely by managers. In most corporations, a sense of urgency is considered a business virtue, but one seldom hears of a sense of quality. There is always time do it over, but no time to do it right. Interestingly, research has shown that companies that introduce a non-pioneering market leader usually talk about their brand as the market pioneer. The first entrant is usually discontinued and so its voice is not heard anymore.

Companies that pride themselves on the superiority of their products and advertising ignore or deny external evidence that suggests that their product or advertising is below average and tend to manufacture their own 'facts.' Positioning and advertising are magical factors managers like to celebrate at the expense of more mundane, though usually more effective, factors such as distribution, media spending and price promotions.

> *A team tested a new initiative in a concept and product test. After-use reaction was positive but concept scores were poor. Management was not discouraged and said 'we can fix the concept when we develop the copy.' The learning that it is extremely difficult to develop strong advertising out of a weak concept was not internalized. Copy results came back poor, as would have been predicted by the concept scores. After several rounds of testing, the ad agency was changed. A new copy was developed deviating from the original concept and copy. The launch failed.*

Objectivity or 'heads I win, tails you lose'

'Most men, when they think they are thinking, are merely rearranging their prejudices.'

Knute Rockne

Objectivity means giving equal weight to information that confirms our hypothesis as to that which contradicts it. In reality, we often assign excessive weight to confirmatory data at the expense of contradictory data. This usually involves two mechanisms: first, we often quote anecdotal cases that support our beliefs and ignore those that don't, and second, we exercise 'optional stopping' or 'satisfying' in the pursuit of data when the early data supports our convictions, but continue the search for more data when early indicators do not support our predictions (Janis and Mann, 1979 p. 25; Sutherland, 1992 p. 259). This is a kind of 'I always find lost things in the last place I search for them.' If results of a first test are positive, we move ahead with our project. If they are not, we run more tests hoping to obtain better results. Thus, our biases influence the quality and the quantity of information we seek. In everyday life, this is often known as 'self-fulfilling prophecy.' We seek the quantity and quality of information that confirms our preconceived ideas: 'Seek and ye shall find.'

One way of slanting the data to support our point of view is to seek the opinion of experts and consultants who agree with our point of view and disregard those who don't. If we are interested in stressing the importance of building brand loyalty or niche brands, we would probably not invite a marketing consultant who does not believe in the viability of niche brands or increasing brand consumption among current brand users. We want to hear what we want to hear.

Darwin '. . . followed a golden rule, namely that whenever a new observation or thought came across me, which was opposed to my general results, to make a memorandum of it without fail and at once; for I had found by experience that such facts and thoughts were far more apt to escape from the memory than favourable ones (Gilovich, 1993 p. 62).'

When looking at equity or image information, we often look for the signs of significant differences (-s-) and draw firm conclusions around those differences. We ignore the lack of significant differences on most equity and image attributes. Our brands are often significantly similar to other brands. The same goes for trend data. We focus on change and ignore the fact that in many categories things are amazingly stable.

Asymmetric evaluation

'It is the peculiar and perpetual error of human understanding to be more moved and excited by affirmatives than negatives.'

Francis Bacon

Managers should always check if there is evidence to the contrary of what they are advocating, and address it.

In a research seminar, I gave my audience a popular objectivity test. You are shown four cards that have letters on one side and numbers on the other side and are asked to determine the minimum number of cards you need to turn on the other side to confirm this statement:

All cards with vowels on one side have odd numbers on the other side.

The four cards are: A, B, 3, 4. The most common answer is that you only need to turn the A card to 'confirm' that this vowel A has an odd number on the other side. Very few realize that we also need to turn the 4 card to see if it has a vowel on the other side, thus 'disconfirming' our hypothesis. It is a habit of the mind to seek information that confirms our beliefs but not that which denies it. Incidentally, a few managers also suggest we should turn the 3 card to see if it has a vowel or a consonant. However, the 3 card is irrelevant since we are not making any statements about consonants (Wujec, 1989; Vos Savant and Fleischer, 1991; Sutherland, 1992 pp.137–138; Paulos, 1995).

Asymmetric evaluation is one special type of the lack of objectivity involving observing and citing occasions when an event occurred and a specific outcome resulted, and overlooking all other event/outcome combinations.

A believer in astrology will cite cases of correct predictions as evidence of the validity of astrology but will ignore or even forget false predictions. Lottery organizers give wide publicity to the few lucky winners and say nothing about the vast majority that gain nothing. We remember the few dreams that seem to have come true and forget the many that didn't. Similarly, a manager will refer to the one example where his strategy worked and ignore all cases when it didn't.

A rational way to address the asymmetric evaluation bias is to build a two-by-two table to count the incidents when input was used or not used, and the incidents when an outcome was obtained or not obtained.

In everyday life, we often 'feel' that the telephone only rings when we are in the shower. In reality, we are more likely to recall times when the phone rang while we were showering than times when it rang when we were not showering, or did not ring while we were showering.

	I was in shower	*I was not in shower*
Phone rang		
Phone did not ring		

In business, an advertiser may insist on using a celebrity in a TV commercial because he recalls a successful ad that had a celebrity. He is unlikely to recall successful commercials that had no celebrities or unsuccessful commercials with a celebrity.

	Commercial with celebrity	*Commercial without celebrity*
Successful		
Not successful		

Even professionals are influenced by how options are framed to them. Doctors opt for different routes, operation vs. medication, depending on whether the probabilities of success are framed positively (80% will survive) or negatively (20% will die).

We should also provide future predictions in both positive and negative terms. For example, a sales forecast should indicate the likely revenue in case of in-market success, and also the likely loss in case of not meeting objectives. Put differently, for our internal transactions, we should frame our propositions in both positive and negative terms.

False dilemma

'The absence of alternatives clears the mind marvellously.'

Henry Kissinger

Managers need to seek new directions beyond either/or options.

'Are you for everyone's right to own a gun or do you want to have criminals run the country?' This is how the National Rifle Association frames the issue of gun control. This is a flagrant example of a false dilemma, because only two unfavourable alternatives are presented, when in reality there are a variety of policy options for gun control, ranging from stricter ownership controls to tougher penalties for illegal ownership (Gilbert, 1996).

Companies often set 'Go/No Go' decision stops for product initiatives. For example, a company's action standards for an initiative may stipulate that if the new product or advertising obtains a specific score in testing, it will be introduced. Otherwise, the project is shelved. This puts a manager in a situation where he has to make a tough call: 'Should I approve the heavy investment or kill the project?' Moreover, when people's careers are at stake, every effort is made to lead top management to a 'Go' decision, even if the facts suggest otherwise. This situation often represents a false dilemma, or an incomplete specification of possibilities, because in reality there are more than two choices (Dawes, 2001 p. 55). There is usually a continuum of decision-making with 'Go' and 'No Go' only being the extreme points. Managers may opt to step back and refine the product idea or formula, do more consumer work, pilot the plan in a test-market, combine the initiative with another one, launch it on a smaller scale, etc. Many faulty product launch decisions are driven by a simplistic and limited comparison between launching and 'doing nothing'. The fear of losing market opportunity by not launching a new product often has a stronger persuasive power for action than the potential savings of not making the wrong launch decision (Pratkanis and Aronson, 2001 p. 95). Managers need to think black, white and grey (Pratkanis and Aronson, 2001 pp. 99–100).

Pennsylvania Dutch

'It ain't so much what people don't know that hurts as what they know that ain't so.'
Artemus Ward

Managers should know the origins of their beliefs, rules and practices so they can use them appropriately. Large numbers of people in the United States believe, erroneously, that the founders of Pennsylvania came from Holland, as they hear references to the 'Pennsylvania Dutch'. The truth is that it was the Germans who settled in Pennsylvania in great numbers. Due to the difficulty many have in pronouncing 'Deutsch' (or German), the term was distorted to 'Dutch' (or, from Holland). This is an extreme form of a communication phenomenon known as 'sharpening and levelling' in which the speaker emphasizes what he considers to be the key points of the message and ignores the details or caveats. As kids, we encountered this strange phenomenon when we played the telephone game, in which we sat in a circle and each one whispered a sentence in his neighbour's ear. By the time the circle was completed, the message was unrecognizable to its author.

In business top management, the ultimate decision-maker is often exposed to heavily 'sharpened and levelled' recommendations. Results of a small-scale test are often sharpened by omitting to mention the base size or ignoring the fact that the differences were not statistically significant. Worse, nonsignificant results of several small-scale tests are lumped together to produce an artificially significant win. Product test wins among the current brand users in a directed interest test are quoted out of context, giving the impression that the test was run among a representative sample in a blind context. A manager in charge of a project to restage the existing brand with new advertising reports that the plan will increase sales by 30%, and neglects to say that this requires increased spending and that at equal spending to current levels, the sales increase would be less than 10%. Management is often given the good news only: the truth but not the whole truth, and not nothing but the truth. This sharpening and levelling effect is often illustrated by the popular business anecdote about workers who evaluated a new product and judged it to be a crock of shit, took it to their supervisors who considered it a pail of dung, the managers assessed it as a container of excrement, but their directors thought it was a vessel of fertilizer. By the time the news reached top management, the product was considered to be an object that promotes growth.

> The product test showed a nonsignificant advantage for the new for-mula over its main competitor among a small group of the past three months' users of a related product category in a copy-aided blind test. That's what the official summary said. The next piece of com-munication ignored the 'nonsignificant' part. The next presentation left out the breakout part. What top management heard was that the new formula had a great win against competition in product testing.

The past is history

'*The most honorable action is always that of ceasing to honor dishonorable commit-ments.*'

(Pratkanis and Aronson, 2001 pp. 235–241)

Managers should assess the soundness of their financial decisions, ignoring past investments.

A common form of financial irrationality is known as the *sunk cost error*. In its simplest form, a person who buys a theatre ticket for an extremely boring show will torture himself by watching it to its very end. Instead of minimizing his losses by making better use of his time, the person thinks he is 'getting his money's worth.' In business, managers will refuse to abandon a failing initiative because the company has already invested so much in it. This is a thinking error, because what counts are the future gains and losses. The past is irrelevant (Dawes, 1988 pp. 24–27; 2001 pp. 22–25).

Interestingly, the sunk cost error has its reverse side. A person who buys a theatre ticket for $10 and loses it will refuse to buy a new ticket for $10. Again, whether he had bought a ticket in the past or not is irrelevant. If the show was worth paying $10 for in the first place, it should be worth paying the same amount again, unless of course one runs out of money, which is rarely the case. In business, whether money has already been spent on a project or not is irrelevant to an assessment of a project's future cost/benefit analysis (Sutherland, 1992 pp. 99–101). The claim that we should spend more to salvage what has already been spent should be attacked as a rationale for throwing good money after bad money.

> *The attempt to salvage an historically strong but now declining brand made little progress. The concept was not above average and the product failed to score higher than competition, but the price was higher. The decision to launch was difficult given the test results. But the decision to stop the project was equally difficult given the past spending. Eventually, the 'doing something is better than doing nothing' logic prevailed, and the product was launched, unsuccessfully.*

Hypotheses and conclusions

'Our brains are designed to be brilliantly uncreative. They are designed to form patterns on every possible occasion on the future.'

Edward De Bono

Managers should not confuse hypotheses with conclusions.

As thinking expert Edward De Bono suggests, our brain is not a thinking organ. It is a pattern-forming machine, from an evolutionary perspective – man sees beast, man runs away (or beast eats man). There is no need to break such a pattern from a survival point of view. Even in our current day-to-day life, routine action is more common and necessary than conscious thinking. We find a route to get to work and follow it for years. The tendency to look for order and to spot patterns is a natural, and often a healthy, one. However, when data are ambiguous, we should suspend judgement and treat our newly formed patterns as hypotheses and not as conclusions or facts. Such a distinction is often blurred as we seek to use whatever information we have at hand to make decisions. Tolerating ambiguity is often a key step towards breakthrough changes. Unfortunately, tolerating ambiguity is not a business virtue, and what starts as a hypotheses becomes, if unchallenged, a conclusion. The essence of market research is making decisions based on probable hypotheses and likely theories, not on proven facts or guesses. Market research is science applied to marketing. It is not perfect mathematics, but it is not astrology either.

Piccadilly explanations

'I can't think now, I am working.'

Garfield cartoon

Managers should resist superficial bases for decisions, especially under time pressure.

Many companies attempt to study their past successes and failures to draw lessons for future application. Results of these analyses are often at best superficial, and at worst misleading, though for different reasons. For successes, it is usually the manager in charge who conducts the analysis. The purpose is usually to sell to top management the person's marketing or product development genius, with the hope of obtaining a promotion and salary increase. The analysis usually provides good material for an annual meeting presentation, but it hardly ever provides adequate perspective for reapplication. No wonder very few companies manage to reapply their in-market successes.

Extraneous factors for success, such as government regulations, as well as nondramatic marketing variables like distribution or pricing, are often ignored and emphasis is put on the person's or team's marketing genius. In cases of failure, if any post mortem analysis is done at all, the person who conducts the analysis is not the one who was in charge of the initiative, simply because that person is usually not around anymore. The review is again superficial and focuses on the previous manager's stupidity, wrapped in business jargon. The new manager is more interested in selling his new plans to management than in providing an objective assessment of the failing project. He is unlikely to conclude that the project was bound to fail because it was not based on a real market need or due to internal company politics.

Importantly, the root causes of success or failure are never explored. Detailed descriptions of what happened are given instead of explanations. This is known as the 'the Piccadilly explanation', after the famous road and circus in London. The 'explanation' given for giving that road such an un-English name was that a tailor who lived in that road used to make collars called piccadills. No explanation was given as to why the collars were called piccadills in the first place (Jones, 1995).

It often strikes me that airlines announce the late departure of a flight due to the late arrival of an incoming flight. I am often tempted to ask why the incoming flight was late to begin with, but I expect the answer to be the later arrival of the previous flight, and so on.

> *An internal company analysis concluded that the key to success was offering a product that consumers truly wanted and supporting it with persuasive advertising. But don't all marketing recommendations say that consumers truly want the product and that testing shows that the advertising is persuasive? What is different this time? For failures, it is a similarly simple explanation, such as 'We did not have deep understanding of the consumer,' or 'The advertising did not give consumers a good reason to buy the product.' Why not?*

The illusion of control

In our complex world, there is usually a huge gap between our actions and the outcome of those actions, whether we are talking day-to-day behaviour, political decisions, sports endeavours, business activities or simply the toss of a coin. Results are influenced by circumstances, the actions of others and many unforeseen factors. The interaction of these factors may be simply referred to as luck.

The illusion of control refers to attributing to our skill and effort positive outcomes, and to luck or circumstances negative outcomes. A corollary of this phenomenon is attributing to skill positive outcomes of our own actions, and to luck those of others. In its simplest form, the illusion of control is observed when gamblers roll dice softly for low numbers and hard for high numbers, or when we think that lottery tickets chosen by us have higher chances of winning than lottery tickets given to us.

The primacy effect provides more power to the illusion of control. Those who guess early tosses of coins right, or are made to think so, gain more confidence in their ability to predict future tosses of coins than those whose early luck is less fortunate.

In business, many managers assume that new product launches will produce the results they anticipate and desire. Assuming a 50/50 chance of success, managers with an early success record will hold stronger beliefs about their ability to succeed in the future. Less successful managers will discount past failure as a result of chance and circumstances. The illusion of control is a major factor in our inability to learn from past successes and failures, and in the predominance of the hindsight bias.

> *A global team expanding the launch of a new product, successfully launched in the parent country, to new regions dismissed research evidence that the launch was unlikely to succeed in other countries due to different consumer habits, competitive landscape and regulatory environment. The team insisted that as they had made it work in one market, they would make it work in others.*

EMOTIONAL REASONS

Lake Wobegon effect

'The average person thinks he isn't.'

Managers need to see the similarity in different things as much as they see the differences in similar things.

In his fictional community of Lake Wobegon where 'the women are strong, the men are good looking, and all the children are above average,' Garrison Keillor draws our attention to a peculiar form of irrationality; that of everyone thinking he or she is above average in favourable characteristics or skills. Research suggests that we all live in Lake Wobegon. In a survey among one million high school students, 70% thought they were above average on leadership ability and only 2% thought they were below average. On getting along well with others, all students thought they were above average and 60% thought they were in the top 10%. Students learn from their teachers. A survey among university professors showed that 90% of them thought they had above-average teaching capabilities. This Lake Wobegon effect applies to the future as much as it applies to the present. Although only 25% of the total population thought the United States as a whole would be financially better off in the next year, 54% thought they would be better off (Gilovich, 1993 pp. 77–78). The Lake Wobegon effect also seems to be a global phenomenon. In a survey among British motorists, 95% thought they were above-average drivers (Sutherland, 1992 p. 240).

In business, the simple laws of probability suggest that most new product introductions will fail, given the large number of such introductions into predominantly stable markets. This is the same Murphy's Law logic that explains why the other line in a supermarket seems to move faster than our own line, simply because there are more 'other' lines (Matthews, 1997).

Research suggests that objective assessment of new products by external consultants indicates a much lower proportion of truly innovative products, compared to self-assessment by managers for products launched by their firms (ACNielsen BASES and Ernst & Young Global Client Consulting, 1999; Schneider/Boston University, 2001).

On a more personal level, young managers come up with the same ideas and products their predecessors tested unsuccessfully, and expect different results. When queried about their rationale for expecting success, they usually refer to changing circumstances, when they secretly think that they will make the proposition work because they are different. Every manager thinks his company, product category, brand or situation is different. True, we are all unique, just like everyone else.

A variant of the Lake Wobegon effect is the belief that high risks and probabilities of failure, even though valid in a statistical sense, would not apply to me, be it a risk of lung cancer due to smoking, AIDS due to unsafe sex or new product failure due to research findings (Pratkanis and Aronson, 2001 pp. 241–243).

> *A respectable business forecasting firm mentioned to me that when one of their clients did not like the volume forecast for their new lemon squared soap, they challenged the forecasting firm, asking, 'Have you ever done any forecasts for lemon squared soap in Bingoland before?' The forecasting firm explained that they had done many forecasts for similar products, but the client insisted 'No, lemon squared soap is different.'*

Limbic management

'Where id was, there ego shall be.'

Sigmund Freud

'How could an intelligent person like him do something as stupid as that?' is a common expression of astonishment at obviously irrational behaviour from apparently rational people. This includes the famous politician caught in a sex scandal, a sports star involved in a street fight or simply a normal and calm person getting mad because someone cut in front of him at a supermarket checkout counter. These occurrences cannot be interpreted in rational terms alone. They are due to the fact that our brain operates at three levels: reptilian (shared with reptiles and regulating basic unconscious functions such as body temperature) limbic (emotional, shared with mammals) and cortical (rational). The id is a term often used to describe our basic emotional drives and instinctual reactions, compared to the ego (rationality) and superego (morality and ideals). The id is impervious to awareness, logic or time. This explains phrases such as 'I just wasn't thinking at the time,' which, in psychological terms, means the emotional limbic brain overtook the rational cortical brain.

The limbic brain is induced to action via five basic drives: Power, Territoriality, Sex, Nurturance (relationships) and Survival, which developed over millions of years of evolution. In business, all five drives are present in disguised forms, some of which are more relevant to new product launch decisions. A manager may want to launch a product as his only way to get a promotion and attain power, or even to survive. Agreeing with one's boss on a wrong decision is one way to foster nurturance. Territoriality, in the literal sense of a larger office, or in the more abstract sense of broader geographic responsibility, is often a driver of business decisions. Sex is probably the strongest of all five drives, yet the subtlest in our modern life. Sex may be seen as a potential reward for achievement driven by a bold decision, or as a driver of that decision (Weiner and Hefter, 1999).

The testosterone effect

'*Doubt is not a pleasant state but certainty is a ridiculous one.*'

Voltaire

Research shows that senior marketing executives are perceived, by younger marketers, as people who make rush decisions relying on focus groups and intuition, are focused on short-term results, pay too much attention to competition and are always in a rush. They find it easy and appealing to make major decisions, leaving the execution to their subordinates. Importantly, males are perceived to exhibit these flawed decision-making characteristics to a higher degree than females. Women are more thoughtful in their decision-making process and are better at building consensus. A joint study released by Copernicus Marketing Consulting and Research and Gazelle International at the Conference Boards 1998 Marketing Conference indicated that men's and women's approach to marketing decision-making differs greatly, and that a harried approach to marketing decision-making may be a significant factor in the poor performance of most marketing programmes, according to Dr. Kevin J. Clancy and Douglas Calhoun, CEO and President, respectively of Copernicus and Gazelle (Copernicus Marketing Consulting and Research and Gazelle International, 1998).

GROUP REASONS

'The initiative has no clothes' or business group think

'Where all men think alike, no one thinks very much.'

Walter Lippman

Managers should encourage individual thinking and voicing of unpopular opinions.

Disastrous decisions are often made by teams concerned with maintaining consensus and taking action to such an extent that individuals do not voice their concerns. As each person silences his reservations, the group as a whole adopts a false feeling of the correctness of its decisions. Group think is characterized by an illusion of invulnerability, discounting early warnings, extreme optimism, putting pressure on those who express opposing opinions, suppressing one's own doubts to conform with the group and unquestioned belief in the group's morality (Janis and Mann, 1979 pp. 130–131). The main danger of group think is that, by diffusing responsibility among group members, it allows teams to make irrational and hasty decisions which they would not make as individuals. People assume that with a group of smart managers, good decisions follow automatically. After all 'we can't all be wrong.' This, in turn, leads to a *de-individuating* effect on team members that inhibits them from expressing their opinions or trusting their judgement. As the cynical creator of the Dilbert character put it, 'Remember, you can't be wrong unless you take a position. Don't fall into that trap (Adams, 1996).' A serious consequence of this attitude is known as the '*Bystander effect*', whereby individuals refrain from taking an action in the presence of others, which they would take if they were alone. In its extreme form, it was found that individuals are more likely to come to the aid of victims of accidents or crimes when they are the only witnesses than when others are watching. The same phenomenon seems to be true of business accidents and crimes (Sutherland, 1992 pp. 59–60).

Research shows that people give more wrong answers when exposed to previous wrong answers by others than when they answer individually. This tendency is aggravated when a group is promised a monetary reward linked to the number of group members who answer correctly. In business, lower ranking managers are influenced by comments made by their superiors, and often suppress or change their opinions.

Group dynamics in hierarchical organizations also suffer from projection, where executives overestimate the proportion of managers who share their opinion (Gross and Brodt, 2001). This is either due to the executive insecurity that drives them to believe in the commonness of their perceptions, or to their non democratic management style that makes them end up surrounded by conforming subordinates.

Truth, lies and market research

'Market research can be conducted and interpreted to prove any desired conclusion.'
The Law of Predicted Results

Managers should be trained on the basic principles of market research before they use its findings to make business decisions.

Market research is a critical element in the qualification of new introductions to the marketplace. Million-dollar decisions are based on consumer research findings. Unfortunately, many managers lack a deep understanding of the basic concepts underlying consumer research methods and interpretation. But very few have the audacity of David Stockman, Reagan's Budget Director, who admitted in 1981 that 'None of us really understands what's going on with all these numbers (Dewdney, 1993).'

Below are a few observations on some of the most common errors in using market research findings.

- **Representivity** – managers are often given research data that show that 'consumers' gave a high rating to the product, but are not always told that the test was run among a narrow group that represents only 20% of the population and is difficult to reach in reality (e.g. users of a certain product subsegment who think that a particular product attribute is important).
- **Validation** – an advertising agency may play a piece of advertising and present data that show that 80% of consumers said they would buy the advertised product, without mentioning that no correlation has ever been found between results of such a question and in-market results. That is, the technique and question asked are not validated. The research world is overflowing with consumer research techniques that measure the effects of advertising, packaging, pricing and promotions

on brand sales. However, very few of these techniques are predictive of market results.

- **Statistical significance** – consumer research data are based on samples of the total population ranging between 100–1000 people, in most cases. Thus, unlike results based on the total population, consumer research numbers carry with them a margin of error. This is analogous to the difference between results of opinion polls and those of actual elections. Statistical significance testing is conducted to indicate a level of confidence in the data. Results are declared significant if the possibility of them having occurred by chance is extremely low (e.g. 5–10%). Unfortunately, many managers quote research numbers without indicating whether the higher rating for product A vs. product B is statistically significant or not. Moreover, significance, because of its literal meaning, is often confused with importance. Significance, statistically speaking, only means that the difference between two numbers is likely to be real, but not necessarily important. The total population may indeed prefer a red pack to a green one, but this does not mean that more of them will buy the product in the red pack.
- **Benchmarking** – in consumer research, all numbers are relative. To say that a product received an average rating of 65, or that 40% said they would buy a product, is meaningless. Are those numbers high or low? Compared to what? Good research design and interpretation require reliable benchmarks. Benchmarks could be another product in the same study or historical norms within a category or country. Failure to define a benchmark, especially for a new category, is one reason for misreading consumer reaction. A company that develops a low-caffeine coffee may not know whether to test it against regular coffee or decaffeinated coffee. What would you test Post-It pads, a 2-in-1 shampoo and conditioner or a notebook computer against? Another common misleading benchmark is to compare the same product among different consumer groups and conclude that it is more accepted by one group vs. other groups. For example, results may show higher ratings for a new toothpaste among older consumers vs. younger consumers, leading to the conclusion that the old like it more than the young. In reality, however, it could be the case that older consumers tend to rate any product higher than younger consumers. The right benchmark would require testing another product among both old and young consumers.
- **Ceteris paribus** – ensuring that 'everything else is equal' is a vital requirement of sound research design and interpretation. Measuring

single elements of an initiative as single variables is the only way to analyse a proposition's strengths and weaknesses. Testing two products that have different formulae and perfumes does not allow us to understand the differences in acceptance, due to the 'halo effect', which results when one variable influences consumers' acceptance of other variables. *Ceteris paribus* also applies to business analyses. An analysis of product acceptance compared to market share may suggest that better product acceptance leads to higher market share. This may be true, but not necessarily. A third factor may be at play. For example, it is possible that better product acceptance encourages a company to spend more money behind the new initiative and, hence, the new brand achieves higher awareness and distribution, which, in turn, lead to a higher market share. A single variable test would compare different products at similar spending levels, or vice versa.

- **Correlation** – a simple look at advertising spending compared to a brand's dollar sales may show a very strong correlation, suggesting that by increasing its advertising spending, a brand can grow its dollar sales. The reality of the matter is that many companies allocate their advertising spending as a percentage of their dollar sales – the higher a brand's sales are, the more money it gets to support its advertising. In other words, the causation is reversed – high dollar sales cause higher advertising spending (Clancy and Shulman, 1995 p. 135).

> '*OK the data's lousy, but it's all we've got.*'
>
> Gerry Gill

The above are just a few examples of how and why business thinking goes wrong. In reality, different types of thinking errors take place simultaneously and are aggravated by emotions, reward systems, workload pressure, urgency, massive firings, business politics and inefficient organizational systems and processes.

> '*There is no such thing as a classification of the ways in which man may arrive at an error, it must be doubted whether there ever can be.*'
>
> Augustus De Morgan

In this chapter we split decision-making errors into cognitive, emotional, group and those related to misuse of market research. This is simply to isolate and explain such factors. However, in reality, these different factors are often combined into a kind of exponential Murphy's Law. A manager is given a new product launch project to which his next promotion is attached (emotions). He leads a team whose career and emotions are attached to the new product. They conduct early qualitative research and abuse it beyond its original purpose (misuse of market research). They benefit from the effects of availability error and the anchoring effect (cognitive errors). The team, mostly men, moves quickly from exploration to execution under the pretext of preempting competition, driven by a heavy dose of testosterone. Final launch decisions are made in a hierarchical group with all the classic faults of group think (group errors). And all these irrationalities are taking place in the middle of a complicated reality where the only sure thing is future uncertainty, with too many data floating around and too many competitors and opponents.

Corrective action needs to address all these dimensions.

WHAT CAN WE DO?

'The ideal businessperson is a realist when making a decision but an optimist when implementing it.'

J.E. Russo and P.J.H. Schoemaker

It is bad news that we are not the rational beings, or managers, we like to think we are. The good news is that there is something we can do about it. Market researchers should take the lead in improving the marketing decision-making process in their organizations. Marketing is too important to be left to marketers. Market researchers should also introduce cultural changes in their organizations representing the consumer voice. They should also play a more active role in functional and corporate training. Here are a few suggestions for managers.

Process

- Create a devil's advocate rotating position for new product evaluation, assigned with the task of identifying all weaknesses in a new initiative without being responsible for addressing them. The assigned person should be changed regularly to avoid labelling him and eventually dismissing his input.
- Use Edward De Bono's Six Thinking Hats (use different thinking approaches to cover a topic from different angles using an analogy of hats, where a blue hat represents the process [blue is sky], a white hat represents facts [white is neutral], yellow represents optimism [yellow is sun], green represents creativity [green is fertility], red represents emotion

[red is blood] and black represents negativity [black is judgement])
approach to ensure innovations are assessed from positive, negative,
rational and emotional perspectives by all involved.

- Allow managers to provide anonymous assessments on initiatives before
  launching them.
- Run double-blind tests to guarantee managers' objectivity in inter-
  preting research results.
- Ensure diversity in decision-making teams, particularly on gender.
- Reverse engineer new product successes and failures.

Training

- Provide formal training in critical thinking, covering the areas of logic,
  fallacies of thought, data analysis, statistics and probabilities.
- Provide basic and advanced training on the use of market research for
  business decisions.

Learning

- Run formal 'post mortems' on failed initiatives, by outside consultants
  or a special group within the company to maximize the company's
  ability to learn from its mistakes without pointing fingers. Minimize
  'hindsight simplifications,' – 'In the past we were stupid, now we are
  smart,' – and 'blamestorming' by studying launch recommendations
  carefully.
- Run objective assessments of success models by outside consultants or
  managers not involved in the project to ensure objectivity.

Culture

- Create an environment that encourages rapid reporting of bad news as
  much as good news.
- Analyse and improve the decision-making process, not just the new
  product launch process.
- Ensure rewards and promotions encourage in-market success, not just
  initiative launches, and long-term commitment to the brand.
- Keep this topic of initiative success a priority, seek feedback and share
  learning regularly.
- Develop new day-to-day work habits: in meetings, let the lowest ranking managers speak first, then the next lowest, and so on. Ask questions to disconfirm your hypothesis. Frame proposals positively and

negatively. Use intuition for hypothesis and framing, not for decision-making.

'It has been said that man is a rational animal. All my life I have been searching for evidence which could support this.'

Bertrand Russell

ACKNOWLEDGEMENTS

Thanks to Mahmoud Aboulfath, Jim Bangel, Mitch D. Barns, Drayton Bird, Annelilly Cone, Nigel Conway, John F. Cook, Andrew Ehrenberg, Anne Favrelle, Laura Hanslik, Lisa Hillenbrand and Chris Warmoth.

REFERENCES

ACNielsen BASES and Ernst & Young Global Client Consulting (1999), *New product introduction. Successful innovation/failure: a fragile boundary*.

Adams, S. (1996), *The Dilbert Principle*. HarperBusiness, p. 36.

Barker, J. A. (1993), *Paradigms – The Business of Discovering the Future*. Harper Business.

Boyer, P. (1995), Ceteris Paribus (All Else Being Equal), in Brockman, J. and Matson, K. (Eds). *How Things Are – A Science Tool Kit for the Mind*. William Morrow and Company Inc.

Cialdini, R. B. (1993), *Influence – The Psychology of Persuasion*. Quill, William Morrow.

Clancy, K. J. and Shulman, R. S. (1995), *Marketing Myths That Are Killing Business*. McGraw Hill, Inc. USA.

Cooper, R. G. (1993), *Winning at New Products*. Addison-Wesley Publishing Company, USA.

Copernicus Marketing Consulting and Research and Gazelle International (1998), *The Testosterone Rush – A Study of Senior Marketing Executives' Decision-making and Management Styles*. Joint study presented at the 1998 Marketing Conference October.

Dawes, R. M. (1988), *Rational choice in an uncertain world*. Harcourt Brace College Publishers, USA.

Dawes, R. M. (2001), *Everyday Irrationality*. Westview Press.

De Bono, E. (1986), *The Mechanism of Mind*. Penguin Books.

De Bono, E. (1988), *The Use of Lateral Thinking*. Penguin Books.

Dewdney, A.K. (1993), *200% of Nothing*. John Wiley & Sons, Inc, p. 95.

Ehrenberg, A. (2001), Marketing: Romantic or realistic? Setting unrealistic goals gives marketing a bad rap. *Marketing Research*, Summer, pp. 40–42.

Gilbert, M. A. (1996), *How To Win An Argument*. John Wiley & Sons, Inc, pp. 130–133.

Gilovich, T. (1993), *How We Know What Isn't So*. The Free Press.

Golder, P. N. and Tellis, G. J. (1993), Pioneer Advantage: Marketing Logic or Marketing Legend? *Journal of Marketing Research,* **30** (May), 158–70.

Gray, W. D. (1991), *Thinking Critically About New Age Ideas.* Wadsworth Publishing Company.

Gross, R. L. and Brodt, S. E. (2001), How assumptions of consensus undermine decision making. *Sloan Management Review,* 01/01, pp. 86–94.

Hutlink, E. J. Hart, S. Robben, H. S.J. and Griffin, A. (1999), *Launch decisions and new product success: an empirical comparison of consumer and industrial products.* Elsevier Science Inc.

Janis, I. L. and Mann, L. (1979), *Decision Making – A Psychological Analysis of Conflict, Choice, and Commitment.* The Free Press.

Jones, S. (1995), Why Are Some People Black? In Brockman, J. and Matson, K (Eds). *How Things Are – A Science Tool Kit for the Mind.* William Morrow and Company Inc.

Kahneman, D. Slovic, P. and Tversky, A. (1993), *Judgement Under Uncertainty: Heuristics and Biases.* Cambridge University Press, USA.

Lin, L. Y.-S. *BASES – New Product Sales Forecasting Model.* National Chung-Hsing University—Research Institute of Agricultural Economics, Taichung, Taiwan.

Lukas, P. (1998), One-man focus group – The ghastliest product launches. *Fortune,* 03/16.

Macrone, M. (1994), *Eureka! What Archimedes Really Meant.* Cader Books.

Matthews, A. J. (1997), The Science of Murphy's Law. *Scientific American,* April.

McMath, R. M. (1998), *What were they thinking – Marketing lessons I've learned from over 80,000 new-product innovations and idiocies.* Times Business/Random House, USA.

Ormerod, P. (2005), *Why most things fail.* Faber & Faber.

Ostrom, G. F. (2001), *Why smart people do stupid things.* Writer's Showcase, USA.

Paulos, J. A. (1989), *Innumeracy – Mathematical Illiteracy and Its Consequences.* Viking.

Paulos, J. A. (1995), *A Mathematician Reads The Newspaper.* Basic Books, p. 73.

Plous, S. (1993), *The Psychology of Judgement and Decision Making.* McGraw-Hill Inc, USA.

Pratkanis, A. and Aronson, E. (2001), *The Age of Propaganda – The everyday use and abuse of persuasion.* W.H. Freeman and Company.

Rackham, N. (1998), *From Experience: why bad things happen to good new products.* Elsevier Science Inc.

Russo, J. E. and Schoemaker, P. J. H. (1990), *Decision Traps.* Fireside Books.

Schneider/Boston University (2001), *New product launch report – executive summary.* Schneider & Associates.

Sternberg, R. J. (Ed.) (2002), *Why smart people can be so stupid.* Yale University Press.

Sutherland, S. (1992), *Irrationality – The Enemy Within.* Constable.

Taleb, N. N. (2005), *Fooled by Randomness.* Random House Trade Paperbacks, USA.

Tellis, G. J. and Golder, P. N. (2002), *Will and Vision – How latecomers grow to dominate markets.* McGraw-Hill, USA.

Vos Savant, M. (1996), *The Power of Logical Thinking – Easy Lessons in the Art of Reasoning . . . and Hard Facts About Its Absence in Our Lives.* St.Martin's Press.

Vos Savant, M. and Fleischer, L. (1991), *Brain Building In Just 12 Weeks.* Bantam Books, pp. 84–86.

Weiner, D. L. and Hefter, G. M. (1999), *Battling the Inner Dummy – ID The craziness of apparently normal people*. Prometheus Books, pp. 25–86.

Wilkie, J. and LeComte, M. (1997), *The Effect Of Brand Proliferation On Consumer Purchasing Of Fast-Moving Consumer Goods (FMCG): How The Changing Rules Of The Game Affect STM Models*. Unpublished paper.

Wujec, T. (1989), *The Complete Mental Fitness Book*. Aurum Press, p. 168.

Chapter Seven

When Good Researchers Go Bad – Cautionary Tales from the Front Lines

Stephen Needel[a]

> *Consumer insights, as often practiced, may not be very insightful. This is attributed to pressures to provide insights and an increasing inability to conduct and evaluate marketing reasearch properly.*

INTRODUCTION

'Consumer insights' has become the catchphrase of the new millennium in market research. The rise of insights has come from a number of sources, including overly high expectations for scanner data, a desire to bring the consumer back into marketing research, the availability of quick and inexpensive Internet surveys and a need for researchers to have a seat at the management table.

This chapter suggests that the emphasis on insights, as opposed to an emphasis on research, *can* produce shoddy research that produces poor insights. After a series of examples of research gone bad, and researchers gone bad, we identify two problems brought about by the rise of consumer insights. First, we are giving less and less thought to the quality of our research, with an increased emphasis on providing an insight (correct

[a]Managing Partner, Advanced Simulations, LLC.

Market Research Best Practice. Edited by P. Mouncey and F. Wimmer.
© 2007 John Wiley & Sons, Limited.

or not). Second, there is a growing reliance on consumers' stated opinions in response to direct questions.

We discuss why these problems exist and provide some initial guidelines to keep good researchers from going bad.

The proliferation of scanner data in the 1990s allowed marketing research to shift its emphasis to what we might call *marketing efficiency*. Most of the things we researched in the '90s were not about building strong brands and delivering to consumer needs. Instead, we were focused on *optimizing* our marketing actions, our logistics, and our research. The growth in popularity, and in the amount of detail of both store-based scanner data and household panel data, permitted us to relegate the immediate consumer to secondary status. We interpreted consumer behaviour en masse, at an aggregate level of analysis, often with complex statistical models. It is important to note that we, as an industry, were not particularly successful in modelling scanner and household panel data. The models that were created were not very useful to marketers, and researchers found the low levels of variance explained by these models unsatisfactory.

In this new century, we have seen a rebirth of interest in the consumer among marketing researchers. The term 'consumer insights' is now used as both an extension of and a replacement for the term 'marketing research'. Many companies no longer have marketing researchers, but rather consumer insight managers knowledge managers and shopper insight managers (just a few of the titles we glean from our business card collection). What the consumer has to say is treated with great respect by marketers and researchers these days.

This renewed interest in consumers can be attributed to a number of factors (recognizing this list is most assuredly not complete or in order of importance):

- The realization that excluding the consumer from any part of our research activities is antithetical to all of our training in marketing and in research. Whatever definition of marketing one accepts, it involves consumers and their needs or wants.
- The cyclical nature of a young science, where we focus on a research problem for a time, leave it for a while when a solution does not appear and come back to it again (Kuhn, 1962), hopefully advancing our learning with each new pass. In marketing research's case, the general failure of statistical modelling of scanner data in the 1990s led to a paradigm shift back to the consumer.

- The availability of Internet-based research has made it relatively quick and inexpensive to obtain consumer opinions with large amounts of respondents. With double-digit growth in US online spending over the past four years (Gold, 2005), asking consumers for their opinions is an activity forecast to continue to grow for some time to come. This growth comes despite early issues of sample representivity, which may no longer be relevant, and current issues of 'professional' respondents (Fulgoni, 2005).

- Market researchers have always had a deep-seated desire, as a group, to improve their status within their organizations, yearning to have a 'seat at the table'. An organization can ignore or minimize *research results*; it is harder to dismiss a '*consumer insight*'. The theory is that changing our name changes the organization's perceptions of what we do and what we can offer.

GOOD RESEARCHERS GONE BAD

We believe that bringing the consumer back into the research world is certainly a positive trend for our science. At the same time, we do not think that 'consumer insights' as practiced is necessarily about the consumers, nor are the 'insights' necessarily insightful. We see two disturbing trends in marketing research these days relative to consumer insights:

- There is a significant amount of pressure on researchers to provide an insight, even when the research data does not warrant one. When we were marketing researchers, we could say things like, 'The data are inconclusive or contradictory'. Now, having a seat at the table as consumer insight managers, it's more difficult to say, 'We don't have an insight into the consumer.' The paradigm shift back to the consumer has not been accompanied by new theory or by truly innovative methodological advances (although we grant that technical improvements continue). We are not necessarily improving our understanding of the consumer compared to years past, yet we are quicker to deliver a conclusion.

- In our search for insights we may be accepting more research at face value and not on the basis of reliability, generalizability and projectability. We have observed a tendency to have fewer technically trained researchers, those with a deep understanding of research methodology and statistics, in favour of those who can bring insights to the table.

Recently, a well-known FMCG manufacturer, who will go nameless, reorganized its research department. In this new table of organization there are nine director slots. Only two of the directors have any market research experience at all; seven have *no* research background. We are forced to wonder (a) how they are going to evaluate the quality of a research project and (b) why any talented researcher would work for them, seeing that the career path is limited by the nature of their talent.

As if life isn't difficult enough, we now have academics blaming market researchers for the death of marketing (Schultz, 2005). Schultz's thesis is that marketing succeeds when the marketer understands the consumer, and that marketing research is not delivering this understanding.

We see the manifestation of these problems and pressures as an increasing reliance on listening to the consumer – asking their opinions and taking the results at face value. Whether it is the pressure to provide some level of insight or whether it is a lack of understanding about the quality of the basis for that insight, the consumers' responses from a focus group or survey are being given more weight and less critical consideration than in the past. We believe this has the potential to become a pervasive problem for our industry. Good researchers will do bad research and we won't provide the quality of insights necessary for marketers to function well.

In this chapter, we want to point out areas where we have seen frequent disconnects between what consumers say and what consumers do. Using virtual reality shopping as our behavioural technology, we will show case studies from a number of research areas that highlight this disconnect. The frequency of such cognitive-behavioural disconnects leads us to believe that focusing on consumers' opinions to the exclusion of consumers' behaviour is not in the best interests of those seeking consumer insights. We will discuss why these problems in understanding the consumer arise and offer suggestions about how to avoid them in the future.

PRICING RESEARCH

Understanding how to price an FMCG product used to be a significant research endeavour, especially in the 1990s when scanner data enabled more detailed analyses at the store and shopper levels. This type of research has become less popular lately, at least in the United States, as Wal-Mart's everyday low price strategy has retailers afraid of appearing expensive and marketers skittish about raising prices. Of course, marketers miss the point when they let the retailer set or limit the prices they can charge. As far back as 1986, Dixon and Sawyer showed that consumers do not recall prices charged for products they have just purchased. The implication of this well-known study is that prices are relative and, to the extent that price influences purchase decisions, it is a comparison that is made within the retail environment at the time of purchase. A shopper may choose to go to a store because the chain has a reputation for low prices (e.g. Wal-Mart or Aldi). Once there, a product's price may be important within the context of that shelf set. The opportunity for increased sales and/or profits within a channel or within a chain, by better pricing policies, should not be ignored.

To overgeneralize a bit, pricing research comes in three flavours:

- **Bucket analyses** – stores are put into buckets based on the actual price they charge for a product or on their relative price level. We then look at the average sales per store (adjusted for store size) and develop an elasticity curve. The problem here is obvious – this technique assumes that any store has an equal chance of being placed anywhere along the sorting criterion spectrum. This random assignment assumption is usually not true; chain format (EDLP vs. High–Low) and regional factors can easily skew the data, making the product appear to be more price sensitive.
- **Scanner-based analyses** – as we became more sophisticated in our modelling capabilities (Box-Jenkins, logit modelling) and as scanner data became ubiquitous, the promise of being able to predict sales changes through statistical modelling was alluring. Unfortunately, the models we created rarely succeeded in providing accurate forecasts of pricing effects. These models suffered the same homogeneity problems as bucket analyses. Moreover, the lack of a sufficient number of price changes over time and multicolinearity with category trends tended to yield little usable information. Logit models based on individual household purchasing patterns had difficulty integrating price as a decision factor and were unwieldy enough to make their common use unlikely.
- **Price meters** – price meters, in any of various forms, go directly to the consumer in order to gauge reaction to prices. In their oldest form, consumers are shown a price and asked their purchase intent for the product at that price. They then proceed through a series of prices, giving their purchase intent at each level. The cruder versions of

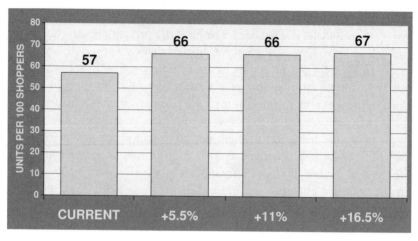

Figure 7.1 Snack product sales.

this methodology are fairly obvious to the respondent; they generate an elasticity curve that is as much a reaction to not wanting to pay more for a product as it is to true elasticity. Some price meters are less obtrusive, such as the Van Westendorp technique, but these also lack academic validation.

Let's consider an example of how asking consumers for their input on pricing decisions can go wrong. A snack manufacturer in the Netherlands ran a price meter study on a 200 gram package because the cost of goods had risen by 5%. The price meter showed that a 5.5% increase in price would lead to a meaningful decrease in sales. As part of a follow-up study looking at changing the size of the package, they ran a price test using virtual reality shopping. The results of this shopping exercise, shown in Figure 7.1, dispute the price meter data. Sales actually improve as we go up in price by 5.5%, stabilizing at +11% and +16.5%.

These counterintuitive results made more sense once we looked at data from the less-obtrusive Van Westendorp technique, which was run after the shopping exercise. As shown in Figure 7.2, the prices we tested (1.79fl to 2.09fl) are all seen as homogeneous to the consumer. Moreover, the prices are well below the point where the product is seen as expensive. Our recommendation was to test higher prices for the product instead of leaving money on the table.

The point of this example is that research methods that rely on the face value of a consumer response can lead to a poor marketing decision.

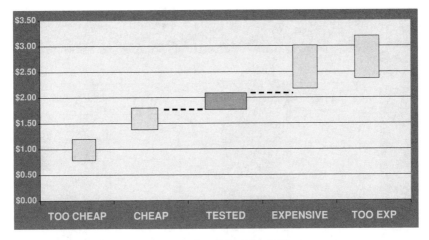

Figure 7.2 Snack food – inner quartile ranges (25%–75%).

When we talk about pricing to a shopper, nobody wants to pay more for a product and that's what they tell us. A research technique that too easily permits the respondent to respond this way can lead to lower prices and lower profits than is necessary.

PURCHASE INTENT

Purchase intent is the measure that first comes to mind when we think of new product research. This measure has achieved exalted status in spite of research that suggests the relationship between intentions and actual behaviour is hardly isomorphic. For example, Sheppard, Hartwick and Warshaw (1988) show a correlation between intention and behaviour of 0.53 across a wide range of behaviours. This slippage is not as big a problem as one would expect for new product forecasting. The research industry has learned how to adjust purchase intent and include exogenous factors into its new product forecasting models with a great deal of success. However, the lack of success of new product introductions suggests we may not be adjusting as well as we should.

Chandon, Morwitz and Reinartz (2005) discuss the biases in purchase intent measures, suggesting that using this as a discriminating measure can be misleading. In addition to sensitizing shoppers and making them more likely to purchase as a result of the act of asking the question, purchase intent is very sensitive to social desirability and interviewer-pleasing

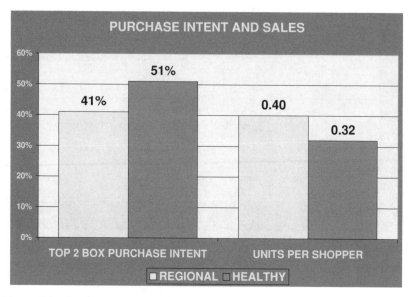

Figure 7.3   Purchase intent and sales.

behaviour. We conducted a study of a line extension for a brand of meal extender products; you add chicken or beef or seafood to the packaged product and get a much larger meal at a relatively low cost per kilo. Rather than follow the old pattern of just introducing new flavours on a periodic basis, the manufacturer decided to introduce a new subline, one that would be ripe for its own future extension. They created two different lines: one based on regional recipes and one based on health concerns (low sodium). The latter is especially interesting as this product is heavy on the salt – it contains about 40% of the daily recommended allowance of sodium in one relatively small serving. The goal of the study was to determine which subline was better for the brand to introduce.

On a total brand basis, sales do not differ by subline. However, the separate sublines show an interesting phenomenon. When we look at purchase intent for the sublines, top two box scores heavily favour the healthy version (see Figure 7.3). This is contradicted by sales, in which regional flavours outsell healthy flavours by 25%. The purchase intent data does not match the sales data. Our hypothesis is a simple one: it is hard for consumers to say, 'No, I'm really not interested in a product that is healthier for me and my family.' It is not that they are lying to the interviewer (or to the interviewing computer program) – they are just being human.

A great deal of new product research, with purchase intent the key measure, is done in the absence of a context for the product. With purchase intent a relatively weak measure to begin with, better methods for collecting probability of purchase, methods that are unobtrusive, contextual and nondirectional, are required. Techniques exist that meet these requirements – good researchers can increase the return on their information investment by employing them.

PACKAGING

There is often an implicit assumption in packaging research that the more consumers like a package, the more likely it is that they will buy the product. No company goes out of its way to design an unattractive package for its products. However, basing a decision to choose new packaging or change existing packaging on attractiveness or consumer liking can lead to a poor marketing decision.

We have discussed some of the problems with attractiveness in previous publications (Needel, 1994; 2000). To update this research, we now have 69 cases where we've tested packages in a virtual reality shopping simulation and have collected attribute ratings after shopping. The results, shown in Table 7.1, remain discouraging for those who favour consumer evaluations as the criterion for package selection.

What we see from this table is:

- Two-thirds of our studies (44 of 69) show a sales difference when testing new packaging.
- When the simulation shows no sales difference between packages tested, 56% (14 of 25) of the studies confirm this lack of difference with attribute ratings, 44% (11 of 25) would show a different conclusion.
- When the simulation shows a sales difference, we see confirmation from the post-test survey results in 55% of the cases (24 of 44). However, 30% of the cases show no differences in survey results and 15% would show a reversal of effect.

Table 7.1 Results of 69 packaging studies.

Attribute ratings showing:	*Studies showing no difference*	*Studies showing sales difference*
No difference	14	13
Difference – confirm	0	24
Difference – Disagree	11	7
	25	44

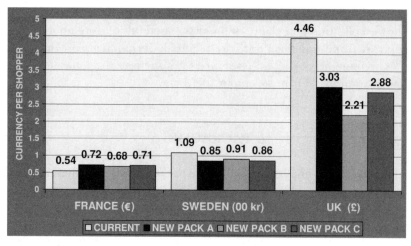

Figure 7.4 OTC product sales.

- Another way to look at these numbers is that in 38 of the 69 cases (55%), we see agreement between attribute ratings and purchasing in the simulation.

There are a number of potential causes for this mismatch between purchasing behaviour and shopper evaluations of packages. One of the most important reasons is, we think, a lack of understanding of the drivers of the purchase decision with respect to packaging. As an example of this problem, consider a recent study we conducted in France, Sweden and the UK for an OTC product. The goal of the package redesign was to make the product appear more contemporary, look more like a leading brand, be seen as premium quality and be trustworthy. We tested three new packages against current and generally achieved these evaluative objectives – in most cases the new packs were at parity or better on these four attributes. However, as shown in Figure 7.4, sales were generally weak for the new packages relative to the current package. This was true for Sweden and the UK; in France, where the test product was new and has weak distribution, the sales did not differ across the four packages.

We wondered why the sales were so weak for new packaging when the evaluations were good. We correlated the four attributes with purchasing (yes/no) of the test product. The results, shown in Figure 7.5, reveal a set of very weak correlations between the four attributes and whether a shopper bought the test product. The conclusion we draw is that these attributes are not what drive consumers to make a purchase decision

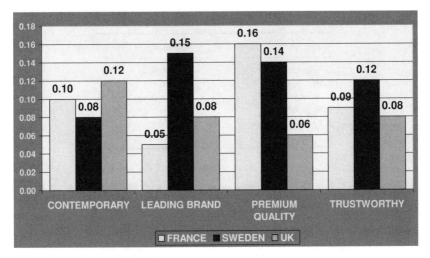

Figure 7.5   Correlation of attributes with purchasing.

about this product. While we may have designed to the attributes, the consumer doesn't care.

PURCHASE DECISION HIERARCHIES

Consumer insights have become very fashionable in connection with category management initiatives. One area of use that has been particularly popular is to create the purchase decision hierarchy, then translate that into new shelf sets. We have found a number of potential pitfalls in this process (Needel and Bean, 2002). Sometimes the translation from hierarchy to shelf layout is not as clean as one would like; the consumer doesn't get the pattern at the shelf. Other times, rearranging the shelf just doesn't matter; consumers know what they want and as long as you haven't hidden their product, you can put it in many different locations without impact.

Where we saw the biggest problems, though, is in faulty purchase decision hierarchies. These hierarchies lose their utility when there are data collection problems and/or when there are data interpretation problems. In an example of faulty data collection, our client, who manufactures skin care products, intercepted shoppers in the skin care aisle after they made a purchase. They asked buyers what was the most important factor in their purchasing decision, next most important, and so forth. From this data, they generated a purchase decision hierarchy and changed their

Table 7.2 Hierarchy of purchase decision factors.

In-store intercept	Shelf simulation
1. Solution	1. Solution
2. Brand	2. Price
3. What it does to solve	3. What it does to solve
4. Ingredients	4. Ingredients
5. Price	5. Brand
6. Form	6. Form

marketing to reflect this hierarchy. As part of a shelf set simulation we were conducting, they asked us to confirm this hierarchy. In the 4^D *Shopper* simulation it is possible to take any product selected for purchase and have it become out-of-stock, allowing us to see what the shopper will buy when their preferred item is not available. This switching data can be turned easily into a purchase decision hierarchy (assuming the data has a well-ordered pattern to it).

We found an interesting difference between the in-store intercept and the simulation results (see Table 7.2). Based on the in-store intercept, where we ask shoppers to explicate their hierarchy, brand is a critical factor. When you actually look at how shoppers substitute products, however, price is critical and brand drops to the bottom. It should be obvious to the reader that a marketing strategy revolving around price level is different from one focused on branding.

Sometimes the problem is more one of data interpretation; while there is a lot of science to the statistics of hierarchical clustering, factor analysis, correspondence analysis, etc., there is also a fair amount of artistry to the interpretation of the results. Our European client manufactures sanitary protection products. Its main competitor began making the rounds of retailers with a new shelf set based on a recent purchase decision study it had conducted. The key to the new shelf set was that it was arrayed by *absorbency*. The belief was that women first selected the absorbency of a product, and then would use other factors to complete their choice.

This was news to our client, who began work of its own to confirm this. What they found was that absorbency was a necessary condition for a product to be considered and that absorbency really means protection – the product won't leak. What they also found was that women in Europe consider *all* products on a shelf to be absorbent, otherwise they wouldn't be there. This led our client to conduct a two-phased study. In the first phase, we ran a substitution test in order to determine the decision

Table 7.3   Loyalty measures.

	Segment loyalty	Brand loyalty	Absorbency loyalty
Full pad buyers	87%	83%	57%
Ultra pad buyers	81%	94%	61%
Tampon buyers	97%	83%	49%
Liner buyers	84%	82%	N/A

hierarchy. The results showed that primary loyalty was to one of the three sanitary protection segments – tampon buyers substituted tampons (97%), pads/napkins buyers substituted pads/napkins (93%) and liner buyers re-purchased liners (84%). The relative strength of brand within segment and the weakness of absorbency within segment are shown in Table 7.3.

The second phase of this study was to test a new vertical seg-ment/vertical brand set and the absorbency set proposed by the com-petitor against the current horizontal set (tampons on top, then liners, then pads/napkins). The results of this study are shown in Figure 7.6. For pads/napkins and liners, the new vertical set is as good as the current set. However, the absorbency set is significantly weaker than either current or vertical. For tampons, both new shelf sets are good and, it turns out, both are identical in layout.

The key point to be made is that an insight relying solely on the voice of the consumer giving us a purchase decision hierarchy would lead you to a poor marketing decision.

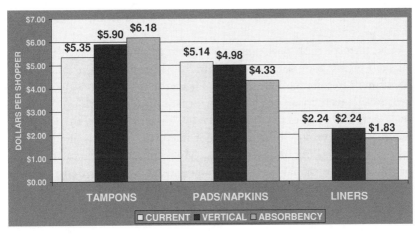

Figure 7.6   Sanitary protection product sales.

WHY DISCONNECTS OCCUR

Each of these examples shares two problems that have led to the disconnect between what people said and what people did:

1. They assumed that people can tell you effectively what they are thinking.
2. They assumed an implicit model of consumer behaviour without testing the model.

What consumers say

A problem running through our four examples is a reliance on (a) asking consumers questions and (b) believing the answers. There are any number of reasons why we should not believe the answers that consumers give us – the two most important reasons being social desirability and the introspection problem.

Rosenthal and Rosnow (1969) present a number of articles which detail the tendency for respondents to behave [verbally] in ways they believe will meet the approval of an interviewer. The interviewer wants to hear different responses to prices, the interviewer wants to hear that one shelf set is better than another, the respondent wants to look like a health-conscious, environment-friendly consumer; all lead to responses in a survey that are not necessarily true. Social desirability does not always lead respondents to lie, but it can certainly distort the truth. Worse though, respondents feel pressured to deliver an answer, even if they do not have a good [true] one to give; this gives rise to the introspection problem.

The introspection problem is considered less commonly, but may be an even bigger issue for consumer insights. Introspection assumes that a consumer can call up from memory or from the subconscious the thought process that went into a product evaluation or purchase decision. Without reviewing 125 years of psychological research, let us just say there is every reason to believe that humans are not likely to do this well, especially when we are asking about FMCGs. Much purchasing is unconscious or subconscious or habit-based, meaning we as shoppers don't need to spend a lot of effort thinking about our behaviour. This is why we keep on advertising – to build and/or reinforce the buying habit (Bill Wells used to say this better than me). We see estimates of time spent at the shelves shopping that are often incredibly short – a matter of seconds.

This is because we often don't think about what we are buying and why; we let the habit take over. In such a cognitive environment, it *should* be difficult for the consumer to consciously recall and replay the complex process that generated a purchase. The introspection barrier is exacerbated when we consider category management research; consumers do not think about shelf sets and assortments, even though they may exhibit differential responses to shelf variations. Asking them questions about the shelf sets elicits responses, but these are often of little use, because it is not something consumers normally think about.

Implicit models

Whether we explicate it or not, all research assumes a model of consumer behaviour. Ignoring the implicit model inherent in a research design or methodology can cause some of the problems in generating valid consumer insights that we've been discussing. Adopting a consumer insights world view *currently* demands a rejection of a strict behaviourist model of consumer behaviour, one in which the stimulus (say, a package design), directly elicits a response (say, purchasing). However, a consumer insights approach does not rule out a deterministic model with intervening variables. Most thinking in marketing research involves some form of *mediational* model (as opposed to a *moderational* model – Baron and Kenny, 1986). Let's use a packaging research model as our example, one that we first described in Needel (1994). This model, shown in Figure 7.7, posits that a product's package design is mediated by a number of

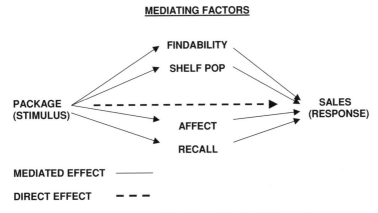

Figure 7.7 Packaging response model with mediated and direct effects.

psychological processes before a purchase decision is made. These processes may be degrees of ease of finding the product, the extent to which a product pops off the shelf, how the shopper feels about the product and what information the shopper retains from the package; more likely it is some combination of the above. Without arguing the merits of this particular model's specification, we want to make the point that this is generally how market researchers think about what packaging does.

When we test packaging, we often measure whether we've made the package pop more, whether it is easier to find, whether shoppers can remember more about a new package and whether they like the new package better. However, we tend to do this research in isolation, focusing on the mediators, making the assumption that if we improve a product's performance on measures of the mediators, then we will increase sales. Indeed, we as an industry often go so far as to ignore sales, making the assumption that the mediators are an analogue for sales, rather than an antecedent of sales. Some researchers (for example, Young, 2002) even argue that sales are not the relevant measure when discussing packaging research.

This use of implicit model mediators as surrogates is, we believe, contrary to the goals of marketing and marketing research. Marketing's goal is to sell more stuff – research's job is to help them sell more stuff. At the end of the day, we should evaluate a new package based on whether it will sell more product, make pricing decisions based on profit considerations, make new product decisions based on sales potential, and category management recommendations based on sales impact. An implicit model that ignores sales in these situations is a catalyst for failure – good researchers will generate bad research; research that fails to deliver a true consumer insight.

REFORMING GOOD RESEARCHERS GONE BAD

Whenever we write a chapter/paper such as this one, we need to step back a bit and note that there is a lot of good consumer insights work being conducted. ESOMAR's 2004 Congress in Lisbon contained numerous examples of consumer insights generating good marketing decisions. There are a lot of good researchers out there who have donned the consumer insights mantle without a problem, without compromising their research, while still playing a key role in marketing decisions. From them, we offer the following suggestions to improve the application of consumer insights to marketing decisions:

- Regardless of our roles or our titles, we are essentially marketing researchers. We are expected to employ sound methodologies and good interpretation skills to provide guidance. We are expected to be the experts when it comes to research and we need to act like that. We need to know the advantages and disadvantages of the research techniques we use and need to be able to convey that information to our organizations. This may mean we ourselves need to continue our education, either formally or informally, in order to keep abreast of current technology. We may also need to invest in training on how to position research within our organizations.

- We need to understand that an insight gained from mediocre research is a mediocre insight. For example, the growth of the Internet has made it all too easy to do quick and dirty surveys on issues that are best understood with more advanced methodologies. We need to stand up to the low-cost/low-quality bid approach to life when it is the wrong way to research an issue. We need to educate our clients about the ROI of information.

- As the experts, we need to clarify the nature of the insight for our clients. Whether we are on the corporate side or the supplier side, we need to use our expertise to ensure that the possibilities and limitations of the insights are clear to the client. That means explaining the strengths and weaknesses of the technology used to gather the data, and interpret the data and the implicit assumptions of the model that drove the research. If the trend toward corporate-side researchers being less technically proficient continues, even more pressure will be placed on the suppliers to provide this service. We will need to see the more senior staff at suppliers spending more time on 'hand-holding' on these issues.

- Finally, we need to resist the temptation (or the pressure) to provide an insight when we the data are ambiguous. We need to stand up and say, 'We don't know' when we don't know. We need to be clear that research doesn't always reveal the answer, and that sometimes marketing judgement is required to fill in the gaps. Consumer insights is not always about telling marketing what to do; it is often about helping them assess the risks and rewards of a given action. Sometimes, research will have a huge impact on that evaluation and sometimes research is not going to help much at all.

As Dudley Ruch, then head of Marketing Research at Quaker Oats, stated in an American Marketing Association speech (Ruch, 1981),

'Regardless of charters, organizational charts and corporate policies, *the role market research gets is the one it earns.*' In the end, we will achieve the goal of being part of the management team when we bring better insights to the management table, when we know more about what we are doing and are able to communicate that to our marketing and management teams.

REFERENCES

Baron, R.M. and Kenny, D.A. (1986), The moderator-mediator variable distinction in social psychological research: Conceptual, strategic and statistical considerations. *Journal of Personality and Social Psychology*, **51**, pp 1173–1182.

Chandon, P., Morwitz, V.G. and Reinartz, W.J. (2005), Do intentions really predict behaviour? Self-generated validity effects in survey research. *Journal of Marketing*, **16**, 1–14.

Dixon, P.R. and Sawyer, A.G. (1986), *Point of purchase behaviour and price perceptions of supermarket shoppers.* Marketing Science Institute, Cambridge, MA: working paper no. 86–102.

Fulgoni, G.M. (2005), *The professional respondent problem in online survey panels today.* Marketing Research Association Annual Conference, June.

Gold, L.N. (2005), *Inside Research*, **16**(7), 1 July 2005.

Kuhn, T. (1962). *The Structure of Scientific Revolution.* The University of Chicago Press.

Needel, S.P. and Bean, J.W. (2002), *Advances in category management – a user's perspective.* Esomar Congress 2002, Barcelona, September.

Needel, S.P. (1994), *Virtual reality comes to marketing research: implications for understanding packaging.* Technical Association for the Paper and Pulp Industry.

Needel, S.P. (2000), The sale's the thing. *Marketing News*, **20**.

Needel, S.P. and Bean, J.W. (2002), *Advances in category management – a user's perspective.* ESOMAR Congress 2002, Barcelona, September.

Rosenthal, R. and Rosnow, R.L. (1969), *Artifacts in Behavioural Research.* Academic Press.

Ruch, D.M. (1981), *The role of market research in the corporation.* Ama Market Research Conference.

Schultz, D.E. (2005), MR deserves blame for marketing's decline. *Marketing News*, 15 February

Sheppard, B.H., Hartwick, J. and Warshaw, P.R. (1988), The theory of reasoned action: A meta-analysis of past research with recommendations for modifications and future research. *Journal of Consumer Research,* **15**(3), 325–343.

Young, S. (2002), Packaging design, consumer research, and business strategy: The march toward accountability. *Design Management Journal*, Fall, pp. 10–14.

Part Two

Knowledge Management

Chapter Eight

Striking Gold in the Qualitative Mine: A New Approach to Build Vision and Generate Insight to Impact Business

Jem Wallis[a] and Vanessa Briese[b]

This chapter proposes a three-step approach to help companies understand consumers. Critical to the model is the development and use of a qualitative database to generate more powerful insights.

INTRODUCTION

This chapter proposes a three-step model to understanding the consumer's world beyond the category. It proposes this more sophisticated approach generates more meaningful and powerful insights for the clients. Critical to the model is the development of a qualitative database the clients can mine to strike gold for their brands. We will demonstrate what kind of work can be generated by mining this database, what is required to build the database and how it has been mined by clients and researchers working as a team to generate new and different insights.

[a] Managing Director, Heartbeat Trends Australia Pty Ltd.
[b] Social Researcher, Heartbeat Trends Australia Pty Ltd.

Market Research Best Practice. Edited by P. Mouncey and F. Wimmer.
© 2007 John Wiley & Sons, Limited.

THREE STEPS

In order to build vision and generate strong insights to impact business, we propose there are three steps researchers should advocate and clients should embrace.

Step 1: Instilling a 'top-down' approach

Traditionally, marketers think of qualitative research as a means to explore their brands and categories. They expect qualitative research to answer the 'why' and the 'how' questions they have. Along the way, they also hope to understand more about the consumer and even gain an insight or two. This is a 'bottom-up' way of thinking and forms the basis of most ad hoc projects.

With ROI now driving marketing thinking, ad hoc projects with narrow and measurable objectives are increasingly the starting point for all work. Marketers are drilled into believing that researching the brand or category will improve their marketing position. It's difficult to get budget approval for a study that doesn't have as its goal the next television commercial or line extension. Imagine going to your Marketing Director and asking for US$30 000 to 'explore the world of the consumer to see what you can find'! You wouldn't have much luck in today's tightly controlled fiscal world.

Yet, we believe trying to gain true insight into the world of the consumer as some kind of by-product of an ad hoc project is far from optimal. It's like trying to map the moon using a microscope. People's attitudes to a brand evolve not only because of shifts in the category, but because of broader societal influences such as changes in social values, attitudes and beliefs. Marketers' current 'bottom-up' approach treats brands like islands rather than cities within a country.

Not surprisingly, marketers dread the next international visitor arriving, because they're ill-equipped to show them how local consumers look and feel today. They find it difficult to show R&D and Sales what the consumer is all about so they can better understand why Marketing has adopted a certain strategy. Marketers get frustrated when creative departments lack creativity, but they don't have the tools to help them break through.

We advocate a 'top-down' way of thinking to gain more broad based and powerful insights; insights to help overcome these problems. Understanding the drivers and effects of change, i.e. the context in which your consumers think, feel and act, ensures brands are touching something meaningful in people's lives and reflect unfolding social reality.

Heartbeat and its social monitors (www.heartbeat.com.au) were developed with this in mind. We start with the consumer and explore their world, mapping the issues and attitudes, lives and behaviours that are important to them. Once we have this map, we can work with our clients to overlay their brand knowledge to pick the parts of the consumer's world that are most relevant to their brand and marketing initiatives. This is equivalent to mapping the moon with a telescope.

Of course, it would be remiss to claim top-down research is a new approach unseen in the industry. We acknowledge there have been, and still are, clients requesting one-off, broad-based studies. Some of these studies use a bricolage methodology to help gain new insights into the consumer's world. Sadly, these types of studies are spasmodic, testament to the concern with ROI and the trend to narrower and narrower ad hoc studies.

We applaud the brave companies who commission these types of studies. While their broad remit is certainly a good initiative, we believe these studies are too few and far between. Their one-off nature limits their value. They are little more than a 'moment-in-time' look at the broader consumer's world. It is hard from even the most well-designed one-off study to see all the patterns and causal factors that affect people's behaviour and shape their attitudes.

We believe the optimal approach to gaining rich insights that impact business is to conduct large-scale, broad-based qualitative studies more frequently. That is, we propose researchers should conduct large-scale studies with enough regularity to enable them to develop a qualitative database which clients can mine. The brave companies that have already taken this path have reaped great rewards.

'I often feel when we do research, we go out and do one study and we come back and we feel we know it all, but it's really not until you've put layer upon layer upon layer that you're building up this picture of the consumer and what's happening in their lives and their aspirations. And I think Heartbeat acquires that data, in various ways to build that picture.'
Barbara Edwards, Consumer Insights Manager, Unilever

Step 2: Developing a qualitative mine

Quantitative researchers are used to data mining and comparing quantitative data. Qualitative data are fundamentally different. There are words not numbers, perceptions, interpretations and attitudes not statistics, formulae and precoded questions. Qualitative research has long been criticized for its inconsistency, how can it be built into a robust database?

We propose that qualitative researchers should apply themselves to the task and work out how to create databases they can mine and cut in different ways in just the same manner as their quantitative brethren.

The first hurdle is to convince clients that it's possible to build a consistent qualitative database worthy of mining. When clients commission one-off, big-picture studies, often several years apart, despite the best of intentions each study takes on a different colour. Different researchers, different brand managers, different research companies, all with different viewpoints, often translate to different objectives, specifications, methodology and, eventually, incomparable data. So, even though the intention may be to 'replicate' a previous study, too often human nature causes the study to change significantly. No wonder clients struggle to see how a consistent database can be built.

After compiling nearly 50 syndicated qualitative studies in Australia and Brazil with consumers aged seven to 70 years over the course of seven years, Heartbeat has developed a qualitative mine (Figure 8.1). The mine is like a data network. Each of the 50 studies taps five data fields: Countries, Demographics, Life Topics, Socio Demographics and Media/Advertising. Some of these fields, like the Socio Demographics field, give the mine its breadth, while other fields, like the Life Topics field give the mine its depth.

Building the mine was no easy feat. It took commitment, investment and vision. The first key ingredient to building a database of value is to ensure consistency. Without some kind of fixed reference points, data comparisons are impossible due to the number of interrelated factors at play. For our mine, consistency begins with the demographics. We conduct regular studies on the following fixed demographics: Kids, Teens, Youth (18–26 year-olds), New Women (mums 30–45 years old) and Baby Boomers.

A consistent approach to methodology is also required. There must be enough consistency in the data to allow valid comparisons at a later date. In quantitative terms, we need to keep within the standard deviation. For our database, the sample structure remains fairly rigid. For example, variables like age range, number of groups and the metro regional splits remain the same and are only allowed to vary slightly depending on the topic selected.

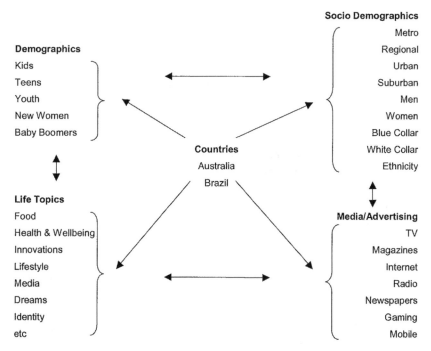

Figure 8.1   Qualitative mine.

We use a bricolage approach mixing ethnography, video-research techniques, other projective techniques and a wide range of qualitative skills. Within this research menu we ensure the methodology for each study has sufficient commonalities with previous studies to allow meaningful comparisons. We acknowledge the degree of variation we see as permissible is subjective rather than formulaic. However, when we started we were rigid in replicating the exact approach each time and only later did we experiment with slight variations, gradually, carefully and one at a time, to ensure consistency was not compromised.

Adopting a consistent methodology across each of our five fields allows us to isolate the causal factors that influence attitudes and behaviour. These are complex and interrelated, but include the following:

- **Country and its culture.** As you can see from Figure 8.1, developing a database can stretch overseas as well. The key is to ensure the fields and subfields are replicated across the various markets. When Heartbeat partnered with Enfoque in Brazil last year to produce regular Brazilian monitors, the same fields and subfields were deliberately adopted so, we could look for patterns or differences in the data and isolate the causal factors. For example, having researched the Youth demographic in Brazil and Australia on the topic of Identity, one can compare the impact respective cultures have on their identities.

- **Life topics.** Our topics range from food to lifestyle to dreams and so on (Figure 8.1). Covering such topics on the one demographic over time is necessary to build up a thorough understanding of all aspects of the consumers' lives and see what the relative importance is of each, not to mention the influence they have on each other. For example, understanding Baby Boomers' attitudes towards food also requires understanding their attitudes towards wellbeing and their attitudes towards lifestyle. Topics are only repeated when there has been a significant shift in people's attitudes and feelings worthy of comment. For example, in the late 1990s, health and wellbeing for Australian New Women was all about physical wellbeing. Today, the focus is more on emotional wellbeing. Hence, the need to revisit the topic.

- **Intergenerational influences.** Being able to look at generational shifts and influences outside of the target group can shed new light or greater understanding on an issue. For example, mining young women can help clients better understand why and how female Baby Boomers' priorities and aspirations are changing. Now the kids have left home, they have the opportunity to do everything they couldn't do before, such as travel, study and have a career. They are adopting the values, ideas and endorsements of their daughters. It is essential to know what their daughters' values are.

- **Socio demographics.** Contrasting variables like urban versus suburban, blue collar versus white collar can have a significant influence on a topic or media. For example, looking at Youth Wellbeing, we saw a world of difference between rural and urban Australia. While many young people dream of a healthier rural lifestyle, in reality the reverse is true. Poor health is endemic and is accepted as part of their lifestyle. They feel depressed because they don't have as many opportunities, so they give up trying to be healthy, which makes them more depressed and, in turn, more unhealthy.

- **Media/advertising.** Media and advertising in all their forms play a large role in influencing how the various demographics think, feel and act. For example, the media Baby Boomers choose to embrace is markedly different to that of their grandkids. This has an enormous flow-on effect in terms of their leisure and entertainment habits. An important part of each study is a considered analysis of current media and advertising and how it is seen by our target.

There are two main benefits in developing a mine with fixed reference points on a variety of topics over time. First, clients can identify shifts in consumer attitudes and behaviours, spot patterns, predict trends on the horizon and plan accordingly. All of which is imperative in an increasingly competitive landscape. Without the consistency and depth of data, the ability to see trends emerging would be difficult. Secondly, through the mine marketers are able to see the bigger picture, they can put things in greater perspective and are less likely to misinterpret data as a result. The data become a tool in their armoury, providing a benchmark against which to evaluate hypotheses and a springboard to develop new ones.

Building a qualitative database is no easy feat. It requires consulting regularly with clients to ensure the mine is generating relevant data. But above all, developing a mine necessitates adopting a consistent approach. Once this is achieved, striking gold for clients is only one step away.

> 'The reality is, you cannot have really good insights unless there is a good mechanism for measuring it. And Heartbeat is a key mechanism for us in keeping that pulse on the key target audiences we have and to understanding how that pulse is changing and what is interesting the consumer, day in day out, month in month out, and year by year.'
>
> Ian Alwill, Director, Marketing Communications, Nestle

Step 3: Striking gold

Once the mine is constructed, the way to strike gold is to fuse the expertise of the researcher with the knowledge of the marketing team. For the client, this requires a leap of faith to shift from commissioning proprietary, ad hoc research to solve a problem to mining a qualitative database which originates from syndicated research. For the researcher, it requires skills more akin to an agency planner than a pure market researcher. In most cases, the questions raised by a client cannot be answered simply by pulling one of the big-picture studies off the shelf. The insights need to be gathered from the database and do not come straight from the original research data but from interrogating it to answer a specific client problem.

Once the client's objectives have been agreed, the researcher begins the analysis. This involves looking for the most relevant subfield(s) within a field, searching for patterns and themes and then comparing all of this against any possible interrelated causal factors. The data combinations are enormous. Here are just some:

- demographic and lifestyles by country;
- advertising on a specific demographic;
- urban versus suburban lifestyles;
- a specific life topic across all demographics.

Naturally, the more studies in the database, the richer the data and the more ways the data can be mined and interpreted to generate new and different insights for the client. The researcher looks for patterns in the data to identify the causal factors. These patterns are pieced together to find the code that answers the client's questions.

The rich consumer insights generated from the mining process can then be presented or discussed in a creative workshop environment. The goal could be to help shape, and facilitate a next research phase, which, might be a piece of ad hoc research specific to the brand or category; it could be to aid idea generation and communication; or to stimulate new product development.

We would like to use two case studies to showcase the type of insights that can be found when mining our qualitative database.

CASE STUDIES

We have mined our qualitative database for many companies like Arnott's, Reckitt Benckiser, Nestlé, Unilever, GlaxoSmithKline and Coca-Cola. The following are just two examples of insights that have been applied to clients in the area of new product development and advertising.

1: Future of the home

Aim: To help a major multinational company generate insightful, consumer relevant new product ideas that match their strategy in extended home care solutions.

Illustrating: Mining a topic.

Fixed fields and subfields: Countries — Australia
                                Demographic — New Women,
                                Baby Boomers

Proposed interrelated causal factors: Demographic – Kids
                                          Life Topics subfields
                                          Socio Demographic subfields

Mining the data: this involved mining two demographic subfields –
New Women and Baby Boomers - and examining the interrelated causal
factors for each, namely:

- the influence of kids;
- the influence of Socio Demographics, such as urban versus suburban
  and men versus women;
- the influence of various Life Topics, such as health and wellbeing,
  lifestyle, relationships, and so on.

Striking gold: from the data we identified eight codes that could affect
the future of the home. Using the results we ran a two-day workshop,
structured as follows:

Stage 1: Consumer immersion

- The eight codes were presented over the course of two days as stimulus
  for the idea generation session.
- Each code represented a distinct consumer segment in Australia.
- We recruited eight consumers to participate in the workshop (one
  consumer representing each code).
- Consumers were asked to talk to the group about their lifestyle within
  the context of each code.

Stage 2: Consumer insight and needs generation

- In order to generate NPD ideas that were both relevant and appealing
  to consumers, the group was asked to focus on the different consumer
  segments' needs and priorities
- These were developed by splitting into teams and brainstorming the
  needs that the consumer segments would most likely have.
- Over 100 needs/priorities were developed.

Stage 3: Idea generation and development

- From this list, eight 'key' needs were chosen as final 'consumer prob-
  lems/needs' from which innovative NPD ideas were developed (with
  eight teams brainstorming one core need each) into an ideas template
  for presentation to the group.

- These ideas were then developed into concepts for research testing, in order to gauge feasibility and potential for development and launch in various markets around the globe.

2: Advertising Baby Boomers' love

Aim: To identify the advertising codes for clients interested in communicating with Baby Boomer men and women in the Australian market.

Illustrating: Mining media/advertising by demographic.

Fixed fields and subfields: Countries – Australia

Demographic – Baby Boomers

Media/Advertising – TV, magazines,

newspapers

Proposed interrelated causal factors: Life Topic subfields

Mining the data: this was done in a variety of ways:

- examining all the Baby Boomer Life Topics to understand what their attitudes and feelings, priorities and aspirations are and how this transfers to advertising;
- trawling through the 'advertising' sections across all our Baby Boomer life theme studies to examine what advertising is cutting through the clutter and why;
- focusing purely on a specific Life Topic – Media and Baby Boomers.

Striking gold: the result was the development of eight powerful advertising codes that are used as guidelines by marketing teams wishing to develop their next piece of creative.

CONCLUSION

We propose that researchers should start thinking about qualitative research using a quantitative ideal: to develop consistency in approach and methodology to make the data more robust and comparable. Achieve this and you can build a qualitative database containing insights worthy of mining and comparing year on year.

Developing a qualitative mine does take investment, commitment and vision, but the benefits far outweigh the costs. Clients are assured they have things in greater perspective and are not misinterpreting data. They are able to spot trends on the horizon before their competitors do.

They can check specific hypotheses and use the data to generate new hypotheses, making every piece of ad hoc work more effective.

Perhaps the true value of the mine is the way it can be re-examined to answer a variety of questions. Different researchers will look at the same data from their own unique perspective. The semiotician will find something different to the psychologist. One researcher will see a different pattern and identify a different code. There is no 'right' answer to a client's question. The richness of the data allows it to be cut and interpreted in different ways: different insights depending on how and where you look. This is a strength of the data not a weakness.

We are not saying this new approach to insight generation should supersede all others. We don't want to start an ad hoc vs. database debate. We see it as complementary to ad hoc research, which is still required to answer more specific questions pertaining to a client's brand and category.

We acknowledge that not all researchers can adopt this approach, and not all clients have the time and money to embrace it. However, we do strongly request that clients should not fool themselves that a one-off, big-picture study is the same as a serious commitment to building a long-term understanding of the consumer's world.

'*We knew as an international team that it would be quite a challenge to pull together some coherent research that would be, believable for the senior management team and leverageable for other marketing teams. So we really jumped at the chance to be able to get access to the Heartbeat material, because it filmed and had a dialogue with real kids in a real environment talking about things that they loved . . . Not only do we use it in trade literature and presentations to senior management teams around the world, but we also included key clips, verbatims and the commentaries from your influencers in an intranet site.*'

James Ward, Regional Director, J&J

Chapter Nine

Improving Honeywell's Market Research: Combining Online Surveys, Traditional Interviewing Techniques and Web-based Reporting

Karl G. Feld[a] and William K. Stone[b]

This chapter examines the application of multiple data collection disciplines to solve data collection error and satisfy Six-Sigma quality standards. Overall, this technique delivers improved customer satisfaction and increased ROI.

INTRODUCTION

Honeywell replaced its international telephone data collection and paper-based tabulation and reporting with blended telephone, online and e-interviewing data collection and real-time reporting. It did so because the company's Six-Sigma quality control process quantitatively demonstrated that while neither telephone interviewing nor self-administered online surveys could sufficiently control sources of error in data collection, a hybrid approach using both modes combined with live interviewers and

[a]Research Manager, D3 Systems.
[b]President, WKS: CSM Consulting, Inc.

Market Research Best Practice. Edited by P. Mouncey and F. Wimmer.
© 2007 John Wiley & Sons, Limited.

their traditional skills could. Together with web-based reporting tools, this combination delivered improved customer satisfaction measurement and service benefits and increased ROI that neither of the individual data collection modes or the more traditional reporting systems could realize.

Now that a broad cross-section of market researchers and end users have had a chance to experience the effects of poorly and well-executed online data collection, we have all come to understand the shortcomings and benefits of the mode for quantitative research. Online research, just like any other mode, has shortcomings. It also has tremendous advantages. Researchers who fit and blend modes of data collection carefully to the research project at hand can garner significantly improved data collection and reporting processes over the CATI or self-administered methods of the past. These improvements in turn increase research influence in the management process as well as return on the market research investment (ROI).

Honeywell's division of Industrial Automation and Control (IAC) is one such group of market researchers. IAC recently went through a Six-Sigma-driven exercise to establish a research-driven customer value process (CVP) that would identify service defects, measure performance against competition and track customer-defined attributes which affect customer value and influence purchase/repurchase decisions amongst Honeywell's customer base.

Six-Sigma is a widely recognized, data-driven philosophy used by companies like Lockheed Martin, GE/AlliedSignal, Motorola, 3M, Dow and DuPont to drive management decisions and action across their organizations. It improves quality by reducing degrees of variance in any process – from manufacturing to transactional and from product to service. The objective of the Six-Sigma process is to create quality of near-perfection: 99.9997% perfect.

Honeywell's specific version of Six-Sigma is a customization of the premise of Six-Sigma methods. That premise is that sources of variation can be identified, quantified and mitigated by control or prevention by examining those elements responsible for process variation known as the '6Ms' (Man [people], Machine [equipment], Material, Method, Measurement and Mother Nature [environment]).

Honeywell's customizations assume that 100% inspection of the 6Ms is in itself inefficient. The company therefore devolves responsibility to management and its role in continually improving the business process. Effective management can control and reduce elements of process variation constantly through numeric measurement. Unquantifiable variables cannot be controlled and can impact process efficiency negatively. Management should therefore attempt to quantify all variables.

At Honeywell, customer satisfaction and value metrics have been a long-standing corporate priority. The current CVP survey process includes a variety of measurements such as customer value assessment and 'report card' surveys. The survey process is relied upon to keep management and the organization abreast of issues concerning service defects, performance against competition and tracking ability of the organization to deliver to customer-defined attributes.

The current measurement process has been in place since 1995 and has relied on B2B CATI. Significant investment has been made to create a process which features highly refined survey questionnaires, collects detailed evaluations from customers, is dependable and customer accepted and supports a closed-loop corrective action process for tracking and promptly addressing concerns, which is an important component in understanding and building customer loyalty.

HONEYWELL'S MEASUREMENTS OF SHORTCOMINGS OF STANDARD COLLECTION AND REPORTING TECHNIQUES FOR THE CUSTOMER VALUE ASSESSMENT

Until the advent of online research, Honeywell had difficulty achieving additional process improvements in data collection and reporting for its customer value assessment research of B2B customers, of which the CVP is a part. No available mode by itself provided enough cost and time efficiencies *and* control of the sources of non-sampling error to move the process closer to a Six-Sigma level. By nature, the process as it existed could never comply with the control parameters necessary for Six-Sigma compliance.

Six-Sigma exercises clearly pointed out the data gathering and reporting process before the use of web technologies was impacted by many previously 'uncontrollable' or 'noise' 'variables'. These variables created numerous 'hidden rework loops' that adversely affected process efficiency. Completion of a failure modes and effects analysis (FMEA) confirmed how failure could occur within each aspect of data collection. A number of new or misunderstood causes were identified.

Some of these causes were a result of mode. The CATI mode used up to the time of the CVP exercise was, by nature, shot through with many potential sources of error. Honeywell customers tend to be increasingly mobile, busy executives scattered across the globe. Often they work away from an 'assigned' office and cannot complete surveys in regular hours. Telephone surveys often suffered both poor response rates and high costs as a result of electronic filtering, preference for e-mail/web based communication and the multiple languages spoken by the respondents. This was particularly significant as the universes surveyed are usually small, making the positive participation of each respondent critical.

Other causes of the uncontrollable or noise variables were a byproduct of the static reporting system used by management. The system delayed delivery of results to decision-makers and account managers, reducing control of the customer satisfaction process.

Evidence of the problems created by the data collection and reporting techniques was visible in stagnant financial growth, unchanging satisfaction scores, changing customer characteristics/requirements, a lack of current value discriminators, <46% of customer value benefits and <22% cost factors, talking to the wrong customers, poorly identified customer segments, sample populations incorrectly aligned with organizational segments and weak competitive information.

HONEYWELL'S DECISIONS: BLENDED MODE RESEARCH TOOLS

To control the variables identified by the FMEA, IAC moved much of its quantitative research to the web. It was believed this would help IAC achieve Six-Sigma standards in its data collection and reporting processes. The cost efficiencies and unique combination of controls over sources of non-sampling error which conducting research online delivers, as well as the improved analysis and reporting tools, made this the preferable mode for data collection.

The use of web-based research and reporting for Honeywell's customer universes addressed problems in response, interviewer and respondent error, as well as reporting delays for management. For example, the universe measured by the CVP relies on e-mail and web-based information for receiving customer service orders. They generally prefer e-mail to telephone for communication. The written word is especially preferred by respondents for whom English is not their native language.

However, IAC was very careful in selecting its online research tools. Previous experience had made its market researchers very aware that online research, as a self-administered instrument, is also fraught with sources of potential respondent error. A simple comparison of CASRO Standards and Best Practices in Data Collection to the capabilities of self-administered online research made this clear.

There was also the problem of non-response bias due to respondent mode preference. Of particular concern was potential respondent error due to the unwillingness of busy executives to complete the lengthy Customer Value Assessment (CVA) survey, or the substitution of an executive secretary. Often, respondents do not want to spend time filling out the detailed responses to open-ends necessary to provide sufficient data for the Six-Sigma model. Sometimes they fly through long surveys without paying much attention to the questions. Occasionally, respondents cannot get web-based surveys to function properly.

IAC decided to use **human**voice's award-winning, e-interviewing product Surveyguardian® to counteract the sources of potential error in online research, guaranteeing the statistical gains in data and process quality, which were the reasons for the move to online research in the first place.

e-interviewing is an online research service which combines the features of common 'help desk' packages used in e-commerce with unique technological functions programmed into a survey engine. These e-commerce features include:

- instant messaging;
- click-for-call-back options;
- co-browsing or application sharing;
- database use by interviewers;
- digital pictures or streaming video;
- incoming contact management and distribution;
- supervisor and client interview monitoring;
- Voice-over Internet Protocol;
- productivity management tools, etc.

The technological functions combine para- or metadata generated by the survey engine about the interviewing process itself with database information about the sample point and statistically predicted behaviours for that sample point. The data are then used to cue interviewer intervention in the survey process as necessary.

Most of the technological functions of e-interviewing are designed to enable interviewers to take various kinds of action when respondent behaviour warrants it (i.e. when some form of behaviour occurs which could cause any of multiple forms of respondent error). Some of these functions include, but are not limited to:

- completion of open ends;
- clarification and coding of unaided awareness questions;
- exceeding degrees of variance on list questions or a series of range questions;
- attempting to move backwards through a survey;
- spending too little or too much time on a single survey page;
- submission of responses which don't match previously recorded or reported data;
- particular punch responses to questions which clients want clarified, probed and recorded on occurrence, etc.

Once the source of error is identified, the e-interviewer interface gives a well-trained interviewer the ability actually to *enter the survey* and take all sorts of actions, including observing respondent mouse behaviour on screen, controlling page progression, reviewing, changing and updating respondent data, cross-checking responses with databases and other forms of administrative and supervisory activity. The 'help desk' features themselves, combined with knowledgeable interviewer use of their personal skills and databases, deliver statistically significant higher cooperation rates by fostering a personal relationship between interviewer and respondent. The technology in both survey and interviewer interfaces delivers the ability for interviewers to control respondent error and data variance. It is this technology which caused Honeywell to adopt Surveyguardian as the preferred means for completing its Internet research.

The addition of e-interviewing to the research process eliminated respondent error problems and some sources of researcher error. The problems addressed included respondent inability error, ineligible respondent error, respondent unwillingness error and measurement error. At the same time, the unique nature of web research eliminated many of the sources of error commonly associated with interviewers, including respondent selection error, cheating error and recording error.

e-interviewing allowed respondents to change survey modes at will with a degree of mode effect that was controllable. Respondents experiencing technical problems received e-interviewer assistance. Respondents and interviewers built relationships through their interactions. These factors reduced non-response error.

e-interviewers also screened out secretaries completing surveys for their executives. Given pre-written probes, e-interviewers were able to elicit full responses to open-end questions with controlled and uniform probing. They also monitored respondent progress, modifying some behavioural sources of respondent recording error.

It is important to note that accurate narrative and qualitative data, unaffected by interviewer interpretation and recording, is critical to the Honeywell quality process. These data are heavily relied on to provide specific problem definition to drive process improvements (cycle-time, on-time delivery, etc.), assess important contributors to customer satisfaction not measured at high levels, identify key subsegments of the customer base and provide the detailed information necessary to drive appropriate corrective action and determine effective resource allocation to 'get the most bang for the buck.' The use of e-interviewers to probe and clarify respondents' responses online, but not enter respondents' answers themselves, was a process improvement unique to the e-interviewing medium. Honeywell did not completely eliminate the use of the telephone for interviewing. To eliminate potential sample frame coverage, as well as response bias created by mode, Honeywell used follow-up phone calls to the e-mail recruiting process to reach respondents who either would not or could not respond online during the study's fielding period. This was especially important given the international nature of the research, as respondents in different countries and time zones have different mode and scheduling preferences. In some cases, respondents were provided with a toll-free telephone number to call at the time of their own choosing, significantly improving the response as well as cooperation rates of this B2B population. The respondents who selected the telephone mode included people who chose to be contacted by telephone while inside the online survey, preferring to change survey modes midstream.

But IAC also needed to reduce its delivery time of reliable data to management. The Six-Sigma process also accounts for time insofar as it impacts customer satisfaction. The existing process just took too long for data to be actionable. For this reason, IAC also web-enabled the collected customer data, with a predictive behavioural model used by Honeywell to forecast customer value trends and develop proactive sales and management strategies.

Honeywell believes that to be effective, the measurement of customer satisfaction must use a comprehensive system based on a hierarchical model of customer behaviour. The concept of the model is that given a choice of products from different companies, most customers will pick

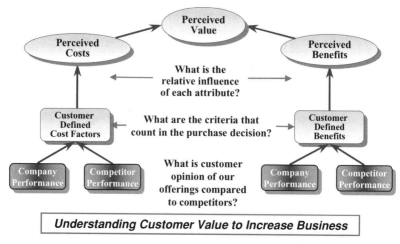

©WKS:CSM Inc. Proprietary

Figure 9.1   Understanding value.

the one that they feel will maximize their benefits versus their costs. In other words, they will select the one that gives them the best value relative to competitive offerings (Figure 9.1).

The tenets of the model are that customers' satisfaction with key expectations drives their perceptions of *overall value*. In turn, improved value will cause the desired behaviour in customers to continue doing business, increase business when able to do so and feel compelled to recommend the client to others based on their experiences.

The sum of this behaviour will assist in achieving customer satisfaction and loyalty. In concept, the behavioural model may be diagrammed as shown in Figure 9.2.

For the model to yield accurate data, customers must identify critical expectations and respective characteristics. This information is obtained through qualitative interviews and examination of existing data (prior research findings, service logs, etc.).

This model is translated into specific survey questions and linear regression techniques are applied to establish the impact ('weight') of each critical expectation on perceived performance. This makes the process diagnostic, i.e. not only is performance measured, but more importantly, the importance of most critical expectations is clarified.

This model supports the strategy that customer delight is an achievable goal and is built on the foundation of measuring and understanding

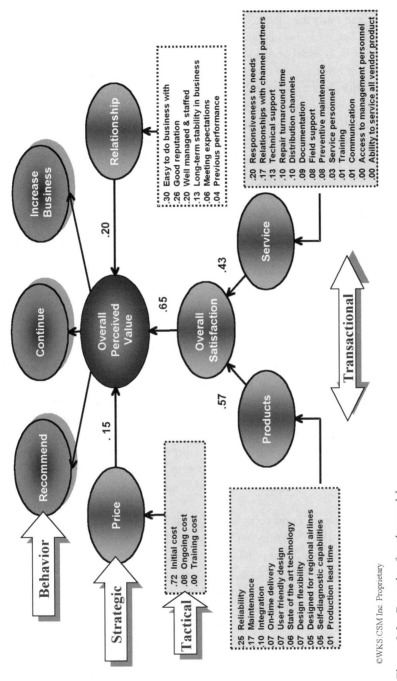

The elements shown in the figure include:

Relationship
- .30 Easy to do business with
- .26 Good reputation
- .20 Well managed & staffed
- .13 Long-term stability in business
- .06 Meeting expectations
- .04 Previous performance

Service
- .20 Responsiveness to needs
- .17 Relationships with channel partners
- .13 Technical support
- .10 Repair turnaround time
- .10 Distribution channels
- .09 Documentation
- .08 Field support
- .08 Preventive maintenance
- .03 Service personnel
- .01 Training
- .01 Communication
- .00 Access to management personnel
- .00 Ability to service all vendor product

Price
- .72 Initial cost
- .08 Ongoing cost
- .00 Training cost

Products
- .25 Reliability
- .17 Maintenance
- .10 Integration
- .07 On-time delivery
- .07 User friendly design
- .06 State of the art technology
- .07 Design flexibility
- .05 Designed for regional airlines
- .05 Self-diagnostic capabilities
- .01 Production lead time

Overall Perceived Value — Relationship .20 — Overall Satisfaction .65 — Service .43 — Products .57 — Price .15

Behavior, Strategic, Tactical, Transactional

Increase Business, Continue, Recommend

©WKS·CSM Inc Proprietary

Figure 9.2 Example of a value model.

customers' satisfaction with key decision making criteria within each area of interface with the client. Typically, areas of interaction include sales, products, services, business relationship and price.

Moving the model online and using data collected online improved the accuracy of information used, calculations completed to deliver accurate model results in a timely fashion and degrees of variance in the delivered data. Six-Sigma promotes efficiency and speed as measures of quality. Moving Honeywell's predictive modelling engine to the web allowed for reporting with a much lower level of researcher and data analysis error while improving speed and efficiency. Providing Honeywell managers with direct access to information also increased transparency and confidence in the information itself, promoting its usage. Managers' access to the modelling engine, reported data as they were collected and 'action comments' instantly delivered to their desktops increased the speed of Honeywell's communication process; one of the objectives of Six-Sigma and the CVA studies.

STUDY DESIGN

The study used to test the qualitative improvements in collection, analysis and reporting quantitative research data online was one of a series of periodic CVAs. The survey collects detailed evaluations from customers concerning known value differentiators. This information is used to improve customer value perceptions and satisfaction significantly. It is also used to create a dependable process to assure changing customer focus in the marketplace is identified promptly to target and execute customer loyalty maintenance activities in a timely fashion. The process itself is Six-Sigma compliant and is identified as an industry best practice.

The CVA study consisted of two parts. The first part used extensive qualitative work to identify true customer value criteria to use in the quantitative portion. This portion of the study used mixed methodology, in that portions of data were collected via personal interviews, e-mail and a small percentage were web-based.

The quantitative survey used the universe of over 1000 international executive clientele to create a sophisticated, stratified sampling frame. As segmentation was necessary for analysis, the final sample frame cube had 90 cells. Records were applied to multiple quota cells based upon responses to questions. Final n size was over 300 completed records.

humanvoice sent e-mail invitations in the name of Honeywell's CEO to all sample points in the universe. The e-mail body contained an active link and URL address to the questionnaire and a unique PIN number. Each also contained a toll-free number and call-scheduler respondents could select to complete their surveys by telephone. Each sample point without a completed survey received a reminder e-mail message four days later. Reminder notices by e-mail and telephone were completed thereafter to respondents in unfilled quotas who had not started or completed their surveys. Respondents could exit the survey and return to it at any time, either by telephone or online – continuing from the point where they left off. They could also change survey modes during completion of the instrument. The study was available to respondents from February 15 to March 28, 2001.

Honeywell relied on **human**voice's integrated web survey/CATI survey software to execute the survey instrument. The software is equipped with all the capabilities expected of today's leading CATI and web survey packages. Honeywell also used **human**voice's Survey-guardian e-interviewing utility described above. **human**voice provided e-interviewer and toll-free telephone interviewer staffing 24 hours a day, seven days a week in the various languages of the study.

humanvoice built a web-based behavioural modelling engine using Honeywell proprietary forecasting methodology to report collected data. Designed to integrate primary and secondary data, the engine allows Honeywell managers to forecast behavioural patterns with a greatly enhanced degree of accuracy. It is used for all customer-driven decision-making within the organization. The slight mode effect observed in the data was controlled using comparisons to previous results as the data was processed within the engine.

The collected data were reported online in real-time using the **human**voice engine customized for Honeywell needs. All data could be displayed, aggregated and cross-tabulated as they were collected on any web browser open to the proper URL.

RESULTS CONFIRM REASONS FOR THE CHANGE

Honeywell went online to better reach respondents, achieve more valid and reliable measures, accelerate and direct exposure to information internally, use the new technologies to make predictive modelling more valid and reliable and provide a more effective and credible method for reporting research outcomes to management.

Following completion of the blended mode data collection, an analysis of pre- and post-process defect rates was conducted. A review of the process maps was also completed (Fugure 9.3). Results clearly indicate process steps were reduced greatly and the sigma level improved. With the use of e-interviewers and online predictive modelling tools especially, the use of blended research modes eliminated most sources of respondent, interviewer and researcher error that have plagued both telephone and self-administered research for the last twenty years.

Since moving the model online there has also been a significant increase in management confidence and use of the process data. Results are being used at the corporate and business unit level to 'pilot' the organization and drive corrective actions. This has resulted in significant improvement in customer satisfaction and, perhaps more importantly, has continued to provide a dependable process by which customers are assured their concerns are registered and will be resolved promptly.

Speedy reporting of data, diffused use of the modelling engine and the decentralized customer feedback process through 'action comments' sent directly to managers' mailboxes brought the closed-loop, corrective action cycle into compliance with the timeframe demanded by Six-Sigma standards. As the speed of corrective action is the whole purpose for Honeywell conducting the CVA studies, this benefit is especially advantageous. Similarly, respondent rating history, individual comments and service history were tracked to determine if previously reported problems had been resolved. Each could then be addressed immediately because of the increased reporting speed.

Moreover, comparison of pre- and post-process metrics revealed significant improvement and reduced variation in CATI-related variables, including appointment scheduling and re-scheduling, screening activities including gate keepers, respondent cooperation, respondent comprehension, global implementation across languages, compliance with the B2B interviewing time window and interviewer recording. It also substantiated decreased variation in process variables such as contact data, labour requirements, quota control, data turn time and sample management.

Comparison of pre- and post-process metrics revealed no improvement, loss of efficiency or increased variation in required contact information, duplicated efforts, questionnaire design, programming cost, sample management, data aggregation and data comparability.

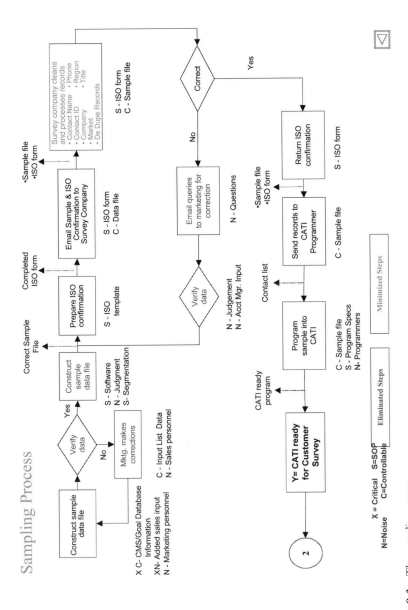

Figure 9.3 The sampling process.

Cost reduction is also a feature of successful Six-Sigma processes. Here again, the blended processes used made significant improvements. Use of blended mode data collection and the reporting tools introduced above reduced the cost of CVA studies by more than 20%.

In summary, the process improvements realized were:

- minimum ROI gain in excess of $5 million;
- annual metrics process cost reduced by 20%;
- management acceptance of CVA thinking;
- key value drivers identified by market segment;
- monitoring system in place;
- CVA process controls in place.

Honeywell's use of the Six-Sigma process to improve its research techniques is a first for both Six-Sigma and market research. Six-Sigma is a highly regarded standard of quality in the corporate world. The use of blended research modes and e-interviewing as a replacement for other modes to achieve it provides this method with new status among Fortune 100 companies. This is especially true of those who have been unwilling up to now to adopt online research because of its lack of credibility.

FURTHER READING

Balm, G. J. (1992), Benchmarking – Nicety or Necessity? *Tapping the Network Journal.* **3**(1), 6–8.

Beebe, T. J., Harrison, P. A., McRae, J. A., Jr., Anderson, R. E. and Fulkerson, J. A. (1998), An Evaluation of Computer-Assisted Self-Interviews In A School Setting. *Public Opinion Quarterly*, **62**, 623–632.

Bell Canada (2001), *How Your Intranet Can Be A Strategic Research Management Tool.* Presented to the Professional Market Research Society Annual Conference. April 24, Ottawa, Ontario.

Bourque, L. B. and Fielder, E. P. (1995), *How To Conduct Self-Administered and Mail Surveys.* Sage Publications, Inc.

Burr, M. A., Levin, K. Y. and Becher, A. (2001), *Examining Web vs. Paper Mode Effects In a Federal Government Customer Satisfaction Study.* Presentation for the 56th Annual AAPOR Conference. May 19, Montreal, Quebec.

Cantor, D., Schneider, S. J., Malakhoff, L., Arieira, C., Segel, P., Nguyen, L. and Guarino, J. (2001), *An Experiment Comparing Computer-Assisted and Paper Modes of Data Collection for the Short Form in Census 2000.* Presentation for the 56th Annual AAPOR Conference. May 19, Montreal, Quebec.

Chadwick, S. (2000), *Betting The Firm*. Presentation at the CASRO Annual Conference, San Diego, California.

Clark, R. (2000), *Impact of Notification Methods On Response Rates For Web-Based Surveys*. Presentation at the American/World Association for Public Opinion Research 2000 Annual Conference. 17–21 May, Portland, Oregon.

Comley, P. (2001), Getting It Right Online. Research Guide To The Internet. *Research Magazine*, pp.10–11.

Conrad, F. G. and Schober, M. F. (2000), Clarifying Question meaning in a Household Telephone Survey. *Public Opinion Quarterly*. **64**, 1–28.

Council of American Survey Research Organizations (1998), *Survey Research Quality Guidelines*.

Couper, M. (2000), *New Developments in Computer Assisted Interviewing*. Presentation at the (2000) Nebraska Symposium on Survey Research. 13–15 April. Lincoln, Nebraska.

Couper, M. P. and Rowe, B. (1996), Evaluation of A Computer-Assisted Self-Interview Component In A Computer-Assisted Personal Interview Survey. *Public Opinion Quarterly*, **60**, 89–105.

Couper, M., Traugott, M. W. and Lamias, M. J. (2001), Web Survey Design and Administration. *Public Opinion Quarterly*, **65**, 230–254.

Crabtree, S. (2000), Untangling the Web. *Quirk's Marketing Research Review*, **XIV**(7), 62–68.

Crawford, S. (2000), *Web Surveys: Perceptions of Burden*. Presentation at the American/World Association for Public Opinion Research (2000) Annual Conference. 17–21 May, Portland, Oregon.

de Leeuw, E. (2002), The Effect of Computer-Assisted Interviewing on Data Quality: A Review of the Evidence, in J. Blasius, J. Hox, E. De Leeuw and P. Schmidt (Eds) *Social Science Methodology in the New Millennium*. Leske and Budrich.

de Leeuw, E. and Collins, M. (1997), Data Collection Methods and Survey Quality: An Overview in L. Lyberg, P. Biemar, M. Collins, E. De Leauw, D. Trewin, C. Dippo and N. Schwartz (Eds) *Survey Measurement and Process Quality*. John Wiley & Sons, Inc., pp. 199–220.

Dillman, D.A. (1978), *Mail and Telephone Surveys: The Total Design Method*. John Wiley & Sons, Inc.

Dillman, D. A. (2000), *The Rise of Intelligent Survey Organizations in the 21st Century*. Presentation at the (2000) Nebraska Symposium on Survey Research. 13–15 April. Lincoln, Nebraska.

Feaver, M. (2001), *e-Commerce Customer Relationships: The Essential Role of Qualitative Research in Developing Evolving Competitive Advantage Strategies*. Presented to the Professional Market Research Society Annual Conference. April 24, Ottawa, Ontario.

Fletcher, J. and Schmidt, D. (2001), *Measuring Response Bias in Survey Research: An Analysis of Age Characteristics of Early Respondents and Resistors*. Presentation for the 56th Annual AAPOR Conference. May 19, Montreal, Quebec.

Green, M., Krosnick, J. and Holbrook, A. (2001), Data Quality Impact from Shifting In-Person Interviews to RDD Telephone Samples. *Research Conference Report*. August. pp. 1–2.

Hughes, D. (1991), Motorola Nears Quality Benchmark After 12-Year Evolutionary Effort. *Aviation Week & Space Technology*, **135**(23), 64–65.

Iconocast (2000), *Internet At A Glance.* http://www.iconoclast.com. Winter.

Jeavons, A. (2001), *Paradate: Concepts and Application.* Presentation at the CASRO Technology Conference in June, New York City, New York.

Krosnick, J. (2000), *Peering Into the Future of Thinking and Answering: A Psychological Perspective on Internet Survey Respondents.* Presentation at the (2000) Nebraska Symposium on Survey Research. 13–15, April. Lincoln, Nebraska.

Krosnick, J. and Chang, L. (2001), *A Comparison of the Random Digit Dialing Telephone Survey Methodology with Internet Survey Methodology as Implemented by Knowledge Networks and Harris Interactive.* Presentation for the 56th Annual AAPOR Conference. May 19, Montreal, Quebec.

Kuhn, K. (2001), Challenges of Internet Research. *Alert!* **39**(4), 24–25.

Last, J. (2001), End User Forum. *Alert!* **39**(8), 9 and 14.

Liu, K. (2001), *Validity Issues In Web Derived Survey Data.* Presentation for the 56th Annual AAPOR Conference. May 19, Montreal, Quebec.

Lukaweski, R. (2001), A Transition From DBI to Online – A B2B Case Study. *Imprints.* PMRS, p. 18.

Luth, R. (2000), *Marketing Research Service In (2005): A View From the Data Collection Side.* CASRO Annual Conference, San Diego, California.

MacElroy, B. (2000), Variables Influencing Dropout Rates In Web-based Surveys. *Quirk's Marketing Research Review,* **XIV** (7), 42–47.

Macer, T. (2001), Get Connected. *Research Guide To The Internet. Research Magazine* January, pp. 5–6.

Magee, C.G., Straight, R.L. and Schwartz, L. (2001), *Conducting Web-Based Surveys: Lessons Learned and Keys to Success with Known Populations.* Presentation for the 56th Annual AAPOR Conference. May 19, Montreal, Quebec.

Mallet, T. (2001), *Retaining Virtue in a Virtual World: e-Surveys in Public Policy Research.* Presented to the Professional Market Research Society Annual Conference, Ottawa, Ontario.

Manfreda, K. (2000), *Design Issues In WWW Surveys.* Presentation at the American/World Association for Public Opinion Research (2000) Annual Conference. 17–21 May. Portland, Oregon.

McNeish, J. (2001), *Using the Internet for Data Collection – Just Because We Can, Should We?* Presentation for the 56th Annual AAPOR Conference. May 19, Montreal, Quebec.

Mehta, R. and Sivadas, E. (1995), Comparing Response Rates and Response Content in Mail versus Electronic Surveys. *Journal of the Market Research Society,* **37**, 429–439.

Miller-Steiger, D. and Abraham, S. Y. (2001), *Changing Patterns of Web Usage Among Elite Populations in a Multi-Modal National Survey.* Presentation for the 56th Annual AAPOR Conference. May 19, Montreal, Quebec.

Minyard, E. and Deitemeyer, A. (2001), Mixed Mode Survey Provides Well-Rounded Results. *Alert!* **39**(1), 10–11.

Mitton, C. (2001), *Preventing the Click-Out: Assessing Web Site Usability.* Presented to the Professional Market Research Society Annual Conference. April 24, Ottawa, Ontario.

Moon, Y. (1998), Impression Management In Computer-Based Interviews: The Effects Of Input Modality, Output Modality, And Distance. *Public Opinion Quarterly,* **62**, 610–622.

Nicholls II, W. L., Baker, R. P. and Martin, J. (1997), The Effect of New Data Collection Technologies on Survey Data Quality in L. Lyberg, P. Biemer, M.Collins, E. De Leeuw, D. Trewin, C. Dippo and N. Schwartz (Eds)*Survey Measurement and Process Quality*. John Wiley & Sons, Inc.

Niemes, J. (1999), Taking Sales Success To New Heights With Six Sigma. *National Productivity Review*, **18**(4), 29–32.

Palmquist, J. and Retzlaff, L. (2000), The Merging of Database and Marketing Research. *CASRO Journal 2000*, pp. 29–32.

Park, J. (2001), *Out of the Ivory Tower and Into The Fire*. Presentation at the CASRO Technology Conference, New York City, New York.

Park, J. M. (2001), *Response Differences from Internet-enabled Respondents in Surveys Fielded via Internet and via Mail*. Presentation for the 56th Annual AAPOR Conference. May 19, Montreal, Quebec.

Poynter, R. (2001), *A Guide to Best Practice in Online Quantitative Research*. Presentation at the Association for Survey Computing Conference 'The Challenge of the Internet'. 11–12 May, London, United Kingdom.

Rivers, D. (2000), *Probability Sampling And The Internet*. Presentation at the 2000 Nebraska Symposium on Survey Research. 13–15 April, Lincoln, Nebraska.

Saris. W. E. (1991), *Computer-Assisted Interviewing*. Sage Publications.

Schwarz, N., Strack, F. Hippler, H.J. and Bishop, G. (1991), The Impact of Administration Mode on Response Effects in Survey Measurement. *Applied Cognitive Psychology*, **5**,193–212.

Semon, T. T. (2000), Better Questions Means More Honesty. *Marketing News*, August 14, p. 6.

Sheppard, J. (2000), Interviewers Are the Key to Respondent Cooperation. *Alert!* **38**(5), 2–3.

Smith, C. (1997), Casting the Net: Surveying an Internet Population. *Journal of Communication Mediated by Computers.*, **3**(1), available at http://www.usc.edu/dept/annenberg/vol3/issue1/.

Smith, R. M. (2001), *Drawing Inferences From Data Obtained From Self-Selected Respondents*. CASRO Technology Conference. New York.

Sorensen, H. (2000), A statistical approach to security/past participation problems. *Quirk's Marketing Research Review*, **14**(3), 28–31.

Stone, W. and Thomas, J. E. (2001), *Online Research in Managing Customer Value and Satisfaction*. Presentation at the Online Market Research and Web-Based Surveys Summit of the International Quality and Productivity Center. 23–24 October, San Francisco, California.

Sudman, S. and Bradburn, N. M. (1987), *Asking Questions: A Practical Guide to Questionnaire Design*. From the *Jossey-Bass Series in Social and Behavioral Sciences*, Jossey-Bass Publishers.

Terhanian, G. (2000a), *Understanding How To Solve the 'Selection Bias' and 'Learning Effects' Problems Associated with Internet-Based Research with Proprietary Panels*. Presentation at the 2000 Nebraska Symposium on Survey Research. 13–15 April, Lincoln, Nebraska.

Terhanian, G. (2000b), *How To Produce Credible, Trustworthy Information Through Internet-Based Survey Research*. Presentation at the American/World Association for Public Opinion Research 2000 Annual Conference. 17–21 May, Portland, Oregon.

Teitler, J. O., Reichman, N. E. and Sprachman, S. (2001), *Cost–Benefit Analysis of Improving Response Rates For a Hard-to-Reach Population*. Presentation for the 56th Annual AAPOR Conference. May 19, Montreal, Quebec.

The Edge Strategies (2001), *The revolution of (CAPI) Computer Assisted Personal Interviewing*. Presented to the Professional Market Research Society Annual Conference. April 24, Ottawa, Ontario.

Tims, M. (2001), Access for All. *Research Guide To Internet Technology*. Marketing Research Society, p. 8.

Totten, J. W. (2000), *Use of E-Mail And Internet Surveys By Research Companies*. Presentation at the American/World Association for Public Opinion Research 2000 Annual Conference. 17–21 May, Portland, Oregon.

Tuckel, P. and O'Neill, H. (2001), *The Vanishing Respondent in Telephone Surveys*. Presentation for the 56th Annual AAPOR Conference. May 19, Montreal, Quebec.

Whelchel, N. (2001), *Paper or PC? Design, Implementation, And Success Of A Mixed-Mode Survey*. Presentation for the 56th Annual AAPOR Conference. May 19, Montreal, Quebec.

Wright, D.L., Aquilino, W. S., and Supple, A. J. (1998), A Comparison of Computer-Assisted and Paper-and-Pencil Self-Administered Questionnaires In A Survey On Smoking, Alcohol and Drug Use. *Public Opinion Quarterly*, **62**, 331–353.

Wygant, S., Olsen, D. and Feld, K. (2001), *Comparative Analysis of Telephone, Web and e-Interview Survey Techniques*. Presentation at the Online Market Research and Web-Based Surveys Summit of the International Quality and Productivity Center. 23–24 October, San Francisco, California.

Chapter Ten

Creating Competitive Intellectual Capital: The Henkel Case

Hans-Willi Schroiff[a]

This chapter the value-added process between a business information need and the consumer-centred decision support via professional market research approaches. There is special emphasis on the interaction between corporate research functions and research institutes.

INTRODUCTION

As organizations evolve from multi-domestic to transnational, they need to develop new ways of obtaining, sharing and acting upon marketing information. The technological advances that led to the 'marketing information revolution' now provide firms the opportunity to develop new approaches to creating strategic and competitive marketing intelligence. This chapter describes how Henkel has generated a vision for knowledge management designed to create new sources of competitive intellectual capital.

Apart from benchmarking the current processes of knowledge management, the creation of a transnational data warehouse as the foundation

[a]Vice President, International Market Research, Henkel KGaA.

Market Research Best Practice. Edited by P. Mouncey and F. Wimmer.
© 2007 John Wiley & Sons, Limited.

is key. The process of creating competitive knowledge by generating integrated (i.e. across sources) and international (i.e. across countries) insights is described. The chapter describes steps from standard reporting of one information source to data mining across many information sources, and the consequences these changes represent both for marketing and market research functions inside a company.

Let me ask you one crucial question: how many of you are working in a company where less than 30% of the revenues are coming from your domestic market and the rest is coming from all over the world?

The reason why I am asking this question is quite obvious. Those of you who gain profits predominantly from a huge domestic market – e.g. the United States – might find some parts of my chapter puzzling. Why should you want to harmonize your databases, why look at whether measure definitions are the same across countries, why try to integrate information across different sources, etc? Are we not getting it that way anyhow? So why bother?

Let me tell you that for a global company such as Henkel the situation is different, particularly as Europe is not yet a unified whole, and languages and cultural contexts including markets are quite different. But keep in mind that what is happening in a Henkel context today could become *your* working environment tomorrow, as more and more businesses are turning global. Therefore, I believe our experiences and findings are relevant even for those happy campers among you that are not yet confronted with the opportunities of global marketing and global information management.

CHALLENGES FOR THE YEAR 2000

Several years ago we were reviewing the challenges that Henkel would have to face in the year 2000 and thereafter. We came up with a lot of topics, a lot of ideas and a lot of suggestions. In the end it all boiled down to three major issues:

- changes in organizational context;
- exploiting information technology;
- creating competitive intellectual capital.

I will refer only briefly to the first two and concentrate on the third.

TRANSNATIONAL ORGANIZATIONS

About ten years ago, Henkel was a typical *multi-domestic* organization. The headquarters in Düsseldorf was exerting some financial control, but basically every subsidiary was allowed to work according to its own procedures, regulations, benchmarks and its own definitions. This was mainly due to the fact that across the years, in common with many other companies, Henkel had grown through a series of acquisitions.

Looking at the organization today, Henkel is determined to get very close to the ideal of a transnational organization (Figure 10.1). The transnational model that is so brilliantly described in the monograph of Bartlett and Goshal (1991) is a bare necessity for companies competing in a global marketplace. These companies typically consider differences between their various subsidiaries as opportunities – not as threats. In an environment of shared mental models about business decision-making, the headquarters makes use of distributed specialized resources and capabilities and employs expertise wherever it comes from.

However, what the transnational model implies are *common rules of conduct* – a sort of 'Euro currency of mind', a common workflow, common definitions. Everyone has to accept a joint way, for example, of viewing the markets, viewing the competitors and evaluating their own performance and those of their competitors in these various contexts.

As we Europeans can testify, harmonization of a currency is difficult to achieve – let alone harmonization of thinking or a 'meeting of minds'.

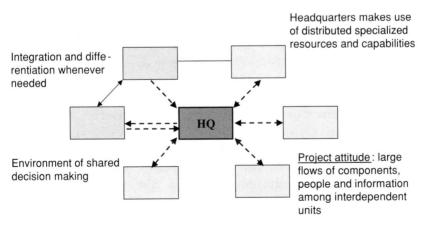

Figure 10.1 The transnational organization. Adapted from Barlett and Goshal, 1991.

Companies are still suffering from 'not invented here' syndromes and the 'hidden agendas' of local managers who cannot see the forest for the trees.

The barriers we have to overcome in order to create a transnational company are not geopolitical barriers, but the mental obstacles which hinder the flow of information and are detrimental to the generation of competitive intelligence and decision-making. Political borders are easy to cross in Europe these days. The real challenge is to tear down the barriers within people's minds by making them think along common mental models that everyone shares.

It is the 'Euro' currency of minds that we are after. This may be difficult to grasp for companies who still rely on their performance in a large home market. In a multi-country environment, such as Europe, our vision is a must for economic success.

The first and most important prerequisite for turning this vision into reality is that the company adopts a transnational mindset. If it remains multi-domestic beneath the surface, all the efforts described later in this chapter will be in vain. So the imperative is:

Change the mind of the people first and then change your databases.

THE COMPETITIVE INTELLIGENCE PROGRAMME

It is self-evident that competitive advantage can best be gained by a superior use of information sources. We are absolutely convinced that it is not the sheer mass of data piled up in a market research department that matters, but how these pieces of information are integrated into business scenarios, solutions, and strategies. The old doctrine of Gestalt psychology also applies here: *The whole is more than the sum of its parts.* It was absolutely key that international market research as a transnationally operating unit was charged with this task and adequately empowered to drive the important process of knowledge management.

It has become even clearer during the past two years that the generation of intellectual capital is going to be the prime contribution and represents the real added value of the research function. The added value of the research department rises and falls according to the degree to which we are successful in producing and utilizing intellectual capital.

Internal benchmarking studies

How did we go about defining and fine-tuning a programme for knowledge management and the generation of intellectual capital? First, we looked critically at ourselves. Henkel performed two large-scale studies among its managers.

The first study addressed the questions of which informational sources they used and how often, which analyses were typically performed on which data and which decisions were usually taken in the light of which evidence.

A second study was related to the first but approached the topic in a 'top-down' fashion. It referred to the characteristics of mental models that decision-makers were employing regarding the dynamics of the market. The diagnosis of mental models – how comprehensive, how true, how elaborate they are – is key to the design of a successful internal intelligence system. You have to know where you stand before you can leap.

The knowledge pyramid

After having diagnosed carefully where we were, we were developing some thoughts on where to leap.

In the book of Vince Barabba and Gerry Zaltman entitled *Hearing the Voice of the Market* (1991) we discovered a chart that best seems to summarize our thoughts and ideas. We called it the *knowledge pyramid* (Figure 10.2). The knowledge pyramid is a good analogy for describing

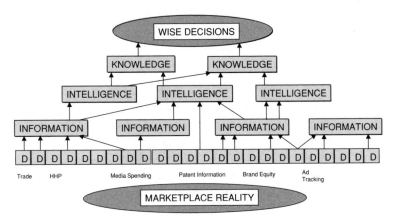

Figure 10.2   The knowledge pyramid. Adapted from Barabba and Zaltman, 1991.

the several steps of the basic task: how to get from a complex market reality to a wise company decision.

The basic layer is the data layer. This comprises the binders that sometimes collect a lot of dust in market research departments. Companies usually buy masses of data on shares, consumer panel, ad tracking, media spending, print promotions, etc. They are basically worthless unless they are transformed into information by established data production procedures – different pieces of information can be translated successfully into intelligence by integrating them across countries and sources. Repetitive insights or intelligence can be turned into sound knowledge which finally can be used as a basis for enabling wise company decisions.

A very simple and pragmatic model, but it comprises almost everything that we have achieved in the last two years in order to provide Henkel with a successful knowledge management system. It became the agenda for our working programme.

You can tie the different layers to notions that you might know. Data warehouse approaches are quite common these days, we all know the classic mono source information systems like In*Fact from Nielsen or DataServer from IRI, just to name two. We are also aware of some knowledge-based systems which pretend that they can integrate and incorporate knowledge from different sources. And finally we are also aware of many ways to improve decision making.

Listen, learn, lead

We can also tie this to three commandments that Vince Barabba mentions in his book *The Meeting of the Minds* – The Listen, Learn and Lead (Figure 10.3). What do we mean by that?

To *listen* to the market is a comparatively simple task. The questions raised here can be answered by the standard classical reporting systems. They basically answer questions like what happened? and thus represent a retrospective evaluation of past performance.

More interesting to us are valid answers to the question why did it happen? This already has a lot to do with the readiness to *learn*. An elaborate intelligence system must be able to come up with a series of valid explanations as to why things happened as they did. This already requires a more comprehensive look at reality than most of us can imagine, particularly those who always try to explain reality from a look at two

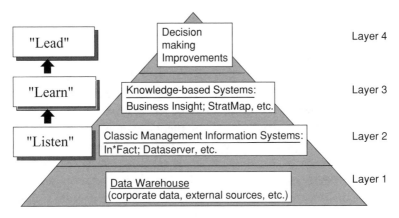

Figure 10.3   Business intelligence – a systems approach.

to three measures from the classical bimonthly trade audit in Europe, or from weekly trade scanner data in the United States.

The ultimate objective is to provide managers with answers to the question 'how can I make it happen?' The prerequisites are very clear. We here refer to sound knowledge that has been generated inside the company, provided by analyses that look behind the phenomena, that come up with valid explanations as to why certain categories have moved and others not. This knowledge can be used to lead by superior knowledge, and by acting upon it you are able to outflank your competitors – you are able to be first, etc.

IMPLEMENTING THE HENKEL INTELLIGENCE SYSTEM

Now what did we do in order to turn this vision into reality? Following the different layers of the pyramid, we started a giant harmonization programme. Harmonization refers to:

- the *data*, particularly their format;
- the *analysis tools* that are used across the Henkel universe;
- the *analysis techniques*, which incorporate the definition of standardized reports and analysis techniques.

Let us take a look at these efforts one by one. I will not refer in detail to the more or less technical requirements that modern data warehousing efforts entail, but will concentrate on the core issue in data warehousing, which is the business data model used to define the organization of data.

Data harmonization

Our business data model is laid down in several strictly confidential documents: the 'White Books' for the single product categories.

The White Books provide the overall market definitions and structures for the respective category. It applies to all internal and external marketing information sources – i.e. it not only covers external data like Nielsen shares or advertising tracking data or media spending figures, but also internal data on shipments, on revenues or whatever else you can think of.

The central idea is to have all business-relevant data aggregated along one data model – one transnational data warehouse. It took little effort to make this chart, but it took a giant effort inside a multi-domestic company to arrive at a common view of markets and structures. It was a major business re-engineering effort, but, having survived this period of blood, sweat and tears, I am ready to admit that this is a *must* for every global company that wishes to operate effectively and efficiently.

Please be reminded that I am not just talking about some sheets of paper providing people with an overall definition. This also has deep consequences for your data suppliers. The Nielsens, the IRIs, the Millward Browns and everyone else supplying data to Henkel have to adhere to the data model and have to deliver data in a specific format required by the model. This is a little tough, because it is equal to demanding a Coke in a square can instead of in a round one, but, after initial hesitation, our business partners have agreed that it makes a lot of sense to look at data the Henkel way.

Harmonization of measures, reports and analyses

What applies to the data also applies to the measure definitions. A second document describes the internationally harmonized measures. Some of you might be surprised at this point – isn't there one way to measure distribution in India and New Zealand? Or in Switzerland and in Poland? I have to tell you that there is not! And I know what I am talking about. The same multi-domestic characteristics that applied to companies like Henkel also apply to companies in the market information business, like Nielsen and IRI or GfK or Millward Brown. Data harmonization without harmonization of measure definitions is a useless enterprise.

Once data have been harmonized and once agreement on the definitions of measures has been reached, one can think about setting up standard reports and analyses. Again, this may strike some of you as odd, but when you look at the variety of ways to do a new product control report you will become converted to the harmonization society immediately. Please be careful: having a common control report across countries on the basis of nonharmonized data and nonharmonized definitions will also get you into trouble. All the prerequisites have to be matched in order to produce meaningful insights. In order to do meaningful analysis you again need two things: first, a powerful and comprehensive analysis tool that is capable of digesting gigabytes of data; and second, the necessary business intelligence in order to use this front end tool effectively.

IDIS – the front-end tool

Let us look at these two points now. Selecting or designing an appropriate front-end tool for data reduction and analysis is a critical issue. Henkel has gathered huge experience in this arena in the past five years, resulting in the insight that none of the existing offers in the market would meet the requirements of the data warehousing problems we were anticipating. I cannot be too detailed about this point, but I can tell you that, finally, an internal system called IDIS was created. IDIS is able to manage the data volumes associated with an integrated and transnational data warehouse on the one hand, and with sufficient statistical power on the other hand. So the problem of data management and data analysis could not be solved by using an existing data software package. However, we are sure that technological advances will create standard solutions very quickly.

Business intelligence

The next issue is the most important of all: how do you capture the existing knowledge and know-how inside the company, transform it into meaningful analysis, train people on these analysis and the mindset in the background, and turn the insights gathered from data analysis into wise company decisions?

In order to exploit the existing knowledge most comprehensively, the Business Intelligence Team (BIT) was set up. The Business Intelligence Team is a group of people who are temporarily taken out of their line jobs in order to collect explicit and tacit knowledge about business intelligence procedures. According to the *best practice* doctrine, they search for and select the most appropriate and most advanced procedures, transform these procedures into standardized approaches and implement them as standard business intelligence modules within the IDIS front-end tool.

Setting up the Business Intelligence Team has probably been one of the investments of Henkel with the highest payoff. The team has provided major input regarding analyses, concepts and suggestions. The team continuously develops and tests guidelines and procedures for marketing and sales in the form of shared analyses that can be accessed easily by every brand manager, marketing director or strategic business unit manager.

Reporting, screening and 'roadmapping'

Of course I am not permitted to share with you the details of what these analyses look like, but we can glance at the general structure of such an analysis system.

According to the various layers of a knowledge pyramid, we start out with what we call *shared reporting*. In a fast and easily accessible intranet environment, the individual manager has the possibility to get a quick overview on key performance indicators of brands, markets, countries and businesses. One of these criteria can, for example, be the market share.

A built-in *alert reporting function* indicates where and when major movements of this criterion have occurred. Let us assume that you have detected a decline of your brand on your most important performance criterion. A more detailed screening chart is just a click away. Here, you can look at the respective decline and find a number of explicative parameters along with it. The next stage you can then enter is a set of guided analyses that we call *road maps*, which help you to isolate the reasons for brand success or brand failure. To put it in simple terms, the basic principle behind our concept of guided analysis is:

- to identify critical developments in the *reporting* mode;
- to generate hypotheses about possible causes in this *screening mode*;
- to confirm hypotheses in the *roadmapping* mode.

Now let us look at these three modes in depth.

Reporting and screening

Figure 10.4 represents schematically the reporting and screening modes, providing the hierarchy of different business perspectives that an individual can adopt. Whether it be the brand manager or the country manager

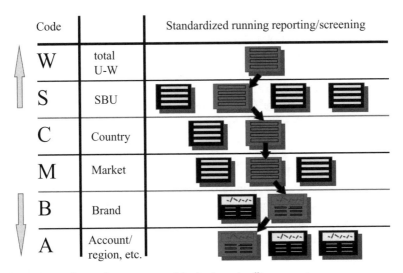

Code		Standardized running reporting/screening
W	total U-W	
S	SBU	
C	Country	
M	Market	
B	Brand	
A	Account/ region, etc.	

Figure 10.4 Reporting structure of the business intelligence system.

or an SBU manager, everyone finds his or her information needs satisfied on a respective level by this intranet offer.

Let us assume that you are the Executive Vice President for detergents. You would start out with a view that shows the performance of Henkel detergents vs. P&G, Colgate, Lever and whoever else is out there. Just a click away is the view of the various SBUs. Here we have cleaning, toiletries, detergents, etc. A click away from the SBUs are the countries, divided into several categories. A category is divided up into several brands, and a brand can be looked at under various account splits and/or regional splits.

This is all represented in a very straightforward intranet solution that we at Henkel call the *Factbook*. The full information content of the Factbook is updated every four weeks in a European environment with a retrospective look at weekly developments for scanner-based input. As you remember, all the different data sources have been conceptually aligned and they are represented in the Factbook with an equally aligned four-weekly period.

The two bottom layers represent the *screening mode*. The basic principle of the screening mode is to generate hypotheses about possible reasons for brand growth and brand decline. In order to narrow down the multiple analysis parts, you are provided with a number of key indicators that provide possible reasons for these developments. Of course, we are referring to some classical time series of mono sources that we usually look at, but the Henkel integrated approach allows you to combine information from several sources in a meaningful way and group it according to its significance in the market, and not according to the type of source it comes from. The way we do it is, of course, strictly confidential, but I think Figure 10.4 at least provides an idea of what can be done to *really* narrow down the reasons for brand success or failure.

Roadmapping

Let us now assume that you have observed a share decline of your brand. The screening mode suggests that this is due to declining penetration. Our *roadmapping* procedure gives you recommendations to follow a 'best practice' path for in-depth analyses, making full use of integrated information across sources.

What it illustrates is the journey through a series of predefined and standardized best practice suggestions that allow you finally to confirm or reject your initial hypotheses about your brand's performance. Not only that – a thorough and guided analysis also enables you to narrow down possible indicated actions. In that sense, we are getting very close to the ideal of enabling wise company decisions by using the analytical power of a superior system based on a truly transnational dataset.

So, what roadmap algorithms do is simply to try to identify as quickly and intelligently as possible the sales and cost drivers in your marketing programme. Of course, roadmaps are not established to sit there forever. International market research is monitoring closely the methodological developments, analytical efforts that are published and experiences within our company in order continuously to revise the existing procedures – because once you stand still, you fall behind.

Let me recap briefly what we have done.

SUMMARY OF OUR WORK TO DATE

We have to be aware that setting up a knowledge management programme is a major business re-engineering project. From our experience it involves at least three major components:

1. I talked about a *mapping of the current processes*. This is a must to establish a baseline – to find a point from where to start. The next important

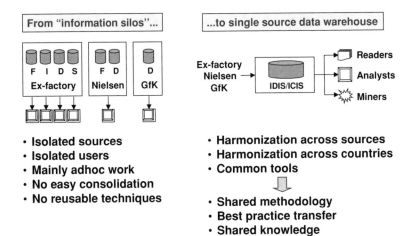

Figure 10.5   From local informational silos to transnational competitive intelligence.

issue is, of course, the question of where to leap, and here we have been leaping in basically two directions.

2. We have been building innovative intelligence procedures on the basis of a transnationally harmonized data warehouse. This not only includes the design of best practice roadmaps, but also the creation of a joint mental model about market dynamics. This model serves as a guideline for the design of all analyses and their sequences. One set of analyses focuses on classical and innovative approaches for better ROI evaluations, leading to better evaluation of monetary investments in marketing mix factors.

3. We have tied this to major changes in the work processes. With the help of modern information technology we were able to tear down the informational silos of a bygone era and to establish a yet unknown horizontal information flow (Figure 10.5). Everything is based on the concept of transnational management.

It is quite easy now to imagine what benefits emerge; what the perspectives are for the marketing function of such a programme:

● More transparent *international reporting* due to an alignment of market definitions, periodicities, etc. provide strategic management with a previously impossible 'bird's eye view' of the global market.

- One of our internal research programmes is focused on measuring the *effectiveness and efficiency of marketing activities* such as promotions, pricing and, particularly, advertising. Here, huge progress will be made in the next decade due to our unique data warehouse and more and more sophisticated analysis procedures.

- *Integrated and transnational analyses* on a harmonized database will permit new performance measures, providing managers with competitive knowledge. The measures are linked to respective decision parameters in pretests.

- *Data mining exercises and meta analysis* will further lead to yet unknown insights and establish empirical generalizations across gigantic datasets, contributing to our company's knowledge base.

The added value is coming from the transition of national information silos to a truly transnational single-source data warehouse. Isolated users that performed ad hoc analyses on isolated sources which could not be consolidated or shared broadly are being replaced by employing shared methodologies on harmonized sources. We also take into account that there are different classes of users. For the simple reader we offer a basic intranet reporting, for the analyst we supply standardized analysis templates, and the data miner can use our shared services unit inside international market research.

CHANGES FOR THE MARKET RESEARCH FUNCTION

It is also easy to imagine what this means for the *market research function* in companies. We will have to develop into an overall knowledge management function very quickly – the sooner, the better. The function clearly has to develop from a *local tactical messenger service into a transnational strategic intelligence function*. The transition from reporting to internal consulting will require a different type of researcher who is capable of acting as a part of a business core team.

The objective is to improve the way we collect, share and effectively use information about markets, customers and competitors, but to do this in an integrated and transnational fashion. Purely national market research departments restricted to geopolitical boundaries will vanish from the business arena.

I think it is perfectly clear what the final objective is in order to really generate intellectual capital: it is the establishment of a corporate knowledge management function where the most important asset of a company in the future is managed by 'knowledge professionals'. I hope I have left no doubt in this chapter that this is a highly formalized process – starting with data warehousing and ending at the moment of data mining.

PERSPECTIVES

The ultimate vision of the business intelligence project is definitely the establishment of a fully-fledged knowledge management system inside Henkel marketing units. In order to gain maximum value from intellectual capital, the knowledge circulating in the business system must be generated, captured, codified and circulated. This process is what we call *knowledge management*. Knowledge management incorporates both 'asking systems' and 'answering systems,' which are linked by the market research interface.

Of course we are aware that this process must be highly formalized and it must be managed by knowledge professionals. Sharing of information in today's environment can only be accomplished by modern technology – for example, a Lotus Notes environment or, more commonly, Internet technology.

Finally, one thing is inevitable: top management sponsorship for the knowledge management function is based on the recognition that intellectual capital drives efficiencies, customer relations and innovation.

Henkel is only just starting this process, but we are totally committed to becoming the competence leader in this particular area. From local data managers to top management, we all want this because we believe that here we have a fair chance not to try harder or to be bigger, but to grow in competitive strength by trying *smarter*.

If you are facing a similar challenge today, or if you are contemplating whether you should be in this kind of business, please keep in mind that this is a train you should not miss. Make up your mind. Making up your mind is not easy – make sure it is not just a cosmetic act. It must be a basic commitment of your company to business re-engineering. With that in mind, I would like to share with you the motto of our project that has been accompanying me as a screen saver over the last two years:

The journey of a 1000 miles begins with a single step.

REFERENCES

Barabba, V.P. (1995), *Meeting of the Minds*. Harvard Business School Press.

Barabba, V.P. and Zaltman, G. (1991), *Hearing the Voice of the Market*. Harvard University Press.

Bartlett, C.A. and Goshal, S. (1991), *Managing Across Borders*. Harvard Business School Press.

Blattberg, R.C., Glazer, R. and Little, J.D.C. (1994), *The Marketing Information Revolution*. Harvard Business School Press.

Chapter Eleven

Getting Research Noticed at the Corporate Top Table

Ioannis (John) Dimopoulos[a],
Jonathan Rabson[b] and Daryl Maloney McCall[c]

> *Putting research assets in a client portal can help research move from a reactive to a strategic role.*

INTRODUCTION

Over recent years, a great deal of research industry discussion has focused on the concern that research is being underutilized at the corporate top table by decision-makers, and that researchers' advice is not being sought at a senior strategic level.

This chapter provides a case study overview of how Reckitt Benckiser's Market Research function has positioned itself as a key contributor to both tactical and strategic decisions within the business, and how the implementation of a web-based Market Research Department (MRD) portal has provided a vehicle for establishing this positioning.

The chapter can be seen as a series of sections that discuss:

[a]Senior Vice President, Global Director Market Research, Reckitt Benckiser plc, UK.
[b]European Director, Insight Marketing Systems.
[c]Director, Insight Marketing Systems, Australia.

Market Research Best Practice. Edited by P. Mouncey and F. Wimmer.
© 2007 John Wiley & Sons, Limited.

1. The parties involved.
2. The rationale for the implementation of the system, based on the objectives and structure of the Reckitt Benckiser market research function.
3. The key requirements of the MRD portal, based on the business's objectives and organizational structure.
4. The criteria used to determine 'who and how' the system would be developed.
5. How the system has been implemented and refined.
6. A brief overview of how the system currently works.
7. Key benefits to date.
8. Future development intentions.

THE PARTIES INVOLVED

Reckitt Benckiser plc

Reckitt Benckiser plc (RB) is the world leader in household cleaning (excluding laundry) and a major player in Health & Personal Care, with operations in 60 countries, sales in 180 countries and net revenues in excess of £3.5billion. Supporting the Marketing, Sales and R&D functions within the organization, the Global Market Research function (MRD) comprises over 30 managers located across more than ten countries.

Due to a range of issues within RB, including:

- the increasing complexity of global MR,
- the necessity for faster information access for competitive advantage,
- an increasing reliance on electronic documents,

the MRD set out to establish an MR portal to capture and index global and local market research projects and documents. It was expected that the library would comprise research back to the year 2000 and would grow by approximately 1000 projects per annum.

E-Tabs

E-Tabs provide specialist software, consulting and services for the electronic delivery of market research tables to research firms and end users. Their flagship 'E-Tabs' software boosts the productivity of research professionals using fast indexing, automatic charting and integration with any tabulation software. E-Tabs software has become the worldwide standard for archiving and delivering research tabulations.

E-Tabs are based in London and Chicago and are an approved distributing partner for *Research Reporter*.

Insight marketing systems

Insight Marketing Systems (IMS) are the developers, owners and distributors of *Research Reporter* – a marketing information management system that provides large and mid-range enterprises with the ability to:

- control access to and re-use high value, knowledge-rich information;
- track and communicate information on multiple projects;
- automate project management processes.

IMS developed *Research Reporter* using a combination of competencies in marketing research, strategic planning and application development. The system was released in early 2001, and has since been adopted by a broad range of large and mid-sized enterprises around the world.

DEFINING THE OBJECTIVES OF THE RECKITT BENCKISER MRD

Traditionally, the objective of a market research team has been interpreted within the context of an individual research project. The emphasis has been on the research outcomes for the discrete business problem(s) a project was designed to address. As a consequence, research has typically been seen as an expense, or an insurance policy to help guard against poor decisions. It was treated as a 'consumable' that once used had little residual value beyond the original business problem.

This internal positioning does little to ensure researchers have a seat at the decision-making table, as they are regarded as having a very narrow frame of reference relating only to the project at hand, rather than an accumulated knowledge of market dynamics built up over time.

For Reckitt Benckiser, the paradigm shift was in recognizing research not as a series of one-off 'expenses', but as a continuing investment in intellectual property, a cumulative strategic asset from which the company could generate a greater return.

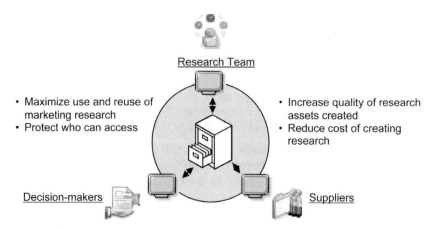

Figure 11.1   MRD objectives.

The business needed to expand its focus to consider not just the narrow objectives of a single project, but to focus on how to maximize the return from the company's ongoing investment in market knowledge.

At a strategic level, the focus on research ROI by the Reckitt Benckiser MRD also allowed the articulation of four key objectives (Figure 11.1):

1. Maximize the use, and re-use, of market research knowledge.
2. Protect the value of the research asset for the business.
3. Increase the quality of the research assets created.
4. Reduce the cost of creating and maintaining the research assets.

These MRD objectives provided the context in which the idea for developing an MRD portal system was conceived. They were also paramount to specifying its requirements.

At a more tactical level, the business benefits sought via the MRD portal included:

- increased consumer knowledge within the organization;
- increased integration of research knowledge within the innovation process;
- faster circulation of market research results;
- quick access to consumer research history;
- access to research from anywhere in the world, 24/7;
- a one-stop location for authoritative reference to all the key briefs associated with each project/brand;
- decreased potential for research duplication and the associated costs;

- decreased potential for decisions being taken in the absence of data that may already exist, but are not known or easily accessible.

Some of the key requirements to ensure the success of an MRD portal within RB were identified to be:

- international applicability and access;
- ease of use (simple archiving and search);
- quick access;
- archiving of all kinds of documents (electronic files, hard copies);
- simple exchange of documents via e-mail functions.

MRD structure

The RB market research function is a global organization (Figure 11.2) spread across more than ten country locations, servicing the following areas:

- geographic regions;
- global categories;
- syndicated data.

Whilst there are reasons for this departmental structure, it can lead to suboptimal return on research investments as:

1. Multiple information storage points restrict the potential for re-use of market research to the local business unit.
2. Multiple information storage points potentially require duplication of infrastructure, security and access protocols, resulting either in increased expense or increased risk to intellectual property.
3. The sharing and adoption of best practices across the team occurs on a more adhoc, rather than systemic, basis, making standardization and efficiency more difficult across the global team.
4. Limited recognition and utilization of suppliers outside of the local team leads to duplication of supplier capabilities.

Figure 11.2 MRD structure.

However, the advantages of this structure outweigh the disadvantages, in quality if not in number:

1. Research teams can work closely with their internal clients, and can respond quickly without the inevitable bureaucracy that would normally exist with a single, centralized MRD.
2. Research teams can develop a deep understanding of the local research issues and industry, and can provide information to assist local decision makers within the business.

The MRD portal system should, therefore, be subordinate to the current structure of the MRD. However, it would be required to overcome the shortcomings of this structure in helping to maximize research ROI within the broader business.

FRAMEWORK FOR DETERMINING MRD PORTAL REQUIREMENTS

Research objectives

The MRD's objectives provided a top-level framework for determining the requirements of the MRD portal as follows:

1. Maximize the use, and re-use, of market research knowledge within the business.
   System requirements:
   - internal clients and researchers should be able to search for and display research information collected from previous studies to assist current decision-making;
   - an ability to search based on a broad range of criteria (e.g., location, product category, market segment, supplier, methodology), as well as words or phrases contained within a report.
2. Protect the value of the research assets for the business.
   System requirements:
   - restrict access and distribution of research information to authorized users;
   - restrict the ability to update or add research based on predetermined authorities.
3. Increase the quality of research assets.
   System requirements:

- provide access to shared resources across the MRD to propagate research team best practices;
- maintain a supplier project register to identify suppliers' project performance, costs and capabilities.

4. Reduce the cost of creating and maintaining research assets.

System requirements:

- automate repetitive tasks to reduce research team administrative overhead;
- incorporate supplier electronic collaboration to reduce 'double-handling'.

Organizational structure

A globally accessible system was therefore required. However, the ability to update and maintain information would need to be performed at a local level.

1. Local vs. central storage and access.

System requirements:

- allow local researchers to update and maintain research projects and documents;
- allow internal clients access to projects and documents, regardless of the geographic location of the study.

2. Project access rights.

System requirements:

- restrict access to personally identified project team members (including suppliers) while project is in progress;
- set global access rights upon project completion to allow RB staff to access information based on their product category, geographic area of responsibility and/or position (seniority) within the business.

3. Adoption of best practices.

System requirements:

- provide local researchers with access to central repository of research techniques, disciplines, templates, research terms and methodologies (Stage 1);
- Incorporate best practices into project workflow processes, to be integrated into the application (Stage 2).

4. Recognition and utilization of supplier capabilities.

System requirements:

- provide a global supplier register of offers, capabilities and preferential status, along with an inventory of projects completed by each supplier;
- include collation of supplier performance measures across projects.

'WHO AND HOW' CRITERIA TO DETERMINE THE DEVELOPMENT OF THE MRD PORTAL

The development and launch of an MRD portal shares many parallels with the development and execution of a research project. Also, like a research project, trade-offs need to be considered with respect to cost, timing, risk and quality of solution.

To establish the 'who and how' criteria for building the system, the MRD drew on its experience in managing market research projects and established the following criteria against which risk, timing, cost and quality of solution could be evaluated.

End user requirements and specifications (the brief)

While the research team had developed a series of briefing templates for specifying market research projects, no such precedent existed for specifying the requirements of an MRD portal.

In the same way that RB internal clients utilize the expertise of the MRD to help specify their research needs, one of the criteria to be used in evaluating a potential partner/developer for the portal would be that partner's ability to assist the MRD to think through all the information requirements for the system, how this information would need to be captured, collated and retrieved, and how these requirements would need to be documented in a way that could be understood by whoever was to build or provide the system.

Communication time (the briefing process)

For a research project, the time spent in communicating with and briefing a research supplier is dependent on that supplier's experience with the methodology required, and their understanding of the business.

While an understanding of database methodology and web technology was a prerequisite for determining who would develop the system, it was also recognized that an understanding of the MRD's function (the dynamics of market research, and the needs of MR stakeholders such as internal clients, research project managers and suppliers) would also be a critical factor affecting cost, timing and risk, and, most importantly, the quality of the solution.

System specification (questionnaire design)

System specifications are akin to the writing of a questionnaire. By drawing on their experience, good researchers have an understanding of how to phrase questions appropriately, set response fields to protect the validity of the information entered, and use skips, jumps and conditional responses to help the operators navigate through a questionnaire.

In a similar way, the MRD recognized that experience in specifying these areas of the MRD portal, including fields for project metadata, explanatory labels and system navigation, would be critical to ensuring the integrity of information entered into the system, and the ease and speed of data entry and access.

Development (CATI programming)

System development costs, like CATI programming costs, depend on the expertise of the programmer, and the capabilities of the underlying software on which the system is to be built.

Similarly, the criteria for determining who could develop the MRD portal would draw on the previous experience of the developer and the underlying software the portal would utilize.

Testing (the CATI pilot)

In the same way that a CATI questionnaire is first audited and then tested with a small group of respondents, the MRD portal would first need to be tested to ensure it met the system specifications, and then evaluated to ensure it met the pragmatic requirements of the users. Inevitably, some changes and fine-tuning would be required.

Selection criteria would therefore also focus on the speed and ability to change the MRD portal's navigation, instructional text and information fields, based on both internal testing and user feedback once the system had been launched.

Controlled publishing capabilities (data collection)

One of the system criteria for determining who would develop/provide the MRD portal was an assessment of the underlying software's ability to allow online collaboration between Reckitt Benckiser and its chosen research suppliers, in order to eliminate double handling (Stage 2).

Ease of use (presentation of results)

Market research is only of benefit to a business if the data captured can be converted into information that can be accessed and understood by decision-makers. Good researchers understand that it is their role to present research results in a format that can be understood quickly by people who often have no experience of the technical aspects of a research project.

Similarly, criteria for determining who would develop the MRD portal would also include an assessment of their ability to provide a solution that presented information to both researchers and internal clients using intuitive and easily understood navigation and presentation of results.

IMPLEMENTING AND REFINING THE MARKET RESEARCH MANAGEMENT SYSTEM

Having established the objectives, requirements and criteria for moving forward, the initial implementation and refinement progressed through the following stages:

- choosing a technology partner;
- initial scoping/configuration;
- development (configuration) and testing;
- data back-loading.

Choosing a technology partner

Reckitt Benckiser's first implementation step was choosing a technology partner. The options included:

1. Using internal IT to build an application.
2. Purchasing a third-party generic application.
3. Purchasing a third-party market-research specific application.

An internal IT build

The 'in-house' option had been considered after reviewing existing applications and technologies. Although considered a 'safe' option, to develop in effect a bespoke solution would probably have resulted in a longer timeframe and required additional resources, from both the IS/IT and MRD perspectives.

Purchasing a third-party generic application

A review of generic products indicated that, although they had the functional capability required, the ability to configure these applications to meet Reckitt Benckiser's specific market research requirements was compromised by:

- an underlying inflexibility in these generic applications in dealing with the complex nature of marketing research projects, processes and information formats;
- a lack of knowledge of market research among the third-party consultants charged with the responsibility of configuring the application.

Externally purchased applications included offerings from major research agencies and 'stand-alone' providers. Although the larger research agencies had both the technical capabilities and the understanding of research processes, their systems created a linkage between content provider and system provider, which was believed not to be in the long-term interests of the business.

Purchasing a third-party market-research-specific application

It is not the purpose of this chapter to promote or recommend any particular supplier or system; however, through the market research software specialist E-Tabs, Reckitt Benckiser chose '*Research Reporter – the market research management system*' from Insight Marketing Systems (IMS).

As a web-based technology, *Research Reporter* combines knowledge management, document and project management and collaboration rolled into one highly configurable system and *designed specifically for corporate market research buyers and their internal clients*.

The decision to use *Research Reporter* was based primarily on four factors:

1. Direct experience by E-Tabs and IMS in providing other large corporations with MRD portals. The RB MRD was keen to leverage the experience of Insight Marketing Systems and E-Tabs to ensure the best solution for Reckitt Benckiser.
2. The fact that this was a prebuilt, externally hosted application. The MRD did not want to waste time and resources discovering programming bugs, or having to deal with internal IT infrastructure issues and timeframes. The *Research Reporter* application had been available since 2001 and was being utilized by many Fortune 500 companies around the world. Also, because the application is delivered over the Internet, no additional support or infrastructure (or accompanying internal recharges) were required.
3. *Research Reporter* has a highly flexible underlying application. This was seen as critical because:
   - it was highly likely that initial specifications would change once data loading started and user testing began;
   - if successful, the information parameters for the system could be expected to expand over time (e.g. to include competitor intelligence);
   - the structure of the MRD organization could also be expected to change over time. The system would, therefore, need to change to reflect any new organizational structures.
4. This involved system 'rental', rather than a lump-sum purchase. The option to rent, rather than buy, the system was seen as an advantage because:
   - there is no high cost capital outlay;
   - it maximizes the solution provider's service levels – knowing that Reckitt Benckiser can choose not to renew the annual contract provides some leverage in ensuring high service levels throughout the year;
   - it provides the flexibility for Reckitt Benckiser to change solution provider at a later date. As part of the contract, the supplier provides annual password-protected CDs containing all research data in the system. This information can then be imported directly into another system should the business choose to change providers at some future date.

System requirements

From a technical and nontechnical perspective, the resources required for the *Research Reporter* roll-out were minimal.

- no software needed to be installed on any RB server or end user PC;
- access to the portal was immediate, and available 24/7 from anywhere in the world;
- requested changes to the system were available to all end users immediately, without any installation;
- IT/IS involvement focused on the application and infrastructure security and bandwidth requirements;
- End users' only requirements are Microsoft Internet Explorer version 5+ and Internet access.

Initial scoping of the system

Initial scoping was broken down to cover:

1. What information was to be stored?
2. How would this information be entered and updated?
3. How would people access this information?

When considering what information was to be stored, the key criteria were speed and simplicity.

For each piece of information to be stored, decisions had to be made to identify how this information would benefit users in quickly finding the 'golden nuggets' they sought against the cost of collecting, publishing and storing the information.

Information to be stored could be broken down into two groups:

1. **Search and filter fields** – used to find and create lists of projects and/or documents based on the selected search criteria, so that a user could locate relevant information quickly.
2. **Descriptive data** – which would allow a user to decide quickly whether to spend more time looking at a project or document.

Data fields chosen to be stored are shown in Table 11.1.

Configuration and testing

Fortunately, because the *Research Reporter* application already existed, there was no requirement to develop an application or review code bugs. Configuring the *Research Reporter* system based on initial requirements was completed over 5–6 days, allowing the MRD to critique the configured application and begin user testing.

The application would have three types of users:

Table 11.1 Example data fields.

Example fields \ User type	Search/filter fields		Descriptive fields	
	Researcher	Internal client	Researcher	Internal client
Project vs. document	4	4	7	7
Type of project/document	4	4	4	4
Category	4	4	4	4
Region/country	4	4	4	4
Date	4	4	4	4
Researcher	4	7	4	4
Supplier	4	7	4	4
Status	4	7	4	4
Size	7	7	4	4

1. **Internal researchers** – who would use the system most regularly and would be responsible for maintaining information.
2. **High-level decision-makers** – internal clients of the MRD who would use the system to find information on a more intermittent basis.
3. **External research suppliers** – who would access information about Reckitt Benckiser, and the MRD, and update elements of their projects' details (Stage 2).

Testing for decision-makers and external suppliers focused on the intuitive layout and instructional text required to ensure information could be found quickly, while testing for researchers focused on the ease with which information could be entered and updated.

Data loading

Before introducing the application to the business, historical project data and document files needed to be back-loaded. Decisions had to be made as to what information should be back-loaded, based on the potential benefit for decision-makers in being able to access the information, against the cost of loading the data in the first place.

Reckitt Benckiser conducts more than 1000 projects every year. Previous to the MRD portal, all project documents had been sent in manually and stored in a central location, then filed using a standardized coding layout. A project database that listed all projects, research agency, project category and country had also been maintained. The solution provider could import this information directly into the application.

HOW THE SYSTEM CURRENTLY WORKS

The Reckitt Benckiser *Research Reporter* is structured to ensure that each target audience can realize maximum benefit from minimal effort. There are seven main areas (menus) with different visibility for each target group, as shown in Table 11.2.

Table 11.2   User group access.

User groups	*Main areas (menus) accessible*						
Internal researchers	1	2	3	4	5	6	7
Internal decision-makers (internal clients)	1	2	3	4			
External research suppliers	1						7

Main areas (menus)

1. **Home** – provides an overview of the application and access to administrative functions (i.e. change your password) and FAQs.
2. **Learning centre** – provides insight into the theory, terminology and practice of market research (for the uninitiated). It can be used as a reference resource or as the basis for further research training.
3. **Research libraries** – the main point of access to past and current research projects and research documents.
4. **Best practice libraries** – access to best practice MR techniques, including white papers and other links.
5. **Publishing** – where researchers can add and update research project details and publish research documents (i.e. briefs, proposals, reports, data files, etc.), as well as other information (i.e. conference papers, training materials).
6. **Supplier resources** – access to the latest information about our key suppliers, including their credentials and past work.
7. **RB suppliers** – to help key research suppliers understand the way the Reckitt Benckiser MRD functions and the expectations it has of them. It also allows suppliers to access and update elements of their research projects, including reports.

Clearly, the most beneficial elements of the system are the research libraries. These libraries have been structured in a way that allows decision-makers to access the information they seek most rapidly. This ease of use is a combination of simple and structured navigation and relevant and meaningful information fields and labels.

The navigational structure recognizes that the user may only visit the site on an occasional basis, and, therefore, an intuitive interface is critical. Designed in a similar way to a website, the Reckitt Benckiser *Research Reporter* requires minimal training and learning for the user to be able to gain access to the information sought.

Information fields have been structured along similar lines to internal Reckitt Benckiser business units. This means research can be searched across product categories or geographic regions, allowing a category manager to go straight to their domain of interest and a regional manager to search across all product category research conducted within their region.

In addition to this 'self-serve' functionality, research can be 'pushed' out to target audiences by the research manager. This allows project stakeholders to be kept informed and even receive their research via a series of 'branded' e-mails.

One or more internal 'administrators' manage all system administration via the online application. This system administrator's role is a nontechnical one and is assumed by key research managers.

KEY BENEFITS OF THE MRD PORTAL TO DATE

Whilst it is still early days (the system was only implemented in 2004), business benefits flowing from the implementation of the RB portal can be summarized as:

1. Repositioning the MRD from reactive to strategic via increasing consumer and market knowledge within the organization.
2. Improvements in the MRD's efficiency and quality.
3. Decreased potential for research duplication and the associated costs.

Repositioning the MRD from reactive to strategic

The provision of a comprehensive, centralized library of market research that allows users to access market research simply and conveniently has undoubtedly increased the awareness and utilization of market research within the organization.

Access to and circulation of research is now easier and faster, allowing for its more timely use at the decision point. Research can be accessed by users from anywhere in the world at any time, without referral to the MRD. This is strengthening Reckitt Benckiser's culture of information-based decision-making.

Quick search, both on full text or specific inquiry by category or region, allows the user to assess quickly whether there is information (current or historical) on a particular area of interest to the business. Previously, this was dependent on the memory of individuals and limited to a manager's sphere of influence (e.g. a specific region or category).

More informed and effective decisions are being executed as a result of this greater access to internal consumer knowledge, while it has significantly reduced the need for, or risk of, research duplication.

A related benefit from the implementation of the Reckitt Benckiser *Research Reporter* has been a general enhanced profile for the MRD within the broader organization. This has provided greater opportunities for market research to be utilized proactively at a strategic level, as the ease with which research can be cross-referenced has expanded its applicability in decision-making and led to greater insights.

Improvements in the MRD's efficiency and quality

The sheer volume of research information managed by the Reckitt Benckiser MRD had previously meant that individual research managers were sometimes at risk of being reduced to 'administrators' and 'librarians'.

Research managers have had to juggle the dual roles of managers of their research suppliers and suppliers to their internal clients. This 'middleman' role was often a simple communication medium. *Research Reporter* now allows all stakeholders to access the same updated project details, as research managers are able to input live projects directly. This has also removed the need to resend material within the organization. Research managers can auto-deliver project information directly to relevant project stakeholders (internal and external) as it happens.

On another level, assisting internal clients in finding and repackaging information from previous research, and addressing administrative requests such as the status of a project, was time-consuming, distracting and not the positioning sought by a highly skilled researcher. This, in turn, can have a detrimental effect on the managers' pursuit of higher personal objectives and their ability to add value to the business.

Decreased potential for research duplication and the associated costs

There is the famous quote most often attributed to Lew Platt, previously of Hewlett Packard, that goes, 'If only HP knew what HP knew!'

The ability to access a comprehensive, centralized library allows RB to find out easily what is already known within the business. This has been of considerable value to Reckitt Benckiser's internal research managers, as the potential for addressing internal clients' information requests by 'raking over the coals' has increased, and can now be performed in hours rather than days.

Whilst it is still too early to assess this benefit fully, there are signs that this could amount to 5–10% savings in primary research costs – costs that can now be applied to furthering researchers' knowledge rather than duplicating it.

FUTURE DEVELOPMENT OPTIONS

The roll-out strategy for the MRD portal has been based around its three major user groups:

1. Internal researchers.
2. High-level decision-makers (internal clients).
3. External research suppliers.

Similarly, future developments can be considered around each of these groups.

Internal research managers

In line with research management best practice and feedback from the research managers charged with the responsibility of managing their projects within *Research Reporter*, future developments will centre on workflow processes that will streamline the project management protocols and further improve the communication lines, both internally and externally.

This may include the further utilization of 'push and pull' technologies: functionality that allows the research manager to 'push' relevant information and communications automatically to the appropriate audiences, and 'pull' technology that allows the internal decision-maker to establish auto-feeds of information and communications based on areas of responsibility.

It is recognized that there is significant potential to utilize the work-flow capabilities of *Research Reporter* to match project requirements with potential suppliers. Examples of this may include:

1. Access to online focus group capabilities as an option when managing a qualitative study.
2. Posting of online surveys via third-party functionality.
3. Specific data analysis capabilities via third-party tools (e.g. E-Tabs Interactive to investigate, analyse and create data tables online).

Decision-makers (internal clients)

Future developments for internal clients will further focus the application on tailoring, and then remembering, the method of accessing information and content available to the individual's preferences.

It is accepted that some (generally senior) managers will rarely visit the portal. For them, information must be generated and delivered automatically (generally via e-mail) to them on demand and/or in real time. This additional subscription service must not place any additional burden on the research managers, but must run without their input.

Other information consumers are more advanced – often referred to as 'power users'. Developments for this group will endeavour to personalize the content made available by 'remembering' their information and formatting preferences. An example of this is a personal electronic bookshelf where the user can store references (links) to re-search found in the libraries, providing future shortcuts to the same research.

External research suppliers

Over time, Reckitt Benckiser's key research suppliers will be asked to play an increasingly important role in the upkeep of the research libraries. To ensure that this process is not any more onerous than absolutely necessary, future developments will focus on single-source publishing and automatic communications between supplier and RB.

Other developments

As the domain of the market researcher broadens to include other, non-traditional market research information sources, so too will there be a need to incorporate other data sources into the RB portal. It is possible that these could include the competitor intelligence and NPD domains.

Chapter Twelve

How to Ensure One Worldwide Heineken Brand Dashboard

Sjoerd Koornstra[a] and Gert Jan de Nooij[b]

The Heineken Brand Dashboard is a worldwide measurment, storage and reporting system of all the essential Key Performance Indicators of the Heineken Brand.

INTRODUCTION

The crown jewel of the Heineken Company is the Heineken brand. Heineken is marketed in more than 170 markets, and the brand is managed internationally via the Global Heineken Brand Team. This team:

- defines the brand positioning (brand values, essence, architecture, proposition);
- defines rules and guidelines;
- develops and executes (in cooperation) international marketing activities, e.g. international sponsorships, new packaging;
- monitors and controls the brand health.

[a]Senior International Knowledge Manager, Heineken International.
[b]Managing Partner, Scanmar.

Market Research Best Practice. Edited by P. Mouncey and F. Wimmer.
© 2007 John Wiley & Sons, Limited.

The Heineken Company has a strong, decentralized organization structure. The local markets are responsible for all their business activities within the given rules and guidelines. Market research is also a local responsibility. Some guidelines for brand monitoring have been made available, but markets have adapted these over the years to local circumstances, due to more intensified brand tracking. This has led to divergent solutions. Parameters were measured in different ways (e.g. brand image in one market was monadic whereas in another market it was on an associative scale). Also, definitions could differ between markets; this could lead to confusion and misunderstanding in meetings.

Two years ago, a major reorganization took place within Heineken. One of the aspects of this reorganization was to develop a more fact-based management and measurement style. One of the key projects was to develop a *Heineken Brand Dashboard*. The main reasons for developing this were:

- the lack of transparent insight into the performance of the Heineken brand;
- pressure for more insight in to commercial effectiveness;
- the current focus on bottom line rather than where the profit is coming from or on future earning power;
- a lack of a universal equity measurement system;
- the fact that a focus on organic growth implies a more systematic, goal-oriented organization. This means that KPIs (key performance indicators) are indispensable for target-setting and for monitoring progress;
- a lack of benchmarking of the performance of Heineken between markets.

THE HEINEKEN ORGANIZATION

The organization consists of:

- 7 single-market opcos (SMOs). These are markets with considerable sales volumes.
- 7 multi-market opcos (MMOs). These opcos cover all the markets within a region (small to large, except the single-market opcos).

The single-market opcos are fully self-supporting and have professional supporting staffs. These markets all have comprehensive brand-monitoring systems in place. This is also the case in some markets belonging to the multi-market opcos. However, within the multi-market opcos, the view of the Heineken brand performance in their region can differ by market.

THE PROJECT TASK AND ORGANIZATION

A project team was installed to secure that the Heineken Brand Dashboard was operational within a year (December 2004). The assignment was also to create this in cooperation with, and the commitment of, the markets. The objectives of the Heineken Brand Dashboard (HBD) project were:

- to create a more systematic, goal-oriented organization, needed for a focus on organic growth;
- to create a universal equity and overall business measurement system;
- to create transparent insight into the performance of the Heineken brand;
- to enable benchmarking of the performance of Heineken between markets;
- to provide more insight into commercial effectiveness.

The multidisciplinary project team consisted of:

- Project leader/Market research specialist;
- ICT expert;
- Controller, responsible for internal data flows;
- Project support manager.

To realize this ambitious system, the following crucial steps had to be taken.

1. Define the KPIs and Dashboard content, and establish a company-wide agreement on these topics.
2. Reorganize, partly reshape and standardize the worldwide data collection process and system.
3. Put an IT system in place to manage the data-inflow and KPI/Dashboard-outflow.
4. Ensure an ongoing data-delivery and feeding process.

Given the worldwide structure of the company, a great deal of commitment from all company stakeholders would prove indispensable during this process. Overall, it required project management skills which mirrored the role of the traditional researcher. Special attention will be given to these aspects of the project.

Each of the above steps will be discussed in the next sections of the chapter.

Selection and definition of KPIs and Dashboard elements

Heineken already had a tradition of measuring brand performance. Based on this experience, we decided the KPIs should consist of indicators measuring Heineken brand performance in the areas of consumer performance (CPIs) related to brand equity, sales/marketing performance (S&MPIs) and financial performance (FPIs) related to the profitability and investments of the brand (Figure 12.1).

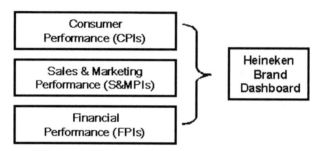

Figure 12.1   Components of the Heineken Brand Dashboard.

A comprehensive benchmarking process was conducted with other FMCG/beverage companies. This benchmark focused on:

- how other worldwide companies were organizing brand monitoring;
- what kind of dashboards other companies were using, and which measures were included;
- whether there were any integrated systems for consumer performance, sales and marketing and financials.

We focused especially on the way *consumer performance* is organized, looking at the following:

- What is measured (awareness, usage, quality perception, satisfaction, loyalty)?
- Frequency of measurement (measured continuously or in dip sticks).
- How it is measured (e.g. which scales are used).
- How data are delivered (one research agency worldwide or local agencies).

- How information is shared (infrastructure outside the company or internally; accessibility levels).
- Frequency of sharing information (timescale of publishing information).

This benchmark gave us a profound understanding of how brand performance measurement in other companies is organized. It gave us new ideas and contributed to what could be useful for the Heineken Company on several aspects (especially on the means and frequency of measurement and the organization). The outcome was the starting point for the system. The benchmark results were also used tactically to convince people about the necessity of more frequent and standardized monitoring.

The Heineken Brand Team, the single-market opcos and the multi-market opcos are the main stakeholders of the project. From a functional perspective, stakeholders are commercial management and market research. Therefore, an international, multifunctional team was installed to participate in the design of the Dashboard system. The Project leader facilitated the meetings to achieve a first consensus about the system. This consensus contained:

- the key performance indicators (KPIs);
- the definitions and composition of the KPIs;
- the grouping of KPIs, plus naming;
- the means of measurement (cost effective, comparable in time and between markets);
- the frequency of measurement by different types of markets;
- the manner in which competition is included.

The composition of the consumer KPIs was driven by the following criteria:

1. **The company view on measuring brand equity.** Several alternative ways of measuring brand equity have been reviewed. These alternative ways consist of models offered by research agencies as well as internal views and experience. Several pilots have been conducted to achieve a uniform way of measuring. The developed brand equity modelling is integrated within the KPIs.
2. **The Heineken positioning and brand architecture model.** The Heineken positioning is the role of Heineken in a brand portfolio and in the competitive arena. This role depends on the brand stage. The brand architecture model describes what the brand Heineken stands for and wants to be for consumers. This framework explains,

amongst others things, the values, personality, offered benefits and brand proposition.

3. **The ease of extending to other brands.** The Dashboard should be operational for the Heineken brand, but should also be easily applicable for other international, as well as local, brands. This means that the selected KPIs should, on one hand, cover the specific Heineken marketing elements (coming from positioning and brand architecture). On the other hand, the KPIs should also be uniform and generic, in order that these can be relevant for other brands as well.

4. **Internal know-how and experience.** More than 30 years of consumer tracking had contributed to significant learning and research insights. This experience was, of course, used as relevant input. The aforementioned competitive benchmark also contributed to it.

The consumer KPIs are composed of the following blocks:

- brand impact (consisting of communication effectiveness measures);
- brand imprint (consisting of image measures);
- perceived value and quality;
- brand (desired) personality;
- brand awareness;
- brand usage;
- brand appreciation.

The ordering is influenced by the different stages that can be distinguished in the brand-building process. These different stages also determine the KPIs to which focus should be given. The stages run from launching the brand (starting to make noise around it) until the stage of a sufficiently loyal and satisfied consumer base.

The composition of the sales/marketing and financial KPIs is based upon sales and market share disclosure by channel and key marketing measures. The key marketing measures are related to distribution position, pricing, promotional volume (obtained from retail tracking) and media exposure.

Organization of the worldwide data collection process

The next step in the process was the organization and set-up of the different data sources to feed the system. In general, many of the data sources needed for the system were already in place, but had to be adapted to fit the Dashboard system requirements.

Consumers' performance indicators

Reorganizing this part of the measurement system was one of the most challenging parts – ensuring a worldwide uniform measuring model over 80 markets in the world.

In many local markets, brand-monitoring surveys were (and are) conducted. As mentioned, the differences in the local measurement models created problems in understanding. Also, the processing of the data was a local activity and an organized data stream was not in place.

For the consumer performance indicators, a standard questionnaire was composed to measure the variables upon which the CPIs were calculated. This basic questionnaire can be extended to meet specific local needs. As mentioned, within Heineken, the markets have a lot of autonomy in organizing their market research. This also means that they have the freedom to work together with their preferred suppliers. In some markets, intensive relationships exist for years. The research agency selection is delegated to the local market. The worldwide scale of this operation suggests that an international research partner could be considered. Given the 'independence' of research in local markets, this has not been an option. The local market selects and briefs the research agency. Besides the standard questionnaire, local markets and research agencies have to adhere to a number of guidelines.

Sample size and type of sampling

Markets with a sufficient Heineken brand share ($x\%$) should conduct the survey among a representative national sample. Markets with a low Heineken share should conduct quota sampling to guarantee sufficient observations within relevant target groups.

Frequency of measurement

Quarterly measurement is prescribed for high-volume Heineken markets and emerging markets. All other relevant Heineken markets are measured once a year.

Timing of data delivery

Quarterly data must be delivered before a specific day at the end of every quarter. Yearly data must be delivered before a specific day at the end of the calendar year. These timings synchronize the data delivery with the quarterly performance reports and yearly planning cycle.

Deliverables

All consumer data are delivered as cleaned raw data files instead of processed result files. This guarantees more control over the data quality and ensures that CPI calculations can be performed in the central database in a uniform way. Besides this, it creates more flexibility to define Dashboard analysis in the future. To secure this dataflow and to handle and control the automated data processing at the Heineken site with minimum effort, the research agencies have to deliver:

- a data file in a specific format/layout optimized for batch processing and flexible towards market-specific variations (e.g. a set of measured brands) and future enhancements in the measurement system.
- for control purposes, a file with processed frequency tables to match these outcomes with the processed data in the system.

A uniform coding system was set up to synchronize brands, markets and time, which are also common dimensions for the other KPI data sources (S&MPIs, FPIs).

Sales/marketing and financial performance indicators

Sales and marketing data used for the KPIs have their origin in a diversity of data sources, like retail tracking and audits, local market studies, national beer trade organizations, etc. In each country, the data source for specific KPIs can differ. It is impossible to collect the data centrally from their original sources. Also, the depth and quantity of the needed data is far less than the CPI data. That is why it was decided to make the local commercial organizations responsible for collecting all the relevant data by means of a standardized input system. To guide the users in this data collection process, an extensive manual can be used, in which the calculation or estimation procedure to arrive at the requested figure is described (Figure 12.2).

Sales and marketing performance data are collected for the Heineken brand as well as for the market and segment leader in the particular market. The input system is also used for collecting the financial data, from which the financial KPIs are derived.

With this design and set-up of the data collection process (CPIs, S&MPIs and FPIs), we expect to have realized a manageable uniform data collection system and have tackled most of the 'technical' weak spots in such a process. A major topic we also had to deal with was the cooperation of all parties in this process.

2.3.1. Numerical Distribution On Premise

KPI	NUMERICAL DISTRIBUTION ON PREMISE (%)
Definition	The number of On-Premise outlets where the brand is available for sales, as a percentage of the total number of On-Premise outlets in the market specified
Frequency of Measurement	Yearly (Q4)
Data source(s)	This figure can be obtained from retail audit-tracking studies. If these are not available the figure can be obtained from a trade census.
What if unavailable	Estimate
Ways of calculating	Another way to make an estimate is to take the total number of points where the brand is sold from the sales administration (internal plus distributors), divide this by the total number of On-Premise outlets and multiply by 100.
Competition	Same procedure as for Heineken brand

Figure 12.2   Example manual: definitions and suggestions for data collection S&MPIs.

Ensuring cooperation regarding the dataflow

Failure and success of a complex data-oriented system depends mainly on an ongoing, smooth, correct data-delivery process. Although the technical part of the data system is quite relevant, mostly systems fail because of a lack of cooperation and discipline of the data suppliers.

Three elements stimulated cooperation in this process:

1. The commercial managers were made responsible for the data-delivery process. They were asked to appoint ambassadors for both data streams. These ambassadors are the contact people for the execution, but the commercial manager stays responsible.
2. The timing and frequency is the same as the quarterly business reporting process. This implies that the same data are used in the quarterly reporting as in the dashboards, and that everybody uses the same data.
3. The top seven KPIs are also included in the quarterly business reporting process. This means that the company needs to have some consumer performance indicators available at the reporting date.

Putting an IT system in place

Concerning the IT system, and especially the front-end side, a functional design for the system has been produced. The main requirements were:

- interactive analyses of KPIs over markets, brands, time, and representing KPIs from different perspectives (e.g. changes over time or related to market leader);

- a web-enabled system with standard reports and easy navigating functionality with an attractive interface;
- that standard reports should be easy and flexible to adapt or to produce from a central server site;
- authorized access for different parts of the information (e.g. restrictions on countries and financial KPIs);
- special folders for different types of users;
- that it should be easy to extend to other Heineken brands;
- storage and display of explanations about the data (annotations) or the research (e.g. this period is a rough estimation, or the sample for consumer research is limited to the four big cities).

Based on these requirements and already known future requirements, like extending the system to other Heineken brands and delivering detailed market research analytical functionality at local market level,[1] a data warehouse and OLAP solution was chosen.

The system is build by Scanmar, a specialized software and solution provider in marketing intelligence systems. In technical terms, the system consists of:

1. A presentation layer that presents the dashboards in the web browser.
2. An analytical layer, performing online KPI calculations depending on the query.
3. A data storage layer storing the data and some precalculated KPIs.
4. A data processing layer to manage both the CPI and the S&MPI processing.

The system is implemented with MarketingTracker – a standard OLAP tool already in use at Heineken. It is based on Oracle multidimensional technology and it can cope with multi-country consumer survey data as well as internal data. The first three layers are realized with the standard product functionality. The data processing layer was custom-built with the standard application development tools that go with the software.

THE DASHBOARD'S DEVELOPMENT

After convincing the IT department not to use a top-down approach in the development of the system, a prototyping approach was used.

---

[1] Although only Heineken, the market leader and the segment leader for a particular market are shown, almost the complete set of local brands is available in the data warehouse.

User group meetings were organized with several representatives (SMOs, MMOs and the Heineken Brand Team). Based upon prototyped dashboards and functionality, it was easier for the users to make up their minds and express their wishes. Two comprehensive user groups settings were organized:

- At the beginning of the building process, a meeting in which a prototype was shown. The users expressed their wishes on report layout, navigating functionality and analysis possibilities.
- At the end of the process, we let them play with the pilot system. They gave their wishes for modification and fine-tuning.

This involvement of the user group created a lot of commitment. The participants in these sessions became owners of the system and started to sell the layout and functionality (Figure 12.3).

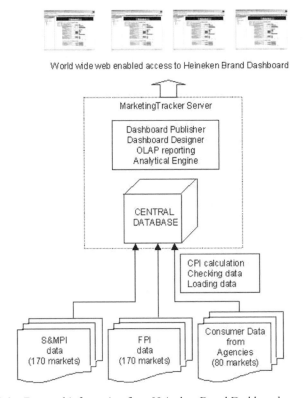

Figure 12.3 Data and information flow, Heineken Brand Dashboard system.

IMPLEMENTATION OF THE SYSTEM

The implementation consisted of the following elements: training, manuals, getting connected and installing a maintenance organization.

More than 300 users were to be connected to the system; this meant that within two months, these users had to be trained. We chose a 'Train the Trainers' approach. Commercial managers were asked to appoint responsible people within their opcoss. Several 'Train the Trainer' sessions have been organized worldwide. These meetings are all introduced by top managers. The importance of the system is emphasized, as well as peoples roles as ambassadors and trainers for the opco. The presence of top management also gives them the feeling of being really important. The training covers system usage, a case study, learning styles and organization of the course. Newsletters accompany the whole process. The timing of the system implementation, as well as the training approach, was explained carefully. This also ensured that people were aware of being connected or invited for training.

Comprehensive, attractive and user-friendly manuals have been written. One manual explains the Dashboard, the interpretation and usage of the indicators and system usage. Another manual concerns the research design for the consumer indicators, as well as the means of data delivery, and is used to brief the research agency. A third manual contains the sales, marketing and financial indicators. This manual explains how to treat different sources and how to estimate market indicators from sources that have partial coverage.

A maintenance organization has been put in place. This maintenance organization:

- maintains the list of people having access (access level, passwords, etc.);
- monitors usage of the system;
- supports the users when they have questions;
- is responsible for uploading sales, marketing and financial data;
- monitors the compliance in data delivery;
- checks the quality of the performance indicators (ensuring that garbage does not get into the system);
- communicates with the responsible ambassadors;
- passes responsibility to the commercial managers when compliance is behind schedule.

For the research agencies, a helpdesk has been organized within Scanmar to handle questions around data delivery.

The maintenance organization and the helpdesk are indispensable in ensuring execution. You need to track, check, monitor and urge.

Embedding the system in the organization

The Dashboard has the same timing and frequency as the business reporting process. The top KPIs are also included in the governance cycle. The usage of the system is stimulated via the following processes:

- The performance of the Heineken brand is on the agenda in the quarterly meetings between the management team for each market and the responsible executive. This means that the Heineken Brand Dashboard is an integrated part of the governance cycle and of the quarterly business discussions.
- A Global Dashboard Performance Report is made twice a year. This report is shared with the top management of the company. On several levels, the results are discussed with the local market (general manager, commercial manager, marketing manager and brand managers), as are the kind of measures/activities to be taken.
- When visiting a local market, the Global Heineken Brand Team always carries with it the latest Dashboard. The results are discussed and mirrored against the planned marketing activities.
- For the local Heineken brand managers, targets are put on indicators from the Dashboard. These brand managers monitor the development carefully during the year.

Obtaining commitment from the various stakeholders

From the beginning of the project it was understood that commitment from all stakeholders was essential for its success. The top of the company strongly supported the project. This implied that the general managers were kindly requested to cooperate during international platform meetings. This group could not oversee all the consequences in practice. But in meetings with other stakeholders, we could always refer to their endorsement.

One of the main stakeholders to get on board was the market research community. The uniformity of consumer measurement would cause changes in their systems. Although an international, multifunctional team facilitated by someone from the corporate department designed the Dashboard, the research community perceived it as a corporate proposal.

The representatives of large markets in particular have difficulties in accepting the changes in consumer measurement:

- 'we have a tailor-made system, this will cause a trend break,'
- 'we do not see the advantages for our market. We are not going to compare the results with other markets since our market is different,'
- 'when the corporate is paying we can do it additionally, but we will stick to our system.'

The research community was given its possibility to give its input, but there was some mistrust towards corporate ('I can give my comments, but what are you doing with it?'). Several additional meetings had to be organized to get everybody aligned. The setting in these meetings was, on one hand how we could support them in following the new structure, in which comparisons with the past were still possible. On the other hand, they were confronted with the question: if you were in our situation, how would you approach/solve it?

From this time-consuming process we learned the following. Instead of the project manager presenting the proposal in an international setting, we should have introduced it via a top executive, who explained the necessity for it in advance.

The commercial managers are involved in the start-up stage to give a go/no go decision. They are also part of all important milestone decisions, e.g. the content of the Dashboard. Communication with subordinates was supposed to be done by the commercial managers. This communication had different levels of intensity, which meant that the brand managers or market managers did not have the same level of information. For this reason, communication was intensified via presentations at international regional meetings, as well as at international Heineken brand meetings where Heineken brand managers come together.

THE ROLE OF THE RESEARCHER

A lot has been written over the years about the role of the market researcher within the company. The way the internal researcher has to change from a brief-taker to a business partner to create more impact is also valid in this case. In this project, the researcher can play different roles. He can take on the traditional role, which is focused on methodological aspects and the research organization, or he can play a more business-oriented role or the 'doer' of the project. The latter role offers a lot of opportunities and challenges. It means that you have to play the role of the project leader, which requires more management skills. This type of project also requires skills that are quite close to the daily work of research, even though the research manager is not always selected to do the job:

- facilitating meetings (although general knowledge of the business is needed);
- communicating the advantages to commercial managers (requires being a business partner);
- structuring data systems and steering ICT;
- training people in using and interpreting results;
- writing manuals.

Besides the above-mentioned, some other skills are needed for this job which are less close to the daily work of the researcher:

- getting and organizing the commitment of several types of stakeholders (ensuring that these people are influenced by yourself or others);
- making use of massive communication around the progress of the project.

As market research played such an important role in this project, it took a great deal of the workload. The project team members had limited knowledge of brand strength measuring or market research in general. These people were selected because of other skills and experience. Given the fact that market research plays such an important role, and the difficulties people had in understanding the content, a lot of time was needed to make them understand and feel at ease.

CONCLUSIONS AND SUMMARY

The system was finalized and in place at the end of December 2004. It is too early to draw conclusions concerning the full realization of the expected business benefits of the system. The system has already contributed to speaking one 'consumer' language. We have, however, realized all the implementation goals of the system.

1. The project was finalized within a year due to a lean and mean project organization. This gave the possibility of re-using experience within the Heineken organization, but also contracting experienced partners in, amongst others, system development.

2. Clear and transparent project planning has been important to manage all the stakeholders. Milestones have been planned for taking decisions that could not be discussed afterwards. These milestones are, amongst other agreements, about the content of the Dashboard (KPIs), organization of the consumer research and navigating/browsing through the system.

3. Communication has been key in getting substantial support and commitment within the company. Newsletters, presentations, posters, manuals and training have been indispensable for making it a success.

4. Incorporating and integrating the Dashboard within the governance cycle has stimulated the implementation and the status of the Dashboard.

5. Nearly all markets involved in consumer research have set up their data delivery, and the processed data and Dashboards are available and in use. For some research agencies with less advanced data-processing technology, it took a while to meet the data delivery requirements.

FURTHER READING

Aaker, D. A. (1996), *Building Strong Brands.* The Free Press.

Ambler, T. (2003), *Marketing and the Bottom Line.* Prentice Hall.

Sherington, M. (2003), *Added Value.* Palgrave MacMillan.

Kaplan, R. S. and Norton D. P. (1996), *The Balanced Score: Translating Strategy into Action.* Harvard Business School Press.

Schroiff, H. W. and Borrell, J. (2002), *Where Do You Go To My Lovely?* Esomar 2002, Barcelona.

Pendse, N. (2005), *The OLAP Survey 4.*

Part Three

New Methodologies

Chapter Thirteen

Possibilities for Ethnographic Research: How to Raise the Validity of Findings and to Facilitate a Better and Deeper Understanding of your Products and Customers

Ji-Seun You[a] and Edeltraud Kaltenbach[b]

This chapter outlines both the fundamentals and the impact of ethnographic research to fuel strategic marketing decisions. It gives a chance to jump into the respondent's life and to take part in particular situations and relevant actions.

INTRODUCTION

Truly understanding your customers and potential customers in the relevant markets and countries . . . does this sound like a dream or can it become reality? I guess it is safe to say that it is definitely not an easy task.

This chapter describes how ethnographic research can help to overcome the barriers of traditional methods, as it is a method that provides

[a] Product Planer, LG Electronics Inc., Germany.
[b] Associate Director, Maritz Research.

Market Research Best Practice. Edited by P. Mouncey and F. Wimmer.
© 2007 John Wiley & Sons, Limited.

clients and market researchers with the possibility of jumping into the respondent's life and taking part in particular situations and relevant actions. It is a way to participate directly and, therefore, to achieve more authentic information than can be obtained by other means. 'Being there' for us means taking part in the person's life in order to participate and learn from him/her what we need to know. There is no better way to explore how a target group behaves in certain situations than in real life.

BUSINESS CHALLENGE

Imagine the case when, say an Asian company wants to explore and pervade the foreign market of Europe. Not as easy as it may sound.

LG Electronics, one of the five main manufacturers of electrical appliances worldwide, wants to further open up the European markets and faces the challenge of gaining a deep understanding of the general behaviour in the main European countries, with a focus on household appliances and their specific usage. A European office for Product Planning and Development was established in Willich (Germany), mainly with managers from the headquarters sent to the European office. A difficult task lies before them: to gain market share in the already quite saturated market of white goods in Europe.

To reach the objectives, a true understanding of the market and its peculiarities is crucial to answering some important questions:

- Which concepts can be transferred from Asia to Europe?
- Which new ideas might create a winning strategy and why? Is it about different technological acceptance and standards, or is it about different behaviour structures and different sets of values, etc?
- How can we distinguish ourselves from competitors in the desired way?
- Which market positioning strategy should we follow?

Sometimes it is not easy to understand the consumers from your own country, even though you share the same culture. Hence, everybody can imagine how difficult it is for a foreign company to understand the European market with all its fine cultural and historical differences. As education, family, culture and even history have an impact on behaviour, and, what was more interesting for us in this setting, the behaviour of consumers regarding household appliances, we had to find a method that covered all these points. What definitely made the job even harder was the fact that the European countries differ, and understanding one does not necessarily mean understanding all the others!

It would help to live in different households and countries for awhile, to observe and understand how they behave and to get an idea of what is important and why. As this proved difficult, if not impossible, for many reasons, one had to find other solutions.

Which strategy did LG Electronics choose? We believe a very good one. LG decided that it needed to research and gather relevant information as much as possible in this phase of understanding the respective cultures. It developed a strategic 3-year plan and divided the main countries into groups in order to focus, not on all countries at the same time, but successively. The first group was formed by Germany, France and the UK, the second by Spain and Italy and the third by Sweden, Hungary and Poland. In this 3-year plan, different kinds of research are scheduled, ranging from product-specific usage and attitude, through exploration of satisfaction, to more general trend research, including both qualitative and quantitative methods. In the remainder of the chapter, we will focus only on qualitative research, and in particular on ethnographic research and its impact on reaching given business objectives.

RESEARCH POINT OF VIEW

Basic principles

'Traditional' research methods like in-depth interviews, focus groups or group discussions have a limit, especially when everyday, habitualized behaviour plays an important role. Why?

The challenge herewith is habituation! Behaviour is no longer perceived consciously in the necessary detail, let alone possible to talk about. To a great degree, certain behaviour has become an aspect that is taken for granted. As a consequence, precious details in everyday behaviour are not accessible merely by asking. The same is true when it comes to unconscious motivators and drivers for certain behavioural patterns. What can be done when the relevant questions require an even greater in-depth analysis of the situation, as is the case especially when investigating highly emotionally positioned product categories? In these cases, traditional qualitative approaches, such as focus groups or in-depth interviews, are insufficient. Other methods are needed to get the results required for a meaningful marketing decision.

Nontraditional research methods like ethnographic approaches can help to get an holistic picture. Looking 'behind the facades' and spending a lot of time with people in their natural, individual environment allows one to understand actual lifestyles, values and expectations in detail. Knowing the customers thoroughly is essential for success. Ethnographic research is an important aid to gaining better and deeper understanding, and this is especially relevant when one seeks to open up new, foreign markets or to reach new target groups – therefore when being faced with the challenge of deeply understanding the general behaviour and specific usage.

Ethnographic research involves examining a group's culture and daily way of life. It relies heavily on up-close, personal experience and possible participation, not just observation, by researchers trained in the art of ethnography. Its origins lie in anthropology. The word itself holds a clue: 'ethno' means people and 'graphy', as we all know, means describe. Ethnography takes research to the people, allowing them to describe their world in their own terms and observing them in their home, their office, their car or in their supermarket.

Ethnographers often work in multidisciplinary teams. The ethnographic focal point may include intensive language and culture learning, intensive study of a single field or domain, and a blend of historical, observational and interview methods. Typical ethnographic research employs three kinds of data collection: in-depth interviews, personal observation and documenting.

An indispensable requisite is the camcorder – everything is recorded either by a cameraman, by fixed installed cameras or by the respondents' family or friends.

It is also important that the participants are not observed and analysed in a rather sterile and 'foreign' environment, such as a test studio, but at home in their natural, authentic surroundings. A direct advantage of this is that interactions of friends and family members can be observed as well.

Ethnographic research is a method that provides market researchers with the possibility to see into the respondent's life and to take part in particular situations and relevant actions. It is a way of participating directly, and, therefore, achieving more authentic information than can be obtained by other research methods. 'Being there' is how we usually describe this, i.e. spending more time in a very intensive way with less people. 'Being there' allows one to find out about needs which are not obvious to the participants, and to understand which dissatisfying aspects are more important than others.

The advantage is obvious: there is no better way to explore how a target group behaves in certain situations. It does not matter if we are talking about accompanied activities – such as sports, shopping, having fun – about video diaries of certain activities, or just watching consumers at the point of sale, at home, etc., the objective always is to learn about consumers' behaviour by observing instead of merely asking questions. In addition, the client obtains visual material that demonstrates the findings clearly and that can be significant for internal communication: based on visible behaviour, all the people involved in the project speak the same language.

Even though ethnographic approaches are not the same as living with the people for a while, they are definitely a step in the right direction in terms of getting a deeper and better understanding.

Here are just some of the general questions to which ethnographic research can find the answer:

- **Understanding usage behaviour** – how are products actually used? What development and optimization possibilities follow from this?
- **Understanding the market** – which needs and requirements are relevant and important in certain markets, how can they be accomplished and which positioning possibilities can be drawn from this?
- **Understanding expectations** – which factors contribute to satisfaction and dissatisfaction towards products, and what possibilities do they have for concept development and strategy?
- **Understanding emotional drivers** – which are the relevant and important emotional triggers? How can the communication strategies based on brand and product be optimized?

Methodology

A drawback of ethnographic research is always being part of a test: even though one is accompanying the respondent's everyday life, being continually filmed reminds the respondent that they are in a test situation. Also, even if the participants have learned to cope with the 'TV-situation', there is verbal or subconscious nonverbal communication with the cameraman going on. So the behaviour is influenced by at least two crucial factors.

Our solution is 'non-presence while being present', using the following two methodologies to overcome these common obstacles of ethnographic research.

Video diaries

This approach is a combination of in-depth interviews and the installation of fixed cameras at respondents' homes, usually for a period of 5–8 days, focused directly on the relevant appliances. It is used mainly if habitualized, subconscious behaviour needs to be researched and analysed in its authentic environment by keeping external influencing factors as low as possible.

Participating observation

The basic idea behind this methodology is that in order to find out and learn about other people, it is best to go and spend time with them, to do what they usually do and to understand them through that experience. This can even mean that the camera, notebook and pencil are put aside, and the researcher joins in whatever is going on, being at 'eye-level' with the participants.

Overall, observing behaviour either for a week or in an 'eye-level' situation for a longer timeframe has, as expected, the positive effect that the respondents get used to the situation of being observed. Furthermore, the observation seems to be forgotten totally by the participants after a short while. It is nearly impossible to behave differently than usual if you do a routine behaviour for a longer period. So, even if the first few minutes might show more socially expected behaviour, this will change automatically to natural behaviour after a while.

Although we cannot guarantee that the behaviour we film by applying these two methodologies is 100% authentic in every single situation, these research designs are a further step towards getting even closer to reality than before.

It is important to stress that observation always needs to be supported and enriched by in-depth interviews to get an holistic picture and understanding.

Factors for success

As fascinating as ethnographic research is, it is also quite different from well-known traditional methods. There are some important issues which one should keep in mind when planning to conduct ethnographic research, because they can strongly influence the success of the research.

Recruiting

To put it delicately, not everyone favours the idea of being filmed, and especially not for a whole week, particularly by installed video cameras. It is important to convince participants that it is not like Orwell's vision of 1984. Building up trust is the key not only with the actual participant, but also with the whole family – their acceptance is crucial.

It is very helpful during recruiting to be as transparent as possible when explaining the goal of this research to the respondents. It is quite easy to explain that the time and energy of our project team will not be wasted on participants' pyjamas or what they look like in the early morning without wearing make-up, and that our client is definitely much more interested in other aspects of their daily life. Of course, all of them receive an official confidentiality agreement and, if they wish, they can come and visit us in our office to see who we are and what we look like.

Also, during installation of the equipment, the building up of confidence is an important factor in making respondents feel comfortable with the situation. Our technician explains everything in detail, showing how cameras will be fixed without scratching kitchen walls, demonstrating that we focus the camera only on the appliances of interest and that the surroundings are cut out. The same goes for the initial interview: talking with our participants and explaining the research objectives in more detail is important for them to lose anxiety. All participants are given a hotline number and have direct access to both the technician and the project manager during the whole period of field time.

Technical issues

Especially when applying the methodology of video diaries, in order to keep the amount of video material within manageable limits, we equip the cameras with a motion detector, so that recording is only done if there is some kind of action at/with the appliances. A web cam-based solution would be best, but this limits the target too much, as not many households in Europe have the necessary technical equipment at home at present. The option of a digital video camera with a PC and hard drive combines the good picture quality of a digital video camera with a local hard drive where the video material is stored, without the necessity of changing tapes. Changing tapes would remind them constantly of the test situation, and that is exactly what we want to avoid.

A standard digital video camera is sufficient if the filming is done hand-held. The cameraman should know his job very well, as light conditions always change and the people do not stand still. Shaky video sequences at the end of filming are no real help for the analysis, so it is worth investing time and money in training the cameramen at the outset. As a guideline, we established a visual booklet with explanations and examples of dos and don'ts.

Editing of film sequences

Watching and editing large amounts of video material is a challenge, and requires not only a team of up to ten people, but also an expert for all the required software programs! Not to mention the need for enough space to allow the whole editing team with their PCs to sit and work together.

We often have more than 600 gigabytes of packed film material that needs to be watched, analysed and finally selected to present the most relevant research findings per country. Usually the material is scanned twice: once to filter out those video sequences that do not show any relevant action, and then to select relevant sequences, which are copied into the specific folders per appliance. Afterwards, these are analysed more deeply.

After the editing phase, the client receives a selection of the most significant behaviour patterns on DVD and one hard drive per country, with all analysed video sequences selected per appliance so that each product manager gets those files that are important to him/her. What makes a DVD so useful is that it shows several subcategories and all involved countries side by side – you can click on one country in a subcategory/problem area and see several video examples, click on the next country and see examples of the same problem area, etc. So you get a very complex and compact visualization of problems.

We strongly recommend that the clients are involved as much as possible during the editing phase, which should include not only their market researchers but also the experts responsible for product innovations.

Teamwork

A very important aspect when conducting ethnographic research is the extensive discussion between researcher and project team on the client's side to get an equal level of understanding of the consumers. On this basis, the team of researchers and product developers, planners and managers can discuss and share ideas to enhance the survey results and match all the different needs and expectations.

The perceptions of researchers and product planners, i.e. experts for each product, are, or often can be, different. The product experts, who have several years of experience within their product category, often have a different sensibility regarding usage, problems, etc. Their method of analysing consumers' behaviour and methods of resolution are sometimes quite different; they sometimes 'see' something a researcher does not 'see'. Ethnographic research, from our experience, enables the whole team to have a common perception. This is a good basis for discussion between the research institute and product planner. It provides a basis for everyone involved to reach a better understanding of the consumers, their lifestyles, their wants and, most of all, their hidden needs.

Before using ethnographic research, a detailed briefing is very important. This is not to outline how to do the research, but rather to discuss the products, sensitizing for the product, its usage, etc. It's not done just by giving a questionnaire to the researcher and then receiving the answers at the end. An extensive briefing and discussion at the beginning and during the whole research is essential. This also helps to recognize problem areas and to structure them.

Logistics

International research always involves the shipment of technical equipment, if necessary, in order to keep the same technical standards. So you need to be prepared to ship large cargo from one country to another: e.g. 12 PCs, 30 cameras, two screens and hard disks, loads of cables, scotch tape, multiple socket outlets, ten expandable telescope bars with a length of 1.90 metres each, etc.

Furthermore, it is crucial – and easily forgotten – to allow enough time for shipping between the countries. Also bear in mind that sometimes shipments do not get to the correct address or even country, and it is often time consuming to redirect or find the lost shipment.

Moderation

Observation with cameras is important, but is only one part of the research. It is always combined with intensive in-depth interviews up to four hours in length. Therefore, you need highly experienced moderators who not only ask the right questions but are able to integrate into the surroundings and atmosphere of the participants' home.

To share the findings and to compare country-specific results, intense face-to-face briefings before and after the research with all moderators are even more important than with traditional qualitative research.

Analysis

Always very challenging and time intense! During the analysis phases, the client's project team should be involved as much as possible in the project. This includes not only their market researchers but also the experts responsible for product innovations. Half-day interim meetings should be held to share first insights.

LG ELECTRONICS' POINT OF VIEW

For us as product planner and developer, the most important point is to know and understand our consumers, especially their 'relationship' with household appliances.

We wanted a method that went far beyond the traditional qualitative methods like focus groups or in-depth interviews. We wanted a method through which we really could understand and get to know the consumer. Not only his/her obvious needs and wants, which could be communicated to us in focus groups or in-depths, but something which revealed even the needs the consumers were not aware of.

Traditional qualitative methods limit the insights one can get. Even if the respondent is honest and tries to describe 'reality', one cannot exclude the possibility that the respondent is describing what her/his expectations are, i.e. how she/he actually would like to be. The risk is that we get socially correct answers and not the information we need for product planning and improvements.

Let's take the in-depth interview for example. Even if we try to be as creative as possible and cover all possible aspects that could be interesting for product planning, we can never guarantee that we have done so. Another important fact is that the respondent just gives us answers to our questions. Aspects such as how a consumer really behaves in certain situations, how he/she really uses an appliance, the problems faced while using an appliance, how these problems are solved by a consumer, what is satisfying and, more important, what is dissatisfying and has to be improved to make consumers' lives more convenient cannot be exposed in the necessary detail by interviews.

We needed a method which answered our questions, revealed obvious and hidden needs of consumers and even aspects we did not think about. It was clear that traditional research methods could not meet our needs.

Ethnographic research is a tool which allows us to get insights into the reality of our consumers – their real lives. Taking part in consumers' lives gives us, as product planners, the possibility of getting answers far beyond the obvious. It reveals aspects even the consumer himself/herself is not aware of. Ethnographic research is a way of discovering the hidden needs, the *real* usage of and behaviour with household appliances.

The most important advantage for us, as a foreign company, is that we obtain visualized information. There is a significant difference between analyses from traditional research methods and analyses that are underlined by visual material. Visualized information makes it much easier for a foreign company to understand consumers with different cultural backgrounds. It is also easier to comprehend all the major and minor differences of each country. Viewing the video material is like immersing oneself in the respondents' world.

However, it should not be forgotten that it is very time consuming to watch all the video sequences. In the case of our washing study, where we implemented video diaries for seven days, we had over 200 hours. For the cleaning study, we used participating observation with just two filming sequences, but we still had over 100 hours! So you can imagine how many days it takes to see all the film sequences.

Therefore, 'pre-work' with the researchers is very important, because they do the preparatory work. They view all the video material and select, cut, glue, categorize, etc. This preparatory work eases one's own analyses immensely – everything is sorted according to your own wishes. Besides the process of how an appliance is used, the most important aspects are the problem areas and unexpected points. The best ways to show the video results are hard disks and DVDs.

After we got the survey results we were able to get answers to our questions, the points we were interested in – real usage, problems and users' ways of solving them, behaviour, etc. But the most interesting fact was that some points were not the way we thought they would be. The problems from our point of view were not the problems for a user, and vice versa. Even some respondents are not aware of their *real* problems. A user might think she/he has this and that problem, but behaviour sometimes reveals completely different aspects. These are the interesting *hidden* needs.

Product improvement or the creation of new products means, of course, meeting needs and wants independently if customers can express them directly. But it is more important, in the realm of household appliances, that improvements or new products make customers' lives more convenient, sometimes without their knowing about this effect.

Coming back to the results, we tried to generate ideas which met both kinds of needs – the obvious and the hidden ones. For the obvious needs it was sometimes easier to generate ideas, because these were the problems we had already thought of before conducting the survey. For the hidden needs it is more complicated. Often, hidden needs show us problems that we as experts didn't think of. This demands a high level of creativity. A really big help with this kind of problem solving were the visual results. In some cases we didn't have to think about a solution at all, because the respondent showed us the idea.

Solving a problem or meeting hidden needs the way a customer does has a positive effect on market communication, too. It is much easier for a customer to understand new concepts, identify with them and, more importantly, understand and see the benefits, if we as a company communicate through the same pictures, i.e. situations.

RESEARCH EXAMPLES

We would now like to outline how we reached the objectives and provided insights for product improvement and product innovation.

We used a bricolage of methodologies – it was a fluid process without being limited to a preset programme. Instead, we were able to adjust the research methodology according to the specific research needs.

In the area of ethnographic research, we conducted three large international projects within the last year: one was to find out about the behaviour in European kitchens with regard to electrical appliances and workflow, the second looked at the whole laundry process and its perception, i.e. from sorting dirty clothes, through the washing and drying process up to ironing, and the third was to do with both wet and dry floor-cleaning habits. So, faced with the task of exploring habitual everyday behaviour as well as product usage, ethnographic approaches were the only feasible way to achieve the required results, as the necessary precious details in everyday behaviour are inaccessible by in-depth interviews alone.

Besides the need to understand authentic usage and behaviour, a further important objective was to explore satisfying and dissatisfying factors with the different appliances with an eye to product improvement and innovation, and to generate insights that would help to increase market share and make us distinctive in the European market.

And we might say that we now understand the usage and expectations regarding household appliances in the segment of white goods quite well!

Project: kitchen

For the kitchen study we implemented the method of video diaries and installed several video cameras in Germany (Hamburg), the UK (London) and France (Paris), with ten households each for a period of 7–9 days. The main objectives were:

- to explore insights about user behaviour in the kitchen while using different appliances, including refrigerator, dishwasher, oven, hob, hood, microwave oven, etc.;
- to find out about inconvenient points and generate ideas and solutions to make everyday life and work at home more comfortable and enjoyable.

Besides the desire to participate, the respondents needed to fulfil the following screening criteria:

- a mix of families, couples without children and singles;
- all had to have bought a built-in kitchen system from a kitchen speciality shop within the last two years;
- the kitchen had to be equipped with a refrigerator, dishwasher, electric oven, hob and hood;
- the minimum spent on these electrical appliances had to be EURO 3000;
- they had to cook at least once per day.

Not the easiest job, which was one reason why only very few institutes sent a quotation apart from us. We had some initial problems in finding the right people due to the rather strict quota restrictions, but also because of the idea of being filmed in the kitchen. Overall, through, it was easier than we had feared. Most respondents who qualified for the study regarded our approach as interesting and funny – we believe that the tendency in the last few years towards normal people being stars in 'reality' TV programmes definitely helped.

We installed 4–5 cameras in each kitchen, directed at the relevant appliances, which originally were oven, hob, refrigerator and dishwasher, but widened during the course of the study to include sink, hood, microwave and small electrical appliances such as electric knives (where applicable). This was definitely a very interesting and challenging project with regard to all aspects, through from recruiting actual fieldwork up to the analysis of loads of packed film material.

Project: laundry

The laundry project was conducted in Germany (Hamburg), Hungary (Budapest), Sweden (Stockholm), Spain (Madrid) and the UK (London), with ten households each using the method of video diaries for a 5–7-day period.

The main objectives were:

- to gain a general understanding of dealing with laundry, its perception, importance, impact on role allocation within the household, etc.;
- to view washing and drying behaviour and to gain insights into how the relevant appliances could cause inconvenience and problems when ironing;
- to identify trends for clothing, materials, etc.;
- to identify the exact usage of specific electrical appliances in this process, satisfying and dissatisfying factors, problem areas, etc.;
- to find inconvenient points and needs in order to generate ideas or solutions for product development;
- to gain insights into lifestyle and potential trends.

All participants who qualified for this survey met the following criteria:

- they were generally households with more than two members, only a maximum of two households per country could be a two-person household;
- they used their washing machine at least three times a week (the more frequent the better);
- they ironed for at least 90 minutes per week;
- the relevant appliances (washing machine, dryer if applicable, electric iron) were are not older than two years.

To find quite new irons was the most difficult part. The filming was not an obstacle, as, unlike the kitchen survey, there was no permanent filming but rather 'controlled' bursts when doing a certain activity, like loading/unloading the washing machine and dryer, putting clothes on the clothes line or ironing.

To research the whole laundry behaviour we used a mixture of various technical solutions: to observe the usage and behaviour for washing machines and dryers we installed fixed cameras equipped with motion detectors – the only problem was if these appliances were located in a bathroom or toilet area. No one fancied the idea of having a fixed video camera with a motion detector in these rooms. We solved the problem by offering to allow the respondents to switch the camera on manually whenever they used the appliances. We ensured that this would not be forgotten by using lists where they wrote down the time and date of the usage of the respective appliance and by putting red 'remember smileys' on and near the appliances. We were also interested in the whole process of drying the laundry manually, i.e. by using a clothes horse or clothes line or any other self-invented strategy, both inside and outside, and in the last step – the ironing. To be able to observe these actions as well, we adjusted the technical equipment and location of the video cameras according to the particularities of the individual and household. For example, in the case that some of the behaviour could not be filmed easily – as in drying the clothes on rooftops or between two houses, which is a common behaviour in Spain and Italy – we chose manual filming by our researchers during the two intense in-depth interview sessions.

Project: vacuum cleaning

The vacuum cleaning project was conducted in France (Paris), Hungary (Budapest), Spain (Madrid) and the UK (London) with 15 households each applying the method of participating observation.

The main objectives were:

- the identification of common grounds and distinctive features in attitude and user behaviour within the researched sample;
- the evaluation of cleaning habits (workflow) and insights about the storage situation;
- the identification of different user types in each country;
- to gain suggestions and hints for optimization regarding the 'ideal' vacuum cleaner and method of vacuuming.

The quota requirements were:

- that we studied the person in the household mainly responsible for cleaning;
- all households had a vacuum cleaner purchased in the last three years (minimum price: EURO 50);
- in each country a good mix of canister, upright and bagless vacuum cleaners in the UK and France there were about 50% upright and 50% canister vacuum cleaners, the other countries were more canister-focused;
- among the households a mixture of middle, middle to high and high incomes.

Fixed installed cameras would not be of much use, as the participants move around while vacuum cleaning, and observing the whole house and apartment was not really an option. Therefore, we chose the method of participating observations, which were embedded in two 3–4 hour sessions at the respondents' homes to show us any regularities or repeated behaviour, etc. We observed how vacuum cleaning is really done for about 45 minutes per visit – quite interestingly, the observed behaviour differed in some aspects from how the respondents had told us they clean.

FINDINGS

When editing the video material we discovered some astonishing be-haviour – behaviour most participants denied, so that they were often very surprised when confronted with the video evidence in the follow-ing in-depth interview. This subconscious behaviour, which added up to approximately 25%, had already become such a habit that it was stored in the unconscious mind, although the problem which caused this be-haviour rather disturbed them.

Our findings mainly covered four areas:

1. **Understanding usage patterns**. We received an authentic picture of behaviour and usage of appliances to the necessary degree of detail. Watching households over a whole week enabled us to see differences between morning and evening, situations of being in a hurry or having time, and even the secret midnight snack! A more comprehensive portrait of daily life is difficult to get.
2. **Understanding the market**. We could discover relevant needs and trends based on the respective cultures in the researched European

markets. Whereas, for example, in Germany the health issue is very important, impacting the perception of technologies as well as cleaning issues (no strong chemicals, especially not when there are children in the house), in France, the convenience aspect is more important, displaying itself in a high acceptance of 'aided' technology (self-cleaning ovens, etc.) as well as a higher readiness to buy new appliances if they are more convenient and trendier than the ones on the market. So, we were able to identify needs in certain markets and generate first concepts of how different desires, as well as the options for positioning of new technologies, could be realized.

3. **Understanding expectations**. We could generate different consumer types with their specific needs and expectations. Analysing satisfying and dissatisfying factors of usage, which are of course influenced by the cultural expectations and lifestyle of the households, played an important role in understanding. Moreover, the comparison of the watched behaviour with the information gathered during the interviews also displayed subconscious and hidden needs. It was astonishing, often only after having shown certain scenes to the participants did the presented problems come up to the surface of consciousness and reveal important insights. For example, despite the fact that households we are concerned with saving energy and water, the actual times that refrigerators were left open or water was left running contradicted this environmental attitude, and showed room and a high acceptance for alarm functions in cases of energy being wasted.

4. **Understanding emotional triggers**. Finally, the 'emotional relationship' to and importance of the researched appliances could be explored. Taking together the insight of all three areas explained above, emotional triggers regarding different appliances in different countries could be generated and grouped. These also provided important insights for promising communication routes aimed at the emotional benefits of the product and brand for the respective consumer types: i.e. 'the rather cautious woman who allows housework to dominate her', or 'the careless, uninterested' or the 'very organized with strict time planning, who is quite self-confident'.

So, what did we 'discover' exactly?

In the kitchen study, we were astonished to see such individuality in storing food in the refrigerator. Every participant had his/her own way of putting items in, rearranging or taking them out, especially if large or bulky items had to be stored. And everyone is probably convinced they have found the optimal way to store items in his/her specific refrigerator. We as manufacturers have to provide for much more individuality – especially regarding storage.

Observing cooking was quite interesting as well, because there are several aspects or problems while cooking that a user himself is not aware of – for example sliding pots on the hob. Both hands had to be used for agitating, and in terms of using energy efficiently, it is most important to have a pot in the right place. We saw how pots were pushed all over the hob in order to turn a fried egg. Obviously, it is important for us to give more guidance and help regarding the surface of the hob.

Another aspect was overboiling while cooking. Nobody wants milk to boil over, it just happens sometimes during the process of cooking – usually while the person is doing something different or standing somewhere else. Then you see how this person jumps to the pot and lifts it – quite difficult and painful if the pot has a plastic handle. We will try to find a technique to prevent overboiling in the next generation of our hobs.

A family consists of different members. All are of different ages, different body heights, etc. These aspects have an influence on their usage, and show us producers which demands an appliance has to fulfil. For example, we observed quite a few times how a tall person (usually the husband) in the household bumped his head against the hood, which was installed at the right height for the smaller wife. To produce a flexible hood height is easy, an important precondition is to know about inconvenience.

We were surprised that people still rinse dishes before putting them in the dishwasher. The reason for this surprise was our knowledge that consumers ask for ecological and economical appliances which grant very good results. One reason for purchasing a dishwasher is water saving, so we produced a dishwasher which makes a preliminary rinse unnecessary and still guarantees washing while saving water. So why do people still rinse? This case showed us that we have to change or enforce communication: it seems that not everyone is really aware of all the advantages his/her appliance offers.

Can you imagine how often someone rearranges plates in order to add another item into the dishwasher? We have a pretty good idea now! We also learned that it can take up to five minutes to put in one small bowl. Another point observed by us was that every family member has a different method of filling the dishwasher, especially different from that of the mother. So, nearly every time someone else fills the dishwasher, the mother rearranges it! We need to offer a dishwasher which makes this rearrangement unnecessary, e.g. by using an easy guidance system.

In the washing study, we learned that doing the laundry and sorting clothes are aspects which strictly go together. People doing laundry either separate directly into different baskets or in front of the washing machine before starting a washing cycle. One lady, for example, had six baskets where she stored her dirty laundry. For this reason, laundry claims a lot of space; even sorting in front of the machine needs space. But we also had respondents living in apartments with spatial restrictions. This requires a solution which avoids sorting.

Another example was a woman treating stains on her sweater for about 15 minutes. That's definitely too long for us. So we found a way for our washing machines to avoid this waste of time.

Do you know what people do if a washing machine is just half full? They go around and look for something they can wash to fill up the machine. Or they take out, for example, the white laundry and replace it with the bigger black load. A machine which is not full seems to evoke, remorse, so it is our job to find a technique which enables an economical and ecological wash, even when the machine is not fully loaded.

After a washing cycle, they check/control each item to see if it is clean and shake it out. We could observe that, in order to avoid ironing, clothes were shaken out properly and hung on hangers. We are thinking of a system or programme which makes this shaking out of laundry obsolete and at the same time facilitates ironing.

A further problem area we discovered by observing the video sequences was the loading and unloading of laundry, due to the small door of the washing machine. We will provide a solution to make this step of the laundry process more convenient.

After analysing the video material, we found out that the level of reliability of dryers is very low. The participants applied very strict separating rules as to what went into the dryer and what not. Apart from their individual rules, material requirements also sometimes make it impossible to put certain items into the dryer. Our task is to develop a particular technology to increase reliability, and one which allows drying for many, and in the best case for all, materials.

It was unbelievable for us to see the huge amount of fluff in the fluff filter. If I myself had this amount of fluff after each drying cycle I wouldn't use a dryer! So we focused on how we could solve this in the sense of less wear off.

Overall, the trend to bagless vacuum cleaners is still quite slow. One reason for this was to be seen on the video files in our cleaning study. While changing bags there was a disturbing cloud of dust, which was more than just disliked – as we could see clearly in the facial expression and body movement. After seeing this we know we need to solve this problem for our bagless cleaners.

It was also amazing to see the heights someone tries to clean with the vacuum cleaner, or which items. We found out that almost everything is cleaned by the vacuum cleaner: beds, couches, books, computers, TVs, etc. We learned that we need to offer more suitable accessories and flexibility for vacuum cleaners.

This is only a small selection of important aspects we learned by observation – many of which we would not have discovered merely by asking.

IMPACT

It was more than exciting – both for us and the responsible project team of LG Electronics – to be able to watch the participants directly. We were astonished to discover behaviour and problem areas which had not been addressed at all in the intense in-depth interviews. For example, the pans often slide on the ceramic surface of the hob, how often the door of the refrigerator was actually opened during one day or how long the door of the refrigerator stayed open (a behaviour the participants totally denied), how many times they re-grouped the dishes in the dishwasher each time they put something new in, or the differences per country, especially regarding cleaning of the appliances (the French women definitely do not like to get their hands dirty, they very much prefer ovens with a pyrolysis self-cleaning function), which strategies they invented to dry clothes in order to facilitate ironing, the different techniques to sort laundry, both for the washing machine and dryer, what can happen during ironing, or what the vacuum cleaner can clean besides floors!

The main impact and advantage of the three ethnographic approaches was definitely that they made the results 'visible' – in the true sense of the word. To get the chance actually to observe behaviour and have all this information stored on DVD so that it can be watched over and over again whenever one likes, including in a year or two, provides the basis to understand foreign cultures – it is something similar to a 'reference book'. One important advantage for LG Electronics was that all product managers involved were provided with a large amount of video material structured according to behaviour and particularities of behaviour, allowing them to participate in their customers' everyday lives and analyse them from the expert perspective as well. Result wise, our client received a tool to make all internal team members, ranging from product management through marketing to sales and the management, speak the 'same language' based on visible behaviour. The possibility to observe actual behaviour was, without doubt, very convincing to the project team – a behaviour quite different from that in Korea sometimes. It was a possibility for the whole project team to share the findings and to understand, by seeing with their own eyes, what problems the participants had to face and which different strategies were used in each country.

The detailed exploration of the observed behaviour combined with the in-depth interviews and especially the comparison of what was being said and what was being done, provided us with valuable insights about hidden needs and improvement ideas, and presented tangible approaches for product development. The results delivered an overwhelming amount of new information: they were extremely detailed and displayed both relevant differences in usage behaviour between countries and improvement ideas for product innovation.

We could draw many aspects for improvement and innovations for each product category, covering all different aspects of convenience, performance, practicability, security, individuality, efficiency, design, etc. Besides this, important insights for communication strategies and indications for product positioning, both on product and country levels, could be drawn. The results of such research, which are both verbalized and visualized, are very 'precious'. They assist further steps in product development in this manner, for internal as well as external communication.

Even if we have the best ideas, they are worthless if they do not meet consumers' needs. It is also a fact that from the development of new ideas until their mass production is a long and very costly process. So it is understandable that top management wants secure data from which we generate our ideas.

The results of ethnographic research not only assist us in understanding our consumers better, therefore generating adequate ideas, the visual results also provide important back data to convince top management and other related departments (R&D, engineering, design, marketing, etc.) of our ideas. Receiving the visual film sequences increases mobility and makes internal presentations of the research findings easier and articulate. During meetings with experts from other departments especially, the selected film sequences proved to be very convincing. Sometimes you don't have to say a word, you just show some examples. Visual explanations are more persuading than verbal ones.

Another positive effect is that nearly every department extracts its own benefits, e.g. marketing gets ideas for how it could trigger special target groups, etc. Considering all aspects, several parties can take advantage, of ethnographic research.

From our point of view, it is an optimal tool to share learning and information among countries. Everybody has the same information and sees the same – even the basis for discussion is the same. At the end we have generated many ideas based on several analyses from different points of view. It is also a big help that not everybody has to read all the written results. It is much more efficient and time-saving to share the visual results.

Hard disks are good for internal work and analysis – you get a load of information and can pick single sequences according to your needs and implement them in your report. These hard disks per country are assets which you can always have a look at, or use to look up something. They are a resource that a company has and can always use, and because they are small and easy to handle, they can be carried around without any mobility restrictions. Important here again is communication with the research team and the product experts to guarantee a standard which supports the workflow. Besides the structure, naming and coding of sequences have to be cleared, and the paths agreed.

SUMMARY

Processes regarding product development and product innovation might be different in each company, but idea generation has to be done by every company. Just put aside the questions of whether an idea is technologically possible or not and all the other questions and challenges. Let's just focus on ideas.

For us as product planners, working life consists of product improvements, innovations and concept developments, besides all the economic figures. The bases for all of these are the results of market research: idea generation and the input to bring something forward.

The results of the studies provide the frame world for our own creativity, and the method a company chooses influences which kind of information you get, and in which way you get it. Selecting and using a method with a positive influence and at the same time easing idea generation has priority. That's why we have chosen and will continue to choose ethnographic research methods in the future.

Negative aspects like high costs, long survey duration, logistical obstacles and long analysing times are outweighed by the following benefits:

- You get the right answers!
- You get answers to questions you've not thought of.
- You get authentic information about respondents' living environment.

The complete result material was used to form idea patterns. Whereas the analyses of the researchers were considered to provide a better understanding of psychological aspects, the video material was the real working material. The idea exhaustion times from this material differed between the appliances – for the product category *oven* we could generate noticeably more concrete concept ideas than for the product category *refrigerator*, although the minimum of ideas generated at the first step was 25 for each appliance. Besides a relatively high quantity of product improvement ideas for each product, we could also generate product innovations.

The 'crop' of ideas depends on the level of satisfaction with an appliance. That means if the level of satisfaction with a product is generally high, the need for better or new products is correspondingly low. If a company in such a market situation uses a 'normal' research method like face-to-face in-depth interview and asking respondents about inconvenient points, necessary improvements, etc., they will answer that everything is fine, there is nothing a producer can do or needs to do. If a respondent directly mentions an inconvenient point, this is an interesting and important aspect for us. But this answer is based on conscious needs and perception, and we often need to know the subconscious, hidden needs.

Ethnographic research delivers both the conscious and subconscious answers. You get to know about aspects even the respondent is not aware of – and not just about the socially desired behaviour, but behaviour the respondents might not like to reveal to a third party consciously. By virtue of all this, we had a frame pattern to create more detailed concept ideas which were closer to actual need states, and therefore of better quality for us.

The next step in product improvement, development and innovation is concepts. Hence, ethnographic research and its results strongly determine concept generation. How the results look and how far they help us to do our work is an essential factor.

Ethnographic research is a tool we don't want to overlook anymore. Its results assist creativity, facilitate work, make it easier to understand respondents and their living environments and function as back-up to convince top management.

OUTLOOK

Ethnographic research can be very powerful in exploring how products are really used and what significance they have. What other kind of research would actually be able to provide film material of kids trying to hide inside the oven, or a lady ironing banknotes!?

We believe that ethnographic research provides great consumer insights for many product categories. Some might be less suitable, even though it would be very interesting to find out how body lotion or toilet paper is actually used!

Chapter Fourteen

Video ergo agnosco – From Observation to Insight

Nic Hall[a]

This paper illustrates how even the most mundane observations can lead to some interesting new marketing initiatives and product concepts. The overall conclusion is that the key to success is in the process used to drive insight from observation.

INTRODUCTION

Direct consumer contact programmes – in which people from all levels of the organization aim to meet the 'real people' who use their products and services – are all the rage. It is generally accepted that this is a 'good thing'. This chapter will review whether or not this fashion really is a good thing given the investment in time and the logistical difficulties it involves. Using some primary research done especially for the chapter, we will illustrate how even the most mundane observations can lead to some interesting new marketing initiatives and product concepts. The overall conclusion is that the key to success is in the *process* used to drive insight from observation.

The famous French philosopher and mathematician, René Descartes said: 'I think, therefore I am'. There is an increasing tendency in

[a]Global Head of Consumer Understanding, Research International.

Market Research Best Practice. Edited by P. Mouncey and F. Wimmer.
© 2007 John Wiley & Sons, Limited.

marketing and market research circles to paraphrase this and claim: 'I see, therefore I know'.

One of the key drivers of this trend is the increasing number of relatively inexperienced people involved in doing primary 'research' with consumers. We deliberately put the word research in inverted commas because what passes for research may be well beyond the boundaries of long-established methods, conducted by people who have potentially had minimal training and little experience. We hesitate to add that this is not necessarily a bad thing! On the contrary, done well, fresh approaches through new eyes can lead to real breakthroughs in consumer understanding. They can put client teams in touch with people they have only ever 'seen' through the eyes of a research report or through a one-way mirror.

Imagine the value to the client's understanding of consumers in the following two scenarios:

- The marketing manager of hair care products aimed at black women is, herself, white. She is responsible for marketing a range of hair relaxant products. Hair relaxing is a complex process, involving time, effort and even some pain to carry out. The marketing manager goes to a hair salon and has her hair relaxed whilst talking to black women in the salon.
- The product development manager for nappies has no children himself. He spends the day first at a prenatal class for women who are talking about what nappies they are going to use and why. The next day he spends some time with a woman who has a 3-month-old baby, assisting her in changing the nappy several times during the day.

Almost every major multinational has in place, or is putting in place, a system of direct contact between employees of the company and users of their products and services. The success of these programmes ranges from claims of groundbreaking insights through to mountains of unusable information. In our experience, it is all too easy to end up with hours of videotape which no one has time to go through, or does not understand if they do. Similarly, we have seen observations take place where the information obtained has been lost due to the pressure of work.

One of the key messages we would like people to take from this chapter is that obsession with observation does not lead automatically to insight. We aim to demonstrate the difference between observation and insight and propose solutions to achieve the goal of consumer insight. We show that successful insights come from a programme of training, observation, insight generation sessions and databasing of findings. They do not, or very seldom, come from sudden flashes of inspiration after walking around someone's home.

FROM OBSERVATION TO INSIGHT

In some cases, observations can lead immediately to obvious actions. The observation that people use the length of their toothbrush to 'measure' how much toothpaste to use, leads directly to a decision to make longer toothbrushes (and perhaps sell more toothpaste).

But, in the worst cases, observations of consumers' lives are taken at face value and acted upon. Watching mothers add extra ingredients to their ready-made bottled pasta sauce might lead to the launch of a range of sauces with 'added ingredients'. The fatal flaw in this scenario is that the observation of people adding more ingredients is not an insight. The insight is that mothers add extra ingredients so that they feel like 'I made it myself'. You need consumers to comment on their behaviour in addition to observing their actions. At the very least, you need to think long and hard about the motivations behind the actions you observe. In this example, a far more useful action would be to add recipes to the labels of the pasta sauce. The use of the sauce is then extended into other areas (for example, as a soup base or an ingredient in casseroles), but the emotional benefit to the consumer of 'I made it myself' is also maintained.

The insight of 'I made it myself' is not a new one. Many product categories have picked up on this idea and developed the basic emotional need to fit the parameters of their category. Ikea seems to have taken this same observation of pride in 'making it myself' and turned it into the whole basis for its business. Despite the fact that Ikea furniture may not be the most cutting edge or even the highest quality available, we may hypothesize that the satisfaction consumers gain from assembling a piece of furniture themselves more than compensates for any shortcomings in these areas.

Similarly, whilst it may be technologically possible to make a complete cake mix, Betty Crocker realized long ago that mums need the satisfaction of adding an egg to their cake mixes. This helps them to feel like they have put that bit of extra love and care into making a cake for the family. It doesn't need consumer immersions and a client awayday to realize that love from the family is a basic emotional need of mothers.

In our experience there are many of these 'universal' emotional motivations that occur in many categories, albeit expressed in different ways. The real trick is to adapt the motivation in the most appropriate way for your category.

It helps to have a definition of insight so that you can recognize what is an insight and what is simply an observation. One useful definition of an insight is that it discerns underlying human truths. Insights are usually obvious and intuitive when brought to life. If they seem obscure, they are probably not a real insight.

SOME EXAMPLES OF OBSERVATIONS TO INSIGHTS

The best cases take observations and turn them into really groundbreaking insights. There are numerous examples of these. The following two examples are based on fairly simple observations which have been used in a highly effective way.

The first example is the 'Got Milk' advertising campaign. The simple observation that people are most likely to have milk top of mind not when thinking about health issues but when they run out of it, led to a breakthrough campaign. In the advertisements, consumers were shown in various typical scenarios where one runs out of milk. This struck an instant chord with consumers and an increase in consumption followed.

The second example is the Marmite 'love it/hate it' campaign. A very simple observation exercise would have demonstrated the passion amongst people asked to use Marmite. It is immediately obvious that people fall into one of two camps – you either love it or hate it. There is no middle ground.

Marmite recently celebrated its 100th birthday. A campaign based on heritage and tradition may certainly have been one approach. However, it is our belief that the 'love it/hate it' campaign was far more effective, because it goes right to the heart of how consumers feel about the brand.

Insights matter because they provide the point where a truth of the consumer's life meets a truth of the brand, product or category, creating a bond between them. They also give a perspective on the consumer's behaviour or belief, which can be leveraged to convince him/her that the brand, product or category is meeting his or her needs.

So if we recognize that using true insight can lead to much stronger emotional reactions from consumers, how do we go about generating insights from the everyday observations of consumers' lives which we make?

IS THERE A WAY TO TURN OBSERVATION INTO INSIGHT, AND WHAT CAN WE LEARN?

To bring the process alive, we will present the previously unseen results of some self-funded research. We started by selecting some video clips of everyday observations taken from real consumer contact programmes. The clips were generated from extended ethnographic observation and interview work in consumers' homes. In reality of course, these clips come from editing hours of videotape down to these short scenes. So already we have been through a detailed process of seeking the true insights from hours of observations.

It is our contention that before one even attempts to do observations of this sort, whether they are in-home, in-shop, in the street or wherever, there is a very important first stage of the process. This is the 'training stage'. We take it for granted that market research people have been trained in the necessary skills to do consumer observations. However, the demand now is for people within client organizations to conduct the same kind of observations. These people are not necessarily even drawn from marketing or market research teams. At the very least, this requires training in areas such as:

- how to ask questions;
- how to listen;
- understanding the role of body language and how you dress/present yourself;
- understanding the role of the location of the interview;
- understanding the role of the gender, ethnicity, social class, politics, etc. of the observer versus the consumer.

This training needs to be done before setting out to do observations.

THE PROCESS OF OBSERVATION TO INSIGHT

Assuming, however, that you have gathered your observations, it is our contention that you need a *process* for turning these observations into insights. This is the process we used for turning these video-clip observations into action-based insights.

A core team involving an ethnographic researcher, a director of our innovation business and the author as consumer understanding specialist viewed these clips and made our first conclusions. Each of the clips shows consumers using brands in new and unexpected ways. Our initial conclusion, at least for children, was that brand usage is a voyage of discovery, in which the children adapt their use of brands and how they are used so as to best fit their need to discover their own way to fit a brand into their world.

We took this basic idea of brand usage being a voyage of discovery and applied the concept to a product field that we had not observed (in this case, oral care). The rationale behind this was to prove the idea that stimulation for insight need not necessarily come simply from observing usage of one's own category. It illustrates the point that real insight is about opening your eyes to the whole consumer and not simply focusing down on a narrow world which interests you.

In the next step, we used a group of specially selected and trained creative consumers to explore the process of turning this observation about brand discovery into real insights for oral care. As input to this group, we used the two clips of kids interacting with their favourite brands as stimulus. The group consisted of the creative consumers, mothers with children and an innovation expert. A director of our innovation business facilitated the whole process. Our experience is that these mixed groups of people are often more successful at generating insights than homogeneous groups drawn purely from the product's target market. The inclusion of relevant 'experts' is often invaluable. Examples of experts would be teachers, nutritionists, disc jockeys, travel agents, washing machine manufacturers, etc. Use your imagination to choose relevant experts for your category.

Finally, we used this same group of people to look at how these insights may be turned into real marketing ideas for dental/oral healthcare products for children aged 8–12.

GENERATING INSIGHT PLATFORMS

The first thing we needed to do was to check our on going hypothesis that 'brand discovery' was a key insight arising from these observations. As we expected, a diverse range of ideas poured out, which was fantastic, but many of the responses were not insights tapping into a deeper truth about kids, they were simply descriptions of what was happening in the clips.

There is a lot of work to do to pull together the responses to the observations and then to group these into insight platforms. This is where the skilled qualitative facilitator plays an invaluable role. In our experience it is a mistake for this kind of session to be run purely internally, using only client teams. Too many preconceptions are involved and often politics plays a strong role.

The strongest insight platforms – listed below – were those which resonated with the team itself. For example: *Ritual* – being able to take this thought and recollect your own rituals as a child and to understand and explain the significance of this. The following insight platforms were recorded:

- **'Play'**, described as
  - o 'take it to the edge' – taking the brand and doing crazy and unexpected things with it;
  - o adapting for own play value – playing with the brand to get maximum fun and enjoyment out of using it;
  - o food as entertainment;
  - o boys (likely to interpret this idea as pure play), for example in the idea of building something;
  - o girls (likely to describe it more as experimentation), for example with personal care products.
- **'Discovery'**, described as
  - o curiosity – a need to test and enquire constantly, typical of a child's view of the world;
    Note also that the manufacturer can anticipate subversion of brand and deliberately build in opportunities for discovery.
- **'Boredom'**, described as
  - o invention to allay boredom – coming up with new ways to use the brand to make sure it is always a fresh experience;
  - o own rules – having your own rules and not following those laid down by the manufacturer (which may be perceived as boring either right away or over a period of time);
  - o novelty for its own sake – changing the way of using a brand simply for the sake of it.
- **'Ritual'**, described as
  - o Creating one's own rituals is part of children's way of managing the world and creating familiar pleasures.

- **'Experimentation'**, described as
  - experience – gaining new experiences by using the brand in a different way;
  - to talk about – being seen as cutting edge or 'cool' by one's peers; the first to try something new and, therefore, a talking point.
- **'Rebellion'**, described as
  - subversive – either versus parents/control figures or versus the brand.
- **'Autonomy'**, described as
  - you decide – using the brand to suit me, not using it as the manufacturer dictates that it should be used;
  - a means of controlling a small part of a big world.

Clearly these insight platforms show a degree of overlap, but they help to flesh out and expand on the basic idea of brand discovery so that, going into the next stage, it is better understood. Since we had already chosen the insight platform of discovery as an in going hypothesis, there was no need to prioritize the platforms at this stage. However, clearly in some cases there may need to be a stage here at which the insight platforms are prioritized.

One problem we encountered in this particular exercise was that insights are open to wide interpretations. So, in this case, the idea of 'discovery' was interpreted by different participants in three rather different ways, as follows:

- 'I'll find out for myself;
- 'It's a wonderful world – every day is a new adventure;
- 'I'm not going to be told what to do – I'll do it my way.'

Each can send the team off in a different direction. It is essential, therefore, to make time to word the insight in detail so that there is no ambiguity later on. Even then, there are people who still forget or reinvent. We need to reinforce the basic insight again and again. Our experience in this regard is that before you proceed further, it is useful to capture the essence of the insight in a few clear, unambiguous sentences before continuing.

INSIGHTS TO IDEAS

The first exercise was to establish what are perceived to be the current barriers to tooth-brushing, particularly as related to the child having 'discovery' opportunities. These were seen as the initial barriers:

- **Boredom** – it's no fun to brush my teeth and it's exactly the same every day.
- **Motivation** – other than my mother saying I have to do it, I have no real motivation to brush my teeth.
- **No flexibility/ fixed routine** – I cannot change the way I brush my teeth, where I brush them, how I brush them, what type of product I use. It is always the same.
- **Bed follows** – I know that once I have brushed my teeth I have to go to bed (usually a negative for children, unlike for adults).
- **Have to do it/moaned at** – my mother complains if I don't brush my teeth.
- **No immediate benefit** – I can't see or feel anything happening. How do I know it's working?
- **Taste** – I don't like the taste of toothpaste, or all toothpaste tastes exactly the same.

Given the above, what then are the ideas which can overcome these barriers? We took the barriers one at a time and ran a free-form idea generation session, designed to generate ideas to overcome the barriers. At this stage there is no judgement of good or bad ideas.

Boredom

Like to watch TV, play computer games, draw. Doing this can overcome boredom.

Ideas

- A mobile system to do teeth anywhere.
- Integrated role play – tooth-brushing becomes part of a wider game where the child is playing a role, with tooth brushing part of this role.
- A print-out linked to a computer showing things like how long the teeth were brushed for, how many strokes were used, etc.
- A diary in which to record details such as time of day brushed, number of times brushed, how long for.
- An electric brush made interactive in some way – for example with a timer speaker.
  The head changes colour after you brush (versions of this idea are already in use by manufacturers).

Motivation

Educate the child as to the benefits of brushing, make it relevant to them.

Ideas

- Make a model of the child's own teeth – show how teeth fall out if they are not brushed.
- Give a reward, e.g. a fluffy animal, based on the number of times brushed.
- Give proof/feedback that brushing really makes a difference.
- Children have a fear of braces/plates – incentivize them to wear braces by making it 'cool' to have them when none of your friends do.

No flexibility

Introduce flexibility by changing the 'rules'.

Ideas

- Let children share tooth-brushing occasions with friends/change the time of day.
- Chewing gums rather than toothpaste (again, an idea in use and several successful product launches. Aimed largely at adults though, rather than children).
- 'Bomb' dispensing machine in the bathroom – dispensing perhaps chewing gum balls.
- Exploding pellets – tooth-cleaning pellets, maybe with fluoride, provide a mouth sensation.
- Variety pack – several different flavours, so child can choose a new one every day.
- Squirtable cream/canister – child squirts product directly into the mouth, foaming action means no brushing required.
- Sponge to wipe over the teeth, which cleans and abrades at the same time.
- Pens to 'write' on the teeth and clean at the same time (rather like a Tippex pen). This idea could be extended to a whitening pen.
- Finger hat – small hats to put on the fingers. Product is applied to the hat and the teeth are brushed with the finger. In many parts of the world, brushing with the finger is the norm.
- Collectables – offered as a 'reward' as child completes a routine, a number of brushes or perhaps a tube of toothpaste.
- Nail polishing – taking the idea of nail polishing to the teeth. Painting the teeth with a brush and then removing the paste. Potentially using different colours to make it more fun.
- Customized toothbrush – personalized or customized to the child in some way.

Bed follows

Ideas

- Keep in kitchen and let the child brush teeth in the kitchen.
- After meal – brush right after the meal so that the child does not have to go to bed immediately.
- In any room – allow the child to brush in any room.
- In bed – allow the child to brush in bed. This and the idea above require a delivery system that probably works without water.
- Part of the dessert – gums or sweets that clean the teeth may be a fun way to end the meal.
- Eat the toothbrush – an edible toothbrush that cleans, massages the gums and flosses between the teeth as you eat it.

Have to do it

Ideas

- Instant incentive – dispenses a gift/prize/reward every time you brush.
- Next day/immediately see results – a clear indication that something has happened (we already have products which show the plaque removed from teeth as you brush).
- Stamp on chart – get a stamp on a chart every time you brush your teeth. See it building up to a stage where you get a reward.
- Dentists – provide a reward scheme linked to going to the dentist regularly.

Taste

Ideas

- Dishwasher/massage action – a paste/gel that actively moves around the mouth creating a massage action. Mouth sensation is key to this idea.
- Cream that expands into a foam in the mouth – this is the basis behind products like Imperial Leather Foam Burst or shaving gels.
- Unexpected flavours like orange, vanilla, chocolate, McDonalds.
- Limited edition flavours that the children actively seek out.
- No flavour at all.
- A mouth sensation – popping, fizzing when using the product.
- Replace the paste with a drink that tastes good.

As with all exercises of this nature, the list of ideas generated is far too long to have practical marketing application. Hence, the next stage of the process is to shortlist the ideas and try to word them in more concrete terms.

GENERATING SPECIFIC IDEAS AGAINST THE IDEA LIST

Taking the concept of brand discovery, we now asked the team to apply this insight platform to oral care and tooth-brushing. It is important to note that we kept on reminding people all the way through this stage of the process that the key insight was *discovery* and that all ideas generated needed to relate back to this basic insight. This helps the ideas from straying too far away from the basic human truth of discovery, which we learned from the observations.

The team was split into pairs to develop new ideas in oral/tooth care using the initial ideas (above) as inspiration. Again, they were reminded that they had to work to ideas that met the insights identified at the start. The top four ideas from this session were as below. Note that whilst they relate to the various different insight platforms described above, they all have discovery at the heart of the idea.

Mouth sensations (Figure 14.1)

Insight

Ritual – 'I like what is familiar to me and develop my own private rituals which make routines pleasurable and help me to control my world.'

Benefit

To activate the product you must swill it around your cheeks for several minutes – this does the cleaning and turns the mousse into liquid. There is also a colour change for visible proof that the product is working.

Product features

- Mouth sensations – squeeze or pump into mouth, two shots of mousse are enough for complete oral hygiene.
- Flavour isn't the point – tingling sensation and colour is.

Figure 14.1

'Dentyls' (Figure 14.2)

Insight

Novelty – 'I want constant novelty to keep me interested'.

Benefit

A game keeps the children interested.

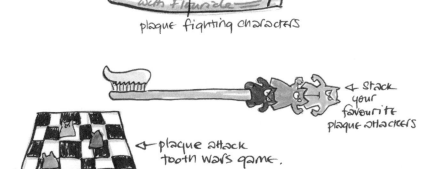

Figure 14.2

Product features

- Toothpaste – 'Tooth wars' – plaque-fighting characters embedded in the paste.
- Brush – stack your favourite plaque attackers on the end.
- Plaque attack – tooth wars game for which child can invent own rituals and play.
- Dispenser for different pastes, brushes and plaque attackers.

'Frank the hip hop rabbit' (Figure 14.3)

Insight

Discovery – 'I do it my way'.

Benefit

Encourages children to clean teeth because hip hop is fun and breaks the adults' rules.

Product features

- He's a video game character who goes on missions round the neighbourhood – skateboarding and cleaning teeth in different ways to get out of trouble.
- Video and game offered in PC and Gameboy.
- Stickers, CDs from newsagents, guerilla marketing.
- Interactive, subversive, fun.
- Unconventional, rule-breaking, individual.

'Cocktails' (Figure 14.4)

Insight

Experimentation – 'I need to experiment and try things in different ways'.

Benefit

No need for a toothbrush, plus a different experience every time you clean your teeth.

Figure 14.3

Figure 14.4

Product features

- Cocktail bar of flavours and sensations and optional delivery systems:
  - bomb – mix of flavours and textures;
  - syringe/squirting dispenser – squirt into mouth, brush with finger, covers with different tastes and textures;
  - pens with textured nibs that you can dip in different flavour sensations.

The strongest idea generated by our piece of research for this chapter seems to be 'Mouth sensations', because it works from such a strong insight. The raison d'etre is the ritual of application and swilling, which then achieves the goal of cleaning teeth and rewards the child with the tactile and visual sensations. It also allows the child to discover new and exciting ways to experience tooth-cleaning.

In contrast, 'Dentyls' were inspired by a much looser insight of a child's need to play – and it shows. Built-in obsolescence is the major weakness. In addition, the parents will only recognize 'play value' as its justification, not efficacy. The parents need to believe in the efficacy of the product if they are to support its purchase.

'Frank the hip hop rabbit' also draws on a genuine insight about kids, but it is a more familiar one. As such, any marketing communications agency plus their media shop would have no difficulty in hitting upon this sort of idea to motivate kids' interest – simply because the insight is quite obvious and has been played out in many ways before. The danger is that it is not new and may therefore not distinguish itself from many other products using the same insight.

To sum up, 'Mouth sensations' leverage a profound insight about the way kids interact with their world and in so doing will satisfy both parents and children. This idea satisfies two criteria we feel are important: it is both fresh and inspiring.

At this stage of the process we have four rough concepts, which may be taken through to further concept development and, potentially, testing. Since the purpose of this chapter was simply to demonstrate the process of turning observations into insights, we have not taken these ideas further.

THE FINAL STEP IN THE PROCESS

Assuming that the scenario of training, observation and insight/idea generation had been followed up to this point, there is one remaining step worth mentioning. It is our experience that the process of direct consumer contact between staff in an organization and consumers can lead to the generation of a vast amount of 'data'. These data can be in many formats including video, collections of artefacts, photographs, and so on. In addition, many of the 'data' simply exist as the experience of those taking part, they may therefore only exist in the heads of those who have collected them.

There is, therefore, an essential step of collecting and collating the data in a meaningful and logical way. This is not only so that others can access the information, but also so that a long-term database of continuous learning can be generated. Whilst it is beyond the scope of this chapter to detail how this step may be achieved, it is a major task in itself. Its importance should not be underestimated in the whole process of driving long term insight from observation.

CONCLUSIONS

Our belief is that generating insight from observation needs discipline, time and focus – using experienced leaders. It is essential that those undertaking observations have some formal training up front if they are to be really effective. This is not a simple process. Creative consumers and indeed internal marketing, research or other teams are good at running away with product ideas, but you can't necessarily expect them to have the experience to develop insights. This skill requires training and time to develop – and not everyone is good at it. So it would be a mistake to assume that every brand manager who goes out into consumers' homes will automatically be able to generate amazing insights. If they don't, then not only is this a failure of the consumer contact programme, it is also damaging for the individual, since they may feel inadequate for the task.

Following on from the first stage of the observation process, insight-generation sessions need to be run as dedicated events – not simply as a group of people having a quick chat around the coffee machine. This seems to be very important and also gives time to reflect on the output before going on to ideation. Time needs to be taken to pause for this stage properly.

At the idea-generation stage, careful control by a very experienced facilitator is essential. Insight platforms (headings) are a great start, but there are many different interpretations of a word – like discovery – so we should only ideate against insights that have been worked through and pushed to the extreme, so there is no ambiguity. It is tempting to stray away from the insight and certainly easier to come up with an 'idea' and then try to justify it. A parallel to this idea would be production-led new product development, where products are made because they can be, rather than because they are needed or relevant to consumers.

So, going back to the initial question posed by this chapter – are consumer contact programmes a good thing? The answer is yes and no. Handled properly, the evidence is that such programmes deliver quantum leaps in consumer understanding and insight. Handled properly though, they can take up a lot of time, lead to vast amounts of data and result in not much more than a few people feeling they have a slightly better grip on how their consumers think. It is worth it if you get it right. Fresh and resonant insights can lead to breakthrough thinking.

Chapter Fifteen

Build Strong Brands and Develop Communications: An Argument for Using Consumer Need States over Values

Michael O'Donohue[a] and Tamsin Addison[b]

> *In this chapter we highlight why consumer need states provide a better platform for understanding consumers' behaviour and their brand relationships.*

INTRODUCTION

Many Asian markets, particularly though not uniquely FMCG markets, are often characterized by an unusual degree of single brand dominance. A common experience is that Usage & Attitudes studies frequently reveal that one brand has 40–50% market share. Moreover, it is often the case that the market structure has remained relatively stable over a considerable period of time.

[a]Marketing Science Specialist, McKinsey.
[b]Managing Director, Decision Science.

Market Research Best Practice. Edited by P. Mouncey and F. Wimmer.

Within the last few years there has been a substantial interest in market segmentation in many Asian markets, with an increasing number of companies now looking to market segmentation as an important means of increasing market share and reducing the dominance of market leaders. As a consequence, the output of market segmentation is being used increasingly to shape brand positioning and determine the right brand values – with considerable implications for marketing and communication activities.

Mirroring trends in other parts of the world, a substantial proportion of market segmentation (though certainly not all) employs consumer-values-based variables, such as attitudes, psychographics (VALs) and lifestyle, as the main variables (notable exceptions include the Conversion Model^{TM}, which segments the market based on brand commitment).

In this context, it is important that there is a clear understanding of the drawbacks and limitations of using these variables. Equally, alternative approaches to segmentation should be borne in mind, particularly when the objectives are intended to drive branding and communications decisions.

This chapter falls naturally into two sections. Initially, it will outline the drawbacks and limitations of segmentation using values-related data, such as attitudes, psychographics and lifestyle data. The second section will define and explain need states. Through this we hope to highlight, using a number of examples, why consumer need states provide a better platform for understanding consumers' brand choice. This section will also outline how need states can be leveraged in the creation of brand values and advertising communications.

THE DRAWBACKS OF VALUE AND LIFESTYLE SEGMENTATION

It should be made clear from the outset that it is *not* our view that market segmentation using values, lifestyle or psychographic data is wrong. Rather, our considered view is that, specifically in the context of building stronger brands and developing marketing communications, these variables often have inherent drawbacks that mean they are less relevant.

The trouble is that using purely values-related variables, such as attitudinal, lifestyle or psychographic variables, as the starting blocks for explaining brand relationships and behaviour is inherently limited. This reflects the fact that the output will focus necessarily on identifying groups with similar or different values, attitudes or lifestyles, and not on identifying groups with different brand relationships.

In the end, the output tends to describe the customer accurately, but rarely does it serve to describe the relationship between the customer and the brand. Therefore, there is a gap between the data in hand and the desired output. In this gap is the danger that the output is segments which, though heterogeneous, do not really vary in terms of their relationship to the brand (Riquier, Luxton and Sharp, 1997).

To compound this problem, in bridging this gap it is often the case that (questionable) assumptions are made about the relationship between these attributes and differences in consumer reaction to different marketing. As Paul Feldwick has been quoted as saying in an article reviewing the output of a lifestyle segmentation, 'it's easy to get the numbers and to massage them'.

We certainly don't question the need to understand who the consumers are. However, understanding the consumer does not mean that we understand their relationship with the brand. Moreover, we would argue strongly that without the understanding of the customers' relationships with the brand, it is impossible to develop the relationship further or to enhance commitment effectively.

SEGMENTATION IN ASIA: FURTHER COMPLICATIONS

In addition, we would argue strongly that the Asian context further compounds the difficulties in undertaking segmentation studies using values-related data.

One of the most notable differences between Asian and Western societies is that they are considerably more consensual than individualistic in orientation (Robinson, 1996). Cooper and Pinijarom (1996) use the term 'IC' dimension (individualism and collectivism) to summarize fundamental differences in values. By collectivism, they mean that behaviours and values are more often determined by the collective group of which people are members – family, work groups and social networks. By individualism, they refer to the fact that behaviours and values are more often determined by the individual through personal choice and individual orientation.

The consequences for brand development of this difference in orientation are outlined in a paper by Robinson (1996), which provides an overview of the cultural dimensions and a framework for thinking about cultural implications in a marketing context. While this is important, we believe that it also has considerable implications for the use of segmentation based on values-related data in Asia.

Our experience suggests that segmentation based on lifestyle and attitudinal data in Asian markets tends to reveal that attitudes and values are often very similar across socio-demographic/economic groups; more so than in Western markets. This reflects the strong degree of homogeneity that is inherent in Asian society and the degree to which values are created and shared collectively – collectivism. The consequences of this are that when a segmentation on values-related data is performed, there are actually few (meaningful) points of differentiation between clusters.

A longer-term problem is the absence of stability over time, since attitudes do not present a consistent base from which to start. This manifests itself in difficulties in replicating results and, in extreme cases, substantial changes in the relative size of clusters within a short timescale.

Cautious design of attitudinal questions and batteries does ameliorate the problem to a certain extent. But this does not remove the essential point, which is that Asian societies tend to be more homogeneous and that data derived from values does not effectively discriminate amongst consumers.

Robinson (1996) also points to a potential procedural problem in collecting psychographic, lifestyle and attitudinal data using face-to-face interviewing in Asia. He suggests that when collected using a face-to-face methodology, the data are often contaminated by 'face'.

> *'The whole question of "face" ensures that not many Asian respondents will honestly admit to personal feeling about oneself. . . Such data have to be collected by a more confidential (e.g. self-completion) approach, or one is simply not getting the truth from an Asian respondent.'* (Robinson, 1996)

AN ALTERNATIVE APPROACH

An alternative approach to segmentation using values is through the use of *consumer need states*. The advantage of need states thinking is that it acknowledges that people consume in different ways. It takes account of the fact that consumers have different need states, which vary according to numerous factors such as the environment, the occasion and their mood. Thus, the same observable behaviour may be the result of different need states. Since need states are related strongly to consumer behaviour, they can be leveraged strongly in the creation of meaningful brand values. Moreover, the learning from consumer need states can be applied to consumer communications to enhance brand relevance and affinity.

DEFINING CONSUMER NEED STATES

The starting point for need state based research is that all consumption behaviour is not the same. At first glance this is a fairly innocuous and self-evident statement. Perhaps so, but our belief is that this statement has profound and considerable implications for how we understand consumer behaviour. Moreover, we would posit that it is significantly at odds with widely held marketing perspectives in which the consistency of behavioural motivation is an inherent assumption.

Marketing as a discipline has embraced some of the psychological work on motivational drivers. Most are familiar with Maslow's hierarchy of needs. Maslow suggests that after basic physiological needs have been taken care of, desires and wants take over. Clearly, today's consumers can be seen to be operating at the higher end of the hierarchy.

While useful, armed only with Maslow's hierarchy we are clearly ill-equipped to deal with the complexities of the modern consumer. To begin to understand these complexities requires a larger framework – a framework in which the consumer, the context, the product and the brand are reflexive. We believe that in consumer need states, we have the beginning of such a framework.

Understanding consumer need states means examining the complex web of moods, emotions and cognitions that impinge on and inform product choice and product consumption. However, this is not all. It also means understanding behaviour within the context and environment in which it is taking place. The basic assumption behind need states thinking is that people feel and behave differently in different contexts and on different occasions.

Let us take the example of the use of make-up and cosmetics. To understand the different need states, we employed a combination of qualitative and ethnographic techniques using a series of depth interviews and individual observations. On initial examination, we found that most women had a routine when making-up. This routine facilitated a consistency of results and finish. However, a closer examination revealed that this 'routine' had many variations within it. Sometimes these were subtle changes that the woman was not even aware or conscious of – a change of shading or colour. Sometimes they were more obvious – using different brands. Need states thinking helped us to understand the behaviour and its implications fully.

We found that on different occasions women would vary their behaviour. Having identified all of the types of occasions, we classified them into three main types:

1. Daily routine – e.g. before going out to work in the morning.
2. Socializing – e.g. going out with friends.
3. Special occasions – e.g. going to dinner with a boyfriend.

Clearly, one of the main purposes of making-up is to enhance attractiveness. Another obvious benefit is the increase in self-confidence that women feel when they are wearing make-up. Delving deeper, we learned the greatest need when making-up prior to going to work is the need to look professional and feel confident. Laddering this back, we discovered that for many women, making-up is 'part of the armour a woman uses to protect herself'. Some office environments are male-dominated and, as a consequence, women often feel uncomfortable and insecure. A well made-up face serves as a mask behind which some women feel they can hide or cover up their insecurities.

One of the consequences of this is that women pay particular attention to the colours they choose. In particular, women tend to choose less vibrant (more conservative) lipsticks and eyeliner. We also noted that prior to important business meetings they would spend significantly more time on their make-up.

However, going out with friends yields a whole different set of emotional responses – anticipation, excitement and good humour. The main need state associated with this is the need to feel young. This reflects the environment and also the fact that sometimes friendships are tinged with an element of competitiveness about looking young. In particular, women do not wish to age faster than their contemporaries and strive to maintain youthful looks.

On these occasions we noted that women paid particular attention to foundation, often cleansing and toning before applying foundation. It was also evident that women were choosing younger and brighter colours. To a certain degree on these occasions, women are 'playing' with their make-up.

On the other hand, going out with a boyfriend stimulates a woman's need to be loved. When elaborated on further, we discovered that this had three prongs. First, the desire to look good because it makes her feel good. Second is the desire 'to look good for your partner'. Third, the desire to make her partner feel good about himself. In effect, these desires are part of a large virtuous circle – feeding into one another. These occasions were characterized by spending a substantial amount of attention and effort, and little expense was spared. Here, women chose more expensive cosmetics and high-class and sophisticated brands.

What this example illustrates clearly is that behaviour does not have a single, either cognitive/rational or emotional, source. Rather, to understand consumption behaviour we must understand both the inner influences (cognitive and emotional) and the context in which a behaviour is taking place. Leith and Riley (1998) sum this up neatly as 'the inner and outer influences (or triggers) impacting on an individual'. In essence, understanding the context in which a behaviour occurs is critical to understanding fully the behaviour itself.

DEVELOPING BRAND MESSAGES AND COMMUNICATION FROM NEED STATES

Understanding the need state can contribute to our understanding of the relationship between the brand and the consumers. We can give an example from the alcohol market in Korea. Korean traditional liquor is called soju. It is very powerful, usually around 23%, and its main characteristic is that it results in inebriation very quickly. It is usually drunk in social gatherings with relatives, friends or colleagues. While brand loyalty appeared to be high, we discovered that most consumers operated a repertoire of brands, which changed depending on the context. Need states helped us to understand why, and the different relationships consumers had with each brand.

Brand A: 'I drink this when I am with my very close friends. We are very relaxed together, we talk and we want to get very drunk very quickly.'

Brand B: 'I drink when I am with work colleagues or in front of seniors – because this is the most popular brand in the market and everyone drinks it.'

Brand C: 'I drink this occasionally, when I am with my girlfriend, because it is very mild.'

Probing further, we discovered that the relationship between Brand A and the consumer was based on heritage. This is the brand consumers drink when they are with their friends, feeling nostalgic and reminiscing about old times. On the other hand, the relationship with Brand B is mediated through the need for social approval. This, and other brand imagery data, helped us to understand the decline in Brand A's market share and suggested the need for refreshment and invigoration of the brand's values.

In terms of developing brands and marketing communications, the primary benefit is that when working with need states, one is working with 'the raw stuff of human needs and motivation' (Goodyear, 1996). This facilitates the creation and development of an entirely customer-driven perspective. Since need states are related strongly to consumer behaviour, they can be leveraged strongly in the creation of meaningful brand values, and the learning from consumer need states can be applied to consumer communications to enhance brand relevance and affinity.

In the cosmetics example, need states helped us to a deeper under-standing of why women choose and consume specific products. In a subsequent quantitative phase, we undertook to:

- measure the prevalence and frequency with which different need states occur;
- determine the perceived values and positioning of different cosmetic brands.

When the findings from both qualitative and quantitative stages were synthesized, the output had significant implications for the client's brand positioning and communications. In particular, positioning to address a need state enhanced brand relevance and affinity. In addition to this, the finding also contributed to initiatives in other areas of the marketing mix:

- in-store promotions;
- packaging;
- pricing;
- product formulation.

CONCLUSIONS

In conclusion, we believe that segmentation based on values-related vari-ables can provide us with a valuable understanding of the consumer. However, segmentation based on these variables provides an inherently limited picture of the relationship between the brand and the consumer. Therefore, its utility in building brand values and developing communi-cations is limited.

We would argue that when the brand is the focus of attention, alternative approaches to segmentation on values-related data ought to be considered. In particular, we believe that need states, which place an emphasis on the interaction between inner and outer influences, contribute to the formation of a better understanding of the relationship between consumer and brand. This provides a better platform to drive the development of brand values and marketing communications.

REFERENCES

Anschuetz, N. (1997), Building brand popularity: The myth of segmenting to brand success. *Journal of Advertising Research*, **37**(1), 63–66.

Cooper, P. and Pinijarom, J. (1996), *The role of qualitative research in Asia*. Proceedings of the 1st East and South East Asian Conference, ESOMAR. Marketing in Asia: The contribution of research. pp. 31–45.

Goodyear, M. (1996), Divided by a common language. *Journal of the Market Research Society*, **38**(2), 105–122.

Gordon, W. (1994), Taking brand repertoires seriously. *Journal of Brand Management*, **2**(1), 25–30.

Forsyth, J., Gupta, S., Haldar, S., Kaul, A. and Kettle, K. (1999), A segmentation you can act on. *The McKinsey Quarterly*, **3**, 6–15.

Leith, A. and Riley, N. (1998), Understanding Need States and their Role in Developing Successful Marketing Strategies. *Journal of the Market Research Society*, **40**(1), 25–32.

Maslow, A.H. (1954), *Motivation and Personality*. Harper & Row.

Riquier, C., Luxton, S. and Sharp, B. (1997), Probabilistic segmentation modelling. *Journal of the Market Research Society*, **39**(4), 571–587.

Robinson, C. (1996), Asian culture – the marketing consequences. *Journal of the Market Research Society*, **38**(2), 55–62.

Chapter Sixteen

Cross-media Measurement: The New Medium Necessitates a New Approach to Marketing Mix Measurement

Rex Briggs[a]

Cross-media and ROI measurement is critical for marketers contending with the Internet and increasingly fragmented traditional media. Return-On-Marketing-Objectives (ROMO) has proven to be a breakthrough, providing accurate answers that older systems (econometric models and brand tracking) haven't.

INTRODUCTION

The Dove Nutrium Bar Cross-media Return-on-Marketing Objective (ROMO) case study represents a breakthrough in marketing mix measurement–it answers the question of where 'online' fits into the marketing mix. In answering this question, the case study applies a combination of best practice research techniques, which this chapter will review. The study, led by the author in partnership with Unilever, MSN, the ARF and the IAB, provides a real-world, side-by-side, dollar-for-dollar

[a]CEO, Marketing Evolution.

Market Research Best Practice. Edited by P. Mouncey and F. Wimmer.
© 2007 John Wiley & Sons, Limited.

comparison of television, magazine, radio, and online effectiveness. The methodology has now been replicated and refined for dozens of additional marketers and expanded to measure radio, out-of-home, events, direct mail, e-mail, websites, planned PR, wireless/mobile, in-store display and more. The findings shed new light on the complementary nature of on-line and offline advertising and reinforce the idea of 'surround sound marketing.' However, the purpose of this chapter is not to review the findings. Rather, the purpose of this chapter is to examine the use of best industry practice to develop this breakthrough research approach. The chapter begins with the history and challenges of cross-media measurement and then dissects the groundbreaking ROMO methodology and analysis used to overcome these challenges.

MARKETING MIX TAKES THE STAGE

Billions of dollars are spent each year promoting brands through a range of media, including television, magazines, radio events, out-of-home and online advertising. What if balancing the marketing mix could make this investment 5% more efficient in achieving the marketer's goals? Even a small improvement in marketing productivity could be worth millions.

The hope of improving results within the same advertising budget is the core argument that has fuelled the growth in marketing mix modelling. Think of a marketer with annual sales of $400 million dollars. A 5% increase in sales is $20 million dollars, without spending any more on marketing. But many marketers lack the tools to sort through marketing ROI in the complex media environment of today.

Many of the market research tools to measure marketing were developed in the 1960s and 1970s, when the conditions studied were simple. Marketing research such as matched-market tests, regression models and telephone, tracking studies has made some contribution to helping marketers understand the proper balance in the marketing mix, but all the old approaches have fallen short of properly measuring online advertising's contribution.

Why do these older methods fail to measure online's contribution? What has been done to date to measure online's role in the marketing mix? What new research methodologies can we devise to answer marketers' nagging question of where online fits in the mix?

We will first address the research efforts to measure online's contribution, and the objections to the previous research. We will then turn to a discussion of why the old research approaches (designed to measure traditional mass-media) do a poor job of measuring the relatively new medium of online. The balance of the chapter addresses the solution to the measurement challenge and details the ROMO methodology and analysis by using Dove Nutrium Bar as a case study.

A BRIEF HISTORY OF MEASURING ONLINE VERSUS OFFLINE (1996 TO 2001)

The first web advertisements began appearing in late 1994 on websites such as HotWired. Within less than two years, marketing researchers responded to marketers' need for quantitatively understanding the value of these new ad units with the first advertising effectiveness study. Over the next five years, several studies would tackle the thorny question of how online advertising compares to offline advertising. Figure 16.1 provides a timeline of these key studies.

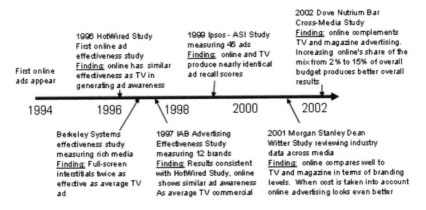

Figure 16.1 Timeline of studies comparing online and offline advertising.

I had the privilege of developing and leading the first research effort to measure online advertising effectiveness back in 1996. The main goal of the 1996 HotWired Advertising Effectiveness Study was to measure the effect of online ads in the real world using a classic exposed/control experimental design.

The way the study worked is that we randomly sampled those visiting the Hotwired homepage. Before the homepage loaded, a survey invitation took over the page. After completing a very brief survey, which collected an e-mail address and basic demographics, users were 'returned to their regularly scheduled programming'. All respondents were returned to the same page; however, half were blindly given the 'exposed' ad and half the 'control' ad (by blindly, we mean that consumers experienced exactly the same in both control and exposed groups and neither was aware that the ad they were seeing was part of research).

We followed up a day later with an e-mail invitation to answer 'a few more questions'. The surveys were exactly the same for 'control' and 'exposed' respondents and measured the brand relationship metrics (awareness, brand image, purchase intent) for the 'exposed' brand. The control group provided the baseline branding level and the exposed group showed if there was a statistically significant lift in the key metrics (Briggs, 1996).

By virtue of the gold standard experimental design, we could isolate the effects of offline from online marketing, thus precisely quantifying the independent value of online advertising. While this gave us a best practice for measuring the independent contribution of an online advertisement to the overall branding levels, we wanted a point of comparison to traditional advertising. In sum, this research had taught us that online advertising could increase branding metrics; the question that remained was, 'how do these results compare to television or magazine advertising performance?'

From the beginning, we stretched to compare the results of online to magazine and television advertisements. Thanks to a colleague's innovative thinking, we compared the three online ads we measured in the HotWired study to a database of real-world magazine and television ads (Briggs and Hollis, 1997). Specifically, Millward Brown had a measurement of television and magazines' effect on ad recall based upon the first exposure. Our measurement of ad recall for the online ads paralleled the methodology and they felt we could compare the data. The finding was that these three online ads compared quite favourably to the averages of offline ads in terms of ad recall.

This research process and online/offline comparison was repeated in 1997 with four full-screen 'interstitial' advertisements (Briggs, 1997) and then again for twelve online banners measured in the 1997 IAB Advertising Effectiveness Study (Briggs and McDonald, 1997). Comparison of the online ads to the average for television and magazine ads again showed favourable results for online advertising.

While this approach provided an innovative comparison of online and offline advertising, it had its share of problems. In particular, two problems concerned me.

First, we were comparing online and offline against 'advertising recall,' the only comparable variable Millward Brown had available across media. Most marketers seemed less interested in advertising recall and would have rather seen data on sales, brand image or brand awareness – but that was beyond Millward Brown's measurements.

Second, and more seriously, we were comparing specific ads to averages for television and magazine advertising. While comparing norms is a common practice, critics are correct when they complain that such a comparison of norms is not precise. Each brand has unique characteristics in the marketplace, and therefore a proper side-by-side study of the same brand advertising across media is a better answer to the relative effectiveness of online versus offline. In other words, the marketers were asking for a side-by-side comparison of the same brand across online and offline advertising to answer the question of online/offline advertising effectiveness.

Side-by-side comparisons: Ipsos-ASI responds

While I was hard at work developing real-world measurement for online advertising, the research firm Ipsos-ASI was hard at work retooling its 'laboratory setting' television pretest to work for measuring online advertisements.

What the laboratory setting of television pretest research lacks in real-world measurement, it adds in greater control of the consumer experience. By directing consumers to do something specific, like watch a television programme, the research may bias the attentiveness of the consumer (so called memory priming effects), but the benefit is inexpensive side-by-side measurement of one advertisement versus another.

Typically, the side-by-side comparison has been used to determine whether one television advertisement would work better than another for the same brand. To get a mental picture of how these studies work, imagine that you are strolling through a shopping mall and a perky interviewer asks you if you'd like to answer some marketing research questions in exchange for 10 dollars. You agree.

You and a few dozen people are put in one of two rooms. In the front of the room is a large television. You watch a thirty-minute television programme and then are given a survey about the television commercials. You are asked questions such as 'Do you recall seeing advertising for Brand X?' At the same time you were watching your programme, the same programme was playing in the next room, however, a different commercial for Brand X was playing. By comparing the two groups, the marketing research firm suggests they can judge which advertisement is stronger.

Now imagine the same two rooms in the research facility. This time, instead of a television in both rooms, the second room contains computers. Half the respondents are directed randomly to the room with the television, and the other half are directed to the room with the Internet.

You are part of the second group and find yourself in the room with the computer. You surf a website and are then asked the question about whether you recall an ad for Brand X.

The results from those in the room with the Internet are compared against the respondents in the room that saw the television advertisement. The researcher judges the relative effectiveness of television versus online advertising.

Such a study comparing online to television was conducted on 45 different advertisements, for major brands such as Gap, Ralston-Purina and Kraft. In a presentation to the ARF, the report's author concluded:

> *'If we put ten people in a room, show them a television programme, turn it off and ask them how many remember the ad for Brand X. . .four will. If we put ten people in a room, show them some content on a website, turn it off and ask them how many remember the ad for Brand X. . .four will.'*

> (Foley, 1999)

In other words, the study found that online ad recall is about the same as television ad recall. This 1999 research by Ipsos-ASI answered the client's request for a side-by-side comparison of online and offline advertising for the same brand. The research was ground-breaking in its own right.

However, those wishing to dismiss the conclusions found it easy to point to the fact that the research was conducted in an artificial research environment – not the real world. The critics reasoned that perhaps the results might be different if the television and online advertisements were measured in the real world, as opposed to forcing prescreened people to watch the ads in a research room.

What these critics wanted was a 'real-world', side-by-side comparison of online and offline advertising – not side-by-side forced exposure 'pre-test' of the ads. Furthermore, they wanted to know the dollar-for-dollar comparison of the two media – not just a comparison of ad recall percentages. In other words, they wanted to know if I invest in online, what is the ROI, and how does it compare to the ROI from television, magazine or other advertising?

Enter Morgan Stanley Dean Witter

In February 2001, the investment firm Morgan Stanley Dean Witter completed an exhaustive study of the financial value of online and offline advertising and direct response vehicles. The basis of the study was the collection of advertising effectiveness metrics, cost data, response rates and so forth. According to the report:

> 'We have conducted an in-depth analysis of data gathered from many studies by AdRelevance, Avenue A, The Cable Advertising Bureau, C.E. Hooper, Inc., The Direct Marketing Association, Dynamic Logic, Media Dynamics, NCH, The magazine Advertising Bureau, and Nielsen Media Research to form our conclusions.'

The report was certainly a milestone in that it drew from so many sources in an attempt to provide an answer to the question of how online stacks up against offline advertising. Furthermore, it broke new ground by doing what financial analysts do so well, and that is making a dollar-for-dollar comparison.

The conclusion is best summed up by quoting from the report directly:

> 'Our primary conclusion is that Internet advertising banners are a cost-effective branding tool. . . Banners exceed or are as good as magazines, newspapers and television in generating brand recall and brand interest. . . When branding is considered in terms of cost effectiveness, banners look even better.'
>
> (Morgan Stanley Dean Witter Equity Research, 2001)

This research was certainly intriguing. But, by comparing averages from a variety of sources, it was difficult to say with certainty the relative effectiveness of a specific online advertisement versus a specific offline advertisement.

Despite the converging validity of the 19 real-world ads measured in the HotWired, Berkeley Systems and IAB studies that I had worked to create, and the 45 measured by Ipsos-ASI and the exhaustive Morgan Stanley Dean Witter analysis, critics would claim that the 'Holy Grail' for quantifying online within the marketing mix is a real-world, side-by-side measurement of ads for the same marketers running in online and offline vehicles at the same time.

In the author's opinion, it would be beneficial for research to go beyond 'online versus offline' and begin to look at online alongside offline advertising – to see how the two might complement one another and provide a more balanced and effective marketing mix.

FROM ONLINE VERSUS OFFLINE TO ONLINE'S ROLE IN THE MARKETING MIX

The previous research compared online to television and other media. In the 1999 ESOMAR paper that Horst Stipp and I presented at NetEffects (Briggs and Stipp, 1999), we argued that we should strive to measure online advertising in context with offline advertising. We suggested that there were hints of online and offline synergy in the early research studies. The challenge was how to measure online's contribution to the marketing mix.

This is the challenge that a collection of dedicated marketers and researchers would rise to address with the Dove Nutrium Bar case study. But, before we discuss how the Dove Nutrium Bar case study provided a 'real-world', side-by-side, dollar-for-dollar comparison of online and offline advertising, let us address the broader challenge of measuring online's role in the marketing mix. Specifically, let's address why older marketing mix measurement approaches generally fail to measure online's contribution (and why we needed to develop a better measurement approach).

The failure of traditional marketing mix measurement and the need to create a new measurement system

With the growth of online advertising, some marketers (including myself) have turned to the old tried and true methodologies in the hope of shedding some light on the value of their online marketing investment relative to their offline spending.

The problem is, these 'tried and true' methodologies fail to measure online's contribution in all but the most specialized of cases. The simple reason is that the older methodologies, designed to measure television, are not well suited to measuring online advertising. In fact, if marketers are looking to have a bright spotlight focused on the value of the online spend, the best that these old methodologies can yield is a dim, flickering candle.

At the heart of the problem is the fact that online is simply a small part of most marketers' current advertising plans. To measure online's contribution properly, the researcher must know who has been exposed and who has not. Consider for a moment the traditional approaches, and the unique challenges of measuring online. Regression models, matched markets, telephone tracking – each suffers from key limitations when it comes to measuring online advertising's contribution.

At the heart of the measurement problem is the need to identify who is exposed to what media at a respondent level. Most of the old marketing mix methodologies side-step this issue by measuring at the population, rather than respondent, level – and with mass media that works just fine. If there were attempts made to measure respondents' opportunity to see, the probability of exposure calculations were very simplistic and inaccurate. We needed a more sophisticated approach.

There are solutions to this conundrum. For each of the traditional research approaches, we will highlight how to update the methodology to measure online's influence.

Modelling of advertising and sales data

The idea of econometrics (or marketing mix modelling if you prefer) is to take the marketing inputs, such as the level of spend, and regress them against the outcome variables, such as sales. Whether one uses multiple regression or more complex neural, Liseral, Bayesian, or another modelling technique that looks at the total marketing inputs versus outputs, each runs into a common challenge. The challenge is that without knowing who specifically is exposed to online advertising, and who is not, the tiny amount being spent to deliver online ads to only a few consumers simply washes out of these models as a rounding error. I call this the 'small investment problem'.

This is not to say that modelling does not hold promise, however. Since online represents only about 2% of most advertising budgets, it is too small to be meaningful when modelled against the variance inherent in weekly (or daily) sales figures from aggregated store or panel-level data.

Regression modelling (and its analytic cousins) can be made to work if one of two conditions is met:

1. The marketer makes online a significant portion of their budget (such as 20% or more) so that the model can better detect the influence.
2. The marketer determines which respondent is exposed to which media.

Determining who is and who is not exposed to online ads is probably more palpable to an advertiser who may be reticent to plunk down 20% of the budget on online for the purposes of conducting a proper marketing mix model analysis. Determining who is exposed, and the influence on sales, will probably entail some type of empanelment approach. Such an approach can link sales to respondents for whom online advertising exposure is known. For example, based on some of my consulting advice, IRI and DoubleClick linked IRI panelists with DoubleClick's ad server, thus enabling exposed/not exposed experimental design for online advertising. We've repeated this approach for Kraft, Procter & Gamble, Nestlé and others, using a variety of sales panels and frequent shopper card databases. This can be combined with offline advertising data to perform a proper marketing mix analysis on the influence of sales among those not exposed to online ads, thus providing a full picture of online and offline advertising's influence on sales.

Matched markets

Matched market measurement has been used for many years to evaluate television, radio and other marketing programmes. Rather than spending nationally, marketing programmes can be cost-effectively tested with a small investment. The way this works is, rather than spending 20% of the marketing budget nationally, certain markets are chosen so that media can be *heavied up*, thus allowing the marketer to measure the impact on sales compared to the control matched market.

This approach has worked for offline media, but it fails to work for online advertising. It does not fail for the typical problem of actually finding well-matched markets (which can be a problem with matched-market studies). It fails because online's regional targeting capability works well for avoiding advertising waste, but generally is limited when it comes to helping the marketer *heavy up* a specific market.

Yes, there is geographic targeting for online ads, but it works differently than geographic targeting for traditional media. Currently, online publishers who sell geographic targeting do so to avoid waste. In other words, if I buy online ads only in the New York City ZIP codes, the online ad server sends ads only to those web browsers that can be *confirmed* to some degree of certainty to be in New York City. If the ad server cannot tell where the user is based (which is a big chunk of the time), it simply skips over the user and does not serve them the regional ad, even if the person does, in fact, reside in New York City.

Why might the ad server skip over someone? Let us say the user dials into America online. Unless the user has provided declared data on where the user is based, the ad server reads the user location as Dulles, Virginia, which is where AOL is based. The ad server has been programmed to skip over AOL users that lack declared data, since it cannot determine where the user is really based. Or, if consumers use their company's corporate network, their location may appear to be at corporate headquarters in one city, even if they are based in another office a thousand miles away. The online local ad serving is a godsend for those marketers wishing to avoid waste. The consequence of this technology solution for avoiding waste is that a marketer generally cannot *heavy up* online to the degree necessary in the market for the purpose of research.

The geographic ad-serving technology is great if I want to avoid serving ads to people outside of New York City. Even though many people within New York City are likely to be skipped over, the marketer gets those that the ad server can determine with certainty are based in New York City. But if I want to get the highest possible online reach within New York City for purposes of a matched-market test, then *skipping over* those that cannot be identified as living in the city makes it very difficult, perhaps impossible, to heavy up a market without contaminating the control market.

Therefore, given the current state of geographic targeting online, matched markets aren't an option for cross-media measurement. As with regression modelling, we can overcome this challenge by devising a strategy to measure at the respondent level who is exposed to online advertising and who is not exposed. If online ads can be served to panelists based on location, then matched markets can be used to detect different media combinations. For one of Marketing Evolution's clients, radio ads were in ten cities and online was national, but included a control group. We could therefore measure the combined effect of online and radio and compare it to the effect of radio only or online only, but we were only able to execute this analysis because we were using a special technology that could detect on a respondent level who was and who was not exposed to online ads.

Telephone tracking

Telephone surveys have been used for decades to examine points in time prior to a television ad airing and the points in time after. The innovation more than thirty years ago was to shift from waves of surveys to continuous surveys. Moving averages of branding metrics were trended against advertising levels. Periods of hiatus offer the opportunity to measure the pre-campaign versus the post campaign effects. Can telephone-tracking studies be used to measure online or other smaller-reach media contributions? The answer generally is 'no'. Telephone tracking does not measure online or other smaller-reach media advertising accurately.

The telephone tracking approach runs headfirst into the *small investment* problem. If only one in ten consumers is exposed to online ads, how can telephone tracking detect it? Even if exposure to online ads boosted sales by 10 points, the tracking measurement would only measure a one-points gain (10 point × 10% reach = 1 point). And, given the typical sample size of 50 to 100 respondents per week, this increase of one point would fail to pass statistical significance testing.

In other words, unless the reach of online (or other small-reach media) is in the 45% or greater range,[1] the top-down telephone-tracking approach will mask the effect of online advertising exposure, even if online's effect is substantial.

This is not just a problem with online advertising; magazine, radio, and newspaper promotions are also penalized by the telephone-tracking bias toward *big-reach* television advertising campaigns.

The solution to the small investment problem is to determine who is and who is not exposed. For online, we can determine who is and who is not exposed by moving the survey online and *tagging* all online ads.

Tagging ads is a procedure that results in a cookie being set each time an advertisement is delivered. This cookie can be read automatically when a consumer is surveyed randomly. For each respondent, we can simply observe whether or not he or she has been exposed to the advertisement. This now allows us to measure the effect of online exposure, even if the online campaign is relatively small.

Continuous sampling with cookie ad-tracking

Online surveys to measure real-world effects of online advertising have been in practice since 1996. The approach has been executed on hundreds of campaigns by a variety of research firms and has received wide industry support. Expanding this proven research approach to measure cross-media campaigns holds tremendous promise.

---

[1] The 45% is based on 75 interviews per week over three months, and uses 10% lift from online as the minimum level statistically significant at the 90% confidence level (using a one-tailed test). A marketer calculates the percentage reach by calculating the online reach (45%), the measurable lift from online (let us assume 10%) the starting branding level (let us assume 50%) and the total sample size over a period of time (let us assume 900–75 over 12 weeks). The calculation is as follows: 50%) baseline × 10% online lift × 45% reach = 2.25%. Statistical significance is calculated as 1.28 × square root of PQ/n – that is: 1.28 × square root of 50% × 1–50%/900 = 2.1%. A marketer can use this same equation to solve for other scenarios to ensure adequate sample size and reach levels.

There are three key benefits of conducting the survey online, and one potential drawback. First the benefits: not only can we measure online's contribution, even if the spending level is fairly small, but another wonderful benefit of moving the survey online is the ability to measure magazines' impact more precisely.

Magazine campaigns typically have lower reach than television and are often more difficult to measure properly. By conducting the survey online, we can show respondents covers of magazines and ask 'Which of the following magazines have you read or looked through?' This cover-recognition-based measure links back to the vehicle reach and is consistent with the way that magazine advertising is bought and sold.

A third benefit is the ability to achieve larger sample sizes than could be achieved with telephone, face-to-face or mail surveys. For the Dove Nutrium Bar study, we surveyed 12 990 consumers over six weeks. The cost of conducting such a survey via telephone would have been many times more expensive.

The one downside of conducting the survey online is that we are systematically excluding those that don't use the Internet at all. How big of an issue is this? Not very, because it is easy to address. We can calculate the degree to which this sampling approach might bias the results through sensitivity analysis, or we can add in a telephone fill-in sample to double check trends among those without online access. Since the potential for sample frame bias is an issue, let us address the question directly.

Addressing the issue of sample frame bias

If the purpose of the study is to quantify the value of online advertising among those with online access, then sampling those with online access is ideal.

However, if the goal is to understand the effect of both online and offline advertising among the total target population, then we must examine the effect of only surveying those with online access. To calculate the degree to which our findings are sensitive to the sampling frame bias, we begin by measuring the percentage of the target audience we are excluding by using an online sample. This is an important place to start, because the smaller the excluded percentage, the smaller the potential bias (the potential for difference in the excluded group to change the overall results is proportional to the excluded group's population percentage).

According to the UCLA random digit-dial-telephone survey of the US population, conducted during the same time that we were conducting our survey for Dove Nutrium Bar, 82% of women aged 25–49 used the Internet either at home, work or some other location (excluding e-mail). Nielsen Net Ratings estimates the percentage using the Internet at closer to 60% (though, unlike the UCLA study where the enumeration methodology is documented publicly, it is not entirely clear exactly how Nielsen's enumeration studies count usage and locations of access). For argument's sake, let us suggest that the percentage of the target population that uses the Internet is at the mid-point between the two estimates: 70%. This would imply that we are systematically including 70% of all consumers and excluding 30%. Since we are including 70%, we can feel confident that our data is projectable to most of the target audience. What we need to consider is the potential impact of the 30% we excluded.

Consider the impact on purchase intent. The baseline measure *pre-campaign* is 8.7%. We examine those people that did not see any online ads. In other words, these people only have an opportunity to see television and magazine advertising, in this case only about 5% of the target audience was reached by online, so most consumers will only have the opportunity to see television and magazine ads. This is the only type of advertising exposure that the 30% of non-online users would have.

Fast forward a couple of weeks in the campaign, beyond the pre-campaign. If we look at those in our survey that saw only television and magazine advertising, we find purchase intent at 11.5%. That is a three-point gain over the *pre-campaign* measurement in the six weeks of tracking – a very respectable increase from television and magazine advertising that would lead most brand managers to congratulate their advertising agency on a job well done.

We could assume that this same increase if observed among the 70% of the target audience that accessed the Internet within the past month would be projectable to the 30% of the audience that also saw television and magazine advertising, but do not have access to the Internet. In other words, if we make the assumption that the two samples have similar reactions to television and magazine advertising, then our results are generalizable to the entire target audience.

But what if those that don't access the Internet are more likely to want to buy a product advertised on television and magazine advertising than those that do access the Internet? If this is the case, then we need to examine the impact on our overall results and recommendations to determine the practical implications of the difference between our sample population and the non-sampled population. We can examine the potential impacts with parallel telephone tracking of those without online access.

In the early years of the methodology, a number of the marketers we worked with opted to run parallel telephone-tracking studies. While these telephone parallel studies add significant cost, they are a definitive way to address the question of sample frame bias.

In performing the analysis of the offline sample versus the online sample, we screened those in the telephone study to only include those without online access. We also removed those in the net-user sample that had seen online ads (to remove the incremental branding effect) and weighted both populations back to the United States Census population targets for age and sex. This provided an apples-to-apples comparison of the Internet users and non-net users.

We compared the two datasets and found that there were no statistically significant differences between net users and non-net users for unaided awareness (first mention and all mentions), nor were there any differences on aided brand awareness. However, we did find a difference on aided product awareness. This difference is caused by the fact that an online survey question showed a product shot while the telephone study simply provided a verbal cue. This led to much higher recognition among those seeing the product shot versus those simply provided with a verbal cue over the phone, without the visual aid of a product shot.

Since the rest of the survey was based on whether a consumer was aware of Colgate toothpaste, the two datasets were not compared easily. This challenge notwithstanding, we attempted to compare brand attitudes and purchase intent among those aware of Colgate Total within the two datasets. We found the following:

- Net users and non-net users have nearly identical purchase intent levels, but net users have a slightly more positive brand perception overall than non-net users.
- Non-net users show a slight down-trend in the last week of television advertising, while net users show a continued gradual increase in positive brand perceptions in the last week of television advertising. On this metric, the net sample shows a more intuitive trend against television advertising weight and timing.

In summary, the similarities between the datasets lead us to conclude that using a net-user sample balanced to United States Census targets would produce very similar data to that of the telephone methodology, with the exception being in the area of product recognition, where visual stimuli used in the online survey produce a different measurement than a less cognitively rich verbal prompt read over the telephone.

Kleenex also performed a telephone comparison study. Kleenex's goal was a quick check of validity of the online sample, and was therefore not as rigorous as Colgate's parallel study. Kleenex has an ongoing telephone-tracking study which trends key metrics such as brand awareness. The trends observed in this telephone tracker paralleled the trends observed in the online-based study.

The Colgate and Kleenex platforms are representatives of what we have observed across each of the parallel studies we performed. These points of converging validity give us confidence in the use of online-based samples, weighted to census targets, to produce nationally projectable data for 13 to 64 age targets. However, certain targets, such as the elderly (65+), we are more cautious about, since we know that the population is less likely to have Internet access compared to their younger cohorts – and as the ratio of offline to online increases, the risk of a nonrepresentative sample increases. But for mainstream marketers, the online sample approach not only allows accurate measurement of online advertising (which is not possible without conducting the study online), it also allows better measurement of offline media, such as magazines, and provides larger samples more cost-efficiently.

There is an alternative method to accessing the potential for sample frame bias which does not require an expensive parallel telephone-tracking study. We've detailed this alternative approach in another paper (Briggs, 2003).

INTRODUCING DOVE NUTRIUM BAR, THE FIRST REAL-WORLD CAMPAIGN MEASURED ACROSS TELEVISION, MAGAZINE AND ONLINE ADVERTISING VEHICLES

In the fall of 2001 we completed a six-month effort to develop the first real-world, side-by-side measurement of a branding campaign running online and offline advertisements. The research represents the collaboration of the marketer (Unilever), its online and offline advertising agencies, a key publishing partner (MSN), industry associations, including the ARF and the IAB, and researchers at Marketing Evolution. Marketing Evolution's measurement approach has been described as 'best practice' through-and-through, and received a nomination from ESOMAR for Best International Research of the year. Before we delve into the methodology, let us recap the objective.

The 'Big Question' we all worked together to answer is, 'Where does online fit in to the marketing mix?' online has grown faster, both in terms of the potential reach and time spent with the medium, than any other advertising vehicle to date, but does that mean a marketer should use online advertising to help achieve her goals? At the time of the Dove study, consumers in the US gave online between 10 and 15% of their total time with media,[2] yet advertising spending as a percentage of the total budget was at a mere 2% on average.[3] Is this level appropriate given the advertising effectiveness of online relative to offline? This research was designed to answer that very question, and, more broadly, to deliver a methodology to measure the entire mix so that marketers could improve their payback from marketing.

As we developed this methodology, we were mindful of the previous research and attempted to answer critics by:

- conducting the research in the *real world* (as opposed to conducting a forced exposure study);
- using *one brand* advertising *across media* (as opposed to comparing norms across media);
- using a side-by-side, dollar-for-dollar comparison (as opposed to comparing branding metrics in a vacuum without consideration of ROI);
- measuring a range of brands spanning multiple categories (as opposed to conducting a single study in one nonrepresentative category – Dove is the first of two dozen brands participating).

In response to the measurement objectives, we refined and adapted proven measurement techniques and, where necessary, developed some new approaches.

What are the key findings of this breakthrough research? What are the implications? online is a potent complement to television and magazine advertising. Adding online allows marketers to increase the productivity of the marketing investment, but online is not the most important medium in the mix. Generally, television is. In addition, magazine is often underleveraged. In sum, marketing profit is increased by getting the balance of media right.

---

[2] Knowledge networks, Scarborough and UCLA.
[3] IAB, PWC report.

We found that overall branding results could be increased by 14% for purchase intent and 8% overall for Dove Nutrium Bar by increasing online's reach and frequency to more optimal levels. This 8% gain in branding effectiveness is achievable without increasing budget. Instead, if marketers reduce television and magazine frequency slightly (leaving reach alone), enough dollars can be freed to boost both online reach and frequency levels.

Achieving expanded reach for online and optimal frequency would require increasing online spending to 15% of current budget. We have found justification for similar increases in budget for Colgate, McDonald's and Kleenex, to name a few. We continue to expand our analysis to examine other brands. The published case studies can be found at www.marketingevolution.com and in the book What Sticks (Briggs and Stuart, 2006).[4] The implication of the research is that marketers should make it a priority to measure whether they too can achieve better overall results by expanding online's role in the marketing mix, or not.

The objective of this chapter is not a discussion of the findings and implications of this research. Instead, the purpose of this chapter is to continue the discussion of the research approach for holistic measurement of a cross-media advertising campaign. The goal is to communicate the *best practice* approaches used to develop greater support of this methodology.

What gives these results legitimacy? Why should you believe these findings? There are at least two reasons for taking heed of these findings. First, the study represents an impressive use of best industry practice to quantify properly the impact of advertising across each medium. Second, the collective effort of a diverse and brilliant team from Unilever, its advertising agencies, the ARF and Marketing Evolution ensured a media neutral measurement and analysis that yields replicable results grounded in a precise measurement of a variety of advertising effects.

The heart of the measurement examines cause and effect. We measure whether exposure to advertising *causes* increases in branding metrics. So how do we measure exposure? What do we define as *branding* effects? First, let us talk briefly about how we define branding, then we will turn to the critical question of *how* we measure the impact of each medium. We will then discuss some of the key analysis, such as the impact of increasing reach and frequency and the calculation of dollar-for-dollar impact across media.

---

[4] www.what-sticks.com

Measuring the branding metrics

We begin with the brand manager's marketing goals. We bring the marketing team together to arrive at an unambiguous definition of success. We translate the goals into survey questions and use the data collection design of exposed and control groups to examine consumers' responses to the branding survey questions to quantify the impact on each branding metric. The measurement is called ROMO, which stands for Return-on-Marketing-Objectives.

We can, at the client's request, connect the ROMO measurement design to actual purchases. Dove was satisfied to measure core branding measures specifically. We measured three standard core branding metrics:

1. Brand awareness (unaided and aided).
2. Positive brand image.
3. Intent to take action (such as purchase the product).

While we did not measure sales directly, it is certainly possible to extend the methodology to measure sales, as later Marketing Evolution studies have done for Procter & Gamble, Kraft, Nestlé and Johnson & Johnson in fast-moving consumer goods, Warner Brothers in theatrical movie releases, Ford and Volkswagen in automotive, Philips in consumer electronics, Target in retail and Motorola in cell phones. In this case, the client opted to use its purchase probability measure as a proxy for sales. Since the survey question of intent to purchase is, by itself, media neutral, the measurement should provide a relative measure of the influence on sales by each medium independently and in synergy.

By surveying new groups of consumers continuously over time (while the advertising weight levels wax and wane based on media schedules), we can trend the consumers' branding levels over time. We then link-up consumers' assignment in the ROMO design of experiments to advertising to determine the effect.

Measuring impact

Given the low-involvement nature of advertising, how can we really be certain of which medium is causing an effect? The answer is to recognize that observing changes in opinions and behaviours using the scientific practice of *design of experiments* is the path to enlightenment. Here's another way to think about it. In the best-selling book, *Freakonomics*, the award-winning economist Stephen Levitt shares the example of a small business owner who sells bagels in company lunchrooms using the honour system. You want a bagel; you put your money in the payment box and help yourself. Except, some people help themselves without paying. The business owner might be interested to find out which signs (advertisements, really) affixed to the bagel and payment box reduce white-collar theft and produce the highest profit. How can one know which signs work best? Should we ask if the consumer 'recalls the sign?' No, that doesn't yield insight as to whether the message worked or not. Should we ask a consumer, 'So, which sign makes you less likely to steal?' No, we're not likely to get an accurate answer from that self-reported direct question approach.

Instead, the bagel owner has a broad enough customer base that he can (and did) deliver *different* messages to a randomized list of customers and observe which messages work best. This scientific practice of creating an experiment by randomizing the assignment of the population to exposed and control groups has been a cornerstone of scientific inquiry, and it can and should be applied to advertising (in fact, this gold-standard approach is the basis of our research).

Don't ask, because consumers can't tell: the pitfalls of asking consumers to introspect on advertising's influence on them

The point that observing changes in consumer attitudes and behaviours is the way to measure message effectiveness leads us to confront a second common mistake in advertising measurement, and that's the practice of asking consumers to state directly if advertising influenced their attitudes or behaviour. The truth is, consumers can't introspect on how advertising and marketing influences them. Our brains aren't wired that way.

Dr Gerald Zaltman of Harvard, in his book *How Customers Think*, noted: 'In actuality, consumers have far less access to their own mental activities than marketers give them credit for.' Zaltman backed up his point with several examples, including Dr Lowenstein's quote: 'Self-reporting methodologies ... that rely on conscious reflection might not provide any substantial insight into what really motivated a particular action or decision.'

Dr Krag Ferenz of Marketing Evolution, with a PhD in Psychological and Brain Sciences, supports this idea, as expressed in the following:

Table 16.1 Results for the P&G experiment.

Advertising recall	Control (n = 271)	Exposed (n = 1162)	Δ	Advertising recall	Control (n = 228)	Exposed (n = 1609)	Δ
TV	77%	82%	5%	TV	39%	51%	12%
Radio	9%	7%	−2%	Radio	8%	5%	−3%
Internet	9%	9%	Not Sig	Internet	10%	10%	Not Sig
Billboards	5%	5%	Not Sig	Billboards	3%	3%	Not Sig
Newspaper	9%	7%	2%	Newspaper	3%	4%	Not Sig
Magazine	27%	29%	2%	Magazine	26%	27%	Not Sig

'If you really want to get an accurate and powerful read on how consumers are influenced by advertising, you need to adhere to the scientific method. You need to establish exposed and control groups beforehand and measure differences in consumers' attitudes and behaviours carefully between groups, rather than relying on consumers' memories of what they saw and how it made them feel.'

Dr Ferenz's point makes clear the insight of neuroscience to marketing and underscores Dr Zaltman's and Dr Lowenstein's point nicely.

Research from P&G on the implications of misattribution is eye opening. In a carefully controlled field experiment, we measured online advertising for a couple of P&G shampoo brands (the results are shown in Table 16.1). The only difference between the exposed and control groups of respondents was the exposure to online ads. And yet, when consumers were asked 'where did you see ads for brand X?' it wasn't Internet ads that were attributed to the increase. Instead, it was television advertising and magazine advertising. To reiterate, there was *no* difference in TV or magazine between exposed and control groups. Therefore, if consumers could self-report ad recall accurately, there should have been no difference between exposed and control groups for TV and magazines, but there should be a difference for online. In fact, for one of the brands, TV wasn't even on air. The only difference between exposed and control groups was that the exposed group was delivered *online* advertisements while the control group was give a placebo ad. And yet, consumers' self-reported data don't accurately reflect the source of ad exposure.

The explanation for these results is that advertising isn't important enough to consumers for them to make a careful mental note of 'I just saw shampoo brand X advertised, and it was being advertised on the Internet.' If you work for the brand, maybe you would make that mental note, but your consumers won't. So, when a survey asks consumers where did you see the ad, the consumer might be aware that they have indeed seen an ad, and they will likely *guess* where they might have seen it. But it's a *guess*, and not a very good one. In this case, most consumers *guessed* television was where they saw the ad – wrong, it was the Internet.

The implications of the P&G research are a warning call. If a marketer were to use consumers' self-stated ad recall by media, then the Internet ad (which drove effect) would not get credit. Using this erroneous data, the marketer would eliminate the Internet and increase magazine and TV spending. But that change in budget allocation would actually undercut marketing effectiveness, because it was the Internet ads that were producing the effect (television and magazines were simply gaining credit because of consumers' inability to report accurately where ad exposure comes from).

We've seen this misattribution work the other way too. In another study, this time for a high-tech consumer electronics product, out-of-home and local market television (spotTV, as it's called) were misattributed to Internet ads. In other words, in the cities where these offline ads were running on billboards and on television, consumers reported seeing more Internet ads, even though the number of Internet ads was constant.

Marketers who rely on self-stated recall of ads by medium, or who rely on consumers' self-stated answers to 'which medium made you buy the product? are likely to draw *incorrect* conclusions about what is truly influencing consumer attitudes and behaviours. Worse, the evidence suggests that relying on such data to make budget allocation decisions across media will actually hurt marketing ROI rather than help it. P&G did not make this mistake. Instead, they used the *design of experiments observation* of differences between exposed and control groups to understand how advertising influences a range of brand attitudes and beliefs (including the perception of where the consumer saw the advertising). As a result of their research, we have an important insight about advertising misattribution, and the dangers involved in using it for advertising effectiveness analysis. And, to be clear, the research for Dove uses observation rather than recall.

What do we learn when we apply the proper design of experiments observational approach to marketing effectiveness measurement? Let's look closer at the Dove Nutrium Bar study and how we can put these principles into action.

Advertising measurement in the real world

The approach of observing responses in the real world is considered a gold standard in advertising measurement. It avoids the artificial conditions of directing consumers to watch a certain programme or visit a website, and therefore avoids the memory-priming problem inherent in forced-exposure studies. It also avoids the self-reported misattributions found in the P&G experiment. Design of experiment observation is a powerful approach to unravelling the effects of advertising.

Discussion of Key Branding Metrics

Brand awareness
Brand awareness is measured in two different metrics. We analyse unaided brand awareness and aided brand awareness. To measure unaided awareness, we ask consumers to type in the soap brand that first comes to mind. If the goal of the marketer is to become more 'Top-of-mind' and salient, then this unaided awareness question is a good measure of that branding goal. The other way we look at brand awareness is to measure 'aided brand awareness.' This means we provide the consumer with a list of several brand names, such as Dove Nutrium Bar, and ask consumers which of the following they are aware of. If the branding goal is to generate higher overall brand recognition, then this is a good measure of that goal. As with each metric, we interpret the data by looking for change over time and between exposed and control groups.

Positive brand image
Often, the marketer's goals go beyond brand awareness. The goal is to create a positive brand association. If we are talking about the beauty bar soap, we want people to be informed that our product 'contains Vitamin E', for example. And we want them to agree that the product will 'nourish their skin.' We also want the consumer to internalize the message and agree that the brand is 'for people like me.' These brand image statements allow us to hone in on whether or not advertising is creating the right kind of awareness and association. For the Dove Nutrium beauty bar, we measured five key statements.

Intent to take action
Our final branding metric is intent to take action. The goal of all marketing is to generate sales at some point. We don't expect that the television ad, magazine ad or online ad will result in people jumping out of their chairs and running to the grocery store to buy the product the instant that these ads are shown. Nor do we expect them to clickthrough, or dial an 800 number and order immediately. That is an unrealistic branding action in the context of this product. We do expect purchase action at some point in the future will result from these ads. For Dove Nutrium Bar, Unilever opted to use the standard purchase probability question 'How likely are you to purchase this brand?' The choices included 'definitely,' 'probably,' 'might or might not,' 'probably not,' 'definitely not.'

Considering our branding measures for awareness, brand image and intent to purchase, you'll probably agree that we have a fairly comprehensive measurement of advertising success. Now, the key question: how do we observe consumers unobtrusively in the *real world* to measure whether or not these advertisements move the needle on key branding metrics?

Measuring exposure – an impression by any other name

Since our goal is to make dollar-for-dollar comparisons of the effectiveness of marketing elements, it is critical to measure advertising impact so that it can be linked to what the advertiser uses to pay for each advertising vehicle. Why is this so critical?

For better or worse, the definition of what constitutes an ad impression paid for by the marketer varies from one medium to the next. If we fail to account for these differences, we cannot link back to the financial data on media cost. This may be an intuitive point, but it is such a key point, allow me to elaborate.

Consider the potential difference between an online, a television and a magazine impression. Each is used as a media currency and advertisers talk about the CPM (cost per thousand) as the denomination of their currency. For better or worse, 1000 television impressions means something slightly different from 1000 online impressions or 1000 magazine impressions.

Let us start with television. Purchasing 1000 television impressions for, let us say $20, does not necessarily mean that 1000 people will sit through your 30-second television commercial with rapt attention. In fact, in the United States, the behavioural ratings that define the audience size are not based on measuring consumers watching a specific ad. Instead, they are based on the average viewing audience within the quarter hour that the ad appeared.

Is it possible that some of these 1000 people, for whom the advertiser paid, did not actually see their ad? Yes. If I am a viewer during that quarter-hour and I leave the room a minute before the ad starts and return a minute after the ad finished playing, I'd still be counted as part of the 1000 users.

Is this a problem for us and our attempt to measure the value of television exposure? No, it is not a problem at all, so long as we link back to the cost paid versus the *impact* when comparing the media.

In other words, if we are asking, 'What impact does $20 spent on advertising in a given medium produce in terms of impact (such as increases in sales, or the number of people aware of the brand, or another definition of success)?' then ROMO provides the right measurements in place to answer this question. So, for instance, if $20 spent on television ads results in 60 people becoming aware of the brand (the increase over the pre-campaign level), then it is really beside the point whether 1000 people really saw the ad and listened to every moment of the television spot, or whether the number is slightly different. The costs are the same and the results are the same, regardless of the 'true' number of actual attentive viewers.

Certainly the savvy researcher will be interested in the qualitative experience of the user included in the 1000 medium defined package. We might be interested to know how many of these 1000 impressions count people in the room. How many of these people watch the entire commercial? How many of them press the mute button and how many of them listen to the sound? How many of them are watching only the television commercial and not multitasking (eating is a popular activity while watching television)? There are plenty of qualitative questions that will influence the overall effectiveness of television (or any medium for that matter). But if we want to do a proper dollar-for-dollar comparison, these issues are not relevant to arriving at the cost per impact of different media in our particular analysis.

The key issue is what the advertiser paid, and what the advertisers got in return for their investment. The bottom line is to focus on measuring the impact of the media based on the same framework – and that gives us the ability to analyse the data properly in a medium–neutral manner.

I have used television as an example for the qualitative viewing versus media–buying definitions, but this same principle applies to magazine and online advertising.

ROMO studies apply experimental designs as a core approach to isolating individual medium effects. The population base for the experimental design ranges from individual respondents to aggregations of respondents based on postal code 'markets'. For example, radio advertising is randomized among a list of markets where 80–90% receive the advertising and up to 20% of the markets are held out as control. The frame of reference is the entire market – ROMO avoids trying to determine who within the market is exposed and who is not (since measuring radio with self-reported data is less reliable). By analyzing the entire exposed market compared to the control markets, a proper experimental design is achieved. ROMO projects the effect to arrive at the total incremental impact of radio. The following equation is useful:

Total number of people impacted
= (Branding% exposed − Branding% control)
× 10 000 000 population (entire exposed markets)

Online advertising uses individuals, rather than markets, as the units of experimental control. The moment before the ad is delivered, the individual is assigned to an exposed or control cell based on a random number generator. If the individual has already been assigned to the exposed or control group, that assignment is maintained. A cookie is placed and that person is designated to receive the advertising for the brand under study (exposed) or a public service placebo ad (control). When individuals are selected for the survey, the presence of the cookie and its numeric value are noted and responses from 'ad-exposed' individuals are assigned to the 'ad-exposed' cell and those from the public service placebo ad are assigned to the 'control' cell. Those not exposed to either are assigned to the 'not reached' cell.

In evaluating online campaigns, the random assignment of 'exposure' or 'non-exposure' is made at the individual respondent level, while for radio or newspaper compaigns, the control is exercised at the market level. When using an individual-level design, adjustments must be made to the individual data to match the actual level of reach that would have been achieved in a market, while the reach level is measured directly in the market-level design.

For magazine advertising, the definition of an impression is tied to those reading or looking through the magazine vehicle. Does the magazine consumer actually look at your ad? Do they read through it? Those are research questions that are addressed by qualitative companies, but they are non-germane to the return-on-investment analysis. We can focus simply on the cost per impact of magazine advertising. Magazine measurement uses a respondent level calculation of exposed and control. While selective binding (experimental design among subscribers or regions) is offered in ROMO, only one of the public studies has used this approach. The rest have opted for a less costly quasiexperimental design. For each magazine used in the advertising campaign, Marketing Evolution shows the cover image of the magazine and asks if the respondent has read or looked through this issue and compares the effects of (potential) exposure to the campaign among readers of the issue(s) in which the campaign ad(s) are placed, with readers of issues in which the ad(s) did not occur. Marketing Evolution measures magazine ad impact with the following method:

1. All those who read any issue of the magazine (by showing consumers the current issue and the two previous months' issues, or five previous weeks' issues in the case of weeklies, using the actual magazine covers) are classified as 'readers'
2. The number of issues read is calculated to arrive at a total number of issues read.
3. The media plan data are then overlaid and readers are divided into 'exposed' and 'unexposed' based on whether they happened to read an issue containing an advertisement or not.
4. 'Exposed' and 'unexposed' respondents are balanced, based on the total number of issues read, demographics and the median date of survey completion.

Because many people read or look through some, but not all, issues of a magazine, and because marketers buy ad insertions in some, but not all, issues of magazines, the respondents grouped into 'exposed' and 'control' can be compared with a low likelihood of bias or contamination.

The accumulation of reach and frequency is not modelled explicitly in the ROMO analysis, because, unless the duration of the study is too short, which we advise against, the pre–post, repeated-survey design captures the majority of the cumulative print impact as well as it does TV. Therefore, modelling reach and frequency is unnecessary.

Television is measured in much the same way that a continuous-tracking study measures the impact of a TV campaign. Wherever possible, a baseline measure is gathered prior to the launch of a brand, or new campaign for a brand. This allows for pre- and post-advertising comparisons, as well as analysis of flighting, changes in creative and competitive spending effects.

To separate out the effects of television, other media that can be isolated through experimental design are subtracted, leaving the underlying effect of television to be assessed.

In sum, for each medium we use the cost versus the impact to ensure an accurate measurement of the contribution of each medium.

With the definitions and rationale of the analysis as cost per impact, let us talk specifically about the ads we measured. Let us look at target audience, as well as the reach, frequency and timing of the ads and how we translate an actual campaign into measurement of impact and ROI.

Dove Nutrium's ad buy

Let us discuss where you, as a consumer, might have seen the ads. The first question is whether you are part of the target audience. Defined in media-buying terms, the Dove Nutrium Bar's audience is women aged 25 to 49.

For those readers who are in the United States, female, and 25 to 49, over the six weeks in October and November 2001, when we were measuring the campaign, based on the information provided by the advertising agency, about 85% of you would have seen the television advertisements. On average, you would have seen six ads. About half of you would have seen the magazine ads, and, on average, you would have seen the ad three times. About one in ten of you would have seen the online ads, and, on average, you would have seen the ad two times according to reach and frequency calculations.

Now, this does not necessarily mean that you will recall seeing any of the ads, or that you will have ever looked at them, but these are the exposure reach and frequency numbers for which the advertising agency paid.

We can measure the effect of the campaign by comparing the post-campaign branding levels to the pre-branding levels before the campaign. In other words, if we survey someone before the campaign starts, we can get a measure of where the brand stands, pre-campaign. If we conduct surveys every day among a new set of consumers, then as television, print and online advertising starts, we can see if the advertising lifts the branding level by trending the combined branding effect of the advertising over time. Specifically, we can determine if the campaign increased key branding metrics over the pre-campaign levels.

This type of measurement typically is referred to as 'continuous tracking'. It was first introduced to advertising measurement in 1976 and has gained wide acceptance since then. In fact, of the top 100 advertisers, over one-third use continuous tracking to gauge their advertising effectiveness. It is a proven approach geared almost exclusively to measuring television campaigns.

The innovation of the ROMO research approach was our ability to look, not only at the combined effects of the ad campaign, but also at the separate effects of online, print and television.

Typically, continuous, tracking studies survey only a few hundred people, and it is not possible to look at subgroups such as those exposed to magazine ads only. We surveyed many times more than the typical tracking research number. We surveyed 12 990 for Dove over six weeks. This gave us more than enough people to analyse the effects of each medium separately and in combination with one another.

How did we pull apart the independent effects of television, online and magazine advertising? We did not want to bias consumers' answers to our branding question by prompting consideration of media habits, so here is what we did: *we surveyed consumers randomly and asked our branding questions first*. This gave us a 'clean' read on how branding levels trend over time, and among exposed and control groups in our factorial design of experiments.

Later in the survey, we could ask media consumption questions to allow us to determine advertising exposure levels using the same 'currency' definition used by the media. We experimented with so-called 'probability of exposure' and found it lacking – probability of exposure really isn't accurate enough for ROI conclusions. It provides directional insight at best. Therefore, we ensured that we could create control and exposed groups to quantify the total number of people impacted by each medium.

When we designed the sampling structure, we ensured that we had a large random sample of consumers. We augmented this sample with a random over-sample to create large 'control' and 'exposed' groups to better measure the precise effects of online advertising relative to television and magazine advertising. Let us go through each medium and discuss our measurement of the exposed and control groups for each medium (or factor) in the campaign. To see how each medium was translated into ROMO's factorial design of experiments, please see the appendix at the end of this chapter.

Our approach to collecting advertising exposure data for each medium represents a harmonization with the industry accepted currency. We came to this measurement approach after consultation with the ARF, the client, the advertising agency and other industry experts. magazine ratings tell us that the average frequency over the Dove Nutrium Bar campaign is about three. But if a researcher chose to use a different qualitative definition of what constitutes an impression – such as a decision rule requiring the consumer to have looked at the headline and some of the text body, then maybe the count would really be 2.5 or 3.5. Regardless of qualitative definitions, we link back to what the agency *pays* for the impressions that will generate the three, and therefore we want to align our analysis with the 'currency' of the media buyer – which is precisely what we did. The measurement is therefore neutral. And, because we

tie back to what the marketer pays, the approach does not favour one
medium over another.

Analysing cause and effect

Let us turn to how we apply this exposure information and branding
metrics to our analysis. If we look over time at the Dove Nutrium Bar
campaign (see Figure 16.2), you can see that, starting on the left of the
figure, on October 11th, we began surveying consumers.

Other than a few old magazines that were still gathering their last bit
of reader accumulation, the campaign was dark. There were no television
spots or online ads. By removing the few people who indicated that they
read or looked through one of the old magazines that we coded as having
contained Dove Nutrium Bar ads, we were left with a pure read on the
'pre-campaign' branding levels (see Figure 16.2a).

A baseline level[5] from which we can measure the branding gain is
important. For purchase intent, for example, the level is 8.7% (definitely
will/probably will buy).

As we continued to interview consumers in the next week, new magazine ads began to appear within the new issues of titles such as *Glamour*
and *InStyle*. online ads also began to appear. We separated consumers
that saw online ads, and did not read or look through magazines that we
coded as containing Dove Nutrium Bar ads. This allowed us to analyse
the branding effects of those who were exposed to online ads only (see
Figure 16.2b).

We could apply the same principle to print ads. We could look at people
who read or looked through magazines that we coded as containing Dove
Nutrium Bar ads and subtract those we observed as having an opportunity
to see online ads. This would tell us how magazine advertising performed
on its own (see Figure 16.2c).

As we continued to survey consumers in the following week, television ads hit the airwaves. To analyse how television performed on its
own, we subtracted the impact of magazines based on the difference
between exposed and control groups, and we subtracted the impact of
online advertisements. This left us with people who were only affected by
television advertising. When we subtract the incremental effect of online

---

[5] The 'dark' period is not essential to the measurement, but to the extent that a brand goes off-air,
   it provides a unique opportunity to see how introducing (or reintroducing) ads in different media
   combinations affects consumer attitudes.

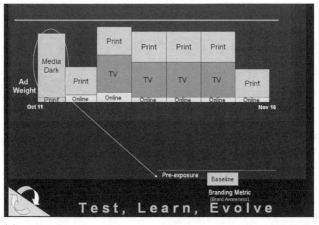

(a)

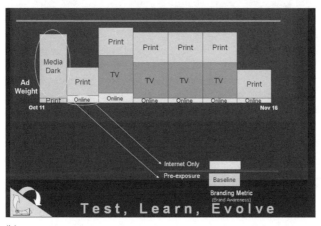

(b)

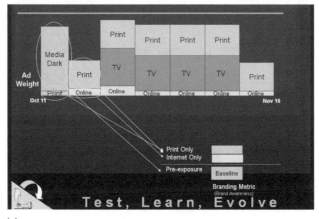

(c)

Figure 16.2 Dissecting advertising effects – the Dove Nutrium Bar campaign.

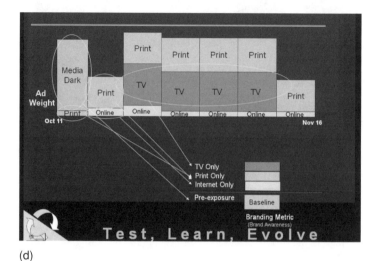

(d)

Figure 16.2   (*Continued*)

and magazine, it is television which is the first effect to be measured, and additional media have the burden of producing an incremental effect above and beyond television's effect. By removing the incremental effects of other media, we can then assess how television performed on its own in terms of moving the branding needle (see Figure 16.2d).

Each of these analyses is very powerful. They tell us how each medium performs on its own. Furthermore, we can combine the cost data for each medium to get a measure of relative efficiency in achieving branding goals.

Understanding how each medium performs independently is insightful, but we were very interested in understanding how media complement one another and work in synergy.

Figure 16.3 charts how we measure advertising synergy. In the second week of data collection, we examined those who were exposed to *both* online and print ads. Since television advertising had not yet begun, we could look at the interaction of magazines and online without the influence of television advertising. This analysis allowed us to better understand the synergy between the two media (see Figure 16.3a).

For example, the online banners and the magazine ads both contained the very clear pink and white Dove embossed beauty bar. However, while the print ad had a clear 'Nutrition Bar' headline along with 'Dove Nutrium Bar,' the online ads only had a small reference to 'Nutrium Bar' in the very last frame.

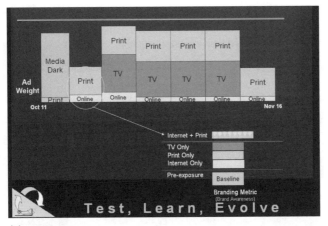

(a)

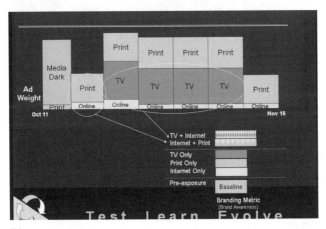

(b)

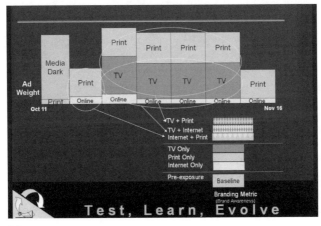

(c)

Figure 16.3 Measuring advertising synergy.

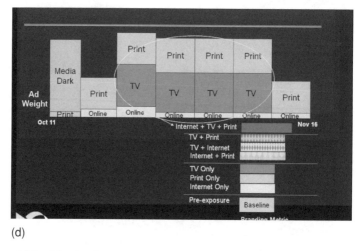

(d)

Figure 16.3 (*Continued*)

Not surprisingly, we found that the online ads increased awareness for Dove, but had little effect, on their own, in improving awareness specifically for the Nutrium Bar.

By examining the advertising synergy, we found that the combination of online and magazine ads was far more successful in driving awareness of Dove Nutrium Bar than the magazine ad alone. This suggests that the consumer was keying in on the pink and white bar. Seeing both the magazine and online ads really reinforced brand awareness substantially.

Synergy is an important part of our analysis. We looked at each combination of 'online and print', 'online and television', 'print and television', and all three together (see Figure 16.3).

This analysis was very insightful. Not only did it underscore the generally held belief that all three media perform better than any one medium on its own, it provided insight into how a properly balanced media mix can improve overall branding results.

Cost-efficiency analysis

We have observed synergy between offline and online advertising. How do we know that it is 'synergy' as opposed to simply the effect of added advertising weight? There are two ways to make this determination: one is cost-efficiency analysis and the other is weight-adjusted branding impact.

Cost-efficiency analysis takes the cost of the advertising and divides it by the absolute branding increase from pre-campaign levels. This produces the cost of affecting each person on average.

For example, if Dove spent \$1 000 000 on the television ad campaigns and the television advertising increased purchase preferred by 1.5% among the target of women aged 25 to 49,[6] we could calculate the average cost per person affected.

We first project the total number of people affected by multiplying the total US population of women aged 25 to 49 by the branding increase (1.5% × 52 674 822 = 790 122).[7] We then divide the total spend by the total number of people affected to arrive at the average cost for television to affect each person, which is \$1.22 (\$1 000 000 / 790 122 = \$1.22).

We can calculate the incremental branding effect of adding online ads, and calculate the incremental cost. By performing the same cost per branding effect calculation, we can determine if adding online ads is more cost efficient or less cost efficient than using television alone. If there is no synergy, then adding incremental media will add incremental branding increases at an increased cost (because there are diminishing returns). If there is synergy, the incremental cost per person affected will decline. In Dove's case, we found that adding online ads was 32% more cost-efficient compared to television and magazine advertising alone – which is a powerful argument for using online advertising in addition to television and magazines.

The second approach to confirming synergy is *weight-adjusted branding measurement*. Since this analysis relies on measuring frequency, let us return to weight-adjusted forecasts after we have discussed the role of frequency thoroughly.

Role of frequency

We've talked about our objective, our definition and measurement of 'branding,' our tracking of online and offline advertising exposure, and our analysis of the relative effects of television, print and online advertising. Now let us turn to our last area of analysis, the effects of frequency and diminishing returns.

---

[6] These cost and branding levels are not the actual Dove figures, these figures are used to illustrate the calculation only.

[7] Census QT-P1 report 2002.

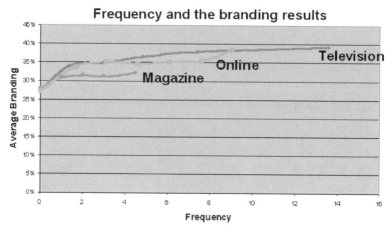

Figure 16.4   The effect of changing frequency.

The previous analysis, which examined the relative effectiveness and synergy of offline and online advertising, led us to conclude that online is often more cost efficient in terms of improving overall branding results. The implication to marketers is this: increase online's reach so that you can get these improved branding results among more people.

There is another dimension to optimizing branding results, and that is frequency. We wanted to understand the value of increasing (or decreasing) television, print and online advertising frequency in terms of the core branding results. Here is how we approached this measurement.

For online, we looked at the number of deliveries of the online advertisements using the ad serves count and then broke people into one or more impressions, two or more impressions, three or more, and so forth. We then looked at each branding metric against these frequency levels and plotted the curve.

What you can see in Figure 16.4, an example for Dove Nutrium Bar, is how increasing online frequency from the current 1.7 level boosts overall branding. However, increasing television from the current level of 6.0 (over five weeks) produces very little incremental effect. The point is this: the methodology allows us to look at the value of increasing (or decreasing) frequency for television, print and online ads.

How do we determine frequency? For online, we can use the observed count of ads served. This matches back to the currency for which online is bought and sold.

For magazines, we can use the self-reported data of the number of magazines read, and match back to the ratings data. This match back allows us to ensure that we are aligned with the magazine impression level corresponding to the frequency for which the advertising agency purchased and paid.

For television, we use a quintile analysis of respondents. That is, we divide the population that has an opportunity to see television advertisements into five groups, from heaviest exposure to lightest exposure, for each day of the study. We do this based on cumulative daily quintile figures provided by the agency. We base this quintile analysis on the amount, daypart and television programming each respondent reports watching. We then match back to the ratings quintiles for the actual average frequency levels to our self-reported quintile. We cross-check the data from respondent level with population impact figures to ensure the respondent assigned frequency is consistent with the population figures. Deciles or other frequency groups can be used.

Frequency analysis is not only useful in terms of gauging the incremental branding from additional advertising impressions, we also plug-in the cost information. For example, Figure 16.5a shows that there is clearly value in increasing online frequency from, say, six impressions over six weeks to twelve impressions over six weeks in terms of improving brand image. But increasing frequency by this amount implies additional cost. The next part of our frequency analysis looks at the cost per branding increase at different frequency levels.

Cost per branding increase

Here is how the analysis works. Take the positive brand image frequency trend we discussed before as an example. For Dove Nutrium Bar, the pre-campaign average positive brand image level was 30.7%.

At 6.1 impressions over six weeks, brand image jumped to 42.1%. That is an eleven point increase. In other words, if we talked to 1000 people, we would find that 307 of them would agree to such statements as 'Dove Nutrium Bar nourishes your skin' *before* we started this new ad campaign. *After* online ads run at a 6.1 frequency level, brand image increased. Now, 421 people would agree with the same brand image statements. That means online advertising made 114 (421 − 307 = 114) more people agree with the desired perception of the brand (see Figure 16.5b).

How much did it cost to make these 114 people agree with the statements? Based on the CPM, it cost about $45.75 per thousand at the frequency of 6.1 over six weeks. But let us translate this into a cost figure that means more to a marketer. How much does it cost, on average, to

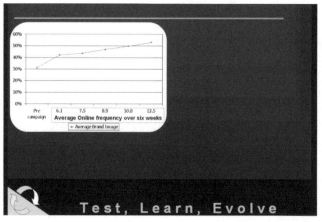

(a)

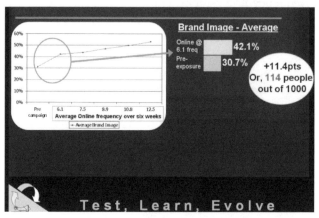

(b)

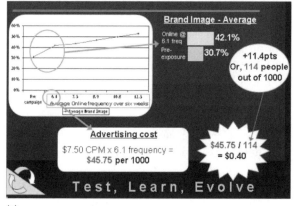

(c)

Figure 16.5 Calculating cost efficiency.

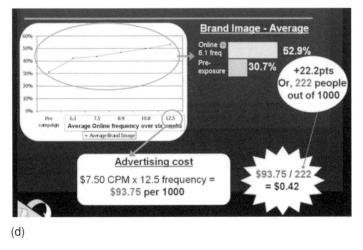

(d)

Figure 16.5 (*Continued*)

make someone agree with the key brand image statements? Taking the cost and dividing it by the effect (among 1000 people), we find that it costs about forty cents to make each person agree with the brand image statement (see Figure 16.5c).

Now, let us look at a higher frequency level of 12.5 impressions over six weeks. We see that brand image increases from 42% at 6.1 impressions (over six weeks) to 53%. That is a big increase. Clearly, a higher online frequency produces better brand image results. Out of 1000 people, online advertising would now make 222 more people agree with the branding statements. But increasing frequency costs more money. In fact, the cost per thousand at this effective frequency level is $94.75. Is this extra frequency worth it?

Let us look at the cost per branding effect. What we find is that the cost, on average, for each new person agreeing with the branding statement is now $0.42 (see Figure 16.5d). An increase over the $0.40 we found at a 6.1 online frequency.

We can plot the cost per branding effect at each frequency and determine the optimal frequency level. We call this chart the cost per effect curve. The point of this analysis is to get very precise about the cost and benefit of increasing the frequency of online and offline advertising. Armed with the cost per effect curve, the marketer can now make a better decision about the appropriate frequency levels.

Depending on the most important branding objective to the marketer, different frequency levels may be selected. In this example we focused on brand image. Had we focused on brand awareness, we would have found that the diminishing returns set in earlier and a lower frequency over six weeks may have been more prudent. The point is not to suggest an optimal frequency for all brands to achieve all metrics. Rather, the point is that this ROMO research allows marketers to examine the role of frequency and diminishing returns in relationship to differing branding objectives.

We've talked about online ads to illustrate this analysis, but we also performed exactly the same analysis for television and print. We found that television produces very little incremental benefit from increasing frequency beyond the current levels of 6.0 over four weeks. Moreover, because the cost is greater, there are steep diminishing returns.

The story for print is similar. In some cases, increasing print advertising produces bigger effects, but the increase in costs tends to outpace the branding improvements. Also, in print's case, those who indicated that they read or looked at more women-oriented magazines tended to have a more favourable brand rating for Dove Nutrium Bar.

Figure 16.6 demonstrates that magazine advertising certainly works – as those who had an opportunity to see the magazine ads had more favourable branding levels than those that did not have an opportunity to see the magazine ads. However, the figure also indicates that increasing

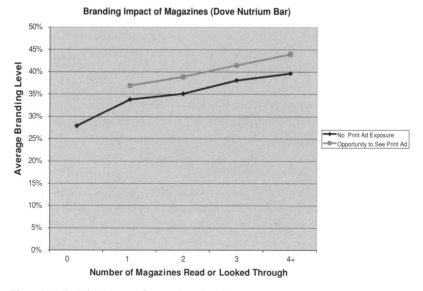

Figure 16.6   The impact of magazine advertising.

magazine advertising frequency does not produce that much of an incremental gain above those reading a similar number of magazines (but not exposed to the Dove Nutrium Bar ads). In other words, there is a 'heavier reader bias' that should be subtracted to get a more accurate view of the role of frequency in this campaign. Heavier media user bias can be examined for each medium.

To reiterate an earlier point: our goal here is not to suggest that there is an optimal frequency for all brands revealed in this study. Rather, our point is that a marketer can examine results at different frequencies for each medium against specific branding goals and use this learning to improve the overall performance of the marketing mix.

Weight-adjusted branding measurement

Now let us return to the question of synergy versus added advertising weight. Are incremental branding gains caused by synergy when adding an additional advertising medium, or are they caused simply by additional advertising weight? Weight-adjusted branding measurement is a direct way of answering this question. While determining the value of adding advertising from another medium, such as online, based on whether the cost per branding effect decreases is one sound and logical approach to addressing this question, weight-adjusted branding measurement is another answer to the question. The weight-adjusted measurement approach does not require any assumption about diminishing return. The two approaches taken together provide converging validity.

In the case of the cost per branding effect analysis, we assume that putting more money (or weight) into television will produce branding increases at the same cost per branding effect level (or at a less efficient level because of diminishing return). Therefore, if adding online is more cost efficient than television, we conclude that the right decision is to increase online advertising.

If we need to trim back television slightly to free up money for online advertising, we examine the cost per branding frequency curve for television to calculate the point at which television's cost per branding effect is equal to online's cost per branding effect. Provided that we are not cutting television beyond this 'cost-balance' point, we have produced a more optimal mix.

Weight-adjusted measurement takes a different approach. We calculate the curve linear equation to describe the exact branding results we observed by frequency. The equation is custom derived as a near perfect fit ($R^2 = 0.99\%$) of the observed data. The equation includes television alone and television and online combined. This equation allows the analyst to input specific weight levels and receive, as output, the exact observed branding levels and cost.

This means that we can determine if adding a dollar to online and removing the dollar elsewhere produces better overall results, while factoring in that the dollar must be subtracted from another medium, resulting in a decrease in impact. The analysis determines how to get the highest overall impact within the fixed budget. Specifically, weight level is controlled by trimming down television when online is added. The overall branding results of television alone and television plus online therefore represent a comparison of equivalent weight levels.

The conclusion from the weight-adjusted measurement is the same as the cost per branding increase. Adding online to television produces better overall results.

SUMMARY

The ROMO research study is a landmark analysis that gives us a chance to peer into the actual branding effects of a cross-media approach – in this case television, print and online. The ROMO research has been extended across several brands and product categories. Marketers that invest the time and effort in this type of measurement can finally get a handle on where online fits into the marketing mix. The indication from the studies conducted since the ground-breaking Dove study is that there is a substantial opportunity for improved marketing efficiency. We hope that this discussion of the methodology helps clarify the mechanics of our measurement and encourages others to manage ROI across all media.

APPENDIX

Television

For television, we knew the exact start date of the advertising, as well as the reach and frequency. We applied this information to those surveyed while television advertising was running. If we surveyed 100 respondents on day four of the study, we knew the opportunity to see (OTS) television ads from this campaign was zero – television ads hadn't started appearing yet. If we surveyed 100 respondents on day 42 of the study, we knew that the marketers' spending was well under way and respondents as a group had an opportunity to be affected by the campaign. Based on prorated spending, we knew the amount invested as of day 42. television's campaign reach was 80% as of day 42, which meant 80 of the 100 people had an OTS for the television campaign.

Our approach gives us a good measure of the opportunity to see television ads across the population surveyed after television advertising starts, but trying to convert this population-wide figure to an individual probability of exposure is guaranteed to be inaccurate. Simply put, we advise caution on respondent level exposure calculations for television. Therefore, we avoid fallacious projections to include exposure for TV, and instead focus the analysis at the population level. The baseline for purchase intent is 8.7%. If that level is increased by 1.3% to 10% among those *not* exposed to magazine or online advertising when television has a reach of 80%, then we calculate that the true effect of television is 1.6% (or an increase of 10.3).

We arrive at this conclusion by observing that only 80% of those surveyed were reached by television according to the agency. Note, we are not trying to determine which 80% were exposed, but rather leaving the observation at a population (or 'market' level.) If we know the observed market level impact and we know the amount paid out, and if we divide the branding increase by 80%, we arrive at the branding increase among those reached by television.

Since the calculated 1.6% increase is a population-based figure that required no assumption or modelling of exposure, we are extremely confident in this number.

As a diagnostic approach to provide greater analyses of television effects, we can define an individual's opportunity to see the television campaign by arraying respondents based on their self-reported number of hours of television watched yesterday, in the past week, times of day watched over the past week, specific programmes and channels watched each day over the past week, etc. – but, this 'probability of exposure' can only be used with caution and should *never* be used for ROI calculations. These media habits were measured at the end of the survey and allow us to calculate a probability that any given respondent was reached by television (based on daily cumulative reach) and the frequency of exposure (based on cumulative quintile frequency). Someone who watches lots of television during the same dayparts Dove advertises in is calculated as more likely to have been reached than someone who watches very little television, or who never watches during the dayparts Dove advertises in. The accuracy of the assignment of individual television reach and frequency *must* be cross-checked by comparing the population-reach-adjusted average to the respondent-assigned exposure probability.

Magazines

For magazines, we had similar reach and frequency data. To figure out the population-level effect for magazines, we first defined which consumers were reached by magazines. We showed consumers covers of 27 magazines and asked respondents to indicate which they had 'read or looked through.' We also gave respondents an opportunity to fill in additional magazines they read or looked through in open-ended fields, so that no respondent would feel compelled to 'choose the closest magazine'. The approach of asking consumers to indicate the magazines they had read or looked through is fairly consistent with how the reach ratings that the agency uses are derived. In fact, using the actual magazine covers exceeds current best practice in magazine measurement.

Because magazines accumulate over a longer period of time, we went back about two months and included titles that were still accumulating readers. We also updated our magazine list the day new issues hit the newsstands. Some of these twenty-seven magazine issues contained ads for Dove Nutrium Bar and some did not.

In fact, over the course of the study, about one-third of the magazines we included in our list contained Dove Nutrium Bar ads. Therefore, we could code respondents that indicated that they had 'read or looked through' any of the magazines that contained Dove Nutrium ads as those the marketer paid to have an opportunity to influence with print advertising for the brand. Note that we did not ask the consumer if they recalled the ad. The focus was on exposure to the medium.

Online

For online, we used the industry definition of ad request impressions. Thanks to an ad tagging system, every single advertisement that Dove served online included a transparent pixel. Serving this transparent pixel allowed us to record the exact time and location that every ad was served. When we surveyed consumers, we simply examined this behavioural data and used it in our analysis.

We could see, for instance, that one consumer did not see any advertisements for Dove Nutrium Bar, while another consumer had an opportunity to see seven ads over the past three weeks. But comparing exposed to non-exposed would be a flawed analysis. So we delivered placebo control ads, so that, as with magazines, we could compare exposed and control groups for accurate calculation of effect.

ACKNOWLEDGEMENT

This research would not have happened without the intellectual contribution of Charles Newman of Unilever research; Jim Spaeth, President of the ARF; Joanne Bradford, Stephen Kim, Piya Panyavetchawat, Mike Sigenthaler and Heide O'Connell of MSN, whose unconditional support allowed us independently to create a media-neutral methodology; and Greg Stuart of the IAB, whose experience as an ex-advertising executive inspired him to replicate the Dove research so marketers could know, rather than guess at, their advertising ROI.

REFERENCES

Briggs, R. (1996), *Hotwired Advertising Effectiveness Study*.
Briggs, R. (1997), *Berkeley Systems You Don't Know Jack: The Netshow Study*.
Briggs, R. (2003), *Excellence in Research*, Cross Media Measurement, ESOMAR, Amsterdam, pp. 359–404.
Briggs, R. and Hollis, N. (1997), Is there response before clickthrough? *Journal of Advertising Research*, 37, 33–45.
Briggs, R. and McDonald, S. (1997), *IAB Advertising Effectiveness Study*.
Briggs, R. and Stipp, H. (1999), Net Effects.
Briggs, R. and Stuart, G. (2006), *What Sticks: Why Most Advertising Fails and How to Guarantee Yours Succeeds*, Kaplan Publishing.
Foley, M. (1999), *Ipsos-ASI report*. Paper delivered at the 1999 ARF Conference.
Morgan Stanley Dean Witter Equity Research (2001), *Does Online Work? Yes, But . . .* , February.
Zaltman, G. (2003), *How Customers Think: Essential Insights Into the Mind of the Market*, Harvard Business School Press.

Part Four

Modelling

Chapter Seventeen

A New Generation of Brand Controlling: Evaluating the Effectiveness and Efficiency of the Complete Marketing Mix

Siegfried Högl[a] and Oliver Hupp[b]

> This chapter presents an approach to brand performance measurement which takes two perspectives into account and which helps management executives to allocate future marketing budgets effectively and efficiently.

INTRODUCTION

Without a doubt, brands currently represent the *most important factor in determining business success*. This is suggested by a survey of businesses carried out by PricewaterhouseCoopers and Sattler (1999), which found that, on average, the asset consisting of the brand itself made up more than 50% of total business value. In future, this figure stands to grow even further. Consequently, the assessment and control of brands (carried out

[a]Managing Director, GfK Marktforschung, Germany, and Member of the Board, GfK Custom Research Worldwide.
[b]Division Manager, GfK Marktforschung, Brand and Communication Research, Germany.

Market Research Best Practice. Edited by P. Mouncey and F. Wimmer.
© 2007 John Wiley & Sons, Limited.

as frequently as possible) is of exceptional importance in terms of ensuring long-term business success.

Similar to other assets, brands demand high investment in order to secure and build their value in the long run. This investment consists of continuous and specifically conducted marketing activities, such as the running of commercials and print ads, an enlargement of distribution or the use of price promotions or other promotions.

The profitability of this investment can be evaluated from two points of view. On the one hand, one must evaluate to what extent the investment can satisfy the main objectives of brand leadership (reaching an attractive positioning for the consumer and distinguishing the brand from competitive offers – profiling and differentiation). Furthermore, the marketing investment has to be assessed according to its orientation towards profit. This means that the return on brand investment should not only be assessed from a qualitative point of view, but also from a financially oriented quantitative perspective.

Against this backdrop, particularly over the past ten years, business practitioners and researchers alike have taken an increasing interest in brands, brand assessment and value-oriented brand management. A great many instruments have been developed with a view to helping brand management executives in the fields of brand planning, control and assessment. Still, definitive brand controlling (*brand performance measurement*) remains beyond the scope of the instruments currently available. Thus, in their landmark research on the work of devising a brand performance measurement approach, Meffert and Koers (2002, p. 404) put forward the criticism that the approaches taken to date have more the quality of stand-alone systems for brand–value measurement and brand-presentation optimization. In keeping with this, studies conducted at the University of St Gallen show that, in Germany and Switzerland, as well as in America:

- brand performance measurement is practiced primarily on the basis of key business figures, and based to a lesser degree on brand-relevant indicators of success (Reinecke and Reibstein, 2001, p. 144 ff. and Diagram 3);
- at many companies, the instrument most important to successful brand management – advertising (on this point see Högl, Twardawa and Hupp, 2001), is either analysed very sporadically for its effectiveness or not at all (Reinecke and Tomczak, 2001, p. 79).

Added to this is that, to date, no instrument designed to aid brand performance measurement has succeeded in locating and quantifying the interdependent relations which arise from the use of such individual instruments.

Therefore, the aim of this chapter is to take up the call of Meffert and Koers for *a comprehensive, effective brand performance measurement system*, which furnishes a definitive assessment of brand performance while at the same time providing a planning and control concept for the optimization of brand presentation. As a comprehensive controlling tool does not just allow for the controlling of past activities, but should also establish the planning of future measures, a model which is based on the statistical instrument of causal analysis is developed. This model helps management to allocate the future marketing budget effectively and efficiently for the different marketing instruments.

The centerpiece of the chapter is the introduction of the so-called *Brand ASsessment System (BASS)*, a newly developed research approach which:

- provides a complete measure of brand strength via attitude- and behaviour-oriented criteria;
- enables evaluation of the efficiency and effectiveness of all marketing-mix instruments;
- provides indications for an optimal allocation of the future marketing budget.

According to Meurer and Panella (2002), many companies currently lack transparency concerning the magnitude and distribution of their marketing budgets. Frequently, the allocation of the marketing budget among the individual instruments of the marketing mix is based not on considerations of profitability, but rather according to rules of thumb, gut instinct or on the basis of what has always worked in the past. This may result in misallocation in marketing planning, i.e. budget amounts are directed to the wrong use. With the BASS technique, we will outline a research system which enables the consequences of alternative measures for the brand value to be assessed, as well as helping to identify which value-improving steps to take. As a planning and control concept, BASS explains how a company's resources can be allocated efficiently and effectively across the various mix instruments.

BRAND ASSESSMENT IN THE BRAND ASSESSMENT SYSTEM

According to Meffert *et al.*, brands represent an *unmistakable image* of a product, service or shopping source, a representation *solidly anchored in the consumer psyche.*[2] If this image is positive in nature, then the prerequisites for lasting market success, i.e. for a strong brand, have been satisfied: the consumer finds the brand attractive and he or she can be expected to purchase the product and to develop strong ties to it, even if it is offered at prices higher than those of other products.

The causal chain suggested here, which leads from the consumer's impressions of a brand to the development of brand attractiveness, purchase, brand loyalty, higher price acceptance and thus, finally, a corresponding financial brand value, has now been confirmed in a series of empirical studies (Twardawa and Hupp, 2000; Högl, Twardawa and Hupp, 2001; Hupp and Hofmann, 2002). The causal chain thus represents a sound foundation for the BASS (Figure 17.1).

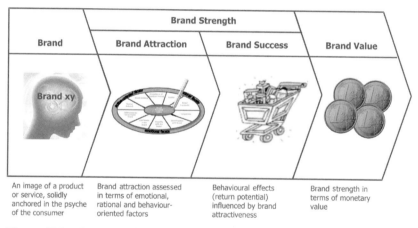

Figure 17.1 Connection between brand, brand strength and brand value.[1]

Thus, proceeding from the definition proposed by Meffert *et al.*, it would appear well-grounded to measure brand success in equal measure via the attractiveness of the brand for the consumer and via the

---

[1] Following the work of Caspar and Metzler (2002).

[2] For this connection, see Meffert, Burmann and Koers (2002). On translating brand strength in to a financial brand value, see Sattler, Högl *et al.* (2002).

behavioural patterns to which this attractiveness gives rise. The latter reflect the brand's revenue potential.

In the ideal case, the BASS provides a valid display of a brand's revenue potential with the help of data from consumer or retail panels. As possible indicators for a brand's behavioural strength, we might cite:

- **the brand's penetration** – i.e. the size of the set of buyers who have purchased the brand at least once;
- **the size of the set of first choice buyers (FCB) of a brand** – these are those buyers of a product category for whom the highest individual market share (measured in terms of value) devolves to this brand (taking multiple purchases into account);
- **the first choice value** – this is the share of sales which first-choice buyers contribute to total sales for the brand;[3]
- **the market share which the brand attains** – this is the result of the indicators of success considered above;
- **the price premium which this brand can achieve over weaker brands** – e.g. a private brand.

The importance of penetration and market share to marketing management is sufficiently well known and needs no further elaboration here. The *first choice buyer* and *first choice value* concepts are performance figures newly developed by GfK Panel Services to enable a more expressive depiction of buyer loyalty and the associated stability of a brand's revenue potential. This can be illustrated in the case of the Jacobs brand (Figure 17.2). In 1999, this brand had a buyer range of 49%. The share of FCB among people who had purchased Jacobs at least once was 42%. Extrapolating to the population of Germany, this means that in the year 1999, 6.8 million German households purchased Jacobs as their brand of preference for roasted coffee. According to evaluations of the GfK consumer panel, however, this small group of buyers accounts for 78% of total sales at Jacobs. This value is the first choice value: a brand's loyalty-related sales potential.

The higher this value is, the more firmly established and stable a brand becomes in its competitive environment, and the fewer the sales promotions needed to maintain the market position achieved. Brands with a high first choice value thus enjoy a much calmer market-share trend, while brands with a low first choice value are subject to pronounced

---

[3] For the detailed derivation and significance of the first choice buyer and first choice value indicators, see Twardawa and Hupp (2000).

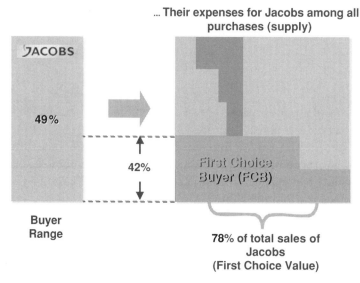

Figure 17.2 First choice buyers and first choice value.

market-share fluctuation and are forced to launch such sales promotions (Hupp, 2000a).

The *price premium* can be measured in a consumer as well as a retail panel, based on the difference between the price of a particular brand and the price of a private brand or some other brand towards the bottom of the price scale. The price of the reference brand represents that particular product's basic utility. The difference between this basic utility and the price of a particular brand, then, represents the additional utility which this brand carries with it. The magnitude of additional utility, in turn, determines the maximum price which a consumer is willing to pay – which is by no means, however, the same as the financial value of a brand.[4] To that extent, it is more fitting to speak of a *premium bonus of the brand*.

Without a doubt, the hard indicators of success revealed by panel research, as described above, represent important economic targets for strategic brand performance measurement, particularly since they also suggest points of departure for optimization of the operational marketing mix. In this regard, according to the above-mentioned study by Reinecke and Reibstein (2001, p. 144 ff.), these criteria also dominate worldwide marketing control. Still, these indicators focus *exclusively on the observable behaviour of consumers*. They can thus provide only limited information

---

[4] On the problems of the price premium as an indicator for financial brand value, see the extensive treatment in Sattler (2002) and Högl and Hupp (2001).

about the individual causes behind this behaviour or about the motivations of consumers. Here, the factors determinative of behaviour include, for example, the emotional and intellectual estimation of a brand ('Share of Soul®'). They thus complete the analysis of brand performance. Beyond that, they convey quite concrete indications for the selection and design of individual marketing measures and represent – unlike consumer behaviour – rather stable factors in the long term, which can only be modified through extensive learning and empirical processes. Within the framework of a meaningful brand-performance measurement approach designed to provide information relevant to planning, decision-making and control in equal measure, *soft success indicators* (performance drivers) localized in the human psyche *are to be measured on a par with the hard success factors* outlined above (core results values) (Högl, Twardawa and Hupp, 2001; Meffert and Koers, 2002, p. 409). According to the study by Reinecke and Reibstein mentioned above, the corresponding brand-strength indicators are 'nevertheless' used by only some 5% of businesses for controlling purposes (Figure 17.3).

In marketing controlling sales are dominating while brand values are only used to a very small extent

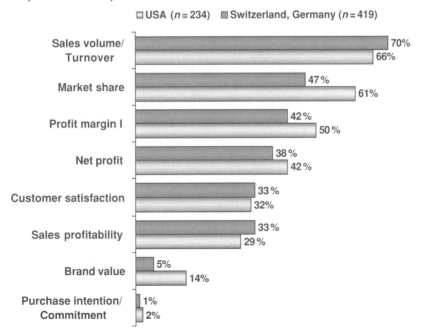

Figure 17.3 Importance of different success indicators in brand-performance measurement.

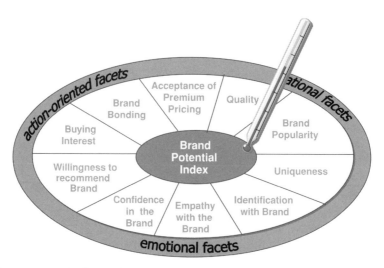

Figure 17.4   The facets of the Brand Potential Index.

Under the BASS approach, the psychological brand strength, i.e. the Share of Soul®, is gauged with the aid of the Brand Potential Index (BPI®). Consonant with the relevant academic literature on brand-value measurement, this index measures brand strength based on a total of ten facets. Using statements, respondents are queried regarding their rational and emotional attitudes with regard to a brand, as well as various kinds of behaviour planned concerning that brand (Figure 17.4). In addition, a painstaking analysis of the validity and reliability of the measurement instrument involved ensures that the Brand Potential Index captures, in objective fashion, a brand's attractiveness and concomitant strength.[5] Corresponding quality tests were carried out for fast-moving consumer goods and for services and durable utility goods in more than 50 countries. The results indicate that the Brand Potential Index measures brand strength in a fashion which is both valid and free of measurement error. An essential prerequisite for a meaningful brand-performance measurement approach has thus been satisfied (Meffert and Koers, 2002, p. 409).

---

[5] The process for validating the Brand Potential Index as a measure is documented in detail elsewhere (Hupp, 2000b). For the first time, in the analysis of the quality characteristics of the measure, second-generation validation procedures are invoked based on the application of a confirmatory variables analysis. These testing methods represent the highest academic standard to be found today. To date, however, among the familiar brand-assessment models, only the Brand Potential Index has been subjected to a comparably elaborate quality examination.

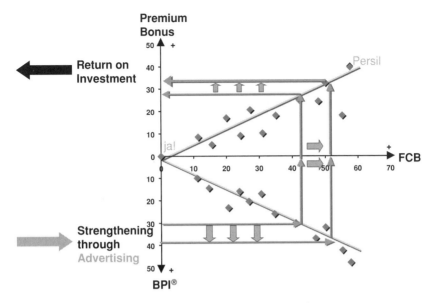

Figure 17.5 Correlation between brand attraction and brand success.

Time and again, and regardless of the industry involved, close correlations were confirmed between the BPI® as performance driver and revenue-oriented brand-strength criteria, such as market share, the share of first choice buyers and the price premium. As a consequence, and as the following example from the heavy-duty detergent market makes clear, brands with a high Share of Soul demonstrate a correspondingly high economic market success as well. The correlation between brand attractiveness and the core results values of market share and premium bonus based on the case of the heavy-duty detergent market is shown in Figure 17.5.

If one looks at Figure 17.5, starting from BPI® and working counter-clockwise, it becomes clear that a brand such as Persil, which enjoys a high share of first choice buyers based on its high level of brand attractiveness and the associated additional utility, is also in a position of realizing a higher price premium. Thus, it demonstrates a higher price difference over other retail brands (in this case Ja! by Rewe).

Based on this system, some preliminary points of reference can be derived for the profitability of brand investments in advertising commitments. If, for example, stepping up advertising commitments leads to strengthened brand attraction, in future this will lead to enhancement of the share of first choice buyers. This, in turn, permits the assertion of a higher price premium in future and, with it, realization of a higher return on brand investment.

The applicability of the system sketched in Figure 17.5 is inextricably linked to a correlation between current brand attractiveness and the future development of core results values. This can be demonstrated for the case of the German chocolate bar market. As can be seen in Figure 17.6, significant advantages in the brand attractiveness of the Lindt brand compared to Sarotti and Trumpf in 2001 contributed to corresponding market-share developments in 2002: Lindt managed to add considerably to its market share, while Sarotti and Trumpf each were forced to put up with losses in market share. Developments of a similar nature for first choice buyers are shown for the detergent market in an article by Högl and Hupp (2001).

The BASS provides a graphic compilation of the results of psychological brand strength and the economical evaluation of market success in the form of a kind of brand scorecard (Figure 17.7). The case presented illustrates, for a client brand, very positive results for the emotional, rational and behaviour-oriented facets of the Brand Potential Index relative to the competition. The client brand also demonstrates pronounced strengths in terms of revenue-oriented indicators. Only the price premium currently realized by the brand must be rated as average. In future, enhancement of brand attractiveness could also lead to improvement in this indicator of success.

In the ideal case, the brand-strength assessment shown in Figure 17.7, based on pre-economic indicators of success (psychological brand strength) along with economic core results values (behaviour-oriented indicators), is tied to the existence of panel data. The survey data are then linked with the panel data by means of fusion to create a single data record.[6]

For markets such as the automobile industry, however, and for services as well, data of this type are frequently unavailable. In such cases, the economic core results values are to be measured via surveys. To achieve a similarly valid pool of data for brand assessment, matching along with, where indicated, a weighting of survey data are recommended, based on

---

[6] In a data fusion, for each person surveyed, a kind of partner within the consumer panel is sought who demonstrates the greatest possible similarity in terms of select behavioural data, such as the brands purchased or the shopping location used, and in terms of socio-demographic factors as well. Once suitable partners have been identified, the information obtained through the survey can then be transferred over to the panel database (on this point, see the extensive treatment in Wildner, 2000).

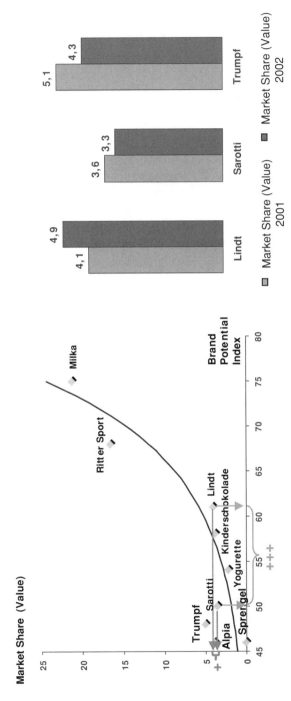

Figure 17.6   Correction between BPI® and market in the chocolate bar market.

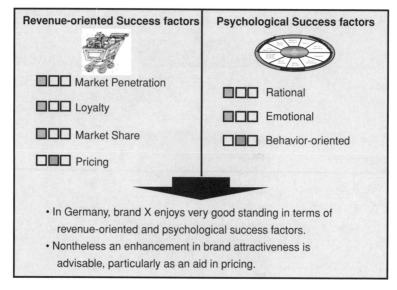

Figure 17.7   Classification of the results of the brand assessment with a brand scorecard.

available secondary statistics such as, for example, results of the regularly-conducted New Car Buyer Survey (NCBS) or existing scanning data available through retailers.

DEMANDS UPON A DEFINITIVE BRAND-PERFORMANCE MEASUREMENT

The individual marketing policy instruments, such as the policy pertaining to the product, service or communications, serve as a means of ensuring successful brand positioning and brand leadership, and therefore the success of a business. Their usage can be considered as a marketing investment. This is emphasized by Doyle (1989, p. 79): 'Like most other assets, brands depreciate without further investment. If management fails to reinvest in enhancing quality, service and brand image, then the brand will decline.' Against this backdrop, Meffert, Burmann and Koers (2002, p. 404) predict that, in the future, the success of brand leadership will not only be assessed from the perspective of profiling and differentiation, but also in terms of results. Even against the backdrop of the prevailing tough economic climate in many European countries, *brand investment* should, in future, be determined more than it previously has been by *profitability considerations* (Caspar and Metzler, 2002; Meurer and Panella, 2002). Consequently, effective and efficient brand control requires that the contribution made by *all* marketing instruments to the current success of the brand in the sense of a *return on brand investment* be ascertained and assessed with regard to future brand leadership.

A core task for brand performance measurement, therefore, is to represent the effects of alternative marketing measures on the economic success of the brand in order to identify those measures which enhance the value of a brand, and to channel the company's resources to these measures. (Spreemann, 1991; Hammann, 1992).

As already suggested, action must also be taken to ensure that the application of the marketing mix and the combined effect of the various instruments is appropriate with regard to *content*, i.e. it qualitatively strengthens the brand positioning (*effectiveness of resource application*). As far as that goes, a further task of brand-performance measurement is the assessment of the qualitative contribution to the marketing objectives made by the individual marketing policy instruments. In addition to the efficiency assessment, sound impact analyses for the brand-performance measurement of each individual marketing instrument used – embedded in the context of the overall marketing mix – can provide valuable indications for the optimization of the entire portfolio of measures.

At first sight, the consideration of all marketing policy instruments within the context of brand-performance measurement appears to be self-evident. With reference to existing brand-performance measurement instruments, however, it is not pure speculation that leads Meffert and Burmann to speak of stand-alone solutions, whereby individual aspects such as the image or specific marketing mix instruments are made a core issue. A recent Internet study conducted by leading market research institutions shows that consultancy work carried out on this connection is based on either:

- analysing the impact and success of *selected* marketing mix instruments on *qualitative* impact variables (e.g. advertising tracking) such as image, brand recognition or brand preference;
- *or* modelling the effects of the *entire* marketing mix on *quantitative* impact variables (usually market share), which are measured with the aid of panels.

However, in order to make sound and objective-oriented decisions regarding the future allocation of the marketing budget to the individual mix instruments, the contribution made by all marketing policy instruments to the overall success of the brand must be assessed in terms of efficiency and effectiveness. It should subsequently be shown how the demands detailed here upon a definitive brand-performance measurement instrument are fulfilled by the BASS.

EVALUATION OF THE EFFECTIVENESS AND EFFICIENCY OF MARKETING MIX INSTRUMENTS USING THE BRAND ASSESSMENT SYSTEM

To provide an illustration of the concrete procedure followed under the BASS approach in evaluations of the effectiveness and efficiency of marketing measures, the individual analytical steps will be illustrated based on the case study of a German manufacturer of electronic entertainment equipment. This manufacturer produces television sets, video recorders and hi-fi equipment, among other products. As a result of the very high level of quality of its products, this manufacturer occupies an absolutely prime position in the various markets in which it is active. The high prices of its products also clearly set it apart from the national, and especially the international, competition.

In late 2001, this manufacturer was faced with the question of how to optimize its instruments of marketing policy in future, with a view to solidifying its market position even further at the expense of other providers of high-quality products.

A first concern in this regard was to identify the relevant fields through which this producer of entertainment electronics could position itself as distinct from the competition in the eyes of consumers. Generally these positioning fields are functional product attributes or emotional product associations, which – from the consumer's point of view – have the potential to increase the success of the brand. In times of low consumer involvement, brand positioning should concentrate on as few dimensions as possible, and specifically on the most harmonized dimensions. Only then is it possible to convey as clear and as accessible a brand image as possible to the consumer. Any attempt simultaneously to achieve a successful contrast of several positioning dimensions usually fails. The customarily passive uptake of information by consumers with a low level of involvement does not allow them to absorb a greater amount of different information and to bond with the brand (Esch, 2002).

Information about relevant positioning fields may be derived from a general corporate strategy or a formulation of the brand core based on objectively logical considerations. In the case study under consideration here, however, it was possible to derive which fields were relevant to market positioning, based on an empirical positioning study which had been conducted previously. This study had identified 'innovative technology', 'exclusivity' and 'leadership in quality' as dimensions relevant to market positioning. According to the positioning study, compared with the competition, the brand in question demonstrated pronounced strengths in consumers' perceptions with regard to the last two of the three characteristics. At the level of 'innovative technology', on the other hand, the brand is viewed as merely average.

For the operationalization of the three positioning fields, a set of suitable indicators from the previously conducted positioning study was selected for each field, which were then brought to the fore within the context of an ongoing brand tracking study. This study was concerned with typical image items that were linked to a seven-point rating scale. The dimension of quality leadership was operationalized, for example, in the statement, 'produces equipment with outstanding performance'. An indicator for the dimension of 'exclusivity' was the statement, 'is a brand which one enjoys being seen with', and the 'innovative technology' dimension was operationalized using the item, 'brand which offers the most progressive technologies'.

Since the objective of the study was an assessment of the efficiency and effectiveness of the marketing mix instruments used within the context of brand management, such as price, advertising, product policy and distribution, a great many qualitative and quantitative indicators to measure the perception of these marketing mix instruments were also incorporated into the survey.

The operationalization of the advertising impact in the existing study is undertaken using traditional indicators from advertising tracking, such as the ability to recall certain advertising campaigns in various media, how the advertising presentation was liked, its uniqueness, etc. The distribution was operationalized by means of questions concerning availability as well as the positioning at the PoS, among others. Where price entered in, an explicit distinction was made between strategic pricing ('especially inexpensive equipment', among other things) and limited-period promotional pricing (e.g., 'part of a promotional sale in the shop'); this enabled greater fine-tuning in evaluations of the effects which these instruments had displayed.

A discerning view of the effects of product policy is reflected through indicators of quality ('produces equipment of very high quality') and design competence ('offers attractive and superbly designed equipment'). The quality of after-sales service was measured as well ('brand which offers excellent service', 'offers a particularly long warranty period', among other statements).

Furthermore, the brand strength was operationalized in accordance with the points listed above, using the Brand Potential Index (BPI®) on the one hand and consumer behaviour. Since consumer-panel data are not a reliable measure for electronic entertainment products, the data-fusion procedure usually applied to products in the fast-moving consumer goods segment could not be used here.

A corresponding catalogue of questions was designed, for which responses had to be given within the framework of a CATI study in four waves of 300 people each. The surveys were conducted in the first, second, third and fourth quarters of the 2002 calendar year. Respondents were limited to those people who had purchased an electronic entertainment device over the course of the prior three months. This procedure ensured reliable recall of the various factors which influenced the purchase decision. Respondents were required to indicate the brand or brands they had chosen in each case, and to rank these and other brands within the purchase-decision-making process (renown, relevant set, repeat or supplemental purchase). In order to achieve an agreeable allocation of interviews over the entire year, the interviews were distributed at equal intervals over several weeks for each group. In this way, we conducted 1200 assessments of client brands and selected competitors over the entire year.

To ensure that the distribution of purchases within the tracking study corresponded with real market trends, a weighting was made to reflect actual market shares measured within the retail panel.

The chosen procedure ensures, on the one hand, that the development of brand perception, brand strength and success can be demonstrated over the whole year depending on the marketing activities introduced for a short period of time (e.g. price promotions), as well as those marketing activities that are being implemented continuously (e.g. product policy). These results are displayed in Figure 17.8 in the format of the well-known time series diagrams.

At the same time, the design of the study provides a reliable database for evaluation of the marketing mix efficiency and effectiveness: the analyses are carried out based on the pooled database as obtained over the four waves of surveying, thereby ensuring a volume of cases sufficient for complex analyses to be carried out.

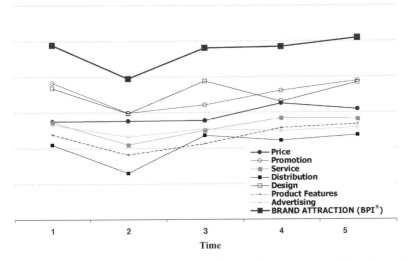

Legend within figure:
- ● Price
- ○ Promotion
- ■ Service
- ■ Distribution
- □ Design
- Product Features
- Advertising
- ■ BRAND ATTRACTION (BPI®)

1   2   3   4   5

Time

Figure 17.8   Performance of different marketing mix instruments and brand attraction (BPI®).

Before the methodical procedure for assessing the effectiveness and efficiency of the individual marketing mix instruments is presented here, the terminology must first be limited in terms of content. To our understanding, the *effectiveness* of a marketing mix represents the extent to which this instrument succeeds in strengthening the positioning of a brand. *Efficiency*, on the other hand, refers to the degree of impact achieved by the marketing mix instruments with regard to revenue-oriented key figures such as market share, consumer loyalty or price premiums.

In accordance with our approach, the first undertaking is to identify the instruments in the marketing mix that have the strongest leverage on the positioning of the brand, i.e. those having the greatest impact. The second step is then to enhance this qualitative assessment of the marketing mix by adding an analysis of the impact of individual instruments on the market success of the brand. With regard to the efficiency analysis, it is therefore a question of selecting those instruments which will achieve maximum success with a given budget.

The 1200 evaluations for the client brand permitted a meaningful application of developed estimation procedures, such as *causal analysis*.[7] The causal analysis represented the basis for the determination of correlations

---

[7] Causal analysis is a complex, static data analysis procedure, which is reminiscent in its character of a regression analysis. In contrast to a regression analysis, a causal analysis allows an estimate to

between the perception of certain marketing measures, the positioning fields, as well as brand appeal and brand success.

A variation of this methodology can be used when indices are created to quantify the perception of the various marketing mix instruments: the indices that express the perceptual quality of the individual marketing mix instruments are estimated in a causal model using *formative indicators*. As opposed to the traditional causal analysis, this procedure abandons the assumption that the endogenous constructs observed (e.g. advertising quality or distribution quality) are responsible for the development of the indicators which underlie them. Instead, this analysis advances the theory that these indicators cause the development of the endogenous variables. This assumption typically is true of the creation of indices.

The establishment of a corresponding causal model is based on the following assumptions concerning the model:

1. The relevant positioning fields for the client's brand are innovative technology, exclusivity and quality leadership.
2. The stronger the relation between a positioning field and the appeal of a brand, the more important this positioning field is from the consumers' perspective. The marketing management should therefore focus its efforts on those positioning fields which have the greatest influence on the brand attraction – and will therefore enhance the future success of the brand.
3. The marketing mix instruments used have varying degrees of impact upon the various positioning fields of a brand. The greater the (causal) correlation between the perception of a marketing mix instrument and a positioning field, the more effectively the respective instrument is able to develop the corresponding positioning.
4. Marketing mix instruments may not actually impact upon the positioning fields of a brand; instead, they may exert a direct influence on the success of the brand.[8]
5. The efficiency of a marketing mix instrument is derived from the sum of all direct and indirect impacts made by the instruments upon the consumers' purchasing behaviour via the brand attraction (*total effects*).

---

be made of the correlation between non-observable variables, such as images, and the appeal of a brand within the framework of multistage models (Homburg and Hildebrandt, 1998, p. 26 ff.).

[8] Behind this assumption lies the consideration that certain marketing campaigns, such as the use of price promotions, do in fact bring about success in the sense of increased sales, but have no significant direct effect on the perception of the brand.

On the basis of these considerations, a multistage causal model can be formulated which reproduces the impact of individual marketing mix instruments on purchasing behaviour (via the various positioning fields). For illustration purposes we concentrate in the following example on just one purchasing behaviour variable. We do not illustrate the effects on the price premium, which were estimated too. The estimated results given by such a model are presented below. For reasons of clarity, the individual module components are discussed one by one. The model estimate, however, refers to the entire model.

Step 1: Analysis of the effectiveness of the marketing mix

By estimating the influence of each positioning field on the attraction of the brand (BPI®), the most important positioning fields for the brand from the consumers' perspective can be identified. In the present case, the dimensions are quality leadership and exclusivity, since they have been calculated as having the greatest effect on the brand appeal. This positioning field presents itself for the future as a strategic lever which is able further to develop the current market position in the consumers' mind (*therapeutic variables*) (Figure. 17.9).

Innovative technology, on the other hand, has no effect on brand appeal that merits a mention; it does, however, have an indirect impact

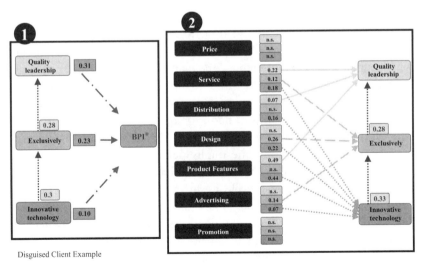

Disguised Client Example

Figure 17.9 Determination of important positioning fields for brand success and the impact of marketing mix instruments upon brand positioning.

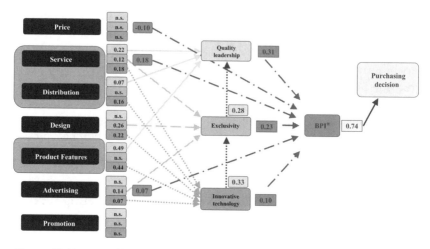

Figure 17.10   Overall model for the analysis of the effectiveness and efficiency of the marketing mix.

by way of exclusivity. In a similar vein, the exclusivity dimension also has an indirect influence upon brand attractiveness, the intervening variable being quality leadership (the more exclusive the product's positioning, the more intense the experience of quality leadership). This being the case, the three positioning fields examined constitute a harmonious brand core.

In order to develop the brand attraction to the maximum extent possible (and therefore also brand success), those marketing mix instruments which support the development of the quality leadership and exclusivity positioning field are to be prioritized. Figure 17.10 clearly shows that the mix instruments with the shaded backgrounds (on the left hand side of the figure) have the greatest impact upon the quality leadership positioning field, and that they therefore work effectively with regard to optimizing consumers' perception. The mildly negative effect of the price on the BPI can be interpreted to the effect that a price reduction would adversely affect the general level of esteem in which the brand is held. Thus, price seems to play a role of key information for the client brand. The academic literature on the subject refers repeatedly to an effect of this nature (Kroeber-Riel and Weinberg, 1996, pp. 298–301).

In the sense of a maximum possible return on brand investment, it was now necessary to filter out those marketing mix instruments which best contributed (based on revenue) to the brand's success from those marketing mix instruments with a high level of effectiveness. For this optimization decision, an indicator variable was built which displayed for a respondent the client brand's position within the purchase-decision-making process (brand renown, component of the relevant set, actual purchase, brand loyalty in terms of repeat or supplemental purchase).

Step 2: Analysis of the efficiency of the marketing mix

Information can be gained regarding the efficiency of the mix instruments highlighted as being effective using the total effects (Figure. 17.11), which are generated by the causal modelling approach (Figure. 17.10).

Figure. 17.10 and 17.11 clearly show that after-sales service, coupled with perceived product quality, has the greatest impact on the actual consumer behaviour (purchase, loyalty, etc.). When considered from an investment theory perspective, improving the design of the equipment should not be a primary objective, even though this aspect exerts a more pronounced influence upon exclusivity than after-sales service and product quality do. Investments in the latter marketing mix elements would lead to a greater return on brand investment.

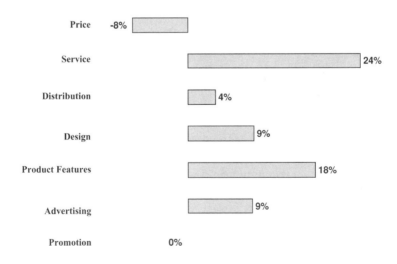

Disguised Client Example

Figure 17.11 Total effects of the marketing mix on the individual market share.

Given the results shown in Figure 17.11, distribution, design and advertising can provide only flanking support for the client brand.

The critical role played by price is worth repeating. Both lasting changes in pricing policy and intensified use of price promotions should be rejected in light of investment-theory standpoint considerations. For the provider of electronic entertainment products under consideration here, these instruments are not suited to significant enhancement of sales-oriented brand success. Strategic pricing exerts, as shown in the figure, an immediate influence over the esteem in which a brand is held, and thus over the brand's very success.

SUMMARY AND FURTHER PROSPECTS

The Brand Assessment System (BASS) presented in this chapter fulfils the central requirements to which a comprehensive brand-controlling approach must measure up. The approach avoids stand-alone systems, as the strength of the brand is measured equally by means of a psychological and a sales-oriented component. Whenever possible, the sales-oriented component is measured with the aid of valid panel data.

In addition, the focus is not directed at the image or individual marketing mix instruments, as is the case in classic brand-tracking instruments. Brand positioning is considered explicitly, and on its own terms, as is the complete marketing mix.

Alongside a pure diagnosis of marketing effects, the approach presented here permits an analysis of the effectiveness and efficiency of the individual mix instruments, thereby enabling prioritization and the accompanying optimization of future budget allocations.

For derivation of concrete recommendations for action, one must go back to the indicators which underlie the various indices for the quantification of the effects of marketing mix instruments. These indicators permit concrete recommendations for action in matters such as whether advertising intensity should be stepped up and/or whether a revision of current advertising is advisable.

By way of a caveat, it should be noted that the efficiency analysis is made based exclusively on sales-oriented considerations. A company's in-house brand-controlling approach, however, can build upon these results and, for example, compare prognoses of market-share growth with the costs for the optimized marketing mix, thus arriving at a more reliable evaluation of the return on brand investment.

REFERENCES

Bekmeier, S. (1994), Emotionale Bildkommunikation mittels nonverbaler Kommunikation. Eine interdisziplinäre Betrachtung der Wirkung nonverbaler Reize, in Forschungsgruppe Konsum und Verhalten (Eds.) *Konsumentenforschung*, pp. 89–104.

Caspar, M. and Metzler, P. (2002), *Entscheidungsorientierte Markenführung: Aufbau und Führung starker Marken*, Münster.

Doyle, P. (1989), Building strong brands: The strategic options. *Journal of Marketing Management*, **1**, 77–95.

Esch, F.-R. (2002), *Strategie und Technik der Markenführung*, Munich.

Grimm, M., Högl, S. and Hupp, O. (2000), TARGETPOSITIONING: Ein bewährtes Tool zur Unterstützung der strategischen Markenführung. *Jahrbuch der Absatz- und Verbrauchsforschung*, **2**.

Hammann, P. (1992), Der Wert der Marke aus betriebswirtschaftlicher und rechtlicher Sicht. in: Dichtl, E. and Eggers, W., (Eds) *Marke und Markenartikel als Instrument des Wettbewerbs*, pp. 205–245.

Högl, S. and Hupp, O. (2001), Neue und weitergehende Wege in der Markensteuerung. *Markenartikel*, **4**, 22–27.

Högl, S., Twardawa, W. and Hupp, O. (2001), Key Driver starker Marken, in: GWA, (Ed.): *Key Driver starker Marken – Gibt es Regeln für erfolgreiche Marken*, pp. 15–59.

Homburg, C. and Hildebrandt, L. (1998), Die Kausalanalyse: Bestandsaufnahme, Entwicklungsrichtungen, Problemfelder, in: Hildebrandt, L. and Homburg, C. (Eds) *Die Kausalanalyse*, pp. 16–43.

Hupp, O. (2000a), Markenwert und Markenführung. *Planung & Analyse*, **6**, 60–63.

Hupp, O. (2000b), Die Validierung von Markenwerten als Voraussetzung für die erfolgreiche Markenführung. *Planung & Analyse*, **5**, 44–47.

Hupp, O. and Hofmann, J. (2002), Was ist eine starke Marke? *Markenartikel*, **5**.

Hupp, O. and Schuster, H. (2000), Imagegestützte Positionierung von Einkaufsstätten als Ansatzpunkt zu einer Verbesserung der Wettbewerbsfähigkeit des Lebensmitteleinzelhandels in Deutschland, *Jahrbuch der Absatz- und Verbrauchsforschung*, **4** (46).

Kroeber-Riel, W. and Weinberg P. (1996), *Konsumentenverhalten*, München.

Meffert, H., Burmann, C. and Koers, M. (2002), Stellenwert und Gegenstand des Markenmanagement, in: Meffert, H., Burmann, C. and Koers, M. (Eds) *Markenmanagement*, pp. 3–16.

Meffert, H. and Koers, M. (2002), Controlling des Markenmanagement, in: Meffert, H., Burmann, C. and Koers, M. (Eds) *Markenmanagement: Grundfragen der identitätsorientierten Markenführung*, pp. 403–428.

Meurer, J. and Panella, A. (2002), Fundamentaler Wandel. *Markenartikel*, **5**, 12–22.

PricewaterhouseCoopers and Sattler, H. (1999), *Industriestudie: Praxis von Markenbewertung und Markenmanagement in deutschen Unternehmen*. Frankfurt am Main.

Reinecke, S. and Reibstein, D. (2001), Marketing Performance Measurement–Einsatz von Marketingkennzahlen in den USA und Kontinentaleuropa, in: Reinecke, S., Tomczak, T. and Geis, G. *Handbuch Marketing-Controlling*, St. Gallen/Wien, pp. 144–166.

Reinecke, S. and Tomczak, T. (2001), Einsatz von Instrumenten und Verfahren des Marketingcontollings in der Praxis, in: Reinecke, S., Tomczak, T. and Geis, G. *Handbuch Marketing-Controlling*, Thexis/Ueberevter, pp. 76–88.

Sattler, H. (2002), Grundlagen und praktische Umsetzung der Bewertung von Marken aus Sicht des Marketing, In: GWA (Ed.) *Der Geldwert der Marke* (edition Erfolgsbeiträge der Werbung, vol. 5), pp. 19–34.

Spreemann, P. (1991), Streit um Kunden, *Wirtschaftswoche*, **45**(39), 90–96.

Twardawa, W. and Hupp, O. (2000), Die Bedeutung der Werbung für die strategische Markenführung. *Planung & Analyse*, **3**, 32–37.

Wildner, R. (2000), Messung von Werbewirkung mit fusionierten Paneldaten. *Jahrbuch der Absatz- und Verbrauchsforschung*, **3**, 242–260.

Chapter Eighteen

The Impact of Consumers' Commitment to Existing Brands on New Product Launch Strategies

Jan Hofmeyr[a] and John Rice[b]

Thousands of new products are launched around the world every year and almost all of them fail. One of the reasons is the failure of existing research methods to take into account people's prior commitment to what they're already using.

INTRODUCTION

Concept and product testing have become increasingly accurate over the years as a means to forecast new product sales. So much so that by the early 1990s, marketers in most developed countries no longer had to guess whether or not their new product ideas would be successful. Yet, as Bennett and Davis report (1996), the failure rate for new product launches continues to be extraordinarily high. In the United States alone, up to 60% of new grocery products fail at the test market stage.

In a world in which forecasting techniques are quite accurate, one of the reasons for continuing failure may simply be that not all new products

[a]International Director of Innovation, Synovate (Brand and Communication).
[b]Co-founder, Research Surveys.

Market Research Best Practice. Edited by P. Mouncey and F. Wimmer.
© 2007 John Wiley & Sons, Limited.

get tested. In 1998, for example, 25 181 new 'packaged goods' products were launched in the United States (*Marketing News*, March 1999). It is hard to imagine that all of these were tested. But a second reason for failure is almost certainly the failure to implement appropriate launch strategies. It is not enough to know that a product has a chance of succeeding. It's also essential to know what needs to be done to *maximize* its chances of success.

This chapter involves a very simple proposition: if you can understand the nature of consumers' commitment to the brands that already exist in a market, you can both sharpen your analysis of new product launches and develop strategies which enhance the prospects of success. Let us see how.

CONCEPT AND PRODUCT TESTING: A SUMMARY OF CURRENT APPROACHES

Typically, concept or product tests have the following structure:

- expose a sample of respondents to the new product or concept;
- measure their response to the product/concept in some way;
- estimate rates of trial and repurchase on the basis of the response;
- predict likely sales, using a formula.

Bennett and Davis (1996) describe the typical formula as follows:

Sales = population × % awareness × % trial × % repeat × buying rate

The above kind of formula would be applied for a time period, say the first year of sales. The 'buying rate' would then be the mean number of times that consumers can be expected to buy a brand in that market during that time.

Marketers make important inputs into the model. They have to estimate the levels of awareness they expect to achieve. In addition, trial estimates depend on both the results of the test and on the marketer's estimates of likely distribution. If sales forecasts are not met, the blame for failure can be sought in a number of places – for example, failure in the test or failures in various aspects of the launch strategy.

Although many variations of the above approach to new concept/product testing exist, they can usefully be classified into two broad categories: those which are 'externally' and those which are 'internally' calibrated.

The need for 'external calibration' arises whenever forecasting techniques are used in which respondents tend to overstate how positive they are about the new product. A typical example of this is any technique which uses 'purchase intent' measures. We know that respondents' claimed likelihood of purchasing a new product is subject to varying degrees of overclaim. We therefore have to downweight such claims by calibration with our empirical experience of subsequent real-world sales.

One of the difficulties with externally calibrated techniques is that the extent of overclaim varies by country and product category. Within countries it can also vary by demographic factors such as location (in mainland China, for example), or levels of sophistication and education. For this reason, externally calibrated methods need a substantial database to be accurate for sales forecasting. BASES is probably the best known externally calibrated sales forecasting product.

'Internally calibrated' techniques try to avoid the problem of overclaim by building calibration methods into the research itself. One of the ways in which they do this is by trying to replicate features of the real world in the testing environment. Respondents may be confronted, for example, with a 'shop shelf' and asked to 'buy' things. Constant sum measures are also used in many of these approaches. In this way, researchers hope to measure respondents' implicit product preferences and avoid overstatement. ASSESSOR was one of the first proprietary techniques of this kind. The main problems with this sort of testing are that it is relatively cumbersome and can be expensive to implement.

Since 1993, we have been using a measure of commitment and availability in our concept and product tests as a way to simplify and reduce the cost of new product testing. Our approach combines the measures typically used in externally calibrated approaches (e.g. purchase intent) with a measure of commitment. By doing this, we have found that there is less of a need for external calibration. In addition, it is less costly than internally calibrated methods. In a sense, by combining commitment with purchase intent measures, we are introducing a form of internal calibration to what have traditionally been externally calibrated methods.

COMMITMENT: WHAT IS IT AND HOW SHOULD IT BE MEASURED?

Back in 1969, Day showed that a consumer could buy a brand loyally (i.e. again and again) and yet rate it poorly on a variety of attitudinal measures (reported in Jacoby and Chestnut, 1978). In other words, it was possible to be behaviourally loyal, yet attitudinally disloyal.

We use the word 'commitment' to refer to what Day called 'attitudinal loyalty'. More specifically, we use it to refer to the strength of the psychological relationship between a consumer and a brand. Behavioural *loyalty* is simply the tendency of a person to buy a brand again and again. *Commitment* exists when that buying is backed by genuine enthusiasm for the brand. How then should commitment be measured?

Clearly, if we are to measure the psychological attachment that people have to their brands, then the measuring instrument itself should only contain psychological questions. Since 1989, we have been using just such a measure. And we have argued that there are only four questions that need to be asked to establish the commitment of a person to anything. The four questions are:

1. To what extent does (whatever) satisfy that person's needs/values?
2. Is the (whatever) something that matters to that person?
3. How does the person rate other (whatevers)?
4. If they rate other (whatevers) highly, which way do they lean?

These questions are not arbitrary. They are based on a theory of commitment and conversion that was first written about in 1985 (Hofmeyr, 1985), and has since been operationalized and validated extensively in the marketing research world (Hofmeyr, 1989, 1990; Rice and Hofmeyr, 1990; Ceurvorst, 1993).

Let us unpack the theory briefly. Like most marketing researchers, we argue that someone who is happy with their brand choice in a particular market will tend to be committed to that brand. Quite simply, satisfied customers are less likely to switch brands than dissatisfied customers.

But customer satisfaction is only one dimension of what makes for commitment. We all know that dissatisfied customers sometimes don't switch, while satisfied customers sometimes do (Keaveney, 1995). Since 1989, we have argued that the failure to take into account two further factors is what causes the measurement of customer satisfaction by itself to be a weak predictor of defections (Hofmeyr, 1995). They are:

- **involvement** – the extent to which the consumer cares about that particular brand choice;
- **attraction to alternatives** – the extent to which the consumer is attracted to competitor brands in that market.

Let us take 'involvement' first. I shower every day. I'm perfectly happy with the brands of soap I use. But it's not a product category in which I am especially involved. For this reason, I have never developed a psychological attachment to any particular brand of soap. I am perfectly satisfied, but uncommitted. It takes very little to get me to buy a different brand of soap.

By contrast, my banking relationships are something I do care about. But consider what I do when something goes wrong. I do not simply close all my accounts and switch to a competitor bank. Because I care, the first thing I do is give my bank an opportunity to fix things. I can be dissatisfied, yet committed. This is not merely due to the hassle factor associated with switching. For a case that unwittingly illustrates the importance of psychological relationships in delaying brand switching, see Reichheld (1996).

Broadly speaking then, when people care about a relationship (with whatever it is), they tend to be willing to tolerate a certain amount of dissatisfaction if things go wrong. This is because their preferred strategy will be to try to fix the relationship rather than to look for an alternative. By contrast, people who do not care about a relationship never really develop commitment to it. As a result, no matter how satisfied they may be, their commitment may remain shallow and they can be switched easily.

The second factor which must be plugged into a measure of commitment is what we call the 'attraction to alternatives'. Let us think about this. Imagine a person who is very good at and loves their job. But then they hear about a friend doing a similar job and getting paid more. Suppose now that they were offered a new job at their friend's company for better pay. The cumulative effect of these events would most likely be to undermine their commitment to their current job first, because of the pay issue; and second, because they were actually being offered an attractive alternative.

Some time ago, Jones and Sasser (1995) wrote in the *Harvard Business Review* that 'only extremely satisfied customers' could be counted on not to defect. But they had no theory to explain this. The theory of commitment and conversion explains the phenomenon easily. We now know that two conditions are required for people to report 'extreme' satisfaction. First, nothing else must be appealing to them, because if something else appeals it tends to undermine satisfaction, even if only just. Second, it must be something that is really important to them, because people simply do not get 'extremely' satisfied with anything unless they really care about it. Involvement is what generates those levels of 'satisfaction intensity'.

Table 18.1   Description of the 'commitment' and 'availability' segments.

	Commitment to brands used		Availability to brands not used
Entrenched	Strongly committed. Least likely of all users to convert.	Available	Closest of all the non-users to conversion to the brand
Average	Also committed, but not as strongly. Also unlikely to convert.	Ambivalent	The new brand appeals, but so does their current brand.
Shallow	Uncommitted. Relatively close to conversion. At risk.	Weak unavailable	Unavailable for conversion, but not far away from it.
Convertible	Least committed of all users. Most likely to convert.	Strong unavailable	Of all non-users, the least likely to convert to the brand.

Note: The above segmentation has been reported on extensively at conferences and seminars since 1989. Over thirty-five conference papers or articles have been published about the segments and their use.

Using our approach, the mind of a committed person can be described easily: they are happy with their brands. The brand choice matters to them. And there is nothing else in that arena of choice that appeals to them especially strongly.

By contrast, low commitment (i.e. a poor psychological relationship with a brand) can be due to any one, or a combination, of a variety of factors. Each one can be present in varying degrees. First, and obviously, it may be caused by low satisfaction. But second, it may be caused by low involvement and, all other things being equal, the level of satisfaction at which conversion actually takes place will vary as a function of the degree of involvement. Finally, commitment is undermined when an alternative is more appealing.

This approach leads to a fourfold classification of consumers according to how committed they are to the products or brands they are currently using. We then use 'the attraction to non-used competitor brands' as one of the inputs to segment non-users according to their availability for conversion to the brands they're not using. We describe the full segmentation in Table 18.1.

WHY DOES COMMITMENT MATTER WHEN IT COMES TO NEW PRODUCTS?

It stands to reason that people who are committed to the brands they already use may be difficult to win over for new brands. It therefore follows that the higher the aggregate levels of commitment in a market, the more difficult it may be to launch new brands successfully. It is one thing to think this, however, and quite another to demonstrate it. Let us therefore turn to a closer examination of what happens when a commitment measure is included in a conventional concept test.

Showing that commitment works to calibrate and identify the best prospects

To demonstrate the effect of a commitment measure on conventional concept and product tests, we simply add it in to such tests. This involves establishing commitment upfront and then repeating certain key questions after exposure to the concept or the product.

In more detail, commitment before exposure is measured by asking respondents to:

- rate the brands they use on a 'satisfaction' scale;
- rate the importance of the brand choice on an 'importance' scale;
- say whether they are leaning towards or away from their brands;
- rate all the brands in terms of how they feel about them.

Then the respondent is exposed to the new concept or product and we ask them the conventional purchase intent or constant sum questions. In addition, however, we re-ask the 'attraction to alternatives' question for that concept/product (i.e. the fourth question). We use a simple seven point 'favourability' scale to do this.

A typical result of this kind of approach, taken from one of our first case studies, is shown in Figure 18.1. As can be seen, the measure of availability, which takes into account both the respondent's response to

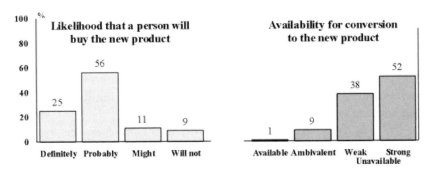

Figure 18.1   Comparison of measure of purchase intent with measure of availability.

the new concept and their prior commitment to existing brands, yields a much lower projected market potential for the new concept than the measure of purchase intent. Whereas 25% of the respondents claimed they would definitely buy the new product and 56% claimed they would probably buy it, only 1% were found to be available for conversion, while another 9% could be considered realistic prospects because they were at least ambivalent.

Using a typical 'purchase intent' measure, 25% of the respondents said they would 'definitely' buy the new product. Another 56% said they would 'probably' buy it, for a total of 81% who indicated an interest in trying the new product. By comparison, when consumers' prior commitment to brands was taken into account, only 1% of the respondents emerged as 'available for conversion' to the new product. Only 10% could be considered realistic prospects for it.

Since then we have repeated this sort of result in over seventy concept and product tests worldwide. When prior 'commitment' is built into the test as a means of internal calibration, the overclaim is reduced.

Recently, in a concept test conducted in Europe we took the method a step further. In this case, our 'purchase intent' measures were combined with both the measure of 'commitment and availability' and a simulated test market measure (STM). This case provided striking confirmation of the power of adding commitment as a way to reduce overclaim. The outcome of the test is summarized in Table 18.2. Note that all the numbers in Table 18.2 have been changed by multiplying them by a constant factor. In this way we have preserved the relationships between the numbers, but protected client confidentiality.

As the results show, the 'commitment/availability' approach yielded virtually identical results to the STM method for both trial and repeat purchase. While the former predicted a long-term market share of 3.2% for the product, the latter predicted a long-term market share of 3.4%. Both methods were obviously better at giving something more realistic than purchase intent.

The fact that we can use the 'commitment/availability' method to reduce overclaim suggests that by overlaying purchase intent scores with the 'availability' segments, we should be able to identify true prospects more easily. Those who say they will 'definitely' buy the new product, but who are found to be 'strongly unavailable' to it, may then be taken to be the most likely 'overclaimers'. Similarly, for respondents who say they will 'probably buy' the new concept we eliminate likely 'overclaimers'. We illustrate the principle, again from a real-world case, in Figure 18.2.

Table 18.2   Purchase intent compared with a measure of commitment/availability and an STM approach.

Purchase intent (pre and post trial)			Availability (pre and post trial)			STM approach (pre and post trial)		
	Pre %	Post %		Pre %	Post %		Pre %	Post %
Definitely	13	26	Available	3	11	Positive	10	32
Probably	39	52	Ambivalent	7	19			
The rest	48	23	Unavailable	90	70	Negative	90	68
Total	100	100	Total	100	100	Total	100	100

Notes:

1. Pretrial results are based on concept exposure and simple response questions in the case of the first two methods. The STM result is based on a simulated shop measure.
2. If we apply a typical 'rule of thumb': take all the 'definitely buy' and one-third of the 'probably buy' then we get trial rates of about 25% using a measure of purchase intent.
3. By contrast, by taking the 'available' plus 'ambivalent' segments at concept stage, we get exactly what we get for predicted trial when using STM, namely, 10%.
4. The post trial result for the purchase intent method is based on only exposing those who said they would 'definitely' or 'probably' buy the product at concept stage, to the new product.
5. Post trial results for the 'commitment/availability' and STM methods are based on exposing those who were 'available' or 'ambivalent' to the concept, to the new product.
6. If we assume that repeat rates are indicated post trial by the 'available and ambivalent' or 'positive' responses, then we get predicted market shares of 3.2% and 3.4% respectively from the latter two methods, using a simple Parfitt Collins equation.

Bennett and Davis have written a detailed account illustrating how adding individual-level commitment measures to 'purchase intent' questions helps to develop a more accurate profile of who is truly available for the new concept or product and who is not (Bennett and Davis, 1996).

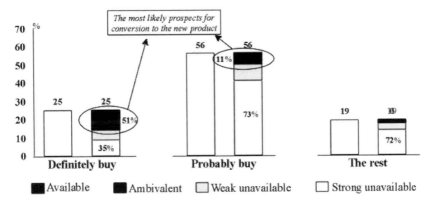

Figure 18.2   Illustration of how the measure of 'availability' helps to identify over-claimers.

At every level of purchase intent we find both 'under' and 'over-claimers'. Among respondents who say they will 'definitely buy' the new product, 35% were strongly unavailable for conversion to it because of their commitment to their current brands. This proportion rose to 73% of those who said they would 'probably' buy it. By contrast, 51% of those who said they would 'definitely buy' the new product were measured as being realistic prospects for conversion to it (i.e. either 'available' or 'ambivalent'). Only 11% of those who said they would 'probably' buy it were measured as being realistic prospects for conversion to it.

How the measurement of commitment achieves these results

In order to understand why our approach works as a means of internal calibration, we need to look at more examples of commitment in action. In Tables 18.3 and 18.4, we highlight two relationships that exist between the commitment that consumers have to their brands on the one hand, and their current and subsequent behaviour on the other.

As Table 18.3 shows, the halflife of a committed consumer is significantly longer than that of an uncommitted consumer. In other words, it takes significantly longer for half of the committed consumers to become

Table 18.3   Defection rates in three countries and five product categories.

| | | Strength of commitment to brands being used | | | | |
		Entrenched %	*Average* %	*Shallow* %	*Convertible* %	*Period*
United States	Pharmaceutical	5	24	44	60	1 year
	Personal care	17	35	62	78	1 year
	Cigarettes	33	54	59	79	2.5 years
Canada	Financial	4	7	20	31	1 year
	Beverages	4	15	36	54	1 year
S. Africa	Financial	3	5	16	44	6 months
	Beverages	13	17	51	58	9 months

Notes:

1. These results come from longitudinal studies. Respondents were recontacted after their initial classification. The period between contacts is shown in the last column.
2. Defection rates are shown for each level of commitment. So, 5% of the respondents who were entrenched users of their brand of pharmaceuticals had defected to another brand a year later.
3. To calculate the halflife of a consumer, do the following: (i) calculate the mean retention rate; (ii) iterate the retention rate until half the consumers have defected.
4. The halflife of committed (entrenched + average) users of pharmaceutical brands in the United States is about 4.5 years. The halflife of uncommitted users is about 0.96 of a year.

Table 18.4 Commitment and its impact on 'share of wallet' (nineteen countries, two product categories).

		Strength of commitment to brands being used			
		Entrenched %	Average %	Shallow %	Convertible %
Product One	Philippines	88	78	48	32
	Singapore	92	82	60	32
	Thailand	82	70	40	30
	Pakistan	74	60	62	44
	Hong Kong	90	88	58	36
	Malaysia	92	82	70	44
Product Two	United Kingdom	68	70	36	34
	Netherlands	70	68	56	44
	France	76	52	30	24
	Germany	66	50	28	18
	Poland	70	56	32	28
	Romania	80	74	36	28
	Turkey	88	60	40	26
	India	80	66	36	12
	Australia	94	70	52	30
	Canada	84	60	44	28
	Mexico	94	84	50	30
	Brazil	76	78	36	26
	Columbia	68	52	32	20
	Mean	81	69	45	30

Notes:

1. In each market, the 'share of wallet' was calculated for a 'midrange' brand, i.e., not the market leader but also not a small brand.
2. Interpretation: in the Philippines, 88% of what 'entrenched' consumers buy in this market is the brand to which they are entrenched.
3. The 'mean' is the simple, unweighted mean within each level of commitment across both product categories and all countries.

non-users than half of the uncommitted consumers. Table 18.4 shows that entrenched consumers devote close to three times as much of their 'share of wallet' to the brands to which they are entrenched than convertible consumers. In over 1800 studies in 160 product categories worldwide, we have observed these effects consistently. In fact, the relationship is found so reliably that it has become the basis for the way we approach brand valuation (Richards, 1998).

Quite simply, committed consumers behave in the way they do because of what is already in their minds about the brands they are using. They are single-minded, happy, involved and disinterested in alternatives. In order further to demonstrate the force of this mindset, we conducted a nonproprietary study in seventeen countries in the laundry detergent

Market Research Best Practice

Table 18.5 Comparison of the advertising awareness of consumers committed to a brand vs. those strongly unavailable to it.

Brand	Big brands	Total %	Relationship with brand Unavailable %	Relationship with brand Commited %	Smaller brands	Total %	Relationship with brand Unavailable %	Relationship with brand Commited %
United Kingdom	Persil	23	17	32	Persil (v2)	15	12	27
Netherlands	Ariel	21	14	40	Witte Reus	12	8	17
France	Ariel	43	29	59	Xtra	5	4	10
Germany	Sunil	44	64	36	Omo	25	20	83
Poland	Vizir	79	57	87	Tix	21	12	55
Turkey	Alo	74	71	89	Persil	31	28	50
India	Surf Excel	71	38	83	Ariel Bar	33	45	20
Philippines	Breeze	81	74	92	Pride	50	45	64
Japan	Super Top	76	48	75	Ariel	39	16	88
Canada	Tide	46	32	59	Ultra Cheer	41	33	60
Romania	Ariel	71	27	84	Tide	54	36	71
Mexico	Ace	82	66	100	Viva	53	36	76
Brazil	Omo	84	85	89	Quanto	19	14	37
Argentina	Skip	49	29	54	Gramby	30	21	56
	Mean	60	46	70	Mean	31	24	51

Notes:

1. The table shows the percentage that claim that they have seen advertising 'recently' for the brands in question. The first half of the table is for market-leading brands, the second for midsize or smaller brands.
2. At individual brand level, the base sizes are relatively small. Nevertheless, the pattern is consistent. The mean score for each table clearly shows the pattern.

category at the beginning of this year (see Table 18.5). We chose laundry detergent because it is common to both developed and developing markets, and because it is characterized by an almost endless attempt to persuade consumers that innovation is taking place.

We tested our hypothesis in the following way: we have argued that committed consumers will tend to be unavailable to alternative products and brands, including something new. One of the ways we should expect to see this played out is in the failure of unavailable consumers to be aware of advertising for the brands to which they are unavailable. In Table 18.5, we show the results of this research.

In the same study, uncommitted but involved consumers were found to be aware of an average of 3.7 advertisements for brands in the category, 32% more than uncommitted, uninvolved consumers.

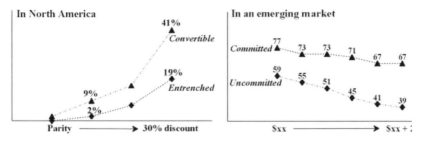

Figure 18.3   Relationship between commitment and price sensitivity.

There are obviously variations both across and within countries as a function of adspend and media penetration. The latter point applies particularly in the developing markets.

The results are clear: unavailability depresses the likelihood that advertising will be seen. In fact, the impact of what is already in a consumer's mind extends beyond the mere likelihood that the advertising will or will not be seen. As Rice and Bennett (1998) have shown, the poorer the relationship between a consumer and a brand, the less likely it is that the adverts, even if seen, will receive a positive response.

Of course, new product launches seldom rely on advertising alone. Often, they will involve instore promotions or sampling, coupled with introductory discount prices. In this way, the marketers of new products hope to achieve trial, and so break through the barrier of 'unconsciousness'. The problem is that it is not just the minds of the committed consumers that are closed. It is their 'hearts' as well.

Figure 18.3 shows the results of a conjoint analysis combined with a measure of commitment in two markets – one in North America and one in Asia. In both cases, the client was concerned about the impact that discount pricing from new brands would have on their market share. In the North American case, the new brands had not yet been launched. In the Asian case, they had, but there was little understanding on the client's part of the pricing dynamics in the market. In both cases, we were able to show that committed consumers were significantly less likely to switch to the new brands than uncommitted consumers, even when the new brands were offered to them at a significant discount to their current brands.

Clearly, one of the reasons that it is difficult to get committed consumers to buy a new product is quite simply that they are not in the market for messages. They are, therefore, less likely than other consumers to pick up the advertising for a new product. But in addition, as our research shows, even if you can make them aware of the new product and offer it at a discount, committed consumers are significantly less likely to convert to it than uncommitted consumers.

The first chart in Figure 18.3 shows the percentage that defect from their brand to take advantage of a discounted new brand. So, when the discount is 30%, 41% of the convertible consumers of our client's brand defected to the new brand, but only 19% of the entrenched consumers did so.

The second chart shows the results of a similar study. In this case, we show the 'share of wallet' retained by our client's brand for different levels of discounting by a new brand. So, when the discount is steep enough that our client's brand is at a 21% price premium, our client's brand still retains 67% of the 'share of wallet' of its committed consumers. By contrast, it only retains 39% of the uncommitted consumers' 'share of wallet'.

We often tell our clients that launching a new product is like trying to break up a marriage: when you aim your product at a committed consumer, it is like trying to break up a happy marriage. If you work hard enough, you can do it. But your prospects for success would be better if you attacked a marriage in which neither person cared about the relationship, or in which both people were unhappy.

BUILDING LAUNCH STRATEGIES AROUND AN UNDERSTANDING OF COMMITMENT

We have argued that building a commitment measure into concept and product tests takes some of the overclaim out of externally calibrated methods and allows us to identify who to target more accurately. It is an inexpensive alternative to internally calibrated methods and helps especially in markets where little prior knowledge or experience exists that can be used to create norms.

We have also shown some of the reasons why a commitment measure works. It is partly because the psychological relationship that committed consumers have with their brands causes them to lose interest in marketing messages. They are, therefore, less likely than others to be aware of new brand advertising. And even if they are made aware of the new brand and offered it at a discount, they are unlikely to take up the offer.

Before we can elaborate on the implications of all these results for new product launch strategies, we need to do just two more things. First, we need to spend more time on the mindset of the uncommitted consumer; and second, we need to look at a real-world example of a successful new product launch.

A more detailed look at the mindset of the uncommitted consumer

Ariel is the market-leading brand of laundry detergent in France. Our nonproprietary research into the relationship between commitment and brand image in this market produced the results shown in Figure 18.4. We look at three states of mind: first, those who are committed to Ariel; second, those who are uncommitted to Ariel and also uncommitted to all other brands, but who think that the brand choice is important; and finally, those who are uncommitted to Ariel and all other brands, but who do not think that the brand choice is important.

- **The mind of the committed consumer** – this is a very clear and expected picture; Ariel is by far the best rated brand on all attributes. It has a clear and strong image. No other brand comes close. In addition, there is no uncertainty in this person's mind – the level of 'don't know' responses is low.
- **The mind of the uncommitted consumer who cares about the brand choice** – although these people are uncommitted, they are not especially unhappy with their brands. They rate Ariel well, but they also rate other brands well. In short, they have clear and strong images of more than one brand. The problem here is not that there is only one brand in their minds. The problem is that they cannot make up their minds – their minds are overcrowded.
- **The mind of the uncommitted consumer who does not care** – the most striking aspect of the mindset of these people is that they do not form strong impressions of any brand, including Ariel. Mostly they say either that they 'don't know' which brand is associated with which attribute, or that 'no brands' are associated with each attribute. The point is because they do not care, they pay no attention.

The effect of these mindsets on advertising consumption is striking. In the first case, as we have already shown, we are dealing with people who are not in the market for messages. In the second, however, we are dealing with people who are involved but uncommitted, and who therefore turn out to be big consumers of advertising. In the third case,

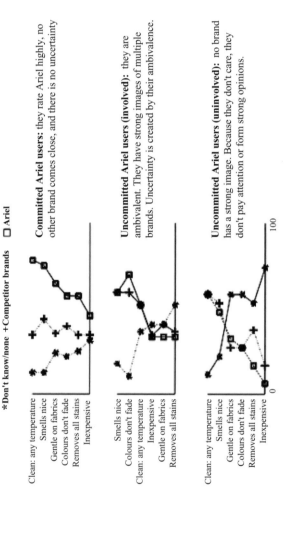

Figure 18.4 Relationship between commitment and brand image.

although uncommitted, we are dealing with people who are uninterested. Their consumption of advertising therefore tends to be relatively low.

We turn now to the real-world example of a successful new product launch.

Lessons from a case study

As we shall see (implicit in Figure 18.5), all markets in all product categories contain all three of the above kinds of consumer. It is just that the number of each kind varies from market to market. We turn now to a case that illustrates a successful launch strategy because the brand marketing team managed to target the correct consumers. Note that the numbers below have been changed to protect client confidentiality, but the essential relationships remain the same. Table 18.6 tells the entire story.

We go back to 1994, before the launch of the new brand. The market was dominated by one brand with over 50% market share by units. A range of smaller brands made up the rest. Store brands accounted for over 15% of the market. No other brand had more than 10%.

We measured commitment in this market prior to the launch of the new brand. Commitment had a dual pattern: commitment to the market leader was exceptionally high but relatively low to all others. Naturally, our client came into this market targeting the market leader. Our message: do not waste your time, focus on the uncommitted consumers of the smaller competitor brands.

The client's brand has grown from zero in 1994 to close to 30% today. But the market share of the market-leading brand has also gone up and

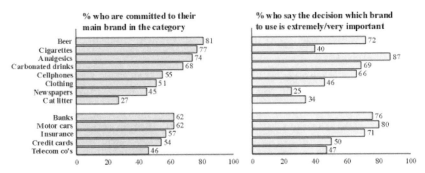

Figure 18.5 Selection of norms for commitment to and involvement in brands across the world.

Table 18.6   Key facts from the history of the launch of new brand B.

		1/95	*1/99*			*1/95*	*1/99*
Commitment	Brand A	85	84	Market	Brand A	56	56
	Store	46	44		Store	18	10
	Others	48	41		Others	10	12
	Brand B	0	82		Brand B	0	22
	Aggregate	68	74		Total	100	100

Notes:

1. All the key numbers have been modified to protect client confidentiality. Brand share has been tracked using Nielsen. Commitment was measured using the Conversion Model.
2. Interpretation: in January 1995, 85% of Brand A's users were committed to it. It had a market share of 56%. In January 1999, 84% were committed and its market share was 56%.
3. Aggregate commitment is the weighted average of the commitment of each of the brands or brand groups. The cell represents the percentage of a brand's users who were entrenched or average.
4. The importance of attributes in the brand choice was established implicitly by ranking attributes according to their correlations with the ideal point in an attribute association. As we note in the text, an attribute that ranked at the bottom of the list in 1995 was identified as a potential market driver. By 1999, it had become one of the most prominent attributes in the brand choice among regular consumers of Brand B.

remains over 50%. Our predictions have been fulfilled exactly. In five years, these two brands have come to dominate the market. How did the market leader maintain its dominant position in spite of the phenomenal growth of the new brand? And how did the new brand achieve its market share in the face of the levels of commitment to the market-leading brand?

The answer to both questions is 'focus' – focus on the consumer target and focus on the key attributes driving brand choice. The new brand launch strategy was simplicity itself: strong distribution, a noticeably different pack, consistency between packaging and advertising, and advertising which drew attention relentlessly to a key benefit of the new brand – a benefit which had been ignored by all brands, including the market leader, up to then.

The market-leading brand adopted a classical defence strategy: it immediately launched 'me too' advertising to reassure its committed consumers. But uncommitted consumers of all brands had long ago made up their minds that they knew what the market leader represented. They therefore paid no attention to the new message coming from the market leader. The 'me too' advertising did its job – it retained the brand's committed users – but it did not attract the uncommitted users of other brands. Instead, they flocked to the new brand.

Prior to the launch of the new brand, uncommitted consumers had consisted largely of people who were uninvolved in the market or who did not think that any brand had a special advantage. They therefore bought on the basis of price and availability, rather than on the basis of brand commitment. The brands of which this was most obviously true were the store brands. After the launch of the new brand, all of these consumers were given a new reason to be interested in the market. As a result, many of them stopped buying on the basis of price and availability. The effect on store brands was dramatic. In a year, between 1996 and 1997, they lost 33% of their market share – all of it going to the new brand.

We have continued to track this market. As the new brand has grown, so aggregate commitment to brands in the market has increased. Before the launch of the new brand, 69% of all consumers were committed to the brands they were using, driven mostly by the very large number of consumers who were highly committed to the market-leading brand. Four years after the launch of the new brand, 75% of all consumers are committed to the brands they are using. Quite simply, because the new brand offers something to consumers that they were not being offered before, it has turned consumers who were previously uncommitted to the smaller brands into consumers who are now committed to it.

The lessons are clear:

- know who to target – the uncommitted consumers;
- understand their mindset – they will be ambivalent or uninvolved;
- identify unoccupied attribute territory – an attribute that matters;
- focus relentlessly on the target and on getting the message across.

Let us now elaborate on these lessons.

Implications for the development of new product launch strategies

In the overcrowded markets of the developed world there is no doubt that achieving success for new products has a lot to do with the difficulty of breaking through the clutter. If there is anything that we've learnt, then it is that there is no such thing as an easy market to launch into. But there is also no doubt that the level of success that can be achieved will be a function of prior levels of commitment coupled with both the accuracy with which new prospects can be targeted and the choice of appropriate launch strategies. Let us therefore summarize our findings in this regard.

1. The more committed people there are in a market, the more difficult it will be to gain trial and win converts for the new product. We have shown that committed consumers are less likely both to see the advertising for a new brand and to respond to discount promotions for it. Literally, when we are dealing with committed people, we almost have to 'force' trial.

2. In terms of launch, therefore, targeting uncommitted consumers of existing brands is the best way to gain trial. That does not mean, however, that it will be easy to establish a stable market share. The problem with uncommitted consumers is that they may remain uncommitted. Stable repeat rates for a new brand depend on turning the uncommitted consumers of existing brands into committed consumers of the new brand.

3. There are two kinds of uncommitted consumer in most markets. There are those who are involved and interested in information about brands on the one hand, and those who are uninvolved and don't really care about the brand choice on the other. The challenge for a new brand will differ depending on which kind of uncommitted consumer is most prevalent or on which kind is being targeted.

Let us consider targeting uncommitted but involved consumers first. The good thing about them is that they are interested in brands and, therefore, that they are on the lookout for information. These are the people whose attention will be easiest to get. The more of them there are, the more appropriate advertising will be as part of the launch strategy. The challenge is stated simply: establish the perception that the new brand has a competitive advantage with respect to an attribute that matters. Ideally, this should be a new attribute.

Targeting uncommitted and uninvolved consumers requires a different strategy. The problem here is gaining their attention in the first place. Unless the advertising is exceptional, advertising per se will not be a good route. These are the people whose attention you have to attract by more 'forcible' means; and the best way to do so is at the point of sale through, for example, instore promotions. The good thing about them is that they tend to be willing trialists. The bad thing about them is that they tend to be fickle. Again, the challenge, although different, can be stated simply: make them care about the brand choice.

Ironically, while the implications for launch strategy may differ as a function of the nature of the uncommitted consumers, the endpoint for a new brand is the same: stable repeat purchase rates based on a committed consumer franchise will only be established if the brand can establish leadership in the mind of a group of people with respect to attributes that those people think are important. The alternative is to go the way of many small brands – namely, to scoop up the uncommitted consumers in a market by virtue of having an advantage when it comes to distribution (as is the case, for example, with store brands), or by offering them low prices. But then the penalty must also be accepted – namely, low margins and an uncommitted consumer franchise.

OVERVIEW OF COMMITMENT IN MARKETS AROUND THE WORLD

Given the importance of commitment levels to the potential success of new product launches, we thought it would be interesting to end our chapter by drawing on our database to show some norms around the world (see Figure 18.5).

81% of all consumers of beer around the world are committed to the main brand of beer they drink. 72% of all consumers think that the decision of which brand to drink is extremely, or very, important.

Some constants have begun to emerge. The first, as the figure shows, is that no matter how mundane or seemingly insignificant the product category, there are always at least some people who are committed or involved. There is, therefore, no such thing as a market in which everybody is uncommitted or in which no one cares about the brand choice.

Second, although involvement is required for deep commitment to develop in a market, not every market in which involvement is high will have high levels of commitment. Figure 18.5 shows, for example, that the motor car market is one in which involvement is extremely high. Yet commitment to motor cars is significantly lower than it is, for example, to brands of carbonated soft drinks. Moreover, the repurchase rates for motor cars as compared to brands of carbonated soft drinks demonstrate this to be true.

Third, no matter what the country, commitment varies systematically with levels of education and income. Broadly speaking, the better educated or wealthier a person is, the lower their levels of commitment will

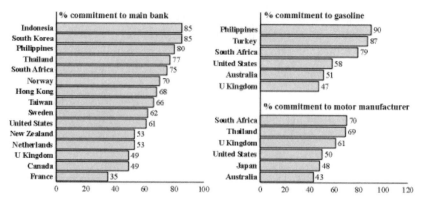

Figure 18.6   Variations in commitment to banks, gasoline and motor manufacturers across countries.

tend to be. We think this has to do with the self-confidence and the lack of risk in decision-making that comes with education and wealth. Poor people cannot afford to make a mistake. Ironically, therefore, poor people tend to be the most willing and committed buyers of premium brands. We've shown norms from three product categories to illustrate this phenomenon at country level (Figure 18.6). Notice how commitment tends to be lower in the wealthier countries, whereas 85% of the customers of banks in Indonesia are committed to their main bank.

Finally, there appears to be no such thing as a 'personality type' which is either committed or uncommitted to everything. In our research of individual consumers across multiple product categories, almost all respondents have been found to be committed to at least one thing (Hofmeyr, 1993). This was so even though the product categories involved a typical list of household goods.

CONCLUSION

When we started on this path to concept and product testing, we had a twofold purpose, neither of which was to create actual sales forecasts. This is because, in the developed world, for example, existing techniques can be used to generate accurate sales forecasts. In the markets of the developing world, on the other hand, we had no empirical basis for knowing what an accurate forecast would be. So our purposes were less ambitious:

1. Whether in the developed or developing world, to increase the accuracy of targeting when an externally calibrated method is being used.

2. Specifically in the developing world, to eliminate some of the overclaim where an absence of experience prevents accurate sales forecasting.

But as we have looked at more and more data about the behaviour of consumers as a function of their commitment, we have realized that by understanding commitment, we can go beyond the relatively limited research objectives we originally had in mind. In particular, we have found that by knowing the level of commitment and understanding the nature of the uncommitted consumer, we can develop more appropriate launch strategies. We are still learning, but we have presented data from a variety of different countries and product categories in both the developing and the developed worlds to show how this is the case.

REFERENCES

Bennett, R. and Davis, R. (1996), Improving new product decisions through the combined use of sales forecasting and brand equity models. *Canadian Journal of Marketing Research*, **15**.

Ceurvorst, R.W. (1993), *The Conversion Model: Measuring consumers' commitment and potential for change*. Presented at the 24th Attitude and Research Conference of the American Marketing Association, Arizona, January.

Hofmeyr, J. (1985), On the factors governing the strength of commitment to a group. Appendix Two of a research report: *Modelling the Interaction of Religion and Society*, Human Sciences Research Council, South Africa.

Hofmeyr, J. (1989), *Mobilizing values to slice up the market*, ESOMAR seminar on Is marketing keeping up with the consumers?, Vienna.

Hofmeyr, J. (1990), *The Conversion Model: A new foundation for strategic planning in marketing*. 3rd EMAC/ESOMAR symposium, Athens, Greece.

Hofmeyr, J. (1993), *Patterns of commitment to products and brands*. Unpublished incidental paper circulated in the network of Conversion Model partners.

Hofmeyr, J. (1995), *Is satisfaction enough?* . . . Paper presented at the conference Measuring customer satisfaction organized by IBA, London, February.

Jacoby, J. and Chestnut, R.W. (1978), *Brand Loyalty*. John Wiley & Sons, Inc.

Jones, T.O. and Sasser, W.E. (1995), Why satisfied customers defect. *Harvard Business Review*, Nov/Dec.

Keaveney, S.M. (1995), Customer switching behaviour in service industries: An exploratory study. *Journal of Marketing Research*, **59** (April), pp. 71–82.

Reichheld, F. F. (1996), Learning from customer defections. *Harvard Business Review*, March/April.

Rice, J. and Bennett, R. (1998), The relationship between brand usage and advertising tracking measurements. *Journal of Advertising Research*, 38(3), May/June, 58–66.

Rice, J. and Hofmeyr, J. (1990), *Segmentation using conversion theory*. Paper presented at the 12th SAMRA convention, Swaziland, October.

Richards, T. (1998), *Measuring the true value of brands: can you afford not to?* Paper presented at ESOMAR, September.

Chapter Nineteen

Predicting the Unpredictable: Agent-based Models for Marketing Research

David G. Bakken[a] and Roger A. Parker[b]

In this chapter, we examine the potential for agent-based modelling in market research. We define key concepts, give simple examples and describe issues and opportunities as this advanced method establishes its place in the researcher's toolkit.

INTRODUCTION

In his best-selling book *The Tipping Point*, author Malcolm Gladwell describes the resurgence of the Hush Puppies brand of casual footwear (Gladwell, 2000). Hush Puppies came to prominence in the early 1960s with comfortable, stylish shoes made from suede pigskin. The shoes were often dyed in bright colours, such as blue or red, and, for a while, became a 'must–have' item among at least some adolescents. The brand was supported with clever and memorable television advertising. However, as tastes in footwear changed over the years, the brand declined. Then, in the 1990s, as Gladwell tells it, some free–thinking individual was spotted

[a]Senior Vice President, Marketing Science/Advanced Analytics, Harris Interactive.
[b]Senior Scientist and Director, Marketing Technology Development, Boeing Commercial Airplanes.

Market Research Best Practice. Edited by P. Mouncey and F. Wimmer.
© 2007 John Wiley & Sons, Limited.

wearing a pair in New York City by someone who then decided he had to have a pair, and then his friends wanted the shoes, and so on and so on. Sales went from a meagre 30 000 pairs annually to 430 000 in 1995 and around 1.6 million the following year. Gladwell uses this example to make an important point. Many phenomena, such as preferences and choices for some products or brands, carry along at a very low level of activity or intensity for some period and then, seemingly without explanation, become 'full-blown' fads or trends. The essence of a 'tipping point' is that it emerges, suddenly and unpredictably, from events that have been occurring in the background for some time.

Gladwell introduced us to an explanation for tipping point phenomena; unfortunately, *post hoc* knowledge of the mechanism by which a tipping point has occurred does not help us predict when and if a tipping point *will* occur. This is a characteristic of an *emergent* phenomenon: the outcome cannot be predicted exactly from knowledge of the starting conditions.

Tipping points are one example of complex processes – the 'butterfly effect' and viral marketing' are two more – that have captured the imagination of marketers in the last few years. Entire businesses have been built around exploiting knowledge of these phenomena. For example, a Boston, Massachusetts-based company called BzzAgent utilizes unpaid volunteers to talk about products with relatives, friends, acquaintances and perfect strangers, in hopes of mimicking, for marketing purposes, the process by which a virus spreads through a population. Procter & Gamble has created a word-of-mouth operation called Tremor that recruits volunteer teenage *opinion leaders* to spread the word about its products.

Traditional marketing research can provide retrospective insight into the success or failure of efforts like BzzAgent and Tremor, but our consumer interview-based methods are not equal to the task of predicting when or where a tipping point will occur, or whether viral marketing will be more effective than more traditional approaches. One challenge faced by traditional *quantitative* research methods is accounting for or capturing the effects of individual interactions between consumers. Most of our methods rely on aggregate statistical analysis and modelling. The mean, median and top two box percentages undoubtedly are the most widely used summary measures in quantitative marketing research. Multiple regression analysis and popular variants, such as logistic regression, are the workhorses of predictive modelling, yet these techniques are limited by reliance on aggregate, rather than individual-level, analysis. On the other hand, qualitative interviewing methods provide rich information about individual differences in consumer preferences, perceptions and behaviour, but also do not enable us to predict the behaviour of a community of consumers interacting in real time with each other, their environment and competing offers.

Outside of marketing research, innovative social and computer scientists have developed a new approach to understanding complex 'nonlinear' phenomena. This approach is known as *agent-based simulation*. Social scientists use agent-based simulation tools to understand complex phenomena such as the formation of social networks. Computer scientists create agents to search the web and to evolve computer programs. A guiding principle of agent-based simulation is that complex phenomena *emerge* from the interaction of multiple agents acting in accordance with rather simple behavioural rules.

Agent-based simulations offer a method for extending market research data (especially data about heterogeneous consumer preferences and decision-making strategies) to dynamic marketplace models that can capture and predict tipping points, formation of communities of interest and competitive dynamics. Agent-based models have been used to simulate the spread of infectious diseases, the emergence of economic trade and diffusion of innovations, among other things. Agent-based models are an alternative to systems dynamics models that rely on sequences of equations or other analytic models, such as the Bass new product diffusion model (we will come back to this topic when we explore marketing research applications for agent-based models).

In the remainder of this chapter, we introduce some basic concepts of agent-based modelling and simulation and demonstrate some ways in which these models can be applied to understanding and predicting consumer behaviour.

SIMULATION APPROACHES IN MARKETING

Most marketers and marketing researchers will be familiar with some form of simulation as applied to marketing. Consider the simple 'What if?' scenario analysis applied to the results from a conjoint analysis, or more elaborate 'war games' in which competing teams of managers (or MBA students) develop and implement strategies in an interactive fashion. Many of us were introduced relatively early in life to a simulated real estate market in the form of the Monopoly® board game.

As a concept, simulation has almost as many meanings as applications, but a central, underlying principle is the representation of one process or set of processes with another, usually simpler in some useful sense, process or set of processes. The Monopoly board game, for example, simplifies a rather complex economic system into a limited set of transactions. Part of the fun of playing the game derives from the degree to which the outcomes (wealth accumulation and bankruptcy) resemble the outcomes from the real world process that is being simulated.

A key concept inherent in this process orientation to simulation is *time*. Processes can be viewed as actions and reactions of components *over time*. This temporal property is an essential characteristic of process-representative simulation, and differentiates the application of simulation as an analytic and scientific tool from many other approaches, such as deductive logic or statistical inference. The central role of time is also an integral part of agent-based model simulations. Perhaps most importantly, we can study the *dynamics* of a system as conditions change over time.

There are compelling reasons to use simulation to study a wide range of problems. In many situations, the scale of the process under study prohibits any other approach. In astronomy and astrophysics, the universe is not available to us for experimental manipulation, but a simulation of important aspects of it is. Similarly, explorations of cultural development or species evolution often cannot be carried out in a laboratory environment, whereas a simulation permits hypothesis testing and inference on a reasonable timescale. In many circumstances, the phenomenon under investigation cannot be subjected to experimentation ethically or safely. The study of disease epidemics, social intolerance and military tactics are obvious examples. Finally, some systems are so complex that traditional experimental science seems hopeless as a research approach. Among these systems we include ecological dynamics, evolutionary economics and the subject of our interest – marketing.

Consider the case of *viral* marketing, or the idea of spreading a message about a product in the same way that a virus spreads through a healthy population. In fact, we might look at an agent-based simulation of viral infection. Figure 19.1 presents a graphic display from a viral infection simulation created using NetLogo (Wilensky, 1998).

Although the image is reproduced here in black and white, when seen in colour, the figures infected with the virus are shown in red, those who are healthy but susceptible are shown in green, and those who have been infected but have recovered and are immune are shown in white. We can imagine a transposition to viral marketing: the infected individuals are 'carriers' of the marketing message; immune individuals have been

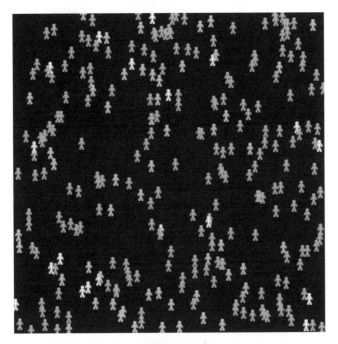

Figure 19.1 NetLogo virus model. (dark grey = infected; light grey = healthy susceptible; white = healthy immune).

exposed but have rejected the message. Individuals who do not recover (and therefore die) are analogous to consumers who 'catch' the message and go on to become purchasers, thus dropping out of the market. As consumers drop out of the market, new susceptible agents enter the field, until the 'carrying capacity' of the environment is reached. For this example, we manipulate three variables to determine their impact on the spread of the virus over time. These include the 'infection rate', or the probability that the message will be transmitted when an infected agent comes into contact with a susceptible agent; the recovery rate, or the probability that an individual will carry the information (and infect others) but not 'succumb' (and make a purchase, in the case of viral marketing); and the duration of time an agent is capable of infecting others. In all cases we start with 150 agents; ten agents, selected at random, are infected at the outset. The agents move at random around the landscape. Figures 19.2a through 19.2d illustrate the results of varying the different parameters. With the relatively high infection and recovery rates (60%) and a short duration (five time clicks of the simulation) represented in

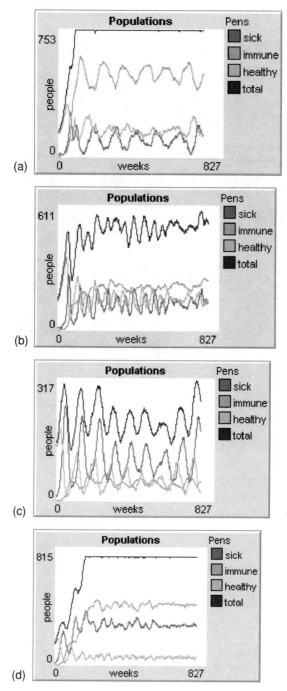

Figure 19.2 (a) Virus model with 60% infectiousness, 60% recovery, 5-week duration; (b) virus model with 60% infectiousness, 20% recovery, 5-week duration; (c) virus model with 60% infectiousness, 20% recovery, 20-week duration; (d) virus model with 60% infectiousness, 60% recovery, 20-week duration.

Figure 19.2a, the population quickly reaches the carrying capacity (more new and susceptible consumers arrive than are eliminated through purchasing or attrition), most of the population becomes 'immune' to the message, and an oscillation in the proportions of infected, healthy but susceptible and immune agents emerges. In Figure 19.2b, we see the impact of changing the recovery rate from 60% to 20%; the total population does not reach the carrying capacity over the course of the simulation (and fluctuates), and the proportions of infected, susceptible and immune agents are more nearly equal, on average. Increasing the time in which an agent is infectious (Figure 19.2c) changes the pattern again. Now, infected agents tend to outnumber healthy and immune agents, but there is also more volatility. In Figure 19.2d, we see the result of resetting the recovery rate to 60%, along with the increase in the duration of infectiousness.

A few interesting themes emerge from these simulations. First, we see that fairly small changes in the starting conditions can lead to dramatically different outcomes. Second, in most of these simulations, a somewhat stable pattern appears to emerge, rather than a state of equilibrium. We get closest to equilibrium in Figure 19.2d, where the oscillations are relatively small.

In this case, we have used the viral model as an analogy for a marketing problem rather than a specific agent-based implementation, but we believe that, even as analogies, such models may shed light on marketing problems, such as the way negative customer experiences might be communicated.

Bounded rationality and emergence

Perhaps the most compelling argument for applying simulation in general and agent-based modelling to marketing in particular comes from two realizations: first, that *individuals* make decisions under conditions of *bounded* rationality, and second, that macro-level behavioural complexity *emerges* from micro-level interactions between individuals.

By *bounded rationality* we mean making decisions under conditions of incomplete knowledge, limited computational resources and limited time. There are a variety of decision processes that people could employ in a specific marketing situation. The idea of rational economic man is essential to neoclassical economics, and to modern discrete choice theory in the McFadden (1973) formulation. While this theory is a wonderfully appealing analytic simplification, there is scant psychological or economic evidence that actual people making actual decisions go about the task by calculating weights for a linear-in-the-parameters utility function. However, there is evidence of framing effects, where the context of a decision process determines the way the decision is made. People also seem to simplify a decision problem artificially, ignoring all but the most important (to them) attributes, without knowledge of the impact of the ignored features. Individuals sometimes look to their own or others' past behaviour in forming decision rules, or simply imitate how the fellow next door behaved in the same situation. This last may be quite important in marketing, since it might account for fad or fashion behaviour. Imitative decision-making by humans may be, at least in part, an adaptation that has evolved over time (people who imitate successful decisions, such as what kinds of plants to eat, increase the likelihood of their own survival).

W. Brian Arthur (1994) presented a problem in bounded rationality that has generated a number of different simulation approaches (named the 'El Farol' problem, after the Santa Fe, New Mexico bar that inspired it). Arthur described a situation in which a local bar provides entertainment every Thursday evening. Because the bar is small, patron satisfaction drops precipitously whenever more than 60 people are in attendance. The problem for the average patron is predicting whether or not the bar will be too crowded on a given Thursday evening. Since each patron has only limited information available, and the type and content of information most likely varies across patrons, there is no *deductive* solution to this problem. Arthur suggests that the only way to explore this problem is with a computer simulation. We constructed a small simulation using a popular spreadsheet program to model patron decision-making under this bounded rationality. Imagine a group of 100 potential patrons. Each patron has a history of Thursday night visits to the bar (unique to the patron). We create a series of decision models for the patrons to use, which will take into account that past history. We assign the decision rules to the patrons randomly; each patron evaluates his or her history in light of the rule and makes a decision as to whether to visit the bar on the next Thursday evening. We might assume that patrons who make 'good' decisions (that is, they decide to visit the bar and there are fewer than 60 people in attendance on that occasion) will be likely to use the same decision model for the next occasion. We update the attendance history of all the patrons who attend, randomly assign new decision models to those who did not attend or whose models were 'bad', and let the 100 patrons make new predictions for the following week. Figure 19.3 shows a time series of the actual attendance. The first twelve weeks are the 'training set.' Each individual has roughly six observations from these weeks. We then run

Attendance History

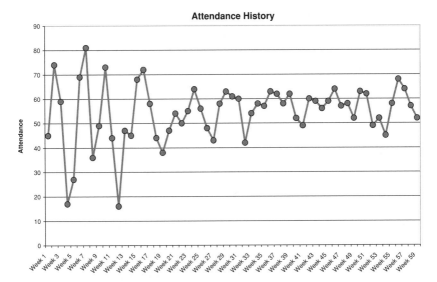

Figure 19.3   El Farol bar simulation.

the simulation out for several additional weeks and observe the simulated pattern of attendance. We observe two interesting things. First, as Figure 19.3 indicates, the week-to-week variability in attendance decreases dramatically and converges around the threshold level of 60 patrons. Second, no single decision strategy dominates. Eventually, all strategies result in a bad decision, and a patron switches to a different strategy.

Emergence is a property of complex systems. We use *emergence* to refer to the *macro* behaviour of the system that results only from the local interactions of the *micro* level components of the system. Just as a 'tipping point' emerges from the interactions of a fairly small number of individuals, complex system-level phenomena such as equilibrium prices emerge from the local interactions of individuals (buyers and sellers in this case). Neoclassical economic theory has resorted to metaphors such as the central Walrasian auctioneer to simplify and explain the emergence of price equilibria, but we know that there is no such central pricing mechanism in most markets. Here is another example: the next time you are driving in heavy traffic on a roadway with hills and valleys, notice the difference in the *collective* behaviour of the drivers when they are travelling downhill compared to uphill. You will most often notice that the traffic *speeds up* while going *uphill*, and *slows down* while going *downhill*. This is the exact opposite of what happens to most drivers when they are alone on a similar stretch of roadway. (The reader is invited to contemplate why this happens, after verifying that it in fact does on his or her next motoring trip.)

Our understanding of emergence has been advanced by a class of agent-based models known as *artificial societies*. The best known of these is perhaps Sugarscape (Epstein and Axtell, 1996). In one example involving combat, a simple change in the conquest rule governing the spoils of war changes an emergent pattern of one tribe eradicating another to sustained trench warfare between two tribes. One of the fascinating aspects of agent-based models in general, and artificial societies in particular, is the way in which simulations produce complex behaviours without resorting to complex explanatory or causal mechanisms. Indeed, one objective in creating an artificial society is to find the simplest possible micro-level behaviours that will produce the macro-level behaviour of interest.

The exploration of the relationship between the micro behaviour of individuals and the emergence of macro-level complexity is of significance, because generally we have macro behaviour data readily available, and we want to build theory that explains the macro-level behaviour in terms of the decisions of individuals. For example, if we are modelling a market, we'd like the predicted supply and demand relationships to look like supply and demand relationships that we observe, or at least theorize we would observe. Emergent behaviour from simulation that matches macro theory can be interpreted to mean that the individual's properties and decision rules explain or account for the macro behaviour. In the study of artificial societies, this is a very important research objective, since by finding (presumably simple) properties of social agents that lead to readily observable macro social phenomena, the causal link between individuals and societies can be explained.

AGENT-BASED SIMULATION MODELS

Origins

Simulation has a long history. The use of scale models – clearly a form of simulation – to guide great construction projects seems to have been present at least since the beginning of recorded history. Simulations involving computation followed the course of development of the mathematical and computational tools needed to support them.

Computer simulations with agent-based models have been enabled by the development of *object oriented programming* languages (OOPs). The OOP programming paradigm rests on the concept of *objects*, which are individual software entities that stand alone within a computer program and interact with the other elements of a program in a carefully defined way. Objects are a successful programming paradigm because they allow complex programs to be built up of simpler, reusable parts that have been tested carefully. (They also naturally clean up a bunch of inherently bad habits by software engineers, habits that make complex software development very difficult.)

Components of agent-based models

So how do we define an 'agent-based' model, and what differentiates this form of simulation from any other? As the name implies, agent-based models are computer simulations where the entities described by the computer program are so-called *agents*. Figure 19.4 shows a general schematic conceptualization of the structure of an agent. Agents exist in an *environment*, which they can sense, make decisions about and affect through actions. The agent perceives the state of its environment and takes actions on its environment based on local circumstances and the agent's internal state. To a greater or lesser extent, agent definitions also include the memory and learning features (on the left of the diagram in Figure 19.4), and logic, experience and beliefs (on the right). In the context of applications of agent-based modelling to marketing, the *actions* of interest will typically involve the making of choices, such as the choice of what to buy or what to sell, or the choice of what market to enter or exit.

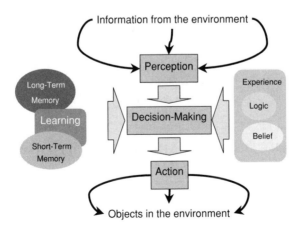

Figure 19.4   Agent structure.

Agents are characterized by at least four essential attributes – *autonomy, asynchrony, interaction* and *bounded rationality*. For agent-based models in marketing, we must add *adaptation* to this list. Autonomy refers to the characteristic that the agents act independently of one another. While the actions of other agents may affect what they do (through the environment, for example), they exist in the computer program as distinct and separate entities that are *not* guided by some central control functionality. Autonomy gives rise to asynchrony, in that the time required for an action by an agent is different for each agent, and does not depend on the state of any other agents in the simulation. While the agents are autonomous and operate asynchronously, they do relate via the interaction they have with the environment, since to each agent, other agents are part of the environment.

While the properties of autonomy, asynchrony, interaction and bounded rationality create a rich context for agent-based experimentation and research, adaptation is an essential characteristic for any agent model that will carry us some distance in the study of marketing. Adaptation refers to the ability of an agent to modify its behaviour in response to the *context in which it finds itself* and *in consideration of its prior experience*. Thus, adaptive agents can learn, forget or become confused. They learn from their mistakes and from the successes and failures of other agents with which they have contact. Adaptation can also occur through inheritance – successful decision strategies can be 'selected for' in a genetic sense, requiring agent 'mating' and 'offspring'. From a computational perspective, genetic algorithms and neural networks are often suggested as means of simulating adaptation.

A particularly interesting form of adaptation, difficult to implement but ultimately of great promise and power, is agent *self-awareness*. Agents can be designed that are aware that they are adaptive, and to a greater or lesser extent can control that adaptation. In this context, it becomes possible to explore self-organizing systems of some complexity, such as societies, governments or business ventures.

MARKETING RESEARCH APPLICATIONS FOR AGENT-BASED MODELS

Up to this point, we have been describing agent-based models and illustrating ways in which they can help us understand phenomena that are difficult to study using other methods. We now turn our attention back to potential applications for agent-based models in marketing research, with emphasis on using agent-based models for both *understanding* and *predicting* the dynamics of consumer behaviour.

Whether we admit to it or not, marketers and marketing researchers are intensely interested in predicting the future. We routinely estimate the probability of future events – most often future purchases made by consumers. And we are most interested in predicting how those probabilities might change as a function of the actions we take in the marketplace.

Unfortunately, our fortune-telling tools are fairly primitive. We are very good at identifying which of several product concepts is 'best' by some measure, but we are relatively ineffective when it comes to predicting what will actually happen when the best concept is released into the marketplace. An obvious reason for this state of affairs is that there is a lot more going on in the marketplace than we can include or represent in the typical market research study. We believe that agent-based models can help overcome this gap.

Consider the introduction of a new consumer durable product as an example. Traditional market research can help us determine if consumers perceive a unique benefit in the product, if they care about that benefit and what they might be willing to pay for it – all in a static environment. One problem we face is that, once a product enters a market, the conditions are no longer what they were when we tested the product through market research. The actual marketing plan for the product might be more or less effective than we assumed in forecasting sales, competitors might take unexpected actions or we might see the emergence of an unforeseen (by definition) tipping point, where sales suddenly take off.

Another problem limits our ability to anticipate or predict emergence in marketing situations. We often know a great deal from market research about the *marginal* distributions of the variables we measure in our surveys. We know far less about the *joint* distributions of many variables considered at the same time. For one thing, as soon as we go beyond joint distributions of more than two or three variables, we are often faced with sparse data, with many of the cells in the joint distribution with one or no observations.

Finally, there are many situations where there are too many *unobserved* factors to develop accurate predictions. One reason that it has proven so difficult to develop models of return on investment for marketing is that it is difficult to measure many of the marketplace factors that influence consumer behaviour.

Before we go any further, we should take a moment to clarify our definition of prediction. When a client asks a market researcher to 'predict first-year sales for this product,' she usually expects a single value (perhaps with some confidence interval around the estimate). We take a somewhat different view, regarding prediction in the sense that might apply to 'predictive modelling' where we want to determine the probability distribution of possible outcomes as a function of changing input conditions. So, in the case of predicting a tipping point, for example, we would like to know how factors under our control might precipitate a tipping point, and, if so, when a tipping point is likely to occur. More importantly, we wish to know if there are some actions that make a tipping point more likely, and some that make it less likely.

To date, there have been few published examples of marketing applications for agent-based models. A significant journal literature on agent-based modelling in the social sciences and economics has emerged (see Tesfatsion, 2006, for a review). Boeing Commercial Airplanes is undertaking a multi-year effort to develop an agent-based simulation for the global air travel market, but that work is still in development.

Word-of-mouth marketing and tipping points

A natural application for agent-based models is word-of-mouth marketing. In order to simulate the spread of word of mouth, we need to locate a population of consumer *agents* on some sort of spatial *landscape*. Moreover, the consumer agents need some way of communicating with, or influencing, other agents. A very simple word-of-mouth simulation can be implemented using a *cellular automaton*. Cellular automata are grids or lattices where the state of each space or cell on the lattice is a function of two conditions – the current state of the cell and the state of one or more of the immediate neighbours of the cell. The agents in cellular automata are limited; they may not be able to move, and they usually exist in one of two alternate states ('on' or 'off').

For our word-of-mouth simulation, we assume that each cell starts off in a state of ignorance. Once one agent obtains information (changing state from 'off' to 'on'), the neighbouring cells become potential recipients of the information.

The probability that any one individual passes a piece of information on to another agent most likely depends on a number of factors, such as opportunity, the importance of the information, the relationship between the neighbours, and so forth. Rather than specify these factors for all agents, we can treat them as a single random variable – a probability of transmitting the information. Moreover, since this probability is likely to vary from moment to moment for any pair of neighbours, we can draw new values from a random distribution for each time cycle of the simulation.

Here's what we have so far – a lattice populated uniformly with agents who have some randomly variable probability of passing along a piece of information once they receive it. It seems likely that agents may vary in their ability to remember the information long enough to pass it on to someone else. We will add a function to generate a probability for forgetting.

Each agent applies two simple rules: if the agent already possesses the information and its probability of forgetting is below some threshold, the agent retains the information through the next cycle; if an agent does not have the information, it looks at each of its immediate neighbours and if one has the information and a high enough probability of passing it on, the agent becomes knowledgeable.

Figures 19.5a and 19.5b show the results of running a simple word of mouth simulation over 50 iterations, starting with two near-neighbour-informed agents selected at random. There are 2500 agents in total, and we can see that, after 50 iterations, somewhat fewer than half have been reached by word of mouth. Additionally, word of mouth spreads more or less uniformly out from the origin, as Figure 19.5c shows. This pattern is reflected in the upward trend in incremental awareness at each time step (Figure 19.5b).

One reason that tipping points occur, according to Gladwell, is that not all agents are equal. Some are *connectors*, who have a greater likelihood of passing information on, and more people to pass it on to. Some are *mavens*, who accumulate knowledge and are especially credible sources with respect to word of mouth. We can modify our cellular automaton to create connector agents, who influence not only their neighbours but other, more remote spaces on the lattice, and mavens, who, by virtue of their credibility, are much more likely to pass on information. Figure 19.6a shows the initial grid with 50 connectors and 50 mavens; 38 of the mavens are already informed. Figure 19.6b shows the same grid after only five iterations.

Figures 19.7a and 19.7b show the results of the simulation with 50 mavens and 50 connectors. Unlike the earlier simulation without mavens and connectors, a clear *tipping point* emerges. Virtually all of the agents have been reached by 20 iterations, and the incremental gain in awareness peaks at the seventh iteration.

So, how is this of value to marketers? Given a limited marketing budget, we might ask whether it is more effective to get the message to mavens or to connectors. To answer this question, we can vary the number of mavens and connectors across several simulation runs. All other things

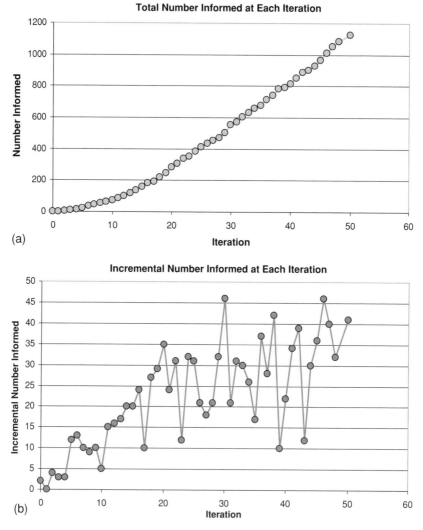

(a)

(b)

Figure 19.5 Simple word-of-mouth simulation.

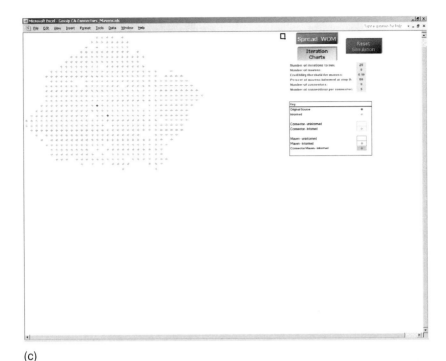

(c)

Figure 19.5 *(Continued)*

being equal, mavens are more effective than connectors, although the presence of either type of agent greatly accelerates the spread of word of mouth.

This example did not rely on any market research. However, we can use market research to make the simulation more realistic. For example, we can conduct surveys to estimate the number of mavens, the number of connectors and the number of connections per connector, and then use these values to initialize the simulation.

Forecasting adoption for a new automobile model

Forecasting sales for new consumer durable goods, such as automobiles, has proven to be one of the biggest challenges for market research. Bayus, Hong and Labe (1989) cite a few reasons for this difficulty, including greater fluctuations in consumer spending on durables, greater variability in the timing of purchases and the fact that markets for durables are not static. Most models for forecasting demand for new durable products are

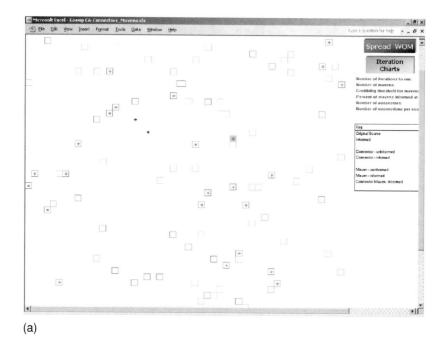

(a)

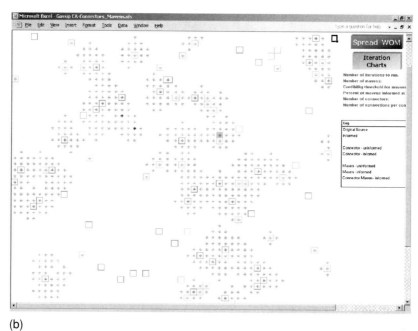

(b)

Figure 19.6   (a) Starting word-of-mouth grid with mavens and connectors; (b) after five iterations.

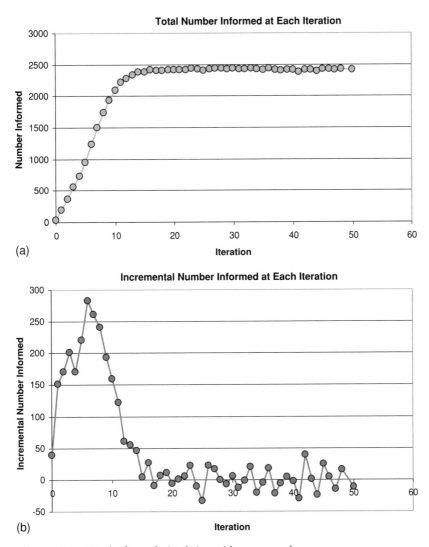

Figure 19.7 Word-of-mouth simulation with mavens and connectors.

based on the Bass (1969) model. In the Bass model, sales are a function of both innovation and imitation. The model is simple and elegant, but requires a number of assumptions. These assumptions create the opportunity for applying agent-based simulation to the problem of forecasting sales for a new consumer durable. For example, the Bass model assumes that market potential remains constant over time, that the diffusion of one innovation is independent of all other innovations, that marketing actions do not affect the diffusion process and that there are no supply restrictions. The Bass model is an aggregate model. Factors that drive individual consumer choices are ignored.

We have seen many advances in market research since Bass first proposed his model. We can now measure, with considerable reliability, the decision-making processes of individual consumers. Consider the introduction of a new car model. Most automakers conduct 'stage-gate' research throughout the development of a new model, refining the concept and resulting product in response to feedback from consumers. We might, for example, have data from a conjoint study that will allow us to estimate the relative utility of the new model for each survey respondent. We can use this as the starting point for an agent-based model to predict the potential sales for this new model.

For this model we will have two types of agents: consumers and automakers (this is a simplification; we would want to include dealers as a third agent class to better reflect the target system). Consumers will have properties (e.g., a 'utility function') and decision rules governing their actions; automakers will have a profit-maximizing function and a different set of rules. Consumers are the *environment* for the automakers; the manufacturers similarly comprise the environment for the consumers.

In order for consumer agents to select a particular car model, they must be aware that it exists and include it in their consideration set. State of awareness thus becomes a property of each consumer agent, and the value for any one car model depends on the marketing efforts of the manufacturer. Awareness for a new model may also depend on the number of vehicles already on the road, as well as whether or not someone in the consumer's social network is aware of, or owns, the model.

For this model, we'll assume that the key drivers of consumer preference are the overall appeal of the model, the consumer's overall preference for the brand and the consumer's 'marginal rate of substitution,' which determines the price differential for one model compared to another for that consumer. We use the conjoint results to determine the joint distribution of these attributes, creating a population of consumer agents that looks like our population of survey respondents with respect to their preferences.

Now that we have a simulated population of consumers, we can enhance the model by adding some additional characteristics. First, we want to be able to specify whether, for each time period in the simulation, a consumer is aware of each specific model. Next, we want to specify a *social network* for each consumer. There are many bases for creating networks.

Table 19.1 Consumer agent 'instance' variables.

Variable	Value
Utility for Brand X	1.555
Utility for Model Y from Brand X	3.426
Utility for Model Y MSRP	−0.145
Aware of Model Y	No
Network member 1	ID 145
Network member 1 owns Brand X Model Y	No
Network member 2	ID 276
Network member 2 owns Brand X Model Y	Yes
Network member 3	ID 566
Network member 3 owns Brand X Model Y	No
. . . repeat for each brand and model in simulated market	

We could use similarity on demographic variables. However, because there are many unobserved factors which determine any one consumer's social network, we prefer to use a random process to generate networks among our simulated population. If we assign each consumer agent a unique identification number, we can then create a string of variables for each agent that contains the unique identification numbers of the other agents in its network. We can use these strings as a way to transmit information between consumer agents. We can even allow the networks to change over time, by dropping or adding agents to the network strings. Table 19.1 depicts the initial *instance* variables for one consumer agent.

The picture is similar, but perhaps somewhat simpler, for the automaker agents. Once a new car model is introduced, the only marketing levers available to the manufacturer are price and advertising. Each manufacturer needs some sort of profitability function for each of the car models it offers. This profitability function will depend on some estimate of variable cost per vehicle and the number of vehicles sold. For a new model, we can add in a fixed cost component (to cover vehicle development). Manufacturers will use this function to determine the price at which they will sell a vehicle. Manufacturers also have resources to spend on advertising, and some indication of the leverage they get (in terms of awareness) from those resources.

To complete our simulation, we need rules that the consumer and automaker agents will implement based on the conditions they encounter in their respective environments. Some of the consumer agent rules are summarized in Table 19.2. Note that we allow price negotiation; both consumer and manufacturer try to maximize a 'welfare function' in arriving at a price.

Table 19.2 Consumer agent rules for making a purchase.

Rule (in sequence)	Description
Rule A1: Awareness formation	For each vehicle, draw a random number from a uniform probability distribution. If the value exceeds the awareness threshold for that vehicle (one of the manufacturer agent's variables) AND not aware of vehicle, set awareness = 'yes'.
Rule A2: Network influence	Survey network members (order determined randomly). If network member owns the vehicle AND awareness = 'no,' flip awareness to 'yes;' if at least one network member owns the vehicle, add X to the utility value for vehicle appeal (where X is a random variable reflecting the strength of the network member's influence).
Rule P1: Calculate marginal rate of substitution	For each vehicle, calculate the total utility (sum of brand, appeal and MSRP utilities). For each vehicle where total utility > 0 AND awareness = 'yes,' calculate the 'marginal rate of substitution'.
Rule P2: Negotiate price	For each vehicle with total utility > 0 and awareness = 'yes', offer price to manufacturer calculated from marginal rate of substitution.
Rule P3: Select highest value alternative	Compare the prices offered by manufacturer for each and calculate the relative value (based on a 'welfare' function) of each vehicle; purchase the vehicle that returns the highest relative value. If no price negotiation exceeds a threshold value for the welfare function, no purchase is made.
Rule R1: Agent replacement	Once an agent has made a purchase, it leaves the market and is replaced with an agent with characteristics selected at random from the utility distributions for brand, appeal and price.

How does the agent-based approach compare to conducting 'what if?' analyses with a traditional conjoint simulator? Consider some of the questions that cannot be answered with a conjoint simulator:

- What will be the *equilibrium* price for this new vehicle?
- How will competitors respond to the entry of this vehicle?
- Where is the point of diminishing return for advertising?
- Will there be a tipping point for this vehicle? If so, what conditions will lead to the tipping point?

Conjoint simulators are designed to estimate demand (for example, share of preference or share of choices) as a function of vehicle attributes and price. In all *static* conjoint simulators, all potential consumers are presented with the same price. In reality, different consumers may negotiate different prices. Some very popular models (such as the Mini Cooper)

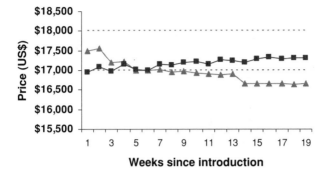

Figure 19.8 Simulated selling prices for two new car models.

may actually sell for more than the manufacturer's suggested retail price. These prices are the result of local transactions between buyers and dealers, and are unlikely to be captured in a traditional conjoint simulator. In our agent-based model, we can introduce price negotiation using each consumer's marginal rate of substitution and each manufacturer's profitability function. For each transaction, a consumer agent and manufacturer agent negotiate a price. In the real world, a manufacturer who consistently fails to make a sale is likely to lower prices for future transactions; we can build a learning or adaptation function into the model to simulate this process. Figure 19.8 shows the average price per time period for two new vehicles. The first vehicle is very popular, and we see that the average price actually rises above the manufacturer's suggested retail price (MSRP). The second vehicle is unpopular, and the manufacturer must ultimately lower the price to move vehicles off dealer lots.

Choice simulators based on individual-level utility estimates are an excellent starting point for applying agent-based simulation to market research. As noted above, the simulation already contains two key agent populations – buyers and sellers. We need only to specify the rules for interaction between the agents over time to create a dynamic agent-based choice simulator. As an example, we used data from a stated preference choice experiment for luxury automobiles. While the objective of the research was to identify the optimal configuration for the client's new model, we used the preference structure from the choice model to simulate the evolution of the luxury car category (which, for the United States domestic market, includes sedans, sport utility vehicles and roadsters). For this simulation, we used a goal-directed method to find the combination of vehicles that would maximize *category* profits. Because we did not have access to every manufacturer's cost data, the results do not reflect the real world. We started with market-based configurations of all existing

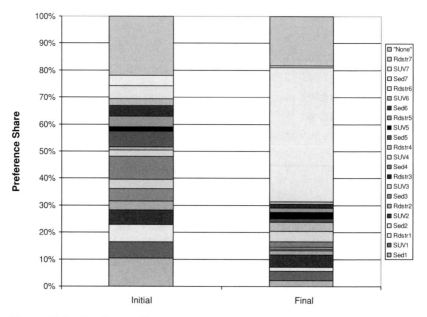

Figure 19.9   Simulation of luxury car category:comparison of initial and final preference shares.

models and, for the new models, configurations with the highest average utility. Since models could 'die' if they did not contribute to category profitability (i.e. total revenue for the model did not exceed total cost for that model), the final vehicle assortment would reflect the preferences and willingness to pay for the market represented by the survey respondents. Figure 19.9 compares the initial distribution of preference shares, predicted from the choice model, with the final distribution. We were surprised to see a dramatic realignment of predicted preference shares.

How can the marketer use this type of information? Earlier we defined prediction in terms of estimating what might happen rather than what will happen (along with estimating the probability of occurrence). Results like this should alert a marketer to the possibility that dynamic behaviour in the marketplace (in this case, on the part of competitors) may lead to unexpected outcomes.

SUMMARY AND CONCLUSIONS

Companies bet billions of dollars on new products, services and marketing strategies. Even the most sophisticated marketing research methods, such as hierarchical Bayesian models for consumer preferences, cannot capture or predict the complex marketplace dynamics that interact to determine the success or failure of these products, services or strategies. Agent-based models, including cellular automata, genetic algorithms and artificial societies, provide a method for investigating marketplace complexities. We can provide only a limited introduction to these fascinating tools in this chapter. We hope that the reader will be intrigued sufficiently by these examples to pursue further investigation of agent-based simulation and potential marketing research applications.

REFERENCES

Arthur, W. B. (1994), Bounded Rationality. *American Economic Review (Papers and Proceedings)*, **84**, 406.

Bass, F. (1969), A new-product growth model for consumer durables. *Management Science*, **15** (January), 215–227.

Bayus, B.L., Hong, S. and Labe, Jr., R.P. (1989) Developing and using forecasting models of consumer durables: the case of color television. *Journal of Product Innovation Management*, **6**, 5–19.

Epstein, J. and Axtell, R. (1996), *Growing Artificial Societies: Social Sciences from the Bottom Up*, MIT Press.

Gladwell, M. (2000), *The Tipping Point*, Little Brown and Company.

McFadden, D. (1973), Conditional Logit Analysis of Qualitative Choice Behavior, in P. Zaremba, (Ed.) *Frontiers of Econometrics*, pp. 105–142, Academic Press.

Tesfatsion, L. (2006), Agent-based computational economics: A constructive approach to economic theory, in K. Judd. and L. Tesfatsion (Eds) *Handbook of Computational Economics, Volume 2: Agent-Based Computational Economics*, North Holland.

Wilensky, U. (1998), NetLogo Virus model. http://ccl.northwestern.edu/netlogo/models/Virus. Center for Connected Learning and Computer-Based Modeling, Northwestern University, Evanston, IL.

ADDITIONAL RESOURCES

Axelrod, R. (1997), *The Complexity of Cooperation: Agent-based Models of Competition and Collaboration*, Princeton University Press.

Center for the Study of Complex Systems, www.cscs.umich.edu.

Kennedy, J. and Eberhart, R. (2001), *Swarm Intelligence*, Academic Press.

Santa Fe Institute, www.santafe.edu.

Part Five

Facilitating Diversity

Chapter Twenty

Managing Global Brands to Meet Consumer Expectations

Malcolm Baker[a], Greet Sterenberg[b] and Earl Taylor[c]

Increasingly affordable information and other technologies allow global brands to be customized for local cultures and other consumers. This chapter sets out a roadmap for choosing between various globalization versus localization strategies.

INTRODUCTION

There is growing consensus that the truth about globalization of brands lies somewhere between the extremes of Ted Levitt's thesis of homogenization (Levitt, 1983) and Naomi Klein's more recent prediction of a 'no logo' backlash (Klein, 2000). To move beyond a sterile debate about globalization, brand strategists need decision criteria based on a typology of brands and environments that they can apply to make informed decisions about whether, when, where and how to globalize or localize a brand.

The ideas presented here are based largely on our Research International Observer (RIO) qualitative study of consumer understanding of

[a]Founder, B/R/S Group and Global Director, Research International Qualitatif.
[b]Global Director, Qualitative Space, Research International Qualitatif.
[c]CMO, Marketing Science Institute.

Market Research Best Practice. Edited by P. Mouncey and F. Wimmer.
© 2007 John Wiley & Sons, Limited.

and reactions to global brands conducted in late summer and early fall
of 2002. We believe this to be the largest and most comprehensive study
of its type ever conducted, involving over 1500 young urban consumers
(aged 18–35) in 41 countries and 52 cities around the world. While over
100 specific global and local brands were included in the study, its purpose
was not to determine consumer images of these brands *per se*. Rather,
extended focus group discussions used a variety of projective techniques
to elicit consumers' feelings and attitudes about the 'globalness' or 'lo-
calness' of such brands. In our analyses we uncover the underlying dimensions along which consumers evaluate brands across multiple product
categories.

Our initial 2002 RIO findings (Sterenberg and Baker, 2002) have
been further analysed to produce a 'roadmap' for brand managers based
on our brand typology and decision criteria for globalization versus localization. A secondary source of data and insights for our current efforts
is a quantitative global survey we conducted recently on behalf of the
Harvard Business School (jointly funded by our parent company, WPP).
This study involved a total of 1800 consumers in 12 countries selected to
represent a mix of developed and less-developed economies and Western
and non-Western cultures.[1]

THE GLOBAL BRAND AT A CROSSROADS

Ted Levitt's globalization of markets thesis asserted that global companies
and their brands would grow inexorably, offering global consumers an

---

[1] Preliminary results of this study (Quelch, Holt and Taylor, 2003) were presented at the Harvard
Business School's Globalization of Markets Colloquium (May 28–30, 2003) on the 20th anniversary
of Ted Levitt's influential paper (Levitt, 1983). The 12 countries included in the study were: Brazil,
China, Egypt, France, India, Indonesia, Japan, Poland, South Africa, Turkey, the UK and the US.
Data collection in the US, UK and France was via Internet panels maintained by our sister company,
Lightspeed Research, while the remaining countries used conventional in-person interviewing.
The six product categories tested were: automobiles, athletic wear, dairy/packaged goods, mobile
phones, petrol/gasoline and soft drinks. Using a split-sample design, 75 respondents in each country
rated three brands in each of three categories (e.g., Ford, Mercedes and Toyota for automobiles).
A total of 20 attributes yielded five distinct factors or underlying dimensions of 'globalness' stable
across all 12 countries. Latent class segmentation and regression analyses were used to determine
the relative impact of each dimension of globalness on brand preference among specific types
of consumers. In order of their overall ability to predict brand preference across all six product
categories, these dimensions are: (1) quality inferred from global availability; (2) country of origin;
(3) status or prestige associated with using a global brand; (4) perceived corporate citizenship; and
(5) embodiment of American values. For further details, see the revised version of the colloquium
paper published by Jossey-Bass in 2004.

unbeatable combination of quality, availability, reliability and low price. He described a Brand Utopia in which tastes and needs would become increasingly homogenized, with successful companies focusing on what 'everyone' wants.

Entering the 21st century, the global brand is at a crossroads. The ubiquity of global brands has become one of the defining features of modern life and one of the core tenets of modern marketing. Yet the issues highlighted by the anti-globalization movement raise questions:

- How local should global brands get?
- Is there consumer-perceived value in globalness *per se*?
- What balance do consumers seek between their need to feel part of a global tribe and their desire to be more individual?
- To what degree do mainstream consumers hold brands accountable for the practices of the companies behind them?

To begin to answer these questions, we need to review a few key findings from our 2002 RIO study.

CONSUMERS LOVE BRANDS

Brands may be constructs created by marketing companies and their agencies that sit on supermarket shelves in the real world. But brands are also ideas and ideals that exist in consumers' imaginations. That's where the real connections are made and where brands are invested with personal meaning and relevance. It is in this platonic, idealized world where brands take on life and where they acquire their redemptive role. (As we shall see, this idealized existence may also prove to be a pitfall for certain types of brands in specific circumstances.)

'If I could I would die for a Chanel suit.' (Argentina)

'My son is obsessed, always wanting Coca-Cola, McDonalds and Nike shoes.' (UK)

'It may be that I have this dream, being like Michael Jordan and therefore I use his sportswear, which is Reebok.' (Colombia)

'I feel close to Starbucks, I believe it is a great and typical American experience.' (USA)

'If I wear Nike there is no need to say anything, if I choose another brand it is as though I am stating something that I have to explain.' (Italy)

'Global brands make us feel citizens of the world and we fear their leaving because they somehow give us an identity.' (Argentina)

CONSUMERS WANT TO FORGIVE AND FORGET

What was perhaps most remarkable in our RIO study was the degree to which consumers feel protective about their brands. Because consumers have such a strong investment in what brands mean to them, they disconnect their idealized world from the real world – as they do the consumer self from the political self. Consumers are reluctant to accept negative messages from the real world that challenge their view of brands. They prefer to make life easy – to forgive and forget. A change in attitude is easier than a change in behaviour. Typical comments reflect a variety of ways in which consumers manage potential cognitive dissonance:

'I assume most, if not all, big companies use "cheap labour", so it's useless to care.' (USA)

'I know about Nestlé and their milk powder scam. . . but at the end of the day, one Kit Kat can't make much of an impact.' (UK)

'I know Nike has sweat shops, like other manufacturers, but at least these people have a job.' (Germany)

'Tommy Hilfiger publicly said that he did not intend his clothes to be marketed for Latin Americans/black people, but I like them and still buy them.' (Black respondent, El Salvador)

'It is so far away from your own situation. It is not your mother who gets exploited, you know?.' (New Zealand)

'As it does not affect yourself, the brand is so important that you forget about it.' (Spain)

While consumers are not actively looking to make a connection between the brand and the company behind it, they may react to information from activists and the media, and will respond to bad company behaviour that cannot be denied. They have thresholds beyond which beliefs get translated into action. These thresholds are lowest on issues dealing with ingredients, contamination and a range of environmental issues; slightly higher for employment practices; and higher still for activities that relate to marketing and general business practices.

AMERICAN BRANDS AND AMERICAN VALUES

While our RIO fieldwork was completed some months before the war in Iraq, controversy about American foreign policy was already widespread, particularly in Middle Eastern and Islamic countries. Nevertheless, in the same way as they separate their political self from their consumer self, most global consumers appear to separate America and American values from American brands. We found little evidence of a widespread rejection of brands that reflect American cultural values. While we did not work in the core Islamic countries of the Middle East, this study did cover Turkey and Indonesia, as well as separate groups with Muslim respondents in India and South Africa. There was little evidence of broadscale rejection of American brands in these cultures. Typical comments included the following:

'*We don't care about America and American politics, we do care about their brands.*' (Panama)

'*I used to go on anti-US rallies when I was still a student, but I never thought about the brand of clothes or shoes I wore.*' (Philippines)

'*We can hate them, we cannot change the world. We need the brands because we rely on them.*' (South Africa)

'*Our political view has nothing to do with our behaviour as customers. If you go downtown you will see many young people handing out documents protesting the capitalistic system, but also wearing Levi's. . .*' (Turkey)

One of the key reasons for this lack of apparent conflict is the fact that many brands have transcended their 'American-ness.' Consumers may know that Coca-Cola is American but the brand's myth is seen as a universal one. The brand's cultural identity, while known, is not central to its appeal. After reviewing our typology of brands and globalization roadmap, we will consider in greater detail the specific reasons why, and circumstances under which, American and other global brands might be vulnerable to antiglobalization backlash.

GETTING THE GLOBAL/LOCAL BALANCE RIGHT

If the antiglobalization movement is not converting the mainstream, does that mean that a global, one-size-fits-all approach is the solution? The answer, unsurprisingly, is no. Even without the impetus of anti-American or anti-Western motives, global consumers may react powerfully against the increasing ubiquity of global brands and their homogenized identities. In assessing a brand's need for localization, marketers must consider four key factors:

1. The type of brand.
2. The nature of the category.
3. The level of aspiration.
4. The nature of the local culture.

Before we can assemble our globalization roadmap, we need briefly to examine each of these factors in turn.

Four distinct types of 'global' brands

Our RIO study revealed four different types of global brand (see Figure 20.1).

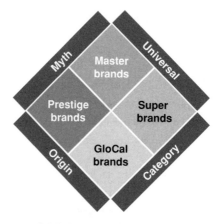

Figure 20.1   Four types of global brands.

Master brands

Nike, Sony and Coca-Cola define their category and are built on powerful myths or narratives (e.g. Levi's theme of independence or Nokia's theme of connection). For these brands, it is this universality of their narrative, rather than globalness itself, that is at the heart of their appeal. Often, these are 'first-mover' brands that define a category. While they can thus leverage their heritage, the corresponding key challenge facing marketers of master brands is the need to keep the myth relevant to each new generation. Coca-Cola has been superbly successful at this; Levi's has been less so. As Coca-Cola also illustrates, master brands can transcend their national origins to be embraced by consumers as truly global brands. They thus require – and permit – little, if any, localization that might threaten to undermine their universality or mythical appeal. Master brands are also less exclusive – and exclusionary – than prestige brands: as one consumer observed, 'it is a status symbol, but anyone can have it.'

'Coca-Cola is for everyone, this gives a feeling of universality and at the same time it considers everyone's individuality.' (Mexico)

'They talk about a product, but also about a specific style, a precise philosophy. . . when you buy it, it is like choosing something with which you identify.' (Italy)

'Brands that have become indispensable and unavoidable.' (Belgium)

Prestige brands

Chanel, BMW, Rolex and Gucci have an appeal built on specific myths of cultural origin or the provenance of a founder or a technology (e.g. Mercedes as the embodiment of German design and engineering excellence). These brands are nearly always in strong display categories with high aspirational value. Like a magic amulet, a prestige brand 'increases the value of the one who uses it.' At the risk of excluding many to appeal to the chosen few, prestige brands actively reject localization. For example, BMW and Mercedes in Japan and Singapore usually will avoid the use of local icons to stay sufficiently aspirational.

'I bought it because it is Swiss, it is high quality just like watches, Swiss means precision and reliability.' (Chile)

'To me, it means differentiation from others. It increases my self-esteem and my self-confidence.' (Germany)

'Not everybody can buy it, then again it is not meant to be for everyone.' (Greece)

Super brands

These are universally available, like master brands. But unlike master brands, super brands are defined more by their category than by a myth or narrative. Examples include Gillette, Pepsi, McDonald's, Shell, Philips and American Express (regular card). In the words of one respondent, they are 'trusted, silver-medal winners.' As such, a super brand may be quite successful and as good as any other in the category without being differentiated on the basis of a distinctive myth or narrative that it 'owns.' Instead, super brands try to become relevant by localizing somewhat (for example, McDonald's adapting versions of local foods to a quick-service environment) and remain relevant by constant product or service innovation (for example, the evolution of Gillette's shaving systems).

'They represent good quality, but are not so unique or universal as Coca-Cola.' (Netherlands)

'The highest level of a brand is reached if it stands for a product category like UHU.' (Austria)

GloCal brands

Dove, Nestlé and Danone are available globally, but marketed locally, often under a variety of local or regional product names (sub-brands). Even where consumers are aware of this global distribution, a glocal brand may 'feel close' and be seen as 'one of ours' – and it is this, rather than its universal availability, that enhances its equity. These brands thus require and permit the greatest degree of localization and are usually, though not always, in categories with weak display value, such as food, household products and personal care. As such, they are brands with the lowest threshold for triggering negative reactions if consumers perceive that their own or their families' health or safety are threatened – see below. We should also note that the potential aspirational value of a given product is relative to local economic conditions; in many less-developed countries and newer consumer societies, a variety of fast moving consumer goods can take on this character.

'They are ours. . . they are homely, approachable, close and warm-hearted. . . they form part of our history.' (Italy)

'As Lipton has a long history in Turkey, it has become like a local brand in our minds and we see Lipton as a local brand.' (Turkey)

The category the brand is in and the level of aspiration towards it

Categories with high display value (or with highly aspirational positioning within a given category) will require and permit less localization. Because they are rooted in local taste, traditional culture and physiology, food, food retail, household cleaning and personal care products will nearly always need more localizing.

It's worth applying the aspirational test to a brand's positioning:

- Toyota, while in a high display category is, for instance, viewed as a local brand in many countries, because its positioning is distinctly everyday and it successfully connects with local values.
- Conversely, Nescafé uses local people for its coffee in India, but puts them in foreign (i.e. aspirational) settings because of the positioning of the brand.
- Nike sponsors a local marathon in Budapest (the 'Footapest'), but is careful to use a spokesperson with a more international standing (Michael Jordan).
- Mika Hakkinen is acceptable as an aspirational role model for Mercedes in Finland, but his wife is rejected as a spokeswoman for Danone.

The nature of the local culture

The final factor required for our globalization roadmap is the nature of the culture in which the brand must operate. Countries included in our RIO study can be plotted on two axes depending on whether their orientation toward brands is individualistic or collectivist, and on whether they are oriented more toward their own culture and values (local focus) or more receptive to global influences (global focus). To avoid confusion, we should emphasize that we are classifying countries qualitatively by *how consumers typically relate to global brands*. This may or may not correspond to stereotypes about specific cultures. Thus, compared to Western Europe and North America, Japan is traditionally thought of as a collectivist society. Nevertheless, *as consumers*, the Japanese share with their counterparts in northern Europe and the Anglophone countries, a desire for brands to relate to them as individuals. These countries are, in turn, differentiated among themselves in terms of their pride in their own culture versus receptivity to others. Here, the Anglophone countries appear

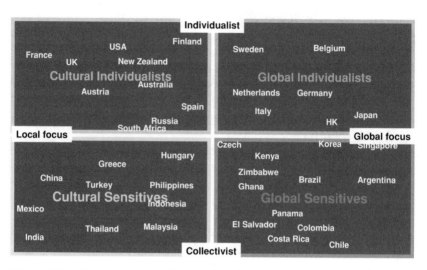

Figure 20.2 Cultural attitudes relating to brands.

much less 'globalist' than the smaller European countries and Japan (see Figure 20.2).

- **Cultural individualists** – these countries have a high pride in their culture combined with strong individualistic values. This requires both localization and an individual connection with local consumers, with the individual connection probably more important than the cultural one (Figure 20.3).
- **Global individualists** – These countries have a weaker interest or pride in their own culture and a correspondingly greater openness to the world. While there is thus a low need for localization (Figure 20.3), consumers in these cultures still have a high need to connect with brands at an individual level (they may thereby feel part of a wider global 'tribe' – see below).
- **Global sensitives** – These are collectivist societies that are open to the world. Connectivity through, and availability of, global brands is often more important than pride in local culture. There is, thus, a medium need for localization in these cultures, more a matter of translation than adaptation (Figure 20.3). A product or brand's origin and where it is manufactured are important.
- **Cultural sensitives** – In these collectivist markets, consumers take high pride in local culture. They expect global brands to understand and respect their culture and, when possible, adapt to local situations, both in terms of communication and product features.

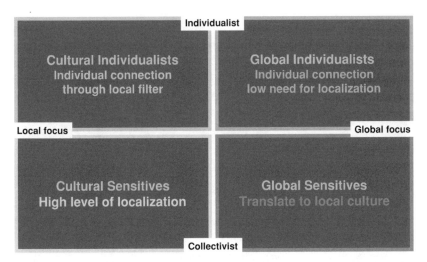

Figure 20.3 Localization required by brand culture.

The relevance of a brand's global identity will also vary geographically. Asian consumers, especially those from Japan and Chinese-based cultures, tend to set a high value on Western provenance for many branded goods, especially those that have prestige value. The same is true for African and South American cultures.

Europeans set less store on global provenance. Less developed countries, many of which have a history of being passed off with second-rate international products, will often want to know where the item is manufactured as well as the provenance of the brand. Thus Kenyan consumers make a quality distinction between Nike shoes made in the USA and those made in China or Indonesia.[2]

---

[2] While our cultural classification is qualitative, it appears to be consistent with findings from two recent quantitative studies. For example, both our Harvard Business School/WPP study (Quelch, Holt and Taylor, 2003) and a separate quantitative analysis of data supplied by Landor Associates and Young & Rubicam (Johansson and Ronkainen, 2003) show that the 'globalness' of brands *per se* matters much less for US and UK consumers than for most others around the world. In our study, with the average impact of the five dimensions on brand preference indexed to 100, the UK has an overall score of 91.0 and the US 93.4. By contrast, the three countries chosen to represent a variety of Islamic societies have the highest scores, with Egypt and Indonesia at 108.6 and Turkey at 107.6. Japan and China also score above average on the overall impact of the five dimensions of 'globalness' on brand preference – especially on perceived quality inferred from global availability and country of origin. While South Africa and Brazil score below average on the overall impact of all five dimensions, both are above average on the contribution that American values make to brand preference.

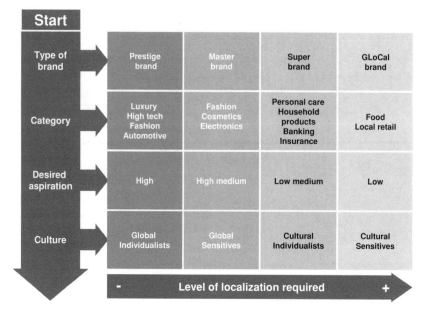

Figure 20.4   A localization roadmap.

THE GLOBALIZATION ROADMAP

Combining these four factors yields a globalization roadmap, or planning matrix, that brand managers can use to assess the need for, or possibility of, localizing versus globalizing a specific brand in specific circumstances (see Figure 20.4). All else being equal, a prestige brand will require/allow the least localization, and a glocal brand the most. Similarly, high-display categories such as luxury, fashion, high-tech and automotive will require/allow the least localization, and food and local retail the most. Independently of these considerations, the more aspirational the positioning of the brand, the less is should be localized. As noted earlier, this dimension is perhaps most context-sensitive, as items that appear aspirational to consumers in less-developed economies will be less so in more mature consumer markets. Finally, countries where consumers relate to brands as global individualists will require the least localization, while those where consumers relate to brands as cultural sensitives will require the most.

If not taken too literally, brand managers should be able to sum localization 'weights' across these four dimensions to determine a brand's overall potential or requirement for localization. The matrix can also point us towards possible interactions among the dimensions and moves across the typology of brands. For example, if we believe our gasoline (petrol) is perceived to be a super brand in most markets, we may wish to link innovation to country of origin when positioning the brand among global individualists who are receptive to superior technology from abroad. In effect, we might want our brand to be seen as 'the Mercedes of gasoline' (assuming this is credible for our target market). The same brand could be positioned among cultural sensitives more in the direction of a glocal brand by emphasizing its longevity in the market and sensitivity to local norms about retail practices, etc. Finally, we might try to move not just the product but the corporate brand itself from a super brand more toward a master brand by engaging a universal myth or narrative. British Petroleum's recent efforts to have 'BP' mean 'beyond petroleum' may be an example of this, an attempt to forge links to a myth of 'sustainability' or 'responsible stewardship'.

As this last example illustrates, our typology of brands is not meant to suggest that a brand simply 'is' a master brand or a super brand for all time. Rather, brands evolve and change their fundamental character in the ongoing dialectic between the companies and the consumers who jointly 'own' them. IBM and McDonald's once defined their categories and embodied myths such as success ('You'll never get fired for recommending IBM') or dependability (the same family-friendly experience, coast to coast). Today, despite past or current stumbles, they are still powerful brands with the potential to reinvent themselves, but they are more nearly super brands than master brands.

Nor should our typology be taken to imply an evaluative hierarchy; each type of brand has its own strengths and weaknesses, its own conditions of and possibilities for success. The next section examines these in terms of the specific dimensions of brand affinity that are most relevant for each type of brand. As we shall see, brand types differ not only in their need for and possibility of localization, but also in their vulnerability to transparency and 'no logo' backlash.

LEVERAGING AFFINITY STRENGTHS BY BRAND TYPES

We can further characterize master, prestige, super and glocal brands in terms of the specific aspects of affinity that each leverages to create brand equity. Research International's Equity Engine[SM] model of brand equity views brand equity as the sum of perceived brand performance (functional

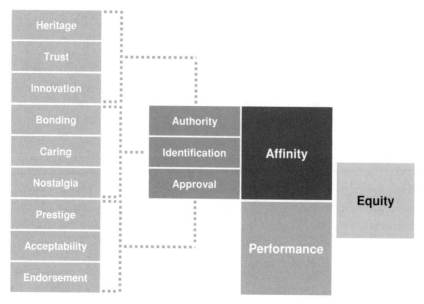

Figure 20.5   Dimensions of brand equity.

benefits) and perceived brand affinity (emotional benefits). While this ranges widely across product and service categories, typically half or more of brand equity derives from affinity rather than performance. Affinity has three basic dimensions, each of which, in turn, has three dimensions (see Figure 20.5).

- **Authority** is the brand's standing among other brands on the dimensions of heritage, trust and innovation.
- **Identification** is the relationship of consumer and brand in terms of bonding (how the consumer currently views the brand), caring (what the consumer believes the brand currently feels about him or her) and nostalgia (past relationships with the brand).
- **Approval** is the consumer's evaluation of the brand through the lens of society at large and specific reference groups in terms of prestige, acceptability and endorsement.

The next four figures show the specific aspects of affinity that are most salient for each type of brand (see Figures 20.6–20.9).

Master brands tend to be strong on at least one aspect of each of the three basic dimensions of affinity. While not all master brands are in fact 'first movers,' they tend to be strong on authority, particularly

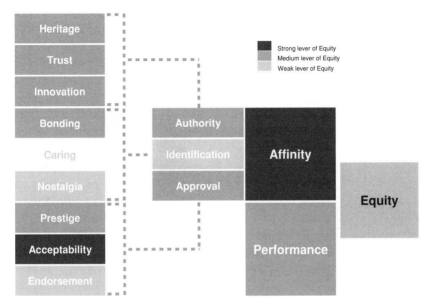

Figure 20.6 Master brand affinity.

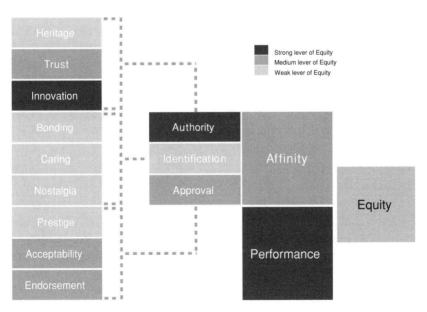

Figure 20.7 Super brand affinity.

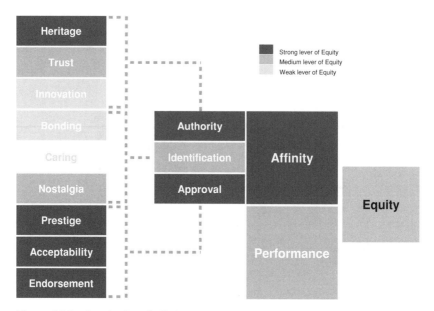

Figure 20.8   Prestige brand affinity.

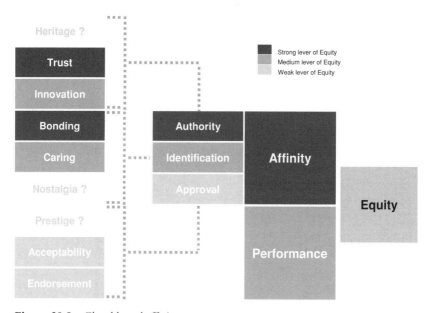

Figure 20.9   Glocal brand affinity.

innovation and trust. This may be in part because of the heritage (actual or presumed) they may claim as (re)inventors of their category. This, in turn, helps explain the nostalgia aspect of identification that master brands can leverage. Importantly, master brands are more 'loved than loving' – that is, they evoke more bonding from consumers than demonstrate caring toward them. Finally, their ubiquity and long-term or dominant presence give master brands particular strength on the acceptability dimension of approval.

Super brands share with master brands strengths in trust and innovation. Since trust is an essential element of all types of brands, super brands attempt to differentiate primarily on innovation – which is defined largely (like super brands themselves) by the category. Because they do not engage a universal myth or narrative in the way that master brands do, however, super brands typically show less strength on the basic dimensions of identification and approval. What strength they do have on these dimensions flows largely from bonding and acceptability, respectively. Conversely, super brands cannot typically leverage the heritage and nostalgia that support master brands' myth or narrative-driven equity.

In keeping with their 'elitest' appeal, prestige brands exhibit the 'coolest' relationship with consumers – allowing themselves to be loved, but reciprocating very little. In fact, prestige brands may selectively appeal precisely to consumers who fancy themselves to be 'above' such common demands, and who are secure in their own identity and self-worth, displayed through their refined choice of such brands. (In this, they resemble – and in fact may be an evolution from – 'tribal brands' discussed below.) Heritage, trust and perhaps innovation yield authority while prestige yields approval – what more could the discriminating consumer ask?

By contrast to the three other types of brands (particularly prestige brands), glocal brands typically demonstrate the strongest identification. They project 'concern and caring' for the consumers they know so well, and elicit in return nostalgia about what these brands have meant to them as they literally 'grow old' together. Like prestige brands, glocal brands thus tend to be strong on heritage and trust, but they trade approval for identification. The distinction here parallels that made by social scientists between modern urban society based on anonymous market transactions (Gesellschaft) and traditional rural communities based on kinship and other close ties (Gemeinschaft). As traditional cultures modernize, personality types and motivations shift from 'inner-directed' to 'other-directed' and social approval takes on a new character. No longer (only) a matter of direct personal relationships, social approval is increasingly mediated through 'virtual communities' defined in part by shared brand experiences (Upshaw and Taylor, 2000). As traditional cultures open to include a wider world, however, the role of glocal brands in maintaining personal and cultural identity remains – and may in fact loom larger as a haven against the perceived negative aspects of globalization.

VULNERABILITY TO TRANSPARENCY AND 'NO LOGO' BACKLASH

One consequence of the different affinity strengths of master, super, prestige and glocal brands is that they are differentially susceptible to threats from 'transparency' – the possibility that consumers will reject a brand because of its parent corporation's perceived bad behaviour. Just as our typology of brands does not imply a value hierarchy, neither is any one type of brand immune to transparency or a 'no logo' backlash. Rather, each type of brand faces its own kind of threat and potential response. To aid our comparisons on this point, Figure 20.10 summarizes the affinity strengths of each type of brand.

As noted earlier, trust is the bedrock precondition of *all* successful brands, but each type can gain (or lose) this trust in somewhat different ways. As Naomi Klein herself suggests towards the end of *No Logo*, brands

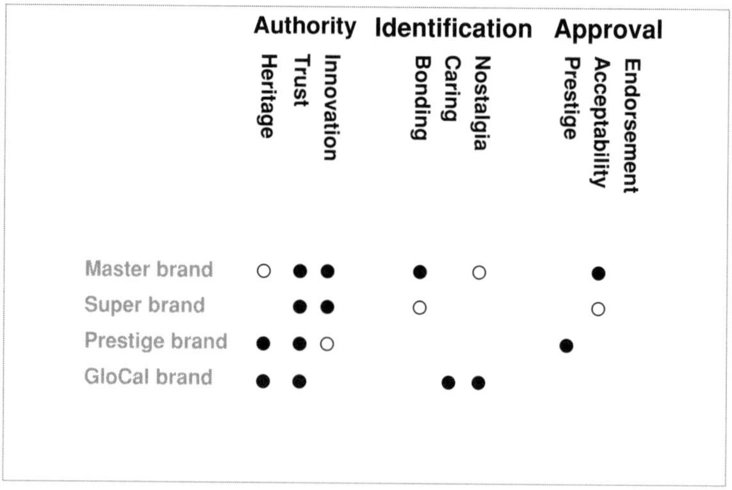

Figure 20.10 Affinity strengths by type of brand.

that are the most visible to consumers and pride themselves on their high moral ground, may be setting themselves up for the biggest fall (Klein, 2000). By appealing to the myth of empowerment, Nike in effect dares consumers to judge it by whether or not it empowers the Third World factory workers who make its products. And as we have seen, one way to avoid cognitive dissonance and continue to love Nike is to decide that, in fact, such workers *are* empowered – if only relative to local conditions, not Western standards.

We find much less evidence of holding master brands accountable than Klein believes is (or should be) the case. Nevertheless, it is precisely the appeal to a *universal* myth that creates Nike's Achilles heel. If empowerment is a universal, rather than a culturally-specific ideal, then Western consumers at least (and perhaps Third World activists) may be inspired to apply the same standard globally, forcing the issue. Potentially offsetting this possibility, if a master brand is truly (increasingly) an ideal accessible to all, it may be able to live its brand promise more consistently. The success of Coca-Cola relative even to other master brands may be an example of this.

As Figure 20.10 shows, master brands and (to a lesser degree) super brands have bonding and acceptability as salient dimensions of their affinity. The potential for a 'no logo' backlash seems inherent in the tension between the consumer's desire to love the brand and to have this love approved by others. If and when the threshold of 'bad' corporate behaviour is crossed, social acceptability may outweigh bonding, and consumers may reject the brand if they believe that others do (or would). Compared to super brands, master brands have heritage and nostalgia with which to buffer themselves against reaching this tipping point. The ability of corporations such as Shell or Exxon ultimately to weather environmental controversies illustrates the power of super brands, but also their susceptibility to such attacks as a function of their ubiquity and more distant relationship to consumers.

Finally, the contrasting vulnerability to transparency of prestige and glocal brands helps illuminate some of the underlying dynamics of potential 'no logo' backlash. While both count heritage and trust as salient aspects of their affinity, prestige brands focus the approval dimension on prestige, rather than acceptability or endorsement. While all three are mediated by society, prestige is the aspect of approval most readily isolated from wider social currents. By definition, prestige brands appeal selectively to an elite that may define itself in part precisely by its ability to ignore the opinions of others 'not like us' (witness the relatively unsuccessful attempts to boycott the use of real furs). Like master brands, prestige brands embody a myth or narrative, but unlike master brands this does not necessarily claim to be universal – at least in the sense of available to all. Rather, a prestige brand's myth or narrative is exclusive and exclusionary, that of a founder or country of origin, the qualities of which not everyone can appreciate. As such, and somewhat ironically, prestige brands may be least susceptible to transparency and 'no logo' backlash. They aim to remain aloof and above the fray.

By contrast, glocal brands may also be less susceptible to transparency than are master or super brands because they are 'beneath the radar.' As noted earlier, glocal brands are the 'warmest' in terms of their reciprocal relationships with consumers. That is, more than other types of brands, their trust is rooted in, and supported by, heritage, nostalgia and concrete demonstrations that they understand and care about consumers on the basis of this long-standing, intimate relationship. Far from embodying a universal or exclusive myth or narrative, they are the familiar, comfortable, 'everyday' brands that share our values; they are felt to be local even when they are known to be globally available. And this is just as well, because glocal brands also tend to be in categories such as food, personal care and household products that can have a direct effect on the health and safety of consumers and their families. If the threshold for 'bad' corporate behaviour to become personally relevant is thus lower, the desire to love the brand is all the greater, even as the potential discrepancy with 'higher' values is less.

Some master brands such as The Body Shop have seemed to embody the myth of Icarus – flying high and aspiring to universal acceptance at the risk of provoking universal rejection. By contrast, glocal brands appear content to fly (or lie) low, keeping so close to consumers that the possibility of a generalized rejection never arises. Glocal brands are far from invulnerable, however.

Using the brand personality typology she developed, Jennifer Aaker, S. Adam Brasel of Stanford University and Susan Fournier of the Harvard Business School have recently reported research which may shed light on the differences between prestige and glocal brands' ability to resist transparency and 'no logo' backlash (Aaker, Fournier and Brasel, 2003). Aaker's experiments indicate that a brand seen by consumers to be 'sincere' may actually have a harder time recovering from a service failure than a brand seen to be 'exciting.' By precise analogy to interpersonal relationships, it appears that consumers put more into – and expect more out of – a 'sincere,' long-standing relationship. When this trust is violated (e.g., by an affair), the damage may be harder to repair. Conversely, less is expected of a casual 'fling.' If and when the other party unexpectedly 'comes through' (analogous to an exciting brand's equally unexpected recovery from a service failure), the individual may re-examine his or her assumptions about the nature of the relationship, and recovery from the let down (service failure) may be quicker and more thorough.

In terms of our brand typology, prestige brands are 'exciting' – aloof and alluring, but consumers may consequently expect little serious commitment from the brand. Conversely, 'loyalty' to a prestige brand may be as much to the *idea of exclusivity* as to the specific brand of the moment, which helps explain the frantic pace of competition in fashion and other prestige categories. Glocal brands are 'sincere.' Prestige brands may escape transparency and rejection on appeal to universal ideals precisely because they are so self-referential and self-validating. Glocal brands may escape a similar fate because they make no appeal to a higher standard other than the fundamental trust they have earned. But if and when this sincere relationship is brought into question (e.g., by a health or safety controversy), the glocal brand may suffer a loss of credibility from which it may only slowly – or never – recover.

THIRD WAVE BRANDING

Thus far we have focused on the need to balance localization versus globalization of different types of brands and their specific strengths and weaknesses in the face of potential antiglobalization 'push back.' We conclude by considering briefly another important theme in our 2002 RIO study: the need to balance the desire for participation in a global consumer society against the desire for individual expression.

Many cultures are still in *Wave One branding* – where brands provide the reassuring guarantee of quality that was their original rationale at the dawn of consumer society in the mid 19th century. Most brands are part of *Wave Two*, where the role of the brand is to enable consumers to make a strong lifestyle statement. More sophisticated consumers increasingly find Wave Two branding too imposing and the brand identities too homogenized. *Wave Three branding* is a counter point in which consumers participate actively in the meanings that brands provide (see Figure 20.11). The consumer selects the brand, not the other way around, and the brand becomes a very individual statement, connecting a social group or 'tribe' based on attitude and behaviour, not age, sex or class. In the words of

	Wave One	Wave Two	Wave Three
Role of brand	Physical quality	Lifestyle projection	Personal projection
Benefit	Trust/ Reassurance	Affinity/ Identification	Authenticity/ Discovery/ Invention
Current geography	Africa/China/India	Developed world	Sophisticated consumers in Europe/Asia/USA
Target	Mass	Mass	Fragmented and proliferated

Figure 20.11   Three waves of branding (thus far!).

one Swedish consumer: 'I don't want the brand to find me; I want to find the brand.' Often, Wave Three branding is used as a rebellion against mainstream brands and their increasing ubiquity.[3]

Examples of Third Wave brands are not limited to, but can include, so-called 'tribal' brands, such as Carhartt, Gola or Quicksilver, and local brands, such as ACNE JEANS from Sweden. The essence of such tribal brands is the experience of authenticity as they are 'discovered' and appropriated (often in idiosyncratic ways) by an avant garde. By definition,

---

[3] Support for the notion of the three 'waves' of branding can be found in our recent quantitative study of the dimensions of 'globalness' (Quelch, Holt and Taylor, 2003). Specifically, we found that the inference of quality on the basis of global availability explained by far the most variance in global consumers' brand preferences, both within and across the six product categories tested. This corresponds to the prevalence of Wave One branding, primarily (though not exclusively) in the less-developed economies and emerging consumer societies that make up the majority of the 12 countries included in our study. As noted above, the UK and US score lowest on the overall impact of this and the other four dimensions of 'globalness' on brand preference. As consumers in such developed countries move through Wave Two towards Wave Three branding, the drivers of brand preference become more diverse, and globalness *per se* matters relatively less. Conversely, the collective impact of the five dimensions of globalness – quality, status, country of origin, citizenship and American values – is relatively greatest for those societies that are arguably most homogeneous and remote from Western consumer values (Egypt, Indonesia and Turkey). Finally, our study also provides support for the notion that brands can be appropriated by consumers in ways that increasingly transcend conventional boundaries. Specifically, there are few differences in the impact of dimensions of globalness on brand preference when the data are analysed by category or by country. Rather, the best mathematical solution was to use latent class segmentation to assign consumers to like groups *regardless of the product category being rated or their country of residence.* The resulting segments are described in Quelch, Holt and Taylor (2003). The point we wish to make here is that our analyses support the idea of consumer segments defined by shared ways of evaluating global brands – 'tribes' if you like – as the most fundamental unit of analysis. Such tribes are distributed increasingly *across* – rather than bound by – different countries and cultures.

tribal brands thus resist heavy-handed corporate control. There are, however, very successful global brands that connect with 'tribes' through limited editions, such as Nike or Sony, and global prestige brands, such as Hilfiger, Rolex or Gucci, that have been picked up as totems of the tribe.

CONCLUSION: THE FUTURE OF GLOBAL BRANDS

While neither Ted Levitt nor Naomi Klein tell the full story, on the evidence of our RIO 2002 qualitative and Harvard Business School/WPP quantitative studies, Professor Levitt appears to be getting the better of the debate. Indeed, the consensus of the recent colloquium held at the Harvard Business School on the occasion of the 20th anniversary of his influential paper, was that Levitt was more right than not.

Importantly, however, the global convergence Levitt predicted has occurred largely (as Marx said of history more generally) 'behind the backs' of consumers. That is, convergence has been greatest on the supply side in terms of management practices, supply chain management, manufacturing (e.g., use of standard global platforms for automobiles) and B2B marketing. Convergence is much less noteworthy on the demand side of B2C marketing. While often overpromised and underdelivered, 'mass customization' is in fact a reality in many business sectors today, allowing convergence in processes to support divergence, customization and localization of the products and services offered to consumers around the world.

The increasing importance and affordability of information technology and the rise of 'permission-based' marketing in more highly developed economies are likely to further, not retard trends toward customization at every level – from country to culture, from 'tribe' to individual consumer. Thus, brand managers are ever more likely to face the twin challenges of localization versus globalization and individualization versus homogenization. While there is no single or simple path to the Brand Utopia Levitt predicted, we hope that our typology of brands and globalization roadmap will provide a useful guide for continuing the journey.

REFERENCES

Aaker, J., Fournier, S. and Brasel, S.A. (2003), *When Good Brands Do Bad*. Paper presented to the Marketing Science Institute Board of Trustees Meeting in Washington, D.C., March 6.

Johansson, J.K. and Ronkainen, I.A. (2003), *The Esteem of Global Brands*. Unpublished draft paper, McDonough School of Business, Georgetown University.

Klein, N. (2000), *No Logo*. St. Martin's Press.

Levitt, T. (1983), The Globalization of Markets, *Harvard Business Review*, May/June, pp. 92–102.

Quelch, J., Holt, D. and Taylor, E. (2003), *Managing the Transnational Brand: How Global Perceptions Drive Value*. Paper presented at the Harvard Business School's Globalization of Markets Colloquium (May 28–30).

Sterenberg, G. and Baker, M. (2002), International Branding: Resolving the Global–Local Dilemma, *Market Leader*, **19**, 42–48.

Upshaw, L. and Taylor, E. (2000), *The Masterbrand Mandate*. John Wiley & Sons, Inc.

Chapter Twenty-one

Audience Measurement in the 'Dual Economies' of Poor Countries: A Case Study from Pakistan

Ijaz Gilani[a] and Mansoor Khan[b]

This chapter introduces the 'duality of economies' prevailing in developing countries such as Pakistan, and the implication this has on advertising and media research.

INTRODUCTION

Why a 'dual economy'?

There are several reasons why we characterize Pakistan as a dual economy. We can name at least seven of them:

1. State-of-the-art, high-tech equipment coexists with extremely primitive technology. The country is fairly advanced in rocket science and missile technology, but bullock-carts are abundant at the same time in rural, and even many urban areas.
2. A small segment of the market consumes world-class branded products in garments, toiletries and household gadgets. However, a large

[a] Chairman, Gallup Pakistan.
[b] International TV Development Director, TNS (UK).

Market Research Best Practice. Edited by P. Mouncey and F. Wimmer.
© 2007 John Wiley & Sons, Limited.

section of the population consumes homemade items, unpacked, unprocessed and, on occasion, exchanged in a barter market.

3. A few corporate-owned large organizations with modern management run alongside hundreds of thousands of micro-enterprises that are owned by individuals and operated from their personal residences. A few large organizations in the private sector employ 20 000 or more people, whereas the majority of enterprises operate on an average of less than five people, including family members (FBS, 1999).

4. The country is a significant exporter of professional manpower such as doctors, engineers and IT specialists and has educational institutions that train them. However, a little over half the population is completely illiterate. Less than 1% of the adult population is qualified from a university (Census, 1998).

5. The country can boast having an advanced fibre-optic-based telecom structure. It has been fairly fast in introducing fax machines, computers, Internet cyber-cafes and cable TV in both urban and increasingly rural areas. However, one-third of rural households do not have electricity so far, and more than 50% do not have a latrine and use open fields for faeces (Gallup, 2001a; 2001b).

6. The country has attracted large international names (or inherited them from the British colonial period) such as Unilever, Shell, Procter & Gamble, Colgate, Nestlé, Coca-Cola, Pepsi and many others in consumer products. It has attracted major international banks as well as fast-food chains. However, annual direct foreign investment remains under half a billion dollars; exports have struggled unsuccessfully to reach ten billion dollars and total advertising expenditure in electronic and print media is so far around 100 million dollars[1] (Aurora, 2001).

7. While two out of three Pakistanis live in small villages and rural areas, one in five homes have at least one person who has travelled or worked abroad. The lifestyle thus combines extremely local features with a touch of globalization (Gallup, 2000). Alongside low levels of foreign investment and exports, globalization is very apparent in the field of advertising, where all of the top ten advertising agencies are now affiliated with global giants in their fields.

---

[1] The country has moved forward on these indicators since 2001. Foreign direct investment has more than doubled during this period. Exports are touching 17 billion US dollars and the expenditure on electronic and print media is estimated at over 150 million US dollars.

Impact of the dual economy on advertising and media

In an attempt to introduce Pakistan from a macro perspective, we ask a relevant question: how does a dual economy affect advertising and media? As a result of its sheer size (160 million people), modern and global economic trends have made inroads into the country. However, a majority of the population is either excluded from it or its participation is very fragile and peripheral in quantitative terms.

To illustrate the point, global soft drinks have penetrated the entire country successfully, but per capita consumption is tiny; Nestlé has introduced a wide range of its food items, but the total turnover from them may be a few million dollars. Half a dozen food and personal care global giants control two-thirds of the entire television advertising, but all of them taken together contribute less than 50 million dollars a year to this activity.

Since TV advertising is so heavily dominated by global players, their management expects globally recognized tools of operation. This is one important reason as to why, despite low levels of foreign participation in investment, manufacturing or trading in the country, the advertising sector has already gone global in a big way. It is from there that we receive the big push for providing television ratings and advertising expenditure research that meets international standards. The inherent duality in the economic environment creates many tensions.

The global marketing companies are increasingly penetrating the entire country, urban as well as rural. Thus, they can no longer focus on a small geographical core. The peripheries present the opportunity, and yet the business generated from them is small in dollar terms.

Advertising has to expand into new markets to realize their promise. Expensive state-of-the-art (international standard) research must be carried out and it will be most relevant if its locus of operation is beyond the traditional narrow geographical core. Thus, it boils down finally to two difficult issues:

1. Money for advertising and advertising research has to come from a narrow revenue base for a vast geographic and demographic mass. An interesting duality!
2. Modern and expensive research needs to be carried out to international standards for a market which is so diverse that some of its members enjoy housing which is comparable, if not superior, to their European counterparts, while at the other end, 30% of urban TV

viewers live in a one-room house which serves as bedroom, living room, kitchen and TV lounge all combined into one (Census, 1998).

The type of house outlined above is electrified, but sockets are makeshift. It may even have a phone that is shared between several complex users of an extended family and may often be out of order because of unpaid bills. It has a TV and possibly a cable connection, but everything is tenuous.

Fragile living conditions rest on a balance that every now and then falls apart. This happens when a new guest arrives and decides to stay for a few days, or events such as a wedding, a funeral or birth of a child happen in the extended family, for which this may be the only available space.

This is not to forget that such fragile and miserable customers may, at the end of the day, be generating more revenue for the products being sold by leading advertisers compared to the upscale consumers. This could be true for tea, soaps, detergents, dental care and many other leading advertising groups.

It is in such exciting and tension-ridden, paradox-laden conditions that brand managers seek advertising budgets that might stretch the limits of what is merited by their revenues. They may find themselves handicapped without providing state-of-the-art research to their global and regional bosses, but still wish to commission it at local miserly amounts.

They may receive excited interest in the peculiarities of local living conditions but fail to convince or receive much attention when it comes to spending resources on how to reconcile local oddities and global standards. The struggle for a researcher in a dual economy is both financial and intellectual; that is, to address difficult and complex research issues that outweigh the complexities in an economically prosperous environment with financial resources that are minuscule in comparison.

Having introduced Pakistan in the topical context of this chapter, a case study now follows of how we initiated and started the process of devising and implementing suitable strategies, so that a viable and modern PeopleMeter-based television audience measurement service could be established in Pakistan – a developing country with its own hard-core set of unique idiosyncrasies (like most countries), coupled with the duality of its economy.

NEW MEASUREMENT TECHNIQUES INTRODUCED THROUGH EDUCATION, NOT BY DICTATING TO THE MARKET

Innovate: To change a thing into something new; to alter, to renew, to bring in something new for the first time; to introduce as new.

Innovation: The action of innovating; the introduction of novelties; the alteration of what is established by the introduction of new elements or form. A change made in the nature or fashion of anything; something newly introduced; a novel practice or method, etc.

(Oxford English Dictionary)

Innovation is defined as developing and delivering products or services that offer benefits which customers perceive as new and superior. The need for innovation arises due to environmental changes plus the changing needs of the customer, or simply because it offers better answers to the present needs through its revamped appearance or a new product altogether.

But why innovate? Today, in this ever-changing world, the pressures are far greater than ever to innovate. In our case, the changes in technology and living standards create new needs, which in turn puts pressure on research companies to update or redesign their measurement products constantly.

The last decade has witnessed dramatic changes in the business environment, but acutely more so in the 'business jungles' of the developing countries, some of the relevant changes being:

- rapid and radical technical developments in computers, telecommunications and information sciences, particularly the explosive growth in the diffusion and impact of television and multichannel broadcasting, cable and satellite reception and, of course, the Internet and intranets;
- globalization of business, including increased international competition and the emergence of regional and global customers and resource markets;
- changing demographics, values, expectations and behaviour of the population;
- increased government and public scrutiny of business decisions, with greater focus on the ethical dimensions of these decisions.

The cumulative impact of these changes and their implications on media research has brought opportunities, challenges and problems for the industry. The media research community is very much on the sharp end of these changes. As fragmentation makes its task harder, the research contracts and budgets are becoming tighter, but the expectation and demand of clients is for ever-more sophisticated data and reassurance that measurement techniques are available that can meet these challenges.

Fuelled by this notion and through the frequent need for innovation, eventually the PeopleMeter, the *de facto* standard methodology for measuring television audiences worldwide, came to be developed and used. It is, for the same reasons, now required in Pakistan and other such comparable countries that have reached a threshold and need to transition from using diaries to PeopleMeter-based technology.

So what is the issue? Technology by itself is rarely a solution. The innovation field is full of new examples of new products that employed exotic technology but failed to achieve customer acceptance or satisfaction, e.g. in the early years of videocassette recorders, JVC's VHS video format 'killed' off the technically far superior Sony Betamax format.

In examining the failure of technologically sophisticated products, one of the major reasons seems to be the pioneer's failure to recognize the importance of the sociotechnological context of the innovation. People do not buy technology; they buy products and services that deliver specific benefits and solve certain problems: an important point that media research service providers might wish to take heed of.

Technology is the facilitator that enables the development of the products and services and helps shape customer's needs and wants. Therefore, understanding the socio-economic and cultural context in which the technology will be used is critical to the design of effective new products and services.

Continuing and keeping this in mind, from our experience and knowledge of Pakistan (readers may wish to draw parallels with other similar countries), there appears a tendency to be 'myopic' in truly knowing the benefits or limitations of new products or services. The reasons can be numerous, but some of the obvious reasons that stand out are the following (this is by no means an exhaustive list):

- high levels of illiteracy;
- lack of quality education and proper training;
- limited financial resources;
- 'blind' product/brand/service loyalty, usually a result of tradition and hearsay;
- language, cultural and religious limitations or prohibitions.

For media research service providers who intend bringing in new technology-based measurement techniques (like PeopleMeters), the implications in not recognizing or addressing these concerns upfront could compromise the success of the service.

From the authors' own experiences whilst interacting with the market, there manifested a general lack of true appreciation in terms of the *real* benefits and the limitations of PeopleMeters. On many occasions, market feedback contained ludicrous preconceived misconceptions like 'PeopleMeters have microphones and cameras inside them'. Televisions are one of the most valued and treasured possessions in Pakistani homes. Rumours were rampant that television sets would need to be taken apart, modified, and there would be many cables sprouting from the back and around the house: all these preconceived notions had to be dispelled, and quickly.

The culmination of what has been discussed till now clearly points to the fundamental and imperative need for developing an effective marketing communication strategy and programme. This needs to be activated and put into motion at the earliest possible moment, delaying this may lead to significant difficulties and possibly prove irrevocable later.

Identifying the target audience (stakeholders), and their relevant importance is the first step. We intend to do this by using and adapting to our needs the stakeholder mapping model, and in particular the power/interest matrix method, as shown in Figure 21.1. This classifies stakeholders in relation to the power they hold and the extent to which they are likely to show interest in the organization's strategies.

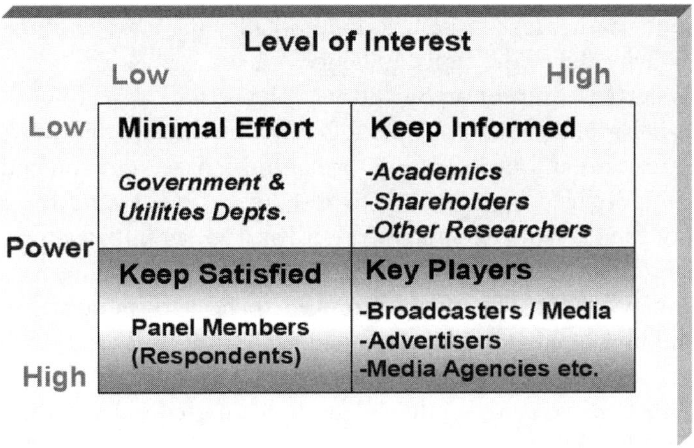

Figure 21.1   Who are the stakeholders? Adapted from Mendelow, 1991.

This map clearly shows that the marketing communication needs to target essentially two groups, the 'key player' (primary) should be given key consideration, and the 'keep satisfied' (secondary) in general are relatively passive but often can prove to be the most difficult.

Next, the need to communicate, educate and influence the following people in each of our target groups will need to be initiated. First, the primary group (media and advertisers) will need to be approached. The secondary group (panellists) should be targeted later, usually at the time of recruitment, and again at the time of PeopleMeter installations, and then by regular intervals thereafter.

If one is to significantly influence key players, it is important to not only build contacts with individuals, but also to maintain them. Hence, this should be considered, when planning suitable communication tools, as part of the marketing communication mix.

The authors recommend from their own experiences the following marketing communication mixes that have proven to be highly effective:

- **Direct visits (media and advertisers)**. According to Knecht's five phases of integrated marketing communication, 'phase 4 involves optimal integration of elements of the marketing mix; the most vital component is personal selling, although price and distribution are also important' (Knecht, 1989). By personally approaching the key people in the primary group and introducing yourself and the technology can pay significant dividends, e.g. lowering mistrust, people relate better to the faces in front of the products, first-hand and prompt removal of any preconceived doubts or concerns people may have, etc.
- **Direct mail**. This is a flexible method allowing a range of messages to be delivered to the target audience.
- **Newsletters and/or cyberletters**. Newsletters especially targeted at panel members offer a cost-effective method to motivate, provide relevant and up-to-date information, quizzes and competitions, and importantly a mechanism to re-educate and remind the panellists of their 'own' responsibilities. In Pakistan, an initiative was taken to target the primary group by cyberletters (monthly Internet delivered newsletter). This method proved to be very popular and successful by keeping key players posted on topical issues and on general media research-related developments and trends. There was such appeal that many in the industry, at that time, considered this to be ground-breaking.

- **Seminars, workshops and informal get-togethers**. Periodic face-to-face contact is one of the most effective ways to get your message across. To maximize this opportunity, seminars, workshops and informal open-session get-togethers are a cost-effective way of getting groups of media people together, not only to explain what you can do but also, importantly, to be able to listen and gain a greater insight into their views and agendas. Hence, in Pakistan we organized periodic 'media research get-togethers and round tables' held in settings ranging from informal social clubs to formal hotel conference rooms. This initiative again proved to be successful and well appreciated.

- **Mass media (television and business magazines)**. If opportunity arises, which we were fortunate to receive, there can be no better medium than using television to impart information to a mass audience. We made a documentary that was featured in a regular business programme, enabling us to target a specific audience. We also featured articles in leading national media magazines.

CHALLENGES IN THE DEVELOPMENT OF PEOPLEMETER-BASED TAM IN DEVELOPING COUNTRIES

Presently, through the many manifestations of the effects of globalization of research practices, there seems to be one prevailing factor – standardization in research methods and techniques. Some good examples of standardization are:

- harmonizing procedures and practices which dictate global quality standards;
- data-capturing techniques, such as the use of PeopleMeters in audience measurement, have become *de facto* standards.

This standardization phenomenon, although prevalent across much of the globe, has a far more accentuated and complex impact and effect on developing countries, hence involvement with such countries requires a higher level of consideration, sensitivity and empathy.

However, this can create a paradoxical situation. Organizations today involved in, or responsible for setting up, television audience measurement services in countries throughout the world are under incessantly growing pressure to deliver services that meet ever-increasing local market expectations and demands, coupled with a tacit requirement from both within the country and externally that the service will at least meet international quality standards, or, in other words, seek standardization.

Organizations exist and function in the context of a complex commercial, economic, political, technological, cultural and social world. For the purposes of this chapter, we intend calling this the *operating environment*.

One of the core principles preached frequently in the field of modern management strategy is that 'the organizations which have been successful and profitable in delivering quality products or services in the marketplace are those that have made concerted efforts in developing and applying strategies designed to maximize the 'harmonization' of their activities with the environment in which they operate'. This is a time-tested concept which holds true to most, if not all, of the different organizational types and their products or services.

Unfortunately, many of today's organizations go into countries with an inflexible approach by having set-standardized mandates by virtue of their heritage and experience in the field, or because they consider they possess the latest so-called future-proof technological products or expertise.

We are not implying all these attributes are not important – they certainly are – but you may seriously run the risk of compromising all of these competitive advantages, and ultimately even the service you intend providing. Therefore, it is imperative that prior and realistic assessment of the recipient country's 'on the ground' realities and challenges are first identified, so that eventually, these can be overcome. In effect, the intention is to try to adjust or modify the standardized approach by incorporating the key environmental factors so that the chance of 'harmonization' is enhanced greatly.

Therefore, the identification of these environmental factors will be critical, developing or modelling an approach that can assist in exploring and seeking out these factors is essential. We will attempt to achieve this by utilizing and adapting established management models, which may permit a more integrated and analytical understanding of the environment. It is also hoped this technique may prove useful for other organizations as well.

ANALYSING THE ENVIRONMENT

The purpose of this analysis is to assess the remote macro areas of the organization (the word 'organization' used in this section applies to organizations involved in, or responsible for, the development or set-up of TAM services). Environmental analysis is essentially an attempt to understand the strategic significance of developments around the organization.

Understanding the nature of the environment

It would be sagacious to begin by addressing the strategic management issue of coping with 'uncertainty':

- How uncertain is the environment?
- What are the reasons for that uncertainty?
- How should that uncertainty be dealt with?

Figure 21.2 suggests that environmental uncertainty increases as environmental conditions become more complex or dynamic. It will be noted that we have positioned the TV media industry as belonging in an environment which is both complex and dynamic, as opposed to the oil industry, for example, which, for comparison purposes only, is categorized as being in a simple and static environment.

In simple/static conditions, an organization faces a relatively stable environment that is not undergoing significant changes; the technology is well established and the competition and markets are entrenched. Changes that do occur are likely to be predictable, so it makes sense to analyse the environment on an historical basis.

In complex/dynamic conditions, organizations have to exhibit proactivity rather than reactivity. Dynamic conditions require organizations to consider the environment of the future, not simply of the past. With

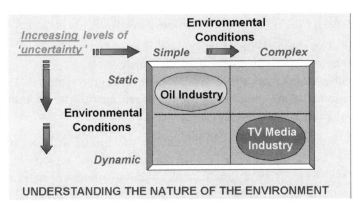

Figure 21.2 Analysing the TV media environment. Adapted from Johnson and Scholes, 1993.

the profusion of TV channels and with different delivery platforms and changing technologies, added to the complex environment of the country's social-cultural and political make-up, one can begin to understand and appreciate how complex and dynamic the nature of the environment really is.

As part of the environmental analysis, assessing the importance of external stakeholder expectations in terms of the power/interest matrix (as described in the previous section 'New measurement techniques introduced through education, not by dictating to the market' as well as in Figure 21.1) may prove very useful; hence, repeating the exercise here is recommended.

Auditing environmental influences

PEST (Political, Economic, Socio-cultural and Technological) analysis is a very useful technique to assess the environmental influences on the organization, and the industry in which it is operating, in terms of identifying long-term drivers of change and the differential impact of external influences. These impacts can be either historical or in terms of likely future impacts that the organization needs to be attentive to.

First, let us begin by reminding ourselves that the notion of environment encapsulates very many influences. The difficulty is in understanding this diversity and its effects on the organization's intended TAM service. The great danger or mistake organizations may make is to rely entirely on a listing analysis approach in attempting to solve the conundrum. We suggest a more active and pragmatic approach to this issue, and in this process devised what we have called a harmonization model (see Figure 21.3). The purpose of this model is twofold:

1. It enables the pick-up of key environmental factors, many of which will be critical elements for the PEST analysis.
2. Feedback of the key PEST analysis factors into the system to assist in harmonizing the activities of the organization with the environment in which it is operating.

The key underpinning requirement for this model to have any real value or use is that it relies on having a 'test panel' set-up. The test panel will basically be a much smaller version (miniature replicate) of the intended full TAM panel. In Figure 21.3, the test panel is shown to be input by what we have called *standardized systems*; these are the 'usual' hardware (PeopleMeters), software (polling/data processing) or other related equipment and materials that are to be used in the set-up

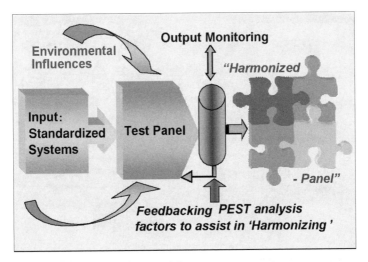

Figure 21.3   Panel harmonization model.

of the TAM service. Once this test panel is up and running, and being exposed to the operating environment, there will then be an important need to closely monitor the output activities of the panel. Some of the key activities that may need to be monitored closely from the test panel include:

- polling systems efficiency;
- data capturing (PeopleMeters) systems behaviour and performance;
- respondent compliance and behaviour;
- viewing data analysis.

Subjecting the panel to this kind of inquisition may yield key environmentally dependent factors. These and other environmentally dependent factors, which may affect the operating of the TAM service, can be termed the PEST analysis factors.

It will be critical to assess these factors in terms of being either positive or negative. We are interested in the identified negative factors. These negative factors will then have to be investigated and worked upon in terms of modification, improvements, or just being more aware or diligent on the part of the service provider. After this has been done, these factors will need to be fed back into the test panel for reassessment. This is a kind of 'iterative' process to achieve a satisfactory level of harmonization.

Once an acceptable level of harmonization has been established, progressing to the set-up of the full panel can then be done with more efficiency, assurance and belief that the intended service will at least meet

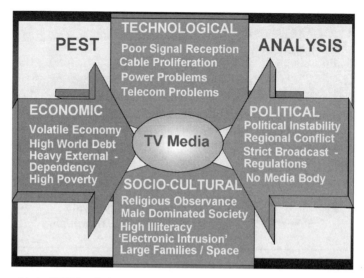

Figure 21.4 PEST analysis.

the needs and expectations of the industry it intends serving. We used this model to a good practical effect in Pakistan. Some of the actual PEST analysis factors pertaining to the country (in 2002) and generated from the model are discussed briefly as follows (see also Figure 21.4).

Political environment

The political environment can affect the organization at a strategic level by creating opportunities and threats. In Pakistan, governmental controls on TV media, historically and recently, have been tight. Presently there is a level of political instability (some may argue stability) in the country, because of an interim military-controlled government. The ramification of this close relationship has resulted in the nation's TV broadcasting environment being entrenched in a state of flux, which has obviously not helped the media research industry at large.[2]

The industry has also not been helped by current regional disturbances. One notable and recent effect of this resulted in the government banning all reception of Indian channels throughout the country. This caused

---

[2] The situation has changed (as in 2006) since the paper was originally written in 2002. The country has gone through an election and is currently governed by a civilian set up closely chaperoned by military authorities. The electronic media has been partially literalized. Private TV Channels now air news and public affairs through cable/satellite. The that extent, and as a result of increasing competition for viewership, opportunities for the media research industry have increased.

significant problems to broadcasters and media research companies alike. For us, lessons had to be learnt and operational contingencies developed for such eventualities. For astute researchers, tracking political moods closely is now a mandatory exercise.

A separate, but still political, theme concerns appropriate industry consultation. At present there is no official TV media research industry consultation body. For developing countries such as Pakistan, where the media industry may be considered as being volatile, such a unifying body representing all key stakeholders may prove to be beneficial in promoting and establishing accountability, equitability and standards in the marketplace.

Economic environment

Economic forces affect most organizations on certain comparable lines. Hence, further detailed differentiation is really not required. Some common influences faced by organizations on their various exchange processes – for example, the price of major resources, both physical and human, the nature of demand and the perceptions and confidence of the business community and of existing and potential customers – are all influenced by the economic environment. Some of the specific key economic factors faced by the nation, which in turn affect the industry, are the following:

- high levels of poverty;
- high world debt;
- heavy external dependency;
- volatile economy.

Socio-cultural environment

Generally, the pace of change in the social environment, which affects such factors as population size and structure, social values and expectations, is slow but inexorable. The case is similar for developing countries, but a tad less slow.

Pakistan's population is predominantly (over 90%) Moslem, the vast majority following their faith to a high observance. The male gender clearly seems to have a more dominant role in society, with the women taking back-stage. This factor became quite evident when we were recruiting and installing equipment in the homes. Although women recruiters were employed, and accompanied installations wherever necessary, still the women when alone seemed to shy away when it came to answering questions or deciding on matters. We subsequently and frequently made appointments when there was a male member also present.

The high illiteracy and low education levels also proved problematic. Whilst trialling our panel member documentation on the test panel, we had to make frequent modifications to ensure a wider range of understanding existed amongst the diverse respondents.

Insecurity and a general lack of trust also prevails in the society. This is not helped when the electronic intrusion of the PeopleMeter is installed in people's homes. The feeling of Big Brother watching you is not uncommon, and many homes will not entertain the idea, but good communication and some persistent but gentle honest persuasion can still work wonders.

Televisions are one of the most prized and guarded possessions in most homes here. Once the people learned that we had to connect our equipment to their television, serious reservations were raised by many. Fortunately, we intended using a noninvasive type of PeopleMeter, which eased concerns considerably.

We also observed a strange viewing phenomenon, or perhaps more correctly 'non-viewing phenomenon', from a noticeable number of homes on our test panel. Particularly in the months of November and December (winter period), we noticed we were unable to collect (poll) data from some homes. After some investigation, what transpired was that marriages were taking place in these homes (time of year for marriages), and it was usual on such occasions to have relatives to stay over for up to a week in many cases. Because of space problems, the TV was 'sacrificed' (disconnected and stored away) to release a room for guests. Although this was genuine non-viewing, and therefore not a research problem, we did, however, stress the point that they should let us know after the marriage was over, so we could ensure everything was reconnected properly.

Technological environment

Pakistan's current technological environment is proving to be very challenging. This was clearly evident from the number of significant factors that we found from our test panel. The following is a brief list of the main factors encountered from our test panel and our responses in dealing with them:

- We improved and tightened meter installation techniques to counter the generally poor and variable reception quality of TV signals (off-air, cable and satellite) being received by the homes.

- We strove continually to improve detection methods and techniques to counter the proliferation of cable systems in cities such as Karachi. A few years ago, cable penetration was non-existent, today it is currently running at over 50% for the entire urban TV viewers, and is around 80% in a city such as Karachi.[3]
- We improved the power supply system in the PeopleMeter. This was done due to experiencing frequent and excessive electricity supply voltage fluctuations (poor power regulation).
- We improved the power back-ups to critical systems. This was done due to experiencing frequent and prolonged power supply shutdowns.
- We improved our polling system and software after experiencing the variable quality of local telephone exchange systems and also because of the variable and poor quality of telephone lines and wiring in the homes.

THE ISSUE OF TRUST AND PROVIDING THIRD-PARTY RATINGS

Some analysts believe that the absence of trust in public affairs is the most distinguishing element that separates an underdeveloped economy from a developed one. If one was to go by this analysis, it is no surprise that most Pakistanis do not repose trust in public institutions.

Public opinion polls by Gallup Pakistan show that there is a low level of trust in the executive, judicial and legislative arms of the government. It is also low in the government-controlled electronic media, as well as in the independent newspapers. The lowest level of trust is in politicians, political parties and the police. Private business does not evoke much trust either.

There is a common unfortunate feeling that fairness and honesty is absent from society. Thus, it is not uncommon for conspiracy theories to prosper and rumours to abound about ill-gotten wealth, hidden motives and under-the-table deals. There is a general tendency to distrust the news in the official media as well as the independent press.

In this prevalent atmosphere of distrust, it is hard for most people to believe that a professional organization would carry out unbiased third-party evaluation. There is a lurking suspicion that ratings would be biased purposefully to hurt or help interested parties. The general argument

---

[3] Figures have been updated for 2006.

runs, 'if ratings can influence big decisions, why would the ratings body not misuse its influence by seeking benefits of one or another kind?' Those who are more charitable believe that professionals might try to play the game more astutely by tampering with samples, weighting schemes, question wordings, and so on.

It is often observed that when people distrust objective methods, their confidence in their own judgement and observation is heightened unduly in the same proportion. Personal observation becomes the reference point to judge 'correct' research from the 'false', and such judgements are held with great emotion and self-righteousness.

Secondly, third-party ratings are a phenomenon that is the hallmark of a vibrant civil society in which the state and non-state institutions are both strong and confident in subjecting themselves to independent scrutiny. A tradition of strong civil society and experience with internal self-governance provides the necessary fertile ground for third party evaluation. Unfortunately, both are weak in a country such as Pakistan.

Thirdly, there are sad past experiences with experiments in self-governance. These failures, whether of parliaments, private associations or cooperative banks, are publicized beyond their merit to further aggravate the lack of confidence in independent self-governing institutions.

Given this prevailing atmosphere, it requires outstanding ability and integrity to inspire confidence in third-party evaluation. Here are some basics, which we have learnt from experience, on how to anticipate the problem and try to pre-empt it by appealing to the following:

- build in systemic checks;
- appeal to credentials;
- appeal to proven track record;
- constant vigilance against rumours and conspiracy theories;
- close interaction with competing interested parties to address their concerns before they become hardened into beliefs.

Let us explain briefly the steps that we undertook to achieve the above objectives. Some of these were taken only after the problem hit us in the face and we bruised ourselves before learning our lesson.

1. Build in systemic checks

It is important to develop a set of highly visible and credible systemic checks about the authenticity and objectivity of the ratings data. We have discovered that high-quality data coupled with meticulous professionalism is not a sufficient check against unmerited objections by those who, for one or another reason, are either dissatisfied with the service or wish to discredit it for other motives. Thus, we have now chosen to appoint a third-party auditing system. A leading international professional firm of auditors is responsible for carrying out an annual quality assurance exercise. It looks into the compliance status of all aspects of the ratings operation. We will also soon have an independent 'ombudsman' whose job would be to investigate any serious complaint about the possibility of bias in the service.

2. Appeal to credentials

Television ratings are a high-profile activity. They may not constitute a large business in monetary terms, but they come under discussion and debate at strategic levels in the leading media of the country. Thus, it becomes necessary that the ratings service should have one or more comparable people of national standing that could interact and engage in debate. In societies where individuals overshadow institutions, it is difficult to defend and create confidence in the validity of ratings without personal credentials and the reputation of its leadership in terms of professional standing and integrity. In Pakistan, our current television audience measurement service has enjoyed this advantage because of our long-standing roots in the academic and professional circles.

3. Appeal to proven track record

The television ratings service influences major financial decisions. It tends to alter well-ingrained methods of allocating media budgets. Thus, when an audience research agency makes its initial interventions in the media allocation process, many eyebrows rise. The technical findings of the researcher are challenged, by referring to the experience of 'old hands'. It is here that the comparable standing and proven track record of the research agency can prove to be a 'counterweight'. The proven track record of the research agency in media research on the one hand and third-party evaluation on the other is particularly helpful. When faced with a challenge from experienced hands, you should provide historical data on the evolution of various media vehicles and channels. These are known and familiar to the challengers, through their own first hand experience. Thus, you begin to connect with them and the relationship becomes more meaningful. Similarly, the assurance that your agency has provided third-party evaluation successfully on other issues to other clients is a reassurance to them that by relying on your ratings they are not venturing into unknown and untested hazardous terrain.

4. Constant vigilance against rumours and conspiracy theories

It is our experience that frivolous slander is not uncommon in the ratings business. The media industry has its due share among the 'chattering class' that loves to pick on others, shock them with their latest discovery or 'inside knowledge', or sometimes be a more blatant cynical carrier of character assassination for interested motives. These people would pick up an odd figure from the ratings data with a cell size of two or three respondents and shock their glamorous audience by their ability to spot such fallacious practices of the researchers, followed soon in hushed tones by insinuations about the motives that might lie behind the evil designs of the researcher. After we had been bruised by such assaults a few times, we decided to go public on the issue. We came to the conclusion that transparent public debate would be the best check against back-room gossip. Thus, we initiated our response to whatever piece of gossip we picked up from the party circuit by explaining our view in the newspapers on those issues. It later triggered us to start our own brief monthly newsletter that began to serve as a vehicle for our point of view. While its first issue was in print, we came to realize that an online version would be equally, or even more, effective for our target audience. That was the beginning of our Cyberletter released on a monthly basis. It has served us well in responding to and even pre-empting some of the mischief of the gossip circles. Our sincere advice to the community of audience researchers is to guard yourself against unscrupulous gossip circles. They will try to hurt you at home and abroad through the time-tested psychological war tool of 'insinuation'.

5. Close interaction with the community of media researchers

Aside from protecting yourself against the mischief of interested parties, it is important to participate actively in the professional forums of media researchers. If none exists, one might attempt to create one. This, in our view, is again a check against the circulation of false information. More-over, it can be a suitable place for exchange of information, discussion and debate. In Pakistan, we initiated for this purpose a media research get-together which meets periodically, bringing together around twenty people from advertising agencies, media planners and media professionals in addition to the research agency people. Together they have formed a lively professional group.

SUMMARY

This chapter concludes that, despite a relatively small current TV advertising market, there are strong pressures and reasons to develop a modern TV-meter-based audience measurement system in Pakistan.

The chapter relates this anomaly to the existence of islands of modernity and globalization amidst a vast and populous periphery of business operations that run on traditional management culture. The periphery, however, is not focused geographically, instead, it runs alongside the modern sector throughout a country comprising over 400 cities, 45 000 villages and 140 million people.

A globally mobile management class, working for transnational corporations, experiences the tensions of working in a dual economy. The chapter listed seven features of 'duality' in the Pakistani economy and explained how the successful introduction of a modern TV audience measurement system is a creative outcome resulting from that tension.

The chapter explained the difficulties of introducing new and modern measurement technology into the challenging environment of a developing and complex country. Some of the issues were political, physical and socio-technological, as well as the relative absence of a civil society in the modern sector of the economy creating sociological conditions in which trust is in short supply and suspicion abounds.

The chapter attempted to show (and to a large extent proved) that these issues could be addressed realistically and overcome by the application of practical methodologies:

- educating the stakeholders through effective marketing – the importance of marketing new measurement techniques and technology tactfully in the marketplace;
- harmonization of the measurement panel through testing – the importance of exhibiting proactivity, creativity and at the same time being pragmatic in approach, so as to help identify and overcome the inevitable challenges in the development of a PeopleMeter-based TAM service in Pakistan;

- creating acceptability of the service through equitability and accreditation – attempting to establish equitability and accreditation by the application of five key objectives.

These lessons, which Gallup Pakistan with the support of TNS, learnt after being bruised a few times, are now passed on to those who might venture to enter similar grounds. Good luck!

REFERENCES

Aurora magazine (2001), special issue, Pakistan, November.

Census of Pakistan, 1998.

Federal Bureau of Statistics (FBS) Pakistan (1999), *Census of Manufacturing Industries and Small Household Manufacturing Industries*.

Gallup Pakistan (2000), *Rural and Urban Market and Media Habits*.

Gallup Pakistan (2001a) *Hygiene and Sanitation in Pakistan*. Study conducted for Unicef.

Gallup Pakistan (2001b), *The status of the IT industry in Pakistan*. Study conducted for the Ministry of Science and Technology.

Johnson, G. and Scholes, K. (1993), *Exploring Corporate Strategy*, third edition, Prentice Hall.

Knecht, J. (1989), *Geintegreerde communicatie*, BvA en VEA, Amsterdam.

Mendelow, A. (1991), *Stakeholder Mapping: Power/Interest Matrix*, Proceedings of the 2nd International Conference on Information Systems, Cambridge, Mass.

Chapter Twenty-two

Jambo Africa: A Discussion on the Challenges and Diversity of Third World Research

Jill Barnes[a] and Solveig Shapiro[b]

> *This chapter aims both to dispel myths about emerging market research (with a focus on Africa) and to provide practical guidelines for conducting qualitative research in this context.*

INTRODUCTION

'*We will just ignore Nigeria because they don't know what they are doing, and anyway, I am too scared to go there. Much better to go to Johannesburg and maybe we can go on safari too.*'
    '*And what an ignorant girl she'll think me for asking*'
(Alice's Adventures in Wonderland)

'*Beware that you do not lose the substance by grasping at the shadows*'
(Aesop's Fables – The Dog and The Shadow)

As market research practitioners in Africa, we have heard similar comments and sentiments all too often. Sadly, it is a clear expression of the

[a] Marketing Intelligence Manager, Tiger Foods.
[b] Managing Partner, The Qualitative Consultancy.

Market Research Best Practice. Edited by P. Mouncey and F. Wimmer.
© 2007 John Wiley & Sons, Limited.

main misconceptions and perceptions of conducting market research in Third World countries, and Africa in particular.

First, there is the perception that working in such countries is dangerous. Dangerous in many ways, but in particular because many countries are perceived to be politically and personally threatening, and because there is an underlying sense of discomfort about having to work in countries in which things are not what they seem.

Secondly, there is the idea that market research capability and capacity in Africa is lacking: '*as far as market research in Africa is concerned, there is South Africa and then there is the rest*' and '*high quality market research is absent in a large number of countries*' (Heeg, 2004). Unfortunate statements such as these contribute to a commonly articulated sense that market research in Africa is often impossible to conduct, of a poor quality and therefore highly unreliable. Further, it places an overemphasis on the role of South Africa – both as a resource and as being used as a valid sample for sub-Saharan Africa.

Thirdly, there is the experience that many clients expect when travelling in Africa – get the company to pay for a safari or something fun, have a quick sight-seeing trip, but at all costs avoid doing anything which will get them too far out of their comfort zones.

This chapter aims to demonstrate that the above is not true. What is true is that market research is a challenge in Africa, not least because of the diversity present in the continent. But research *is* conducted successfully, on an ongoing basis, all over the continent. This directly contradicts the above sentiments. The premise, therefore, is that what needs to be explored in detail are the underlying assumptions made by clients and researchers, as well as the practicalities of conducting research in such markets – and using this exploration to develop a more appropriate understanding of research skills and methods on the continent. In particular, we will demonstrate that a top-down approach will not work in Africa, and that, rather, communication and processes which are based on feedback loops will result in highly effective research. Critically, this will take the research experience one step further – it will not just be another research project but will also lead to increased insight, awareness and personal growth. Conducting research in Third World environments requires a personal investment – but the rewards are immense.

AFRICA

Global marketers are looking increasingly towards Third World markets for expansion as their own markets reach saturation point. Core exploratory markets for expansion include China, India and certain countries in Africa and South America. However, the latter two continents are often perceived to be 'basket cases', and any positive reports on these continents are followed closely by more negative qualifying statements which 'warn' marketers off. There are many horror stories, but what about the successes? What about the potential which undoubtedly exists in these markets?

Facts – the potential of Africa

We will start this chapter off by identifying and understanding some of the opportunities that exist in Africa – specifically by examining economic, political and social facts and figures. It is impossible to taint all of Africa with one brush. The continent runs the gamut from First World cities, such as Cape Town and Johannesburg, to Third World war-torn countries, such as Sudan and Eritrea. In between, however, are numerous emerging and fast-growing economies. For example, cities such as Nairobi and Luanda (Angola) are highly cosmopolitan and consumers aspire to First World products and experiences. Marketers and researchers need to rethink their understanding and comfort zones fast and get out and explore what is happening in what is essentially an increasingly dynamic continent. Where else have consumers gone from completely illiterate to technologically sophisticated in one generation? But, at the same time, this is not a continent which can be treated as a whole, and it is in its very diversity that the biggest research challenges lie.

Some of the facts and figures shown in Table 22.1 will provide an idea of the potential and complexity of this continent. And note, it is

Table 22.1 Facts and figures.

Country	Population size million	Level of urbanization (%)	Literacy (%)	GDP (Billions)	GDP Growth (%)	Per capita GDP ($)
South Africa	44.5	53	82	131.1	3	2941
Botswana	1.6	50	70	6	6.5	3775
Mozambique	19.4	11	40	4.2	10	217
Zambia	10	51	78	3.1	4.7	308
Mauritius	1.2	41	83	4.2	6	3529
Kenya	29.4	32	78	10.7	3.5	360
Uganda	22.8	14	62	6.8	6.3	298
Ethiopia	62.8	13	36	6.5	0	100
Nigeria	130.9	43	52	38.4	2.5	310
Ghana	19.9	46	63	7.5	5.1	377
DRC	53.6	62	77	2.2	5.6	168
Angola	10.4	29	75	9	1	710

not necessarily South Africa (usually regarded as the only viable and First World environment on the continent) that has the highest GDP or economic growth rate. That is happening elsewhere on the continent. Further, can marketers continue to ignore a country the size of Nigeria – regardless of the myriad negative perceptions associated with the country?

There are numerous case studies available covering the success of products and brands in Africa. It is not the objective of this chapter to report on these. We will, however, briefly give an overview of some of the success areas in order to demonstrate the potential of the continent – and in so doing, point out that market researchers need to understand that we *will* have to conduct ongoing research on this continent and in order to do this as a profession we need first to change negative perceptions (both our own and those of our clients) and second, to develop the necessary skills and contacts to work in Africa.

The actual spending power of consumers in Africa is a contentious issue and sparks lively debate. There are only limited statistics available, but in our experience, most marketers assume that about 10% of the total population on the continent has money and some form of disposable income to spend. There are a number of counterarguments to this and we would like to make three points which illustrate an opposing point of view. First, the best estimates of current product purchases by consumers in total across Africa are that about 60% have access to enough cash, aspiration and lifestyle alternatives to become full consumers of a variety of products and categories. Second, Africa is cash rich. Banking facilities are severely limited and cash is king. No one is currently able to measure exactly how much cash is out there, but Nigeria, for example, is the third biggest rice market worldwide in terms of value. And finally, consumers in Africa are highly aspirational. Their emergence is fast, furious and focused. For example, the growth of the cell phone industry took all by surprise and it has taken about eight years for South Africa to achieve extremely high levels of penetration. South African cell phone companies now get up to 37% of their revenue from other countries in Africa, and their products and strategies are recognized as being among the world leaders (Unilever Institute, 2004).

Technology has also been embraced rapidly by consumers in Africa, and, as infrastructure allows, it becomes part of daily life. Cell phones, Internet access, electronic goods, etc. are all taken on board and used – particularly by the youth market. The end result is that these consumers gain entrance into the 'global village' with all the brand and product choices that then become available.

The emergence of the African Union (AU) is a highly positive step. While there are many critics of the Union, they tend not to be Africans or understand the underlying dynamics on the continent. The AU may not be perfect (is the UN?) or able to control and implement all its resolutions and ideals (likewise the UN), but it signifies a growing desire for the continent to take its place in the world and be seen as a political and economic force. There are significant local trade agreements (SADC, UEMOA, COMESA), all of which are cementing economic ties on the continent, and which are also tapping into greater consumer spending power.

We do not ignore the problems, such as war in the DRC and Sudan or Zimbabwe's political intolerance and collapse. We do, however, wish to point out that this is by no means the overall state of Africa at all – and companies such as Coca-Cola, Unilever and Procter & Gamble have all long since recognized the economic changes that are happening and the marketing opportunities in Africa.

MARKET RESEARCH AND ASSUMPTION CLARIFICATION

Segmentation/country clusters – a first step

This leaves us with the challenge of conducting market research on the continent. Many of the multinationals historically embarked on strategies which first allowed them to get their products to market and then work on brand building and consumer insight. Ten years ago, very little consumer research was taking place outside of South Africa, Zimbabwe and Kenya. This has changed with more and more demand for consumer research and insight across the continent. Sadly, many of the misconceptions about the state of market research in Africa have led to projects being shelved, and, as a result, consumer insight is often vague and generalized.

Where research does take place, there is a recognition that it is expensive and, as a result, many clients and researchers have done extensive work on developing country clusters which allow them to understand and group consumers for research and marketing purposes. These clusters are based on a number of factors, including:

- the economic potential of countries/regions;
- geographic proximity;
- psychographic and demographic similarities;
- language;

- consumer sophistication;
- brand sophistication and media literacy;
- access to media.

Broadly speaking, the continent can be clustered into ten significant groups:

1. South Africa, Swaziland, Lesotho and Namibia (generally highly sophisticated with strong brand and media sophistication). Note – Swaziland and Lesotho are included in this segment because they are both completely surrounded by South Africa, and consumers in these countries are exposed to all South African marketing activities.
2. Botswana, Zambia, Malawi (conservative, English-speaking countries, similar levels of brand sophistication mainly derived from exposure to South Africa). To some extent, Zimbabwe is part of this cluster, but it does stand out as a result of the current political and socio-economic collapse and is currently excluded from most marketing plans and investment.
3. Mozambique and Angola (language and cultural similarities and emergence from devastating civil wars).
4. Great Lakes countries (including Congo, DRC, Rwanda, Burundi) (highly unstable and economically challenged despite massive natural resources). There is, however, a recognition of the potential size of these markets (especially the DRC).
5. East Africa including Kenya, Tanzania and Uganda (language – Swahili – and similar consumer psychographics and media/marketing sophistication).
6. Nigeria.
7. West Africa (language, size of market, etc. There are some countries in this cluster which are more stable and attractive, such as Ghana, and others, such as Cote d'Ivoire, which are highly unstable).
8. Sudan, Ethiopia, Eritrea (current disaster zones and severely economically hampered. Show limited potential at this point in time).
9. the Arabic countries (including Egypt, Morocco, Libya).
10. the Indian Ocean Islands (do not necessarily see themselves as part of the African continent and look elsewhere for identification).

Challenging assumptions – the second step

When faced with conducting research in Africa, our experience shows that the first and critical challenge we face is to examine and question the underlying assumptions that exist – by both clients and researchers – when it comes to thinking about and planning research. The following is an-all-too common scenario for us when receiving a brief from either a client or international research supplier:

> '*This is what the research objective is. You will do it in the following way. Our flight schedule is . . . And these are the times the groups must take place because we have other meetings to attend. Also, you must organize a market visit – but we only have an hour to do so. Finally, we would like to experience local culture, so please arrange an evening out – but make sure that we are eating at a very safe place.*'

These assumptions often lead to a number of problems:

- skewed research;
- inadequate research;
- inadequate understanding and insights;
- frustration;
- costs incurred with little or no return;
- a perception that no one in Africa knows what they are doing;
- and, often, cancellation of research or not even starting the research in the first place.

In order to explore these assumptions, we will separate them into a number of practical areas – and in so doing, demonstrate that *flexibility and local understandings* are key to the successful conduct of market research in Africa and other Third World environments.

Infrastructure

The following are often assumed by researchers, both outside and inside the continent:

- there are no available data/information, or, if they are available, they are totally unreliable;
- there is no research capability or capacity;
- there is limited and ineffective capability and capacity.

As a result, projects are often abandoned because researchers do not think they can get what they need to design samples or understand markets. We need to correct and address these perceptions.

The lack of data

It is not true that there are no reliable data or information. The UN has a significant amount of social and economic data available on the Internet, as do companies such as the IDC in South Africa. Data may not be 100% up to date or relevant to certain remote rural areas, but they will definitely be directionally accurate and adequate. The key is to be slightly more flexible with one's requirements. Further, one often has to go to the relevant country and make the necessary contacts to obtain data. For example, while trying to set up a research project in Zambia, the client found it impossible to get the relevant demographic statistics off the Internet or from other sources. But, on arrival in Lusaka, all it took was a couple of hours at the relevant government offices to gain the data. Again, the key is flexibility – less of a reliance on traditional sources and more on researchers doing the groundwork themselves.

In addition, we need to think carefully about the types of data required for various projects. For example, a random sample for a large quantitative study demanded traditional maps and starting points on a grid. The problem was that the study was to be conducted in Luanda, Angola. No current maps existed after the civil war, and the same war had destroyed and damaged much of the existing infrastructure. The solution was to use local expertise and design a rough map of the city and work on designated points on arrival in Luanda.

The lack of infrastructure

Many countries in Africa have come a long way in recent years in developing a solid research infrastructure. Costs (and the previous lack of client spend) have dictated that instead of establishing a market research industry in every country, researchers base themselves in one country and maintain low-cost field workers and structures in surrounding or similar countries. Contrary to previous articles (for example, one published in *Research World* in June 2004), there are well developed research infrastructures in South Africa, Zimbabwe, Namibia, Kenya, Nigeria, Ghana, Egypt, Mozambique and Mauritius, to name but a few. And, contrary to popular belief, the industry works hard to maintain rigorous standards and practices. There are recruiters, moderators, translators, group rooms, viewing rooms, etc. However, as with any emerging industry, there is also a proliferation of untrained and poor-quality qualitative researchers in almost all countries in Africa. It is essential that one guards against using these researchers.

The Research brief

The research brief is frequently and sadly a one-way process and based on assumptions regarding target markets, research tools, infrastructure, etc.

It often comes from a global client or research agency who has little or no understanding of local market complexities. We will discuss each of the issues separately, but it is critical that the brief is developed in conjunction with the local supplier/partner and that socio-economic conditions are kept in mind. Briefs can fail to take into account a variety of factors, all of which may either be highlighted or corrected by local partners. For example, a client put together a brief based on the premise that their particular product had suddenly shown phenomenal growth in consumer sales in the DRC. In fact, the product concerned (canned food) was being bought wholesale by the army for its use. It was virtually unknown by the majority of consumers.

Research topics

It is critical that research topics are relevant to consumers. Assumptions are widely made by global researchers that topics are meaningful – for example, a decision to leverage basketball because '*it is a black youth thing*'. Not true. In some of the countries planned for the research, basketball is not important, is perceived to be very American (a negative) and plays a very poor second fiddle to soccer. Or, an insistence on testing a series of TV ads for a global brand in a country which, at the time, had 5% TV penetration and constant power failures. Or, trying to understand daily consumer behaviour in a country in which government and political interference in daily lives is common, and hence skews not only their behaviour, but their ability to be honest in groups without fear of reprisals.

This is not to say that the research should not happen – rather, a clear understanding of the relevance of the topic should be present, as well as the implications of any findings and their potential for use.

Language

The languages spoken on the continent are numerous. For example, South Africa has 11 official languages and Zambia has 35! Local dialects abound as well. But at the same time, most African consumers will be literate in one of the following: English, French or Portuguese. However, these two facts frequently are misunderstood and misused.

First, by assuming all countries/consumers speak the same version of a language. For example, there is a danger in treating Portuguese-speaking countries as the same. Mozambique and Angola, while both Portuguese-speaking, have different versions of the language and consumers are highly insulted if test material is in either European Portuguese or another country's version. A good example was a concept test in which the product bombed consistently. Researchers were unable to understand why, until, purely by chance, it emerged that while testing in Maputo (Mozambique), colloquial Portuguese spoken in Angola had been used.

The same is true of vernaculars. Swahili spoken in Uganda, Kenya and Tanzania is very different, and nuances and insights will be lost totally if the correct language is not used. Finally, there is a tendency to be patronizing where language is concerned. For many consumers, the use of a European language is aspirational and in fact part of everyday life and communication. An insistence on using a vernacular is seen as down market and inappropriate. In addition to this, we are often faced with incredulity when explaining that in some areas, the vernacular has all but disappeared. Angola, for example, was first exposed to European visitors 1000 years ago, and virtually no traces of the original languages remain.

Story-telling is also a critical component of qualitative research. Linguistic and cognitive structures in many of these markets are circular, and frequently, a story needs to be told or a roundabout route taken before a point is made. Linear logic is not always present, and an insistence on it will lead to frustration and little or no consumer insight.

Target markets

Target market decisions are fraught with many pitfalls. Target markets may not necessarily be defined in a classical sense. Segmentations vary widely and an 'A' consumer in Nairobi will differ from an 'A' consumer in Zambia. Only South Africa has a rigorous segmentation model in place (Living Standards Measures or LSMs) but these must be understood in detail and not applied lightly. Segmentation tools used on the continent include LSMs, ABCD, Hi and Low Density, urban and rural. The following examples illustrate the point:

- An insistence from a client that there are enough whites in Nairobi to justify four groups (based on reliable statistical sources). Yes, there are whites in Nairobi, but they are generally expats whose incomes, lifestyles, brand and product usage are massively different to those of ordinary Kenyans. In fact, white Kenyans tend to live in more rural areas on farms.

- A definition of the target market as 'loyal users'. Fact: due to economic constraints, in this particular product category and region there are no such consumers. They are repertoire users.

Tools and methodologies

It is imperative to guard against assumptions when developing appropriate tools, stimulus materials and methodologies for research. It is not appropriate to adhere rigidly to global protocols and standards, but at the same time, not all consumers in Africa are illiterate or unsophisticated. For example, consider the following:

- An insistence that abstract written concepts cannot be used for research because consumers are not brand or media literate. Fact: consumers in cities such as Johannesburg, Cape Town, Nairobi and Luanda are highly literate, sophisticated and cosmopolitan.
- The assumption that in traditional collective societies, focus groups won't work because 'group speak' will prevail. First, traditional identities are being replaced, and second, any good moderator will get around this. Consumers in urban areas are much more likely to see themselves as individuals and be proud of their opinions and, hence, articulate them.
- An assumption that consumers in Ethiopia must be able to do brand sorts and mind maps of the brands they use. Fact: there are limited branded products available, and no brand imagery has ever been communicated to this society as a whole.
- It should never be assumed that visual aids will be relevant or evoke the desired responses. Some consumer groups are less literate than others, and specific images may be culturally taboo or elicit very different responses to those they would in the First World.

Logistics

When planning research one cannot assume that the logistics will work as they do in more sophisticated environments. Generally, they need to be well thought through and flexible at all times. Do not assume that schedules and arrangements will be adhered to, or that they will happen the way they do in First World countries. When a supplier in Nairobi says that they will meet you at 15:00, they mean this is the time they will leave their office. Depending on the distance of the trip and the ever-increasing traffic chaos in Nairobi, this could mean up to two hours before they get to you.

Group times must be flexible – both in terms of starting times and length. Do not assume that four groups can be conducted in one day. The first group will start late and run late, putting any schedule at risk. Allow time between groups and space them out.

Do not assume that transport and other arrangements are automatic – often, researchers need to arrange for transport for respondents to and from groups. Also, clients cannot just assume that they will be taken care of. They will need to make sure that they have their own arrangements for getting to and from groups.

FROM ASSUMPTIONS TO PRACTICALITIES

We have examined some of the assumptions that underpin research in Africa and will now highlight some of the practical and logistical issues that need to be dealt with in order to conduct successful research. These practical considerations are not just applicable to situations when research infrastructure is either lacking or weak, but also apply to countries where there is experienced research capability. Throughout Africa one needs to be sensitive to two things in particular:

- the difficulties that logistics can and will throw up at you;
- the need to set and monitor standards consistently.

Much of what we have to say follows accepted qualitative practice and standards. But frequently, these fall apart when conducting market research in Africa – mainly due to perceived cost and capability constraints. We too often see, for example, a European qualitative agency insisting on using their own moderators in Africa, in the belief that locals cannot do it. This begs the question – what are they missing/misunderstanding/prejudging? The result of this is that existing prejudices are reinforced, because the assumptions are that it cannot be done locally. We don't really see what is happening because we are too busy looking for constraints rather than being open to the possibilities.

Essentially, we are saying that market research can and should be done locally to avoid diminishing the integrity of the process and of the data. So forgive us if what we are about to point out and reinforce is nothing new to the qualitative industry – the reality is that this breaks down frequently in Africa, and researchers unwittingly land up compromising on accepted research ethics and standards. The following section will highlight a variety of points to consider – although they may also just serve as a refresher course!

The research process

For parts of Africa there is none of the research infrastructure which is taken for granted in the developed world: no recruiting agencies, no discussion rooms handily stocked with paper and pens and glue and Prestick (Blue Tack), no viewing facility, assistants, etc.

What this means is a different level of involvement (for both researcher and client). It requires great attention to detail, flexibility, thinking on your feet and being open to the unexpected. In short, it means submersion in all the nitty-gritty of the research process, with two major consequences:

- cost;
- time.

Recruiting

What happens when there is no recruiting agency or research supplier? Make contact with teachers, with students, with salesmen and saleswomen. But because they are not professionals:

- keep your screening criteria as simple as possible;
- allow time and money for very detailed briefings to ensure they know and understand what we are trying to do and who the target market is;
- remember that demographics alone may be insufficient to identify respondents, so once the locals understand exactly who you are looking for, work with them to develop possible psychographic criteria;
- remember, too, that in certain instances you will be drawing from a small pool of people (say, the A socio-economic group) and the chances are they will know each other and may know the moderator and the interpreter: consider how you will deal with that.

You will need local guidance on the extent to which it is possible to mix different groupings in one discussion:

- mixing genders frequently doesn't work, because in many cultures, women publicly bow to the opinions of men and are not free to express different points of view;

- mixing a wide range of ages can also be misleading, because, similarly, youngsters publicly bow to the opinions of older people;
- mixing people of different language groups or different religious or political persuasions also limits free expression (even where the topic is as apparently mundane as washing powder).

This impacts directly on the sample design: for example, we get asked to cost a project of four groups as part of a global study. By the time you've controlled for gender and age, you already have four groups. What about all the other variables that contribute to the diversity that is Africa? Four groups will not reflect Kenya accurately. Or Nigeria. Or South Africa. Perhaps we need to rethink our sample definitions (and budgets) if we are as serious about Africa as we probably should be. Wrong or incomplete information is worse than no information.

And, of course, always be aware of political sensitivities. These can be such that it is not possible to conduct meaningful research at all (such as at present in Zimbabwe). Or such that one has to do only what one can, even if it means not fulfilling the objectives completely (before the transition to democracy in South Africa, at a time of great instability and violence, we had abruptly to terminate a discussion with migrant workers, who, after 45 minutes, became extremely jittery and announced they were leaving).

Particularly when working outside of major metropolitan areas, be sensitive to cultural issues:

- you need to be introduced to the local head of the community and even, sometimes, to have his permission to interview or recruit;
- sometimes, one needs to get permission from the male head of the household to interview the woman.

The venue

What happens when there are either no group rooms or no viewing facilities? You will need local guidance on a venue which is accessible to respondents and somewhere they will feel comfortable (probably not the 4 or 5 star hotel you may be lucky enough to be staying in!). For example, will the driver be able to find it? Will unsophisticated women who are also housewives be comfortable in a hotel? And what about making young male teenagers feel at home?

View from a room next door via a video link (take your own video camera and plug in to a TV set).

Assume no stationery or recording equipment is available, so travel with your own supplies (particularly batteries and board markers).

Check on catering for both respondents and researchers (Pork? Meat? Halaal? Vegetarian?). And, in the absence of conventional research infrastructure, who is actually going to be organizing the Coke and the coffee?

Transport

For the researcher, it is frequently advisable to hire a local driver who understands routes and traffic patterns.

For respondents, it is almost always necessary that transport is organized to the venue and back home afterwards. This can affect schedules – just one late respondent can delay the start considerably – and can lead to some endearing, if alarming and unexpected, consequences. In Johannesburg, recruiters for different agencies developed over time a central point in the CBD where minibus taxis picked up respondents. Two unexpected results: word got out that if you were at a loose end or wanted an evening's entertainment, you could arrive at that pick-up point for transport to a discussion, meet people and have a nice chat, be given food and refreshments, have transport back home, *and* be paid for it! The other phenomenon was respondent theft, where the driver for one agency would simply 'steal' the respondents for another agency! Needless to say, we now use different pick-up points, and our recruiters travel with the taxi.

Timings

Flexible schedules are the thing, because there is, quite often, a different sense of time in Africa:

- your respondents might arrive an hour early, and then be perfectly content to wait good-naturedly (unlike other cultures where waiting means they would be getting edgy and irritable and threatening to leave);
- equally, they might arrive an hour late (and not understand any stress or urgency you may be feeling, so you might as well not have the agony).

Language and culture differences mean that group discussions can take a whole lot longer:

- Linguistically, some languages take longer to express a concept than English, e.g.
  'Please rate the four products from most to least preferred' (12 syllables)

- translates into Zulu as:
  'Ngicela uphawule lemikhiqizo e-4 ngendlela oyithanda ngayo kusukela koyithanda kakhulu ukuya koyithanda kancane' (45 syllables)

- Culturally, introductions and warm-ups might take longer as one explores the well-being of the extended family. If this is ignored, the group dynamic will inevitably fail or struggle to emerge.

As a rule of thumb, if your discussion lasts an hour-and-a-half in English, expect it to last two hours in many vernaculars.

This influences, too, the number of respondents in a group. The norm in the developed world seems to be eight, and sometimes ten. In our experience, six is probably best: it allows time for everyone to have their say, and to explore various issues in depth. But be aware that in a recruiter's eagerness to please, you may well find 14 respondents waiting outside the door: are you going to cause offence by declining some of them? Do you have enough incentives? Do they, in fact, qualify or are some just eager friends and relatives?

Again, take local guidance on appropriate times and days for doing groups. 18h00 is probably universally a good time (depending on traffic patterns), and 20h00 is probably not...it will start at 20h30, and end at 22h30, and then the driver will still need to take the long route home, dropping everyone off on the way. So, if you want relaxed and giving respondents, the idea of nipping in and doing six groups over three evenings is probably misplaced. Better to plan for daytimes and early evenings.

Moderator

All the best-practice rules apply, only more so. To highlight some to consider:

- **Gender** – in some locations it is not acceptable to have a female moderator for male groups, or vice versa (husbands hovering protectively outside the discussion room can create all sorts of stresses).
- **Clothing** – in some locations women may not have bare arms or wear slacks or have an uncovered head.

- **Demeanour** – the European moderator who decided to get really cosy with her respondents by kicking off her shoes and sitting on the floor, succeeded only in shocking them into uncooperative silence. Taking one's shoes off is regarded as rude and disrespectful.

Transcripts

It's a really good idea to get transcripts back before you leave the country, first to ensure that you get them, but also so that you can check the more mysterious words or phrases in person (remember that for the transcriber/translator English is unlikely to be the mother tongue, so spellings can be refreshingly different). Handy hint: if you can't understand the transcript, try saying it out loud. Here are some delights from recent transcripts into English for our client Tiger Brands (clue: the topics were pasta and sauces):

- *lazania*;
- *nocky*;
- *chubes*;
- *speartime*;
- *immegency*;
- *wooster sauce*.

A point here is that this transcript does not indicate poor quality or a lowering of standards. It is, simply, different. Enjoy the difference.

Language and culture: some practicalities

Colonial heritage and the push towards international communication mean that in many African countries, the language of business and commerce is English or French or Portuguese. But very seldom are these the mother tongue.

When a group or depth interview is conducted in the European language, beware: what you are hearing is not always what it seems.

- Accents can lead to critical misunderstandings. A European researcher heard *when I was a head boy*... and visualized the main prefect in a Western-style school. The respondent was actually saying *when I was a herd boy*... and, clearly, looking after dad's cattle was a very different context for the point he was making.

- Slang expressions can leave one lost and floundering. They come thick and fast, particularly amongst younger respondents, and they change all the time:
  - A *dolphin* in Soweto, 600 kms from the sea? Slang for a BMW 5 series.
  - A *Baby Jake*? We know he's a boxer, but what do they mean? A 250 ml glass bottle of Coke.
  - *Fong Kong*? A cheap imitation of the real thing (probably a corruption of Hong Kong, i.e. cheap imported goods from the Far East).
- Respondents may be able to speak rationally in the European language, but as soon as feelings or emotions are touched, they will lapse into the vernacular.

All of which points to the critical importance of the translator. And the need is for a translator familiar with the local idiom, not just someone who can speak the language. We once used a translator in her forties who spent much of the time in silence, because, although she was fluent in the language, she just could not understand the idiomatic expressions being used by the teens.

Translating is about much more than language:

- it is about interpreting the culture and social issues;
- explaining locations: a '*kaya*' in South Africa can be translated as a home, but it also has a slightly down market implication;
- explaining celebrities: we've probably all heard of Mandela and Madonna, but who is the Felicia or Dare or Daniel they're associating with your brand?
- is the brand they say they're using evidence of overclaim because of its local status connotations?

The very real cultural differences may mean that what you think you see is not what is really there. For example, body language can be confusing: is the avoidance of eye-contact evidence of discomfort or even dishonesty, or is it simply polite? Is the masculine personification of an essentially feminine brand a reflection of status or gender? Is the response '*it's right*' as neutral as it sounds to our ears, or the overwhelming positive that it actually is?

And, of course, this all impacts directly on stimulus material and projective techniques. Although visual images can sometimes get past language issues, beware: literacy and media literacy in Africa varies widely by country and within country, from highly sophisticated to very literal interpretations. Some respondents will be unable to make the leap from rough, hand-drawn storyboards to a finished ad or commercial.

Using visual aids for projective techniques requires especially careful interpretation: a bulldog has very different connotations to a township African than it does to a British citizen.

A concept board might well bomb an idea because of an irrelevant visual detail. For example, an illustration depicting self-service petrol stations was so outrageously wrong in one African country, where the concept of self-service petrol stations does not exist, that respondents could not get beyond this to the main proposition. Hint: be prepared to adjust visual materials to suit the local scene. Similarly, packaging prototypes should be as close as possible to the end result to avoid unnecessary distractions.

Achieving the global objective might well require local tools. For example, personifications might work elsewhere, but describing a funeral will yield richer imagery in those cultures where funerals play a hugely significant role. So, as always, when one technique elicits blank stares, try another.

Literacy, or the lack of it, can be an unexpected issue. Recently, a collage put together by a group included the words 'nits and nasty' – to which the respondent happily offered the explanation *'it's tasty'*.

CONCLUSION

This chapter has aimed at making the following core point:

> *Do not assume that research cannot be done in Africa, and that if is done, it can only be done by researchers from outside the continent. All this does is reinforce two areas: the negative perceptions that exist around the quality and capacity for research, and poor quality research results because they are not truly understood.*

Research can be done, but needs to be true to these core principles:

- Africa is diverse – but diverse does not equal difficult;
- local input is critical to check assumptions, processes and interpretation;
- flexibility;

- on-the-ground involvement;
- a sense of adventure and fun.

Most importantly, do not let it be a one-way street – let the communication flow both ways.

REFERENCES

Heeg, R. (2004), Market Research in Africa, *Research World*, June.
Unilever Institute (2004), *Landscape 2004*, University of Cape Town.

Part Six

Best Practice Case Studies

Chapter Twenty-three

Retail Innovation Learnings from a Segmented Shop Formula: Sunka

Lluís Martínez-Ribes[a] and Xavier Roure[b]

Sunka, a new generation supermarket has been success. The aim of this chapter is to analyse the causes of this success on the basis of the retail innovation method used by its managers.

INTRODUCTION

At the beginning of summer in 2001, Sunka, a new generation supermarket, was launched in Lleida (Catalonia, Spain) and was successful from the start. The supermarket became quite famous in the retail sector.

The aim of this chapter is to present the retail innovation method used by the authors, as well as the Sunka retail mix and its results.

Sunka targets young families with small children in which both parents work, and it offers them a wide range of solutions to meet their daily needs.

The SUPSA Company, the retail company that launched Sunka, is highly innovative, and won the Global Electronic Marketing Award in 1999 for customized vouchers printed at checkouts.

[a]Professor and former Marketing Department Head, ESADE.
[b]Marketing Director, Supermercats Pujol SA.

Market Research Best Practice. Edited by P. Mouncey and F. Wimmer.
© 2007 John Wiley & Sons, Limited.

THE SITUATION BEFORE SUNKA

SUPSA is a Catalan supermarket company which manages some 50 neighbourhood stores under the logo 'Plus Fresc' (see Figure 23.1). Because the company is rather small in comparison to its competitors, its survival has been based on innovation, both in the use of customer information and in the warm shopping experience offered.

Plus Fresc is renowned for its focus on the customer, thanks to both its charming personnel attention at the shop and its customized sales promotions, which are printed on individual vouchers when the customers pay at checkout. These vouchers are designed to target customers according to their past shopping behaviour and preferences – an example of 'one-on-one marketing.' In 1999, SUPSA won the Global Electronic Marketing Award for this customized sales promotions system.

Due to its customer orientation, SUPSA has been the leading regional food retailer over the past 25 years. All the same, the company's competitors have been improving steadily, and SUPSA's position as a leader has been challenged by the Carrefour hypermarket, as well as by other important retailers, including Dia, Mercadona, Champion, Eroski, Caprabo and others.

Figure 23.1   Plus Fresc shop, some years ago.

In 1999, SUPSA decided to monitor its market competitive situation through market research. A research project team was set up, consisting of company managers and consultants.

THE MARKET RESEARCH PROCESS

The first stage was qualitative, and featured the formation of three focus groups run by Rosa Franch (Martinez+Franch Consultores SL), with two main objectives:

1. To define the main hypothesis about SUPSA's competitive advantage.
2. To detect the qualitative changes in the lifestyle patterns of the most important shopper segments.

This qualitative study primarily reflected many customers' constant difficulty in balancing their occupational obligations with their family life. In addition, the winning gap between SUPSA supermarkets and their competitors was decreasing, as the other chains were improving their customer orientation.

As for the quantitative market research, run by the consultancy firm Retail SGC, the team decided to concentrate the fieldwork in only one shop catchment area, as all of SUPSA's main competitors were present there, and the residents of the area were quite representative of regional area shoppers.

As the main goal of the study was to monitor the market situation, 350 food shoppers were interviewed in their homes, taking into account these quotas:

- geographic area;
- shopper's age;
- shopper's gender;
- shopper's activity – job;
- socio-economic class of the household.

The structure of the questionnaire was similar to that of a standard retailing survey, although it featured the following special characteristics:

1. The entire shopping habits block (i.e. preferred food shop, reasons for shop selection, satisfaction and dissatisfaction points, shopping frequency, shopping patterns, etc.) was split into the different food categories: vegetables, meat, fish, canned food, and so on.

2. Consequently, this questionnaire was longer than those used normally, however the questions were answered easily, with no reluctance on the part of those interviewed.

3. The shop variables were chosen carefully and fine-tuned. For example, rather than asking about the overall 'shop staff service quality,' the questionnaire explored more detailed issues, such as 'shop staff knowledge,' 'shop staff readiness to serve,' 'shop staff attitude,' and so on. In the survey findings, these minor variables were extremely helpful in developing a deeper understanding of the different segments.

THE SURVEY FINDINGS

Following the statistical analysis, the survey results were truly interesting. The company chain, Plus Fresc, was still the leader; however, its advantage over the majority of its competitors had decreased over the past four years, as the other retail chains were improving their shops and their services.

There were very different shopping habits for each product category. For example, the preferred shop for meat was not always the same as the preferred shop for canned foods.

Five shopper segments emerged, with very different expectations regarding what a food shop should offer – the shop 'role'. Such disparity was based on the shoppers' different lifestyles. The shopper segments also revealed very different daily patterns – in addition to the obvious time allocation conflicts, areas of dissatisfaction, etc.

One of the segments, called 'Demanding and stressed people', was basically made up of working women under a great deal of stress, due to their responsibilities both at work and at home, particularly when the latter involved young children. These shoppers sought out stores that were convenient and close to home, with a wide range of facilities, and they were very demanding in many aspects (assortment, personnel politeness, cleanliness, lack of errors at checkouts, short queues, etc.). While this segment accounted for 33% of the universe, once its economic relevance was estimated by means of the data warehousing application, the research team realized that the economic importance of this segment was far higher than its percentage implied. Moreover, they also found that none of the supermarket competitors was targeting this segment directly.

Figure 23.2   Plus Fresc shop, current look.

SUPSA'S RESPONSE

After analysing the findings carefully and following an exhaustive internal debate, SUPSA made a set of decisions:

1. **Operational and tactical decision** – the main (obvious) operational decision was to improve the retail mix aspects that were viewed in the market survey as being either unsatisfactory or mismanaged.
2. **Strategic decisions** – SUPSA decided to reinforce its leadership in the region using the 'Market dominance' strategy: to be the regional point of reference in the food sector through many different 'selling machines', and targeting different types of shoppers.
   - SUPSA decided to 'refresh' its Plus Fresc chain, and a redesign process was set up. A team of external consultants (Jos de Vries) and an innovative designer (Pep Valls) were invited to work to update the Plus Fresc shop chain (see Figure 23.2).
   - SUPSA also decided to carry out an exhaustive R&D process. In the retail business, the main research and development activity is to launch new shop formulae. After an internal debate, two new 'selling machines' were launched:

- **Plusfresc.com**, an online supermarket, positioned as 'the most practical supermarket', and characterized by its speed, functionality and shopping convenience. The site was created by the SUPSA Information System Department, using the rather uncommon Citrix software for high connection speed. Senyal web designers were responsible for its visual design.
- **Sunka**, a segmented shop, targeting the 'demanding and stressed people' segment. The SUPSA marketing executives, Martinez+Franch Consultores and the designer Pep Valls formed the Sunka work team, with Monica Aler as the Project Manager. The pilot shop was located in downtown Lleida in an old 900 square metre garage with a high ceiling.

SUNKA'S RAISON D'ÊTRE

The strategic options for any shop format are as shown in Figure 23.3. In food retailing the great majority of chains, both the generalists and the

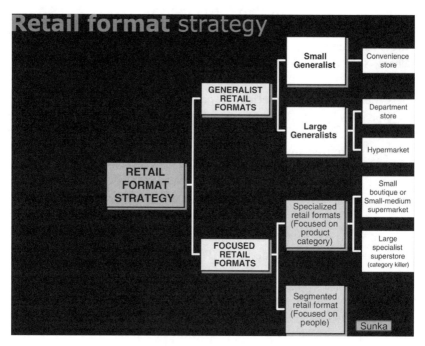

Figure 23.3 Retail format strategic options.

specialists, follow the undifferentiated option, which basically consists of opening almost identical shops, ignoring the profile of the segments existing in each catchment area.

There is a clear lack in terms of the use of the segmented shop format, at least as far as the large retailers are concerned. This option implies that the shop format is designed to deliver almost everything (products and services) that the targeted segment may need or desire. In a certain way, the shop may become the segment's paradise, as the feeling of mutual understanding is very deep.

The entire team (the managers and the retail innovation consultants) decided to create a completely new type of shop, following the segmented shop format, geared primarily to the 'demanding and stressed people' segment.

Its CEO, Rafael Pujol, accepted the risk that some of the other customer segments might not like Sunka (meaning possibly losing a part of the turnover). At the same time, the company managers believed that the loyalty of the 'demanding and stressed people' might compensate for the possible cost of lost customers.

SUNKA – CHARACTERISTICS

Sunka is a Japanese word that means 'take time for yourself' (being yourself despite the stress you are under). The team thought this name very symbolic of the main solution that the shop formula intended to deliver to its targeted segment.

As can be seen in Figure 23.4, Sunka does not look like a standard supermarket, because it is designed as a centre that delivers the perfect solutions to the daily needs of working couples with children.

At the entrance the visitor comes upon a 'deceleration zone', a noncommercial area where s/he can relax and enjoy the works of young artists. Opposite the paintings, there is the 'Butler' desk, where the customers may leave things to be repaired, clothing to be cleaned, shoes to be mended, as well as many other services. In this manner, just at the entrance, the customers are made to feel that there are well-managed solutions for their frequent non-food-related problems.

A supervised nursery is nearby. Parents may leave their young children there to play, and may enter the commercial area at ease, knowing that their children are having fun.

Figure 23.4 Sunka shop.

Before getting a trolley, the visitors pass through a poetry tunnel. If they are decelerated enough, they can read the moving words. If not, there will be more opportunities later on.

The entrance to the typical supermarket area is through the fruit section, so the brightness and colours of the fruits warmly welcome the customers. There is a buffet salad, where shoppers may choose the items they like most, placing them in plastic boxes and paying according to the weight.

Sunka offers its customers two different types of 'meal solutions': the first is the precooked items section and the second is called 'the kits' section. A kit is a container which includes all the necessary fresh ingredients to cook a given recipe, with quantities for either one or two people. The recipe is provided in the back. Some customers prefer this option, because it is fresher and easy to cook in minutes.

The fish section is very important, both in self-service and at the counter. Customers may have the seafood steamed just after ordering it, a service which is free of charge.

Meat is sold through self-service, although shoppers can request a special item, which the staff will then prepare.

The entire shop is equipped with electronic labels that display the price and the promotions, which are linked to the computer and to the checkout counters via radio waves.

In the upper section of the shop, on a sort of balcony, there are three computers for free Internet access. This feature makes the visit to Sunka a pleasant outing for the whole family, as it is a favourite spot for many teenagers.

Nearby there is a rest area, with tables, chairs, newspapers and magazines, where people can sit, read and have something to drink (an automatic vending machine is available).

The first floor is also equipped with a multipurpose room, for occasional cooking seminars, conferences and meetings.

When customers proceed to checkout, their waiting time is enlivened, thanks to the TV sets positioned there for their entertainment.

The checkout staff is particularly warm, well trained and proud of being part of Sunka. Not only do they scan the products, but they also put them into an automatic bagging system, so the customer doesn't have to rush to bag the scanned products.

Customers may also choose to have products delivered to their homes the same day at certain selected times if the packages are heavy, or simply if such an arrangement is more convenient for them.

Sunka prices are in line with those of the ordinary supermarkets within the area, and a bit higher than those of the hypermarkets and discount chains. Sunka's policy is to eliminate the 'price' as a marketing mix variable, or at least to make it a neutral element. Customers need not worry about price, so they can relax when shopping.

THE RESULTS

Sunka communicated its shop in two newspaper adverts (one the day before its opening and one on the opening day). Nothing else was done in conventional communication media.

News of the Sunka supermarket was spread by word of mouth (buzz marketing) and through public relations when organizing conferences, such as the half-day debate about genetically modified food products.

One particularly original medium was the publication of a small hardback book with some personal thoughts reflecting the Sunka philosophy. All Sunka employees, SUPSA managers, city VIPs and journalists received

Figure 23.5   Sunka sales vs. SUPSA stores.

a copy. Sunka's top 150 customers (out of 55 000 active shoppers) also received a copy.

Sunka's sales have not topped out yet, and Sunka has become the sales shop leader among all the SUPSA shops. Sunka's sales in relation to the average of all the other SUPSA stores may be seen in Figure 23.5. The sales data show the first 110 weeks of Sunka's existence, by the end of which it reached 130% sales compared to the other SUPSA shops (source: SUPSA).

Sunka's customer loyalty is also the highest when compared to the other SUPSA shops located in downtown Lleida. This information comes from the internal data warehousing system, as the SUPSA customer card is valid either at Sunka or at Plus Fresc (see Table 23.1). The chart shows the percentage of household shopping expenditure made by customers in their preferred shop.

In April 2003 a new competitor, Consum supermarket (see Figure 23.6) opened its doors just a few metres away from Sunka. Its prices are lower than Sunka's, and the chain is well managed, however Consum has not given Sunka customers a clear reason why they should change

Table 23.1 Shop loyalty shown by each shop's customers (downtown Lleida).

Sunka	85.48
PF Baró Maials	80.13
PF Cap Pont	80.07
PF Mariola	79.88
PF Templers	79.38
PF Boleda	78.41
PF Plaça Europa	75.75
PF Pi i Margall	74.49
PF Pius XII	69.95
PF Clot	68.96
PF Prat Riba	66.84

Universe: SUPSA shops, either Sunka or the Plus Fresc (PF) shops, all located in downtown Lleida. *Date*: August 2003.

Figure 23.6 Consum supermarket, April 2003.

their supermarket. As a result, this conventional supermarket formula is reinforcing Sunka's differentiation.

The pilot shop has demonstrated that the segmented shop formula is working very well and can be expanded to other urban areas where this segment is located.

THE INNOVATION PROCESS FOLLOWED

First of all, it was detected that a shopper segment was showing a profound, yet unspoken, need. Although there were no specific answers in the market survey showing any radical rejection of the conventional food shop format models (supermarket, hypermarkets, discount, and the like), after analysing the findings carefully and combining the quantitative and qualitative studies, the managers and consultants recognized a considerable lack of satisfaction regarding the current food shop formats. This is basically due to the fact that these shoppers need a solution that is more adapted to their needs, given their complex lifestyles.

The second stage was detecting the universes, or worlds, that the new shop belongs to. This is a kind of brainstorming method (Martínez-Ribes, 1978) which guides or influences the decision taking process. This method, moreover, helps in selecting the key world, which may become the positioning axis.

For Sunka, after this exercise, the decision was to build on four worlds: 'Daily needs' + 'Convenience' + 'Simple solutions' + 'There is life beyond supermarket shopping'. A final slogan, which sums up everything mentioned previously, was created: 'Daily life can be different'.

The third source of innovation resides in understanding any shopping transaction, not as an exchange of 'Product for Money', but rather as an exchange of 'Solution the shopper receives' for 'Efforts the shopper has to make' in order to obtain the solution (Martínez-Ribes and Dawson, 1998).

Obviously, the 'efforts' side includes an economic effort: paying the price.

As a result, Sunka is aiming to generate the target shoppers' preference in two ways:

1. By supplying these segment shoppers with real daily *solutions*, rather than simply food. This is the reason why at Sunka, 'services' have become a key part of the common assortment.

2. By reducing the non-monetary efforts this type of shopper is reluctant to make. For example, the automatic bagging machines at checkout are there to avoid a further source of stress.

There are three types of solution that any retailer can provide (Martínez-Ribes, 1980):

1. **Functional solutions.** For example: avoiding stock out, supplying the appropriate product quality, etc.
2. **Symbolic solutions.** For example: with suitable brand meaning, either with suppliers' brands or with the shop's own retail brand.
3. **Sensory solutions.** For example: all the aspects relating to the human senses and to convenience. Hence, the shopping activity is associated strongly with the sensorial experience.

At Sunka, functionality is a must, though it is not highlighted. The symbolic solution resides in the combination of Sunka brand fresh products with renowned canned-food supplier brands. The sensory solutions are rooted strongly in the contemporary shop design, the free nursery, the automatic bagging, the free Internet access, etc. It is quite obvious that some of the sensory aspects also come into play on a symbolic level.

The fourth source of innovation comes only after understanding that any winning shop should be excellent in three aspects:

1. As an effective 'selling machine,' stressing its productivity and monitoring it through KPIs (Key Performance Indicators).
2. As a great communication medium. The shop – and everything that takes place in it – is the main 'retail product.' The first retailer goal is to 'sell the shop', in other words, to try to generate customer traffic to the shop in question. Once the shopper has entered the shop, turnover is probable.
   Once the shop is perceived clearly as 'the product,' the next logical step is to acknowledge the importance of 'product packaging': the shop design and the atmospherics. Retail atmospherics and sensory aspects also convey part of the retail solution to the targeted customers. With colours, textures, music, lighting, smell, and the like, retailers can transmit subtle messages to their target customers. As the targeted segment is made up of contemporary people, with a primarily urban lifestyle, Sunka needs to speak to them in a fresh, cosmopolitan, open-window visual language.
3. The winning shop also has to be a data vacuum machine, or an information exchange site.

With the scanner data and the customer card, the company tracks 87% of the turnover, making it easy to follow the shopping patterns of the different households. This input is key to generating customized sales offers for each customer continually.

Furthermore, Sunka is giving its shoppers 'fresh' information, because it uses electronic labels on the shelves, which are linked to the checkout counters through radio waves. In this fashion, the price the customer sees on the shelf is the same one that s/he pays. There is a further advantage to the use of e-labels: the possibility of creating time-based, noncustomized sales offers. For example, the shop can reduce the price of some fresh products (some retailers call them 'perishable products') half an hour before closing the shop on Saturdays. This is a kind of 'happy hour' promotion. In fact, this is one way of using 'Time' as a retail marketing element.

FINAL INSIGHTS

Although market research is essential when launching new 'products' (shop formulae), managers should not rely solely on the shoppers' opinions if they are looking for real innovation. When customers or shoppers are asked to exemplify their 'ideal' shop, they usually describe something familiar to them, but simply improved. Innovation is a manager's responsibility; improvement may be founded much more on customers' opinions.

Innovation does not stem from a quantitative market survey. This method is only complementary. Managers may rely more on qualitative, and even projective, methods to discover the needs, hopes or desires that are most difficult to express.

It is plain to see that the famous expression 'value for money' seems myopic, as any commercial transaction is an exchange of solution for efforts. Money is only one of the many efforts shoppers must make to obtain their desired solution. If you only think of money, you are forgetting other types of efforts your target may be reluctant to make, without necessarily being too price-sensitive.

FOR FUTURE RESEARCH

A segmented shop is a shop format that is neither widely used nor well known. Some people mistakenly think that a speciality store is the same thing as a segmented shop.

One of the effects to be considered in future studies is the fact that, although the shop has been designed specifically to suit the needs and tastes of the target segment, people from other segments also use this store. Unanticipated visitors may like the shop and buy certain things there, or they may shop there occasionally. For example, some typical traditional housewives visit Sunka early in the mornings on weekdays, and although they like some of the shop's features, they dislike others, like the meat in self-service.

We believe that segmenting with new tools, such as applications based on artificial intelligence, may open doors to new knowledge regarding the concept of segmentation in retail marketing (or in general marketing).

Let us propose one final question: will future marketing managers have to manage ambiguity?

REFERENCES

Martínez-Ribes, L. (1978), *The Universes: A method to guide brainstorming activity*. Document for MBA class discussion, ESADE, Barcelona.

Martínez-Ribes, L. (1980), *Value Added by Retailers*. Case study for MBA discussion, ESADE, Barcelona.

Martínez-Ribes, L. and Dawson, J. (1998), *Retail Marketing: Solution, Efforts and the Creation of Retailer Value*. Document for MBA class discussion, ESADE, Barcelona.

Chapter Twenty-four

How to Make Good Dough: Revitalizing your Product Portfolio by Understanding Consumer Needs

Pia de Wit[a] and Sinéad Twomey[b]

This chapter shows a research framework with a rich blend of methodologies. This, in turn, enabled the business to conjure up new and fresh ideas for both the development and positioning of products within the bakery industry.

INTRODUCTION

[a] Consumer Scientist, Unilever R&D.
[b] Project Manager, SKIM Analytical CPG.

Market Research Best Practice. Edited by P. Mouncey and F. Wimmer.
© 2007 John Wiley & Sons, Limited.

The ability to sow and reap cereals may well have been one of the chief causes leading man to dwell in communities, rather than to live a nomadic life hunting and herding cattle. About 10000 BC, man first started eating a crude form of flat bread – a baked combination of flour and water. Ever since, bread has remained one of the principal forms of food for man. The trade of the baker is, therefore, also one of the oldest crafts in the world, and it would be easy to think that, by now, all possible forms of bread would have been thought of, tried and tested. According to Unilever, this is certainly not the case!

In the early days within Unilever, the results of bakery technical research alone provided the input required for the development of new bakery products:

$$\text{Bakery technical research} \xrightarrow{\text{technology push}} \text{Good quality dough}$$

Although this approach led to the creation of some good quality products, there was a fundamental lack of in-depth understanding regarding what consumers really wanted, and which consumers to target (Reynolds and Olson, 2001). Findings from certain concept market tests revealed that Unilever had an average product which did not really fit into any of the consumers' ideals.

Unilever had great expertise in collecting consumer insights, but it was not common practice to link the consumers' needs, benefits and descriptive attributes in a situational setting, to different bakery products. Unilever then realized that, not only did it need to know more about consumer motivation, but it also, more importantly, needed to translate these consumer needs into technical requirements – i.e. how a bakery product in the eyes of a consumer delivers a certain goal for a specific eating occasion/context.

$$\text{Consumer research} \xrightarrow{\text{market pull}} \text{Bakery technical research} \xrightarrow{\text{technology push}} \text{Great dough that fits consumers' needs}$$

In an effort to gain in-depth insight into the way a bakery product can best satisfy the needs of the consumer on a certain eating occasion (situation/location and time of day) and in a certain context (weather, social context) and subsequently to translate these needs into the technical requirements of the baker, Unilever designed a framework in which all

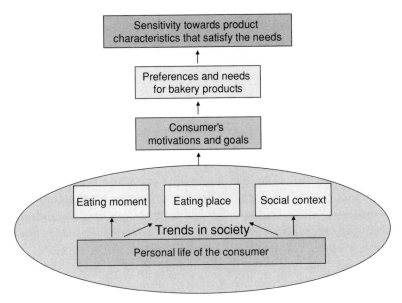

Figure 24.1   How trends in society influence the lives of consumers, and, consequently, their consumption choices regarding bakery products.

these elements we linked. This framework is based on the assumption that, given a certain eating occasion, consumers may have different eating goals, i.e. different desired benefits from a certain product.

Trends in society influence the personal life of the consumer. Moreover, both the general trends and the lifestyle determine the relevant situational context with regard to the consumption of bakery products (eating moment, eating place and social context). This situational context conditions the consumer's motivations and goals, which translate into the preferences and needs that lead ultimately to specific sensitivities for bakery products and their subsequent product characteristics. The underlying paradigm can be expressed graphically as in Figure 24.1.

With this conceptual framework in mind, Unilever embarked on a two-phase multi-country research project – the countries being the UK, Spain, Belgium and The Netherlands. The *first phase* enabled us to define product attributes that effectively describe and predict consumer acceptance of selected bakery products which satisfy a certain need on a given eating occasion within a specific context. The *second phase* focused on linking this consumer information to the bakery technology, i.e. to identifying new consumer-driven technical directions for bakery research in the long term, and inspiring product development in the short term.

PHASE 1

Although we had the conceptual framework in mind from the outset of the study, it was clear that an exploratory phase was necessary to test the model's underlying hypotheses and to provide an understanding of the relevant situational contexts, motivations, preferences and needs with regards to bakery products. As a careful exploration of the hierarchical relations between these concepts was essential, we realized we had to apply a methodology that would enable us to establish this in an holistic way. We decided to use goal derived laddering, a qualitative technique rooted firmly in the Means–End Chain (MEC) theory of Gutman (1982).

The basic assumption of the MEC theory is that each person acts in a certain way ultimately to reach his or her goals. The actions taken, decisions made and products bought all have the same purpose: to satisfy the deeper needs of the person taking the actions, in accordance with their personal motivations and values in life. Goal derived laddering is suited particularly to eliciting the specific product attributes that ultimately satisfy the consumer's end goals, which is crucial in the product development phase of any new product initiative.

By discussing a relevant situational context in a face-to-face interview, each respondent was put into the appropriate frame of mind when completing the laddering exercises.

The qualitative interview consisted of the following sections:

1. Description of a relevant eating occasion.
2. Determination of the eating occasion goal.
3. Elicitation of concrete product attributes.
4. Goal derived laddering.
5. Product associations.
6. Creation of a dream product.

To begin with, respondents were asked to describe a relevant eating occasion by:

1. Choosing a combination of one of the following eating moments and situations whereby eating a bakery product was common to him/her:

   Eating moment   *Situation*
   Early morning   On the move
   Mid-morning   At work/school
   Noon   Leisure time/recreation
   Late afternoon
   Dinnertime
   Late evening

2. Determining the specific eating occasion goal.

   The underlying assumption of the framework is that the eating occasion influences the motivation a specific consumer has for eating a bakery product. The following is an example of an eating occasion, which may have taken place for a male consumer of bakery products.

   It was early in the morning; he was on his way to work. At this point, he was what we would call 'on the move'. What were his physical surrounding? Did he stop off at a petrol station on the way? Was it cold or warm outside? What were his social surroundings? Was he alone in a crowded environment when eating, or with others? In addition to the situation, he also had to describe what initiated or triggered him to eat this product. Was it the occasion? (He had to fill up his car with petrol); was it the smell? (He couldn't resist the smell of the freshly baked pastries); was it out of habit? (He always eats his breakfast on the move); or did he react to a physical signal? (He was hungry).

   This motivation, the eating occasion goal, is part of the means–end chain. Activation of the goal will, in turn, activate the entire means–end chain, i.e. the benefits and product attributes that are linked to the goal, and subsequently the ideal product that is chosen.

   In the study, each respondent was invited to describe the products they would consume given the specific eating occasion, with the objective of eliciting as many concrete product attributes as possible.

   The stylized example of an individual interview shown in Figure 24.2 illustrates how all the relevant subjects were explored and related. The verbatims (in italics) illustrate the framework by presenting an actual interview, which was conducted with a male consumer from the UK.

   The next step was to use goal-derived laddering to link the eating occasion goal with the product attributes mentioned. The objective of using

Figure 24.2 Stylized example of an individual interview.

this specific type of depth interview is to uncover the links between the attributes that characterize the product, the subsequent benefits derived from consuming these attributes and the goal the respondent aims to achieve. Figure 24.3 shows an example of one of the ladders, which resulted from the interview with the male respondent from the UK. He has chosen a bakery product, which has a crunchy texture, with the ultimate aim of indulging himself.

The respondent was invited finally to choose his ideal bakery product. The objective of this exercise was to investigate if any additional attributes, which were not already mentioned, also contributed to reaching his desired goal.

Although the exploratory phase provided Unilever with a wealth of consumer understanding, it also generated many questions from the local technology teams. 'Does the consumer want a crunchy and sweet bakery product, or is it a savoury, crunchy bread that will best satisfy their needs?' It was obvious that these qualitative insights needed to be validated and quantified in order to formulate and fine-tune Unilever's marketing and

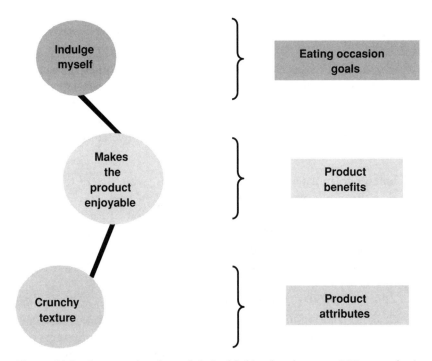

Figure 24.3   An example of a goal-derived ladder, based on one UK respondent's interview.

product development strategies. The next phase would, therefore, require the use of research methodologies which would answer the following fundamental questions:

1. What combination of these product attributes will create the optimal product design?
2. How valid are the links between the attributes, benefits and end goals, and how relevant are the consumer needs overall within our markets?

PHASE 2

The second phase was aimed at gaining more insight into consumers' preferences for product attributes and a quantitative interpretation of the links between the attributes, benefits and goals, which were derived from the explorative study in phase 1. The quantitative interview consisted of the following parts:

1. Selection of product platform and description of eating occasion.
2. Determination of eating occasion goal.
3. Applying structured open association pattern (SOAP) to quantify the hierarchical links.
4. Defining the optimal product design using adaptive conjoint analysis (ACA).

Unilever formulated five product platforms, which were fine-tuned based on the results of the first phase and formed the context of design and analysis in phase 2. They comprised a combination of eating moment, place and social context whereby the consumer eats specific types of bakery products. Each respondent was invited to choose a platform which was relevant to him/her, and determine the specific eating occasion goal (Figure 24.4).

As the laddering served us well in the exploratory phase, we also wanted to use the technique in the quantitative phase. However, as a data collection technique it is more suited for smaller sample sizes. Simply conducting more laddering interviews is rather time consuming and merely identifies new concepts by building new ladders, rather than quantifying

	EATING MOMENT	PLACE	SOCIAL CONTEXT	REMARK	NAME OF PLATFORM
1	Lunch	Out of home	Alone	Replacement	Meal replacement
2	Breakfast / dinner / lunch	At home	With others	Accompaniment	Meal accompaniment
3	Breakfast / dinner / lunch	At home	With others	Meal as a special occasion	Special occasions
4	In between lunch and dinner	Out of home	With others	Impulse snacking	Snack with others
5	Lunch / In between lunch and dinner	Out of home	Alone	Impulse snacking	Snack alone

Figure 24.4 The five product platforms.

the associations between selected concepts. The best-known method to measure means–end chains, validated by Ter Hofstede *et al.* (1998) is the so-called association pattern technique (APT).

This method presents the respondents with an empty matrix of product attributes and benefits, and invites them to indicate the relevant links. Next, they are presented with a matrix of product benefits and consumer goals and are again asked to indicate the links. As this technique provides each respondent with the same stimulus material, a quantification of the results is possible.

We decided not to use the APT technique, because asking at the level of depth required by the APT results in a long interview in which respondents get bored, thus reducing data quality. There are so many possible associations involved that it reduces their ability to be able to focus on every question within the questionnaire. Also, due to the double matrix, the attribute/benefit associations are separated from the benefit/goal association, which severs the links between attributes, benefits and values. As a result of these drawbacks, SKIM Analytical set out to develop a technique which would overcome these disadvantages. The outcome was a new laddering-derived quantification technique: the *structured open association pattern (SOAP)*.

SOAP is essentially a card-sorting exercise. All the relevant product attributes, benefits and goals are printed on cards and the respondents construct complete ladders by means of an interview that closely resembles the traditional laddering interview. Since the data collection process is more structured, the tasks become easier to complete for the respondents. Applying SOAP enables the results to be quantified. Moreover, since the interviewer probes each respondent to explain why he/she has selected the attributes, benefits and goals, the detail and quality of information is increased and is therefore very useful for product innovation. The result of the SOAP research is that we gain insight into the relevance of the attributes, benefits and goals to the overall market.

The following describes the results of the 'Special occasions' platform, as displayed in Figure 24.5.

The general goal of the platform 'Special occasions' (as mentioned in Figure. 24.5) is socializing with friends and family. The platform distinguishes itself on five benefits. In general, it can be said that people look for something extra when they have a special occasion: the product must be teasing ('makes the product enjoyable', 'looks inviting to eat'). It must be 'good quality' or 'nourishing' and specifically

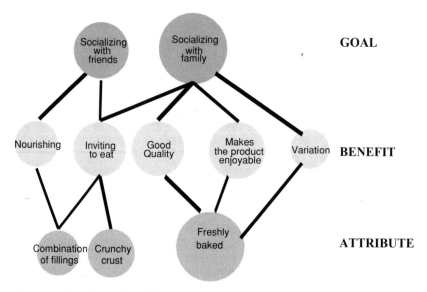

Figure 24.5 The results of the 'Special occasions' platform.

not a junk food. It must provide 'variation'. The distinguishing attributes are 'crunchy crust' and 'a combination of fillings'. When these attributes are defined in a product concept, a good description would be 'a filling in a special jacket'. Freshly baked is not a really distinguishing attribute, but it is important in an absolute way.

We now need to translate these consumer needs into the technical requirements of the product. Unilever wants to find the combination of attributes that is most preferred by the consumer on a specific eating occasion. For instance, in the early morning, consumers mainly prefer their food to be low in calories, soft on the outside and sweet, but not too sweet. In the late afternoon, on the other hand, a low-calorie level is far less important. First of all, it must be warm and tasty.

As mentioned above, the attributes that are generated from the laddering study are 'consumer-driven' and therefore a good starting point for bakery technical research. However, more detail is needed in the specification of the attributes to be able to find the optimal combination. The attributes must be specified in such detail, that we are talking about attribute *levels* rather than just attributes. For example, the attribute 'texture' would consist of the attribute levels crunchy/crispy/spongy/etc.; the attribute 'taste' would consist of the attribute levels sweet/savoury/salty/

neutral/etc. One way in which we can validate these attribute levels is by using Adaptive Conjoint Analysis (ACA). The strength of ACA is that we can investigate which combination of these attribute levels is the most attractive to the consumer. Moreover, as it is model-based, a number of 'what if' scenarios can be explored (Johnson, 2001). For example, it gives the product developer the opportunity to see the effects of different scenarios which could be of interest: Do consumers trade-off 'sweet' with 'high-calorie'? What are the compromises, they are willing to make?

The result of the ACA module was that we gained insight into:

1. The overall *consumer sensitivity to product attribute levels*.
2. The prefered attribute *levels*.
3. The *optimal combinations* of attribute levels for developing new products.

APPLICATION FOR THE UNILEVER BUSINESS

On the basis of the study results, one of the new and 'fresh' ideas the Unilever Bakery Business worked out for product development was a 'special occasion' product, as shown in Figure 24.6.

This mixture of methodologies and a comparable framework is in use successfully today in the other divisions within Unilever, like, for example, soups and sauces.

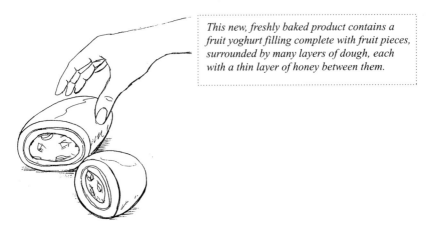

This new, freshly baked product contains a fruit yoghurt filling complete with fruit pieces, surrounded by many layers of dough, each with a thin layer of honey between them.

Figure 24.6   A 'special occasion' product.

CONCLUSION

Relying on bakery technical research alone can result in the creation of products that are only somewhat attractive to the consumer. Certain research methodologies can provide insight into consumers' preferences and needs. However, *mixing* the appropriate research methodologies in solving marketing issues provides for a rich blend of insight and results with regard to what the consumer really wants and which consumers to target. These results, when put into action, can lead to breakthrough product innovations.

ACKNOWLEDGEMENTS

We would like to thank Ria van der Maas (Unilever R&D Vlaardingen), Jürgen Warnecke and Dirk Huisman (SKIM Analytical) for their contribution to the work described in this chapter.

REFERENCES

Gutman, J. (1982), A Means – End Chain Model based on Consumer Categorization Processes. *Journal of Marketing*, **46** (2), 60–72.
Johnson, R.M. (2001), History of ACA. Sawtooth Software, Inc.
Reynolds, T.J. and Olson J.C. (2001), *Understanding Consumer Decision Making: The Means-End Approach to Marketing and Advertising Strategy*. Laurence Erlbaum Associates.
Ter Hofstede, F., Audenaert, A., Steenkamp, J.B.E.M. and Wedel, M. (1998), An investigation into the Association Pattern Technique as a quantitative approach to measuring Means–End Chains. *International Journal of Research in Marketing*, **15**, 37–50.

Chapter Twenty-five

Hide 'n' Seek: Driving Disruption in Skincare

Lyn McGregor[a] and James Potocki[b]

This chapter shows how a creative research design played a critical role in the development of a new global brand strategy and innovation plan. Furthermore, the research yielded nemerous key insights for communication.

INTRODUCTION

This chapter explores a major issue facing brands and organizations: the need to stimulate fresh thinking and prepare for tomorrow's market. We demonstrate how a creative research design involving semiotics makes it possible to understand developments in different cultures, and yet succeed in delivering insight that is of great relevance to the client at a global strategy level. This approach moves beyond static consumer segmentation models to reflect the increasing use of brands by consumers to create multiple identities. The research played a critical role in the development of a new global brand strategy and innovation plan.

[a]Director, Flamingo International, UK.
[b]Senior Consumer Insight Manager, Dove Global, Unilever USA.

Market Research Best Practice. Edited by P. Mouncey and F. Wimmer.
© 2007 John Wiley & Sons, Limited.

THE CHALLENGES FACING UNILEVER

In a number of countries around the world, the global skincare team at Unilever was seeing a clear evolution of body care needs and habits. However, the potential of this evolution was not reflected in the marketplace. In general, products have very blunt targets and benefits – a classic example of brand architecture would include products for normal, dry and very dry skin. As a result, consumers' skin characteristics and needs are generalized to a limited choice.

As a manufacturer, Unilever felt an urgent need to understand and market against a more powerful and precise definition of body care consumers' perceptions and aspirations. We believed that this understanding could guide brand architecture, innovation strategy and communication.

The key objective was to reveal how consumers defined their skin and the real role and impact it had in their daily life (conscious and subconscious). We needed to understand the key factors that influenced and determined their relationship with their skin.

A key challenge was that consumers spoke about their body skin through the language of manufacturers; however, we knew this language did not truly reveal how consumers defined or identified with their skin. This initiative was particularly challenging for the Body Care category, because the current lexicon is very basic (e.g. I have dry skin... and I want soft, smooth skin).

We knew that our existing research learnings could only unveil the most superficial layers of a consumer's beliefs, aspirations and relationship with her skin. This initiative would require a deep dig into consumers' lives and behaviours – a 'qualitative' research project of depth, scope and scale like none other conducted in body care.

It required a profound understanding that is difficult to unveil in traditional focus groups. We knew that we had to push the boundaries of how we traditionally conducted qualitative research. This need for fresh insight required direct consumer contact, observation and provocation. We knew we needed a research agency that would challenge our assumptions and actions. Finally, to meet the needs of the business, we had three months to complete the study.

CO-CREATING A NEW APPROACH

The whole project created a relationship between the agency and the Unilever client team of 'intense partnership', rather than the more traditional client/agency separation in terms of view-ing/participation/debrief. We continued this sense of intensity by work-ing with our research partners in a close collaborative style. This project benefited from a strong sense of dynamic energy from start to finish. No matter where we were in the world – from Brazil to Scandinavia – we were in conversation with the client team every few days throughout the project.

From the outset, key members of the global team suspected that the skincare market was changing dramatically and that the old ways of defin-ing and segmenting the market would not provide the competitive edge sought by Unilever going forward. The strong feeling existed that we needed to develop a new way of thinking about skincare from a con-sumer's perspective, one which would resonate across markets but would also allow for cultural differences.

The problem was that, to date, efforts to research the consumer had resulted in the same tired old language and category conventions being played back. We knew we needed to do something quite fresh and very different if we were going to be able to produce fresh results to satisfy the project objectives. The need for research that helps marketing anticipate the future in rapidly changing times has been recognized by many leading thinkers in the industry (Gordon, 1999; Spackman *et al.*, 2000; Valentine and Gordon, 2000; Desai, 2002; Clough and McGregor, 2003). The ability to achieve this successfully was the difficult part!

We kicked off this project with an Ignition Workshop in Connecticut, involving the global client team and the core team from Flamingo. The Flamingo core team included senior people from our main office in London and our office in the US. The session was led by Flamingo and by the end of the day we had begun to establish what the client already knew – and what we needed to discover!

The brand team had considerable knowledge of the way in which this market had been segmented traditionally. A recent global segmentation study had been conducted that focused on identifying segments using personality and consumer needs as key variables. Inevitably, most of this work had been conducted within the *dominant* cultural context. After looking at this work, we felt that we might find some interesting fresh insights to inform our future model by looking at the market from slightly different perspectives. To meet the project objectives, we would be open to discovering *emergent* themes within skincare – and even the wider cultural context – that may inform the creation of a *future-focused model*.

We agreed an approach that involved semiotics, expert round tables and consumer immersions. The consumer immersions involved pre-task activities, triads and depth interviews, and consumer audio and video recording. These consumer immersions involved skin extremists, leading edge skin consumers and mainstream consumers to understand fully the role of involvement and the rate of adoption of new ideas and innovations in skincare.

Within each of these areas we designed activities that would take us deeper into understanding the changes that might be taking place in consumer values, rituals and emotions within different cultures.

Semiotic analysis

Semiotic analysis is a vital methodology for understanding the broader effects of socio-cultural shifts upon the skincare category. The approach was designed to identify *emergent trends* and to aid in the development of category disruption strategies. At Flamingo, we believe that semiotics is a powerful tool in understanding factors that are affecting consumer motivations. We were keen to use semiotics in this study to help inform the creation of a future-focused brand model.

Our in-house semiotician, working at times with local country partners, reviewed relevant materials from several key countries. This analysis consisted of two main elements:

- **Category context** – an analysis of the language, symbols, images and myths associated with the skincare category. This was achieved by analysing brand communication across the territories (print and film).
- **Cultural context** – this included an investigation into broader socio-cultural shifts and emergent trends in skin and personal care, as well as socio-cultural influences beyond the category.

Part of the challenge for this research was going beyond beauty clichés, ensuring distinctive future communication to move the brand on. By applying both sections of the semiotic analysis, we were able to evaluate how Unilever Skincare might 'speak' and 'behave' differently than its competitors, and how it could communicate a powerful new attitude and spirit.

Semiotic analyses of the category and surrounding culture were extremely useful in stimulating and complementing consumer insight. By understanding the emergent language on packaging and in communications, the trends in the wider skincare environment (such as spas and retail environments) and by examining what we could learn from other related categories such as face creams, as well as the developments in the wider culture, we were able to develop valuable insights that would contribute to future strategy.

The key to making this element work hard within the project as a whole was close collaboration between the semiotics team and the consumer research team.

Changing consumer values

As the culture of a society changes, so do the values that make up the society. To access these emergent themes we wanted to explore *values, attitudes* and *beliefs* held by those who are more involved with their skin across a range of cultures. We wanted to explore if values, attitudes and beliefs relating to skincare were changing, and how this differed across the globe.

Laddering methods would help us to relate current behaviour to deeply held beliefs and the individual's sense of self, with subsequent analysis designed to understand if personality issues are contributing to differences in values. For instance, how do ambitious, career-minded professionals differ in terms of these end-state values from sporty, outgoing, fun-loving extroverts? Do their behaviours and attitudes provide NPD opportunities? How would this learning affect communications? What does this indicate in terms of a model for characterizing the skincare market?

In particular we were interested in understanding the *differences between leading edge respondents* and *mainstream respondents* within each market, and also the differences in the rate of evolution across markets. By laddering-up to values and exploring self-concepts with individuals, we would be able to determine if there were differences that may be associated, not only with involvement, but personality type, lifestages or cultural experiences.

Recognizing the increasing role being played by media in the transference of values within culture (Clough and McGregor, 2003), we realized it was important to examine advertising and editorial items on skincare with consumers. Arguably, consumers are limited in expertise in this area, and so we complemented their understanding of the influence of communications with the expert view of our in-house semiotician, who took our understanding to a level not achievable with consumers.

By combining these approaches we were able to assess the cultural impact of media upon consumer values, attitudes and current behaviours. McCracken (1985) identified the role of the media, advertising and fashion worlds in the process of transferring cultural meanings to products

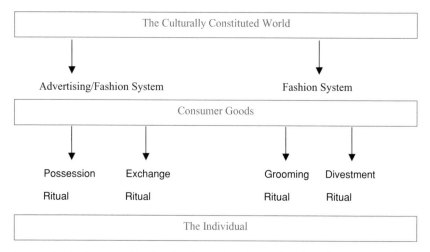

Figure 25.1 The transfer of cultural meaning (Reproduced, with permission, from McCracken, 1985).

(see Figure 25.1). The Grooming Ritual was identified by McCracken as a source of meaning transmission from products to the individual within a culture. We wanted to ensure that we understood consumer grooming rituals and how these might be changing as a result of changes at a cultural level.

Changing cultural grooming rituals

We wanted to explore the acts of current purchase and usage within the category and related categories (possession rituals), including the changes taking place in retail environments. Researchers visited retail outlets and our semiotician also analysed developments taking place at this contextual level.

Specific attention was paid to grooming habits within this category and related categories. Not only were these behaviours explored in pre-task activities and during the immersions themselves, respondents were invited to capture personal experiences *directly on video* allowing greater individuality to be expressed in their own environments. These videos allowed the research team to observe consumers in their own bedrooms and bathrooms, with their own personal sets of grooming products.

We identified linkages between possession and grooming behaviours, different value systems and their cultural contexts.

Fresh fantasies, feelings and fun!

Of particular interest were the *emotions* aroused during ritual behaviours, and pre-task activities were designed to open up the exploration of these emotions within the subsequent interviews. Given that a primary issue for this study was the dominance of well-worn codes and language, one of our initial tasks was to shake things up and prompt new modes of expression.

One way to achieve this is to switch *senses* – asking respondents to see and feel what is normally spoken. In the actual consumer sessions, we employed a toolkit of visual and tactile stimuli designed to help consumers explore their feelings. The power of *metaphor* is also vital in this type of work, and we used a range of sensory stimuli to enable exploration of the relevant emotions. Another method employed was to encourage a free associative and exhaustive stream of consciousness. When the usual words run dry, things often get interesting – and very revealing.

WHO, WHERE AND HOW

The aim was to access deep insights, fresh learning and challenging ideas that broke the paradigm and enabled us to construct anew from a genuinely exciting foundation. The total project involved France, Germany, the US (New York, Los Angeles), Mexico, Brazil and Japan.

We conducted expert round tables, skin extremist depths, and consumer friendship triads, including both leading-edge consumers and the more mainstream. We designed this sample to enable us to understand the emergent themes and the rate of adoption of new ideas across these different cultures.

Expert round tables

The expert round tables included dermatologists, spa consultants, beauty journalists, therapists, etc. To encourage an atmosphere of buzz and dynamic intellectual interaction, we spoke to experts in more creative environments than those normally used for research. This was a dynamic moderated session where the experts were given open forum to dump their knowledge.

Key trigger questions were used to spark provocative and category disruptive discussion, although most sessions generated their own flashpoints given the range of experts we had convened together. The discussion took a deliberate future facing direction.

Consumer immersions – extreme skin interviews and consumer triads

We dissected the consumer's relationship with her skin via a range of pre- and post- interview activities designed to go deeper. These included:

- **'Skin texts'** – these revolved around quite impressionistic and emotive questions designed to get 'under the skin' of people's skin relationships. These 'texts' included photographs and collages created from magazines. Key sections included:
  - Skin biography;
  - Me and my skin – our relationship;
  - The geography of my skin.
- **Skin movies** – we asked some respondents to document their relationship with their skin (filming and narrating what they filmed). We gave them an open-ended list of prompt questions, some designed to orientate us around their current skin world, and other questions that were more impressionistic.
- **Brain dumps** – women were asked to spend ten minutes alone with a dictaphone and a prompt question to give us their 'skin stream of consciousness'.

Approaches in the immersions themselves

We employed a *rolling hypothesis approach*, inputting into the questioning in an open-ended way (as stimulus rather than direction) the hypotheses we were forming on the way.

We employed a range of enabling techniques to go beyond the usual ways consumers describe their relationship with their body skin. These included:

- projectives;
- disruptive language exercises;
- imagery building;
- laddering and ritual exploration;
- cultural imagery;

- product/packaging stimulus.
- the creative challenge: future heaven!

SEEING INTO THE GLOBAL FUTURE

Working closely with our research partners, we achieved a deep level of understanding within the different cultures in the study. At this point we needed to achieve a global level of analysis. Global analysis showed us where similarities and differences existed across cultures between consumer values, behaviours and attitudes.

We employed the learning from our semiotics work in determining the cultural reasons for such differences. We were looking for common themes – dominant and emergent territories. We examined trends and trajectories to determine where different cultures were located currently and where they might be heading – the feedback from leading edge consumers was most important in helping us to map this out.

During this analysis we were able to identify the location and rate of development across the countries of interest. Such analysis would inform the subsequent development of strategy, the introduction of new products/brands and the communications that would strike a fresh chord in the near future.

The global analysis was a core element in developing a model for the future. As a result, this was the point when the senior core team needed to spend considerable time, not simply pulling together the different country results, but determining 'what it all meant' and what it might mean for the development of a model.

Revisiting the dominant segmentation model

At this point it was useful to revisit the segmentation model that had identified the segments relevant for Unilever skincare brands. As Jonathan Clark has commented in *Admap*, consumers are changing rapidly and broad-based segmentation techniques often fail to deliver the insights that lead to marketing success (Clark, 2004).

Sherrington (1998) suggests '*the value in segmentation is not just in understanding how the market currently stands. The real power is in understanding how it can be changed*'. He goes on to point out that brands create segments and new ways to segment can create brand opportunities.

Our aim in revisiting these data was to understand what we had learnt from our work that was fresh and new, and also to identify how our new learning might create new brand opportunities.

The emergent model: moments of identity

As is often the case at this stage in the qualitative process, the research team is looking for different patterns or models that explain what has been seen, heard and experienced during the fieldwork phase, and the complexity of a multi-country study is always challenging in this way. Models are tried and rejected when they do not explain satisfactorily the attitudes and behaviours that have been discovered.

One such model in this study was based around *lifestage*. Although lifestage explains many differences between consumers, we found that it is becoming less useful nowadays as women's attitudes to skincare are not determined solely by lifestage. This was most noticeable in those markets that were experiencing greater levels of cultural change. Static models were proving to be disappointing in their ability to explain the consumer attitudes and behaviours we had witnessed.

We realized we needed to use a new way of thinking about the consumer as 'a subject in search of identity'. According to Valentine and Gordon (2000), '*the 21st century consumer*' is constructing identities constantly:

> '*Rather than being a person who we can get to know – and therefore control – "the consumer" becomes a temporary, precarious point of identity, which is ever-changing, ambiguous and unpredictable. We have called this point the Moment of Identity.*'

Their paper goes on to argue the need for new tools to understand the brand and consumer as 'Moments of Identity'. We realized we had in fact incorporated many of their recommended approaches in our research design – including need state, semiotic and trend analysis. Valentine and Gordon comment upon the need to make these methodologies more mainstream if we are to understand fully the post-modern consumption experience. They quote my own colleague at Flamingo, James Parsons, who pointed out in an earlier ESOMAR paper that the old tools are simply not 'adequate' enough (Parsons, 1999).

After a great deal of internal discussion, and then discussion between the core Flamingo team and the core client team, followed by further reinterrogation of the various country reports, we became firmly convinced that women consider their skins to be affected by a variety of fluctuating factors – from environmental factors to hormonal, lifestyle and emotional ones – not to mention genetic inheritance! The fact that many of these factors are fluctuating and variable mean that they work against the development of a model that is constant. These factors can combine in new and different ways to affect the condition of their skins *at any given moment.*

Attitudinally, some women get more emotionally involved than others in the condition of their body skin, but most experience *situational involvement* rather than ongoing high levels of involvement – i.e. the occasion can temporarily increase their nature and degree of involvement with their skin.

We are suggesting that the *desired identities combined with occasions* would create a better understanding of the emergent, more dynamic consumer behaviour in the body skincare market. There are moments for women when they desire certain functional and emotional benefits (or end states) in certain situations, and there are early indications that they are beginning to purchase different skincare products to help achieve these different desired outcomes.

As Valentine and Gordon point out in their seminal paper, the old ways of thinking about the consumer and their relationship with brands assumes that they are at a *'fixed point in a fixed space in a fixed time.'* They note that this allows targeting, segmentation and the ability to predict based upon the current context. By accepting the new way of thinking we lose this predictability and sense of control. However, by doing so, we make way for the markets of tomorrow rather than simply competing for those of today.

Brand repertoires to meet the needs of the moment

In fact, Mary Goodyear alluded to this 'new consumer' as early as 1996 at the MRS Conference when she pointed out that

> *'Segmentation on an occasion-and-needs-determined basis is now extensively used in the UK and USA. But in much of the rest of the world, consumers are still being identified as if they were stable and predictable types of people.'*

Goodyear identified that, as a market sector becomes richly furnished with consumer choice, consumers tend to become more promiscuous in their behaviour:

> *'They pick and choose which brands they want, deploying a repertoire of products and brands to suit the needs of the moment: the moment of purchase or consumption.'*

POST-MODERN MARKETING	CUSTOMER-DRIVEN MARKETING
Company brands	Brands as icons
Cynical consumer	Saturated marketplace
Needs-based segmentation	Segmentation based on usage
Destructured advertising	Symbolic advertising
Electronic data capture	Creative research

Figure 25.2 The consumerization continuum (Reproduced, with permission, from Goodyear).

Goodyear identifies that different markets can be at different stages of development, and that this affects the marketing approach that is most appropriate. The 'Consumerization Continuum' she identifies moves from Selling to Marketing, and then Classic Branding (heavily reliant on brands as personality), before moving into a new and different phase she calls Postmodern Marketing, and then finally Customer Driven Marketing (see Figure 25.2).

Rapid category change

The body care category is undergoing a period of rapid change, and this sudden acceleration required the application of more creative research methods. In the body care market, key brands are becoming more associated with strong motivational drives allowing consumers to express themselves to society, or simply to reaffirm their sense of identity to themselves.

Eventually, as Spenser and Wells (2000) point out, consumers may use a 'portfolio' of brands. We were finding that in the most emergent markets for skincare, consumers were beginning to use different brands to express 'me at work', 'me as a lover' or 'me as a mother'.

If consumers use brands to create their identity/identities, then the brand must communicate a strong, clear 'lighthouse identity' in the words of Adam Morgan (1999). Whilst this thinking was developed initially for challenger brands, Morgan points out that to stay Number one, you need to think like the challenger as a new generation of market leaders such as Nike, Intel and Microsoft are already doing. In particular, he describes the need to think like a challenger in a category where the rules are about to change rapidly. These are, quite simply, brands that face challenges.

Unilever skincare brands were facing such challenges. Using this work it became possible to begin to build fresh identities to be used by modern consumers.

Moving forward

The research is hailed as a leading example of breakthrough and insightful consumer learning. As such, Unilever plans to conduct similar research in other product categories. Principles and techniques used in this study have been adopted consistently in subsequent research. Most importantly, the key business objectives were met.

The learnings have had a profound impact on the body care business. They played a critical role in the development of a new global brand strategy and innovation plan. In the brand strategy, the research dimensionalizes the future world of body care, category whitespace and key territories for the brand to occupy. In innovation planning, the research inspired the development of new cross-category innovation platforms, as well as a more progressive approach to innovation – one that is no longer problem/solution based. Furthermore, the research yielded numerous key insights for both innovation and communication.

REFERENCES

Chandler, J. and Owen, M. (2002), Brands and the Human Dimension, in Ereaut, G., Imms, M. and Callinghar, M.(Eds) *Developing Brands with Qualitative Market Research*, Sage publications.

Clark, J. (2004), Connecting with Consumers, in Making Sense of Segmentation, Admap, September.

Clough, S. and McGregor, L. (2003), *Capturing the emerging zeitgeist: aligning the mirror to the future*. Award-winning MRS Conference Paper.

Desai, P. (2002), Methods Beyond Interviewing in Qualitative Market Research, *Qualitative Market Research: Principle and Practice*, 3, pp. 6–7, 92–95, 121–127.

Ehrenberg, A., Long, S. and Kennedy, R. (2000), *Competitive Brands' User-Profiles Hardly Differ*. MRS Conference.

Goodyear, M. (1996), *Divided by a Common language: diversity and deception in the world of global marketing*. MRS Conference Papers.

Gordon, W. (1999), *Goodthinking , A Guide to Qualitative Research*. Admap.

McCracken, G. (1985), Culture and Consumption: A Theoretical Account of the Structure and Movement of the Cultural Meaning of Consumer Goods. *Journal of Consumer Research*, **13**, 71–84.

Morgan, A. (1999), *Eating the Big Fish: How Challenger Brands Can Compete Against Brand Leaders,* John Wiley & Sons, Inc.

O'Donoghue, D. and Steele, L. (2004), Is lifestage losing its meaning?, in 'Making Sense of Segmentation', Admap, September.

Parsons, J. (1999), *Me nuh 'ave nuh time for nuh bag a chat,* ESOMAR Seminar, The Speed, Validity and Reliability of Qualitative Research, Athens.

Sherrington, M. (1998), Market segmentation really is cool. *Market Leader,* Spring.

Spackman, N. Barker, A. and Nancarrow, C. (2000), *Happy New Millennium: A Research Paradigm for the 21st Century*, Proceedings of the Market Research Society Conference, March, pp. 91–104.

Spenser, D. and Wells, S. (2000), Qualitative Research and Innovation, in L. Marks (Ed.) *Qualitative Research in Context*, Admap.

Valentine, V. and Gordon, W. (2000), *The 21st Century Consumer – a new model of thinking*, MRS 2000 Conference.

Chapter Twenty-six

Jack in the Tiffin-box: Unconventional Paths to New Product Idea Development

Sangeeta Gupta,[a] Subhransu Rout[b] and Farheen Romani[c]

This chapter outlines how a challenging NPD opportunity ('tiffin-boxes' for middle class school children in India) was exploited effectively. A blend of unconventional research methodologies, including microethnography and semiotics, was employed to yield a mine of exciting new product ideas.

INTRODUCTION

The problem

For many companies today, especially those with large successful brands (market leaders in their category), there is a strong focus on new product development as a means to achieve growth. And many of us also know (sometimes rather painfully) that true successes in this area are rare, particularly in the foods category. As marketers of food products, we search for the right product idea, which can only come from a sound

[a]Independent Consultant, Research, Strategy and Innovation.
[b]Head, Business Intelligence Unit, GlaxoSmithKline Consumer Health Care, India.
[c]Brand Planning Director, LOWE Lintas (India) Pvt. Ltd.

Market Research Best Practice. Edited by P. Mouncey and F. Wimmer.
© 2007 John Wiley & Sons, Limited.

understanding of the socio-cultural needs of the consumer combined with a strong sensorial/organoleptic benefit.

The opportunity

We know that as a child grows, his needs change, and mums keep trying to keep pace with their needs. Recent studies led us to believe that there existed an opportunity specifically in the 'tiffin-box' arena. Mothers struggle every morning to fill their children's lunch boxes with items that are nourishing, satiating, healthy and actually *get eaten*. BUT, the child opens his box at recess time, likes to be surprised and wants interesting foods that can make even his friends envious. A clear gap!

There is a similar opportunity during the bus ride home. The child is hungry, may have the leftovers from the box, or pick up a snack from the canteen. On both occasions, the available options are not entirely satisfactory.

The purpose of this chapter is to examine closely the dynamics of the child–mum–tiffin-box on an everyday basis, the ways a win-win solution can be reached and the development of ideas which address a symbiosis of these needs.

Thus, the objective of our study here has been to reach an *actionable and stimulating brief* to develop a range of NPD ideas to be used by Glaxo-SmithKline's R&D and Marketing teams. We will not dwell long on the *final* product ideas in terms of formats, textures, tastes, etc.

THE APPROACH: A MULTI-BRANCHED METHODOLOGY

While we often marvel at the amazingly perceptive and articulate children we encounter every day, we recognize that they are at their best in this respect in *their* own time and place. In an artificial environment, it is not easy to get children to identify and articulate need gaps. Being creatures of the moment, they are most effectively understood through 'live' interactions.

Hence, we used techniques from ethnography, wherein we studied the child on the actual consumption occasions (recesses and bus rides), and the mums (working mums and non-working mums) at the tiffin-box packing times. To add an expert perspective to our observation highlights, we also conducted a few in-depth interviews with specialists from different fields like nutritionists, doctors and journalists/columnists of food magazines.

The methodology in detail – a mixed 'cuisine' of techniques for the tiffin-box

Step one: Marinating

We began with an attempt to understand the psyche of the child aged 8–12 years. This was done via intensive readings of the works of noted child psychologists, and was an integral part of the initiation into the project to prepare the researchers for the audience that they were to observe.

Step two: Precipitating

The child

Our researchers (a team of two executives) then went out and spent time with children during school recess times and bus rides. There were observations as well as informal chats with various groups of children.

The researcher stayed unobtrusive in the beginning . . . simply looking around and mentally noting various behaviours in the class/play field/bus. The children at this point in time were not really 'aware' of her presence.

Gradually, the researcher attempted to move into the child's world with short interactions, wherein she began chatting casually with the children. There was a lot of joking and laughing amidst the chaos of recess time; there was no formal questioning session.

She then rode back home in the school bus with a group of children. Again, interactions started off being simple observations, moving gradually into chatting sessions while travelling back home together.

At both these times, it is important to note that all interactions happened in *natural and spontaneous groups*. The researcher, after observing various groups would settle naturally into one preformed group of children and strike up spontaneous conversations. Groups formed and disintegrated in a completely natural way. Thus, these were not pre-timed groups; on average, the groups in the bus lasted for about 20 minutes, the ones during a recess about 10 minutes.

The mothers

In order to obtain the mum's perspective, our researcher visited mothers during the morning 'rush hour', when the child is getting ready for school and his mum is packing the boxes while at the same time completing a score of other household chores. To ensure that she did only what was typical, we told her that we were interested in her morning chores, not specifically in the tiffin-box. In some cases, we even dropped in unannounced (Indian hospitality means that we were still welcome!). Our researcher typically stayed with the lady until the children left for school, sometimes a little longer.

Step three adding the flavour

We also met a few school teachers, as we know they have a deep and up-close understanding of child behaviour. We spoke to nutritionists and doctors to get a 'scientific' explanation behind specific observed behaviours. Additionally, we captured the views of columnists/journalists on food magazines to discover trends in this area and to understand certain traditional practices and cultural pretexts to the food habits in the Indian scenario.

Step four: Assimilating and simmering

All observations and recordings were then analysed in depth, employing the 'usual' qualitative research tools like content analyses, cultural analysis, etc.

Step five: experimenting – going beyond

Brainstorming sessions for ideation were then conducted amongst 'creative' mothers and 'creative' children to elicit NPD ideas.

MICROETHNOGRAPHY – A BRIEF INTRODUCTION

We now describe our ethnographic methodology in a little more detail. As is commonly known, ethnography basically involves the researcher in some form of up-close participative observer role in a natural, everyday setting. The mandate is holistic, the ethnographer synthesizes disparate observations to make meaningful 'constructs'. She immerses herself in local conditions as an experiential whole.

We 'customized' these concepts to a more convenient construct to serve our objectives, and conducted episodic observations at multiple sites. Thus, we conducted what is called *microethnography*.

This technique required the researcher to follow a systematic process of study, while ensuring that the flexibility and open-ended nature of the approach still allowed for the creative nature of the output we desired. The process laid emphasis on the following aspects:

- **Seeking out reorienting and disconfirming observations** – while many of us are familiar with the need to 'build' on learnings as we go on, it is even more important continuously to seek out observations that require us to 'reorient' or modify our thinking on the subject under study. One such assumption was that the tiffin-box must mean a lot to the child and must be something that he looks forward to in his entire school day. However, this hypothesis was soon disconfirmed.

- **Revisiting the sites under study** – we visited the identified schools repeatedly to observe recess behaviour on different days amongst the same set of students. We also visited the same set of students at different times of the day to observe the gamut of interactions with their tiffin-boxes and food.

- **Participative role relationships so that inquiry was unfettered** – our researcher was a participative observer, so was able to question many aspects in a natural manner. For example, when our researcher went to meet mothers while they were packing the tiffins, she helped the lady with her chores and in the process was able to probe for reasons for her behaviour and raise topics of interest in an informal and natural way.

- **A wide range of perspectives and groupings** – as mentioned earlier, we met mums, children, teachers, even fathers who were around the home in the mornings, as well as referencing a range of 'experts'.

- **Collaborative 'insider–outsider' effort** – an interesting aspect about this methodology was the team spirit it invoked. We found a high degree of collaborative effort from both the children and the teachers. The 'unofficial collaboration' of a strategically located insider, or the apprentice-like feature of this technique, was inspired by the works of ethnographers Kondo, Gouldner and Barker.

- **Multiple modes of data collection** – we employed artifacts, the boxes themselves, photographs, spontaneous groups, etc.

- **Systematic data transformation** – this included indexing, coding, decontextualizing, memoing, recontextualizing, etc..., ensuring that the data were examined from many perspectives and with due rigour.

Fieldwork was conducted in Delhi over the months of January and February 2004 and August and September 2004, to cover both summer and winter seasons. The first round was conducted during the winter season, while the second phase of the study was conducted during the summer season; thus providing an interesting contrast between needs that differ based on seasons. Delhi is a metropolitan city in North India; please note that not only is the Indian market very diverse when it comes to food beliefs and practices, but even school timings vary considerably across cities and hence, tiffin needs would differ too.

THE INSIGHTS

In this section, we present our findings using a simple narrative structure (the style being as close to typical consumer language as possible), woven with interpretations/explanations as we go along. The narrative is set in normal text, the takeouts are italicized. We depict, sequence by sequence, the roles, thoughts and the behavioural contexts of the mother and the child and how the tiffin-box takes shape and fits into their lives.

We begin the story with the mother starting the day faced with the dilemma of what she should be packing in the tiffin-box, the conflict between her beliefs and the child's demands; we then move to a brief look at the 'box' itself, its meanings and symbolisms; and then, finally getting to the crux, a deep understanding of our hero, the 8–12 year old. This understanding necessarily has to be the very core of our study. We have touched upon his mental, physical, emotional and social compulsions and how they find expression in his school day and his tiffin choices.

We end with a brief word about the possible directions GSK can now take towards developing a range of tiffin products for the Indian market. This section is necessarily brief given the sensitive nature of the activities involved.

For the purposes of convenience and differentiation from the mum, we have used the pronoun, 'he/him' while describing the child. Findings apply to female children as well.

The Mum's Story

Mrs Indu Singh is busy in her kitchen at 5.45 in the morning – she looks harried. She needs to ensure that there is enough drinking water in the house, that she is ahead of time in the preparations for the children's school, that her husband's breakfast is prepared quickly, tea is ready for herself and her husband – all this at the same time! She is also praying that her maid shows up today...she has skipped twice this week already.

Her children are 9-year-old Rahul and 13-year-old Manisha. A challenging combination indeed – the impishness of boyhood and the traumas of an entrant teen lady!

Getting them to start preparing for school is a Herculean task. Indu has to get their uniforms in place and ironed, see to it that their shoes are polished and ensure that the homework is complete – else they may earn a red mark in their diary for not having done it. In the middle of all this there is a knock at the door. Oh God! It must be the milkman; he simply keeps ringing the bell to show he has to attend so many houses early morning, but never realizes that it takes time to wash the milk utensil before attending to him. Anyway, as long as he gets the milk on time every day it is okay. Having taken the milk, Indu heads straight to the kitchen to start preparing breakfast.

Indu does not believe in taking shortcuts when it comes to taking care of her children. And why not, after all, she has so many dreams for her children – that they should succeed at whatever they do, always stay healthy and fit, be the most popular and be smarter than the other kids in their peer group. Therefore, she puts in her best efforts to keep the children healthy, well nourished, happy. Even if it means slaving away to make most things fresh early in the morning.

(The mother is a product of her upbringing and culture, and consequently is ruled by firm beliefs and practices in all activities related to food preparation and serving – an area core to her self concept. A typical Indian meal (or the 'thali') is all about multiplicity – multicomponent, multitextured and multitasting. It comprises a core cereal, a supplement pulse and vegetable, complement yoghurt and a titillating pickle, papad or chutney. Mums try to replicate this concept in the tiffin. She thus ensures that her child takes 'proper food' to school; she must pack at least the core, the obligatory traditionally cooked parantha (a freshly kneaded and prepared pancake like flat bread) and sabzi (a portion of freshly chopped and cooked seasonal vegetable).

The effort actually begins much earlier, when she soaks almonds at night to have them ready to be peeled and given to the kids in the morning. Her mother always told her that almonds sharpen the mind.

The absolute must have, she knows, is the glass of milk, and if her children hate to have it, she thinks of other alternatives, such as some form of milk additive like Bournvita or Horlicks. But there is no way she can let them escape without it; she believes that milk can provide all the essential body requirements, especially after the long gap of the night. After all, it will also keep Rahul full until the break time, since he has not eaten anything in the morning.

(Interestingly, this 'compulsory' glass of milk leads her to believe that even if her son were not to consume the tiffin-box fully, his nourishment needs would be taken care of to a great extent. We also notice here that the beverage occasion in the morning is restricted to milk, and that milk is considered substantial enough to make up for the absence of solid intake at this hour.)

Indu also makes a butter-jam sandwich, neatly cut into two slices so that her son finds it easier to eat. But the sandwich is really not that important, it is just something that is kept alongside, with the hope that a bite or two might be taken.

While she is carefully managing her early morning food preparations, she is calling out constantly to Rahul and Manisha, asking them to start dressing for school. Managing the morning time is solely her responsibility. She worries that they may get distracted while she is busy in the kitchen – it is better that she keeps checking on them. They never keep their things in the right places, so they need her help constantly for little things. She keeps stepping out of the kitchen to provide them that lost sock or belt and then rushes back to attend to the boiling milk, which is ready to surf the stove and add another 10 minutes of cleaning time.

Alongside the breakfast preparations, Indu is also wondering what the accompaniment could be in the tiffin-box along with the 'parantha'. The vegetable can change every day, but of course there is no second thought about packing the 'parantha' – that is the core, after all. They need something substantial to pull them through the day. In any case, by the time the poor kids actually get down to eating their tiffin-boxes, they get only cold and unappetizing food. She is careful, therefore, to use a foil wrap to keep the food warm.

While she is very sure she must pack the nourishing 'paranthasabji', she is only too conscious of the fact that both her children want something quite different – they crave variety and a break from the regular cuisine.

She resorts to solving the dilemma by either giving an occasional break from the regular food with a pizza/burger/sandwich, or she sticks to her everyday menu but adds a bait of 2–3 biscuits or potato chips in a corner of the tiffin, hoping to get some interest generated.

(The mum knows her child wants something different every day, more variety. Regular food like parantha/rotis and vegetables are boring for the child, and other healthy foods like green vegetables/pulses are not liked for their taste. Instead, the child prefers fast food, like pizzas, burgers, unusual cuisines, like Chinese and Mughlai, or fun foods, like chocolate and chips. She knows that the child

wants to titillate his palate and taste buds. In order to overcome this problem she tries a hybridization of the Indian food along with other kinds of snacky items like chips/biscuits).

Indu thinks about the times both Rahul and Manisha have talked about the exotically packed tiffins their friends have had at school, described as having interesting green, red or orange toppings, and creamy layers, sounding nothing less than a Bahamian lay of food. She had always thought that maybe those kids belonged to very rich families who had exotic chefs, or their mums spent lots of money on buying such exclusive stuff. She herself is unable to live up to those standards. But that does not mean that she cannot be smart enough to manage the modern kind of food within her means, just that being able to meet such desires would have been so much easier if only she knew how to get the food looking good, or knew about the more interesting options available, so even she could hope for a compliment as a 'Supermum!'

(One of the key dissatisfiers in the tiffin-box is the complete lack of visual appeal in the food. The Indian mother has been used to traditional dishes which are sombre looking – gravies in browns and pale yellows with layers of floating oil. Thus, while the food may taste good, it certainly looks otherwise. The current practices in tiffin preparation leave her with limited scope to improvise and make food look more appetizing.)

She wishes she could do more to the food that she packs in the tiffin, even if it took more time or was more tedious than her regular cooking. At least it would pay off if Rahul and Manisha had it and enjoyed it.

(The problem is not the physical effort that goes into it, it is the lack of ideas, the absence of amicable solutions, the mismatch between her children's tastes and Indu's definition of healthy food, and the want of ways to package the same healthy food in a different manner that looks very attractive too).

Alas, nothing is good enough and nothing is really ENOUGH! So she comes to the conclusion that children are children and they will eat only as much as they want, but something is better than nothing. She continues to pack the regular tiffin-box. She feels there is only so much that she can do about it, and anyway she can make up for the occasion by feeding more and healthier food during lunch, where she is back in control.

(In order to come to terms with the child's rejection of tiffin food, some mums tend to trivialize the importance of this meal itself. Despite her best efforts (which are actually quite considerable), because she has very little control over the child eating what she thinks is important for him, and is actually quite helpless, she adopts an attitude of 'children will be children, they do not like proper food and are bound to eat some and leave some'. She tells herself she can always make up for it during the remaining meals of the day; after all, she

is at home when he comes back from school. Hence, at times, she simply seems to have 'given up' on controlling this consumption occasion and instead sees the lunch meal, as the key occasion when she can ensure that the child has healthy nutritious food.

The irony in this is that the tiffin occasion is actually a time when the child can consume a healthy and nourishing meal because of the very lively group dynamics at the time. He sees his peers eating, so he feels the need to eat. He is enjoying himself chatting and fooling around with friends, is pleasantly distracted and can actually consume a lot more food, but only if the food available to him is in a form that he likes. This consumption occasion actually holds a lot of promise and its trivialization is a missed opportunity).

Finally, the menu for the tiffin is the parantha, but stuffed with potatoes, and, to add to the taste of the food, pickles are kept in one corner of the box. Indu decides to pack two paranthas in each of the boxes. This is because Rahul and Manisha tell Indu stories about how they eat with their friends and how they finish each other's tiffins. That makes Indu plan the box accordingly – one parantha for sharing and one for Rahul or Manisha to eat. This way, at least they will eat something from their own tiffins too.

(A consistent observation across our study has been that the mum packs in extra food to ensure that her child has at least something from his own nutritious and hygienically packed tiffin).

The next worry on Indu's mind is about ensuring that all her effort is not wasted, so she needs to ensure that both the children have what she has prepared for them and actually carry their boxes with them. She knows very well that children need an excuse to leave the tiffin-box at home and rush to school. So she herself puts the tiffin-box in their school bags.

She also realizes that she needs to sit with Rahul, since he is the more finicky eater. She quickly reviews whatever Rahul has learnt for his class test today, just to be sure that he has done his lessons well. Once he is through with eating and Indu is aptly satisfied, she hurries him to leave for the bus stop; it is almost 7am.

After both the kids have left for school, Indu is by herself. She starts to think about how hectic mornings are. She also wonders how her friend Anita, who is a working woman apart from being a mother, manages just fine.

(Not surprisingly, the working women we met were more receptive to ready-to-eat/ready-to-cook products. Nonetheless, there is a strong desire to feel involved in the food she cooks and serves to her family, and products which offer her this flexibility seem to suit her well. She is also less ruled by stringent 'beliefs' about food practices (which are mostly culturally dictated). She expects a certain amount of independence in her own regimen, and thus allows a certain amount of independence to the child as well).

Rahul's Story

Let us now look at what 9-year-old Rahul's day is like. Rahul shares his room with his sister Manisha. Mum wakes them both up precisely at 6.00am. They are allowed a grace period of ten minutes more, but those ten minutes seem to fly in just worrying that they will be over, too soon. Mornings are typically depressing for Rahul. He has to be up when the whole world is sleeping. It is so dark outside that he needs to put the light on in the room. With eyes half shut, he gets out of the bed thinking, 'yet another day of two maths classes consecutively'. Tuesdays are the worst days on Rahul's school timetable: no games period and an overdose of least-interesting maths, and there is nothing that he can do about it. He heads to the bathroom lazily, only to find it already occupied by Manisha. These girls take an awfully long time in everything they do – they complicate even simple things in life. He stands at the door and keeps knocking until Manisha comes out of the bathroom fuming with annoyance. These younger brothers are such pests – she has been begging Mum for a separate room to herself.

Rahul, unbothered, goes to the bathroom and brushes his teeth in less than a minute. For him it is a mere formality to satisfy the ever-questioning and doubting parent breed. He finishes with his morning ablutions and shouts out for Mum for his uniform – a pair blue of shorts with a white shirt.

Donning his uniform, he wonders when he will be grown up enough to reach the senior classes, so that he can start wearing trousers and not these child-like shorts. After all, does Dad ever wear shorts to his office?

(Child nutrition experts tell us that the 8–12 year old is growing very fast physically, with rapid increases in height and bone formation. Psychologically, he is undergoing a phase of social and emotional development and seeking self-identity. This makes him very sensitive about his appearance; his social acceptance by friends and teachers means a lot to him, whether it is the kind of clothes he wears, the kind of food he eats or the behaviour he exhibits, and thus everything that helps him conform to social norms is important.)

It is amazing to see the transition that happens in Rahul once he is fully up and awake. He is like a butterfly who simply cannot stay still for more than a moment. He is occupied primarily with vicious ideas of how to get on Manisha's nerves, until she whiningly cries out to Mum complaining about Rahul's little taunts. Right now, he is aping her in a funnily distorted way.

There is a restlessness in Rahul which starts early morning and seems to stay for the whole day. He even talks and eats as if there is a spring attached to him, and cannot seem to settle down even for a few minutes.

(From infancy itself, an exploration and testing of boundaries is the basic instinct that helps babies grow and develop. As the child gets older, societal boundaries and restrictions are gradually put into place to protect and nurture him during the growth process. However, this also creates a conflict in the child when he experiences a subconscious need to be released from the 'trap' that he seems to be in. We see this need, albeit a little muted, in the 8–12-year-old as well. He is subjected to many restrictions and is being reigned in to fit academic, social and familial norms whereas his spirit still searches for space and freedom to be.)

In order to get Rahul in a more constructive mode, Indu reminds him to pack his bag as per the timetable, and check if he has finished his homework. Rahul packs his bag and carries his notebook to the kitchen to show Indu the comments his teacher has written in his diary.

Having satisfied her, he asks her where his socks are and Indu directs him to a corner in the closet. He fetches the socks and when he puts on, he realizes that one of them has a little hole at the tip. Now this is not acceptable, he needs new socks. It is very embarrassing when he has to take off his shoes and walk into the computer room with holes in his socks. He can well imagine how everyone will make fun of him. He complains to Indu about it, and she promises him a new pair and asks him to make do for today.

He looks out for his shoes – the white sneakers if there is a games period and the black ones on regular days. Since it is not his lucky day, and there is no games period, he wears his normal black ones.

(Rahul is at an age widely known as the stage of the competence/industry vs. inferiority conflict, as was propounded by Erik Erikson in his study of the emotional development of children. We see him at a stage of heightened self-consciousness. Peers become the key social agent and the child begins to compare himself with others outside of the family. He is very concerned about how his peers see him. That is why if the class laughs at him he feels deeply hurt. We noticed that he worries a lot about his reputation, and searches constantly for encouragement, approval and reassurance).

Rahul, not interested in the food laid out for him, is busy playing with his ball, until Mum comes and stands beside him to supervise him eating breakfast. She instructs him to gulp down the whole glass of milk and show her his homework, just a quick check on whether the tuition teacher is doing her job properly. Just then, Manisha calls out for Indu because she is unable to find her needlework apparatus, and Indu rushes to look for it.

This gives Rahul a chance to get out of his early morning plight of eating. Taking in anything at this hour is just so difficult when everything is so rushed, and especially when you are going to be 'jailed' for four hours in the morning classes in school. The priority, therefore, is to play as much as possible before he is forced to submit to the drudgery of school.

Manisha steps out all ready to leave, Indu following her with instructions on how she needs to tidy up her wardrobe after school today. She continues to complain about Rahul making her late every day and shouts out a loud 'bye' to her father heading straight out of the house towards the bus stop, while Rahul rushes into the bedroom to say goodbye, expecting some quick pocket money if Dad is in a good mood. He manages a neat Rs 5 out of him and then heads off to catch up with Manisha.

Rahul is thrilled about getting the pocket money to buy himself a snack of his choice from the school canteen during break time. But Rs 5 is a big amount, he thinks of all the possibilities he can productively employ the money for – he could trade some more Pokemon cards or a quick puzzle, or even play a video game with the same money at the playstation in a café nearby.

(Children at this age are very fond of collecting things. Owning large collections is a matter of pride, e.g. Pokemon cards, tazos. There is frequent trade, and highly involved discussions on fakes vs. genuine cards, with excruciating detail on the characteristics of the various monsters.)

On reaching the bus stop, Rahul has not much to do but wait for the bus. The other kids who come to the bus stop are neither his classmates nor friends. It is a boring wait, where Rahul has to stay put at one place without having anything to do but wait. He keeps moving about, taking small steps, kicking stones around, and hopping up and down.

(Our early morning bus stop observations indicate a potential eating occasion for children. We noted that some children were accompanied by their mums/domestic help and were actually fed some fruit or packaged dairy milk at the stop.)

Rahul's school is a fairly typical Indian school, with a strong emphasis on discipline. All the boys must be dressed in white shirts and blue trousers/shorts, while girls must wear white shirts and blue pinafores. There are other musts, like neatly cut nails and neatly tied hair – plaits for girls and army-cut hair for boys. These codes are checked before the start of assembly and anyone who defaults pays a fine and earns a scold and a remark in his diary.

At 8.00am sharp, the assembly starts, with all the kids lined up in the playground for a little prayer, followed by some important early morning announcements. Disciplined and streamlined, the respective sections move in lines towards their classes, much like rows of ants.

The classes look 'morose' too. The class teacher who frequents the class more than the other teachers, decides where each student will sit. You count yourself lucky if you get along with your neighbour, if you are made to sit next to a girl, too bad, and there is only so much that you can do about it.

All the kids move to their respective seats, talking to each other about their regular homework and study-related worries. For Rahul, it is really tough luck – he gets to sit in the front row. That's partly because he is a little shorter than the other boys and partly because the teacher doesn't trust him to behave and not fool around unless he is right under her nose.

Everyone takes out their books as well as their other gadgets – pencil boxes, rulers, etc – some have rather fancy looking boxes, either gifted to them or bought by parents after considerable persistence. Rahul's pencil box is also done up dexterously with stickers of a mysterious-looking, blanket-wrapped skeleton face, and a hyper-muscled cartoon character; his friend's box sports WWF characters.

Thankfully, there are no rules about owning any specific types of pencil boxes. Everyone can have their own kind, depending upon how lucky they are. Someone or other in Rahul's class would get a different looking pen/pencil/eraser every day, which grabbed all the attention in the class. And then, for the next three days, they would all dream of owning something like that.

(It is interesting to note here that the pencil box enjoys a very close relationship with the child. From his perspective, the pencil box is his arena – it belongs solely to him. He has complete authority on the constituents of the box and has a wide variety of child-oriented things he can buy for it. It is something that remains with him through his entire school day, sitting on his desk. At school, it is something he can show off, something that is a reflection of who he is. Teachers don't interfere with it. It is entirely personal and he is possessive about it. The contents of the box are rightfully only his, and he protects them passionately.

Compared to this, the tiffin-box does not evoke the slightest feeling of possessiveness. In fact, he has been taught to share the contents of the box. More importantly it is the mother's arena – an adult arena. It is something that his mother stuffs with things of her choice and it lies in a corner in his bag. During the release period of recess it stands for the 'must do' things of life ('You MUST eat the food in the tiffin'!). It normally has boring things in it. It is something that even his teacher may set rules for. After he gets back from home, the box is inspected and it can be a reason for a reprimand if something is found left in the box. After that, the box goes back to the mother and he has no interaction with it.)

When everyone is settled with their things, the teacher enters the class and everyone stands to greet her. There is absolute silence in the classroom, and Rahul and his peers must follow the teacher's instructions faithfully. There are times when she asks questions, which always seem very difficult, considering the short time one has to answer them. These are the times which demarcate the smart kids from the not-so-smart ones in the class. Everyone tries hard to get that four-letter word from the teacher – GOOD – and hopes that she will forever remember who answered correctly.

For Rahul, too, it is very important to be in the good books of the teacher. If he had his way, he would want her to listen only to him, to care for him and to always favour him above the rest of the class. But then there are good times and bad ones. The last time Rahul forgot to finish his homework and the teacher discovered it, he got scolded in front of the entire class and felt he did not want to study ever again – he hated coming to school and felt like burying himself in the ground and not showing his face to any of his classmates. He had gone so far as to think that now his classmates would also label him a failure, someone they had been instructed by their mums not to befriend. Thank God that misery came to a quick end.

(Referring again to Erik Erikson's competence/industry vs. inferiority conflict theory, if the child (6–12 years old) can find pleasure in learning, being productive and seeking success, he will develop a sense of competence; conversely, if not, he will develop feelings of inferiority.)

Each period is quite similar. The bright side is that these 45-minute periods must also come to an end, and the shrill of the bell at the end of each period is the sweetest music to many young ears.

But nothing sounds as sweet as the bell for the much-awaited recess. That's when Rahul can snap his books shut, shout out loud, and run outside the classroom! This is officially his time. The recess time happens sometime around 10:30/11:30am in Rahul's school. It feels like having been in a pressure cooker where the steam has been building up since morning, but now is the time simply to shut his desk, not worry about things that 'have to be done' and dash madly out into the field to play and chat with friends.

(What makes the recess time so interesting is the fact that it is the first time in the day when he can just be himself. The initial hours of school are normally mundane and he is concerned primarily about academic issues and teacher presence and impressions. It is a time for discipline, sitting inside a closed classroom with only the mind being active. The recess time is his first 'release' from the trap of rules and boundaries. The intensity of this feeling of release is amazing, there seem to be great amounts of pent-up energy that the child needs to burn. It is the first moment in his day that is totally 'free'. Therefore, it becomes a time of frenetic activity, and one sees him and his friends running all over the play fields, giggling, fighting, talking loudly and behaving with abandon. The shortness of the 'release time' and the need to enjoy it as much as he can in this time is almost palpable. Not surprisingly, the time spent on the tiffin is short.)

Even though it is short, the time spent on the tiffin-box is not really something that he wishes to do. If he had his way he would not carry any tiffin-box or water bottle. He wonders why he can't be like the other cool dude senior boys, who never carry tiffin-boxes, because carrying tiffin-boxes and water bottles is such a kiddie thing to do. He would see them simply fool around during recess with ties loosened, joking and picking on the other kids, heading straight to the canteen and buying a samosa or sandwiches, which they would feed on while strolling aimlessly. But not so for poor Rahul, who does have a tiffin-box carefully packed by Mum and which could earn him a potential scold if found uneaten on coming back from school.

So, Rahul plants himself near the play field with his friends to finish his tiffin-box. Rahul's tiffin-box is a regular steel round box, nothing could be more common looking than that. But that's okay, most of the boys have tiffin-boxes which are regular and nothing too fancy. Anyway, it is something one needs to get through as fast as possible to get down to play.

(An interesting cultural read shows us that the 'box', though familiar enough, is not an object that Indians are very close to. Not many objects in our homes are box-like, except perhaps a medicine box. Most jars and containers are rounded; most toys in the child's room are stored in the open, a tub or bucket. Rarely are toys or chocolates sold in boxes. Apart from shoes, very few items are actually packaged in boxes. Even our traditional tiffin boxes are round. Moreover, there seem to be shades of negativity around the very concept of a box. It often stands for closed spaces that are stuffy and uncomfortable. We hear this in references to small houses and small cars, which are often disparagingly called 'dabbas'. Boxes are not part of life but more a symbol of temporariness – boxes are what we pack our things in when we are moving. Overall, there is perhaps a lack of affinity with the very concept of a box. Added to this, the tiffin-box is one area where there has been virtually no innovation in style and looks, especially compared to other children's products, like stationery or toys. The tiffin-box continues to be largely a square/round compartmentalized box with at best a sticker or two, or the addition of a ruler or a spoon on the lid, of limited appeal to toddlers.

In sum, the tiffin-box itself appears to be distant from the child. The interaction with the box has not increased over the years. It is something that belongs to the mother, and for the child it fulfils a simple functional need, not an emotional need. Clearly, there exists an untapped opportunity in this area for marketers to exploit.)

Rahul opens his tiffin-box and discovers that the mustard oil from the pickle has seeped through the corners. He needs to be extra careful in opening the box, else there's a good chance of spoiling his hands or his shirt with it. Rahul worries that it might have spilled in the bag where it was kept and stained his books too. He really can't understand why, despite his complaining ten times over, his mother insists on packing these oily things. Last time it was the 'bhindi' (okra) in the box that had played havoc and had actually spoiled Rahul's favourite drawing book. He did not speak to his mum for the whole day that day. And yet, she's just done it again!

On opening the tiffin-box, Rahul finds an aloo parantha (a wheat pancake stuffed with potatoes). Though the pickle is spicy and thus holds some interest, the parantha is something that he is really bored with. He has a small sample of it and then moves on to the small piece of pickle, carrying it in his hand and sucking it slowly.

(Children have a clear preference for tangy/spicy tastes or food with sharp flavours.)

(The prime focus in the lunch hour is on playing and thus foods that allow children to move around and play while eating are definitely found interesting. Clearly, 'mobile' food is a strong need that should be exploited by marketers.)

Parantha is something that Rahul has never really enjoyed. Just because Mum puts it in with a different filling every day does not make it an any more interesting or appealing addition to his tiffin.

(Anything that is everyday is boring and the child wants constant change. We know he loves to be surprised; he'd be delighted with new and different foods. When asked what he would like to have, the list ran into reams ranging from 'junk' to restaurant food, from south Indian cuisine to Chinese cuisine, from party food to fun food.)

He wishes there was something like chips, creamy wafers, cheese balls – all the things that are crunchy and thus good fun to eat.

(Crunchy foods are a big hit with children. For example, the crackle in the 'magic crackle' is unexpected and never fails to evoke enjoyment.)

A few kids with exotic tiffins proudly show off their food and announce their exclusive treasure 'I have got idlis in my tiffin today', and then wait for everyone to pounce on them, trying eagerly to earn popularity. Rahul, knowing his box is uninteresting, also keeps taking intermittent bites from the other children's tiffin-boxes, more than offering his tiffin to others.

Seemingly satisfied with whatever little he himself ate and offered his friends of one parantha, he still manages to be left with some of it. He simply stuffs the leftovers in his mouth, as if he wants to get rid of then, and then heads straight to the play field. It is certainly better to spend the precious time on playing than forcing himself to linger over that boring stuff.

It has been instinctive for Rahul to select his friends from among only boys. Interactions with girls in his class are best restricted to need-based chats. They simply lack the same interests in life. With boys he can do so much more.

He plays games like thief and cop or hide and seek until the bell rings. There are times when Rahul has also stood watching the senior boys play basketball, and has wondered if he could be included in their teams and play like them.

(Needless to say, playing with friends is extremely important because his world has begun to revolve around his friends. He finds it important to gain social acceptance and experience achievement. Secret codes, shared word meanings and made up language, passwords and elaborate rituals are employed to strengthen the bonds of friendship. Close friends are almost always of the same sex. They have fun playing together, learn by watching and talking to each other; in times of trouble they band together, in times of stress give support, cooperate and share.)

Rahul plays until he hears the much-dreaded end of the pleasurable break time. Reluctantly, he moves back towards the class and, on his way, stops to drink water at the school water cooler which is in the long corridor on the way to the class.

(An important observation here is that beverages are noticeably absent, restricted to plain milk (or milk with an additive) in the morning, and plain water during the day. This is also evident in the fact that as a country we are not big consumers of a variety of beverages. It simply does not occur to mums to pack anything but water.)

Recharged and dishevelled, Rahul returns to the classroom with his group of friends. During this half of the school day, he is more distracted, even though overall energy levels are high. There is the knowledge that the school hours are going to end very soon.

Preparations for the end of the school day start in the 'second last' period. Rahul cleverly keeps only a few belongings out in the last period. As soon as the final bell peals, he walks out with his friends, chatting and talking. He resumes the interesting conversation they were having in the break about his best friend having joined cricket classes in the stadium close to his house and his experiences there. Rahul needs to know every detail because he plans to sell the proposition to his parents.

(Since the child is in a high learning mode, he is extremely inquisitive, highly impressionable and in the process of discovery (c.f. Jean Piaget's stages of cognitive development). He tends to learn most about things he is involved with. Food in the tiffin-box currently has very low involvement, it is just a chore. We could create an opportunity here by encouraging higher involvement – if he is involved in choosing his flavours, textures, etc, this would increase his consumption of the contents as well.)

The conversation between Rahul and his friends takes a turn towards fun jokes about sardars and bald men. They find such jokes extremely funny and enjoy embellishing them with little figments of their own. As they pass the canteen, Rahul quickly runs in to buy himself some chewing gum. There is no greater pleasure than blowing the gum, especially in school. All of a sudden school becomes good fun, right when it is coming to a close. Rahul has to part with his friend, when they reach the buses, lined up ready to leave.

In the bus, too, there are some unwritten rules that must be followed. The juniors sit in the front, while the more privileged seniors can occupy the seats at the back of the bus. Rahul goes and sits in the front, looking longingly towards the back where all the action takes place; it is a pity he cannot be there. But no sweat! He still has lots of friends from other sections who are his bus mates. They shout together, tease people on the road and do all the other things that are great fun, but definitely will not simply just sit in one place.

(Once more, the end of the school day is release time, but of a different nature, because there is no boundary on this release. The bus ride is an occasion for frolic; he is very noisy, giggly and jovial at this time. A famished and thirsty child normally gets home by 2:30 or 3:00pm to the hot lunch that his mother has prepared for him.)

EXTRACTING THE KEY GAPS

Over the last few pages, we have observed in some detail the ways in which mums and children interact with the boxes, and have found several areas of opportunity. Here, we first identify the critical ones from the child's perspective that have a direct implication on product development. Food should be:

- **Mobile** – because he needs to release some of that pent-up energy during recess hour, and playing is his priority. Foods that can be consumed while he is moving around and playing will have enormous appeal.
- **Bite-sized** – serving sizes should suit his appetite; he would feel guilty leaving food or throwing it away.
- **Manipulatable** – because he is nimble with his fingers and needs to stretch and enjoy using them.
- **'Whacky'** – since we know that the recess is a loosening from restriction given the current stiff education system we follow, and the term 'break' takes on loaded meaning in the child's day. Thus, food that is *crunchy/munchy* and *playable* is a big hit.
- **Engaging** – something that the child wants to come back to again and again, as is seen in most successful children's products.
- **Surprising** – always a hit with children, and captures the essence of the 'opening' of the box with a sense of anticipation.

- **'Close-to-a-teen's-world'** – since the need to be older faster is critical.
- **Shareable** – since a large part of his world revolves around friends, and it is important to be together at break time.

BRIDGING THE MUM – CHILD DIVIDE

The mum, as we have seen, plays a critical role, and her needs too must be satisfied; hence the brief to the R&D team, which should satisfy both. The needs of the mums and the desires of the children are compared below.

Mum's needs	Child's desires
Nutritious and healthy	Fun
Replication of the 'thali' – a little bit of everything	Not everyday home food
Filling	Mobile food
Should not spoil easily	
Should not be inedible/unappealing on becoming cold	
Not very spicy	Spicy
Should not be messy to eat (e.g. rice with sambhar)	
Attractive shapes	
Hygienic, fresh	
Crisp	Crisp and crunchy
Tangy	Tangy, fruity, chocolatey
	Surprising formats/experiences on consumption
	Should be able to play with it
	Should be able to run around with it
Give lots of food so that at least some is eaten	Smaller portions of many things

Some specific areas where we could begin working include:

- **Hybrids** – hybrids in different foods seem to hold a lot of appeal amongst the kids. So, a cross between Chinese and Mexican, Mexican and Indian and all such mixes and matches were found interesting. A chowmein as a pizza topping, macaroni stuffed in roti or even a noodle sandwich evoked a great deal of interest.
- **Interest in everyday food** – kids seem to realize that their mums are not simply going to give up on the traditional foods, and hence are even willing to make some compromises to make the regular food taste

and look interesting to them. There were suggestions like strawberry jam filled roti or flavoured rotis.

- **Animated/action-packed food** – for children, food needs to move out of its 'passive' state of simply being there waiting to be eaten. There needs to be 'action' packed in the tiffin, which can make it more interesting and fun to have. Thus, there were ideas from kids like *'blinking food, just like stars shiny and bright'; 'food that changes its colours on eating'.*

- **Empower me** – we have seen how children are in an active learning mode, and seek independence and empowerment in their choices. They would enjoy food if they were involved in the making of it at any point; there is a feeling of ownership of such food, and also a feel-good factor of feeting like an adult who can make choices. An oft-expressed desire – 'if we were given a tiffin with different flavours and we could make something on our own'.

- **Playable food** – this is a critical need, and has been observed at several points in our study. Some ideas from children:
  - 'a tiffin with wheels that can be controlled by a remote control. . . it can go to whoever in our group wants to take a bite' – shareable and playable.
  - 'food in the shape of a ball – can play with it easily'.
  - 'tiffins that mean we can play games with the food inside them'.
  - 'a fruit drink like mango in a mango-shaped pack which can be sucked like a real mango'.
  - 'a yoyo shaped "laddu".'

Over and above this, the *beverage* opportunity is significant. Milk is the only beverage that is consumed in the morning. There are, however, occasional indulgences in soft drinks from the canteen, but this is not encouraged by parents. A 'mobile', tasty and 'happening' drink would certainly appeal to the child, if we made it season-specific . . . thirst quenching, light and energizing in the summer, warm, immunity-building in the winter and hygienic in the monsoons – it would have high appeal with the mums too.

THE ROAD AHEAD

Recognizing the big beverage opportunity, which is currently underutilized, GSK has installed vending machines for milk-based beverages in 60 schools across the four metros in India.

In some Western markets, inspired by the child's desires, we see a typical tiffin-box with products like a nutritious cereal bar, a small pack of juice (150ml), a small box of raisins and a small sandwich. This would ensure that a little bit of the goodness of various things is offered to the child in a form that he likes. Note that the cereal bar is easy to have on the run, the pack of raisins gives nutrition, and children can enjoy tossing them into their mouths, the juice is the thirst quencher with nutrition, in a flavour that the child likes, and can have while chatting with friends or on the way back from school. In addition, the sandwich is the 'proper' meal, but if he does leave it, adequate nutrition has still gone in through the other items.

LEARNINGS FOR COMMUNICATION DEVELOPMENT

Apart from the cues for NPD described above, the study has yielded some invaluable insights for communication. For example:

- The 'community' eating and sharing nature of the consumption vs. a single child's gustatory relish.
- The capture of the 'release' feeling, and the subsequent high energy levels and speed of consumption to leave 'enough time to play'.
- Great-tasting and delectable food.
- A great deal of fun in the process of consumption, tactile interaction with the food.
- Participation of a favourite teacher, or 'approval' of some sort from her.
- Humour – in-the-face, slapstick, with a catchphrase that kids can laugh about and repeat at school to look funny.
- Sensitive handling of the mum's tendency to trivialize at times.

CONCLUSION AND FURTHER THOUGHTS

We draw two sets of inferences from this chapter – one, about how we can take this specific topic further, and two, about how our approach worked and where else it can be used.

Ideation for specific product ideas

For this study, we conducted limited ideation sessions amongst 'creative' mums and children. The next step will be working with consumers on some of the ideas generated with the active participation of various stake-holders – R&D, the ad agency, the 'experts', etc., conducting workshop-like sessions at appropriate sites using typical brainstorming methodologies. Needless to say, as in all brainstorming sessions, many ideas will be wild, but the inspiration will not be short. As the next step to this study, we plan to follow this through.

How microethnography helped

Microethnography enabled a deep psychosocial understanding of the child and his environment. It was only by means of the observations that we could understand his disappointments, fears, what insulted him, how big a role various people played in his life, how his mind worked and how he interacted with others, etc. This understanding gave a ref-erential context to the specific issue that we were exploring (i.e. tiffin consumption behaviour).

Specifically, we valued the way we were able to witness the child's community behaviour, his form of play, his energy levels, his restlessness. We understood the magnitude of important issues like his disinterest in food, the ploys to hide leftovers and the criticality of distraction in food consumption, as well as the consumption process itself – his playing with food, his need to chat and gossip while eating, his inclusion of food in his games, the speed of consumption, the act of licking, rolling, etc.

A key advantage of this process was the easy interpersonal dynamics that this method permitted. Despite the fact that we were studying a very young age group and most of our researchers were much older, the breakdown of barriers happened very fast. Children were very relaxed, entertained and not perturbed at all by an adult's presence. It was easy for us to get them to joke with us, sing to us and play the fool with us – all very important in understanding their feelings and attitudes. As a process, both the researcher and the respondents enjoyed it.

Other categories where microethnography could be useful

- **Personal care** – where people are normally hesitant to speak about the real reasons/insecurities which compel them to take certain decisions.
- **Automotive experience** – the driving experience and the factors that go into affecting brand decisions are often not articulated or recalled well in a discussion scenario. Here, again, microethnography could throw up invaluable insights.

- **Baby care** – especially useful because not only is it difficult to persuade mothers of infants into a research venue, but, more importantly, because the entire arena of motherhood and mother's love, and the deep seated worries and insecurities, are issues that would be best understood through participative observation.
- **Cellphone behaviour** – another area which left to the recall of respondents almost always throws up findings that are superficial. Observation of this behaviour would help to understand the real behaviours and motivations therein.
- **NPD for a rural population** – the rural segment is particularly difficult to research for NPD because their lives and worlds are rather distant from ours. This methodology would help us understand their contexts and worlds, and let us observe product consumption and the gaps therein.

REFERENCES

Feldman, M. (1995), *Strategies for Interpreting Qualitative Data*. Sage.
Guber, S. and Berry, J. (1993), *Marketing To and Through Kids*. McGraw-Hill.
Stewart, A. (1998), *The Ethnographer's Method*. Sage.

Chapter Twenty-seven

Becoming Cultural Architects: How to Drive the Influence of Research on Company Culture

Paul Buckley[a] and Hilary Perkins[b]

This chapter describes how consumer research can become an integral and vital part of the business process, underpinning every action and in so doing, actually changing company culture.

INTRODUCTION

Many client-side research groups seek to challenge and change the paradigms on which their businesses operate into more consumer–centric ones. This chapter describes how a single, global segmentation study catalysed one organization into rethinking many of its most important internal processes, including the allocation of resources across countries, brand positioning and the prioritization of innovation opportunities. It contains lessons for others seeking to maximize the cultural impact of their work.

[a] Market Research Director (Europe, Middle East and Africa), Avon.
[b] Head of Research and Innovation, Beam Global Spirits and Wine.

Market Research Best Practice. Edited by P. Mouncey and F. Wimmer.

THE ALLIED DOMECQ EXPERIENCE

Many companies claim to put the consumer (and hence consumer research) at the heart of their business strategy, yet relatively few truly achieve this goal. Allied Domecq is the second largest spirits and wine company in the world, yet, until recently, we did not possess a globally consistent way to look at our business from a consumer perspective. At the centre of our corporate vision for future growth is the provision of better consumer experiences to enable us to build the value of our brands. To deliver on this has necessitated substantial organizational and procedural change, but we have taken significant strides along this road in the last two years. By combining the research skills of our in-house team and those of our agency partners, Research International, we have enabled research to play a prominent part in redefining the framework against which investment and brand strategy decisions are taken.

Prior to 2001, the company had conducted a variety of U&A studies for different drinks categories using inconsistent sample definitions and different methodologies. Whilst providing a patchwork of local insight, there was no ability to address more fundamental questions, and consequently little account was taken of the desires of consumers when key strategic decisions were made. During 2001, the situation changed with the emergence of a more marketing-centric vision for the company, within which the research group would have to become more proactive. It quickly became obvious that more fact-based decision making would require a reassessment of our existing information strategy and this led in turn, to the team drawing up a comprehensive brief that would attempt to answer multiple questions simultaneously.

Within most FMCG sectors there is now an abundant supply of product alternatives, which requires marketers to recognize that the overriding purpose of marketing is no longer about smarter selling, but instead about simplifying and guiding consumer choice. In emotionally driven categories, such as spirits and wines, in which rational benefits rank relatively low on the decision ladder, the brief needed to find a balance between seeking the hard data typically used for resource allocation discussions and the softer data to allow us to build consumer relevance for our brand propositions.

The ambitious aim was to conduct an in-depth quantitative segmentation study which would identify the primary drivers of consumer drink choice across all alcoholic beverages, and provide this at a brand level for the spirits category. There would also be great cultural challenges, as the study would need to be conducted in the 12 countries which collectively made up around 90% of the company's profitability – these ranged from Korea and Japan to Brazil, Mexico, Spain and Germany. As well as the different social relationships that exist with alcoholic beverages in each of these countries, we also needed to overcome the internal perception that no common solution could cater for the nuances of any individual population, and hence that the study would provide little locally actionable information.

There are many examples of grand segmentation study designs that have promised much but delivered relatively little, despite substantial investment of both time and money from the companies concerned, and which subsequently faded from view relatively quickly. There appear to be two primary reasons for the premature demise of these studies. First, some have strictly limited predictive foundations, in the sense that they don't explain current (and hence future) consumption behaviour. Whilst it might be academically interesting to produce a clustering of category users based on psychographic or lifestyle factors, the business benefit is likely to be small if the behaviour across groups is largely similar. Secondly, some solutions that do offer some predictive capacity have little intuitive relationship to the kind of criteria that are typically used to define brand and commercial strategy, and hence getting buy-in and commitment to action from groups outside marketing can be elusive.

What we hope to show here is how a single study has become a touchstone for a consumer orientation that has now permeated the vast majority of processes and departments within a multinational business to become a genuine cultural catalyst. The reasons for success, as we'll discuss, have included excellence in the research process itself, but, significantly more important, has been the communication agenda and the active engagement of as many senior stakeholders from the outset.

In all we anticipated needing 3000 interviews per market. That seemed likely to pose several problems, both logistical and financial. After some initial scoping calculations, a rough project budget of £6 million was arrived at to cover qualitative questionnaire development, quantitative fieldwork, data analysis, multiple presentational workshops and software development. At this stage we were faced with the decision to suboptimize what we considered the ideal design to make the cost more acceptable or to argue to the Board that investment on this scale was justified if we were genuinely to be considered leaders within our industry.

Fortuitously, we had also embarked on developing a new vision for the research group based around the same construct that we use to define

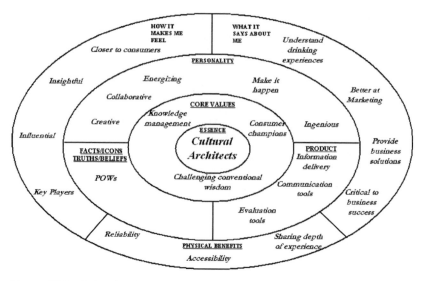

Figure 27.1 Cultural architects.

how our brand positionings will resonate with their target audiences. At the heart of this framework, we aspire to have as our essence shaping a more proactive future by becoming *Cultural Architects* (Figure 27.1). If we were to be true to this vision, we would need to adopt a less risk-averse attitude and demand to be held more accountable to demonstrate the commercial payback that research can bring.

The decision to grant us the funding in full led to the setting-up of a project management team made up of senior members of Research International and Allied Domecq, and an external review panel made up of independent research consultants to provide challenge at key milestones. We also recruited a dedicated project manager to manage the timeline and make certain that agreed actions were followed up promptly.

The first phase was an extensive round of qualitative work based around individual depth interviews to establish the consumer language to describe all aspects of drinking consumption and purchasing behaviour. Rather than adopt a prescribed solution based on predetermined factors, the overall design for the quantitative questionnaires took the more pragmatic approach of including sections of any likely factors that might be important in determining consumer choice.

The final design included psychographics (attitudes to life, attitudes to drinking, etc.), demographics (sex, age, etc.), situational variables (venue, group composition, daypart, mood, etc.) and emotive reasons for choice.

This yielded a questionnaire of 90 minutes in length, so details on purchasing behaviour were incorporated into a separate, leave-behind instrument (which achieved a response rate of over 90% in most countries – this would seem to indicate that respondents found the experience an enjoyable and engaging one).

Following extensive multivariate statistical analysis, the solution that provided the most efficient explanation of brand choice was based on three factors: People split male/female and by age brand (<30, 30–44, 45+); Occasion location/type (in/out of home and with/without a meal); and Want state (a cluster solution of multiple emotive reasons for brand/category choice). The 3-dimensional POW matrix formed by using these as axes has been used as the primary analysis tool for many applications of the study data. (It was also subsequently featured in an article on the front page of the London *Financial Times*.) The word 'POW' now appears in the vast majority of documents that our marketing team produces, both for internal use and in dealings with our agency partners.

In some respects this would appear to resemble a standard needs-based segmentation. However, each of the seven Want states defined by the solution represents a combination of emotive drivers for choice and the overarching mood associated with a particular drinking experience, which, used in conjunction with the other two dimensions of the solution, provides a uniquely holistic explanation for the repertoire consumption behaviour that we observed in the alcoholic drinks category.

At first sight the total of 168 potential POW combinations might appear far too many to analyse fully, but within any one country the bulk of consumption occasions are concentrated in only 20–50 POWs. This still represents a large and complex analysis task, but by no means an impossible one.

To make the solution as internationally comprehensible as possible, we not only gave intuitive titles to each of the Want states, we also gave them each an associated colour. The seven Want states have a set of core values that attempt to convey the primary themes of the choice statements aligned most closely with each:

- Let Loose and Lively (Orange) – excitement, gregarious, fun loving;
- Let's Drink To That (Blue) – special, rewarding, flirty;
- Shedding The Day's Baggage (Yellow) – transformation, changing gears, uplifting;
- Relaxing Comfort (Brown) – soothing, tranquillity, winding down;
- Delicious Delights (Purple) – conviviality, enhancement, treat;

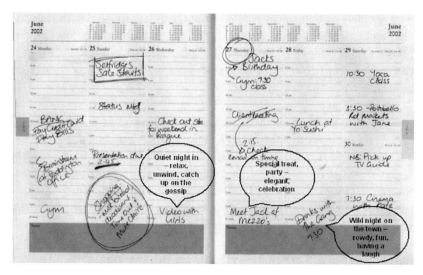

Figure 27.2   Want states revealed by diary entries.

- Social Commitment (Green) – easily amused, free spirited, social awkwardness;
- Subdued Pleasure (Red) – pace yourself, sociable, friendly.

Figure 27.2 shows how several different Want states might reveal themselves for the same person in a relatively short timescale. The week might begin with an informal night at home with friends. At this point they might be in a tranquil, winding down kind of mindset – which typifies the 'Relaxing Comfort' Want state. The following day, they go out for a celebratory meal and they move into the romantic mindset associated with the 'Let's Drink To That' Want state. Finally, they go out on Friday night with a large group and have a much more hedonistic, rebellious occasion driven by the 'Let Loose and Lively' Want state.

The colours have now superseded the text descriptions in the way we refer to the solution internally. Indeed, the notion of getting a bit Orange (the Let Loose and Lively Want colour) is part of the office vernacular when talking about the weekend's activities with colleagues.

The first question that we were faced with was to consider how best to convey the scale and depth of the study to the Board sponsors. Throughout the development process we devoted as much time as possible to presenting the information in a manner that was assimilated more easily by senior management in the business. Crucial to this was a reluctance to talk the language of the research community, and to replace results that talked about sample percentages, etc. by the amounts of money that different opportunities appeared to offer. We therefore converted the survey results into a map of the profit distribution for all the major spirit brands in each country.

For the first time, we were able to articulate the current DNA at the heart of any of our brands in a common way across the globe, by showing the way that the profitability was split across a number of the circumstantial dimensions included in the study (Figure 27.3).

Following a successful initial presentation, we were asked to make a detailed analysis of the data the central focus of two major avenues of strategic review by the company. First, we demonstrated for the local management in each country how the volume of their portfolio was distributed currently across the POW framework and how this might be optimized in the future. Not only did this allow us to see the true competitive set that exists for growth (outside the confines of traditional product composition), it also identified the changes in brand imagery that would be necessary to optimize the fit with consumer desires. For each major brand/market combination in the Allied Domecq portfolio, we have now identified both the key POWs in which we need to maintain existing volume, but also those in which we need to invest to recruit more drinkers to the franchise to underpin future volume growth. This involved extensive analysis, not only of the scale of opportunity that each POW combination represented, but also how accessible that profit pool might actually be given the level of competitive A&P spend from the other prominent brands with significant volume in that POW.

The shift in culture to viewing the competitive arena as being brands with similar consumer Wants profiles also led us to evolve the brand and advertising tracking we conducted across our major markets. We are also now able to measure the degree to which we have improved our association with key defining characteristics underlying the target Want state for our brand through our communications.

The alcoholic beverage industry has one advantage not enjoyed by other FMCG categories, in that the On Trade provides a specific environment where the emotional proposition behind brands can be brought to life. As a manufacturer, we are still faced with several key decisions about where and how to allocate our resources given the huge diversity in the nature of the On Trade universe of outlets. The segmentation study has been instrumental in bringing about a revolution in the way

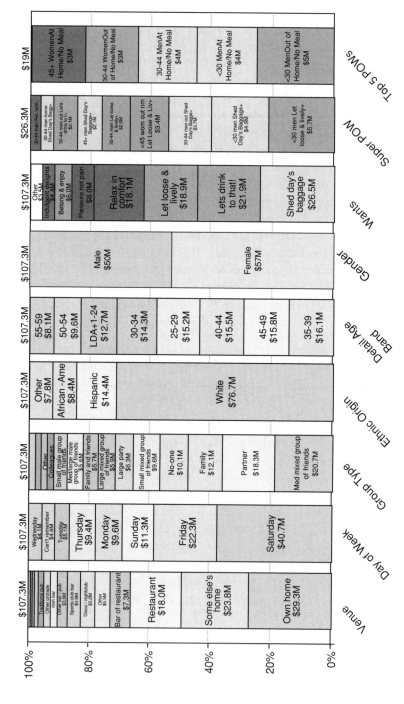

Figure 27.3 Splitting profitability across circumstantial dimensions.

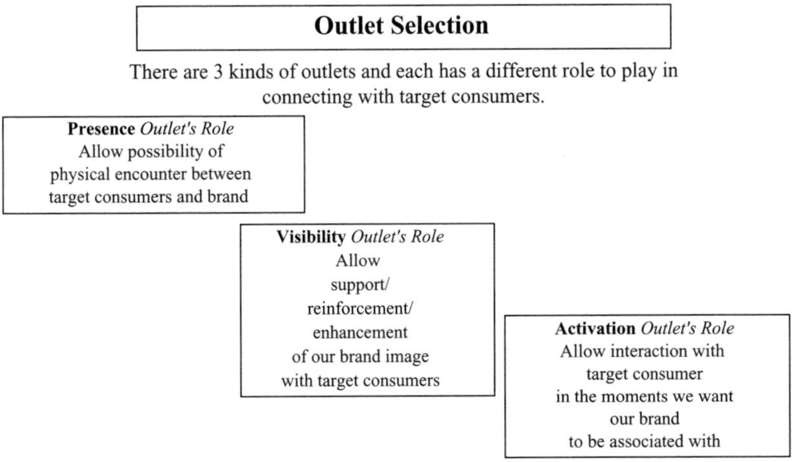

Figure 27.4 A hierarchy of importance for On Trade-driven markets.

that Allied Domecq has thought about this strategically, and also in the way we have organized the activities of our field sales forces around the world. For our major On Trade-driven markets, we have developed a hierarchy of importance that reflects how any given brand will seek to represent itself in that outlet (Figure 27.4).

Using some of the critical distinguishing factors behind each of the segmentation Want states, we have been able to design a short questionnaire for the sales force to complete when they visit an outlet and talk with the owner/bar staff. This has enabled us to classify each of our priority Activation outlets by their predominant Want state, and hence identify which of our brand set we should be targeting at each. It also determines the style of activation, in that the mood of the bar promotion should reflect the mindset and mood associated with the target POW. The development of creative materials to support these types of initiatives has become significantly more efficient and impactful as a consequence.

We also showed how the different cultural associations with alcohol that exist around the world were reflected in our solution, and how this might be used to inform our innovation strategy. This has led to the incorporation of segmentation study data as a mandatory component of all Annual Brand Plan submissions, and as part of the justification for requests for innovation development. A matrix of the most promising multinational POW opportunities has been constructed to focus our product development resources.

As the results were comparable on a global basis, we were invited to assist with a review of resources allocation across countries. For the first time, the future consumer potential of a market could be included alongside more short-term portfolio profitability arguments. As a consequence, we have subsequently chosen to reduce the emphasis of some countries at the expense of those in which the consumer profit pools appear more accessible.

However, the overall success of the project has not been driven by influencing senior management alone. It has been equally important to engage the remainder of the staff, particularly those with only a peripheral understanding of marketing. As a consequence, we have been ambassadors for the work by presenting highlights at many team and regional group meetings. We have also taken every opportunity to get articles published in the in-house magazine (Figure 27.5), and one Head Office conference room has now been decorated with material from the study.

One spin-off of this missionary work was to consider using the data to support our stance on responsible drinking. Allied Domecq is in the forefront of industry efforts to curtail the damage, both social and physical, that can result from excessive alcohol consumption. To aid discussions with both the World Health Organisation and the British Government

Figure 27.5 The power of magazine articles to spread the word!

on the causes and consequences of binge drinking, we converted all the data on drinks consumed on all occasions cited by the respondents into units of pure alcohol. We were then able to identify the common factors that seemed to trigger excessive drinking behaviour across the 12 countries that were included in the study.

Other groups within the organization are now independently using the POW framework to shape their own thinking, by aligning their efforts with the overall marketing vision. For instance, our US Finance team has classified the Want colour for each piece of promotional material that we use to produce a regular summary of the market pressure we are applying with our brand portfolio against the focal POWs in our business. This, in turn, has allowed us to divert monies away from non-core activities so we can better deliver against where we need to.

Becoming noticed as a group that can deliver results that permeate the overall company culture has other benefits. It has now become substantially easier to get funding for more speculative research projects, whereas before there were many in the business who thought of research as a cost rather than as a form of brand investment. We now find it much easier to secure money to talk to our consumers about their lives, rather than concentrating purely on the push of our own manufacturing and branding agenda.

Our key learnings are that for researchers to become genuine Cultural Architects in business, we don't need to borrow the skills of management consultants, we just need to believe more in the value of our own talents and be a little braver in asking for the money to prove it. Finally, we must remember that the life of any research is not run when the report is produced; the onward communication of implications is the overriding responsibility of any 21st century client-side researcher.

REFERENCE

Financial Times Monday September 30th, 2002, p. 1.

Chapter Twenty-eight

Show Me Your Home and I Will Tell You Who You Are, or Building Homes Based on Consumers' Values and Lifestyles

Lena Gilchrist[a], Britt-Marie Eriksson[b] and Olof Eriksson[c]

This chapter will describe how research, along with the use of technology, can be applied to various decision-making processes throughout the different stages of production and marketing cycles of real estate.

INTRODUCTION

This chapter will show how research helped a traditional construction company develop a new approach towards marketing, by gaining insight into the deep meaning embedded in the phrase 'a home'. The company moved its position from mere functionality towards market and consumer orientation.

[a]Country Manager, Ipson, Sweden.
[b]Marketing Manager, Lafarge Roofing.
[c]Marketing Manager Skanska.

Market Research Best Practice. Edited by P. Mouncey and F. Wimmer.
© 2007 John Wiley & Sons, Limited.

By applying a wide range of methods – qualitative, quantitative, observational and desk-research – a wealth of results was achieved. The researchers and client created an interactive intranet reporting system, containing photos, animations, statistics, etc. This scaleable system was designed for continuous and interactive updating and analysis. Furthermore, planners, designers, architects, engineers and other professionals within the client's organization can use the system easily and creatively throughout planning and production cycles.

BACKGROUND

Skanska, a company founded in 1887, is one of the world's leading companies within construction-related services and project development. Skanska had a turnover of approx imately. SEK 125 billion (2005), around 54 000 employees (2005) and is listed on the Stockholm Stock Exchange (now Stockholmsbörsen). Skanska operates in 23 permanent markets, with Sweden, the US, UK, Denmark, Finland, Norway, Poland, the Czech Republic, Argentina and Hong Kong as some of the major ones. Skanska's mission is to develop and service the physical environment for consumers' living, working and travelling needs.

Skanska is one of the leading construction companies in Sweden and had, until 1992, benefited from a stable and relatively competition-free market. In 1992, the Swedish 'housing market' was deregulated, which resulted in a significant change for Skanska and the whole construction business.

Prior to 1992, Skanska's largest customer was 'Allmännyttan' – the housing corporations owned by the city councils. These corporations were formed in order to make it possible for the city councils to provide reasonable housing for their inhabitants. These city-council-owned housing corporations operated without any profit interests and could therefore offer rents below the actual market values. Having Allmännyttan as its major customer meant that Skanska had relatively little need to market its products directly to the consumer.

After the 1992 market deregulation, Skanska found itself in a new position. Since the city councils no longer had the same responsibility to provide housing, Skanska found itself facing fiercer competition and a new market situation. Suddenly, Skanska had to start marketing its projects and services on the 'free' market directly to the consumer. It had to move its position from being a supplier towards becoming a market leader with strong knowledge about its potential customers.

The first few years were years of trial, error and learning. Marketing and consumer insights were scarce within the company, and there were hardly any marketing people employed in key positions within Skanska. Moreover, most of the major decisions, marketing and otherwise, were taken by engineers rather than marketers.

The real-estate development process that was followed at the time had a predetermined route. When an interesting object was found, it was purchased and developed. The housing units that were built were presumed to fit the buyer/consumer, rather than the other way around. As a result, while some housing units sold well, others, without an apparent explanation, didn't sell at all.

This route soon proved to be irrational. The industry could not afford to build houses that no one wanted to live in. Slowly, Skanska, and indeed the whole industry, started to change their strategies towards becoming more consumer- and market-oriented. There was, at the same time, a growing need to individualize housing – to create target-group-specific housing rather than standardized homes.

The evolution of competition has been one of the driving forces in most markets to evolve from competing on product value to competing on service value or solution value. This is discussed in a book by Anders Gustafsson and Michael D. Johnson (2003), and the evolution is presented in a model, as shown in Figure 28.1.

This model is applicable to the housing market, where there has been a need to shift from manufacturing standardized production housing to producing 'homes', with a strong focus on customization. It is very difficult to survive only on the basis of being good at manufacturing.

BUILDING A KNOWLEDGE BANK – AN INTERACTIVE SEGMENTATION TOOL

By 1999, Skanska was carrying out specific market research within various construction projects. The objectives of the different research projects were to understand the market for each housing project separately. However, Skanska soon realized that there was a growing need to coordinate

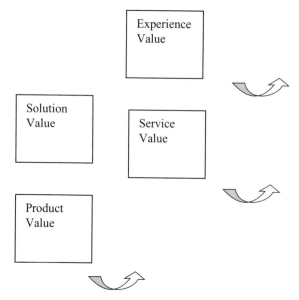

Figure 28.1 The evolution of competition.

the knowledge that was accumulated from different research projects within the organization. By 2000, Ipsos-Eureka and Skanska began to explore the possibility of carrying out a more general segmentation study. Skanska wanted to be able to define and understand the major market segments that should be targeted closely.

With that in mind, and after commissioning this exciting project, a segmentation study was launched. The study was based on consumers' attitudes and values instead of just functional attributes. The approach was based on the notion that houses strongly reflect the values and lifestyles of their owners. A house, indeed a home, is very much a mirror of our own values and aspirations in life. When buying a new home we are not just purchasing a physical house with a roof and walls, but we are also buying into, and defining, a lifestyle. Thus, capturing people's attitudes about living and housing is essential for understanding the arena within which construction companies act.

A large-scale quantitative survey, based on telephone interviews with 1500 individuals, was carried out by Ipsos-Eureka. Thirteen segments were created as a result of the survey. The segments differed in regard to attitudes, values and expectations regarding their homes. Each segment was also described in demographic terms. In Figure 28.2 the important segments are shown with regard to where we find them geographically.

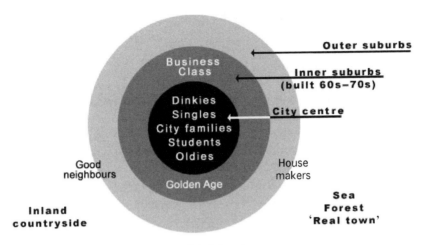

Figure 28.2 Important segments and their locations.

Apart from the information we had about the segments from our study, additional information was added to the segments as they were run through several databases. By doing so, each segment's media habits, specific interests, etc. could be defined. Skanska also used a geographic information system to plot the segments throughout Sweden, in order to know where it would be appropriate to build suitable houses for each segment.

At that point we had a lot of quantitative data about each segment, but we still needed to gain further insight into each segment's future housing plans and aspirations. One of the interesting questions we needed to answer was what each segment would like to change in their housing situation if they could, and how they would go about it. This was a strategically important question for Skanska, since knowledge about people's future needs and dreams could, and should, influence future construction projects.

The next stage of this project was launched. To gain qualitative insight, 120 in-depth at-home interviews were carried out with respondents belonging to 9 (of 13) segments. Each interview took two hours to conduct and was accompanied by observation, photo-taking and video-filming. We covered a range of different aspects of a home, such as:

- choice of geographical area;
- important criteria when choosing a neighbourhood;
- indoor preferences regarding the layout of the house, the design of the kitchen and bathroom, sizing of different rooms, etc.;

- outdoor preference regarding the garden, the exterior, play-area, etc.;
- indoor and outdoor activities around the home;
- lifestyle and values;
- dreams and aspirations for the future.

This vast amount of information had to be analysed and reported back to Skanska. Instead of a traditional report, the idea of an interactive reporting system was formed. With the help of modern technology, an intranet site was designed and all information was then gathered there.

Even if the original set-up cost proved to be higher than a traditional report, the advantages of such a reporting system and knowledge bank proved to be many:

- it was interactive, up to date and easy to upgrade;
- it could bring the consumer alive, with pictures, sounds, colours and emotions;
- it was easier to access for a larger number of people;
- it was scaleable, easy to expand.

The segments were presented to Skanska with a wealth of information about each, complete with sound, pictures, collages, verbatim and analysis.

In addition to demographic and statistical background information, each segment's lifestyle, home preferences, values and ambitions, hopes and aspirations were described. The site captured how people live, work, spend their leisure time, spend time within and outside their homes, attitudes to each room in the house (kitchen, living room, bedroom, bathroom) with words and pictures, sounds and movies.

In the following example we will show some highlights from one segment – Business Class – and a few examples of the presentation on the site regarding this segment.

Business Class

This segment comprises families with high incomes and good careers. They are able to live more or less in the type of house and area they want. They prefer a new house, which needs less maintenance. They can afford to purchase the services they need, for example, gardening and cleaning. This segment leads a busy life, with a lot of interests out of the house – golf, for example. The children in these families attend a lot of activities. The family enjoys travelling and is able to enjoy several trips abroad per year. They often own at least one other property – a villa by the sea or a house near the ski slopes. They have a very active social life and the house must be able to cater for all the needs required when having big functions.

Since they are career-minded and work plays an important role, they must be able to work from a distance, which means that they have high demands when it comes to functionality and technology.

The kitchen is one of the most important rooms. Cooking together with friends at the weekends is quite common, which means that it is very much a social area. The kitchen is a 'show-off' room, where it's obvious that appliances are of a very high class.

Figure 28.3 shows how we mix text and pictures on the site to make it easy to understand the thoughts of the target group. This page (page 1 of 3) is describing the view on kitchens.

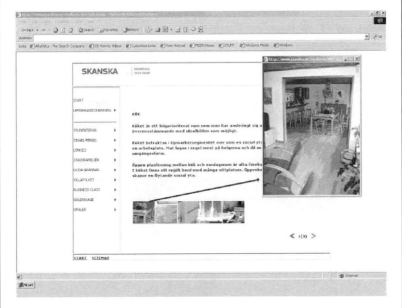

Figure 28.3   The Business Class segments view of kitchen.

All people attending the focus groups produced their own collages, some of the more typical ones are available on the intranet. The one shown in Figure 28.4 was produced by a woman who dreams of material like wood, stone and tiles. The kitchen is described as the most important place in the house and it's filled with the latest kitchen appliances.

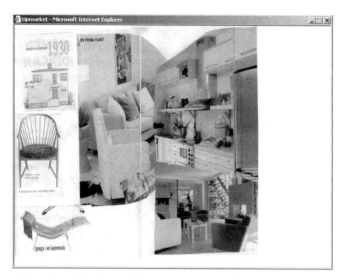

Figure 28.4   One 'Business Class' woman's collage.

The key values found in the collages in this target group were:

Freedom, Security, Intelligence and Style

To make it even easier to understand each segment, one typical person describes his/her own values, lifestyle and dreams in a film, as shown in Figure 28.5.

Figure 28.5   Film footage from a representative of the segment.

Different professionals within the organization have access to the information gathered on the site. Project managers, production managers, architects, interior designers and marketing people can search for specific information about specific segments easily and accessibly. It is also possible for some people outside the organization, such as advertising agencies and professionals within the city councils, to have limited access to the site.

The site/knowledge bank has been developed and changed continuously as new knowledge is gathered and new insights are added. For example, results from a study about attitudes to skyscrapers and a study about environmental issues were added to the site.

A STRATEGIC TOOL THROUGHOUT PRODUCTION AND MARKETING

The knowledge bank/intranet site we built is designed to be used throughout all stages of the production and marketing cycle. From purchasing a site to construction, production and selling of real estate, engineers, architects and marketers are aided by the knowledge provided within this site. With the help of the site/knowledge bank, consumers' needs, demands and lifestyles can now inspire the thousands of decisions that are made throughout each and every construction project. Figure 28.6 illustrates the internal process at Skanska.

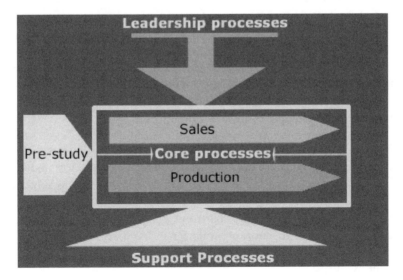

Figure 28.6 Skanska's internal process.

Skanska intends to add all new knowledge to the intranet site/knowledge bank. By making the site dynamic and by creating a common ground for new development, a more market-sensitive approach can be achieved.

Using the site, teams working on each specific stage of a project can look for specific answers. For example, when planning the purchase of a construction site and defining the project, the project team can find information about the potential of the site by asking (and answering) the following question: which segment would be likely to buy a home here, and why?

Throughout the project, the project team can have the following questions as guidelines: how should we design the houses inside and outside with a specific market segment in mind? What does the specific segment prefer, and what are they willing to pay for?

At the next stage, the site can help the sales team better understand how the project can be marketed and sold, and which arguments will trigger a purchase.

PRACTICAL APPLICATIONS

An example of the practical application of the segmentation model and the knowledge bank was the work done with interior design. Three teams of interior designers created three different home interior-design style packages – a traditional, a contemporary and a modern home interior. The concepts were then tested among the different segments using focus groups. The resulting analysis showed how different segments perceive and value different designs, and what kind of kitchens, bathrooms, flooring, etc. each segment prefers and is willing to pay for. Some conclusions seemed to apply to most segments:

- Most homes don't have enough storage space, and there is a great demand for more and better storage possibilities. Skanska is about to launch a project in order to further develop smart storage solutions within the home.
- With the lack of spare time that most families have today, 'easy-to-clean' space is of the utmost importance. As a consequence of this finding, wall-hung toilets have become standard in many new homes built by Skanska.

- Light and light fittings are key issues for the target groups, especially spotlights. Since the Swedish winter is long and dark, it is important to have sufficient light inside the home.
- Swedish people dream of a fireplace. It represents security and cosiness, values that are important to many Swedes.

This information, together with segment-specific conclusions, is accessible to Skanska's architects and designers, and is used when planning future projects.

Another practical example of using the knowledge bank is when a project team recently used the site while planning, executing and marketing a real-estate project.

In the south of Sweden, just outside the city of Malmö, an estate called Fjärilsbyn (Butterfly Village) was developed. Targeting specific segments and creating individualized concepts, the team built 29 houses with three segments in mind (Golden Age, Good Neighbours and Home-makers). The work was based wholly on the knowledge found in the segmentation study. Three distinct types of houses were created to match each specific segment/target group. The project manager, Magnus Carlsson, says:

'We used the insights on the site right through the project definition phase and in all discussions with the architects. We also designed all the sales material with the knowledge as a base. It was very useful and there were many decisions that were made based on this. Before we used to design houses that would suit as many different categories as possible – now we have the courage to make a choice and be more stringent. All houses were sold easily, and when we compare the buyers with the proposed target groups, it was a perfect fit. We have changed our way of working.'

CONCLUSION

By using the segmentation approach and gathering all information about each segment in an interactive knowledge bank, Skanska can now, with much greater accuracy, create homes that fit consumers needs rather than trying to find consumers to fit to homes already planned and built. For Skanska, as for the whole construction industry, it is important to be able to market and launch the right product at the right time for the right target group/segment. The segmentation approach helps Skanska in this delicate process, with the resulting benefits of lower costs and easy-to-sell homes.

There were, of course, some difficulties in introducing the segmentation approach and tool within the organization. In an organisation populated by creative entrepreneurs, used to making their own decisions, there was (and is) a strong concentration on logistics, rather than marketing awareness. The segmentation tool therefore fills an important educational function, as it inspires users to understand the market and the consumers better.

REFERENCE

Gustafsson, A. and Johnson, M. (2003), *Competing in a Service Economy: How to Create a Competitive Advantage through Service Development and Innovation*, Jossey Bass.

Chapter Twenty-nine

Market Research, Accountability, Outcome-focus and Service Standards in the Australian Government Public Sector: How Market Research has Significantly Improved the Reformation of the Australian Government Public Sector

Peter Bycroft[a], Catherine Argall[b]
and Natalie Wearne[c]

This chapter provides an illustrated history of market research in the public sector in Australia, including a case study of the application of market reasearch in the Child Support Agency.

[a]Managing Director, Corporate Diagnostics Pty Ltd.
[b]Chief Executive Officer, Medicare Australia.
[c]TNS Social Research

Market Research Best Practice. Edited by P. Mouncey and F. Wimmer.
© 2007 John Wiley & Sons, Limited.

INTRODUCTION

Like its overseas compatriots, since the mid-1980s, the Australian Government Public Sector has been quality assured, restructured, re-engineered, downsized, continuously improved, delayered, reinvented and performance managed through the balanced scorecard. In some cases these changes have been tokenistic; in many, they have been a source of frustration for public sector employees – exhausted from guru-driven management; in others, the changes have been marginal.

But there have been many successes. As a generalization, the reinvention of the Public Sector in Australia since the mid-1980s has been a success that contains significant lessons applicable to the market research industry internationally.

A key platform of those successes has been the partnership between the market and social policy research industries and the Australian Government Public Sector. This partnership has witnessed the development of a suite of new market research tools in support of a reinvented public sector.

This chapter outlines six case studies that highlight the innovative use of market research techniques to create responsibility for outcomes and in the development of accountability mechanisms linked to improved service delivery to the Australian community. The chapter concludes with a detailed case study from the Child Support Agency, who have been using market research to drive organizational improvement, segment clients and restructure service delivery since the early 1990s.

THE CONTEXT

The emergence of public sector reform in Australia can be traced to the early 1980s and the Quality Assurance and Total Quality Management (TQM) movements. However, as with most public sector reform internationally, the reforms accelerated rapidly in the early 1990s with the publication of many definitive texts on repositioning and redefining the role of the public sector.

The six movements in public sector reform in Australia since the mid-1970s, which have culminated in the rise of market research initiatives across all levels of government in Australia, are:

1. **Downsizing** – derived from the desire to reduce the 'unnecessary' size of government and commenced in the mid 1970s with a

taxpayer/political focus. Usually linked to California Proposition 13, which argued successfully for indexing property tax (rates) to market-based factors, thereby reducing income to local governments. Despite the development of 'downsizing' into a divisive tool in some quarters, its origin was based on the emerging notion of accountability and the appropriate or 'right' sizing of public sector organizations commensurate with their demonstrable, reasonable and relevant access to funds.

2. **Continuous improvement** – emerging from the quality movement and commenced in the mid 1980s' this was influenced largely by the work of Dr W. Edwards Deming. It was a grass-roots incrementalist approach to change, and specifically process improvement. It involved decentralizing power, team-based Total Quality Management (TQM and its many variants) and introduced the notion of cooperative process improvement (Walton, 1986).

3. **Re-engineering** – based on private sector notions of rebuilding organizational processes and structures, this trend commenced with the publication, in 1994, of Michael Hammer and James Champy's book *Reengineering the Corporation*. In Hammer's words, it involved 'ripping the guts out of an organization and reassembling them in the context of today's changing business world.' It involved throwing away the current paradigms and current organizational model and structure, starting from scratch and focusing on the customer through fundamental and radical redesign (Hammer and Champy, 1994; Hammer, 1996).

4. **Reinvention** – based on entrepreneurial government/governance, this commenced with the publication in 1993, of David Osborne and Ted Gaebler's book, *Reinventing Government* and formalized the move from input to outcome thinking and funding in the public sector. It also introduced the notion that the public sector could be entrepreneurial and use multiple methods of service delivery (Osborne and Gaebler, 1993).

5. **Delayering** – based on reducing the layers of management, this commenced with the publication, in 1993, of Doede Keuning and Wilfred Opheij's book *Delayering Organizations*. It was based on reducing information bottlenecks, reducing the distance between 'top and shop floor' and accelerating decision-making by devolving it. It created the conceptual underpinnings for matrix management and 'flat organizations' (Keuning and Opheij, 1993).

6. **Virtual Integration** – based on the organization as a networked web of relationships, this commenced as a result of the impact of

the previous five initiatives, assisted by the significant opportunity provided through technology. It strengthened the move away from hierarchical to decentralized structures and pushed the concept of matrix management towards being a web or network of devolved decision-makers. The virtually integrated public sector organization capitalized on the leverage available through e-commerce to become a 'federation' of smaller 'companies', 'divisions' or 'partnerships' which focused on client and/or market segments. The public sector was seen as more entrepreneurial and could 'mix and match' multiple methods of service delivery, through its partnerships and alliances and through virtual integration (Hedberg, Dahlgren, Hansson and Nils-Goran, 1994; Tapscott, 1999).

MARKET RESEARCH AS THE EMERGING TOOL OF A REFORMED PUBLIC SECTOR

Although there have been many definitive texts and many movements of change, one work has had the most prolonged effect in terms of its impact on the market research industry. *In Reinventing Government: How the entrepreneurial spirit is transforming the public sector* (Osborne and Gaebler, 1993), the concepts of entrepreneurial, customer-driven, market-oriented government with a focus on results and outcomes were first introduced to the public sector.

Historically, in the absence of a profit motive, the public sector had struggled to improve the efficient and effective delivery of services to Australian citizens. By definition, the public service delivers services for the broader benefit of the community – 'the common good'. To introduce reform, it was important that a metaphor for the profit motive be introduced. The metaphor for the profit motive was the delivery of demonstrable outcomes. In the past fifteen years, this has seen the emergence of a range of information-based mechanisms built largely around reliable market and social policy research techniques.

The new market research tools

The simplest explanation of the metaphor for the profit motive is that it needed to create a sense of responsibility for outcomes. Several innovative methods for creating this sense of responsibility have now been in operation in the Australian Government Public Sector for the past fifteen years, and there are now ample examples of how effective these have been. The main methods for creating responsibility for outcomes have seen market research techniques being used to:

- model the structure of service delivery in the public sector;
- segment public sector markets to ensure carefully targeted communications and service delivery strategies;
- continuously monitor and measure citizen, client and customer satisfaction with the public sector delivery of services (internally and outsourced);
- define service standards and link these to market, client and customer perceptions of the quality of service delivery;
- link staff and senior management performance to market, client and customer feedback;
- link collectively bargained agency agreement salary increments to market, client and customer feedback.

The use of market research as a key tool for measuring outcomes and rewarding success is now commonplace in the Australian Government Public Sector. The following case studies are drawn from a wide portfolio of research undertaken for six of the signature public sector agencies in Australia.

CASE STUDIES

1 – The integrated use of market and opinion research in developing and improving service quality

This agency was established in 1988 and immediately instigated a market-driven approach to its management and service delivery. The agency manages in excess of 24 000 facilities around Australia, and within five years had established its own internal market research capability, including the automated production, distribution and scanning of optically read client surveys. The client survey results are used to improve the quality of new facilities, provide real time feedback on building maintenance and to benchmark service quality across its regional offices. The agency also introduced the routine surveying of staff opinions in 1991, and this internal market research and the external market research have now been part of routine business management for sixteen years.

2 – The role of market research in the due diligence process for the sale/outsourcing of government functions

This agency was charged in 1996 with the sale/privatization of six government functions. As part of the due diligence process, the agency commissioned client and staff research to measure the value of each of the government assets in terms of the corporate health of the staff and the loyalty of the existing client base. All six functions were transferred successfully to the private sector and they are regarded as one of the most successful examples of government privatization of selected functions. In addition, the agency built into the contract for sale a provision that the level of service provided after the sale should be comparable to, or better than, the standard as measured prior to the sale. This ongoing monitoring was built into the contract and has been an integral part of the success of the transfer of these functions.

3 – The role of market research in developing service standards and improving staff professionalism

This agency has some 20 000 staff and twenty-one different shopfront offices around Australia. For the past ten years it has commissioned extensive market and opinion research to improve the relationship with its clients, re-engineer internal processes and promote the changing nature of government service delivery.

In 2001, the agency introduced the concept of linking client feedback to staff remuneration. The agency has established a theoretical model of professionalism, and this has been used to train staff as well as monitor their performance in the eyes of clients (see Figure 29.1). Every six months, staff professionalism is measured and the results of this research are linked to staff pay increases under a collectively bargained agency agreement.

4 – The role of market research in cultural change and improving staff morale

This agency is responsible for a sensitive portfolio which is close to government and often in the public eye. It has developed an integrated performance management system – based loosely on the balanced scorecard (see Kaplan and Norton, 1996) – which is linked to its strategic plan. Like all agencies described in this chapter, the use of market research has moved away from being an ad hoc process to a fully integrated component of a

Figure 29.1 How one Australian agency (case study 3) has modelled staff professionalism prior to routine measurement through external market research.

business management strategy. The agency developed a routine staff survey as a performance indicator against its Human Resource (HR) strategy. However, the survey also fulfilled the role of modelling, measuring and monitoring cultural change. The development of the survey included a new model written in layperson's language describing the organization and the key principles it was trying to establish (see Figure 29.2). This model and the terminology within it is part of the organizational culture and is monitored routinely.

5 –The role of market research in client segmentation in the public sector

This agency has developed an annual cycle of market and client research that is linked to its high-level business plan. This market research continuously informs the strategic conversation within the agency about how to gain and implement better insights into its clients and its market. The agency routinely adapts its approach to service delivery based on the knowledge developed from its market research programmes.

A series of citizen insights was gained through market research, and this has resulted in new ways of thinking about the agency's relationship with

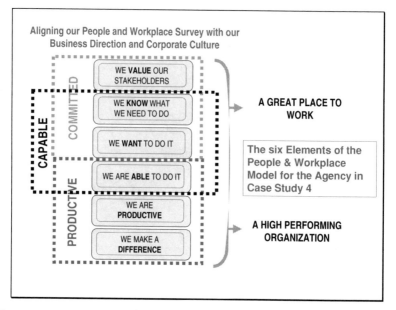

Figure 29.2 How one Australian agency (Case study 4) has modelled its Human Resources Strategy with a view to developing routine measurement and monitoring of its performance.

its clients. The result has been the development of a life-events approach to service provision and intervention (see Figure 29.3).

6 – A detailed case study on the Child Support Agency

About the Australian Child Support Agency (CSA)

The Child Support Agency (CSA) was established in 1988 to administer the Australian Government's Child Support scheme. The scheme aims to ensure that separated parents share in the cost of supporting their children according to their capacity. The CSA's role includes registration, assessment, collection and transfer of child support payments.

The CSA has over 1.4 million clients and facilitated the transfer of AUD$1.94 billion in 02/03 for the benefit of over one million children. The agency has 3000 staff located in 16 offices around Australia, as well as 21 Regional Service Centres co-located in offices with another Government service provider.

As part of the Department of Family and Community Services (FaCS), the role of the CSA aligns with and supports the FaCS's vision of *A fair and cohesive Australian society*, achieved by working with others to help

Developing a life-events client segmentation model

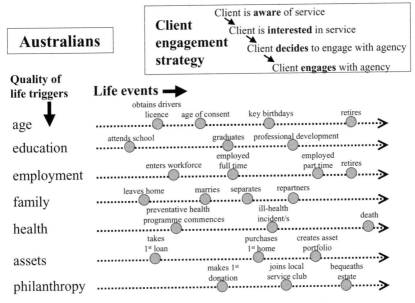

Figure 29.3   A life-events approach to client segmentation (from Case study 5).

families, communities and individuals build their self-reliance and make choices that meet their needs. The CSA's vision is that 'all Australian parents meet their child support responsibilities'. The agency's strategic intent is to encourage parental self-reliance and independence.

Market research, both internal and external, has been fundamental to the development of the CSA's business framework, and is a core process in our evaluation of business outcomes.

Identifying the issues

Approximately 40% of marriages in Australia end in divorce. A couple entering into marriage and having children in Australia today faces a significant risk that:

- the marriage will end before the children are reared;
- the marriage will end against the wishes of one partner;
- the children will then live with only one parent;
- the children will live a significant distance from one parent;
- the children will lose contact with one parent;
- their health and wellbeing will be significantly affected.

Meeting the legislative requirements to collect and transfer child support payments for the benefit of children of separated parents was the primary focus of the Child Support Agency from its inception in 1988 until 1996.

A review of the CSA's service approach in 1996 acknowledged the agency's success as a collection agency, however, this success had been achieved at a cost of parental self-reliance, i.e. parents were becoming increasingly dependent on the CSA. Further, a number of other factors were driving a need to rethink the CSA's strategic approach:

- the high number of complaints to the Ombudsman and Members of Parliament;
- a low satisfaction rating amongst clients;
- a projected strong growth in caseload;
- budgetary pressures to reduce operating costs.

This led to a business conundrum – '*how do we increase client satisfaction and reduce costs whilst maintaining an excellent child support collection rate?*' The answer lay in recognizing that future significant improvements in the payment of child support and client satisfaction were dependent upon improvements in parents' voluntary acceptance of their child support responsibilities, and greater levels of self-reliance.

A major research programme established the following key factors that influence voluntary payment of child support. These were:

- **relationship quality** – the nature of the relationship with the other parent;
- **involvement with children** – the nature of the relationship and extent of contact with the children;
- **financial capacity** – separated parents' perceptions of affordability of paying child support;
- **procedural support** – the level of support provided to parents from the CSA and the family law system.

These business factors and research findings highlighted a need to reduce parent's dependence on the CSA for the collection of child support by actively supporting them to manage their own child support responsibilities, whilst still providing safety net arrangements where private arrangements failed. This approach of addressing wider needs would help maintain cooperative relationships between parents and, therefore, lead to increased voluntary acceptance of paying child support. The CSA would need to play an important role in encouraging and maintaining self-management of child support.

The CSA's strategic framework

To operationalize the strategic intent of maximizing independence, the CSA developed a new strategic framework in 1996, with the vision *All Australian parents meet their child support responsibilities*. The new strategic framework identified six challenges that the CSA would need to work on to move towards this vision:

1. Influence a combined, 'whole of government' approach.
2. Build a community focus.
3. Encourage and support parental responsibility.
4. Refine agency service delivery.
5. Increase our organizational capacity and productiveness.
6. Guarantee a transparent and accountable service.

Over the ensuing eight years, the CSA used this strategic framework as a basis for fundamentally transforming every aspect of its business. This transformation included:

- a comprehensive review of the service offered to clients, which led to a major restructure and the development of a segmentation model with targeted services provided according to client needs;
- development of a client service culture, focusing on outcomes for clients, not just processes and transactions;
- a comprehensive planning approach, which aligned planning, evaluation and reporting from the strategic vision through to operational activities;
- the expansion of our strategic focus to incorporate a broader, whole-of-family law system approach to meeting our clients' needs;
- the fundamental redevelopment of our supporting infrastructure, including new information technology and communications to better support client independence;
- creating and operationalizing a comprehensive human resource infrastructure that has driven cultural change.

Underpinning the strategic framework

Underpinning this new strategic framework was an evaluation strategy, incorporating both an internal and external research programme. Market research is used continuously to measure our performance and to assist in the development of new strategies to meet these challenges.

To date, the external research programme has included:

- research into client compliance – that is, determining the factors which influence parents' ability to meet their child support responsibilities;
- client satisfaction research – including both qualitative and quantitative research;
- research with clients to shape the development and marketing of products and services that support client independence;
- staff satisfaction research based on an holistic model of organizational health;
- research to determine the defining characteristics of high-performing staff;
- research regarding the community perception of the Child Support Agency and the role of Government in the administration of child support;
- client perceptions of e-business and electronic service delivery.

The CSA's research programme includes both quantitative and qualitative research methodologies, including the use of online surveys and automated responses using the telephone system.

The CSA's Client Service Delivery Model

The CSA's market research formed the basis of segmenting our clients into various groups, ranging from parents needing intensive support and assistance, through those requiring a small amount of support, to parents who can establish totally independent arrangements. The CSA's Client Service Delivery Model (see Figure 29.4) is designed to leverage this segmentation. Accordingly, our model recognizes three levels of client independence:

1. **Self administration** – separated parents who have no interaction with the CSA and who make their own child support arrangements. These clients may access the CSA's website for any information they require to manage their own arrangements.
2. **Private collect** – separated parents who transfer child support payments directly between themselves on the basis of ongoing CSA assessments of the amount to be paid. These clients require little involvement by the CSA.

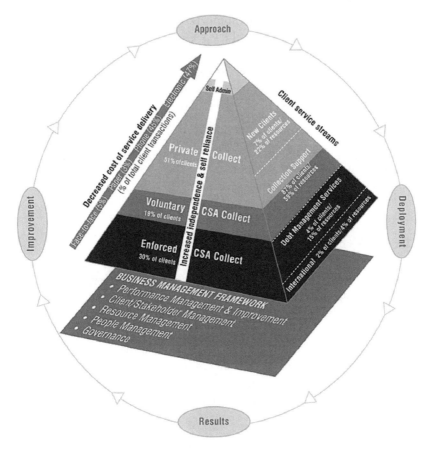

Figure 29.4 The CSA's Client Service Delivery Model.

3. **Agency collect** – separated parents who arrange for their child support payments to be calculated by the CSA and have funds transferred through the CSA. These parents require varying levels of involvement with the CSA, which are dependent largely on the ongoing relationship between the parents and payment compliance. The specific needs of these clients are met through four specialist client service streams.

The CSA's current primary segments are:

• the *New Client Stream*, comprising recently separated parents who are assessed based on holistic needs, with our service responses tailored to those needs. Clients remain in this stream for nine months before being transferred into the second segment for ongoing assistance if necessary;

- the *Collection Support Stream*, comprising separated parents who have an ongoing relationship with the CSA and are generally meeting their child support responsibilities;
- the *Debt Management Services Stream*, comprising separated parents where voluntary child support arrangements have not been established or sustained;
- the *International Stream*, which liaises with other international government agencies, where reciprocal agreements are in place, facilitating the exchange of child support payments when one parent resides outside of Australia.

The CSA's client service delivery channels

The CSA's client service delivery channels are structured to best align client needs with available business resources. The channels have been developed as a result of thorough research into client preferences and needs, aligning these with the CSA's objective of delivering an efficient service.

The service channels provide varying opportunities for levels of interaction to best suit differing client needs. The main service channel used by clients is the telephone, including automated interactive voice recognition systems. These services are provided through a network of metropolitan sites. For those clients requiring more personalized interaction, face-to-face services are also provided throughout regional Australia. Clients who require lower levels of interaction can manage their child support business activities by accessing information about the Child Support Scheme on the website, including using online tools such as the child support calculator to determine their child support payments.

The CSA is refining its service delivery channels continually to provide improved client service at a reduced cost. The CSA is investing heavily in a new telephony infrastructure to manage the growth in call demand effectively. Focus group research has indicated positive attitudes to electronic service delivery, especially amongst our payer clients. Developments in online service delivery will enable clients to achieve a greater level of independence in managing their child support arrangements.

Putting the Client Service Delivery Model in place has delivered significant increases in parental independence, as reflected by the fact that 51.1% of CSA clients were in the Private Collect category (in 2004) compared to the 1996 rate of 39% (see Figure 29.5).

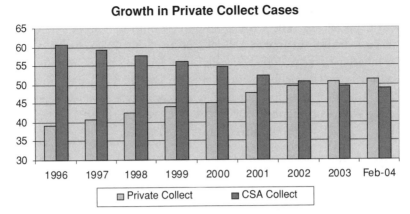

Figure 29.5 Percentage of CSA clients in the Private collect and CSA Collect categories over time.

Client satisfaction in the New Client segment has also been through a transformation (see Figure 29.6).

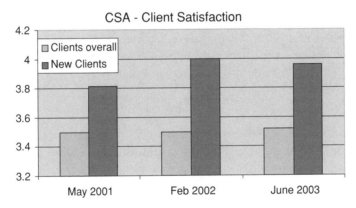

Figure 29.6 CSA client satisfaction ratings over time.

Integration

Client Service Charter – the service commitments the CSA makes to clients

Research into what clients value and expect from CSA service delivery has been integral in the development of the CSA's Client Service Charter (which outlines the service commitments the CSA makes to its clients). This research formed the basis of the first draft of the Client Charter in 1995. From there, further research has been conducted with clients, staff and other stakeholders to realign Charter statements continually with client expectations. The CSA is now in its third iteration of its Client Charter, which is integrated into all aspects of the organization.

A Charter Package, which is a staff tool detailing the behavioural expectations of staff needed to demonstrate the Client Charter commitments, was also developed from this research. These behaviours align directly with, and support, our values, and are embedded across all key operational areas of the business. This includes:

- all CSA's training programmes;
- the performance management framework (including individual performance agreements for staff at all levels);
- the recruitment strategy based on recruitment for values alignment, client service orientation and emotional resilience;
- the Rewards and Recognition programme, which recognizes staff achievements in line with the values and Client Charter commitments;
- a Capability Framework, which defines expectations of CSA staff at each level. Demonstrated evidence against this framework is the basis for promotion in the CSA.

The CSA's success in integrating its Charter commitments and values to drive service excellence has also been recognized through multiple Service Charter Awards in the Australian Public Service.

Client research

The CSA has used market research extensively to understand the needs of clients, in order to provide tailored and appropriate products and services. Ultimately, the aim is to increase the level of satisfaction clients have with the CSA's service delivery, and, therefore, to increase the voluntary payment of child support.

The CSA conducts a number of research programmes on a regular basis to identify and understand the needs of clients. These include:

- quantitative research to benchmark and monitor the level of client satisfaction over time;
- qualitative research to explore issues of concern that may be identified through the quantitative research;
- qualitative research to better understand the needs of clients;
- qualitative research to seek feedback from clients during the development phase of products and services;
- research to evaluate the performance of products and services.

This research is used to address many areas of the business, including the development of:

- new products and services that promote independence;
- satisfaction with national training programmes;
- effective service delivery channels;
- input into the CSA's business planning and improvement processes.

The CSA has used quantitative client satisfaction research effectively to identify areas where improvements in service delivery need to be made, and then translated these findings into action. For example, in 2000 and 2001, little movement in the level of client satisfaction was evident. To better understand why initiatives and improvements weren't having any effect on the level of client satisfaction, the CSA undertook extensive qualitative research. This research revealed many issues and assisted the CSA in better understanding the needs of our clients. As a result of the factors and issues discovered in this research, the CSA developed a national training programme based on realistic client scenarios – Quality Outcomes for Clients.

The research programme has also been fundamental in assisting the CSA to develop tailored products and services that meet the needs of clients effectively. In particular, market research has been used by the CSA to assist in the development of products and services that specifically meet the emotional, financial, legal and parenting needs of clients.

Market research is used throughout the cycle of product development, from identifying the initial need, developing the content and format, to designing the look and feel of the product. The use of market research enables the CSA to produce a product that clients can relate to and use.

In 1998, the CSA and Corporate Diagnostics developed the CSA's model for measuring client satisfaction, known as the Professionalism Index. The Professionalism Index consisted of 20 questions that related to the professional and personal attributes of the CSA staff, the outcomes of the interaction and how the client felt they were treated. This model has been used regularly by the CSA to measure client satisfaction since 1998. This has allowed the CSA to benchmark and monitor performance over time, and identify where improvements need to be made.

The model has also been integrated into the CSA's business by linking the measure to the CSA's enterprise-based pay agreement with staff. An improvement in client satisfaction is one of the key corporate outcomes required in order for CSA staff to receive an annual pay increase.

To complement the client satisfaction research programme, comparisons are made with other organizations (where appropriate and available) and with the CSA's staff perceptions of how well service is delivered to clients.

The Corporate Health Index (CHI) – the CSA's staff satisfaction survey

The CSA worked with Corporate Diagnostics to develop its staff satisfaction survey, known as the Corporate Health Index (or the CHI). The CHI was introduced in 1998 to measure all aspects of the organization's health through a staff census (see Figure 29.7).

The CHI survey has now been conducted five times. The results have been fundamental drivers of annual organizational business planning. The CHI itself has undergone a continuous process of improvement and refinement, including:

- reshaping the model from a standard staff survey to a unique model that communicates what constitutes corporate health in the CSA;

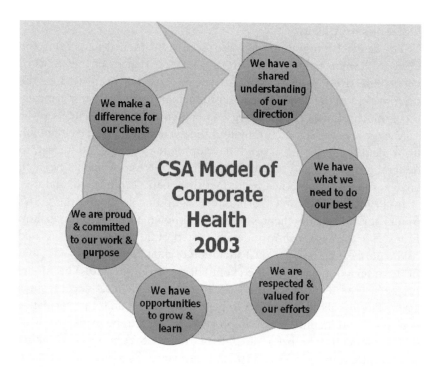

Figure 29.7 The CSA Corporate Health Model.

- supporting the research outcomes with a detailed national communication strategy which includes site and team-based presentations and action planning at national, regional and site levels;
- integration of corporate health into senior managers' performance agreements to provide a level of accountability for improvements to be made;
- inclusion of corporate health as a key performance indicator in the CSA's external reporting.

Human resource strategies

The impact of the CSA's people development strategies is monitored in a number of ways. Two critical areas are:

- staff's perception of the level of support that they receive to deliver quality client service monitored through the Corporate Health Index;
- clients' perceptions of quality of service, measured through the client satisfaction surveys.

From an internal perspective, the Corporate Health Index has enabled the tracking of the CSA's progress against key issues of concern amongst staff (see Table 29.1).

Table 29.1   Monitoring issues of staff concern using market research.

Key priorities in 2000/01 business plan	Corporate health survey themes	2000 average rating by staff	2001 average rating by staff	⇒	2003 average rating by staff
Maintaining a viable operational workplace	Resources to do the job	2.4	3.1		3.1
Managing workload	Time to do the job	2.3	3.0		3.4
Supporting CSA staff	Change management	2.5	3.1		3.1
	Training	2.8	3.3		3.3

The top three staff issues identified in the 2000 CHI became key priorities in the 2000/2001 Business Plan. In the 2001 CHI, these issues were the ones showing the greatest improvement.

Research driving business improvement into the future

Recently, the CSA has been investigating new ways of obtaining feedback from clients that provides more timely and relevant data. With the increasing use of the Internet, the CSA now has an online survey that allows clients to provide feedback at any time that is convenient to them.

Additionally, the CSA is implementing a national programme which uses the CSA's telephony system to gather feedback from clients. In this situation, clients are selected randomly by the CSA's telephony system and asked if they would like to provide feedback at the completion of their call. Those clients who choose to participate are transferred through to an automated survey at the completion of their call with the client service officer. The automated survey asks clients several questions about the service they have just received, and these questions are related directly to the Charter commitments made to CSA clients. This will enable the CSA to measure its performance directly against the commitments made to our clients.

This research will provide the CSA with timely, relevant and detailed data that can be used to improve the service delivery. Client service teams will be able to use these results to develop service improvement initiatives in team plans and coaching strategies. This quality measure will be used with current quantitative data to give a more accurate picture of the CSA's overall performance.

Within the next 12 months, the CSA will be conducting further research to review the vision and the challenges of the organization. This research will be fundamental in understanding the future of the CSA's role as a service provider, and in refining stakeholder expectations, purpose, objectives, performance and evaluation.

CONCLUSION

Since the mid-1980s, the Australian Government Public Sector has made a giant leap forward in the use of market and opinion research to measure, monitor and improve its performance. There is now a key and well-established role for the market research industry in providing the information and the intelligence required by the new Australian public sector. Although the local industry is responding in a sporadic and uncoordinated manner, the market trend is forcing the emergence of a united industry approach.

The market research industry internationally has responded to this shift in emphasis and role. For instance, the 1998 ESOMAR Conference which addressed the wisdom of foresight recognized that 'when

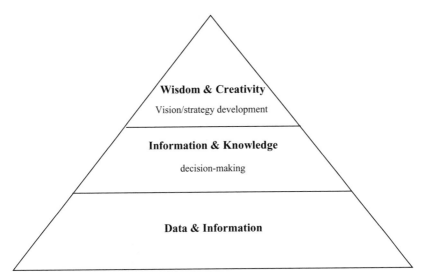

Figure 29.8 The 1998 ESOMAR Model showing the move from research findings to marketing intelligence.

information is transformed into knowledge, it becomes part of the equity of the company and is often shared with important and vital partners' (ESOMAR, 1998).

ESOMAR developed the model shown in Figure 29.8 for strategically realigning the market research industry in the light of these developments, and reinventing itself as a major force in public and private sector governance.

The market research industry is being asked increasingly by the Australian Public Sector to move up the value chain and develop better strategic use of data (see Bycroft and Vasiliauskas, 1998). The Australian Public Sector has established clear leadership in the introduction of many new business management initiatives, including the comprehensive and integrated use of market research.

This leadership provides a watershed opportunity for market leadership from the Australian market research industry. It requires the reinvention of the industry itself. Market researchers will need to move from a focus on engine-room technical provision of services to a greater outcome focus and better understanding of client business strategies. This is a major challenge and cultural change in itself, and it will be ironic indeed if the market research industry cannot meet it.

REFERENCES

Bycroft, P. and Vasiliauskas, E. (1998), *Book-ending the Engine Room: Embedding Market Research in Strategic Management and Corporate Communications.* Keynote address presented at the Market Research Society of Australia (MRSA) International Conference, Melbourne, 14–16 October.

ESOMAR (1998), *The Power of Knowledge – From Research Findings to Marketing Intelligence.* 51st ESOMAR Marketing Research Congress and Exhibition, Internet page.

Hammer, M. and Champy, J. (1994), *Reengineering the Corporation,* Allen and Unwin.

Hammer, M. (1996), *Beyond Reengineering,* Harper Collins Business.

Hedberg, B., Dahlgren, G., Hansson, J. and Nils-Goran, O. (1994), *Virtual Organizations and Beyond, Discover Imaginary Systems,* John Wiley & Sons, Ltd.

Kaplan, R. and Norton, D. (1996), *The Balanced Scorecard: Translating Strategy into Action,* Harvard Business School Press.

Keuning, D. and Opheij, W. (1993), *Delayering Organizations: How to beat bureaucracy and create a flexible and responsive organization,* Financial Times, Pitman Publishing.

Osborne, D. and Gaebler, T. (1993), *Reinventing Government – How the Entrepreneurial Spirit is Transforming the Public Sector,* Addison-Wesley Publishing Company.

Tapscott, D. (1999), *Creating Value in the Network Economy,* Harvard Business School Press.

Walton, M. (1986), *The Deming Management Method,* W.H. Allen & Co.

Chapter Thirty

Research for Innovation: Fitting the Design Process at Philips Design

Monica Bueno[a] and Lucile Rameckers[b]

This chapter is based on Philips Design's 2003 research programme. It describes an approach for design research using rich information from everyday life. From this 'Personas' – fictional characters based on real-life stories – are created.

INTRODUCTION

Philips Design is a global community of professionals, focused on delivering competitive value to its clients through design. We strive for innovation in both our design services and in the solutions we offer.

These services and solutions are based on the latest research methods applied in global markets. We have established a multidisciplinary team of researchers and designers. Over the past ten years, we have been developing projects that deal with current and future values and needs of people, and how design can address these. We develop and experiment continually with the latest methods in design research.

[a]Consultant, Strategic Design, Philips Design.
[b]Senior Research Consultant, Philips Design.

Market Research Best Practice. Edited by P. Mouncey and F. Wimmer.
© 2007 John Wiley & Sons, Limited.

This chapter is based on the 2003 research programme at Philips Design, in which the authors took part. It describes our approach in conducting qualitative research aimed at giving more value to design in our innovation process. In this approach, we combine conventional qualitative research methods with design research methods to gather real-life data. A structural analysis enables us to show the connections between people's values, their needs and concrete solutions in the context of their everyday lives. This information is translated into *'personas'*, which are fictional characters based on real-life stories. *Personas* are used as a tool to communicate the research results to designers. We will illustrate how the use of *personas* improves the innovation process at Philips Design.

We believe that the unique power of our approach lies in combining different disciplines of research and design. A handbook with research guidelines and a tool that helps translate the findings into *personas* have been developed as concrete output that enables designers and researchers to work together more closely.

In our socio-cultural research, we investigate how society is changing. Globalization, multiculturalism, the speed of technology and business innovation are causing people to change and adapt constantly to the world around them. The world we live in is becoming increasingly complex, and we encounter this in our daily lives through the many possibilities offered by technologies and media. The societal knowledge base is transforming rapidly: we have been replacing our structured and clearly arranged lives by ways of living which are more dynamic, varied and difficult to predict. Whether you label this as the Mosaic society, Postmodernism or 'liquid fluidity', these profound changes are influencing the way people function and manifest themselves: we are in constant transformation.

To respond to these changes successfully as a global company, we need to know more about the complexities of people's everyday lives so that we can develop technologies and innovations that suit their needs and add value to their lives in particular contexts, moments and situations. This demands new perspectives in doing 'people research'. We need to move away from focusing on *consumers'* product use and buying behaviour and take a broader perspective. We believe this broader perspective focuses on *people's* needs and values as the leading force.

Moreover, we should realize that it is not enough to focus on the individual person. Rather, we have to focus on how people and their needs are connected to the communities and the groups they live in. Only in this way are we able constantly to 'fine-tune' people's needs, put them in the context of daily life and describe them on a level of human detail that goes beyond a purely stereotypical description of consumer target groups. This is the type of in-depth information that we need as a continuous stream of input into our innovation process. Thus, having moved our focus from product design and technology-driven strategies to the continuously transforming consumer and brand experience, we now have to deepen our understanding of consumers by studying people and their everyday lives.

The first part of this chapter discusses method development in the fields of consumer research and design research, the way these research methods are used in design and what is lacking. The second part describes research directions that are more appropriate for the purpose of design. The third part expands on how to optimize the communication between researchers and designers to get the most out of research projects. Finally, the fourth part indicates how the current approach adds value to the design process at Philips Design. We will introduce a new tool that we are developing, and we will illustrate how we integrate research and design to build this tool and how using the tool enables collaboration between research and design.

CURRENT RESEARCH METHODS

Professionals in the area of design research have begun to recognize the necessity of gathering information on people's needs in the context of real life. We see many of these developments in a variety of research fields. Below, we will describe some examples from the areas of quantitative and qualitative research as well as design research.

In quantitative consumer behaviour research, we have seen an expansion from using experimental settings towards the use of large secondary datasets, such as scanner data and panel data. On the one hand, scanner data provide an insight into people's purchasing behaviour at a retail store level. These data could tell us something about the influence of in-store strategies, like price promotions, on buying frequency. However, it is not possible to track the behaviour of individual consumers. Panel data, on the other hand, focus on the individual consumer. Here, we see an increased focus on the development of psychological constructs. This means that we can explain individual behaviour more and more by the 'softer', complex psychological variables in addition to the demographics and sociographics that were used in the past. There are two ways in which designers use this type of data. First, they use them for designing in the context of the store environment, e.g. store layout or packaging issues. In this respect, scanner data could give some basic insights. Second, designers use quantitative data to derive some first ideas about consumption and usage behaviour with regard to certain products. They do this mainly to scan the area for relevant design triggers. These data are useful at the start of the design process and not at later stages, as direct information on consumption and usage behaviour is lacking. The latter would give designers a better idea of how needs and behaviour are related to each other, and how these needs differ across different situations and moments.

In the field of qualitative research, we experience that businesses increasingly realize the added value of observational research, usability trials with real users and consumer panel evaluations at home. At Philips Design we have been experiencing this as well. This includes longitudinal research by visiting people at their homes several times; involving participants as co-researchers by giving them home work and tasks; and involving participants as co-designers by inviting them to creative work sessions. Data from qualitative research are of major importance to designers for inspiration as well as for a reality check. However, in communicating these data to designers, often only core messages are revealed. The rich context is left behind or made available in unreadable databases or reports. As a solution, designers should be more involved in the research process and researchers should better understand how to make sense of data specifically for the sake of innovation and design (Beyer and Holtzblatt, 1997).

A traditional working tool used in design research for the purpose of innovation and concept generation by designers and researchers is *stereotyping*. This is often done following the 'I-methodology', in which designers create something with themselves or their friends in mind (Akrich, 1992). Following the 'I-methodology', designers will create characters and scenarios that are inspiring because of the personal detail in which they are described. The problem often is that these scenarios can be presented from a functional perspective very much like instruction manuals. Sometimes the psychological, social and behavioural aspects of people are not described, and the context of use is seldom mentioned. Furthermore, there is no direct user participation involved, which provides us with a view of people's lives mainly from the outside. Also, in generalizing about a group of people, the outcome can be quite abstract, in the sense that it does not focus on the deeper user behaviours of the individual. It is these deeper issues, which are often unpredictable, that are inspiring for designers.

To make these methods more appropriate for the area of innovation design, it would be necessary to use real-life data that were very rich and illustrative, showing the subtleties of everyday life. Therefore, designers and researchers started thinking about methods to engage and understand users more in the design and development of new products. Approaches described in the literature that make use of different levels of user involvement are: participatory design, user-centred design, ethnography and contextual design (Kujala, 2002).

Companies like Microsoft and Cooper, a product and interaction design consultancy, have been experimenting by illustrating the richness of real life data in the form of *personas*. *Personas* are fictional people who have life stories, goals and tasks. Scenarios can be constructed around *personas* (Grudin and Pruitt, 2002). Both companies recognize the power of *personas* in creating information for design that is rich, detailed and realistic. However, they focus mainly on *personas* seen from an engineering-oriented perspective, as their work is mainly in the areas of development and redesign of screen applications. They centre on explaining workflow issues and content areas like news, media, music and e-mails. In order to use *personas* for more than product design or screen applications (e.g. strategy development), we would need to keep the richness of the stories and pull them out of the technological context into the daily life contexts of people.

DATA IN THE CONTEXT OF EVERYDAY LIFE

From the previous section we have seen that designers are more and more interested in using data in the context of everyday life. One could question what came first: the need for real-life data or the resources and opportunities to produce real-life data. On the one hand, increased competition has made more and more businesses aware that they have to find their consumer, rather than the consumer having to find them. Businesses cannot expect consumers to search for their product amongst the clutter of brands and products. They must become more active in showing how their brands and products fit into people's everyday lives. To be able to do this they must know the details of people's lives. The current trend of customization and personalization stems from this development. On the other hand, better resources have become available for researchers and marketing and innovation managers. The constant growth in computer power, enabling analyses of large databases, and the

Internet, enabling easy and cheap methods of doing research, are just a few examples. Whatever came first, it is clear that Philips Design, as a global company, must be innovative on all fronts, not only with regard to technological developments, products and solutions that we offer to the market, but also with regard to the methods used to gather knowledge about people.

To address this issue, we developed our 2003 research project 'Pulse'. We tried to combine research methods that stem from the area of design with more analytical approaches from the consumer behaviour area and exploratory approaches from anthropology. With this, we developed an approach that includes co-research and contextual inquiry. Both are explained in detail below.

Co-research

Co-research means that we perceive people as participants who can teach us about their lives, rather than as passive respondents who comply to the questions of the researcher. It also involves people as researchers of themselves. For this project we gave participants the opportunity to research 'themselves' by providing them with a homework assignment ten days before the actual face-to-face sessions. The intention of the homework assignment was to:

- gather information to gain insight into people's lives from the people themselves;
- help us to gather information;
- make participants more aware of their own behaviour and thoughts;
- help participants visualize issues that are difficult to express in words.

We developed two booklets that had some creative tasks and some traditional question/answer tasks. The creative tasks were visual exercises such as maps with stickers and drawings or fun-to-do exercises. The left side of Figure 30.1 shows some statements on which participants could give their own opinions. The right side of Figure 30.1 shows an exercise where participants were given 'money' stickers. They were asked to distribute these stickers over given categories to indicate how much they would spend and what they would spend it on. Creative tasks are based on the idea of cultural probing, which is an inspirational approach that brings the user closer to the design space in a way that is different from conventional observation methods (Lebbon, Rouncefield and Viller, 2003). The intention of cultural probes or creative tasks is to

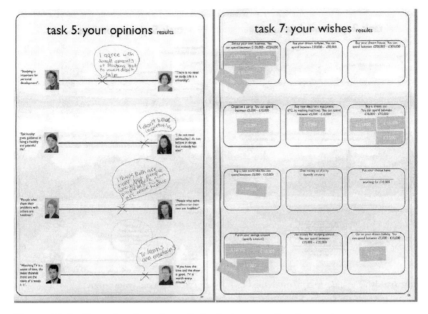

Figure 30.1 Example of creative tasks in the homework assignment.

get a sense of people's feelings with regard to a specific topic in order to explore boundaries for design. Typical characteristics of cultural probes or creative tasks are that they:

- ask for *immediate* action of the participant;
- trigger responses in an *intuitive* way;
- make use of *visual* stimuli;
- are less focused on their purpose (i.e. for participants it is difficult to guess what the researcher is looking for).

Next to the creative tasks, more traditional tasks were included. These were more time-consuming, like taking photographs and commenting on them. Figure 30.2 shows an example of a traditional exercise. Researchers' intentions with these types of exercises were twofold – first, to get descriptive background information on the participant and second to gain insight into people's underlying thoughts and attitudes. Typical characteristics of traditional question/answer tasks are that they:

- allow more *thinking* and preparation time;
- ask for *descriptions* of processes, thoughts, people, going beyond the 'what' to the 'why';

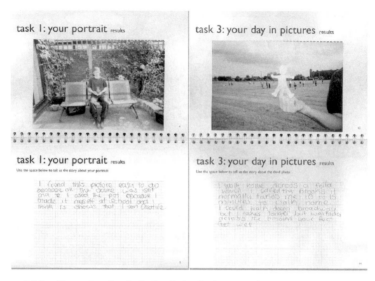

Figure 30.2　Example of analytical tasks in the homework assignment.

- make use of a *question-and-answer* format;
- are focused on their purpose (i.e. participants might more easily guess what the researcher is looking for).

The idea of the booklets was that they were deliberately beautiful and inspiring for participants to engage with them readily, but not too beautiful that people would not want to write in them. Another important aspect in creating them was that they needed to be triggers, inspiring for designers and researchers to facilitate the creation of *personas*, which forms the last part of our approach and is described in the next section. The books were packaged carefully as gifts in separate boxes for each participant, with treats inside like coloured pencils, pens, a disposable camera and different envelopes for photos (Figure 30.3).

Contextual inquiry

The second part in our approach is contextual inquiry, which combines observation and in-depth interviewing in the field. For our research, we focused on a particular market segment called 'Plugged-ins' This target group, which is important for our business, consists of people defined on age and certain attitudes with regard to lifestyle and products. Among other things, Plugged-ins are aware of the latest trends and they find it

Figure 30.3 The data-gathering toolbox.

important that other people see the brands they use. We also focused the research on a specific context, namely the context of home. For doing observational research at people's homes, we selected Plugged-ins that were willing to open their homes to us.

In setting up the research, we first assessed the research topics that were of interest in the context of home. We investigated the information about Plugged-ins that was already available at Philips, and categorized it in different topics. It was our intention to enrich this information. The results showed that the information was available in different levels of abstraction. For some topics we had only concrete facts or solutions, for others we had information on the value level. We 'completed' the information so that every topic included the concrete solution and the abstract value level: the levels used for each topic were those shown in Figure 30.4.

The concrete level was needed as a trigger or starting point for each topic during the interviews. This was necessary because in daily life people are used to thinking at the concrete level.

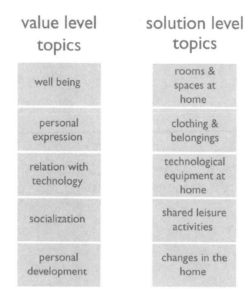

Figure 30.4 'Pulse' research topics.

We also felt that an important part of the context of everyday life is that people are connected to other people. Consequently, in setting up the research, we wanted to involve other people related to the Plugged-ins. To achieve this, we structured the interviews in two parts: first a group session with the Plugged-in and his/her friends and/or family, followed by a session with the Plugged-in only. We studied the social interaction in several ways:

1. By asking the Plugged-ins, via the homework, about their relationship with other people.
2. By asking the Plugged-ins to arrange friends and/or family for a group session. In this session, we asked them about their relationship with the Plugged-in.
3. By observing the interaction between Plugged-in and friends/family during this group session.
4. By asking the Plugged-ins about this interaction in an individual session.

During the sessions we interchanged the techniques used depending on what was most appropriate in the specific situation. Also, as with the homework, we wanted to use the power of both research and design by combining creative tasks with analytical tasks. Sometimes we had informal conversations, other times we asked them to draw a map of their social relationships or to make a video of their homes. However, our overall purpose was to understand the deeper reasons why people like and do certain things or have specific opinions. For this, we used the laddering interview technique, which starts by asking very specific questions like: what is your favourite object? From a concrete trigger such as this, we then try to find out why a person likes that object, identifying the important needs in relation to the object and finally the values that the person lives by.

As described in the consumer behaviour literature, laddering is based on the Means–End Chain theory, which explains the relationship between products and consumers (Reynolds and Gutman, 1988). It is based on the assumption that consumers' deeper motivations drive their behaviour, as this motivation creates certain needs. Consumers choose certain products that offer certain benefits to satisfy these needs. The specific characteristics or attributes of the product offer these benefits.

To extract the most out of our observations, we conducted the sessions with a researcher and a designer together. We also created a research handbook that explains the process and the skills needed in each step to stimulate future research. In addition, we developed interview and observation guidelines, including hypotheses about how Plugged-ins would answer the different questions. Although it sounds contradictory to use stringent guidelines and even hypotheses in explorative research, it gave researcher, designer and participant the freedom to explore things that seemed interesting while keeping focus at the same time. The guidelines are included in the research handbook as well.

COMMUNICATING RESEARCH RESULTS TO DESIGNERS

Having developed a multidisciplinary approach to obtaining real-life data in the data gathering process, we recognized that researchers and designers use different levels of abstraction in their communication, which makes it difficult to understand each other. In our group at Philips Design, researchers focus primarily on values and needs of people. Designers translate needs into benefits and develop solutions to address these needs. Making sense of data and communicating results into the design process is an important pitfall that has to be overcome to prevent the data from being misunderstood (Kujala, 2002). As we work in multidisciplinary

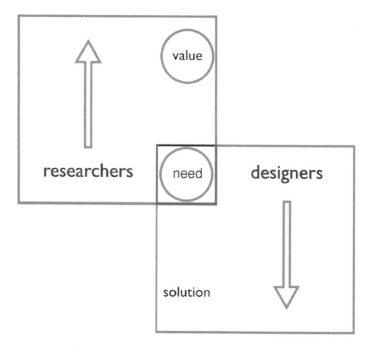

Figure 30.5   Levels of communication of researchers and designers.

teams at Philips Design, this aspect of communication and understanding
by many different people became the second aim of this project.

As it is almost impossible to ask people to change their way of communicating or to learn the 'language' of others, we were looking for
something that would offer a solution. For this we could use the reasoning behind the *Means–End Chain* theory. The theory links different
levels of abstraction by assuming that the concrete things in life, like people's behaviour and choices, can be explained with more abstract levels,
such as people's underlying values and motivations via the benefits they
provide.

In Figure 30.5, it is easy to recognize these three different levels of
abstraction. The most abstract level is the *value* level. This level refers
to people's underlying motivations of behaviour. The value level refers
to the value or (end) goals that people want to fulfil in their lives. The
second level is the *needs* level. It is about the needs people have in a
certain situation. Products or solutions that provide certain benefits can
address these needs. This is a subjective process: different people might
perceive the same product to provide different benefits. The third level
is the level of *solutions*. It is the most concrete level, referring to the

features or attributes of products and solutions that deliver the specific benefits to fulfil people's needs. The arrows in Figure 30.5 illustrate that researchers 'climb up' in the model. During the interview, researchers use the concrete level to start the conversation and, via the needs, they aim to find the value level. Designers, on the other hand, 'climb down' the model: they focus on understanding the needs and aim to find solutions to these needs.

The structure of the three levels has become a common thread throughout the 'Pulse' project. The overlap in Figure 30.5 indicates that the needs level forms the 'common' language between researchers and designers. The model helped to extract the right levels of data from the fieldwork. Figure 30.6 shows the examples of two participants for whom socializing is an important value: one of the participants, a girl (participant x in Figure 30.6), indicates that keeping in contact with her friends is of major importance to her. Another participant, a boy (participant y in Figure 30.6), states that he does certain things because he is convinced that his friends like him because of it. For both participants it is important to belong to a group, and technology supports them in this, but in very different ways. It is her mobile phone that forms the interaction platform with her friends for participant x: her core need is to be online to have the

Figure 30.6 Example of laddering analysis of the needs of two participants.

feeling of being constantly 'in touch' with her friends. The Playstation 2 functions as an interaction platform for participant y: he explains that he tries to be better than his friends in solving games so that he can show off.

Structuring the data according to the three levels ensured that we covered the focus area of researchers (the value level), that of designers (the solution level) and the overlapping area in between (the needs level). The data were translated into a tool that helps to communicate research results to designers. Following the work of Microsoft and Cooper mentioned earlier, we call this tool a *persona* tool.

The persona tool

Once the information is analysed, it needs to be documented in a way that can be used to create *personas*. To facilitate this process, we created a *persona* template. Figure 30.7 shows an illustration of this template. Simple summaries with quotes and source references are key at this stage.

The template helps gather all relevant information for the *persona*, and consists of six parts. How much of the template is needed depends on the nature of the design project in which the *persona* will be used. You

persona
template

research
handbook

Figure 30.7 Research tools.

could, for example, think of *basic personas* with more generic information and *specific personas* with more detailed information.

After completing the template, a *persona* representation has to be made. There are different ways of doing this, from a small drawing or photo of the *persona* with descriptive text, to a video interview. We came up with different ideas for presenting the *personas*. Which representation is appropriate depends on the project and where in the innovation process the *personas* are going to be used. Some *persona* representations are:

- *A persona diary* – a description using the first person singular as subject or 'I-mode'. This is a long quote where the *persona* is telling us who he/she is. This could be mixed with a picture diary, an audio diary or a video diary.
- *A persona interview* – a question and answer interview as text, audio, video or with images.
- *A persona article* – this is a combination of analyses and diary-style ('I-mode') quotes. This is the representation that we have chosen for 'Pulse' and it has achieved its objectives well. It can be done as text, a collection of pictures or a video.

A mood board with pictures and keywords can be added to any of the representations above. For the 'Pulse' project, we developed *personas* such as the one illustrated in Figure 30.8.

To present the results of the research in a way that is understandable and inspiring for designers, we need to show the connections between things people like and use, their important values and the stories that go with them.

The *persona* illustrated in Figure 30.8 is composed of three parts: the main part in the middle consists of the key values of the person. This represents a summary of the character or personality. This part is used in deciding what *personas* to select for a certain workshop, for example, to make sure that all values of interest are represented. The left column contains a subtle mix of information like quotes, opinions and descriptions. It is composed in a way that enables everyone in a workshop, despite background or interests, to pull out information or triggers. The right column will differ depending on the project; in the case of 'Pulse', this is the context of home. This part provides the details that enable designers to make their solution specific if necessary. We found that describing the *persona* in the first person makes the stories livelier, as if the person was talking to you. Pictures and video, if available, could be added to illustrate the *persona* further and make the information more stimulating.

Figure 30.8 A representation of a *persona* based on the 'pulse' project.

To be successful, a *persona* has to fulfil the following criteria:

- it has to be believable;
- it has to tell a real-life story and not be an empty fact sheet – the laddering stories are transformed easily to the storytelling format that is appropriate for this;
- it has to give some elements of reality validated with research data;
- it has to describe the person and his/her values and needs in context;

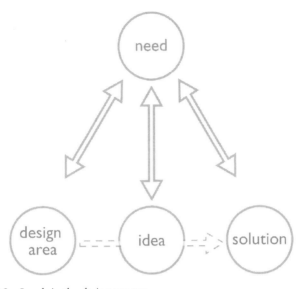

Figure 30.9 Levels in the design process.

- it has to be a recognizable target user, balanced with individual aspects, thus providing a combination of stereotyping segment characteristics and reality;
- the whole has to convey a clear character and personality of the person.

Personas will not be successful if they sum up all kinds of values and needs in a random way – they have to be grounded in reality. The aim of using *personas* in the creative process is to understand those values and needs, and address them with design areas, ideas and innovative solutions. This is done in an iterative way until the most suitable value–need–solution combination is found. This creative process is illustrated in Figure 30.9.

PEOPLE RESEARCH: HOW IT FITS INTO THE INNOVATION PROCESS AND IMPROVES OUR BUSINESS

In this chapter, when talking about innovation we are not only referring to product solutions, but to all kinds of design solutions like products, web concepts, communication services, innovation and experience strategies.

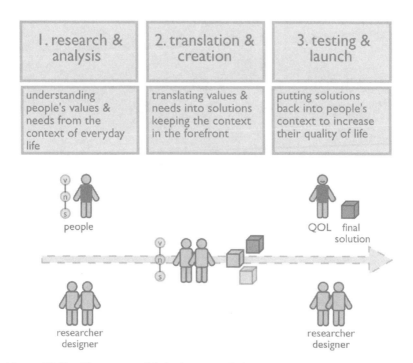

Figure 30.10 The process of designing new solutions.

The generic process of designing new solutions is represented in Figure 30.10.

Figure 30.10 shows three different phases. First, we have a research and analysis phase, focusing on data gathering and understanding values and needs. Researchers and designers work together in taking information from the context of everyday life. They involve the potential user (indicated by 'people' in the figure) for gathering real-life data. These data are analysed, and the core values and needs, including the relationships between them, are identified. The second phase is the translation and creation phase. Designers and researchers translate the values and needs into solutions. It is important that they do not focus on product requirements or needs in isolation, but that they keep in mind constantly the everyday life context in which the values and needs are grounded. Only in this way is it possible to understand the real meaning of values, and thus the real meaning of solutions that they create to improve people's quality of life. These solutions are then fine-tuned and visualized, which is often supported by additional input from researchers. Finally, we have the testing and launch phase. In this phase, researchers and designers take the solution back into the real-life context and observe how the participants experience it and whether it improves their quality of life. It enables them to validate the intended position in the market for the specific market segment that is represented by the participants.

Thus, we have enriched the generic process for designing new solutions in two ways. First, we made the process dynamic by involving both designers and researchers in every phase of the process. This cooperation *within* each phase of the innovation process makes it an iterative loop with constant cross-fertilization of research and design, rather than a static process with linear steps. This new way of working is beneficial for our innovation process, as it facilitates the transition from the research phases into the design phases. Traditionally, designers are rarely involved in the research process and receive hard-to-read and often uninspiring documents from the researchers. These documents have to be redigested by the designers, often resulting in misunderstanding and unnecessary work. On the other hand, researchers often want to be more involved in the later phases of the innovation process to make sure that their research findings are really used and translated optimally into design.

A second benefit of our approach is that we have closed the gaps that often exist between the three steps in the process. We create a consistent thread by taking the everyday life context into the process at the beginning, creating solutions with this context in mind and focusing on a market for which this same context is relevant at the end of the process. Traditionally, potential users are involved mainly in the latter part of the innovation process, during testing and evaluation stages. We have found increasingly that involving users throughout the process of design adds value to the final solution: it validates the concepts earlier in the process, gives designers the opportunity to see the concepts in context and considers values and needs all the way through from the analysis stage to the solution.

We developed a research handbook and a *persona* template that help translate observations into rich descriptions of people's lives. Designers and researchers use these descriptions in their scenarios and the concept development phase. This enriches the generic design process, as *personas* form a direct link between 'people research' and the solutions or design directions that are developed to fulfil the identified needs.

At Philips Design we are using *personas*, with successful experiences, in two of our current projects. In one project, 'Music Flow', we have used *personas* to help us generate future applications for audio. We created 12 *personas* from different age groups and with different interests. We used *personas* to identify needs related to music, and to explore these needs in order to come up with solutions. In another project, 'TV identity', we have used *personas* to develop identity concepts for the 2006 TV range. We identified four key values for home entertainment, and created four *personas* to embody a value each. This helped designers focus on one value at a time and derive an identity element for each.

Other possible ways for using *personas* could be:

- To create future scenarios for illustrating insights from trends studies.
- To brainstorm on solutions, either by using *personas* in drawn scenarios as characters (cartoons) or by role-playing. This helps designers understand the *personas* more and live the experience of use through a *persona's* eyes.
- To validate the experience of use. It is possible to invite the people on whom *personas* were based to keep a consistent thread all the way through.
- To brief advertising agencies for a product launch, packaging and communication. This is useful, as the consistency and focus on certain values and needs is kept from research to implementation and it shows a strong people focus.

CONCLUSIONS

To respond successfully to the continuous changes in society, Philips Design, as a global company, must be innovative in its research methods to investigate people's changing values and needs. In this chapter we describe an approach for doing design research that makes use of rich and illustrative real-life data, showing the subtleties of everyday life. It combines analytical and creative approaches.

The approach also covers the communication of research insight into the design process. It does this by making the levels of communication explicit in different levels of abstraction and translating them into a *persona* tool.

Translating the insights into *personas* helps researchers communicate their findings to designers and clients. With the use of *personas*, we have found a common language for understanding people's needs and values. Even though researchers and designers speak different languages, they talk about the same issues – namely needs – but from different perspectives.

By using *personas,* research work is more likely to be used in the design process and carried through to product development in a consistent way, as it enables designers to link solutions to individual needs, abstract values and the context of people's lives. This also helps businesses to develop sensitive solutions that are relevant to customers and in line with our philosophy as a company.

Our approach enriches the process of designing new solutions by focusing on 'real-life data', which are more realistic, personalized and appropriate to the market, as well as innovative and truly people-driven. By using these everyday life data, we have created a consistent thread throughout the process by taking the everyday life context from the beginning, having this context in mind in creating solutions and focusing on a market for which this same context is relevant at the end.

Our approach also has made the process more dynamic, by involving both designers and researchers in every phase of the process. This stimulates cross-fertilization and mutual understanding between designers and researchers. Researchers and designers understand the relationships between needs and values in the context of everyday life.

ACKNOWLEDGEMENTS

The authors wish to thank all the people involved in reviewing the chapter. Specifically, we want to thank Christina Lindsay and Liesbeth Scholten for their major involvement in the research set-up, management and review of many versions of this chapter. We want to thank Sue Coles and Mili Docampo Rama for their indispensable work during the field period of the research and Juliana Kelly for her help in analysing the data and creating the *personas*. We are very grateful to Steven Kyffin and Josephine Green for their continuous support during the whole project, and Ange Dunselman for her useful comments on the chapter.

REFERENCES

Akrich, M. (1992), The Description of Technical Objects, in W. Bijker and J. Law (Eds) *Shaping Technology/Building Society: Studies in Sociotechnical Change*, pp. 205–224, MIT Press.

Baunt, Z. (2000), *Liquid Modernity*, Polity Press.

Beyer, H. and Holtzblatt, K. (1997), *Contextual Design: A Customer-Centered Approach to Systems Designs*, Morgan Kaufmann.

Grudin, J. and Pruitt, J. (2002), *Personas, Participatory Design and Product Development: An Infrastructure for Engagement.* Proceedings of Participatory Design Conference 2002.

Kujala, S. (2002), User Involvement: A Review of the Benefits and Challenges, in T. Soininen (Ed.) Preprints, Software Business and Engineering Institute, Helsinki University of Technology Report HUT-SoberIT-B1, pp. 1–32.

Lebbon, C., Rouncefield, M. and Viller, S. (2003), Observation for innovation, in Clarkson, J., Coleman, R., Keates, S. and Lebbon, C. (Eds), Inclusive Design: Design for the older population. Springer.

Nail, J., Charron, C., Youen, E. and Lonian, A. (2003), The essentials of integrated marketing. *Forrester*, February 27.

Reynolds, T.J. and Gutman, J. (1988), Laddering theory, method, analysis and interpretation. *Journal of Advertising Research*, **February/March**, 11–13.

Index

'professional' respondents, consumers
165
professionalism improvements, human
resources 606
project management 98–100
projects, holistic approaches 54–65
promiscuous behaviour, consumers
549–50
promotions 100–2, 226, 316, 381–90,
403–4, 410, 625–6
prototyping 258–9
proven track records, dual-economy
third-party ratings 485–6
psychoanalytical-based qualitative
research 8
psychographics 310–12
see also values…
psychology 135–61, 310–12, 369–78,
394–6, 411–12, 445–7, 543–4,
563–8, 625–6
see also emotions
BASS 369–78
bounded rationality 421–4
brand strength 370–8, 445–7
children 563–70
child–mum–tiffin-box dynamics in
India 555–6
commitment 394–6, 411–12, 445–7
irrationalities 135–61
public sector
see also Australian government…
market research 601–22
Pujol, Rafael 517
'Pulse' research programme (2003),
Philips Design 623, 624–5,
628–43
purchase decisions
brands 173–5, 332–4, 336, 337–63,
373–4, 397–414
concepts 100, 169–76, 332–4, 336,
337–63, 373–4, 393–4, 397–414
habits 176–7
hierarchies 173–6
shelf sets 173–4
substitution factors 174–5, 434–5
purchase intent, concepts 169–71, 332–4,
336, 337–63, 373–4, 393–4,
397–414
'push and pull' technologies 246–7, 528–9
pyramids, knowledge 102–5, 217–19,
222–4

Quaker Oats 179–80
qualitative data 3, 8, 11–12, 25–6, 42–65,
88, 98–100, 106, 128–9, 154–7,
201–8, 269–90, 343–63, 379,
416–17, 513–15, 530–7, 540–52,
580–600, 616–21, 626–7
bakery industry 530–7
case studies 190–3
concepts 185–7, 201–8, 269–90,
343–4, 540–52, 626–7
critique 186
current research methods 626–7
database mining 183–93
emerging economies 489–508
Philips Design 624, 626–42
RIO study 443–66
SUPSA company 513–15
Quality Assurance 602
quality factors
bad researchers 163–80
brand leverage 16–19
leadership 381
Six Sigma quality controls 195–208
quantitative data 3, 11–16, 25–6, 42–54,
58–61, 62–3, 68–70, 88, 98–100,
106, 154–7, 185–6, 192, 204–5,
379–80, 416, 533–7, 578–600,
616–21, 625–6
bakery industry 533–7
current research methods 625–6
database mining 185–6, 192
questionnaires 197, 206, 237, 513–14,
581
Quicksilver 464

R&D 55–6, 184, 287–8, 515–16, 554,
572, 575, 624, 632–43
Rabson, Jonathan 229–48
radio media 320–62
Ralston-Purina 324
Rameckers, Lucile 623–44
rationality
see also irrationalities
concepts 135–6, 152, 370–8, 421–4
definition 135
RB *see* Reckitt Benckiser
re-engineering projects 224–5, 602, 603
reactive research, strategic role 244–6
reactivity, proactivity 244–6, 477–8
Reagan, Ronald 154
real estate 589–600